Whales
Of The
World

"And God created great whales, and every living creature that moveth, which the waters brought forth abundantly, after their kind . . . and God saw that it was good."

Genesis 1:21

WHALES
OF
THE WORLD

by
Spencer Wilkie Tinker

E.J. BRILL
LEIDEN • NEW YORK • KØBENHAVN • KÖLN
1988

Bess Press, Inc.
P.O. Box 22388
Honolulu, HI 96822

Printed in the United States of America
First Printing: 1988
Published and Distributed by Bess Press, Inc., Honolulu, Hawaii

Library of Congress Cataloging-in-Publication Data

Tinker, Spencer Wilkie.
  Whales of the world.
  Bibliography: p.
  Includes index.
  1. Whales—Classification. 2. Whales—Anatomy.
3. Whales—Evolution. 4. Mammals—Classification.
5. Mammals—Anatomy. 6. Mammals—Evolution.
I. Title.
QL737.C4T46   1988   599.5   87-70063
ISBN 0-935848-479 (U.S.)

Typesetting and Design: Alice Capelle and Gary Todoki
Artwork: Michelle Chun, Mariane Cooper, Charles J. Dorigan,
Marianne Early, Neil Hickey, Marilyn Kahalewai,
Dianne Rose, and the author.
Cover Design: Donald Bain and Marilyn Kahalewai.

Distributed world-wide by:
E. J. Brill Publishing Company
P.O. Box 9000
NL-2300 PA Leiden
The Netherlands

U.S.A. & Canada
E. J. Brill (U.S.A.) Inc.
1780 Broadway
Suite 1004
New York, N.Y. 10019

ISBN 90-04-08954-3

ACKNOWLEDGMENTS

Most books on natural history are the product of many individuals, both living and dead, who studied the creatures of the natural world and thereafter made their findings available to others through lectures, writings, illustrations, and exhibits.

With the passage of time, much of this information has been collected, stored, and catalogued in large museums and in large libraries, particularly in those which are found in the great universities.

It is from these gigantic reservoirs of knowledge that much of the information on the world's whales has been selected for inclusion in this volume.

The author is especially grateful to Mr. Michael Graybill of Charleston, Oregon, for the many photographs of the skulls of the smaller whales.

Dr. Alan Baker of the National Museum of New Zealand was especially helpful by making some photos of uncommon species from southern seas available for this book.

Dr. Giorgio Pilleri of the Brain Anatomy Institute of the University of Berne, Switzerland, has greatly enlarged the knowledge of whales through his studies and publications; we are greatful that these studies have been available to us.

Dr. Masaharu Nishiwaki of Japan has made his lifetime of studies on whales available to the scientific world through the Scientific Reports of the Whales Research Institute of Tokyo. He has been particularly helpful with the Pacific Ocean species.

The author is also indebted to Mr. Charles J. Dorigan of Great Falls, Virginia, for the drawings of most of the species. Additional illustrations were supplied by Michelle Chun, Mariane Cooper, Marianne Early, Neil Hickey, Marilyn R. Kahalewai, Dianne Rose, and others. The cover design was prepared by Marilyn R. Kahalewai.

Mrs. Alice Matsumoto Capelle set the text and prepared part of the paste-up; the remainder was completed by Mr. Gary Todoki, both of Honolulu, Hawaii.

In addition, the author is grateful for the opportunity to draw upon the libraries and other resources of the following institutions:

The American Museum of Natural History
New York, New York, U.S.A.

The Aquatarium
St. Petersburg Beach, Florida, U.S.A.

The Brain Anatomy Institute of The University of Berne
Berne, Switzerland

The British Museum: Natural History
London, England, The United Kingdom

The California Academy of Sciences
San Francisco, California, U.S.A.

The Carnegie Institution of Washington
Washington, D.C., U.S.A.

Humboldt State University
Arcata, California, U.S.A.

Marineland of Florida
St. Augustine, Florida, U.S.A.

National Marine Fisheries Service
Washington, D.C., U.S.A.

National Marine Mammal Laboratory
Seattle, Washington, U.S.A.

National Museum of New Zealand
Wellington, New Zealand

Oregon Institute of Marine Biology
Charleston, Oregon, U.S.A.

Queensland Museum
Brisbane, Queensland, Australia

Scripps Institute of Oceanography
La Jolle, California, U.S.A.

Sea Life Park
Waimanalo, Oahu, Hawaii, U.S.A.

Sea World, Inc.
San Diego, California, U.S.A.

United States National Museum
Washington, D.C., U.S.A.

University of British Columbia
Vancouver, British Columbia, Canada

University of Guelph
Guelph, Ontario, Canada

University of Hawaii
Honolulu, Hawaii, U.S.A.

Vancouver Public Aquarium
Vancouver, British Columbia, Canada

Waikiki Aquarium
Honolulu, Hawaii, U.S.A.

The Whales Research Institute
Tokyo, Japan

Wometco Miami Sea Aquarium
Miami, Florida, U.S.A.

Spencer Tinker
Honolulu, Hawaii

PREFACE

I wrote *Whales of the World* to gather in one volume enough information on the anatomy and classification of whales so this book could serve as a handbook, a simple reference book, and even a textbook for readers wishing to learn about this fascinating, largely unknown group of aquatic mammals. I hope this book will also be of use to people who, sometime and somewhere, may find a whale stranded on a beach and want to identify and review the anatomical features of the specimen.

Whales of the World emphasizes anatomy and classification because knowledge of these fields will most assist the reader who wants to learn the identity and characteristics of the various species. The book, therefore, contains very little physiology, information on the life habits of whales, or information on whaling. In describing the various anatomical systems of the whales, I usually refer to these systems as they occur in typical mammals and in man. This affords readers a wider point of view, offers a basis for comparing the whales with other mammals and with man, and reminds us of our membership in the great group of the mammals. In addition, I have supplied ample illustrations to give readers visual images of the anatomical structures of the species described.

Considerable confusion and lack of uniformity exists in the use of popular names for the various species of whales. In using popular names, many authors divide the Cetacea (whales) into three groups, namely, whales, dolphins, and porpoises. Here they use the word "whale" to designate the very large species and refer to the remainder as dolphins and/or porpoises. Some authors even refer to all of the smaller species as either dolphins or porpoises which, of course, they are not. Since these animals are all whales, both large and small, it is only logical to use the word "whale" for the entire group and then to use a common name for each species which indicates its family, its distribution, or some anatomical feature. The scientific names are used liberally throughout the text and are usually accompanied by their popular or common names. This is done to force the reader to learn, to use, and to feel comfortable with these Greek and Latin names.

The classification scheme used here follows that of Rice, Dale W. — "A List Of The Marine Mammals Of The World."
U.S. Department of Commerce
National Oceanic and Atmospheric Administration
National Marine Fisheries Service
NOAA Technical Report NMFS SSRF-711. 1977. 15 pp.
This report lists 66 species of toothed whales and 10 species of whalebone whales together with synonyms, distribution, and a bibliography. It contains no illustrations. It is an excellent bulletin.

Over the years, zoological scholars have discovered, studied, described, and named a great many different kinds of whales. These scholars often described and named species of whales which had also been previously described and named by other scholars, thereby causing a single species to have two or more names. As the whales become better known in this century, these duplicate names (synonyms) are being eliminated and the total number of species can be more easily and accurately determined. Some uncertainties still remain because some species of whales have separate groups or populations which live in very widely separated places and never mingle together. In these cases, it is difficult to know whether two similar groups are all of one species, are of a single species with two varieties, or are really of two separate and distinct species. At present, the total number of different kinds of whales seems to be about 77 species, of which 67 species are toothed whales *(Odontoceti)* and 10 species are whalebone whales *(Mysticeti)*. It is these 77 species which are described in this book.

A large bibliography is not included in this book since many comprehensive bibliographies have been printed; furthermore, most of the scientific literature on whales is only available in major scientific or university libraries.

Many scholars, living and dead, have contributed to the information contained in this book. Sources extend from Aristotle (384-322 B.C.) of ancient Greece to contemporaries. Fortunately for us, these scholars and scientists recorded their observations over the centuries and on every ocean of the world to leave a legacy of knowledge for us to use and enjoy.

Spencer Wilkie Tinker
Honolulu, Hawaii

WHALES OF THE WORLD

TABLE OF CONTENTS

—PART ONE—
The Origin and Evolution of The Whales

—PART TWO—
The Anatomy of The Living Whales

—PART THREE—
The Living Whales
Order Cetacea
(Arranged by Suborders, Families, Genera, and Species)

—PART ONE—

The Origin and Evolution of The Whales

— PART ONE —

The Origin and Evolution
of
The Whales

Chapter I

THE DIM, UNCERTAIN PAST

The ancestry of modern whales is uncertain. Although fossil records present quite a variety of forms extending through the last four epochs of the Tertiary Period, these fossil records lack those fossil forms which show the group or groups of mammals from which these early whales originated. Since whales are mammals and since mammals developed as a group of terrestrial animals, most scholars assume that whales have ascended from one or more terrestrial mammalian groups which slowly returned to live in the sea.

The exact identity of the terrestrial mammals which participated in this movement into the sea will probably never be known, but we do know that a great many species formed the long procession which slowly transformed a land mammal into an aquatic mammal. We also know that this move or change from a land habitat to an aquatic habitat took many millions of years.

Since most of the other mammals of the world inhabit the land, one cannot help but wonder why the whales are living in the water; one also wonders in what ancient time and in what ancient land the ancestors of the whales moved from their terrestrial home and relatives and took up a life in the water. The early ancestry of the whales is uncertain and largely unknown due principally to the absence of adequate or even scanty fossil records of the early whales and their whale-like ancestors.

The toothed whales (*Odontoceti*) and the whalebone whales (*Mysticeti*) are so dissimilar in many anatomical features that it is apparent they have been separate and dis-

tinct groups since very ancient times. It is also rather obvious that neither of these two groups gave rise to the other group. Scholars are looking back into the early Cenozoic Era, including the Paleocene Epoch and the Early Eocene Epoch for possible ancestors. Some scholars feel that the anatomical changes which took place between the ancestral land mammals and the earliest whales are so basic, radical, and startling that there is insufficient time in the Paleocene and Early Eocene Epochs for the whale groups to develop their special features by the middle of the Eocene Epoch. Some of these scholars have therefore turned their attention to the Middle and Late Mesozoic Era and are hoping to find there some older ancestral clues in the Late Jurassic and Cretaceous Periods.

Among the ancient whales (*Archaeoceti*), no fossil species has yet been found which would appear to be an early ancestral whale leading to either the modern *Odontoceti* or to the *Mysticeti*. Some scholars are led to conclude that the ancestral origins of the *Odontoceti* and the *Mysticeti* lie farther back in time and that these two suborders plus the *Archaeoceti* all had their beginnings in the Late Mesozoic Era (Late Jurassic and Cretaceous Periods); they thereafter advanced together into the Cenozoic Era as three separate groups to be later found in abundance and diversity in the early Epochs of the Cenozoic Era.

Some scholars have noticed that the embryos of whales have tails of different lengths. The tails of the embryos of the toothed whales (*Odontoceti*) are longer in proportion to the body than the tails of the embryos of the whalebone

2

whales (*Mysticeti*), which are relatively shorter in length. This leads them to speculate that the *Odontoceti* may have developed from mammals with long tails, while the *Mysticeti* may have descended from mammals with shorter tails. So far, these facts have not led to the positive identification of any ancestors.

Early Odontoceti (toothed whales). Some students believe that those whales (*Odontoceti*) with longer-tailed embryos may have descended from the creodonts (*Creodonta*)—an ancient, primitive, generalized order of flesh-eating mammals which lived in the Paleocene Epoch in the Early Tertiary Period. These creodonts seem to have split off from the early, primitive insectivores (the moles, hedgehogs, etc.), which are also believed to be the ancestors of other groups of the mammals. Among the creodonts, a great variety of forms evolved; some resembled dogs, bears, weasels, and other modern families of mammals. It is possible that there may

Some scholars think that a creodont mammal, after moving into the water, might have been the ancestor of some of the whales. *Dromocyon* is an example of a creodont, but it was not the ancestor of any whales. **Drawn from Lull.**

have been a long line or series of aquatic credonts, resembling and possibly related to the flesh-eaters (*Carnivora*) of today, which may have served as a transitional ancestor between the *Creodonta* and the early whales. This relationship would probably be based principally upon the teeth.

Early Mysticeti (whalebone whales). It has been suggested that those whales (*Mysticeti*) which have shorter-tailed embryos may possibly be descended from the *Condylarthra*—an order of early, extinct, herbivorous mammals which was intermediate or transitional between the early insectivores and the early hoofed animals (*Ungulata*).

In searching for the earliest, unknown, whale-like ancestors of the modern whalebone whales (*Mysticeti*), some scholars look back for a possible ancestor among the members of the Family *Mesonychidae*—a family of early primi-

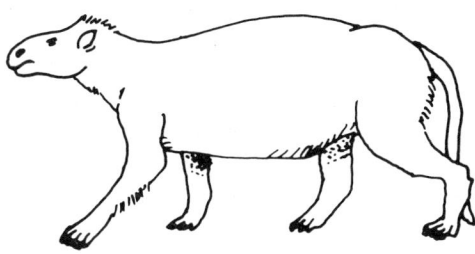

Some scholars think that a condylarth mammal, after moving into the water, might have been the ancestor of some of the whales. *Phenacodus* is an example of a condylarth, but it was not the ancestor of any whales. **Drawn from Lull.**

tive mammals within the Order *Condylarthra*. The *Mesonychidae* were generalized condylarth mammals which resembled the terrestrial ungulate mammals of the Paleocene Epoch and which some scholars believe might have been a connecting link in the long line of species leading from the land mammals of the Early Paleocene to the first whales which appeared in the Early Eocene Epoch which followed.

The *Mesonychidae* include several promising genera, each of which could qualify as an ancestor of the early whales. Although the evidence is incomplete, the members of the *Mesonychidae* exhibit features which suggest they are related to the hoofed mammals *(Ungulata),** and the ungulates in turn show some interesting affinities with the whales. These ungulates, especially the *Artiodactyla,* are believed to be the closest evolutionary relatives of the modern whales, and, among the *Artiodactyla,* some scholars suspect they may be most closely related to the pigs (Family *Suidae*).

Looking Forward. Although the ancestry of the whales is still a biological mystery, scholars are slowly adding "bits and pieces" of evidence which help to shed additional light upon some of these unanswered questions, as well as to raise new questions regarding the relationship of the three great orders of the whales. Scholars continue to wonder if the *Archaeoceti* are the ancestors of both the *Odontoceti* and the *Mysticeti,* if one was ancestral to the other, or if all three orders of the whales arose as separate groups from separate mammalian ancestors sometime in the Late Mesozoic Era or Early Cenozoic Era and thereafter continued onward as three separate groups through succeeding periods of time.

Two new areas of study have developed which are helping to better clarify the relationships between the many groups of the animals. These are studies of the chromosomes and studies of the blood components of various species.

The chromosome or karyotype studies* map, count, study, and finally compare the chromosomes of the cell nucleus of a given species with those of other species. These karyotype studies are one of the most basic and reliable biological markers of a species and have proven to be very trustworthy in determining the identities and relationships of the mammals.

Comparative studies of the blood (seriology)* of various whales and the blood of members of the *Artiodactyla* (hoofed mammals) show similarities in the blood components of these two groups. These similarities suggest relationships which are not obvious in superficial studies and which extend backward into the ancestry of these two groups. In these studies, the blood of the whales resembles more closely the blood of the *Artiodactyla* than it does the blood of any other group of the mammals.

Scholars are expanding their areas of investigation and are now viewing these puzzles of the origin and relationships of the whales from several additional points of view. This new developing evidence is making some theories questionable and is also providing additional proof to support other theories. The few years ahead should see the development of a much better understanding of the origin of the whales.

*The ungulates or hoofed mammals are divided into two groups known as (1) the *Perissodactyla* or odd-toed ungulates (including the horses, tapirs, and rhinoceroses) and (2) the *Artiodactyla* or even-toed ungulates (including the pigs, hippopotomuses, camels, cattle, deer, goats, sheep, etc.).

*See Gaskin, David Edward (1982) listing in the bibliography for references on this subject.

Chapter II

THE EARLY FOSSILS

Fossil Archaeoceti. The earliest fossils of the ancient whales appear in the early part of the Eocene Epoch, about 50,000,000 years ago. These ancient whales, collectively known as the *Archaeoceti,* were already well adapted at this early time to life in the sea. Some were of large size (to 60 feet), they had spindle-shaped bodies with a horizontal tail, and the hind limbs were greatly reduced and disappearing. Their skulls were still bilaterally symmetrical, the bones of the face had not yet begun to slide (telescope) backward over the bones of the cranium, and the nostrils were still located midway along the snout. Their jaws were elongated and contained the 44 basic teeth of the early placental mammals. The teeth in the front of the mouth (incisors and canines) were conical in shape, while the teeth along the sides of the jaws were triangular in shape and were developed into cusps of which the center cusp was the largest and highest; these cusps were aligned in a single series along each jaw bone. However, it is very doubtful that these were the ancestors of either the 67 species of the modern toothed whales (*Odontoceti*) or the ancestors of the 10 species of the modern whalebone whales (*Mysticeti*).

At present, the earliest or oldest known fossil of an ancestral whale, *Pakicetus inachus**, is an incomplete skull which was found about 4 km. northwest of the village of Chorlakki in the Kohat District of eastern Pakistan. It was found in the

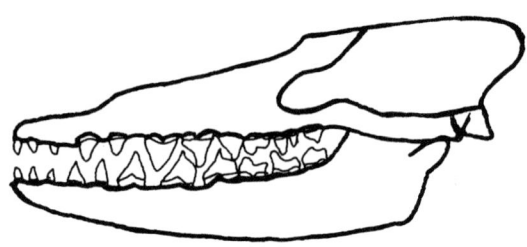

The skull of *Pakicetus inachus*
(Archaeoceti: Protocetidae)

Fragments of the skull of this ancient, primitive, whale-like mammal were found in Pakistan in Early Eocene deposits of about 50,000,000 years ago.
Drawn from Gingerich et alii.

---

*Protocetidae: *Pakicetus inachus* Gingerich and Russell, 1981. See SCIENCE Vol. 220, April 22, 1983, pp. 403-6 (2 figs.).

red sediments of an ancient, prehistoric river bed together with other fossils of various land mammals.

These sediments are of the Early Eocene Epoch of approximately 50,000,000 years ago when a body of ocean water, known as the Tethys Sea, stretched across this area in an east-west direction and separated most of India from the continent of Asia. These red sediments were laid down in river mouths or estuaries at a time when the earth's land masses in this area were shifting and contained many inland

seas, swamps, bays, and estuaries.

The cranium of this early whale skull is estimated to have measured about 30 to 35 cm. (12 to 14 in.) in length and about 14 to 15 cm. (almost 6 in.) in width and to have contained a comparatively small brain. This whale did not appear to have developed any modifications for diving and the ear bones had not developed the adaptations for underwater hearing which are found in the modern whales.

The teeth were strong, well-developed, and suited for the catching of fishes. The teeth of this fossil suggest that this early whale may occupy an evolutionary place somewhere midway between the ancient land mammals and the early whales. These teeth resemble somewhat the teeth of the later whales of the Middle Eocene Epoch and also the teeth of a group of carnivorous land mammals, the mesochelyd *Condylarthra,* from which the whales may possibly have descended.

The ancient whales were well established in the early years of the Eocene Epoch and branched out into a great variety of forms in that Epoch and in the succeeding Oligocene and Miocene Epochs. Although they were truly whales, they were still to undergo many additional anatomical changes before they would resemble the more recent families of whales. These early ancient families of whales lost their identity with the passage of time and slowly disappeared; their disappearance seems to have begun in the Late Eocene Epoch and extended in an erratic and sporadic manner through the Oligocene and Miocene Epochs and on into the Pliocene Epoch. It was during the Miocene Epoch that the whales, particularly the toothed whales (*Odontoceti*), developed a great variety of groups. Although many of the whales which originated in the Miocene Epoch did not continue through to the present time, this Epoch appears to have been the time during which the majority of the present-day families of whales first appeared.

Early Fossil Odontoceti. The toothed whales (*Odontoceti*) first appear as fossils in the later or upper part of the Oligocene Epoch, possibly about 30,000,000 years ago. In the earlier fossils of these toothed whales, the skull is quite elongated and quite symmetrical, the brain is smaller, and the teeth are ragged and shark-like. There were several of these ancient groups of toothed whales in the Oligocene Epoch. One group, known as the *Squalodontidae* because of their shark-like teeth, changed as they passed on through the remainder of the Tertiary Period. Their teeth became less shark-like, their brain slowly enlarged, their nostrils migrated upward and backward toward the top of the head, and their skull developed the twisted asymmetrical pattern of the present-day toothed whales. This twisted skull is a rather recent acquisition and did not appear as a well-developed feature until possibly the Miocene Epoch.

Early Fossil Mysticeti. The whalebone whales (*Mysticeti*) are believed by some scholars to be descended from fossils (*Cetotheriidae*) as far back as the middle of the Oligocene Epoch, which is about 30,000,000 years ago. Although these Oligocene whales still retained teeth, they are regarded by some scholars as one of the possible ancestors of the modern

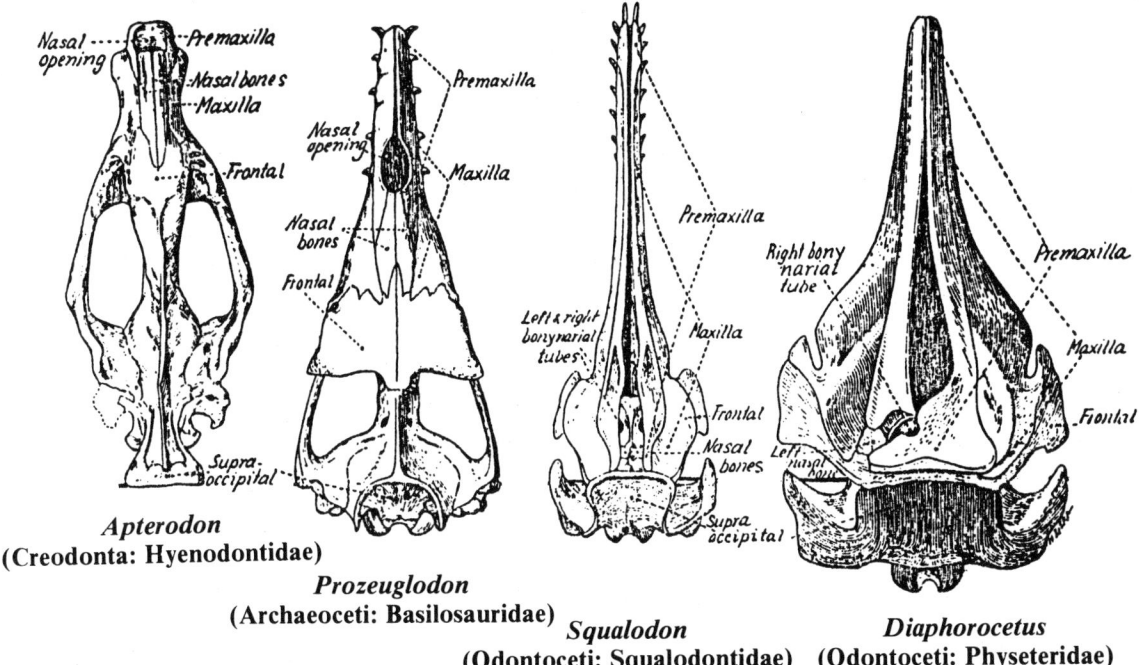

Diagram labels:

Apterodon
(Creodonta: Hyenodontidae)

Labels: Nasal opening, Premaxilla, Nasal bones, Maxilla, Frontal, Supra-occipital

Prozeuglodon
(Archaeoceti: Basilosauridae)

Labels: Premaxilla, Nasal opening, Maxilla, Nasal bones, Frontal

Squalodon
(Odontoceti: Squalodontidae)

Labels: Premaxilla, Maxilla, Left & right bony narial tubes, Frontal, Nasal bones, Supra-occipital

Diaphorocetus
(Odontoceti: Physeteridae)

Labels: Right bony narial tube, Premaxilla, Maxilla, Frontal, Left nasal bone

Diagrams of the skulls of early fossil whales and whale-like
forms in dorsal view showing the movement of the blowhole
toward the top of the head and other specializations.
From Raven and Gregory.

whalebone whales. In the remainder of the Tertiary Period, these early whales were scheduled to undergo some gradual, but significant, changes. Of these changes, the most obvious were the development of the whalebone plates and the modifications of the skull to accommodate them; they also underwent an enormous increase in size in the later part of the Tertiary Period.

Summary. It is not easy to speculate about the changes which might have transformed these ancient toothed whales (*Archaeoceti*) into the modern toothed whales (*Odontoceti*), because there are no good, solid, transitional ("missing link") fossils which help to connect the ancient *Archaeoceti* with the more modern toothed whales. Neither are there strong clues or fossil records which connect the ancient *Archaeoceti* with the modern whalebone whales (*Mysticeti*). Although several groups of primitive whalebone whales are known from the Miocene Epoch, there are no known fossils which clearly, directly, and completely connect any of the modern whalebone whales (*Mysticeti*) with the more ancient primitive ancestral whales of the Early Eocene Epoch. These relationships will only become clearer with the passage of time.

Of the living modern whales, two families have thus far left a very scant, meager fossil record. They are the Narwhal-Beluga Family (*Odontoceti: Monodontidae*) and the Gray Whale Family (*Mysticeti: Eschrichtiidae*). Fossil records of the gray whales have not yet been found which extend backward in time beyond the glacial or Pleistocene Epoch. Fossils doubtless exist, possibly dating back to at least the Miocene Epoch, but to date they have not been found.

Chapter III

THE FAMILIES OF THE ARCHAEOCETI

The whales of the world are usually divided into the following three great groups which are known as "suborders."
 1. Suborder *Archaeoceti* (the ancient whales, all extinct).
 2. Suborder *Odontoceti* (the toothed whales, both extinct and living).
 3. Suborder *Mysticeti* (the whalebone whales, both extinct and living).

There are no living members of the *Archaeoceti;* all are extinct and are known only from fossils; however, both the *Odontoceti* and the *Mysticeti* contain both extinct and living whales. The living whales number about 77+ species; these are discussed in PART THREE of this book. Mention will be made of some of these extinct whales in the pages which follow and in the accompanying charts and tables.

THE ANCIENT EXTINCT WHALES
Suborder *Archaeoceti* Flower, 1883

The ancient whales were descended from land-living mammals which moved into the sea, probably in the Mesozoic Era, and over a very long period of time adjusted their anatomy and their habits to life in the water. Their bodies were long and snake-like and they did not closely resemble the present-day whales, although they did have many whale-like features. Some of these ancient whales may have been the ancestors of other species which later became extinct, and some are doubtless the ancestors of the present-day whales. Many species of these ancient whales were simply passing stages in the evolution of the mammals and did not give rise to any present-day species of whales.

The *Archaeoceti* are divided into three or more groups which are known as "families," all of which end in "-idae." They are the Family *Protocetidae,* the Family *Dorudontidae,* and the Family *Basilosauridae (Zeuglodontidae).* In

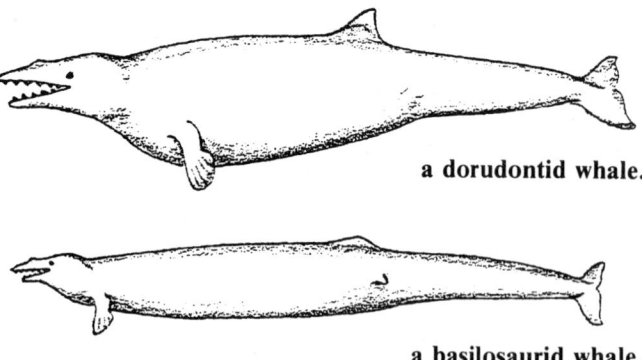

a dorudontid whale.

a basilosaurid whale.

Early primitive whales of the Eocene Epoch as conceived from their skeletal remains.

Redrawn from Maglio, Vincent J. and H.B.S. Cooke — EVOLUTION OF AFRICAN MAMMALS. 1978. Reprinted by permission of Harvard University Press, Publisher.

addition to these three families, there are many other fossils which do not fit comfortably into any of the above three families; these are usually listed as "incertae sedis" (meaning of uncertain place or position) and are not completely classified. Some scholars even add a fourth family, the *Microzeuglodontidae,* which will be briefly mentioned later in the text.

The *Archaeoceti* includes the very oldest of the whales and whale-like mammals and, as such, show many features of both the modern whales and the land mammals from which they were descended. They seem to have appeared in the Cretaceous Period or earlier and in the Early Eocene Epoch (Africa) and to have flourished during Eocene times; they are an Eocene group of which very few lived beyond that Epoch into the Miocene Epoch. They varied in size from the small forms of the *Protocetidae* to the larger forms of the *Basilosauridae.*

Their head was small, their skull, which was symmetrical, had not been shortened in an anterior-posterior direction, and the various bones of the skull had not begun to slide (telescope) over each other. The nasal openings (blowholes) had not advanced very far in a backward direction along the top of the head and the nasal bones were still in place above the nasal passages.

The teeth were usually of three kinds, namely, incisors, canines, and molars. The teeth toward the front of the mouth were usually conical in shape with a single root, while the teeth of the cheek may have had cusps, serrations, and more than one root.

The hearing apparatus was already well developed, indicating their future specialization in this area.

The lower jaw bones were straight, slender, laterally flattened, and were not fused in front at the mandibular symphysis.

Their vertebrae were distributed approximately as follows: C7 + D12-15 + L13 + S1-2 + Ca: many = 55-65. The neck (cervical) vertebrae were relatively long, distinct, and free to move. The sacral vertebrae were still distinct and could be distinguished from the lumbar vertebrae. The sternum consisted of several segments which articulated with the anterior ribs.

The limbs were present but were undergoing radical changes. The pectoral girdle was intact, but the fore limbs had been shortened. The elbow joint was still movable, the movement of the wrist had been reduced, and the bones of the hand and fingers (metacarpals and phalanges) had become slender and elongated. The pelvis was still present but greatly reduced in size, and was slowly moving away from the sacral vertebrae. The femur and the tibia were present as rudiments to the side and below the backbone, and most of the leg bones below the tibia had vanished. The entire hind leg was enclosed within the body and did not project beyond the body surface.

It is possible to regard the following three families of the

6

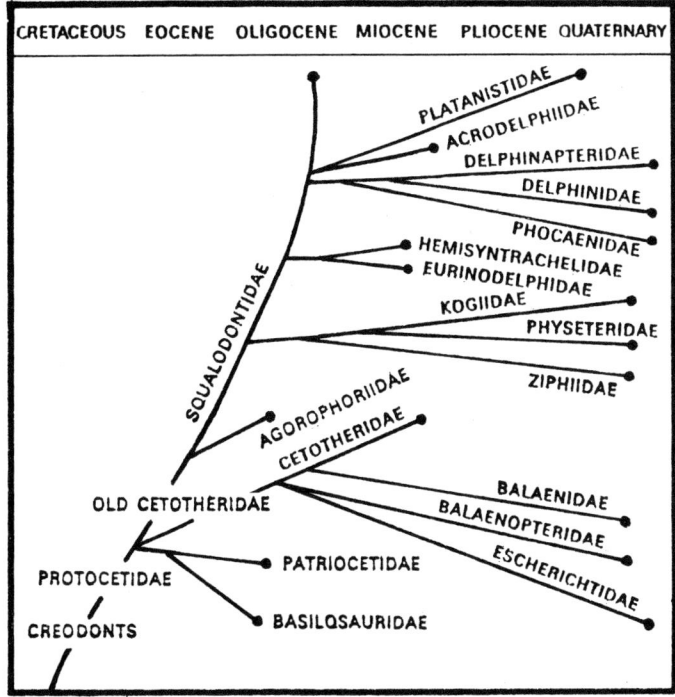

CRETACEOUS EOCENE OLIGOCENE MIOCENE PLIOCENE QUATERNARY

Diagram of a theory showing a possible evolutionary pathway from the ancient mammals of the Cretaceous Period to the modern whales.

Archaeoceti as an evolutionary series beginning with the more generalized and smaller *Protocetidae* and then progressing through the *Dorudontidae* to the larger and more specialized *Basilosauridae*. It should be remembered that, of these three families, only the members of the *Protocetidae* had the evolutionary potential of being the ancestors of the more recent and modern species of whales.

1. Family Protocetidae Stromer, 1908. The *Protocetidae* are the most ancient or archaic of the *Archaeoceti*. Although their ancestry and their descendants are both uncertain, they have for a time been regarded by some scholars as the most probable ancestors of several groups of whales including the *Odontoceti*, the *Mysticeti,* and other groups which are now extinct. Of the ancient whales, this family was probably the most closely related to the land-dwelling ancestors of the *Archaeoceti*. These early protocetid whales ranged in size from small to large. Their vertebral count was approximately as follows: $C7 + D12\pm + L7\pm + S1 + Ca$: unknown $=50\pm$. The neck (cervical) vertebrae still retained two generalized features, namely, they were free to move and they were not compressed. The side teeth of the jaws exhibited various patterns of cusps, from one to three in number, including some which were step-like.

In the Genus *Protocetus,* the animals were small in size; one specimen measured about 2.48 meters (8 ft.) in length. Its skull did not resemble the skull of any of the land mammals of its time, nor did it resemble the skull of any of the whales which are living today. The vertebral count was approximately as follows: $C7 + D15 + L13 + S2 + Ca\ 20\pm = 57\pm$. The bones of the neck were still separate and not compressed, but the pelvis, although present, was much reduced in size and had already disarticulated and separated from the transverse processes of the sacral vertebrae. This ancient mammal was elongated in form and shape and was well adapted for life in the water.

2. Family Dorudontidae Miller, 1923. The members of this family were of small to medium size, short bodied, and probably reached a maximum length of about 6 meters (20 ft.). They possessed an elongated skull which may have reached a length of about 91 cm. (3 ft.) and which ended in an elongated rostrum.

The vertebral count in the Genus *Dorudon* is approximately as follows: $C7 + D15 + L13 + S2 + Ca21\pm = 58\pm$. The vertebrae of the neck were free to move and were scarcely compressed, and those vertebrae in the posterior dorsal region and in the lumbar region were quite normal and little altered. Although this was an aquatic animal, the trunk and tail were not greatly lengthened.

The forelimbs were quite stout, still had hinged movable elbows, and were adapted for swimming. Most scholars do not believe that this family was the ancestor of any group of modern whales; although some have suggested that both the *Odontoceti* and the *Mysticeti* may possibly have come from among the members of the *Dorudontidae*.

3. Family Basilosauridae (Zeuglodontidae). Cope, 1868. The family of the *Basilosauridae* was probably the most specialized of the *Archaeoceti*. Some were of rather large size, measured from about 12 to 15 meters (39 to 49 ft.) in length, and had a large skull which measured about 1.5 meters (5 ft.) in length. The teeth of the cheek were of an unusual serrated type which was specialized within the *Archaeoceti*.

In the Genus *Basilosaurus,* the vertebral count was approximately as follows: $C7 + D15 + L13 + S2 + Ca\ 21\pm = 58\pm$. The vertebrae of the neck were free to move, but they were shortened, and the vertebrae of the trunk and tail showed an elongation of the usual pattern. The pelvic or innominate

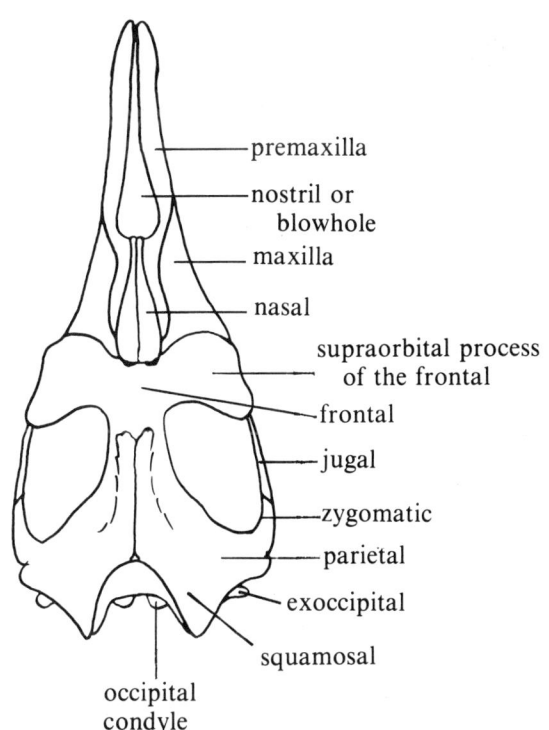

premaxilla

nostril or blowhole

maxilla

nasal

supraorbital process of the frontal

frontal

jugal

zygomatic

parietal

exoccipital

squamosal

occipital condyle

Diagram of the skull of *Basilosaurus cetoides* (Archaeoceti: Basilosauridae) in dorsal view.

Drawn from Kellogg.

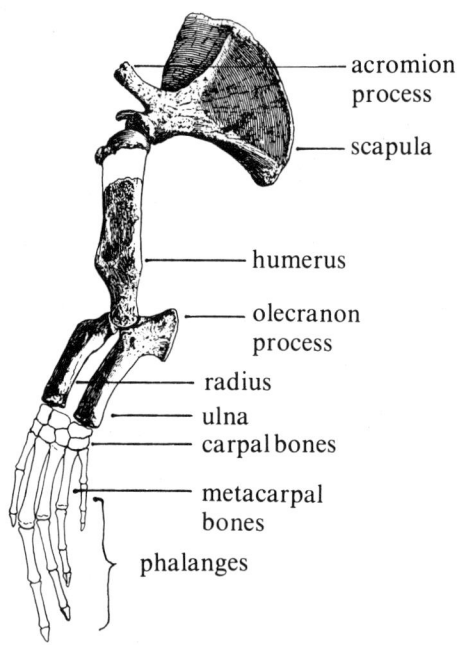

Diagram of the left anterior appendage of *Basilosaurus cetoides* (Archaeoceti: Basilosauridae) in lateral view. Note the enlarged olecranon process at the proximal end of the ulna.

From Kellogg.

4. Family Microzeuglodontidae. Some recent scholars have created an additional family within the *Archaeoceti* known as the Family *Microzeuglodontidae,* based upon a single specimen, *Microzeuglodon caucasicum* Stromer, 1903, from the Late Oligocene Epoch. This fossil whale was discovered on the Apsheron Peninsula on the western shore of the Caspian Sea near the city of Baku. This species was similar to others within the *Basilosauridae,* but was smaller in size; the body was about 4 meters (13 ft.) in length. The teeth resembled those of the *Basilosauridae,* but the molars were more widely spaced along the jaw bone. Most students include this species within the *Basilosauridae.*

Summary of the Archaeoceti. The *Archaeoceti* had their heyday during the Eocene Epoch (duration: 22,000,000± years), but the ancestors of the *Archaeoceti* probably had their whale-like beginnings in the very early years of the Eocene Epoch, in the preceeding Paleocene Epoch (duration: 5,000,000± years), or in the latter part of the Mesozoic Era. It was during this Eocene Epoch that the *Archaeoceti* developed a great diversity and variety of primitive whale-like forms which were to inhabit the seas for over 30,000,000 years. At the end of the Eocene Epoch, the production of new forms and new species had diminished and the older forms were dying off, so that as the Oligocene Epoch proceeded, the species which were disappearing were more numerous than the new forms which were appearing.

At the end of the Eocene Epoch, only a very few representatives of the *Dorudontidae* and the *Basilosauridae* were destined to live on into the Oligocene Epoch. Of these, the members of the *Basilosauridae* seem to have disappeared in the Late Oligocene Epoch and the *Dorudontidae* lingered on until the Early Miocene Epoch, at which time all members of the *Archaeoceti* ceased to exist.

At this point, it should again be remembered that the *Archaeoceti* (with the possible exception of the *Protocetidae*) were not the ancestors of the modern families of whales. The unknown ancient whales, which were ancestral to the families of the modern whales, were already in existence and were developing side by side with the dying *Archaeoceti.*

bones were rudimentary and measured about 23.4 cm. (9 in.) in length; they were located about opposite the sacral vertebrae, but were greatly reduced in size and no longer articulated with the sacral vertebrae.

The femur was non-functional and measured only about 20 cm. (8 in.) in length. The remaining bones of the hind leg were usually absent.

Because of their specialization, most scholars do not regard these early whales as the ancestors of any of the groups of modern whales.

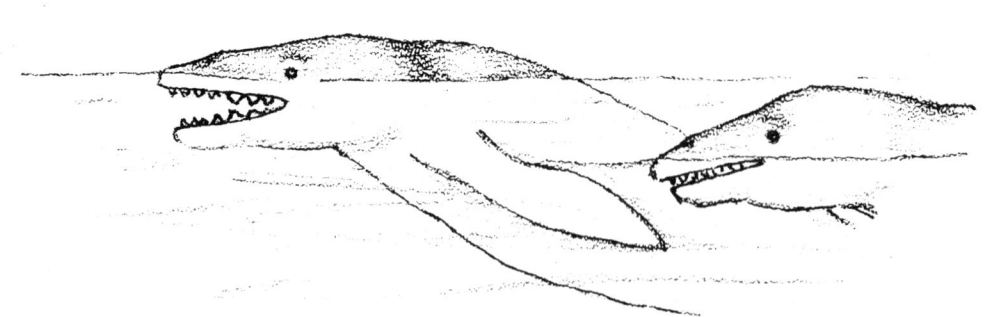

Prozeuglodon was an ancient, primitive whale (Archaeoceti: Basilosauridae) which existed about 40,000,000 years ago in the later part of the Eocene Epoch. It measured about 5 to 6± feet in length and possessed large, serrated teeth.

Chapter IV

THE WHALES IN ANCIENT TIMES

During the Mesozoic Era (The Age of Reptiles), which ended with the Cretaceous Period, there were great changes in the configuration of the earth's surface and in the nature of the animal life, both on the land and in the sea. Among the vertebrate animals, the reptiles dominated the Mesozoic Era and then declined at its end. During the Jurassic Period in the middle part of this era, the mammals first appeared as a new and insignificant group and, with the passage of time, slowly expanded their species and their populations on both the land and in the sea and then passed on into the Cenozoic Era. These events, as they relate to the development of the whales, are outlined in the pages which follow.

THE MESOZOIC ERA
The Age of Reptiles
(Duration: 160,000,000 years)

THE CRETACEOUS PERIOD
Duration: 72,000,000 years

Although the Mesozoic Era is known as the "Age of Reptiles," it is also the era in which the mammals saw their initial development and early specialization. The Jurassic Period seems to have been the time during which the mammals made their first appearance. Although the mammals were overshadowed by the reptiles during both the Jurassic and Cretaceous Periods, they developed along many diverging lines and passed into the Cenozoic Era as a group of considerable diversity including both terrestrial and aquatic forms. These aquatic and semi-aquatic forms from the Cretaceous Period which lived on into the Paleocene Epoch of the Cenozoic Era included the unknown, unidentified, and undistinguished ancestors of the whales. Among these forms were the ancestors of the *Archaeoceti* (ancient whales) and the unknown ancestors of all other extinct and modern groups of whales.

THE MESOZOIC ERA

CENOZOIC ERA	Duration: 65,000,000 years
MESOZOIC ERA	Cretaceous Period Duration: 72,000,000± years
The Age of Reptiles	Jurassic Period Duration: 45,000,000± years
Duration: 160,000,000± years	Triassic Period Duration: 50,000,000± years
PALEOZOIC ERA	Duration: 345,000,000 years
PRECAMBRIAN ERA	Duration: 4,030,000,000 years

THE CENOZOIC ERA
The Age of Mammals
(Duration: 65,000,000 years)

THE TERTIARY PERIOD
The Age of Mammals
(Duration: 63,000,000 years)

THE PALEOCENE EPOCH
(Duration: 5,000,000 years)

The Paleocene Epoch, although of comparatively short duration, was both a transitional and a developmental period. During this epoch, the terrestrial mammals spread widely over the earth and the aquatic mammals, including the ancestors of the whales, were diverging and developing into the ancestors of the basic forms which were to later appear in the Eocene Epoch. Unfortunately, the ancestral whales of the Paleocene Epoch left no fossils which have come to light at this time, and so scholars are as yet unable to identify any early ancestral whales from the Paleocene Epoch.

THE CENOZOIC ERA
The Age of Mammals
(Duration: 65,000,000 years)

THE TERTIARY PERIOD
The Age of Mammals
(Duration: 63,000,000 years)

THE EOCENE EPOCH
(Duration: 22,000,000 years)

Archaeoceti (ancient whales). The Eocene Epoch was the heyday of the *Archaeoceti* and was marked by the development of a great diversity of species in great numbers. The *Archaeoceti* had bodies which were serpent-like; their hind legs were probably enclosed within the body and did not project much beyond the surface; their head was small with a very minimum of telescoping (sliding of the facial bones over the cranium); their neck was distinct and movable; their teeth were differentiated into 3 kinds: conical incisors, canines, and molars; and their nostrils were placed a short distance back from the snout. Although the *Archaeoceti* were true whales, they were not the ancestors of any other known groups. The *Archaeoceti* included, among others, the following families:
1) the *Protocetidae*, which appeared in the Early Eocene Epoch and apparently became extinct in the Late Eocene;

2) the *Dorudontidae,* which appeared in the Late Eocene Epoch and extended through the Oligocene Epoch into the Early Miocene Epoch before becoming extinct;

3) the *Basilosauridae,* which appeared in the Middle Eocene Epoch and extended into the Late Oligocene Epoch before disappearing;

4) and sometime the *Patriocetidae,* although this family is most often listed as a primitive family within the *Mysticeti* (whalebone whales). It is regarded by some scholars as intermediate between the *Archaeoceti* and the *Mysticeti,* and is not usually regarded as an ancestor of the *Mysticeti.*

Odontoceti (toothed whales). Among the *Odontoceti,* the *Agorophiidae* seems to be the first of this group to appear in the Late Eocene Epoch; they disappeared sometime in the Late Oligocene.

Mysticeti (whalebone whales). Within the *Mysticeti,* the first forms to appear as fossils were the questionable *Patriocetidae* which appeared in the Late Eocene Epoch and disappeared in the Late Oligocene Epoch.

THE CENOZOIC ERA
The Age of Mammals
(Duration: 65,000,000 years)

THE TERTIARY PERIOD
The Age of Mammals
(Duration: 63,000,000 years)

THE OLIGOCENE EPOCH
(Duration: 11,000,000 years)

Archaeoceti (ancient whales). In the Oligocene Epoch, the *Archaeoceti* reached their greatest height in forms and numbers and thereafter began to die off. The diversity and production of new species had declined and then ended and the rate of the extinction of species was greater than the rate of creation of new species. This epoch was of short duration and left a poor fossil record of the *Archaeoceti.* The *Proto-*

cetidae were probably all extinct by the Late Eocene. The *Dorudontidae* were to continue through the Oligocene Epoch and to die off in the Early Miocene Epoch. The *Basilosauridae,* which had continued from the Eocene Epoch, disappeared in the Late Oligocene Epoch.

Odontoceti (toothed whales). Within the *Odontoceti,* the *Squalodontidae,* with their shark-like teeth, made their first appearance in the Middle and Late Oligocene Epoch. With the exception of the *Agorophiidae,* which had continued from the Eocene Epoch, all toothed whales *(Odontoceti)* delayed their appearance until nearer the beginning of the Miocene Epoch.

Mysticeti (whalebone whales). Within the *Mysticeti,* the *Patriocetidae* continued from the Eocene Epoch and disappeared at the end of the Oligocene Epoch. Two additional families made their appearance in the Oligocene Epoch. The *Aetiocetidae* appeared in the Late Oligocene Epoch and in turn disappeared before the end of the Epoch. The *Ceto-theriidae* appeared in the Middle Oligocene and were destined to live on through the Miocene Epoch which followed and to disappear in the Early Pliocene Epoch; this group is regarded by some scholars as the first and earliest family of true whalebone whales and the possible ancestor of the modern whalebone whales.

THE CENOZOIC ERA
The Age of Mammals
(Duration: 65,000,000 years)

THE TERTIARY PERIOD
The Age of Mammals
(Duration: 63,000,000 years)

THE MIOCENE EPOCH
(Duration: 12,000,000 years)

The fossils which remain from the Miocene Epoch are quite numerous and varied. These fossils include representatives of groups (*Archaeoceti*) which were disappearing and many representatives of the two groups (*Odontoceti* and

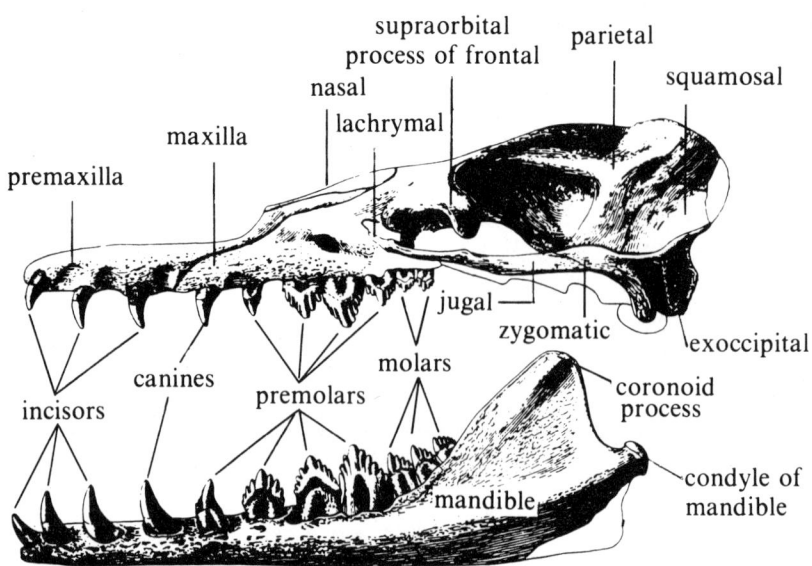

Diagram of the skull and lower jaw of *Basilosaurus cetoides* (Archaeoceti: Basilosauridae) in lateral view.

From Kellogg.

10

Mysticeti) which were emerging to become the dominant types of the modern whales.

Archaeoceti (ancient whales). Only one family of the *Archaeoceti*, the smaller, short-bodied *Dorudontidae*, lingered on into the Miocene Epoch; these few remaining species died out in the Early Miocene Epoch.

Odontoceti (toothed whales). The Miocene Epoch presented a great variety of species of true toothed whales, most of which had their origin in earlier epochs.

1) The *Squalodontidae* continued as a prominent family during the Miocene Epoch. They had a long pointed beak with pointed teeth in front and serrated teeth on the sides of the jaws.

2) The *Eurhinodelphinidae* (*Eurhinodelphis* and relatives) with their long, pointed beaks, appeared at the beginning of the Miocene Epoch, were a prominent group during this Epoch, and disappeared at the end of the Miocene Epoch.

3) The *Hemisyntrachelidae* and 4) the *Acrodelphidae* both appeared early in the Miocene Epoch, continued through it, and disappeared early in the succeeding Pliocene Epoch.

5) The *Kentriodontidae* appeared and developed during the Middle and Late Miocene Epoch. They were generally of small to medium size and dolphin-like in shape. Their special features included:
— a symmetrical skull with some primitive features including large cranial crests,
— a short to medium length rostrum,
— a long mandibular symphysis,
— teeth of a single type with single round roots and rough enamel, and
— unfused cervical vertebrae.

The Genus *Kentriodon* resembles the *Delphinidae*. They are a rather primitive group and are thought by some scholars to be descended from the *Squalodontidae* and also to be possible ancestors of the modern *Delphinidae*. These species are usually included within the *Delphinidae*, although a few scholars have regarded them as sufficiently different to merit a separate family which they call the *Kentriodontidae*.

The following four modern families of the *Platanistidae*, *Delphinidae*, *Physeteridae*, and *Ziphiidae* first appeared in the Early Miocene Epoch and have continued through to the present day.

6) The *Platanistidae* developed in the ocean during the Early Miocene Epoch; they show relationshps with the *Squalodontidae*.

7) The *Delphinidae* had their beginnings in the Early Miocene Epoch, while the true porpoises appeared as small species in the Middle and Late Miocene Epoch.

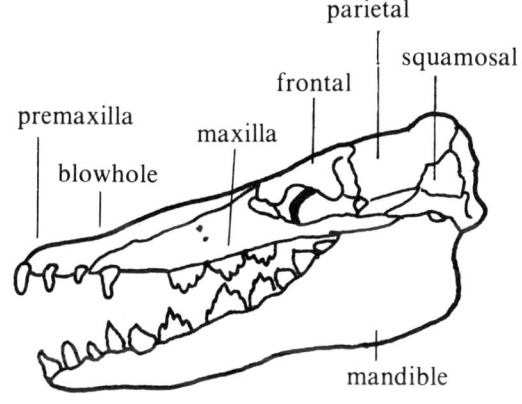

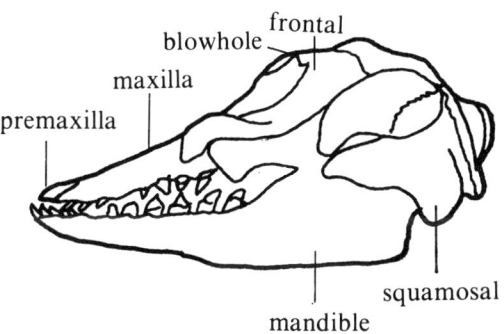

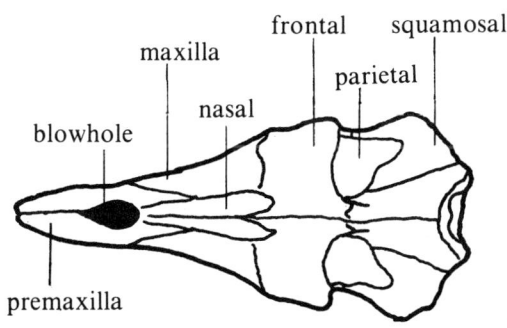

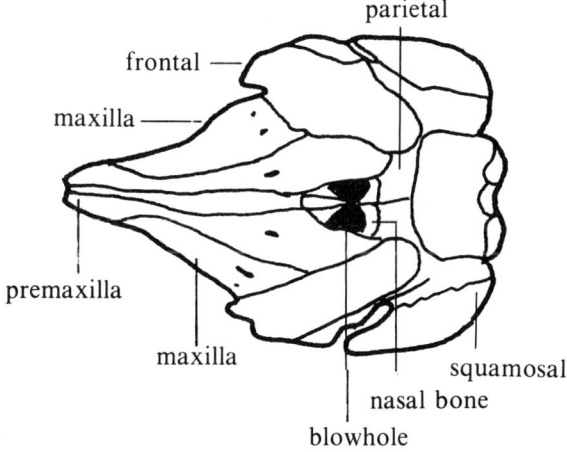

Basilosaurus of the Eocene Epoch shows the blowhole or nostril beginning its backward migration.

Drawn from Young.

Reprinted by permission of the Univ. of Chicago Press from illustrations adapted from A.S. Romer — MAN AND THE VERTEBRATES. 1945. Univ. of Chicago Press.

A **squalodontid** whale of the Miocene Epoch shows the blowhole or nostril aproaching the top of the head.

Drawn from Young.

Reprinted by permission of the Univ. of Chicago Press from illustrations adapted from A.S. Romer — MAN AND THE VEGETABLES. 1945. Univ. of Chicago Press.

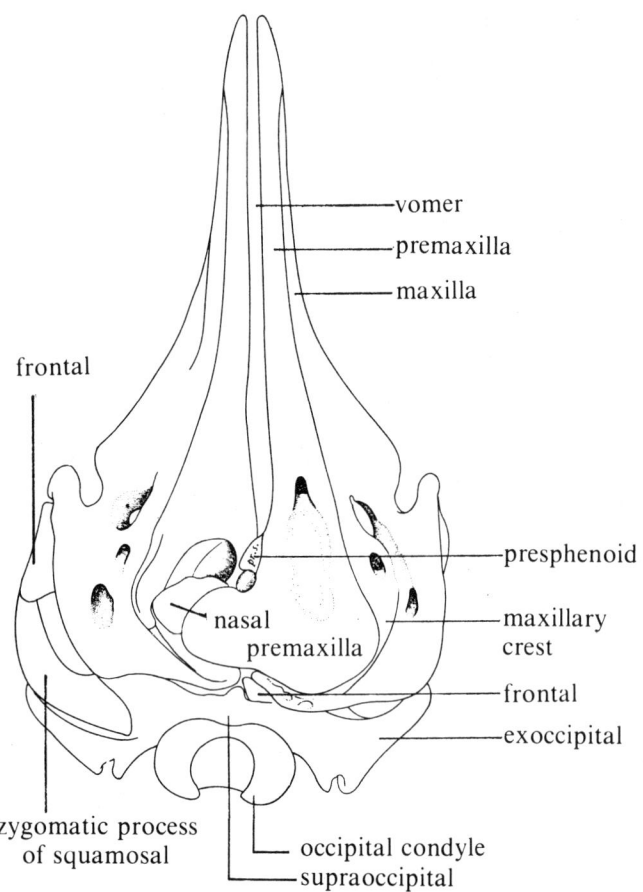

A diagram of the skull of an early sperm whale, *Orycterocetus crocodilinus* (Odontoceti: Physeteridae), in dorsal view. It was discovered in the deposits of the Miocene Epoch in Charles County, Maryland. The skull measured 75 cm. (30 in.) in length.

Drawn from Kellogg.

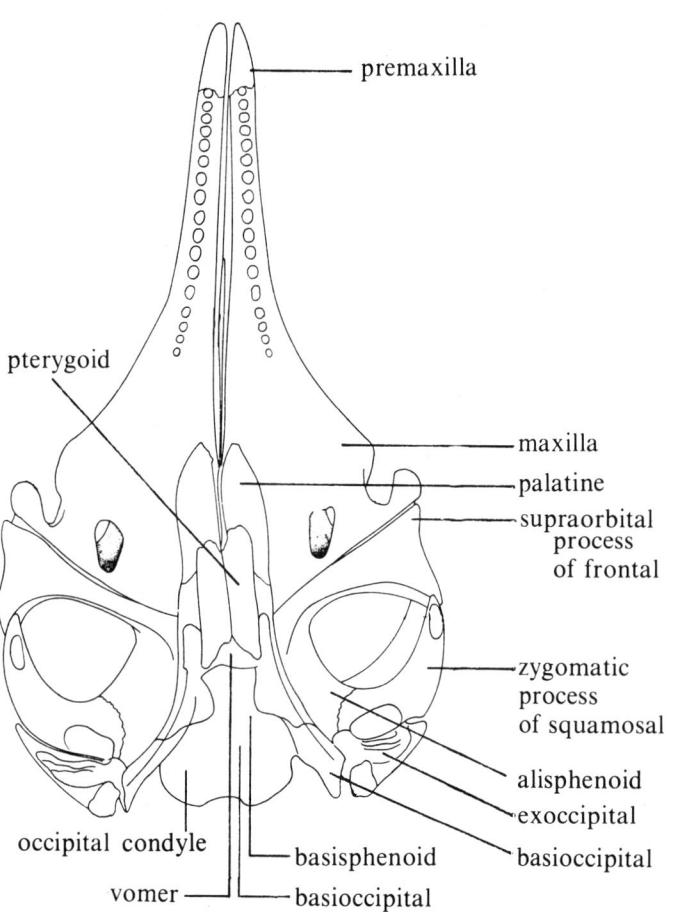

A diagram of the skull of an early sperm whale, *Orycterocetus crocodilinus*, in ventral view, from the Miocene deposits in Maryland.

Drawn from Kellogg.

8) The *Monodontidae* are first known from fossils of the Miocene Epoch from the Pacific Coast of North America, although they doubtless had their origin in earlier times.

9) The *Physeteridae* began as smaller species in the Early Miocene Epoch.

10) The *Ziphiidae* began in the Early Miocene Epoch; they showed a tendency to lose their maxillary teeth, due possibly to their diet of squids, but they retained two or more mandibular tusks in the front of the mouth.

In general, the fossil records of the Miocene Epoch show many new forms of both large and small toothed whales, most of which were abundant and widely distributed.

Mysticeti (whalebone whales). The *Cetotheriidae* were one of the predominant groups throughout the entire Miocene Epoch; they originated in the Middle Oligocene Epoch, continued through the entire Miocene Epoch, and disappeared in the Early Pliocene Epoch. Although some species reached a length of 9 meters (30 feet), most were much smaller. This family had over 20 genera and its many species had short baleen plates. Some scholars think that this group appears to be a possible ancestor of the present-day gray whales (*Eschrichtiidae*).

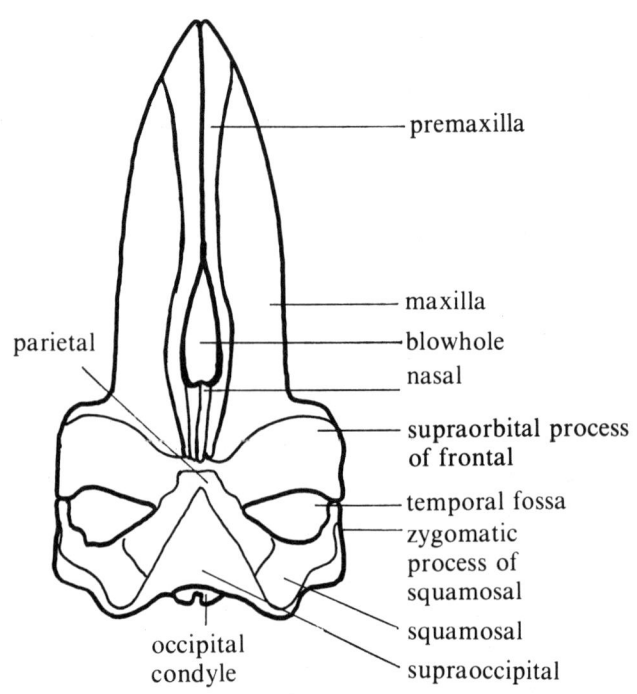

A diagram of the skull of *Cophocetus oregonensis* (Mysticeti: Cetotheriidae) in dorsal view. This is a fossil whalebone whale from the deposits of the Miocene Epoch at Newport, Oregon. **Drawn from Packard and Kellogg.**

THE LIFE SPAN OF THE FAMILIES OF WHALES
In Geologic Time

—— Cenozoic Era ——

—— Tertiary Period —— | Quarternary Period ——

Families of Whales	Paleocene Epoch	Eocene Epoch	Oligocene Epoch	Miocene Epoch	Pliocene Epoch	Pleistocene Epoch (Glacial) 2,000,000 years	Holocene Epoch
	5,000,000 years	22,000,000 years	11,000,000 years	12,000,000 years	11,000,000 years		11,000 years thus far

Families of Whales

ARCHAEOCETI
(The Ancient Whales)

1. Protocetidae
2. Dorudontidae
3. Basilosauridae

ODONTOCETI
(The Toothed Whales)

4. Squalodontidae
5. Agorophiidae
6. Eurhinodelphidae
7. Hemisyntrachelidae
8. Acrodelphidae
9. Kentriodontidae
10. Platanistidae
   (The River Dolphins)
11. Delphinidae
   (The Ocean Dolphins and Porpoises)
12. Monodontidae
   (The Narwhal and White Whale)
13. Physeteridae
   (The Sperm Whales)
14. Ziphiidae
   (The Beaked Whales)

MYSTICETI
(The Whalebone Whales)

15. Aetiocetidae
16. Patriocetidae
17. Cetotheriidae
18. Eschrichtiidae
   (The Gray Whales)
19. Balaenopteridae
   (The Fin-backed Whales or Rorquals)
20. Balaenidae
   (The Right Whales)

15

GEOLOGIC TIME SCALE

Era	Period	Epoch	Approximate Duration	Years Before The Present	Important Events
Cenozoic / Age of Mammals	Quarternary (Age of Man)	Holocene (Recent)		11,000	The ice receded as the climate became warmer and more arid. Some mammals perished. Man develops a more complex civilization.
		Pleistocene (Glacial)	2,000,000	2,000,000	The ice ages. Man first appears. The mammals mix, migrate before the ice, and are later thinned out. Modern whales are well established.
	Tertiary (Age of Mammals)	Pliocene	11,000,000	13,000,000	Mammals reach high development.
		Miocene	12,000,000	25,000,000	Apes develop into many types. Whales are well established.
		Oligocene	11,000,000	36,000,000	Early whales, both toothed and whalebone types, are developing.
		Eocene	22,000,000	58,000,000	Mammals develop into modern groups.
		Paleocene	5,000,000	63,000,000	Mammals undergo a great expansion. Ancestors of ancient whales appear.
Mesozoic / Age of Reptiles	Cretaceous		72,000,000	135,000,000	Dinosaurs wane and disappear. Angiosperm plants expand greatly.
	Jurassic		45,000,000	180,000,000	Birds and mammals first appear.
	Triassic		50,000,000	230,000,000	Dinosaurs first appear on land.
	Permian		50,000,000	280,000,000	Primitive reptiles expand into many forms.
Paleozoic / Age of Ancient Life	Carboniferous — Pennsylvanian (Upper or Later Carboniferous)		30,000,000		Great forests develop which later become coal. Reptiles appear for first time.
	Carboniferous — Mississippian (Lower or Earlier Carboniferous)		35,000,000	310,000,000	
	Devonian		60,000,000	345,000,000	Amphibians first appear. Insects first appear.
	Silurian		20,000,000	405,000,000	Land plants first appear.
	Ordovecian		75,000,000	425,000,000	Earliest known fishes appear.
	Cambrian		100,000,000	500,000,000	Marine invertebrates appear in great abundance.
Pre-Cambrian			4,400,000,000	600,000,000 / 4,500,000,000	Fossils first appear.

Chapter VI
THE FOSSIL AND RECENT FAMILIES OF WHALES
(Order Cetacea)

Suborder	Family Name	Range In Time	Approximate Number Of Known Genera
ARCHAEOCETI The Ancient Toothed Whales	† **Protocetidae**	Early Eocene to Late Eocene	Fossil — 4+ Recent — 0

REMARKS: Includes *Protocetus, Pakicetus, Pappocetus, Eocetus,* and other whales.
Fossils are known from England, Africa, and No. America.
Size was small (2-3 m.); hind legs were absent; skull was not "telescoped"; snout was extended; nostrils had moved half way up the skull; front teeth were rounded and conical, while side teeth were serrated; centra were short.
This family is extinct.

	† **Dorudontidae**	Late Eocene to Early Miocene	Fossil — 4+ Recent — 0

REMARKS: Includes *Dorudon, Zygorhiza, Kekenodon, Phococetus,* and other whales.
Fossils are known from Europe, Africa, No. America and New Zealand.
Size was medium (5-6 m.); hind legs were absent; skull was not "telescoped"; snout was extended; nostrils had moved half way up the skull; front teeth were rounded and conical, while side teeth were serrated; neck vertebrae were not compressed; body was not abnormally long.
This family is not an ancestor of modern whales.
This family is extinct.

	† **Basilosauridae (Zeuglodontidae)**	Middle Eocene to Late Oligocene	Fossil — 3+ Recent — 0

REMARKS: Includes *Basilosaurus, Prozeuglodon, Platyosphys,* and other primitive whales.
Fossils are known from Europe, Africa, and No. America.
Size was large (20 m.); hind legs were absent; skull was not "telescoped"; snout was extended; nostrils had moved half way up the skull; front teeth were rounded and conical, while side teeth were serrated; neck vertebrae were compressed; body, trunk, and tail were abnormally long and slender.
This family is not an ancestor of modern whales.
This family is extinct.

ODONTOCETI The Toothed Whales	† **Agorophiidae**	Late Eocene to Late Oligocene	Fossil — 2+ Recent — 0

REMARKS: Includes *Agorophius,* a primitive toothed whale, *Xenorophus,* sometimes *Archaeodelphis,* and other genera.
Fossils found in No. America.
The hind legs were absent; skull shows beginning of "telescoping"; snout was extended; nostrils had moved up the skull to above the eyes.
This family is extinct; its history was short. It is probably not an ancestor of modern toothed whales.

	† **Squalodontidae**	Middle and Late Oligocene to Early and Middle Pliocene	Fossil — 12+ Recent — 0

REMARKS: Includes *Squalodon,* a primitive toothed whale, and other genera.
Fossils found in Europe, No. and So. America, Australia, and New Zealand. These fossils are quite abundant.

---

† Fossil.

Suborder	Family Name	Range In Time	Approximate Number Of Known Genera
	These whales were porpoise-like. The beaks of some were long and pointed. The teeth were differentiated; the front teeth were long and pointed and the back teeth were flat, serrated, and shark-like. The nostrils were atop the head. It is a possible ancestor of modern toothed whales. This family is extinct.		
	† **Eurhinodelphidae**	Early Miocene to Late Miocene	Fossil — 3+ Recent — 0
	REMARKS: Includes *Eurhinodelphis,* a long-snouted form which is known from fossils from Europe, No. America, So. America, and Japan. All are extinct.		
	† **Hemisyntrachelidae**	Early Miocene to Early Pliocene	Fossil — 2+ Recent — 0
	REMARKS: Includes *Hemisyntrachelus* and *Lophocetus* which are known from Europe and No. America. All are extinct.		
	† **Acrodelphidae**	Early Miocene to Early Pliocene	Fossil — 6+ Recent — 0
	REMARKS: Includes *Acrodelphis* and other genera. Fossils are known from Europe and No. America. All are extinct.		
	† **Kentriodontidae**	Miocene	Fossil — 9+ Recent — 0
	REMARKS: Includes *Kentriodon* and other genera. They were dolphin-like, of small-to-medium size, had a short-to-medium length rostrum, a long mandibular symphysis, and teeth of a single type with single, rounded roots and rough enamel; the cervical vertebrae were free. They were possibly descended from the Squalodontidae and are possibly ancestral to the modern Delphinidae. This family is extinct.		
	Platanistidae The River Dolphins	Early Miocene to Recent	Fossil — 11+ Recent — 4
	REMARKS: Includes the following four living genera: *Platanista, Inia, Lipotes,* and *Pontoporia.* There are five living species. Fossils are known from Europe, No. America, So. America, and S.E. Asia.		
	Delphinidae The Ocean Dolphins and Porpoises	Early Miocene to Recent	Fossil — 25± Recent — 20
	REMARKS: Includes 20 recent genera which include about 39+ living species. It includes small- and medium-sized whales including the dolphins and porpoises. It includes the Stenidae and Phocoenidae of some authors. Fossils are known from Europe, No. America, Asia, and New Zealand.		
	Monodontidae The Narwhal and the White Whale	Late Miocene to Recent	Fossil — 2+ Recent — 2
	REMARKS: Includes two genera, *Monodon* and *Delphinapterus,* each with a single living species, both of which inhabit the Arctic Ocean. Fossil forms are known, but undescribed.		
	Physeteridae The Sperm Whales	Early Miocene to Recent	Fossil — 20+ Recent — 2
	REMARKS: Includes two recent genera, *Physeter* and *Kogia.* There are 3 living species in temperate and tropical seas. Fossils are known from Europe, No. America, So. America, Japan, and Australia.		

†Fossil

Suborder	Family Name	Range In Time	Approximate Number Of Known Genera
	Ziphiidae **The Beaked Whales**	Early Miocene to Recent	Fossil — 14+ Recent — 6

REMARKS: Includes six living genera: *Tasmacetus, Berardius, Indopacetus, Mesoplodon, Ziphius,* and *Hyperoodon.* There are 18 living species which inhabit subpolar, temperate, and tropical seas.
Fossils are known from Europe, No. America, and So. America.

Suborder	Family Name	Range In Time	Approximate Number Of Known Genera
MYSTICETI The Baleen or Whalebone Whales	†**Aetiocetidae**	Late Oligocene	Fossil — 1+ Recent — 0

REMARKS: Includes *Aetiocetus* from the Late Oligocene.
Fossils are found in No. America.
Body resembled the baleen whales, but teeth were present.
This family is extinct; its history was short.

	†**Patriocetidae**	Late Eocene to Late Oligocene	Fossil — 4+ Recent — 0

REMARKS: Includes *Patriocetus* and other fossil genera which are possibly intermediate between the ancient whales and the whalebone whales.
Body resembled the whalebone whales. Nostrils had moved toward the top of the head. Skull showed the beginning of telescoping. Rudimentary teeth were present.
It is not ancestral to modern *Mysticeti.* Fossils are known from Europe and No. America.
This family is extinct.

	†**Cetotheriidae**	Middle Oligocene to Early Pliocene	Fossil — 30± Recent — 0

REMARKS: Includes *Cetotherium* and other fossil genera.
Some reached 10 m. (30 ft.). The neck vertebrae were free; the cranial bones were telescoped; the lower jaw was slender; they had no teeth and possessed a short "baleen filter."
This family included the first true baleen whales and is believed to be an ancestor of modern baleen whales.
Fossils are found in Europe and in No. and So. America.
This family is extinct.

	Eschrichtiidae **The Gray Whales**	Pleistocene to Recent	Fossil — 1 Recent — 1

REMARKS: Includes *Eschrichtius* with one living species.
Fossils are found in the Atlantic Ocean area, although today it lives only in the North Pacific Ocean.

	Balaenopteridae **The Rorquals or Fin-backed Whales**	Late Miocene to Recent	Fossil — 7± Recent — 2

REMARKS: Includes *Megaptera* with one living species, and *Balaenoptera* with five living species.
Extinct genera include *Burtinopsis, Idiocetus, Megapteropsis, Mesoteras, Notiocetus, Paleocetus,* and *Plesiocetus.*
Fossils are known from Europe, No. America, and Asia.
Miocene fossils are scarce; Pliocene fossils are more abundant.
Living species inhabit all oceans.

---

†Fossil.

THE FOSSIL AND RECENT FAMILIES OF WHALES
(Continued)

Suborder	Family Name	Range In Time	Approximate Number Of Known Genera
	Balaenidae **The Right Whales**	Early Miocene to Recent	Fossil — 4+ Recent — 2

REMARKS: Includes *Balaena* with two living species and *Caperea* with one living species.
Extinct genera include *Balaenotus, Balaenula, Morenocetus,* and *Protobalaena.*
Fossils are known from Europe and So. America.
Miocene fossils are scarce; Pliocene fossils are more abundant.
The three living species inhabit the colder temperate and polar seas.

For fossil genera see SIMPSON, GEORGE GAYLORD.
Classification of Mammals. *Amer. Mus. Nat. Hist. Bull.*
85, 1945, pp. 100-105.

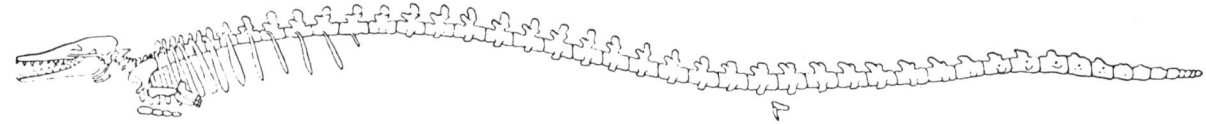

Drawing of a skeleton of *Basilosaurus* sp. (Archeoceti: Basilosauridae) showing the serpentine pattern of the body and the remnants of the vanishing pelvis. After Gidley.

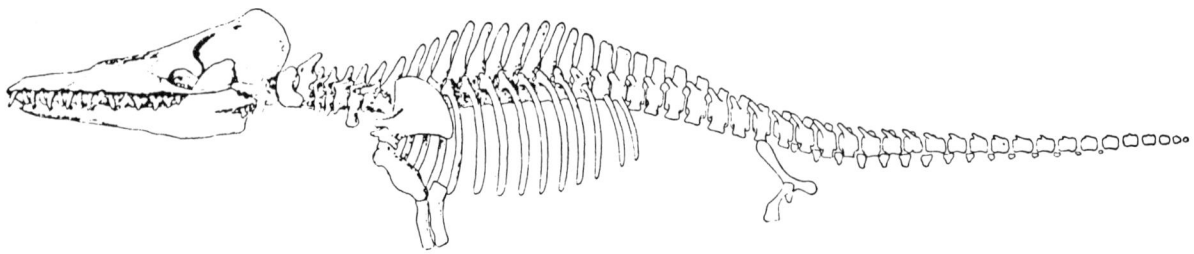

Drawing of a skeleton of a species of *"Zeuglodon"* (Archaeoceti: Basilosauridae) showing its whale-like proportions and the vestiges of the pelvic girdle. After Abel.

Chapter VII

A COMPARISON
OF
TOOTHED WHALES AND WHALEBONE WHALES

Although the toothed whales and the whalebone whales are both groups of the mammals and superficially resemble each other, they do not appear to be closely related. Their differences are so numerous and so significant that it is very doubtful if they ever shared a common ancestor, except in very remote times. After reading the following comparisons of the toothed whales and the whalebone whales, a student is immediately captured by the idea that these two groups of whales are really not closely related at all. It appears that these two groups ascended from two separate ancestors, each of which entered the ancient seas at different times and at different places and thereafter evolved its own group of descendants.

The following tables, adapted from A.V. Yablokov et alii, show the many similarities and differences of these two groups of whales.

Division 1

SOME SIMILARITIES OF
TOOTHED WHALES *(Odontoceti)* AND WHALEBONE WHALES *(Mysticeti)*

Some Anatomical Features of Whales	Remarks
1. General Features	
The body shape	A streamlined body is a feature of all whales.
The tail	The hind legs have atrophied or disappeared. The main organ of locomotion and propulsion has shifted from the legs to the tail.
2. The Skeletal System	
The bones of the face	The facial bones have been elongated.
The neck	The neck bones or cervical vertebrae have been greatly shortened and many are fused to adjoining vertebrae in various combinations.
The sacrum	The sacrum is absent in all whales.
The tail	The tail has been greatly elongated. The caudal spine has been greatly lengthened and bears the V-shaped chevron bones in a row beneath it.
The collar bones or clavicles	The clavicles are absent in all whales.
The front legs	The front legs have been transformed to flippers and all joints are immovable except the shoulder joint.
The finger bones or phalanges	The number of finger bones has multiplied (hyperphalangism).
The pelvis	The pelvis has almost disappeared. Most whales retain small remnants of the ilium, ischium, and pubis.
The hind legs	The hind legs have nearly disappeared. Small, rudimentary remnants of the femur or of the femur and a tibia occasionally appear in some species.
The bone tissue	The bones have become spongy and the spaces within them are filled with oil.
3. The Integument	
The epidermis and hypodermis	These special layers include the blubber.
The hair, sweat glands, and sebaceous (oil) glands	The whalebone whales retain a few scattered vibrissae on the head. Sweat and sebaceous glands are absent.
The mammary glands	These glands have moved to the rear of the abdomen.
4. The Viscera	
The diaphragm	A sloping diaphragm descends from the back toward the front at a gentle slope and then turns downward more abruptly toward the ventral side.
The stomachs	The stomachs are multiple; the compartments number from 3 to 13.
The gall bladder	The gall bladder is absent in all whales.
The caecum	The caecum is present in some species, absent in others.

Some Anatomical Features of Whales	Remarks

5. The Respiratory System

The lungs . . . . The lungs are single-lobed.

The nostrils . . . . The nostrils have moved to the top of the head.

6. The Nervous and Sensory Systems

The olfactory lobes . . . . The olfactory lobes of the brain are reduced in size. The sense of smell is absent or nearly so.

The cerebral cortex of the brain . . . The cerebral cortex is highly differentiated.

The external ear . . . . The external ear is practically absent; only a few vestigial muscles remain.

7. The Reproductive System

The testes . . . . The testes are internal in all male whales.

The penis . . . . The penis is fibro-elastic; the os penis (bone) and the glans penis are absent.

The uterus . . . . The uteri are all two-horned (bicornate).

The vagina . . . . The interior is lined with circular folds.

The corpora lutea . . . . Scars are formed at the site of the rupture of the ovarian follicle; they remain throughout life.

The placenta . . . . The placenta is of a diffuse epitheliochorionic type.

The amniotic fluid . . . . The fluid contains fructose.

8. The Endocrine System

The hypophysis or pituitary gland
of the brain   . . . . This gland is divided into two parts; these divisions are a neuro-hypophysis and an adreno-hypophysis.

Adapted from A.V. Yablokov et alii.

Division 2

SOME DIFFERENCES BETWEEN
TOOTHED WHALES *(Odontoceti)* AND WHALEBONE WHALES *(Mysticeti)*

Anatomical Features of Whales	Toothed Whales *(Odontoceti)*	Whalebone Whales *(Mysticeti)*
1. THE SKELETAL SYSTEM		
Symmetry of the skull	Asymmetrical	Symmetrical
Vomer, temporal, and palatine bones	Development is negligible	Well developed
Pterygoid bone	With a complex system of sinuses	Flat
Margins of the choanae or posterior nares	Formed by pterygoid bone	Formed by palatine bones
Occipital condyles	Face backward	Face upward
Teeth or whalebone present		
In embro	Teeth	Teeth
In adult	Teeth	Whalebone
The wider jawbones	Maxilla	Mandible
Mandibles or lower jaw bones with well-developed mandibular symphysis	Yes	No
Mandibles fused at symphysis	Yes	No
Occlusion or closing of jaws	Complete	Incomplete
Curvature of mandible	Straight or bowed inward	Bowed outward
Hyoid bones	With mobile joints	Massive and solitary
Sternal bones	Several bones	Single bone
Sternal rib segments	Always present	None
Number of ribs articulating with the sternal bones	3+ pairs of ribs, minimum	1st pair of ribs only
Movement of thorax	Mobile	Rigid
Pelvic bones	Columnar	Triangular
Digits in the hand or manus	5	4 or 5 (*Balaena*)
Plates in osseous tissue	General plates present; no macrocircular plates present	Macrocircular plates present
2. THE DIGESTIVE SYSTEM		
Stomach divisions	From 3 to 13	Always 3
Intestine length	Less than 9 times longer than body	Usually over 10 times longer than body
Caecum	Usually absent	Usually present
Colon length compared to entire intestine	10% or more	10% or less
Bile ducts	1	2
Mesentery and its folds	Thick, fine folds	Thin, large folds
3. THE RESPIRATORY SYSTEM		
External blowholes	1	2
Larynx	Tubular	Wide
Larynx with retrolaryngeal sac	Absent	Present
Separation of pharynx	Constant transverse partition	Inconstant separation
Complex supra-cranial air passages	System present	No system present
Tracheal rings	Closed	Open dorsally
Respiratory lung sections	Acinous	Tubular
4. THE CIRCULATORY SYSTEM		
Branches of caudal artery	Pass behind transverse processes	Pass in front of transverse processes
Sphincter muscle on inferior vena cavae	Present	Absent

Anatomical Features of Whales	Toothed Whales *(Odontoceti)*	Whalebone Whales *(Mysticeti)*
5. THE NERVOUS SYSTEM AND THE SENSE ORGANS		
Sensory foveolae (chemo-reception)	At base of tongue	On tip of snout
Ear bones connected to skull	Not directly connected	Directly connected
Ear plug of wax in external auditory meatus	Not present	Present
Echolocation ability	Present	Absent
Sounds emitted	Of wide range, including high frequencies (ultrasonic)	Primarily of lower frequencies including sonic and subsonic frequencies
Sound emission direction	Directional	Non-directional
Sound generated	In the larynx and supra-cranial air sacs	In the larynx and retrolaryngeal sac
System of parotid sinuses	Complex	Simple
Cochlea coils	1.5+ coils	2 to 2.5 coils
Sclera of eye	Thin	Thick
Vibrissae and/or hair in adult	Usually absent, present in foetus	Always present
6. THE EXCRETORY SYSTEM		
Urinary canal	Well developed	Very short
Urinary canal opening	On surface of ridge (crista urethrae)	On surface of urogenital papilla
Bladder size (in cc. per 100 kg. of body weight)	20-50 cc	100-150 cc
7. THE REPRODUCTIVE SYSTEM		
The larger sex	Male	Female
Vaginal ligament	Absent	Present
Plug in cervix uteri during pregnancy	Present	Absent
Ovaries	Smooth, in ovarian sac	Striated, exposed
Ovulations per year (average)	1	2
8. HABITS		
Behavior complexity	Very complex	Not typical
Group social structure	Complex	Simple
Central figure	Adult female	Adult male
Group size	Gathers in small to large groups	Gathers in small groups.
Sexual behavior and play	Complex and diversified	No complex play
9. MISCELLANEOUS		
Food	Squid, fishes, larger animals	Plankton and small fishes
Parasites: the number of genera of helminths specific to the two suborders of whales	23 genera of 47 species	1 genus of 14 species

Adapted from A.V. Yablokov et alii.

—PART TWO—

The Anatomy
of
The Living Whales

—PART TWO—

The Anatomy of the Living Whales

Chapter I

INTRODUCTION

The study of the anatomy of the whales is a very interesting and difficult area in the science of mammalogy. There are really two groups of whales, toothed whales and whalebone whales, which are quite similar in general appearance and shape, but which are really not very closely related. So, in studying the anatomy of whales, a student is really studying the anatomy of two quite different groups of mammals.

Although whales are mammals, their bodies have undergone some very remarkable and very radical changes since they first entered the sea in very ancient times. The loss of the sacrum, the pelvis, and the hind legs together with their supporting muscles, coupled with the backward elongation of the vertebral column and the development of a tail, are among the most unusual and remarkable of all of the many evolutionary developments within the mammals. Add to these the specializations undergone by the front feet, the skull, the respiratory system, the alimentary tract, and nearly all of the other organs and organ systems, and scholars are obliged to conclude that the whales are among the most amazing of all the mammals.

The study of the anatomy of whales is very difficult because the typical mammalian organs and structures are often altered, are not always in their accustomed locations, and are sometimes quite unlike those of other mammals. In addition, the bodies of many whales are so large that they are difficult to obtain, to transport, and to preserve. In most cases, the carcasses of whales, which appear upon beaches, putrify so rapidly that their fleshy parts are not available for study for more than a few hours. For these reasons, more is known about the skeletons of whales than about their fleshy parts.

In the pages which follow, the anatomy of the two great groups of whales (toothed and whalebone) will be presented in a simple fashion beginning with the skeleton. The structure of both the toothed and whalebone whales will be described so that some comparisons may be made of these two groups. The anatomical features of the whale will be compared with other mammals which are more typical of this group and also with the comparable structures in man. This will give the reader a somewhat wider perspective as he or she studies these great mammals.

Chapter II
THE SKELETAL SYSTEM

Division 1
THE AXIAL SKELETON

The skeleton of a whale is the skeleton of a mammal which has undergone some very unusual changes resulting from its adaptations to life in the sea. The skeleton of a whale is therefore not typical of mammals or similar to the skeletons of the mammals with which we are familiar.

In studying the skeleton of any mammal, it is customary to divide this study into two parts as follows:

1) the *axial skeleton,* which begins with the head and which extends posteriorly or backward down the central axis of the body to the tail, *and*

2) the *appendicular skeleton* which includes the appendages.

The *axial skeleton* includes the skull, the vertebral column, the ribs, and the sternum. The *appendicular skeleton* includes the shoulder girdle with the anterior appendages or front legs *and* the pelvic girdle with the posterior appendages or hind legs.

All of these structures, which are typical of the mammals, are found in the whales, although some of them have undergone considerable modification or are missing as a result of their life in the sea.

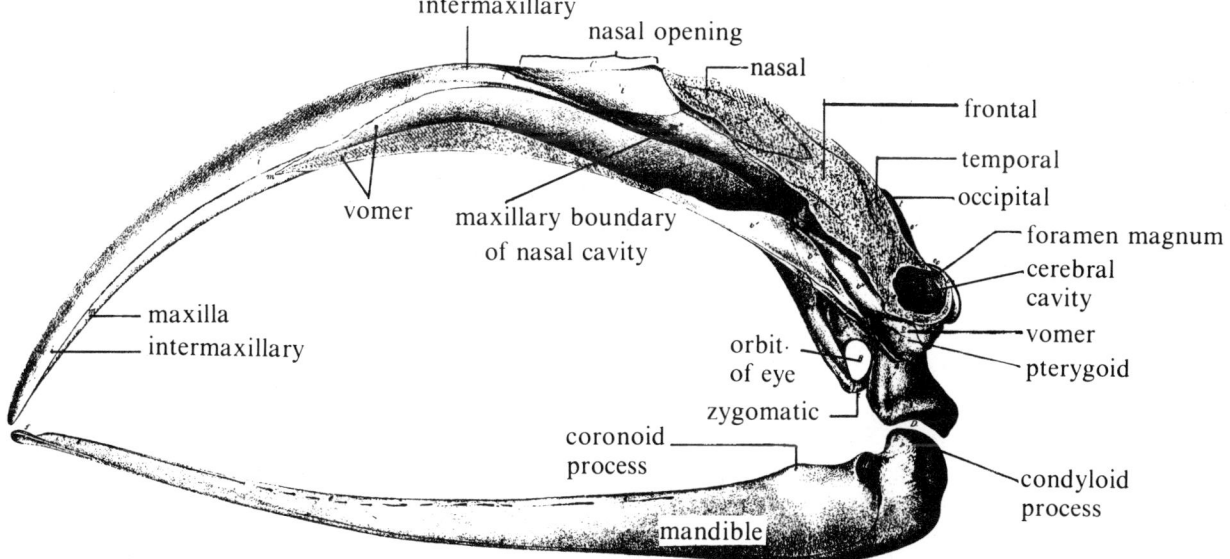

Diagram of the skull of the bowhead whale, *Balaena mysticetus* **(Mysticeti: Balaenidae), in mesial section showing the gigantic development of the jaws to accommodate the whalebone blades.**

From Flower.

Section a
THE SKULL

(1) The Introduction

The skulls of the modern whales have changed in form and shape from the skulls of the ancient mammals which were their ancestors. Their skulls have been squeezed in a front-to-back direction for reasons which are not clearly known. This change is often referred to as the "telescoping of the skull." The cranium of whales and the brain within it are now wider than long; this is a very unusual feature in the mammals and has resulted in changes in the relative size and shape of some of the bones of the cranium. Also, various bones of the face in the whales have been squeezed from front-to-back so that some bones have been forced to slide over or under other bones, thereby disturbing the relationship of these bones as they are usually found in the skulls of other mammals.

In the details of the "telescoping" of the skull, there is a difference between the toothed whales (*Odontoceti*) and the whalebone whales (*Mysticeti*).

In the toothed whales (*Odontoceti*), the anterior bony parts of the skull prefer to override the more posterior parts of the skull. Here the proximal parts of the maxillae spread back over the supra-orbital processes of the frontal bones to the point where they approach and/or meet the supra-occipital bones behind the orbit. The maxillae also spread laterally to roof over the temporal fossae on the sides of the skull.

In the whalebone whales (*Mysticeti*), the posterior bony parts of the skull prefer to override the more anterior parts. Here the occipital and temporal bones have grown forward until the supra-occipital bone approaches the apex of the cranium. The parietal bones have overridden the supra-orbital processes of the frontal bones. The maxillae at their posterior margin simply abut against the supra-orbital process of the frontal bones and do not override it as in the toothed whales.

The cause of this telescoping of the skull is unknown, but some scholars believe that this change was the result of the continual pressure of water against the front of the head caused by swimming. The head was being pushed forward against the water by the vertebrae of the neck and, over millions of years, responded to this pressure by a gradual shifting of the position of the bones of the skull. This shifting of the bones is not a recent development, but was already present in some of the earliest known fossil whales.

The resulting changes in the shape of the skull of whales are easily noted. The cranium or brain box has been shortened so that it is now wider than it is long and the brain within it has also assumed these same proportions.

The nostrils or blow holes have migrated from the front of the face toward the rear and (with some exceptions) now lie much farther backward upon the top of the head.

In the toothed whales (*Odontoceti*), the blowholes have become asymmetrical and the left nostril has developed at the expense of the right nostril. The ancestors of the toothed whales (*Odontoceti*) doubtless had symmetrical blowholes, so the present asymmetry is of quite recent origin and probably developed sometime within the Miocene Epoch (13- to 25,000,000 years ago).

Although the whales possess some features in the anatomy and composition of their skulls which are most unusual and which differ from the skulls of other mammals, they also

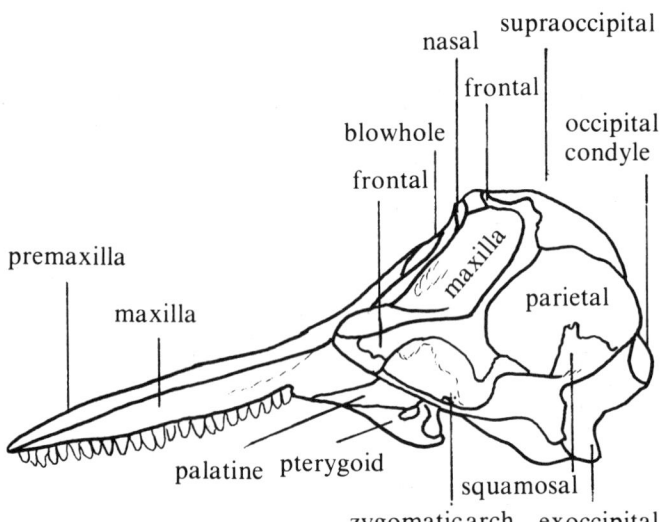

A diagram of the skull and lower jaw of the common bottle-nosed dolphin, *Tursiops truncatus,* in lateral view.

differ among themselves. The toothed whales (*Odontoceti*) with their five families show both similarities and differences when compared with the three families of the whalebone whales (*Mysticeti*). Some of these features* are listed below.

(a) The skulls of whales are basically mammalian in character, but of the two groups, the skulls of the toothed whales (*Odontoceti*) resemble the typical mammalian skull more closely than those of the whalebone whales (*Mysticeti*).

(b) The skulls of both the toothed whales (*Odontoceti*) and the whalebone whales (*Mysticeti*) are usually of great size and are disproportionate to their bodies when compared with other mammals.

(c) In the toothed whales (*Odontoceti*), the skull is asymmetrical; the right half of the facial skeleton is always larger than the left half. This asymmetry is usually not visible or apparent on the ventral side of the skull.

(d) The proportions of the skulls of whales differ from those of other mammals. The facial part of the skull has been greatly extended to form a rostrum composed of the elongated maxillae and premaxillae. Within the toothed whales (*Odontoceti*), this extension is less significant than in the whalebone whales (*Mysticeti*). Within the toothed whales (*Odontoceti*), it is probably most obvious in the beaks of the River Dolphins (*Platanistidae*), the ocean dolphins (*Delphinidae*), and the sperm whales (*Physeteridae*). However, in the whalebones whales (*Mysticeti*), the rostrum has been extended to a great length as a support for the many baleen plates which are suspended from it.

(e) The blow hole or nasal opening (naris; pl., nares) has moved backward as far as possible in both the toothed whales (*Odontoceti*) and the whalebone whales (*Mysticeti*). This backward migration has brought the nostrils up against the brain case and has deformed the two nasal bones and the nasal aperture to the point where they are both vertical in position. The nares are also unequal in size; the aperture of the left nostril is usually slightly larger than the right.

(f) The "telescoping of the skull" has been the greatest anterior to the cranium, where the bones of the face have altered their attachments to the cranium and to adjoining bones. In both groups of whales, the two maxillae and the two premaxillae have spread backward and to the side so as to override the frontal bones.

(g) The two parietal bones have been crowded far to the sides.

(h) The "telescoping" of the bones of the skull has been less severe or marked at the rear of the skull in the toothed whales (*Odontoceti*); here the occipital, parietal, and squamosal bones have not spread over or under their surrounding bones to any extent.

(i) The occipital bones have become flattened and tilted forward in both the toothed whales (*Odontoceti*) and the whalebone whales (*Mysticeti*). In the whalebone whales (*Mysticeti*), the occipital bone has pushed forward to over-ride the two parietal bones and to overhang the inferior part of the two frontal bones.

(j) The single interparietal or post-parietal bone has disappeared in adult whales.

(k) The pterygoid bone (a part of the sphenoid bone) is typically flat in most all mammals, including the whalebone whales *(Mysticeti)*, but it is a very complex bone in the toothed whales *(Odontoceti)*.

(l) The lacrymal bones have become thickened and larger in some of the toothed whales (*Odontoceti*), particularly in some of the species of the beaked whales (*Ziphiidae*).

(m) The ear bones and the mechanism of hearing are vastly different in the toothed whales (*Odontoceti*) and in the whalebone whales (*Mysticeti*).

(n) There are differences between the toothed whales (*Odontoceti*) and the whalebone whales (*Mysticeti*) in the smaller, more complex bones of the face.

(o) A great "frontal basin" has developed in the head of the sperm whale (*Odontoceti: Physteridae: Physeter*) for the reception of the spermaceti organ or case; this development has cramped the cranium and the brain within it.

The skeleton of the head is more complex than the skeleton of any other region of the body. The bones of the head consist of those forming the skull, together with some separate, miscellaneous bones, which, although originally a part of the visceral[1] skeleton, are now associated with the head; these include the lower jaw, the hyoid bones, and the ear bones[2]. For purposes of study, the bones of the skull, about two dozen in number, will be divided into the following four sections: the bones of the cranium, the bones of the face, the bones of the lower jaw, and the hyoid bones.

---

1. The visceral skeleton includes those bones which were originally part of the arches supporting the gills in our evolutionary ancestors. In general, the vertebrates with jaws have seven visceral arches or bars (the mandibular, the hyoid, and five branchial arches) in their embryonic and/or ancestral history.

2. In the mammals, the ear bones are derived from the first two visceral arches as follows:

the malleus is derived from the articular part (plus a small dermal bone) of the 1st or mandibular arch;

the incus is derived from the quadrate part of the 1st or mandibular arch; and

the stapes is derived from the hyomandibular part of the 2nd or hyoid arch.

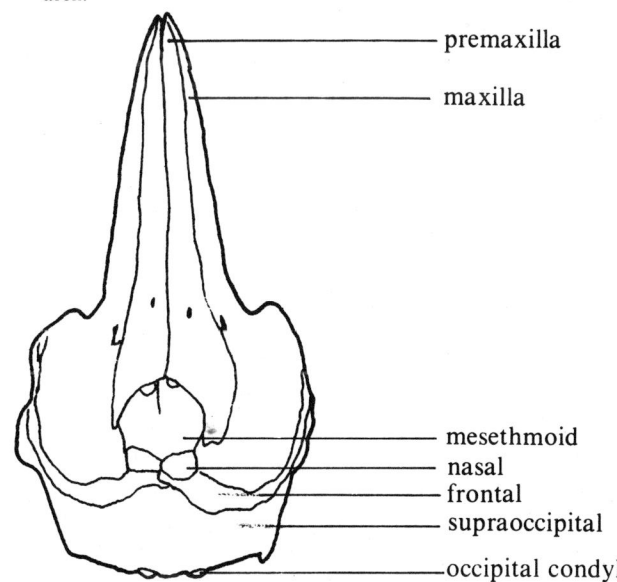

premaxilla
maxilla
mesethmoid
nasal
frontal
supraoccipital
occipital condyle

A diagram of the skull of *Tursiops truncatus* in dorsal view.

---

*From Howell, Yablokov, et alii.

(2) The Bones of the Cranium

The cranium is the box of bone which encloses the brain. It consists of many bones, several of which are thin and flat. The following bones, which comprise the cranium of most mammals, will be briefly described below:

(a) one occipital bone   (f) one sphenoid bone
(b) two parietal bones   (g) one pre-sphenoid bone[3]
(c) one inter-parietal bone   (h) one pterygoid bone
(d) two temporal bones   (i) one ethmoid bone
(e) two frontal bones

A diagram with labels: premaxilla, maxilla, palatine, pterygoid, jugal, frontal, zygomatic, vomer, basioccipital, exoccipital

A diagram of the skull of *Tursiops truncatus* in ventral view.

Reprinted by permission of Louisiana State University Press from *The Mammals of Louisiana and Its Adjacent Waters* by George H. Lowery, Jr. Copyright © 1974 by George H. Lowery, Jr.

(a) The Occipital Bone. The occipital bone *(os occipitale)* is a single bone, lying at the base of the skull where it articulates with the first vertebra *(atlas)* of the neck. It surrounds the large opening *(foramen magnum)* through which the spinal cord passes enroute from the brain to the neck. The occipital bone is composed of four parts which are variously fused: these include a basi-occipital bone below, two ex-occipital bones on the sides, and one supra-occipital bone above.

In the whales, the occipital bone has become flattened in both the toothed whales *(Odontoceti)* and the whalebone whales *(Mysticeti)* and has been greatly tilted forward. In the sperm whales *(Odontoceti: Physeteridae)* and in some of the beaked whales *(Odontoceti: Ziphiidae)*, the occipital bone is vertical in position. In the sperm whales *(Physeteridae)*, this is due in part to the presence of the great "facial or frontal basin" which occupies the upper part of the face. In the whalebone whales *(Mysticeti)*, the occipital bone is less prominent than in the toothed whales *(Odontoceti)*, but the forward tilting of the occipital bone is more pronounced in this group than in the toothed whales *(Odontoceti)*, and is greater than in any other group of the mammals.

The occipital bones are reduced in size in the rorquals

---

3. Not described.

(Mysticeti: Balaenopteridae), especially the lateral parts "which are functionally replaced by the parietal and sphenoid bones" (Yablokov). The occipital bones are not visible in the ventral view of the skull of the right whales *(Mysticeti: Balaenidae)*. The two occipital condyles at the base of the skull, which form part of the "joint" with the vertebrae of the neck, are very large in whales, although they are probably no larger than in a land animal of comparable size if one existed.

(b) The Parietal Bones. The parietal bones *(os parietale)* are paired bones which lie at the top and upper side of the cranium (above and behind the ears in man) and which form the principal covering of the sides and top of the brain. These bones are thin, smooth, and curved and join together in the midline on the top of the cranium. Within the whales, the parietal bones have been depressed laterally and do not assume great importance.

(c) The Inter-parietal Bone. The inter-parietal bone or post-parietal bone *(os inter-parietale, os incae)* is a single, small, smooth, triangular, arrow-shaped bone which forms a small portion of the roof of the cranium. It lies at the rear of the cranium between the parietal bones on the sides and the supra-occipital bone to the rear.

The inter-parietal bone is not apparent in adult whales and is regarded as absent in all *Odontoceti* and *Mysticeti*. However, the inter-parietal bone is present in the embryos of the rorquals *(Mysticeti: Balaenopteridae)*, but merges with the supra-occipital bone in the course of its development.

(d) The Temporal Bones. The two temporal bones *(os temporale)* form the lower sides of the cranium. They are very complex bones and consist of three parts or portions:

- a **squamous portion** *(squamosa)*, lying between the ear and the cheek in man, which includes the zygomatic process with its mandibular fossa for the articulation of the inner end (condyloid process) of the lower jaw;
- a **petrous portion** *(petrosa)*, lying in the area of the ear and including the bones surrounding the organs of hearing; and
- a **mastoid portion** *(mastoidea)*, lying low in the lateral wall of the cranium.

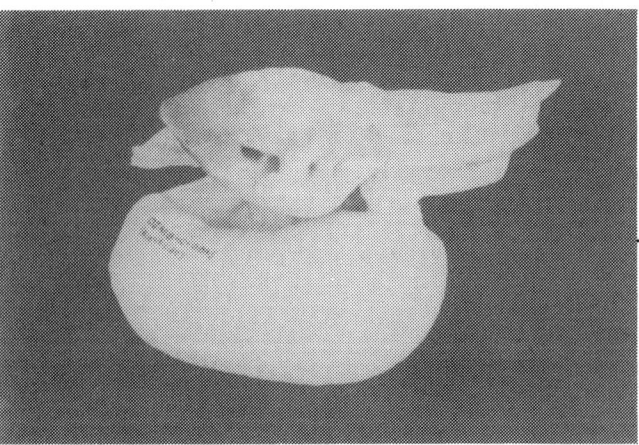

Photo of the interior face of the right periotic bone with the tympanic bulla attached. It is from a lesser rorqual or minke whale, *Balaenoptera acutorostrata* (Mysticeti: Balaenopteridae).

Ore. Inst. Mar. Biol.

In man, the temporal bones are about as described above.

In the whales, the temporal bones are well developed and are among the principal bones enclosing the cranium on the sides. They are better developed in the whalebone whales (*Mysticeti*) than in the toothed whales (*Odontoceti*), although they are well developed in the river dolphins (*Odontoceti: Platanistidae*) and where, as usual, they enter into the formation of the zygomatic arch.

In the whalebone whales (*Mysticeti*), the temporal bones are among the principal bones enclosing the cranium of the rorquals (*Balaenopteridae*). The zygomatic process, extending from the temporal bone to form the posterior part of the zygomatic arch, is large in the rorquals (*Balaenopteridae*) and may account for one-half of the weight of the temporal bone.

(e) The Frontal Bones. The two frontal bones (*os frontale*) form the upper, forward section or roof of the cranium and a portion of its anterior surface; they meet in the midline of the forehead and lie in the area between the nasal bones and the parietal bones.

In man, they have united to form a single bone.

In the whales, the frontal bones are well developed, particularly in the toothed whales (*Odontoceti*), where they are comparatively larger than in the whalebone whales (*Mysticeti*) and where they form an arch curving forward; they are especially enlarged in the family of the ocean dolphins (*Odontoceti: Delphinidae*).

In the whalebone whales (*Mysticeti*), the frontal bones are relatively smaller than in the toothed whales (*Odontoceti*) and form an arch which curves backward in the right whales (*Balaenidae*). The supra-orbital processes of the frontal bones are strongly developed in the rorquals (*Balaenopteridae*) and, in this group, are large, wide, and heavy.

(f) The Sphenoid Bone. The sphenoid bone (*os sphenoidale*) is a single, complex bone which forms a part of the lower, forward wall of the cranium, part of the nasal cavity, and part of the orbit of each eye. Its divisions include a basisphenoid and two, lateral, wing-like ali-sphenoids. In some animals, a pre-sphenoid bone and a pterygoid bone (the internal pterygoid plate of the sphenoid bone) are identified and described in this complex.

In man, the sphenoid bone is a very irregularly-formed, wedge-shaped bone which lies at the base of the skull.

In the toothed whales (*Odontoceti*), the sphenoid bone lies just forward of the basi-occipital and adjacent to it.

In the whalebone whales (*Mysticeti*), the sphenoid bone is small and is overgrown by the vomer bone. It is greatly reduced in size in the rorquals (*Balaenopteridae*) and is often invisible because it is covered by the excessive growth of the vomer.

(g) The Pre-sphenoid Bone. The pre-sphenoid bone is not described here.

(h) The Pterygoid Bone. The pterygoid bone is classified both as an independent bone and also as a part (*processus pterygoideus*) of the sphenoid bone. It is a single, complex, flat plate which occurs in nearly all terrestrial and marine animals. It is present in all whales and within them is more apparent and pronounced in the toothed whales (*Odontoceti*).

In the toothed whales (*Odontoceti*), the pterygoid bone is strongly developed when compared with other mammals. It is well developed in the beaked whales (*Ziphiidae*) and is larger than the palate bone in all ocean dolphins (*Delphinidae*). In the toothed whales (*Odontoceti*), the pterygoid

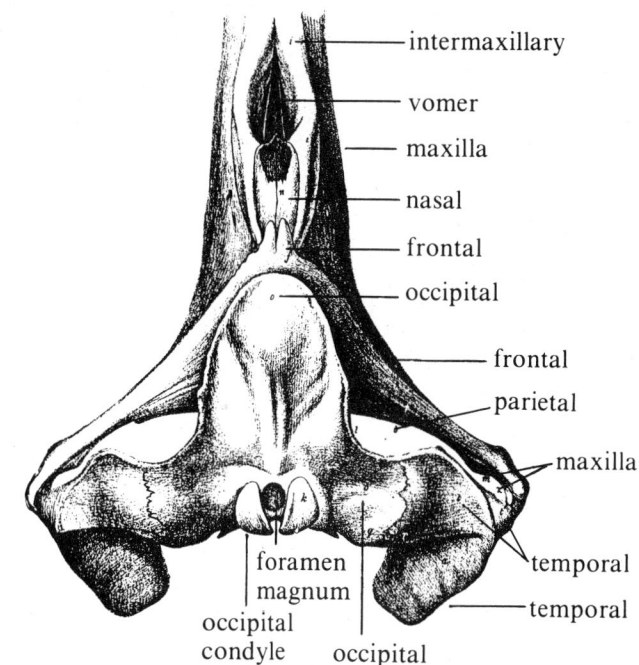

Diagram of the skull of the bowhead whale, *Balaena mysticetus* (Mysticeti: Balaenidae), in dorsal view.

From Flower.

bone often forms the bony margin of the choanae (posterior nares) in the back of the mouth; in the whalebone whales (*Mysticeti*), this margin is formed by the palate bone.

(i) The Ethmoid Bone. The ethmoid bone (*os ethmoidale*) is a single, small bone of complex shape which closes the front of the cranium and occupies much of the nasal cavity. It consists of four parts:

First. The single cribriform plate (*lamina cribrosa*) is the posterior portion of the ethmoid bone. It forms a portion of the forward wall of the cranium and contains the many perforations (*cribriform foramina*) through which the nerves pass enroute from the brain to the lining of the nose.

Second. The single mesethmoid or perpendicular lamina forms a large part of the vertical, median nasal septum which divides the nasal cavity into its right and left components.

Third and Fourth. Two ethmoturbinate or lateral ethmoid bones form a large portion of the lateral walls of the nasal cavity. They each have a cranial portion and a caudal portion, each of which may bear thin, scroll-like bones which are known as the turbinated bones.

The turbinate bones are confusing because they are known in man and in other mammals by different sets of names and because they all border or project into the nasal cavity as parts of different bones.

In the whales, the ethmoid bone remains in the front of the cranial cavity, but the cribriform plate has been altered because the olfactory nerves, formerly passing through it, have degenerated with the sense of smell.

In the toothed whales *(Odontoceti),* the cribriform plate is usually without perforations as in the ocean dolphins *(Delphinidae);* however, it is reported that a single pair of perforations remains in the cribriform plate in some of the beaked whales *(Ziphiidae: Hyperoodon).*

In the whalebone whales (*Mysticeti*), small perforations

still remain in the cribriform plate and small nerves still pass through them. This may indicate the lingering presence of an olfactory sense, although it is greatly reduced or possibly absent.

(3) The Bones of the Face

In the mammals, the bones of the face lie forward of the cranium and above the cavity of the mouth. They are nearly all of complex shape, number more than a dozen, and in most mammals, include the following:

    (a) two nasal bones
    (b) one vomer bone
    (c) two inferior turbinated bones
    (d) two lacrymal bones
    (e) two malar bones
    (f) two palate bones
    (g) two maxillae bones
    (h) two premaxillae bones

(a) The Nasal Bones. The nasal bones (*os nasale*) are two, small, elongated bones which meet in the midline on the surface of the face, where they form part of the roof of the nasal cavity.

In man, they form the bridge of the nose. They also bear the small nasoturbinate bones usually called the superior nasal conchae in man.

In the whales, the nasal bones have been both moved and modified. They have moved far to the rear of the face, have been reduced in size, and now lie just behind and adjacent to the blowholes.

In the toothed whales (*Odontoceti*), the nasal bones are almost vertical in position, although their normal position is a sloping cover for the nasal cavity.

In the whalebone whales (*Mysticeti*), the nasal bones have been reduced in size and also lie just behind and adjacent to the blowholes.

The nasal bones, when viewed from above, are generally rectangular in outline, lie side by side, and are slightly wider at their anterior ends. One set (of 2) of these bones in an adult blue whale (*Balaenoptera musculus*), measured about 27.3 cm. (10.75 in.) in anterior width and about 25.4 cm. (10 in.) in posterior width; their length was judged to be about 30.5 cm. (12 in.).

(b) The Vomer Bone. The vomer bone (*vomer*) is a single bone of complex shape which is situated in the back of the nose. It is closely associated with the ethmoid bone and lies below this region.

In man, a portion of the vomer bones forms the lower and posterior, bony part of the nasal septum (*septum nasi*).

The vomer bone, although sometimes of obscure and uncertain identity, has become greatly enlarged in the whales with the development of the rostrum; it reaches its greatest development in the whalebone whales (*Mysticeti*).

In the toothed whales (*Odontoceti*), the vomer is present in both young and adult animals, where it develops an attachment at its posterior end to the pre-sphenoid and the basi-occipital bones of the cranium. It is greatly extended in a lengthwise direction, forms the bony septum which divides the nasal cavity, and extends forward to end between the two maxillae bones of the upper jaw. It is one of the weight-bearing bones of the rostrum, although it carries a somewhat lesser load in the ocean dolphins (*Delphinidae*). In the narwhal (*Monodontidae: Monodon*), the vomer is large and covers the anterior part of the sphenoid bone. In the beaked whales (*Ziphiidae*), the vomer bone can usually be seen from both the top and bottom of the skull.

In the whalebone whales (*Mysticeti*), the vomer is present, identifiable, and strongly developed. At its forward end, the vomer is greatly enlarged and forms one of the principal weight-bearing bones of the skull of rorquals (*Balaenopteridae*). At its rear, the vomer meets the occipital bone and partially covers it to a small degree.

(c) The Inferior Turbinated Bones or maxillo-turbinal bones. The inferior turbinated bones (*concha nasalis in-*

The Turbinated Bones

Names Used For		Remarks	The Condition In	
Most Mammals	Man		Odontoceti Toothed Whales	Mysticeti Whalebone Whales
1. Nasoturbinate Bone or Superior Turbinated Bone	Superior Nasal Concha or Concha Nasalis Superior	It is a process of the nasal bone (*os nasale*).	Vestigial	Reduced in size. Persists as a vestige in the nasal passages.
2. Ethmoturbinate Bone or Middle Turbinated Bone	Middle Nasal Concha or Concha Nasalis Media	It is a process of the ethmoid bone (*os ethmoidale*). It has a cranial portion and a caudal portion with several scroll bones.	Absent or vestigial	Reduced in size. Persists as a vestige in the nasal passages.
3. Maxilloturbinate Bone or Inferior Turbinated Bone	Inferior Nasal Concha or Concha Nasalis Inferior	This is a separate, independent bone which in man articulates with the maxilla, the ethmoid, the lacrymal, and the palatine bones. There are two bones in man.	Reduced in size. Persists as a vestige in the nasal passages.	Reduced in size. Persists as a vestige in the nasal passages.

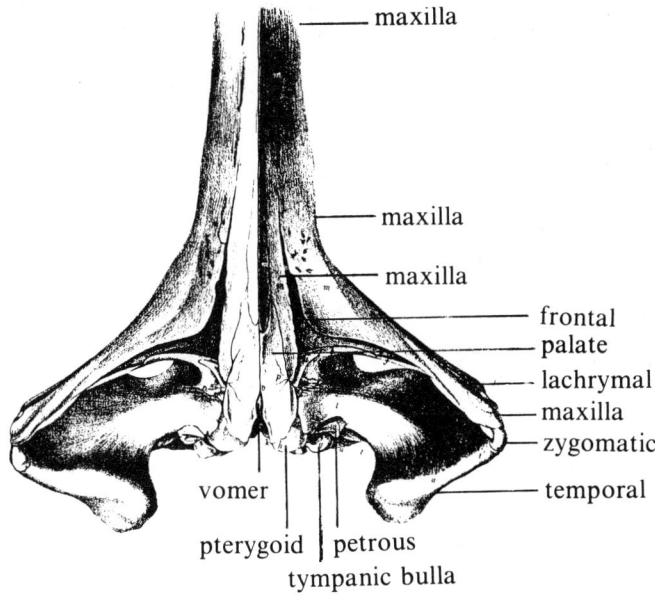

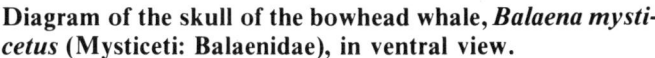

Diagram of the skull of the bowhead whale, *Balaena mysti-cetus* (Mysticeti: Balaenidae), in ventral view.
From Flower.

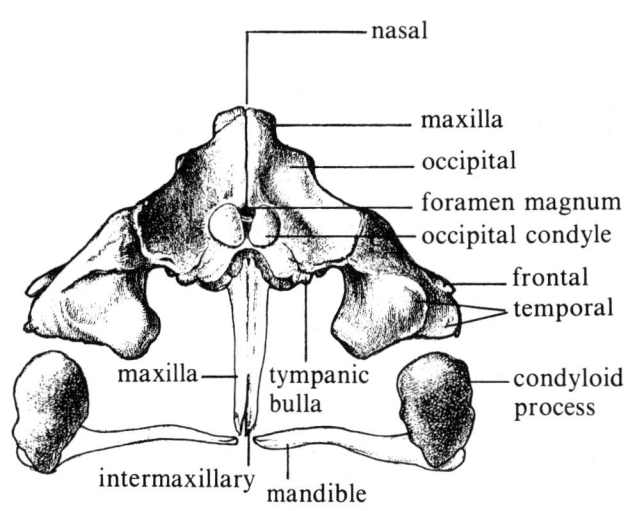

Diagram of the skull and lower jaw bones of the bowhead whale, *Balaena mysticetus* (Mysticeti: Balaenidae), in rear view.
From Flower.

ferior) of mammals are two, thin, paired, porous, cancellous bones of complex shape which are attached to the maxillae and which form a part of the outer wall of the nasal cavity.

In man, the inferior turbinated bones lie along the outer wall of the two nasal fossae or chambers.

In the whales these bones are not as prominent as in other mammals and are proportionally reduced in size.

In the toothed whales (*Odontoceti*), the inferior turbinated bones are reduced in size and persist only as traces.

In the baleen whales *(Mysticeti)*, the inferior turbinated bones are also reduced in size and persist as vestiges in the nasal passages.

(d) The Lacrymal Bones. The lacrymal bones (*os lachrymale*) are two small, very thin paired bones of the face which lie on the medial side of the bony orbit of the eye. Their exterior surface faces into the orbit of the eye and their interior surface faces into the nasal cavity.

In man, they are situated, one on each side of the face, between the nose and the orbital cavity of the eye. They form a part of the canal through which the lacrymal tear ducts pass enroute to the nose.

No special mention is made here of the lacrymal bones in whales, although they are described as hypertrophied (overgrown) in the beaked whales (*Odontoceti: Ziphiidae*).

(e) The Malar Bone. The malar, jugal, or zygomatic bones (*os zygomaticum*) are two heavy, paired, somewhat elongated bones which lie at the sides of the face. Their anterior ends articulate with the upper jaw bones (*maxillae*) and their posterior ends attach to the zygomatic process of the squamous portion of the temporal bones. Between these ends, the malar bone passes beside the eye, thereby forming a portion of the side and back of the bony orbit of the eye.

In the whales, the malar bone is present and well developed and forms the anterior part of the zygomatic arch; this bone extends backward from the maxilla in the front to the zygomatic process extending outward from the squamous portion of the temporal bone. This bone is larger proportionately in the toothed whales (*Odontoceti*) than in the whalebone whales (*Mysticeti*). Within the whalebone whales (*Mysticeti*), the malar bone is larger in the right whales (*Balaenidae*) than in the rorquals (*Balaenopteridae*).

(f) The Palate Bones. The palate bones (*os palatinum*) are two, medium-sized, irregularly-shaped bones which lie above the mouth cavity and toward the back of the face. They derive their name from the fact that they form a part of the hard palate of the roof of the mouth.

The hard palate of most mammals is variously composed of horizontal extensions of three pairs of adjoining bones which meet in the midline to form the roof of the mouth. The anterior portion of the hard palate is formed in part by the two premaxillae or inter-maxillary bones; the larger, central portion is formed by the two maxillae; and the posterior portion is formed by the two palate bones.

In man, the palate bones are roughly L-shaped and form the back part of the roof of the mouth; they also form part of the floor and outer wall of the nasal chamber or fossa and a portion of the floor of the bony orbit of the eye.

In the whales, the palate bones are moderately developed. They are less developed in the toothed whales (*Odontoceti*) and more strongly developed in the whalebone whales (*Mysticeti*).

In the toothed whales (*Odontoceti*), the palate bones are generally reduced in size throughout the group. However, the palate bones are reported as very well developed in the goose-beaked whale (*Ziphiidae: Ziphius*), but are less well developed in the other species of this family.

In the whalebone whales (*Mysticeti*), the palate bones form a plate-like portion of a small hard palate. The palate bones also form the bony margins of the choanae or posterior nares, which in the toothed whales (*Odontoceti*) are most often formed by the pterygoid portion of the sphenoid bone. In all rorquals (*Balaenopteridae*), the palate bone is larger than the pterygoid bone.

(g) The Maxillae. The maxillary bones (*maxilla; pl., maxillae*) more commonly known as the upper jaw bones, are two, large, paired, irregularly-shaped bones which form a part of the front of the face. They lie above and beside the mouth and for this reason form a part of the roof and sides of the interior of the mouth. They usually bear the teeth of the upper jaw, although, in some mammals, teeth are also born on the premaxillae.

In man, the two maxillae usually unite before birth to form a single bone which we know as the upper jaw. Each half of this united maxilla supplies a horizontal extension which meets its opposite extension in the midline of the roof of the mouth to form the greater part of the hard palate. The lower, anterior portion of each half of the maxilla is known as the alveolar process. Together, these two alveolar processes bear the sixteen upper teeth, of which eight teeth are on each side; these eight teeth include two incisors, one canine, two premolars, and three molars. Other portions of the maxillae form part of the floor and anterior wall of the nasal chamber or fossa, the paired, scroll-like maxilloturbinates or ventral nasal conchae,* and a part of the floor of the bony orbit of each eye.

In the whales, the two maxillary bones have undergone considerable change from the maxillae found in other mammals. They still comprise a very important part of the face and, in addition, have grown forward so that they now comprise one of the important bones of the rostrum. They are greatly elongated anteriorly and, at their posterior end, have spread out over the brain case in both toothed and whalebone whales. The maxillary sinus associated with these bones in mammals is present in the whales in a greatly reduced and rudimentary form.

In the toothed whales (*Odontoceti*), the maxillae form a large and important part of the rostrum, although they vary considerably in the different families and genera. In some species, including the killer whales (*Delphinidae: Orcinus*), the rostrum is strong, robust, and firmly attached to the cranium. In some of the ocean dolphins (*Delphinidae: Tursiops*), the rostrum, including the maxillae and the premaxillae, is quite thin and somewhat frail. In the river dolphins (*Platanistidae: Platanista*), the maxillae are placed very close together and have well-developed maxillary crests upon them. Maxillary crests are also well developed in the beaked whales (*Ziphiidae: Hyperoodon*). The most amazing development of the maxillae in the toothed whales *(Odontoceti)* is their backward progression, where they have spread over the brain case and pushed upward over the frontal bones.

In the whalebone whales (*Mysticeti*), the maxillae are unusually long and form a portion of the rostrum of the upper jaw from which the rows of baleen plates are suspended; the maxillae are also very important parts of the structure which supports these plates. Considering the size of the upper jaw and the weight which it is expected to carry, it is regarded by some scholars as very fragile structurally and its attachment to the skull as weak mechanically. At their posterior ends, the maxillae have pushed backward against the skull and have pushed over the frontal bones and, in addition, have pushed some distance beneath them.

---

*Same as inferior nasal conchae in man.

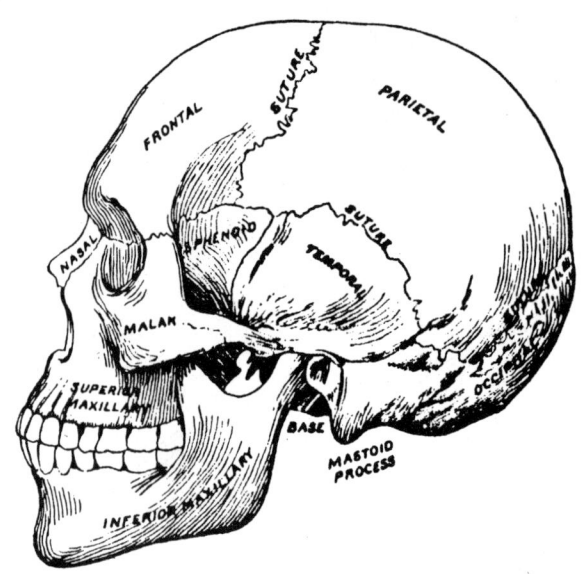

A diagram of the human skull in lateral view, showing the surface bones.

From Pope.

The whalebone plates (baleen) are a new and additional structure (neomorph) which was not present in the ancient, ancestral whales. They consist of many fused tubules of a fibrous material (*keratin*) which originates in the epidermis and which grows downward from it. These plates are suspended from the palate and the great forward extension (or rostral process) of the maxillae.

(h) The Premaxillae. The premaxillary or inter-maxillary bones (*os incisivum*) in mammals are two small paired bones which occupy a median position, side-by-side, at the very front of the upper jaw, between the expanded anterior ends of the maxillae. The premaxillae bear the incisor teeth in mammals and form the anterior portion of the hard palate in the roof of the mouth.

In man, the premaxillary bones have ceased to be independent bones as in most vertebrates and have become fused in the adult with the adjoining maxillae.

In the whales, the premaxillae are closely associated with the maxillae and, like them, are also greatly elongated; these four bones, two maxillae and two premaxillae, have joined together to form the major part of the rostrum.

In the toothed whales (*Odontoceti*), the premaxillae are exceedingly long and form one of the principal components of the rostrum.

In the whalebone whales (*Mysticeti*), the premaxillae are also exceedingly long and slender. At their anterior ends, they extend forward with the maxillae to form a part of the great rostrum of the rorquals (*Balaenopteridae*) and other species and, at their posterior ends, have pushed up over the two frontal bones of the brain case in the same manner as the maxillae.

(4) The Bones of the Lower Jaw

The lower jaw or mandible (*mandibulum; pl., -ula*) of mammals is composed of two paired bones which lie lengthwise beneath the mouth and face and which meet in front of the face at the midline below the mouth where they form the "chin." The right and left jawbones are usually united through fusion where they meet in front at the chin; this

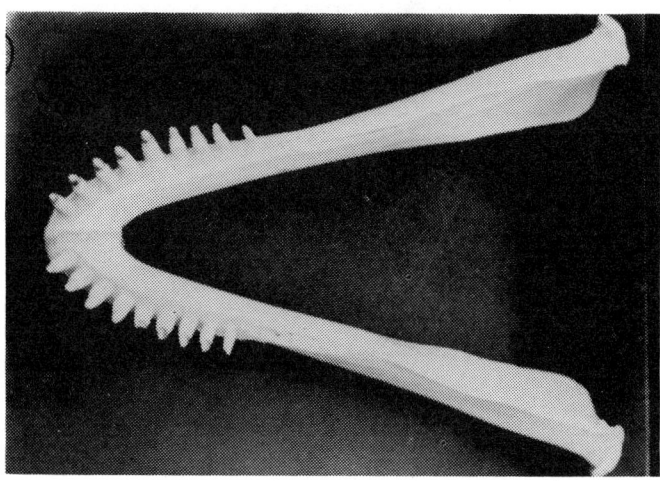

The lower jaw of a pilot whale, *Globicephala* sp. in dorsal view.

Photo by Michael Graybill at Humboldt State Univ.

point of union is called the mandibular symphysis (*symphysis mandibulae*). It is of varying length and the fusion there of the two jawbones is of varying completeness and strength.

The upper or alveolar border of each lower jawbone bears teeth, although not all mammals have teeth in their lower jawbones.

In man, the two bones of the lower jaw are firmly fused together in front at the mandibular symphysis, thereby combining the right and left jawbones into a single unit. In man, the lower jawbones, like the upper jawbones above them, bear two sets of teeth. The first is temporary (deciduous) and includes two incisors, one canine, and two molars on each side; the second set is a permanent set and includes two incisors, one canine, two premolars, and three molars on each side.

In man, the posterior end of each jawbone bears two vertical processes (ramus) or projections. The posterior projection, known as the condyloid process, projects upward and articulates with the mandibular fossa of the zygomatic portion of the temporal bone to form the "joint" between the jawbone and the skull. A second ramus, known as the coronoid process, is located slightly forward of the condyloid process and serves as the attachment for the muscles which elevate the lower jaw.

In the whales, the mandibles or lower jawbones have changed greatly from the form and shape found in their ancient ancestors. In general, the mandibles have become greatly elongated in the whales. The condyloid process, which forms the "joint" between the jawbone and the skull and which fits into the mandibular fossa of the temporal bone, has become reduced in both size and height in both the toothed whales (*Odontoceti*) and the whalebone whales (*Mysticeti*).

In the toothed whales (*Odontoceti*), the mandibles have lengthened to accommodate the long rows of teeth, although some species, including the pilot whales (*Delphinidae: Globicephala*), have very short jaws. In general, the mandibles of the toothed whales (*Odontoceti*) have become very weak in comparison to the size of their skulls or the skulls of comparable land mammals, except perhaps in those species which are aggressive hunters (*Delphinidae: Pseudorca, Globicephala, Orcinus*) and those species of the beaked whales (*Ziphiidae: Mesoplodon*) which bear "tusks" in their jaws.

In the whalebone whales (*Mysticeti*), the lower jaws have become very long in order to accommodate the long rows of baleen plates hanging downward from their upper jaws. Their lower jaws have lost their teeth, have become rounded, gigantic, and bowed outward at their centers; they have also given up the union at the mandibular symphysis (*symphysis mandibulae*), where each mandible unites with the mandible of the opposite side; so today the lower jawbones of these whales no longer unite or even touch in front at the chin.

(5) The Hyoid Bones

In the mammals, the hyoid apparatus or hyoid bones (*os hyoideum*) lie suspended in the flesh at the back of the throat; they consist of a single, central, transverse bone called the basihyal, plus a variety of attached extending bones. Usually, the right and left ends of the basihyal bone each bear two branches or horns (*cornu;* pl., *cornua*). The greater branches or horns, consisting of one bone each, project posteriorly; they are called the thyrohyal bones because they attach by ligaments to the thyroid cartilage of the larynx. The lesser or anterior branches or horns consist of a series of small bones on each end of the basihyal bone; proceeding from ventral to dorsal, these bones are named the ceratohyal, the epihyal, the stylohyal, and the tympanohyal bones. Each of these two anterior branches or horns connects by its terminal tympanohyal bone to its respective tympanic bulla of the skull. In some species of mammals, this series of bones is incomplete and is replaced, all or in part, by cartilage and/or ligaments.

In man, the hyoid appears as a single U-shaped bone which supports the tongue and lies in the upper throat just above the "Adam's Apple." This hyoid bone, consisting of five parts, is located in a horizontal position at the base of the tongue. The body or basihyal bone bears a greater cornu at each side which projects backward; this is the thyrohyal bone. In addition, the lesser cornu, composed of the ceratohyal bone, projects backward and upward on each side.

The hyoid bones are present in all whales, are well developed, and appear in various configurations. They are located in the midline of the body, beneath the larynx, and below the base of the skull. These bones are difficult to locate and to identify; in addition, they vary between the various families and genera of whales in their number, their shape, and their degree of ossification.

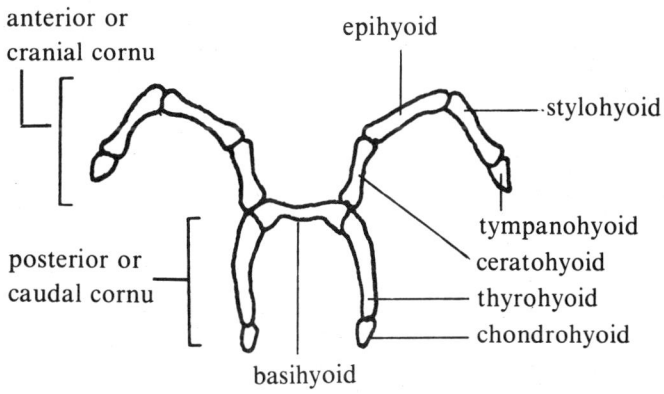

Hyoid Bones of the Cat

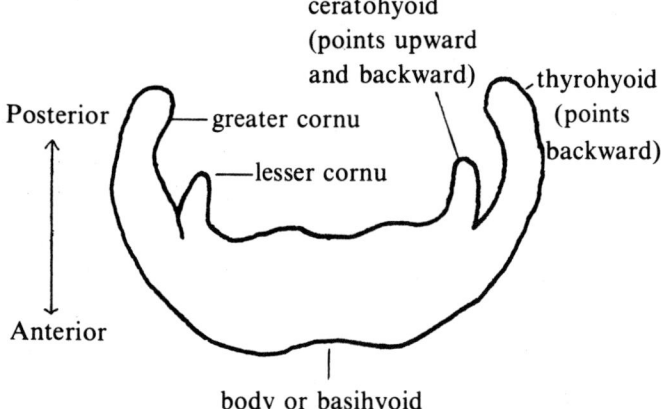

ceratohyoid
(points upward
and backward)

thyrohyoid
(points
backward)

Posterior

greater cornu

lesser cornu

Anterior

body or basihyoid

Hyoid Apparatus of Man

In the toothed whales (*Odontoceti*), the hyoid apparatus consists of the central basihyal bone plus remnants of both the anterior and posterior cornua. In some genera, the two posterior cornua (thyrohyal bones) are fused with the central basihyal bone. The anterior cornua usually retain one or more bony segments adjacent to the basihyal bone.

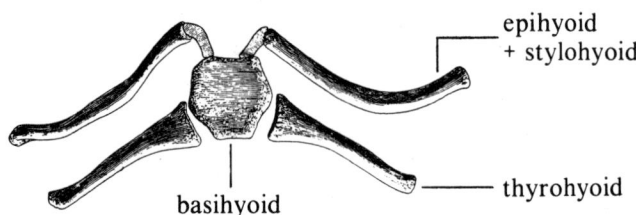

epihyoid
+ stylohyoid

basihyoid

thyrohyoid

Diagram of the hyoid bones of *Basilosaurus cetoides* (Archaeoceti: Basilosauridae) in ventral view.

From Kellogg.

In the whalebone whales (*Mysticeti*), the hyoid apparatus usually consists of a single bone which represents the fusion of the basihyal bone and the two greater cornua consisting of the two posteriorly-projecting thyrohyal bones. This single resulting bone varies within the baleen whales, but most commonly exhibits lateral, wing-like extensions. The two anterior branches or cornua may consist of one bone each, plus their continuing cartilage and/or ligaments, or the bony parts of these anterior cornua may be entirely missing.

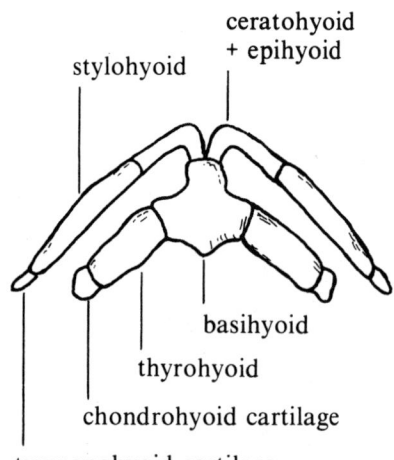

ceratohyoid
+ epihyoid

stylohyoid

basihyoid

thyrohyoid

chondrohyoid cartilage

tympanohyoid cartilage

The hyoid bones of the Narwhal *(Monodon monoceros).*

Section b
THE VERTEBRAL COLUMN

The vertebral column consists of a linear series of vertebrae which extend from the base of the skull to the end of the tail. The vertebrae which comprise this series differ somewhat in their structure and function and therefore are divided for convenience into five regions; these vertebrae are named and numbered according to their position in this series. These regions are named as follows:

cervical	(neck)
thoracic or dorsal	(thorax)
lumbar	(waist)
sacral	(lower back)
caudal	(tail)

The initial letters of these words are used to indicate these regions when recording the number of vertebrae in each region. For example, the domestic cat which has 42 or 43 vertebrae might be described as follows: C 7 + D 13 + L 7 + S 3 + C 22-23 = 42-43. In the whales, there are only four regions in the vertebral column. Since the whales have greatly altered the entire pelvis and hind legs, the vertebrae which formerly formed the sacrum are no longer fused together; they have resumed their generalized structure, are almost indistinguishable from the adjoining vertebrae, and are now counted with the lumbar vertebrae.

It is helpful here to review these five sections of the vertebral column in the whales.

The cervical vertebrae include all of the vertebrae between the skull and the vertebrae which bears the first rib; they are always 7 in number, are reduced in length, and are often fused together in various combinations in the whales.

The thoracic vertebrae are those which bear ribs at their anterior border; although these ribs are associated with a particular vertebra, they usually occupy a position nearly midway between their particular vertebra and the one which is just anterior to it. The thoracic vertebrae end with the last rib.

The lumbar-sacral vertebrae begin with that vertebra which has no ribs and end just anterior to the 1st caudal vertebrae which has a pair of chevron bones beneath it.

The sacral vertebrae cannot be counted accurately in whales, so they are combined with those of the lumbar region and a combined count is given for these two regions.

The caudal vertebrae begin with the first vertebra to have two chevron bones beneath it and continue posteriorly to the end of the tail.

In reviewing the total number of vertebrae in all living species of whales, scholars find that the number of vertebrae in the *Odontoceti*, in general, exceeds in number those of the *Mysticeti*. The greatest total number seems to occur in Dall's

White-flanked Porpoise *(Delphinidae: Phocoenoides dalli)* with about 97 vertebrae and in the Right Whale Dolphin (*Delphinidae: Lissodelphis borealis*) with about 88 vertebrae, both within the *Odontoceti.*

Within the *Mysticeti,* the Pigmy Right Whale (*Balaenidae: Caperea marginata*) with about 41 vertebrae has the fewest number.

The following paragraphs describe the four regions (cervical, thoracic, lumbar, and caudal) of the vertebral column found in the whales.

(1) The Vertebrae of the Cervical Region

Although the standard number of vertebrae in the necks of all mammals is seven, these seven vertebrae vary widely in length, freedom of movement, and other features. Among the mammals, the giraffes have the seven longest cervical vertebrae, while those of the whales are undoubtedly the most compressed in length and restricted in movement.

Among both the *Odontoceti* (toothed whales) and the *Mysticeti* (whalebone whales), the cervical (neck) vertebrae vary in their longitudinal compression and in their freedom of movement from some species in which the entire seven vertebrae are fused into a solid, immobile unit to other species in which the entire seven vertebrae are free and moveable to a limited extent. Both the moveable and the fused condition of the cervical vertebrae is found in both groups of whales.

Mention should be made that the first two cervical vertebrae, called the atlas and the axis, or epistropheus, differ from the remaining five vertebrae, are sometimes fused together, and when free do not articulate very freely with each other.

Within the *Odontoceti* (toothed whales), the cervical vertebrae are often combined in various combinations; examples of some of these combinations are set forth below.

The family of the River Dolphins (*Platanistidae*) has the seven cervical vertebrae completely free and moveable. This permits a slight turning of the head to examine the objects in their habitat; this is a need which oceanic species do not have.

In the Long-beaked Ocean Dolphins (*Delphinidae: Stenella*) all of the seven cervical vertebrae are fused into a single, immobile unit.

In the Saddle-backed Dolphins *(Delphinidae: Delphinus),* the atlas and the axis are fused into one unit.

In the False Killer Whales (*Delphinidae: Pseudorca*), the anterior six (occasionally five) vertebrae are always fused, while the seventh may be fused to the preceding six in older animals.

In the Pilot Whales (*Delphinidae: Globicephala*), the first six (occasionally five) vertebrae are fused into one unit and the seventh is free.

In the Killer Whale (*Delphinidae: Orcinus*), the anterior two or three vertebrae are fused and the posterior two are usually free.

In the Irrawaddy River Dolphin (*Delphinidae: Orcaella*), the first two vertebrae are fused into a single unit and the remaining five vertebrae are free.

Among the True Porpoises (*Delphinidae: Phocoena*), the cervical vertebrae are fused in various combinations from two to all seven vertebrae.

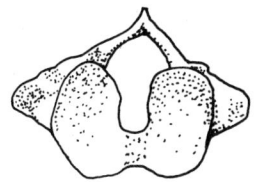

Atlas or 1st cervical vertebra.

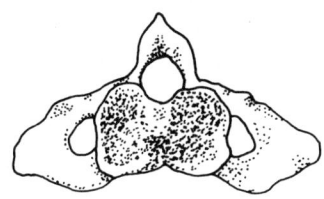

Axis, epistropheus, or 2nd cervical vertebra.

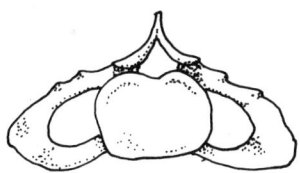

3rd cervical vertebra.

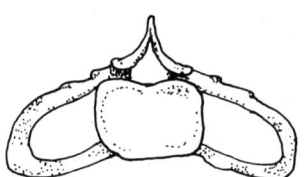

4th cervical vertebra.

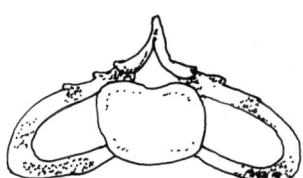

5th cervical vertebra.

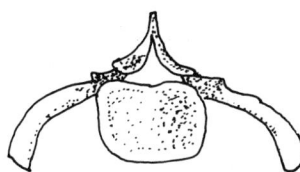

6th cervical vertebra.

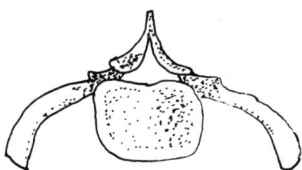

7th cervical vertebra.

Diagrams of the cervical vertebrae of the sei whale, *Balaenoptera borealis.*

Drawn from Andrews.

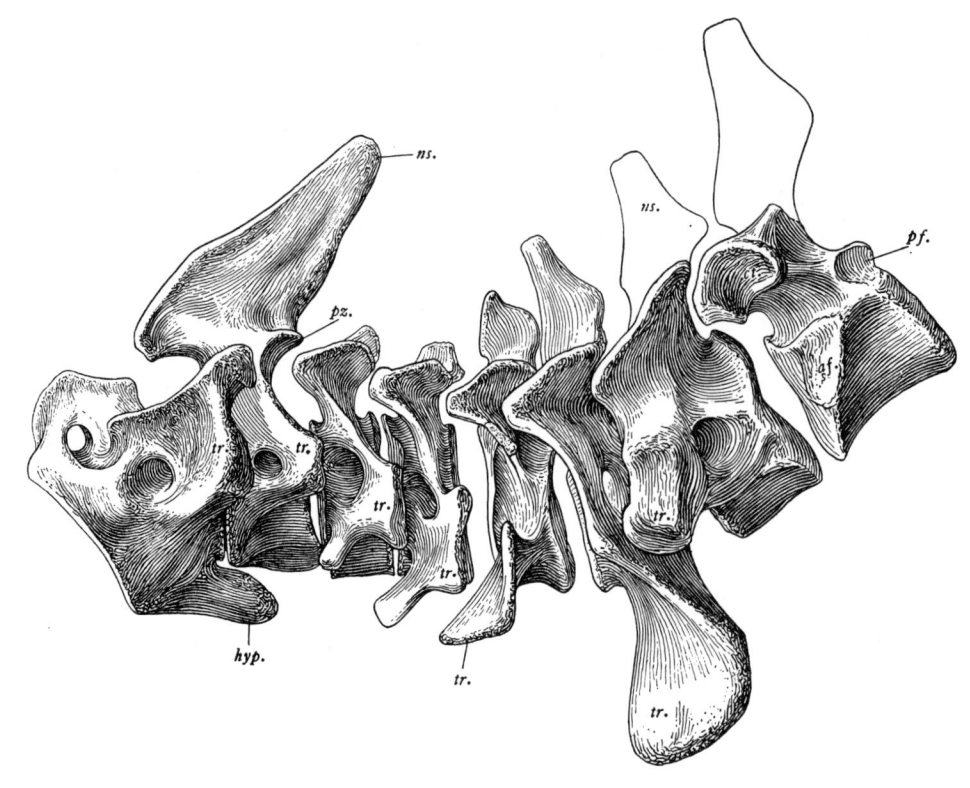

anterior ⟵————————————⟶ posterior

A drawing of the seven cervical vertebrae and the first dorsal vertebra of *Basilosaurus cetoides* (Archaeoceti: Basilosauridae) in lateral view. Approximate length: 51 cm. (20 in.). From the Upper Eocene of Alabama.

From Kellogg.

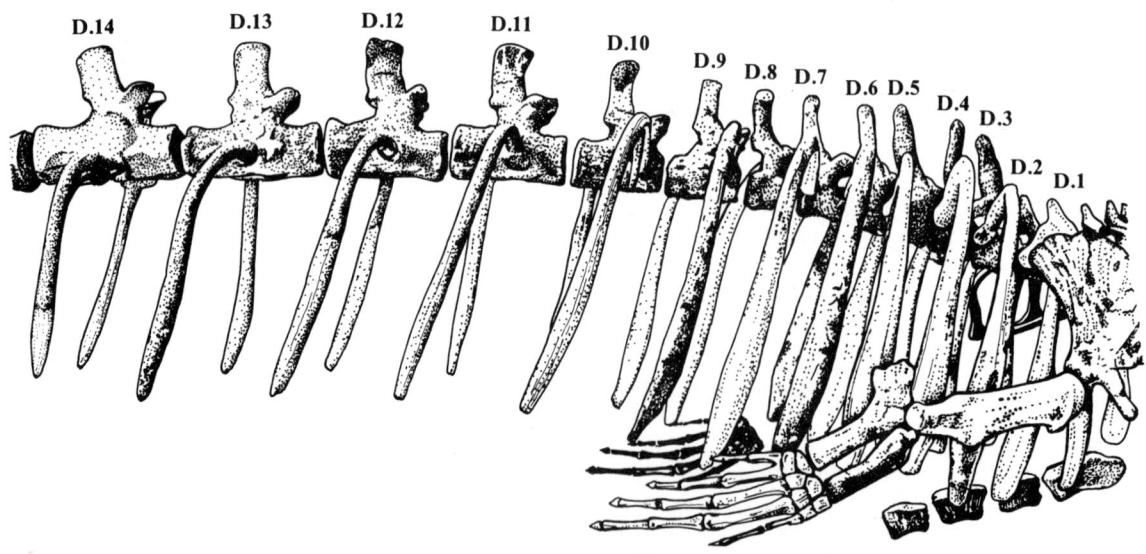

A drawing of the skeleton of the thorax of *Basilosaurus cetoides* (Archaeoceti: Basilosauridae) from the right side showing the vertebral column of the thorax together with 14 ribs and the bones of the anterior appendage.

Approximate length of thorax: 300 cm. (118.1 in. or 9.84 ft.). From the Upper Eiocene of Alabama.

From Kellogg.

In the Narwhal (*Monodontidae: Monodon*) and in the Beluga (*Monodontidae: Delphinapterus*), the entire seven vertebrae are free.

In the Sperm Whale (*Physeteridae: Physeter*), the first cervical vertebra (atlas) is free, but the remaining six vertebrae are fused into a single unit.

In the Beaked Whales (*Ziphiidae*), the cervical vertebrae are fused in various combinations; in *Hyperoodon*, all cervical vertebrae are solidly fused in the adult animals.

Within the *Mysticeti* (whalebone whales), both free and fused cervical vertebrae occur. In the family of the Gray Whale (*Eschrichtiidae*), all seven vertebrae are separate and distinct. In the Fin-backed Whales (*Balaenopteridae*), the seven cervical vertebrae are separate and free in all six species. In the Right Whales (*Balaenidae*), the seven cervical vertebrae are fused into a single, immobile unit.

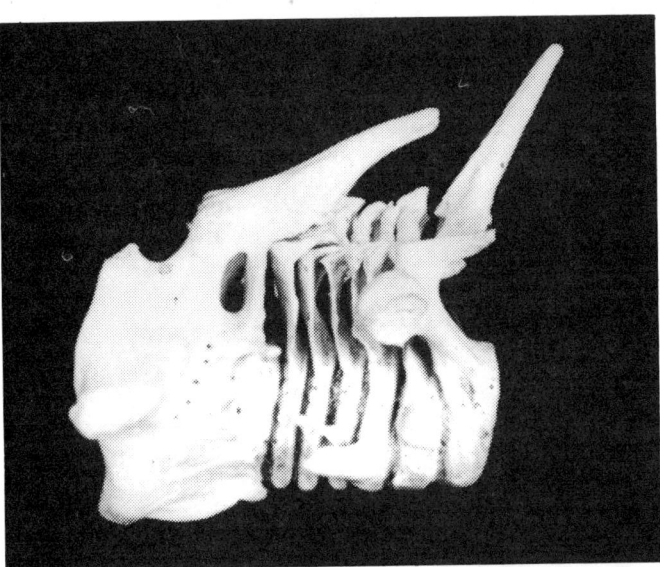

Photo of the cervical vertebrae of the common dolphin, *Delphinus delphis,* in lateral view, showing the seven cervical vertebrae fused into a single unit.

Ore. Inst. Mar. Biol.

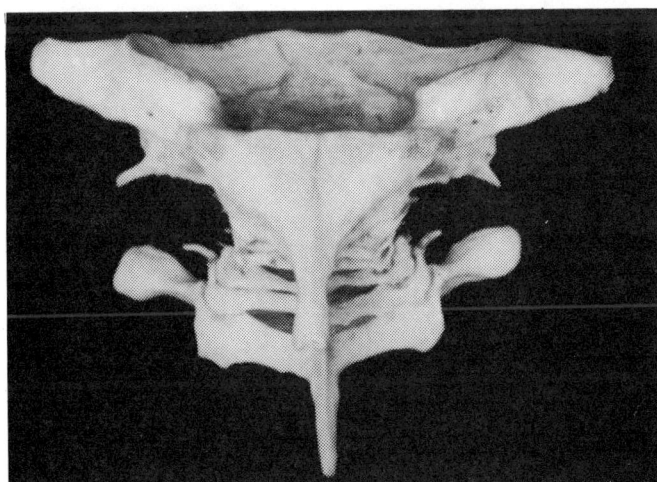

Photo of the cervical vertebrae of the common dolphin, *Delphinus delphis,* in dorsal view, showing the seven cervical vertebrae fused into a single unit.

Ore. Inst. Mar. Biol.

(2) The Vertebrae of the Thoracic Region

The thoracic region of the vertebral column is shorter in whales than in most mammals and is less flexible. The articular surfaces (zygapophyses) of the thoracic vertebrae are poorly developed in all whales and are often missing, especially on the anterior thoracic vertebrae. This means that there is very little movement possible in this region of the vertebral column and whatever movement is possible is probably restricted to the posterior thoracic vertebrae.

Within the *Odontoceti* (toothed whales), the greatest number of thoracic vertebrae is found in Dall's White-flanked Porpoise (*Delphinidae: Phocoenoides dalli*) which has about 16 thoracic vertebrae; the fewest number of thoracic vertebrae is found in the False Killer Whale (*Delphinidae: Pseudorca crassidens*) with about 10 vertebrae and in several ziphiid whales including Cuvier's Goose-beaked Whale (*Ziphiidae: Ziphius cavirostris*) with about 9 thoracic vertebrae.

Within the *Mysticeti* (whalebone whales), the greatest number of thoracic vertebrae is reported to occur in the Pigmy Right Whale (*Balaenidae: Caperea marginata*) which has about 17 thoracic vertebrae. The genus or species with the fewest number is difficult to determine, but of these whales the Lesser Rorqual (*Balaenopteridae: Balaenoptera acutorostrata*) has but 11 thoracic vertebrae and appears to possess the smallest number.

It is usually difficult to identify isolated vertebrae; however, in the California Gray Whale (*Eschrichtiidae: Eschrichtius robustus*), the following suggestions may be helpful. When the thoracic vertebrae are viewed from the side, the neural spines of vertebrae 1 through 6 are inclined forward, the neural spines of vertebrae 7 through 9 point vertically, and the neural spines of vertebrae 10 through 14 are inclined backward.

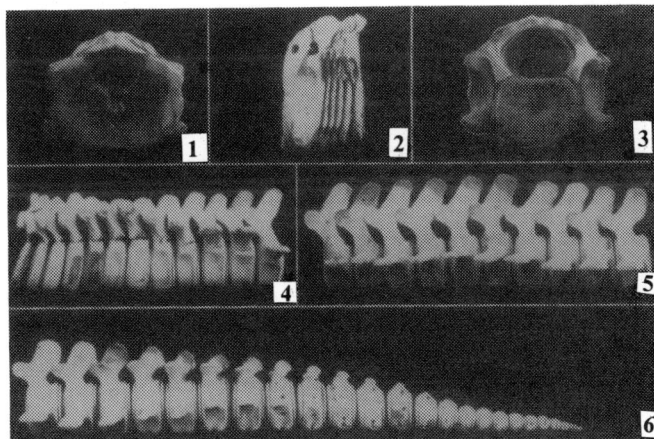

The vertebral column of the bowhead or Greenland right whale *(Balaena mysticetus).* All lateral views have the anterior end to the left.

Photos by Nishiwaki and Kasuya.

1. **The 1st cervical vertebra (atlas) in anterior view.**
2. **The seven fused cervical vertebrae in lateral view.**
3. **The 7th and last cervical vertebra in posterior view.**
4. **The twelve thoracic vertebrae in lateral view.**
5. **The ten lumbar vertebrae in lateral view.**
6. **The twenty-four caudal vertebrae in lateral view.**

In the Sei Whale *(Balaenopteridae: Balaenoptera borealis)*, when the thoracic vertebrae of this species are viewed from above, the transverse processes of vertebrae 1 through 6 are directed slightly forward; those of vertebrae 7 and 8 are directed laterally; and those of vertebrae 9 through 14 are directed slightly backward.

(3) The Vertebrae of the Lumbar Region

In most mammals, there are five divisions of the vertebral column (cervical, thoracic, lumbar, sacral, and caudal), but since the whales do not have a distinct sacral region which can be easily recognized, the sacral vertebrae are counted together with the lumbar vertebrae. This enlarged lumbar area extends from the first vertebra without a rib (a characteristic of the thorax) to the last vertebra without a pair of chevron bones (a characteristic of the caudal region). For the above reasons, the lumbar vertebrae of whales are always more numerous than those of most mammals.

In the evolution of the whales, the lumbar area has undergone an extension in length and an increase in the number and size of the vertebrae. The centrum, the spinous process, and the transverse processes of the lumbar vertebrae are always larger and heavier than those of adjoining vertebrae.

The largest count of lumbar vertebrae is found in the Right Whale Dolphins *(Delphinidae: Lissodelphis borealis* and *L. peronii)* which are reported to possess about 29 lumbar vertebrae.

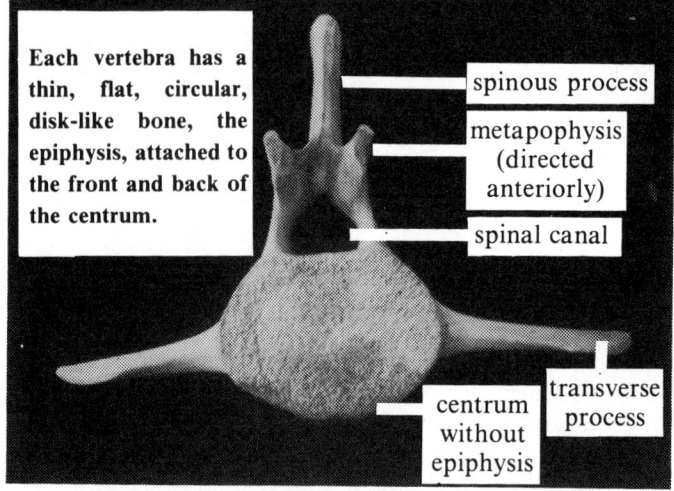

Each vertebra has a thin, flat, circular, disk-like bone, the epiphysis, attached to the front and back of the centrum.

spinous process

metapophysis (directed anteriorly)

spinal canal

transverse process

centrum without epiphysis

Anterior View

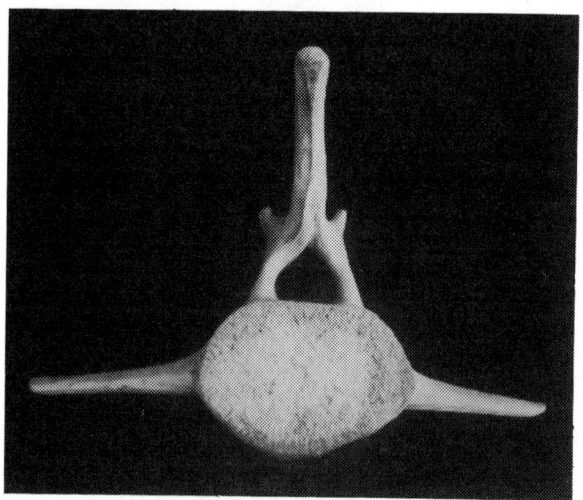

Posterior View

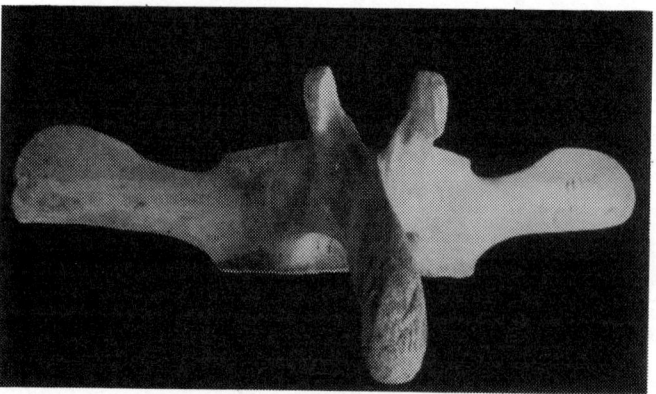

Dorsal View

Photos of a lumbar vertebra of a large whale.

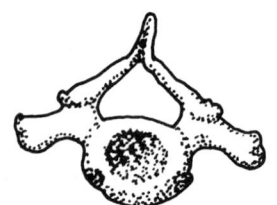

1st thoracic vertebra

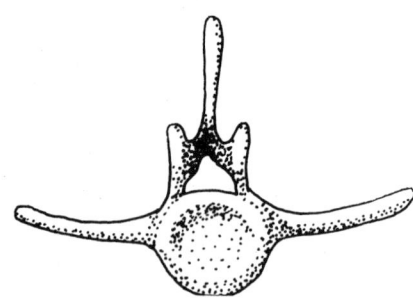

1st lumbar vertebra

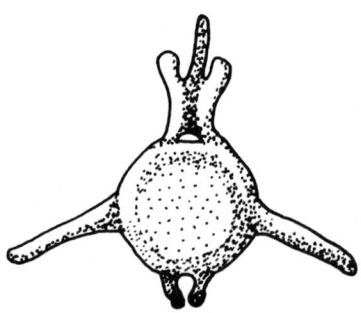

1st caudal vertebra

Diagram of the vertebrae of the California gray whale, *Eschrichtius robustus.*

Drawn from Andrews.

In many species of whales, the lumbar vertebrae have a small, longitudinal keel on the lower side of the centrum. This single keel changes to two keels on the lower side of the 1st caudal vertebrae; these two keels then become the point of attachment for the chevron bones of the caudal vertebrae. This feature can be very useful in separating the vertebrae of these two regions.

(4) The Vertebrae of the Sacral Region

Since the pelvic bones have been greatly reduced in size and have moved away from the vertebral column, it is no longer possible to use them to locate the sacral vertebrae. In other mammals, the sacral vertebrae are modified by their attachment to the innominate bones, but in the whales the sacral vertebrae do not show any modifications which can be used in their recognition. They resemble the vertebrae of the lumbar region so closely that it is impossible to know where the lumbar region ends and the sacral region begins. Scholars believe that the sacral region must have ended just anterior to the beginning of the chevron bones beneath the caudal vertebrae. But since it is impossible to count the sacral vertebrae with accuracy, these scholars have decided to combine them with the vertebrae of the lumbar region.

(5) The Vertebrae and Other Bones of the Caudal Region

The vertebrae of the caudal (tail) region begin with the first vertebra which has chevron bones beneath it. These chevron bones lie beneath the centrum and unite there to form a haemal arch and a haemal canal through which pass the arteries and veins of the tail (*A. sacralis media* and *V. sacralis media*).

The point at which the lumbar vertebrae end and the caudal vertebrae begin is usually very difficult to determine or locate. In addition, the first one or two chevron bones are small and are easily lost in the cleaning process; the 3rd and subsequent bones are larger. Roy Chapman Andrews[*] in discussing the Sei whale (*B. borealis*) states that "The first caudal can, however, be determined regardless of the chevrons themselves, for the inferior median carina, which is present in the lumbar vertebrae, begins to widen posteriorly on the last lumbar and bifurcates upon the 1st caudal, thus forming facets for the chevron attachments. This is a fairly safe, although not infallible, guide for determining the location of the 1st caudal when the chevron bones have been detached from their respective vertebrae."

It could also be noted that, in the California Gray Whale, the first caudal vertebrae has the centrum with the greatest diameter of the entire body. It also has the widest transverse processes of the entire vertebral column; these are directed slightly downward. The transverse processes of the 4th, 5th, and 6th caudal vertebrae are directed outward and forward.

These caudal vertebrae change gradually in character and shape as they continue backward toward the flukes; they become smaller and shorter in size, the spinous process slowly disappears, the transverse processes disappear, the neural canal above the centrum disappears, and the chevron bones diminish and disappear at the flukes. The caudal vertebrae end at the flukes which are lateral developments of connective and bony tissue.

The total number of caudal vertebrae has undergone an increase in number by the addition of a few extra vertebrae (sometimes called the "post sacral" vertebrae) just behind those vertebrae which comprised the ancient sacrum of the whales.

Caudal vertebrae are most numerous in the White-sided Dolphins *(Delphinidae: Lagenorhynchus* sp.), which have about 44 caudal vertebrae and in Dall's White-flanked Porpoise (*Delphinidae: Phocoenoides dalli*), which has about 48 caudal vertebrae.

Caudal vertebrae are least numerous in the La Plata River Dolphin (*Platanistidae: Pontoporia blainvillei*) with about 16 vertebrae, in Shepherd's Beaked Whale (*Ziphiidae: Tasmacetus shepherdi*) with about 17 caudal vertebrae, and in the Pigmy Right Whale (*Balaenidae: Caperea marginata*) with about 15 caudal vertebrae.

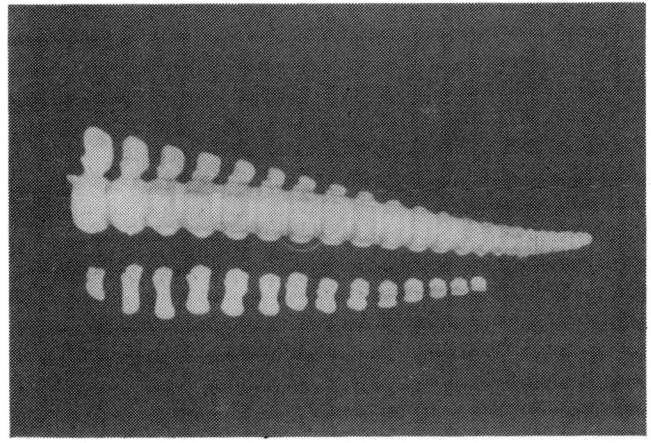

Photo of the caudal vertebrae of a dolphin together with their accompanying chevron bones.

Ore. Inst. Mar. Biol.

---

[*]Andrews, Roy Chapman *Am. Mus. Natl. Hist. Mem.* n.s. 1:6, Mar. 1916, pp. 356-7.

The Number of Vertebrae of Some Toothed Whales (*Odontoceti*)

	Cervical (Neck)	Thoracic* (Dorsal)	Lumbar* (Lumbar + Sacral)	Caudal* (Tail)	Total*
Platanistidae					
Inia geoffrensis	7	13	5	17	41-42
Delphinidae					
Delphinus delphis	7	14	21	31-32	73-74
Grampus griseus	7	12-13	18-19	30-31	68-69
Globicephala macrorhynchus	7	11	12	27	57
Orcaella brevirostris	7	14	14	28	63
Phocoena dioptrica	7	13	16	32	68
Phocoenoides dalli	7	15-18	24-27	44-49	92-98
Monodontidae					
Monodon monoceros	7	11-12	6-10	26-27	50-55
Physeteridae					
Physeter macrocephalus	7	11	8	24	50
Kogia breviceps	7	13	9	27	56
Ziphiidae					
Ziphius cavirostris	7	9	11	20	47

From Nishiwaki et alii.

The Number of Vertebrae of the Whalebone Whales (*Mysticeti*)

	Cervical (Neck)	Thoracic* (Dorsal)	Lumbar* (Lumbar + Sacral)	Caudal* (Tail)	Total*
Eschrichtiidae					
Eschrichtius robustus	7	14	12	23	56
Balaenopteridae					
Balaenoptera acutorostrata	7	11	12	18	48
Balaenoptera borealis	7	14	13	22-23	55-57
Balaenoptera edeni	7	13	13	21	54
Balaenoptera musculus	7	15-16	14-16	26-27	63-64
Balaenoptera physalus	7	15-16	13-16	24-27	60-63
Megaptera novaeangliae	7	14	10-11	21-22	52-54
Balaenidae					
Balaena glacialis	7	14-15	10-12	23-26	55-57
Balaena mysticetus	7	13	12-13	22-23	54-55
Caperea marginata	7	17	2	14-15	40-41

*The numbers are approximate

From authors.

Section c
THE RIBS

The ribs of whales show great variation in their numbers, in their structure and degree of ossification, and in their attachment to the vertebral column and to the sternum.

In whales, the ribs are not as completely ossified as in land mammals and so a greater proportion of their number is partly or completely cartilaginous.

When compared to land animals, the ribs of whales are usually very slender and fragile. However, in the Pigmy Right Whale (*Balaenidae: Caperea marginata*), the ribs differ from those of all other whales; they are broad and strong and form a rib cage which is dorso-ventrally flattened.

In their attachment to the backbone, the ribs of whales show three patterns. The two-headed ribs (anterior ribs) at the anterior end of the thorax articulate with the centrum and with the transverse process of each vertebrae. Farther back on the thorax, the ribs may lose their articulation with the centrum; these single-headed ribs (posterior ribs) articulate only with the transverse process. Toward the posterior end of the thorax, some ribs (floating ribs) may not touch either the centrum or the transverse process and are found simply lying embedded in the flesh in their proper position.

Likewise, there is variation in the manner in which the ribs join the sternum on the ventral side of the thorax. Some ribs articulate directly with the sternum or by bony or cartilaginous extensions (costal bones or cartilages); some ribs are attached indirectly to the sternum by the attachment of their costal cartilage to the costal cartilage of the preceding rib; and some ribs (floating ribs) do not reach the sternum at all, but remain suspended in their proper position without any ventral connection with the sternum.

The beaked whales (*Ziphiidae*) probably have the distinction of having the smallest number of ribs for their ribs are not known to exceed about ten pairs. However, the La Plata River Dolphin *(Platanistidae: Pontoporia blainvillei)* is also known to have as few as ten pairs of ribs. The greatest number of ribs is found in a whalebone whale, the Pigmy Right Whale (*Balaenidae: Caperea marginata*), where the ribs are reported to number as many as 17 or 18 pairs.

In general, it might be stated that the ribs of the whalebone whales are slightly more numerous than those of the toothed whales.

In most of the whalebone whales (*Mysticeti*), the ribs have lost the head (*capitulum*) of the rib and articulate with their corresponding vertebra by means of the tubercle (*tuberculum*). Only in the California gray whale (*Eschrichtiidae: Eschrichtius robustus*) have the ribs retained both the head and the tubercle; in the remaining species of the whalebone whales, the heads of the ribs have disappeared through the processes of evolution.

The Number of Pairs of Ribs Which Articulate with the Sternum

Odontoceti — The Toothed Whales

With Three Pairs of Ribs
  Platanistidae
    Inia geoffrensis 3
  Delphinidae
    Neophocaena phocaenoides 3

With Four Pairs of Ribs
  Platanistidae
    Platanista gangetica 4
    Pontoporia blainvillei 4
  Delphinidae
    Steno bredanensis 4
    Cephalorhynchus commersonii 4
    Pseudorca crassidens 4
    Orcaella brevirostris 4
    Phocoena phocoena 4
    Phocoena spinnipinnis 4
  Physeteridae
    Physeter macrocephalus 4

With Five Pairs of Ribs
  Delphinidae
    Sousa chinensis 5
    Sotalia guianensis 5
    Stenella longirostris 5
    Delphinus delphis 5
    Grampus griseus 5
    Globicephala melaena 5
    Orcinus orca 5
  Monodontidae
    Delphinapterus leucas 5
  Ziphiidae
    Hyperoodon ampullatus 5
    Ziphius cavirostris 5

With Six Pairs of Ribs
  Delphinidae
    Tursiops truncatus 6
    Lagenodelphis albirostris 6
  Monodontidae
    Monodon monoceros 6
  Physeteridae
    Kogia breviceps 6

With Seven Pairs of Ribs
  Ziphiidae
    Berardius arnuxii 7
    Mesoplodon bidens 7

Mysticeti — The Whalebone Whales
Only the first pair of ribs articulates with the sternum in all ten species within the Suborder Mysticeti.

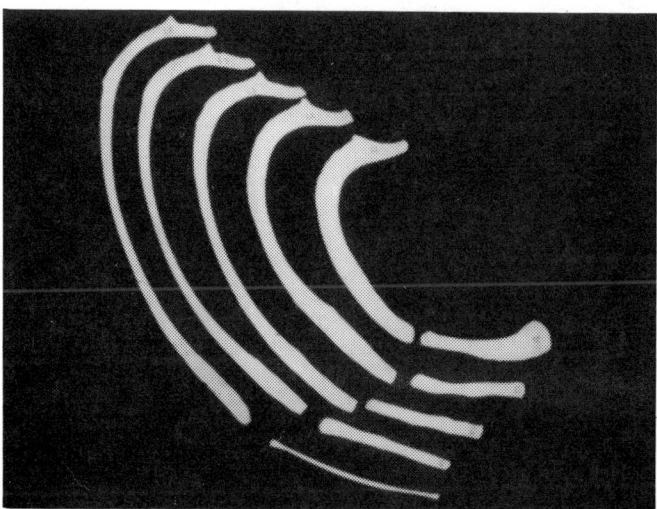

Photo of the five sternal ribs of the left side of the harbor porpoise, *Phocoena phocoena,* in medial view.
Photo by Michael Graybill at Ore. Inst. Mar. Biol.

Adapted from Arvy and Pilleri, 1977, et alii.

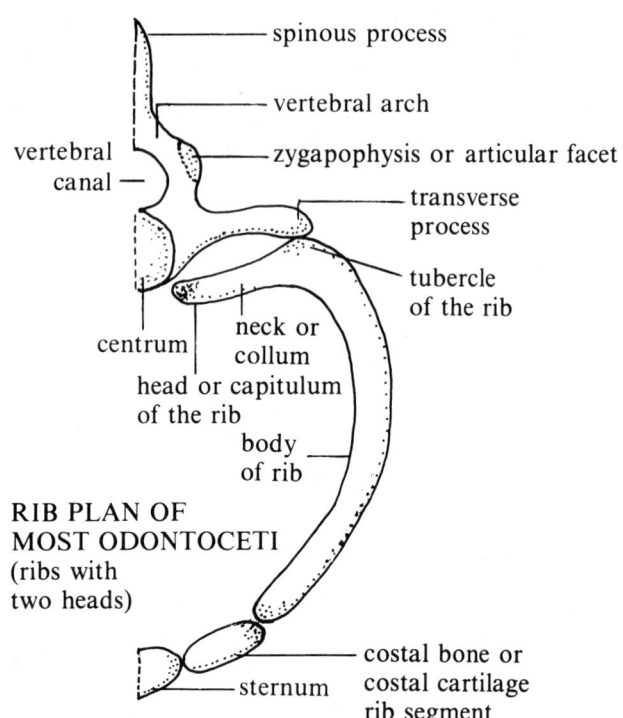

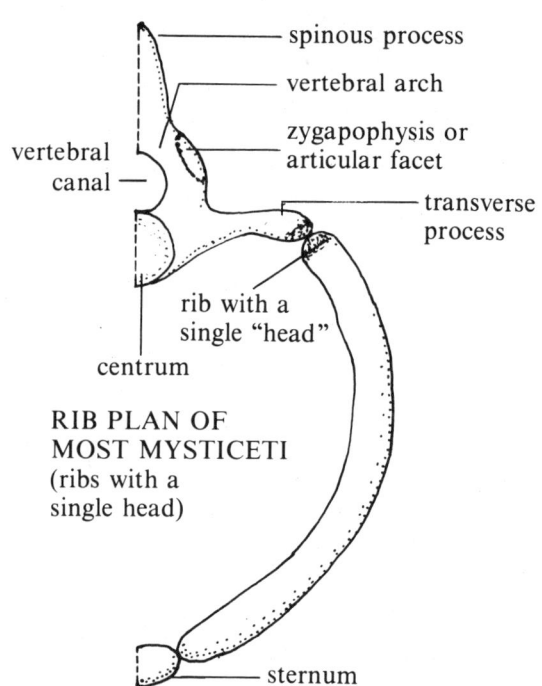

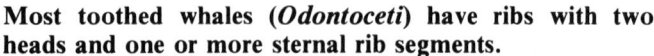

RIB PLAN OF
MOST ODONTOCETI
(ribs with
two heads)

RIB PLAN OF
MOST MYSTICETI
(ribs with a
single head)

Most toothed whales (*Odontoceti*) have ribs with two heads and one or more sternal rib segments.

Most whalebone whales (*Mysticeti*) have ribs with a single head and no sternal rib segments.

Section d
THE STERNUM

The sternum of most mammals consists of a longitudinal series of bones (*sternebrae*) lying in the midline on the ventral side of the thorax; they are usually flat bones and are tapered from their anterior end backward; they contain shallow recesses along their lateral margins to receive the ventral ends of the ribs or their extensions. In the whales, great variation exists in the size, shape, and composition of the sternum and in its articulation with the ribs.

The toothed whales (*Odontoceti*) possess a sternum which is usually segmented, although in some species it is a single bone. It varies between families, genera, and species and, in some instances, the structure of the sternum varies within a species. In the toothed whales, the sternum may be joined by two to seven pairs of ribs depending upon the species.

In the whalebone whales (*Mysticeti*), the sternum always consists of a single bone; it is usually short, broad, somewhat shield-shaped, and may be somewhat soft in texture; here the sternum is joined by only one pair of ribs.

In general, the thorax is more flexible in the toothed whales, in spite of the fact that the thorax of this group contains more bones.

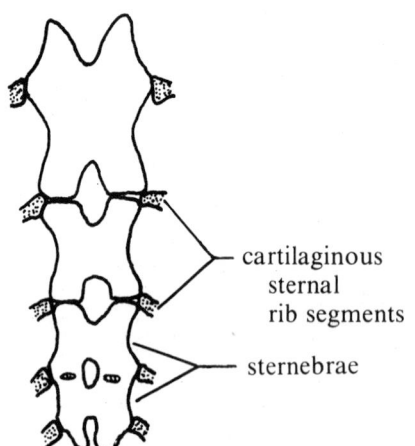

**Diagram of the sternum of *Mesoplodon europaeus*.
Drawn from Raven.**

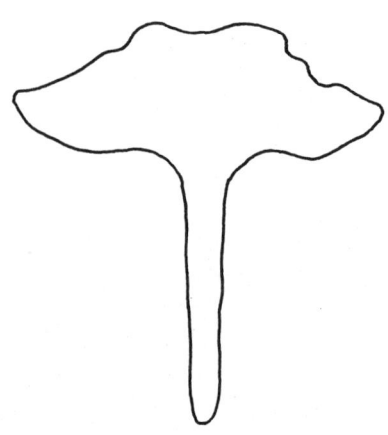

**A diagram of the sternum of the minke whale, *B. acuto-rostrata*.
Drawn from Omura et alii.**

Division 2
THE APPENDICULAR SKELETON

It is the normal and usual pattern for all mammals to have two sets of appendages; this is true of all land mammals and of several of the aquatic mammals. However, in those mammals which have had a long evolutionary history of living in the sea, the rear appendages and their accompanying pelvic girdle have slowly atrophied and partly disappeared. This is true of the whales, the manatees, and the dugong *(Sirenia).* Other semi-aquatic groups *(Pinnipedia),* including the seals, the sea lions, and the walrus, still retain their pelvic appendages, although they show definite signs of modification or atrophy.

Section a
THE PECTORAL GIRDLE
AND
THE PECTORAL APPENDAGES

In the mammals, the skeleton of the pectoral girdle consists of the scapula, the clavicle, and the remnants of the ancient coracoid bone. The bones of the pectoral appendages consist of the humerus, the radius, the ulna, the carpal bones, the metacarpal bones, and the phalanges.

The whales possess most of the bones of the shoulder and of the front legs which are found in the land mammals; however, in the whales, they have been changed somewhat as a result of their life in the water. In the whales, the bones of the shoulder girdle include only the scapula; the clavicle is absent and the ancestral coracoid bone remains as a process near the end of the scapula.

(1) The Pectoral Girdle

The shoulder girdle originally provided for the attachment of the appendages to the body by means of muscles and also allowed the weight of the body to be transmitted to the legs. However, in whales, the front feet have been replaced by flippers and the weight of the body is supported by the surrounding water. The resulting modifications in the structure of the pectoral appendages of the whales are fewer at the proximal end of the appendages of the whales and increase toward the distal or free end of the appendage. The shoulder joint is moveable, but the joint at the elbow has become rigid and immobile. The bones of the arm have become shortened, while those of the hand have been extended with the development of the flipper.

(a) The Scapula. The scapula (shoulder blade) is the principal bone of the shoulder girdle. It is usually wide, flat, and triangular in shape and is placed against the outside of the body above the rib cage, where it is held in place my muscles. It receives the head of the humerus and, in most mammals, transmits most of the weight of the anterior end of the body to the front legs. In the whales, the scapula* is a smaller and simpler bone than in land mammals, because there is less weight involved and the movements required of the front appendages are less complex.

(b) The Clavicle. The clavicle (collar bone or wishbone) in man extends from the acromion process of the scapula to the anterior end of the sternum and thereby connects the arm bones with the trunk. In birds, the ends of the clavicle join in the mid-ventral line to form the wishbone. The clavicle is absent in the skeleton of all whales.

(c) The Coracoid. The coracoid bone was a part of the shoulder girdle of our ancient, evolutionary ancestors and extended from the scapula toward the sternum. It is well developed in reptiles and birds, but it is rudimentary in mammals (except monotremes) and remains as a process extending outward from the scapula near its joint with the humerus. This bone is absent in all whales, although the coracoid process remains attached to the scapula.

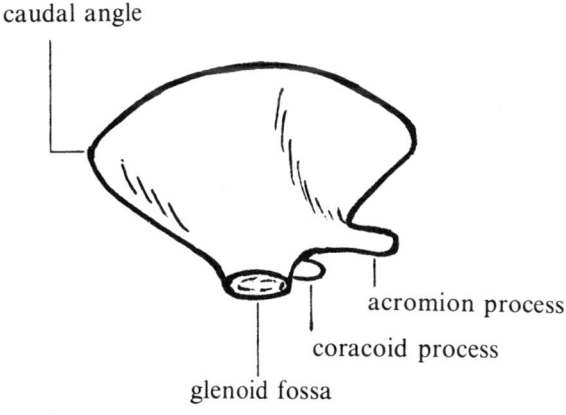

caudal angle

acromion process

coracoid process

glenoid fossa

Diagram of the scapula of the sei whale, *B. borealis* (right side, lateral view).

Drawn from Andrews.

*In a specimen of an adult blue whale (*B. musculus*), the glenoid fossa (shoulder socket) measured 33 cm. (13 in.) by 24 cm. (9.5 in.) in diameter; the acromion process projecting forward from the scapula measured about 40.5 cm. (16 in.) in length.

(2) The Pectoral Appendages

The bones comprising the pectoral appendages are almost standardized within the mammals. Beginning at the proximal end (nearest the body) and proceeding distally, they include the humerus, the radius, the ulna, the carpal bones, the metacarpal bones, and the phalanges. These bones are discussed below in the above order.

(a) The Humerus

The humerus (upper arm) is the single, elongated bone extending from the shoulder to the elbow. Although usually round in cross-section, it has become flattened and generally shortened in whales. In spite of these changes, it is easily recognized.

(b) The Radius and the Ulna.

The radius and the ulna (forearm) are the two elongated bones which lie parallel in the forearm and extend from the elbow to the wrist. In whales, they vary in size, shape, and length, but, in general, they have become considerably shortened and flattened. In addition, they have become fused at the elbow to the end of the humerus and have therefore produced a solid, immobile joint at the elbow without any of the motion which is typical of most of the land mammals.

In some whales, there is a tendency for the radius and the ulna to fuse; this fusion is most advanced in the river dolphins (*Platanistidae*), where the radius and the ulna are solidly fused together.

At the proximal end of the ulna is an extension known as the olecranon process (elbow) which shows great variation in the whales; in some families *(Platanistidae, Monodontidae)* it is entirely absent; in others *(Physeteridae, Ziphiidae, Balaenopteridae)* it has become quite large.

(c) The Carpus

The carpus (wrist) consists of various numbers of small, irregular bones; in man, there are usually two rows of four bones each; in the cat the carpal bones are 7 in number. The carpal bones are present in the flippers of all whales, but they lack the mobility usually associated with these joints.

In the river dolphins (*Odontoceti: Platanistidae*), the carpal bones are fused to the distal ends of the radius and the ulna.

In the Sei whale *(Mysticeti: Balaenopteridae: Balaenoptera borealis),* there are 5 ossified carpal bones arranged in two rows; one proximal row of three bones extends across the end of the radius and the ulna, and the other row of two smaller bones lies parallel and distal to the row of three bones.

(d) The Digits

The "hands" (manus) of whales are not uniform in the number of digits which they contain. Although five fingers is regarded as the usual number, only the toothed whales (*Odontoceti*) are consistent in possessing this number. Among the whalebone whales (*Mysticeti*), some genera possess five digits and some have only four digits; in the Mysticeti, the missing digits may be either the 1st or the 3rd.

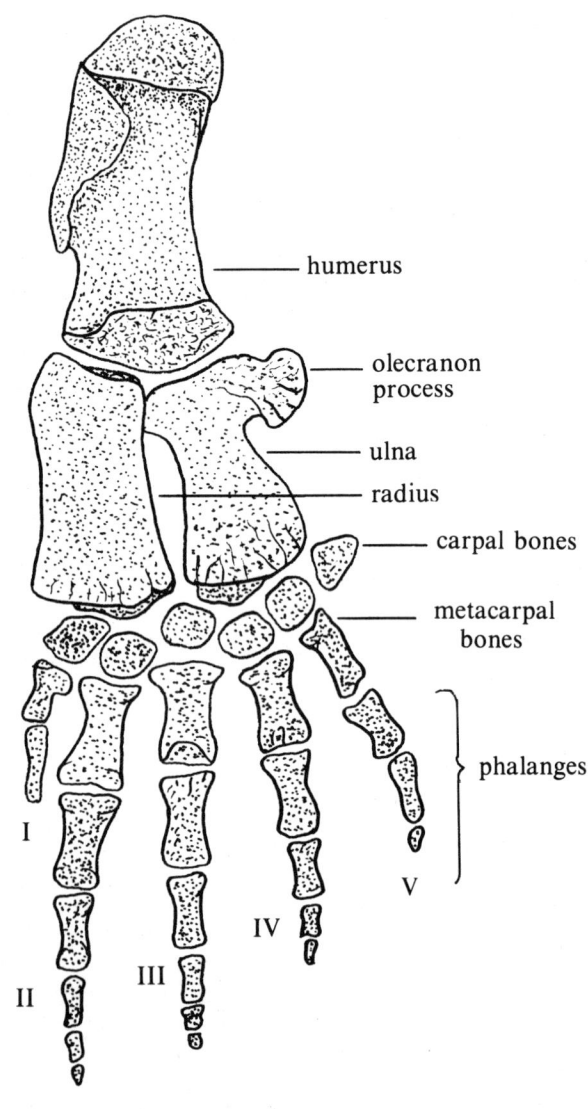

Diagram of the left appendage of the great sperm whale, *Physeter macrocephalus* (Odontoceti: Physeteridae), in lateral view. Note the shortened bones of the upper arm and forearm.

Drawn from Flower.

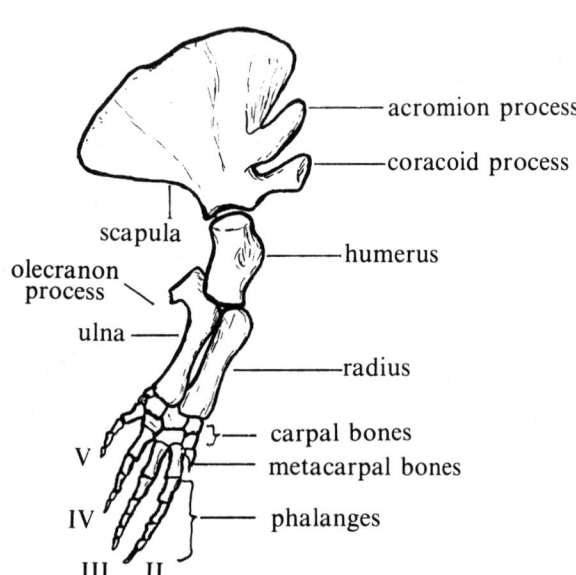

The pectoral appendage (right side, lateral view) of *Mesoplodon europaeus*.

Drawn from Raven.

The Number of Digits in the Flippers of Whales

Group	No. of Species	Total No. of Digits	The Missing Digit
Sub-order Odontoceti	67	5	None
Sub-order Mysticeti			
1. Family Eschrichtiidae			
Eschrichtius	1	4	1st
2. Family Balaenopteridae			
Balaenoptera	5	4	3rd
Megaptera	1	4	3rd
3. Family Balaenidae			
Balaena	2	5	None
Caperea	1	4	

(e) The Metacarpals

The metacarpal bones which form the palm of the hand in man, are present in the whales, but lie buried in the flesh of the flipper. The palm of the hand normally consists of five, slender bones extending from the wrist to the fingers; however, in whales, they have undergone a reduction in their numbers in three families (*Mysticeti: Eschrichtiidae, Balaenopteridae, Balaenidae*). In the gray whales (*Eschrichtiidae*), the manus (hand) of the California Gray Whale has only four digits; the first digit is missing. In the rorquals (*Balaenopteridae*), the manus (hand) of the flipper contains only four digits in all five species of *Balaenoptera*; here the 3rd digit is missing. In the Right Whales (*Mysticeti: Balaenidae*), the third and last family of the whalebone whales, the two species of *Balaena* possess all five digits in the hand of the flipper, but the Genus *Caperea* has only four digits in its flipper.

(f) The Phalanges

The phalanges (fingers) are the bones of the fingers and, in mammals, usually consist of 14 bones (thumb with 2; 4 fingers with 3 each). In whales, there is considerable variation in the phalanges, depending upon the shape of the flippers. In whales with long, slender flippers, the digits lie close together and the phalanges are elongated. Where the flippers are broad, the digits are separated and the phalanges are less numerous. Where the flippers have been elongated, the increase in the number of phalanges has been greatest in the middle three digits. These digits seem to have reached their greatest elongation in the Pilot Whales (*Globicephala*) where the 2nd and 3rd fingers possess approximately 14 and 11 bones, respectively.

There is a tendency in aquatic animals to transform the front appendages into flippers and to increase the number of phalanges in them; this has taken place in the ancient aquatic lizards, the pleiosaurs and ichthyosaurs, and also in the ancient whales (*Archaeoceti*). Modern mammals possessing flippers include the *Sirenia* (manatees and the dugong), the *Pinnipedia* (seals, sea lions, and walruses), and to a limited extent in at least one of the *Carnivora*, the sea otter. This development of a flipper is most always accompanied by an increase (hyper-phalangism) in the number of bones in the fingers, doubtless in an effort to increase the efficiency of the flipper.

Mention should be made of the lack of uniformity in the counting of the phalanges. Some scholars count only the phalanges; other scholars add the metacarpals to the count because they are short in length and otherwise resemble the phalanges.

Section b
THE PELVIC GIRDLE
AND
THE PELVIC APPENDAGES

The pelvic girdle (hips) and the pelvic appendages (hind legs) of whales make a very interesting study, because the whales do not possess all of these bones and, when they are present, they are represented by very small vestigial remnants.

(1) The Pelvic Girdle

The pelvic girdle of the mammals consists of three* pairs of separate bones which are fused together. One set of these three bones lies on the right side of the vertebral column and the other set of three bones lies on the left side of the vertebral column. These three bones, collectively known as the innominate (nameless) bone, are named the *ilium* (located dorsally), the *ischium* (located posteriorly), and the *pubis* (located ventrally).

The innominate bones connect the vertebral column with the hind legs and, in the land mammals, serve to transmit the weight of the body to the hind legs. Each of the innominate bones is attached by the ilium to the dorsal side of the sacral vertebrae; they then descend ventrally in a somewhat circular manner to the midventral line where the right and left pubic bones unite by a ligament to form the pubic symphysis (*symphysis pubis*). These three bones also form a socket (acetabulum) on their lateral surfaces to receive the head of the femur (thigh bone).

In most mammals, the skeleton of the pelvic appendages (hind legs) consists of a fairly standard set of bones. Beginning at the pelvis and continuing distally (outward), each leg includes the femur, the tibia, the fibula, the tarsal bones, the metatarsal bones, and the phalanges. Most of these bones are absent in the whales, and those bones which are present are usually those which are nearest to the pelvis.

---

*A fourth bone, the acetabular bone, is actually present in the pelvis. It is small in size and is of no importance.

(2) The Evolutionary Changes in the Pelvis

The presence of remnants of the pelvic girdle in whales indicates their relationship with the land mammals and also points to the immense period of time which has elapsed since the whales moved from the land into the sea.

The remaining bones of the pelvic girdle are not uniform throughout all whales or even in any of the families of whales. Also, the number of bones which is present varies from one to several bones. Some whales have only the pelvic (innominate) bones; some have the pelvic bones and the femur; some have the pelvic bones, the femur, and the tibia; and still other whales have these bones plus the bones of the ankle, foot, and toes, all greatly modified from their ancestral number, size, and structure.

In most whales, these bones are contained within the body; however, in some whales, these leg bones will project beyond the body wall of the abdomen and appear on the outside of the body as a small, external appendage. In sperm whales, these external "legs" are believed to appear in one of every 10,000 individuals. There is an unusual record of a hump-backed whale (*Megaptera novaeangliae*) captured near Vancouver Island, Canada, in 1919, which was reported to have exhibited hind legs which measured 1.2 meters (3.94 ft.) in length.

In the ancient whales *(Archaeoceti)* the pelvic bones had already separated from the sacral vertebrae and lay buried in the flesh. As expected, the pelvic bones of these ancient whales were larger than in the modern whales and the sutures between the bones were more apparent. The pelvis contained a socket (acetabulum) for the head of the femur and an occasional femur, but the fossils of this period (Early Miocene: 25,000,000 years ago) have not revealed the presence of a rudimentary tibia, although they were doubtless present, at least occasionally.

(3) A Comparison of the Pelvic Bones of Whales

In general, the pelvic bones of the *Odontoceti* differ from those of the *Mysticeti*. Although both of these pelvic remnants are elongated in shape, consist of the same bones with indistinct sutures, and lie isolated in the flesh at some distance from the vertebral column, they are of different shapes in the toothed and whalebone whales. These pelvic bones are compared below.

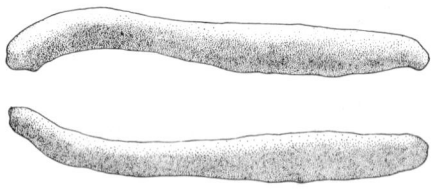

Drawing of the pelvic bones (innominate bones) of the pigmy killer whale, *Feresa attenuata* (Odontoceti: Delphinidae).   **From Pryor et alii.**

Features of The Pelvic Bones	Toothed Whales (Odontoceti)	Whalebone Whales (Mysticeti)
General Shape	Elongated and Columnar.	Elongated and Triangular.
Relative Size	Male pelvis is larger than female pelvis.	Female pelvis is larger than male pelvis.
Other Features	Male pelvis is more costate (ribbed) than female pelvis.	
	Female bones are smoother than those of males and are without sharp crests and notches.	

Adapted from Yablokov.

(4) The Pelvis of the Odontoceti

Nearly all of the toothed whales (*Odontoceti*) have a single pair of pelvic (innominate) bones, although a few show additional remnants; sperm whales, for example, will retain a vestigial femur and tibia.

In some *Odontoceti*, the pelvic bones are found only in the males and are entirely missing in the female whales. This condition occurs in the Pigmy Sperm Whale (*Kogia breviceps*), in the North Sea Beaked Whale or Sowerby's Whale *(Mesoplodon bidens),* and doubtless in other species. This condition is associated with the fact that the penis is attached to the pelvic bones and this connection doubtless accounts for the retention of the vestigial pelvis in the males as well as the smaller size of the pelvis in the females of some species.

(5) The Pelvis of the Mysticeti

In general, the pelvic (innominate) bones of the whalebone whales (*Mysticeti*) lie nearly parallel to the vertebral column, lateral to it, and below it; their position is usually lateral, above, and posterior to the genital opening. In some fetuses, these structures may sometimes be felt embedded in the flesh after the skin and other tissues have been removed. Although these pelvic bones vary in length between the individuals, the sexes, and the species of the *Mysticeti*, they usually measure between about 1% and 2% (or less) of the body length.

In a Sei Whale (*Balaenoptera borealis*), the pelvic bones were found to lie embedded in the flesh near the vertebral column about 30 cm. (12 in.) or more apart and about 25 cm. (10 in.) or more anterior to the anus. Pelvic bones have measured about 50 cm. (19.7 in.) in length in the Gray Whale (*E. robustus*) and about 20 cm. (8 in.) in length in the Sei Whale *(B. borealis)*.

A.V. Yablokov divides the modern whales *(Mysticeti)* into three groups on the basis of the number of parts of the pelvic girdle and appendages which remain buried in the flesh of adult whales.

Pelvic Remnants
In the Whalebone Whales *(Mysticeti)*

The Pelvic Region contains three parts	The Pelvic Region contains two parts	The Pelvic Region contains one part
1. The innominate or pelvic bones	1. The innominate or pelvic bones	1. The innominate or pelvic bones
2. The femur	2. The femur	2. Usually no femur
3. The tibia	3. Usually no tibia	3. Usually no tibia
The Right Whales *(Balaenidae)*	The Rorquals *(Balaenopteridae)*	The Rorquals *(Balaenopteridae)*
1. The Right Whale *(Balaena glacialis)*	1. The Hump-backed Whale *(Megaptera novaeangliae)*	1. The Minke or Bay Whale *(Balaenoptera acutorostrata)*
2. The Bowhead *(Balaena mysticetus)*	2. The Blue Whale *(Balaenoptera musculus)*	2. The Sei Whale *(Balaenoptera borealis)*
	3. The Fin Whale *(Balaenoptera physalus)*	

From A.V. Yablokov.

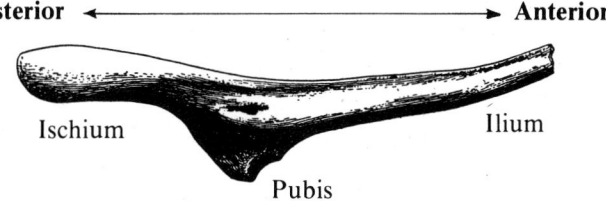

Left innominate bone in internal view.

Right innominate bone in external view.

The innominate (pelvic) bones of a fossil Cetothere, *Cophocetus oregonensis* (Mysticeti: Cetotheriidae), from the Miocene of Newport, Oregon. Approximate length: 24 cm. (9.4 in.)

From Packard and Kellogg.

Chapter III

THE INTEGUMENTARY SYSTEM OR SKIN

The skin or integument of animals is a rather unusual organ and one which is of great importance to all mammals. The skins of the various species of mammals vary considerably in their appearance, but, with a few exceptions, perform the same functions and have the same basic structure throughout this group.

The purposes and functions of the skin, which are about five in number, include the following:

a. The skin serves as a covering for the body and thereby helps to contain it, to protect its delicate structures from injury, and to prevent the absorption of harmful substances into the body.

b. The skin acts as the base and location of many of the sensory receptors of the body. Through these receptors, the skin responds to touch and to temperature and thereby helps the body to adjust to its surroundings. Much of this adjustment is the result of reflex mechanisms which begin with the sensations which are transmitted by the receptors located within the skin.

c. The skin serves as an auxiliary excretory organ by discharging metabolic wastes (water, salts, etc.) which have been carried there by the blood vessels which lie beneath it.

d. The skin is also the opening and the location for the entry of substances from the environment into the body. Many animals which have damp skins absorb oxygen through their skin and likewise release carbon dioxide into their surroundings. The skin can also be the location for the entry of harmful substances into the body.

e. The skin assists in the regulation of the body temperature in most mammals. It is a protection against both the cold and heat and helps to stabilize the body temperature—a function which is of great importance to the mammals.

Division 1
THE STRUCTURE OF THE SKIN

The skin of whales follows the same structural pattern of other mammals and consists of about four layers.

a. **The Epidermis.** The outer or surface layer is very thin in whales and consists of a very thin, outer, pigmented layer which is about 1 mm. (1/25 in.) in thickness. Beneath this pigmented layer lies the thin supporting tissue of the epidermis which, together with the thin outer layer, measures in all about 5 mm. (1/5 in.) in thickness.

b. **The Dermis.** The *dermis,* which lies below the epidermis, is likewise a thin layer and is composed of tough connective tissue.

c. **The Hypodermis.** The next layer, the *hypodermis* or the blubber, comprises the thickest part of the integument and is composed of connective tissue and fat cells. This layer of blubber varies in thickness and density from a thin layer to a layer with a thickness of over 60 cm. (2 ft.), depending upon the species, the age and the size of the whale, the state of health of the whale, the availability of food, and other factors. This blubber reaches its greatest thickness in the Right Whales (*Balaenidae: Balaena*) where it is reported (Slijper) to average 50 cm. (20 in.) in thickness and to reach as much as 71 cm. (28 in.) in thickness on some areas of the body; it may exceed 1/3 of the total body weight of these species. In general, the blubber is thickest on the dorsal and posterior areas of the body. It is comparatively thinner toward the anterior and ventral areas of the body and is reduced to a minimum in the areas around the eyes, the lips, the blowholes, the other body openings, the flippers, and the tail flukes. This layer of blubber is a non-conductor of heat and is the principal layer and organ for the storage of food during their migrations and during the rearing of the young whales. It also enables them to live in frigid climates.

d. **The Connective Tissue.** Beneath the layer of blubber lies the last and innermost layer of the integument. It is a layer of *connective tissue* which lies midway between the layer of blubber and the various muscles of the body. On its outer surface, it is fastened to the blubber and on its inner surface, it attaches to a thin, tough layer of fascia which covers and encloses the muscles of the body wall. This connective tissue, although tough and strong, is loose and pliable and thereby permits limited movement to occur between the blubber and the muscles of the body wall.

The color of whales follows a fairly regular pattern, although there are exceptions to each of the following generalities. Their bodies are usually darker in color above and lighter below. Their colors are nearly always variations of black and white. The colors shade gradually from one area to another and the sexes are of the same color, hue, and pattern. It should be mentioned that Cuvier's Beaked Whale (*Ziphiidae: Ziphius cavirostris*) is usually lighter above than below. The Beluga or White Whale *(Monodontidae: Delphinapterus leucas)* is nearly completely white as an adult, although it is variously grayish, bluish, and/or brownish for a time following its birth.

Although it is the usual pattern for adjoining color areas to blend gradually into each other, there are some species of whales in which the borders between adjoining color areas are very sharp. The white spots of the Killer Whale (*Delphinidae: Orcinus orca*) are an example of this feature. Likewise, in Commerson's Dolphin, also known as the Piebald or Black and White Dolphin (*Delphinidae: Cephalorhynchus commersonii*), and in Dall's Porpoise (*Delphinidae: Phocoenoides dalli*), there are sharply defined color boundaries on their bodies.

Because the skin of most whales is very thin, it has never been found to be of great value as a leather or other raw material and so does not appear as a product of commerce in our society. There are, however, two whales, the Beluga and the Narwhal, in which the skin is thick enough to be suitable for tanning. These skins were formerly tanned and reportedly used as mail bags.

Division 2
THE VIBRISSAE

Although hair is a very conspicuous part of the integument of land mammals, it is almost totally absent in the whales. Following their adaptation to life in the water, whales lost almost all of their hair and today retain only a few scattered vibrissae which are similar to those found in other mammals, although they usually develop hair sometime during their fetal stage. The embryos of various species of whales show vibrissae at some stage in their prenatal development but lack them entirely in their adult stage. Of these, the best example is probably the sperm whale, which has vibrissae upon the foetus, but has no vibrissae upon the skin of the adult. Of the vibrissae retained by adult whales, nearly all are restricted to the top of the head and along the beak, the lips, and the chin.

Within the family of the ocean dolphins (*Delphinidae*), the number of vibrissae is greatly reduced and includes only six or eight short vibrissae scattered over the anterior part of the snout. The beluga and the narwhal seem to be completely devoid of vibrissae at all stages in their life cycle.

Among the whalebone whales (*Mysticeti*), the rorqals or fin-backed whales (*Balaenopteridae*) have four or five dozen vibrissae upon their head. These vibrissae are in four longitudinal rows; one row extends along the margin of each upper lip and two rows extend along the top of the head from the area of the snout backward to the blowholes; of these, a single row lies on each side of the midline.

In the right whale (*Balaenidae: Balaena glacialis*), there may be as many as 250 bristles (Slijper) located upon the top of the upper jaws and upon the chin. Most whales, however, have far fewer vibrissae upon their bodies.

In addition to the whales, hair has disappeared or been greatly reduced in the *Sirenia* (the three manatees and the dugong), in the larger members of the *Pinnipedia* (the seals, sea lions, and the walruses), in the *Proboscidea* (the elephants), and in some of the ungulates.

Division 3
THE GLANDS OF THE SKIN

The sebaceous or oil glands of the skin are absent in both Toothed Whales *(Odontoceti)* and Whalebone Whales *(Mysticeti)*, and also in the *Sirenia*. These are the oil-producing glands which are usually associated with hair and which produce the oil which lubricates both the skin and the hair.

The sweat glands, which are so common in the integument of terrestrial mammals, are also absent in both groups of whales.

Division 4
THE SENSES OF THE SKIN

The skin of whales, like that of other mammals, embodies the sense of touch. This sense is spread over the entire surface of the body, particularly in the very small tactile swellings scattered over the body and also in the vibrissae found scattered over the head and along the lips. The sense of touch in the skin is well developed and the skin is very sensitive over its entire surface. This is evident from the fact that nearly all whales rub each other with their flippers during their mating activities and the smaller dolphins commonly found in various oceanaria enjoy being touched and stroked by their trainers.

Division 5
THE PARASITES OF THE SKIN

Although the skin of whales is exceedingly smooth, it is usually covered with a great variety of scars, spots, cuts, and scratches of various origins. These are the result of scratches from the teeth of other whales and the suckers of large squids, bites from lampreys, sharks, and other whales, and also from the marks of various external parasites.*

---

*For an account of parasitic crustaceans (*Amphipoda: Cyamidae*) on whales see Pilleri, Giorgio — INVESTIGATIONS ON CETACEA. 1982. 13:149-164 (4 figs.).

*For a list of the many parasites of whales and a bibliography, see Ridgway, Sam H. (editor)—*MAMMALS OF THE SEA: BIOLOGY AND MEDICINE*. 1972. 812 pp. There is a very good article in Chapter 9 by Murray D. Dailey and Robert L. Brownell, Jr., titled, "A Checklist of Marine Mammal Parasites" (pp. 528-589) which lists the parasites by parasitic groups and also by host species.

The bodies of whales are host to a multitude of external parasites which seem to be more numerous on the larger species of whales and also upon those species which are comparatively slow swimmers.

These include several species of:

—acorn barnacles (*Crustacea: Cirripedia: Balanidae: Coronula* sp.),

—stalked barnacles (*Crustacea: Cirripedia: Lepadidae: Conchoderma* sp.),

—slender copepods (*Crustacea: Copepoda: Penellidae: Penella* sp.),

—whale lice (*Crustacea: Amphipoda: Cyamidae: Cyamus* sp.), and

—various diatoms which form colonies upon the bodies of whales and impart to each whale the color of that particular species of diatom.

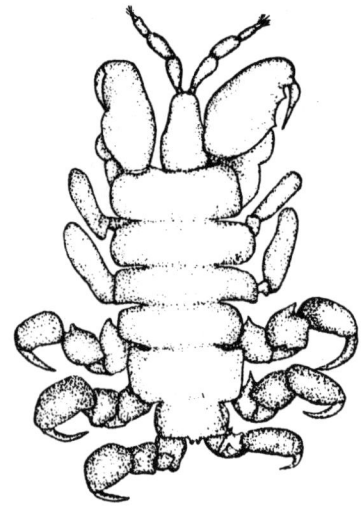

Drawing of a male whale louse, *Cyamus antarcticensis* (Crustacea: Amphipoda: Cyamidae), in dorsal view. Length: 1 cm. (.4 in.).

From: Berzin, A.A. and Vlasova, L.P. in Pilleri, Gregorio — Investigations On The Cetacea. 1982. 13:149-164 (fig. 1C).

Whale lice, a parasitic crustacean, from the "bonnet" of a North Pacific right whale, *Balaena glacialis.*

Photo by H. Omura.

From: Pilleri, Gregorio — Investigations On The Cetacea.

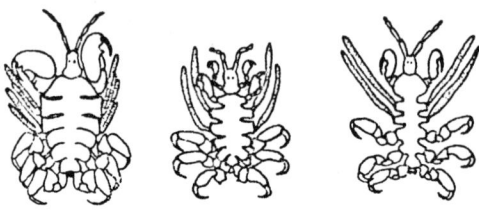

Drawings of various species of whale lice, *Cyamus* species, which are ecto-parasites on the bodies of large whales.

After Rowntree.

From: Pilleri, Gregorio — Investigations On The Cetacea.

Chapter IV
THE MUSCULAR SYSTEM

The muscles of whales are exceedingly difficult to study. Some species are of great size and their capture and preservation is an almost impossible task. Where the carcasses of whales have appeared upon beaches, they are usually destined for decay within hours or days and so cannot usually be dissected in those locations. Scholars have therefore usually resorted to the study of whales which are of smaller size or they have secured a fetus from a large whale aboard a whaling ship or from a beached specimen.

The study of the musculature of whales is also difficult because the muscles of whales depart quite radically from those of the typical mammals which are known to scholars. The musculature of the whales, like that of other mammals, is but an evolutionary extension of the musculature of the reptiles. This same evolutionary process has continued throughout the mammals and has produced within them a very wide variety of forms, each of which has developed and inherited its own particular muscular system.

Nowhere among the orders of the mammals, either ancient or living, has the evolutionary process developed as different and as startling a pattern of musculature as it has within the whales. The muscles of the whales, although basically mammalian in design, have been greatly modified to fit the unusual body needs of whales and the unusual environment in which whales live. This most unusual departure from the pattern of muscles found in most mammals is primarily due to the absence of the pelvis and the hind legs. Although three species of manatees (*Trichechidae*) and the single species of the dugong (*Dugongidae*) likewise lack the hind legs, their departure from the typical mammalian form is not as pronounced as in the whales. This absence of hind legs in whales is compensated by the elongation of the lumbar and caudal regions to form the caudal peduncle and to terminate in the wide tail flukes. This caudal region has undergone a greatly expanded muscular development to furnish the strength needed for swimming.

In the land mammals, the bones serve two purposes, namely, to support the weight of the animal and to provide a place for the attachment of the muscles. Because whales live floating in water, their bones do not have to support the weight of their bodies. For this reason, their bones comprise a smaller proportion and their muscles comprise a larger proportion of their body weight than in the land mammals.

The muscles of the blue whale, *Balaenoptera musculus* (Linnaeus, 1758), are reported to comprise about forty percent of the weight of the animal and the skeleton about seventeen percent (Slijper).

In the sei whale (*Balaenoptera borealis* Lesson, 1828), the muscles comprise about fifty-four percent of the body weight and the skeleton about seventeen percent (Slijper).

This muscle tissue is a very dark red color due to the myoglobin, the oxygen-carrying, hemoglobin-like substance found in these muscle cells.

Division 1
THE MUSCLES OF THE SKIN

The skin of whales contains very little muscle when contrasted with the skin of land mammals. Both of the large, blanket-like muscles, which move the skin of the terrestrial mammals, are not apparent in whales.

a. The Cutaneous Muscle. The large, thin, cutaneous muscle (*M. cutaneous maximus*), which lies immediately beneath the integument and which covers most of the side of the body in many land mammals, is scarcely evident in the whales.

b. The Platysma Muscle. Likewise, the platysma muscle *(M. platysma)*, which covers part of the side of the head and the top and sides of the neck, is not apparent in the whales.

c. The Panniculus Muscle. The panniculus muscle (*M. panniculus carnosus*) is present in whales as a very thin, sheet-like muscle which extends just beneath the skin over parts of the thorax and abdomen or trunk.

In the rorquals (*Balaenopteridae: Balaenoptera*), the panniculus muscle extends from the mouth to the anus, while in the right whales (*Balaenidae: Balaena*) it is limited to the head.

Division 2
THE MUSCLES OF THE HEAD

The muscles of the head of whales vary considerably between the toothed whales *(Odontoceti)* and the whalebone whales *(Mysticeti)* and also between the families and genera within these two groups. The heads of whales vary greatly in size from some which are possibly one-tenth of the length of the body to that of the sperm whale (*Physeteridae: Physeter*) in which the head measures over one-third of the length of the body. In addition, the head assumes various shapes; some are nearly spherical in shape, many are beak-shaped with long jaws; and many others are of various configurations. All of these variations are accompanied by a variation in musculature.

The muscles which connect the head with the neck and thorax are well developed. These muscles extend both dorsally and ventrally from the occipital bone (*os occipitale*) at the back of the skull to the first cervical vertebra or atlas. Other muscles extend from the skull and lower jaw to the neck and thorax below. The muscles of the lower jaw have been reduced in size. These include the masseter muscle (*M. masseter*) which elevates the lower jaw and which is used in chewing. The temporal muscles (*M. temporalis*), also an elevator of the jaw, has been reduced in size and function.

Division 3

THE MUSCLES OF THE NECK

Within the mammals, there are many factors at work determining the nature of the neck bones and the neck muscles. Oddly enough, the length of the neck and the length of the legs appear to be related, since the length of the neck must be long enough for feeding and for the drinking of water. This relationship does not seem to apply where the front feet have been used to bring food to the mouth or where feeding does not require much movement of the head; in these species the neck assumes shorter proportions. The size and agility of the neck depends upon the weight of the head and the need for strength to carry it about and to move the head in its activities of hunting, feeding, fighting, mating, etc.

With the exception of the white whale (*Monodontidae*), the gray whale (*Eschrichtiidae*), the right whales (*Balaenidae*), and the river dolphins (*Platanistidae*), few whales exhibit any visible external signs of a neck. Among the whalebone whales *(Mysticeti)*, the gray whale (*Eschrichtiidae*) has the longest neck and one which is quite mobile.

Since the head of whales has a greater need to move in an up-and-down direction, the neck muscles of whales are the strongest and best developed on the dorsal and ventral sides of the neck; the dorsal muscles of the neck support the whale's head when it appears above the surface and the ventral neck muscles pull the head downward.

Division 4

THE MUSCLES OF THE THORAX AND THE PECTORAL APPENDAGES

When the whales assumed their aquatic existence, they relieved their skeletons of the responsibility of carrying their weight. So those muscles, which related to their terrestrial habitat, underwent a gradual change. These changes included the muscles relating to movement upon land, the muscles which were associated with their legs, and any and all muscles which were involved in any way with the bearing of weight.

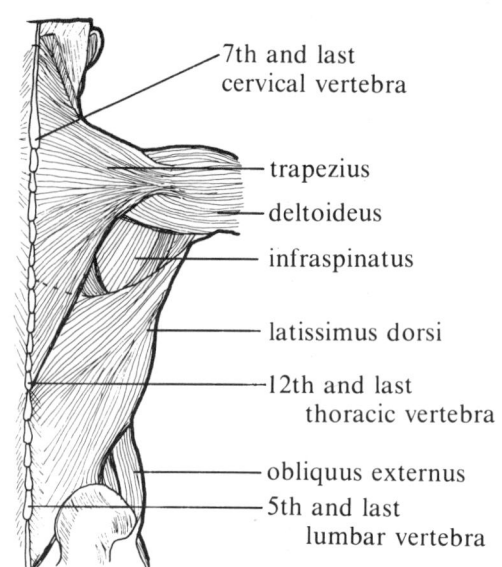

A diagram of the superficial muscles of the human shoulder and back in posterior view.

Drawn from Pope.

The thorax, the region of the body with the greatest weight and body circumference, is covered in part by blanket-like sheets of muscle.

a. The Longissimus Muscle. The longissimus muscle (*M. longissimus dorsi*), a thin, sheet-like muscle, covers much of the upper side of the thorax.

b. The Panniculus Muscle. The panniculus muscle (*M. panniculus carnosus*), another sheet-like muscle, covers a part of the side of the thorax and abdomen.

c. The Pectoralis Muscle. The pectoral group (*M. pectoralis*) of muscles lies below the flippers and extends upward from the sternum and ribs to the

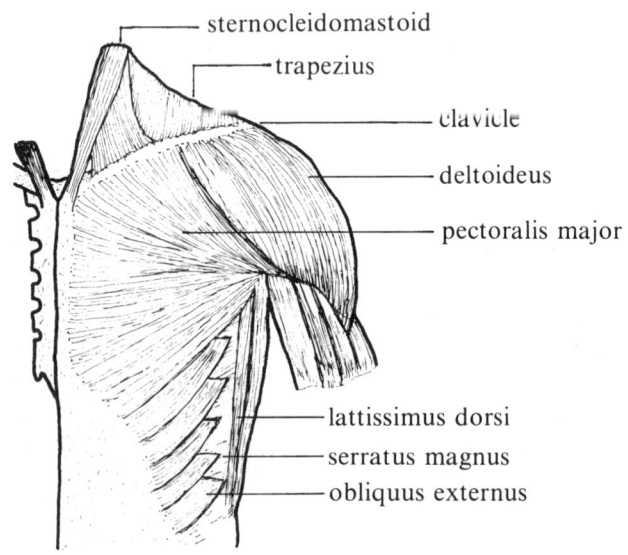

A diagram of the superficial muscles of the human shoulder and chest in anterior view.

Drawn from Pope.

54

humerus bone of the flipper. The area of the thorax below the flipper is covered by various divisions of the pectoral muscle (*M. pectoralis*) and more anteriorly by various muscles connecting to the sternum and to the hyoid bones and bearing compound names indicating these connections (such as *M. sterno-* or *M. -hyoideus*, etc.).

d. The Trapezius Muscle. The trapezius muscle (*M. trapezius*), the broad, flat, triangular muscle which covers much of the back of the thorax in man and other mammals, is absent in the whales.

e. The Rhomboideus Muscle. The back of the thorax above the flippers is covered in part by the rhomboid muscle (*M. rhomboideus*); it is a vertical muscle.

f. The Latissimus Muscle. Farther back the upper side of the thorax is covered by the latissimus muscle (*M. lattisimus dorsi*); it is a diagonal muscle.

The whales inherited their forelimbs via the evolutionary process from the front limbs of their ancestors. They have received nearly the full complement of the mammalian bones and muscles and have adapted them for their use in their aquatic environment. The forelimbs have become transformed from legs to flippers, which may range in outline from paddle-shaped to sickle-shaped. The humerus[1], the radius, and the ulna have been greatly shortened and flattened, the digits[2] have been lengthened and somewhat united, and the entire limb has been fused into a single unit.

Since the purpose of the whale's flipper is not propulsion, but balance and steering, some restrictions have appeared in its movement. For example, the flippers cannot be moved forward beyond an angle of about 90° to the longitudinal axis of the body; in addition, all of the joints below the shoulder, including the elbow, wrist, and fingers, have become fibrous and immobile. These flippers are attached and moved by many muscles of which the several sections of the deltoid muscle (*M. deltoideus*) are probably the most important.

Division 5
THE MUSCLES OF THE TRUNK

The region of the body between the thorax and the pelvis is known by many names including the abdomen, the trunk, and the lumbar area. In the whales, however, it is a bit hard to define the abdomen or trunk because there is uncertainty in knowing just where the ancient sacrum and pelvis were located. The vertebral column is often used as a reference in identifying these regions. In counting the vertebrae of whales, the trunk or lumbar area has been combined with the pelvic or sacral area and includes all of the vertebrae posterior to the thorax and anterior to the caudal region. The thoracic vertebrae end with the last vertebra which bears a rib and the caudal vertebrae begin with the first vertebra which bears a pair of chevron[1] bones beneath it. All vertebrae (lumbar and sacral) between these two landmarks are therefore classified as lumbar vertebrae.

The muscles of the trunk or the abdomen are many. Much of the lateral surface of the abdomen is covered by the oblique muscle (*M. obliquus externus abdominis*); this is a thin, sheet-like muscle which covers nealry all of the lateral surfaces of the abdomen and extends forward to the thorax. The ventral surface of the abdomen is occupied in the midline by the rectus muscle (*M. rectus abdominus*), a long, wide, large, and well-developed muscle which, when contracting, bends the body downward.

A dorsal fin is present upon the back of most whales. It contains neither bone nor muscle, but is composed principally of tough, fibrous, connective tissue. In the smaller whales, the dorsal fin is located quite near to the midpoint of the body, while in the larger whales, it is located nearer to the tail.

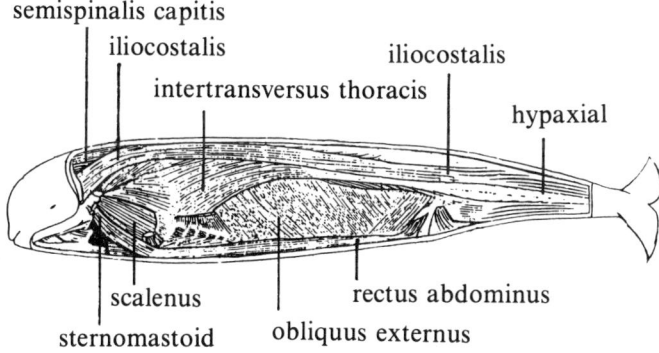

Diagram of the narwhal, *Monodon monoceros*, in lateral view showing some of the superficial muscles.

From Howell.

From: Alfred Brazier Howell — AQUATIC MAMMALS. 1931. Courtesy of Charles E. Thomas, Publishers. Springfield, Ill.

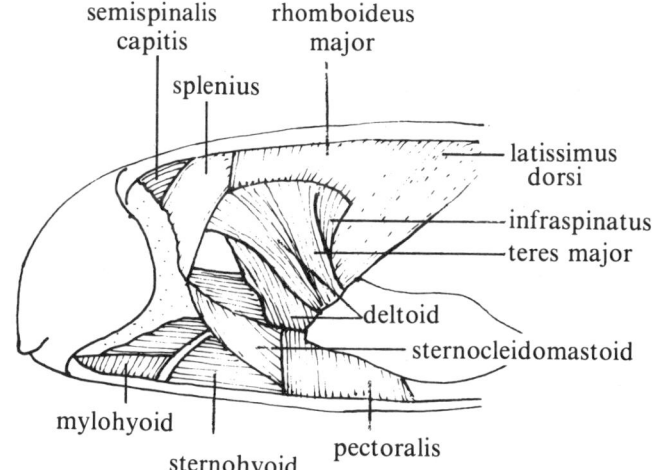

Diagram of the muscles of the left side of the thorax of the narwhal, *Monodon monoceros*, in lateral view.

Drawn from Howell.

From: Alfred Brazier Howell — AQUATIC MAMMALS. 1931. Courtesy of Charles E. Thomas, Publishers. Springfield, Ill.

---

[1]The humerus is shorter than the radius in all whalebone whales (*Mysticeti*) and in *Platanista*, *Pontoporia*, *Physeter*, and *Kogia* in the toothed whales (*Odontoceti*).

[2]All toothed whales (*Odontoceti*) have retained the original 5 digits (fingers) of the hand. In the whalebone whales (*Mysticeti*), only the two species of *Balaena* have 5 digits. *Eschrichtius* lacks the 1st digit (thumb); the five species of *Balaenoptera and Megaptera* lack the 3rd digit; and *Caperea* has but 4 digits.

---

[1]The chevron bones (*os intercalare*) lie below the vertebrae of the tail and form the haemal arch through which the artery to the tail (*Arteria sacralis media*) passes and its corresponding vein (*Vena sacralis media*) returns.

Division 6

THE MUSCLES OF THE PELVIC REGION AND THE PELVIC APPENDAGES

There is no doubt that the ancestors of the whales possessed a full set of pelvic bones together with a paired set of leg bones, each including a femur, a tibia and a fibula, and a full set of ankle and foot bones. Today, there are no external traces of these bones except for an occasional "throw back" in which some useless rudiments appear. However, the whales of today possess a small pair of bones which are remnants of their pelvis[1]; these bones are usually slender, curved in an irregular manner, and lie buried in the flesh of the abdomen somewhere above the reproductive openings.

The ancient ancestors of whales chose to swim with their tails and to trail their hind limbs in the water. These hind limbs became reduced in size and function and had practically disappeared before the modern whales appeared. In the ancient fossil zeuglodont whale (*Basilosauridae: Basilosaurus*) of 40,000,000 years ago (Eocene), the legs were already gone and only a rudimentary femur[2] remained.

The atrophy of the hind limbs led to the atrophy of the pelvis. The ilium and the pubis were probably the first pelvic bones to be reduced in size or to disappear, because they were most closely associated with the muscles of the legs. The ischium, not as closely related to the leg muscles as the ilium and the pubis, would probably remain for a longer time because these bones are the attachments for the perineal muscles *(M. perinei)* which form the floor *(perineum)* of the abdomen and also because they are the attachments for the muscles *(crura)* from each corpus cavernosum of the penis.

Since the muscles of the pelvis, the pelvic area, and the hind limbs have vanished or been reduced to remnants, they no longer contribute to any muscular activity in the whales. With this disappearance of the typical mammalian pelvic muscles, this region of the body and part of the lumbar region anterior to it have really become a functional part of the tail.

---

[1] The pelvis consists of two innominate bones (*os innominatum;* pl., *ossa innominata*), one of which forms the right side of the pelvis and the other forms the left side. Each side or innominate bone is composed in turn of three bones, an ilium (*os ilium*), an ischium (*os ischium*), and a pubis (*os pubis*), which are fused together to form the innominate bone.

[2] Rudimentary femurs are often found in most whalebone whales (*Mysticeti*) and occasionally a trace of a tibia will persist.

Division 7

THE MUSCLES OF THE CAUDAL REGION

In the caudal region of the body, the muscles have undergone a great development to form the extension of the trunk known as the caudal peduncle. This caudal peduncle includes the large and strong muscles which move the tail and its flukes in an up-and-down direction. These muscles and their tendons extend in a very complex series from the lumbar region backward to the flukes.

The most astonishing aspect of the caudal peduncle is its great height and narrow width. The vertical height is the result of the need for very strong muscles to move the tail up-and-down, thereby producing the forward thrust required for swimming. Since the tail is moved vertically, the muscles of the tail which perform this work have increased greatly in size and strength. They are longitudinal in direction, long and tendonous, and terminate posteriorly in tough, white strands of connective tissue. Since there was no demand for any lateral motion of the caudal peduncle, the musculature on the sides of the caudal peduncle is not well developed.

The longitudinal muscles of the back and tail are many and are exceedingly complex. Many of these muscles arise in the lumbar area and terminate in the various caudal vertebrae. Collectively, these muscles above the vertebral column are called the apaxial muscles (above the axis) and those below the vertebral column are called the hypaxial muscles (below the axis). Of these, the chief muscle to elevate the tail is known as the *M. erector spinae,* while the lowering of the tail is accomplished by a combination of several ventral muscles.

The tail of whales terminates posteriorly in two flat, horizontal blade-like flukes, one of which lies on either side at the end of the vertebral column. These flukes contain no true bone, but are composed of exceedingly tough fibrous tissue which has become ossified into flat, bony units. The muscles, as we know them, diminish posteriorly in the caudal peduncle and tail and are there replaced by hard, tough, fibrous connective tissue.

Chapter V
THE DIGESTIVE SYSTEM

The digestive tract of mammals consists of a tubular passageway extending from the lips and mouth backward through the body to the anus. In general, it consists of the same series of organs regardless of the species. These divisions of the digestive tract in mammals include the lips, the mouth, the pharynx, the esophagus, the stomach, the small intestine, the caecum, the large intestine, the rectum, and the anus, together with the associated digestive glands of the salivary glands, the liver, and the pancreas. However, these divisions of the digestive tract vary widely in number, size, length, arrangement of the compartments, and other features. These variations are the result of the ancestry of the whales, their food and method of feeding, their environment, and other factors.

Among the whales, there are differences between the digestive tracts of toothed whales *(Odontoceti)* and whalebone whales *(Mysticeti)* because they seem to be descended from different ancestors, and because their food and manner of feeding are quite different.

Division 1
THE MOUTH

The mouths of whales are of two general types—those with teeth and those with whalebone—both of which are developed around two upper jaw bones and two lower jaw bones. Both are bordered by thin, immobile lips which lack the muscles and the mobility found in other mammals; but within these lips, the differences between these two types of mouths are indeed great.

Section a
THE TONGUE

In the toothed whales *(Odontoceti)*, the jaws within the mouth contain teeth of various numbers and arrangements and a tongue on the floor of the mouth between them. This tongue is of moderate size and has somewhat restricted mobility except for the area at its anterior extremity. During its formation, the tongue develops a normally free distal end, but, as it progresses, becomes restricted in some species to a point approaching uselessness. See page 85.

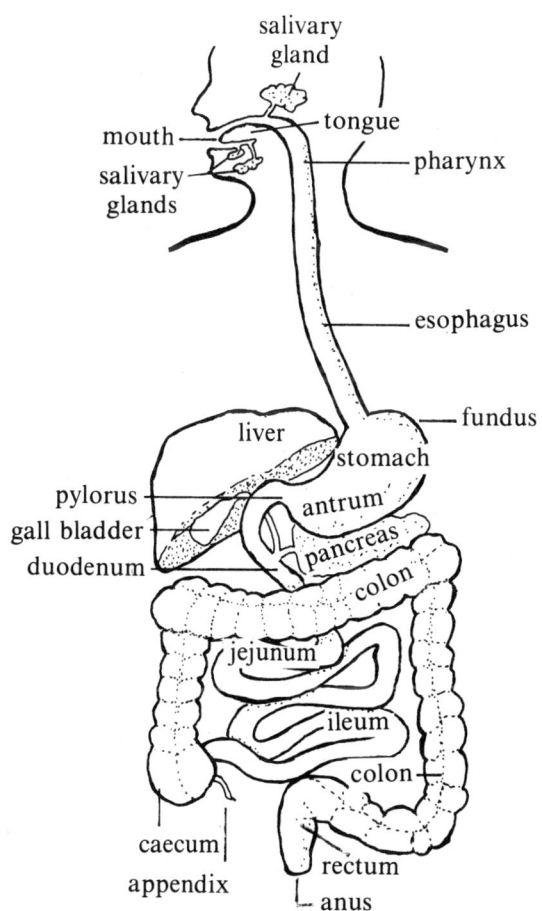

Diagram of the human digestive tract.
From authors.

In the whalebone whales (*Mysticeti*), the tongue is enormous in size and occupies the entire floor of the mouth. The tongue of a large blue whale has been estimated to approach 3,629 kg. (8,000 pounds) in weight and is large out of all proportion to its use. It is composed of a very soft, spongy connective tissue with a minimum amount of muscular tissue. When feeding, the whale swims forward with its mouth open; the water streams in the front of the mouth and outward to the right and left through the whalebone blades and over the lips. During this time the tongue lies upon the floor of the mouth and is only moved at the time of swallowing; at this time, the tongue is elevated to force the water from the mouth and to enable the food which is lying upon the surface of the tongue to be swallowed.

In 1941, the carcass of a female fin whale (*Balaenoptera physalus*) was weighed piecemeal as it was being cut up for processing at the whaling station at Fields Landing, California. The total weight of this whale was 130,942 pounds (59,394 kg.); of this amount, the tongue weighed 2705 pounds (1,227 kg.); this is 2.06% (.0206) or 1/48 of the total body weight.

Section b
THE TEETH

The whales are divided into two great groups on the basis of their teeth; these groups are the toothed whales (*Odontoceti*) and the whalebone whales (*Mysticeti*).

The whalebone whales lack teeth and in their stead have a single series of long whalebone blades hanging downward from the upper jaw bone in a row along each side of the mouth.

The teeth of the toothed whales (*Odontoceti*) show great variation in numbers, size and shape, distribution along the jaw bones, and in other features. They range in size from the small, spindle-shaped teeth of the dolphins (*Stenella, Delphinus*) and the slightly-flattened teeth of the porpoises (*Phocoena*) to the heavy, massive teeth of the sperm whale (*Physeter*) and the long, slender, spirally-pointed tusk of the narwhal (*Monodon*). In addition, there are fine, sharply pointed teeth in the dwarf sperm whale (*Kogia*) and heavy, solid nubbin-like teeth embedded in the tips of the lower jaw bones of some of the beaked whales (*Mesoplodon*).

The teeth of the toothed whales *(Odontoceti)* are usually quite similar in size and shape in each species and do not present the differentiation into incisors, canines, premolars, molars, etc., which is common to many mammals. In addition, whales do not develop the "milk" teeth prior to their permanent set. They get only one set of teeth (monophydont) and those teeth of this permanent set which become lost or broken are never replaced.

Among the mammals, the basic number of teeth is regarded as 44 in all; these include 3 incisors, 1 canine, 4 premolars, and 3 molars in each half of the upper and lower jaws. However, the passage of time, together with both evolutionary and environmental forces, has altered this basic number of teeth in the mammals. Numerous teeth are regarded as an ancestral condition and fewer teeth are regarded as being a more recent and more specialized condition.

The reduction of the number of teeth in mammals is an evolutionary trend which has doubtless been associated with life on land where food is often less abundant, and where this food must often be nipped or cut off, chewed, and partially digested before swallowing. Here the jaws become more active, the jaw muscles increase in size with chewing, and the jaw bones become shorter. In these situations, the teeth in different parts of the mouth become obliged to assume different duties and, in due time, assume those sizes and shapes which are more efficient.

Among the whales, the various species of dolpins and porpoises (*Delphinidae*) tend to have numerous teeth. This condition doubtless developed after their return to the sea and may represent a return to their ancestral condition of numerous teeth; or it may have been brought about by ample food, little need for chewing, and the need of longer jaws with many teeth to assist in the capturing of food in the sea.

Section c
THE WHALEBONE

The whalebone whales (*Mysticeti*) at some time in their ancient lineage slowly cast aside the teeth of their ancestors and gradually developed an entirely new and different mechanism to use in the acquisition of food from the sea. From the tissues of the upper jaw, they somehow developed a row or series of long, giant, feather-like plates which now hang downward from the upper jaw bones and into the mouth cavity along both sides of the mouth; it is through these whalebone plates that they now strain out the small drifting creatures of the sea on which they now feed.

These sheets or blades of whalebone are not composed of bone, but rather of a hard, strong, horny substance known as keratin, a nitrogenous epidermal tissue which is common in the hair, nails, hoofs, and horns of mammals, in the feathers of birds, and elsewhere. These blades are flat, somewhat triangular in outline, are attached by their short side to the jaw above, and hang vertically and nearly crosswise with their pointed end directed downward. These blades have one smooth edge and one edge which is frayed into threads along its entire border; this frayed edge is turned toward the tongue and helps to form the mesh which strains from the sea water the many small creatures on which these whales feed.

These whalebone or baleen plates will range in length from less than one foot to as much as 14.7 feet (4.5 meters) in the bowhead whale *(Balaena mysticetus)*. On each side of the mouth, they will number from perhaps 140 or 150 in the gray whale (*Eschrictius robustus*) to as many as 375 to 400 in the humpbacked whale (*Megaptera novaeangliae*) and in the blue whale (*Balaenoptera musculus*). Needless to say, the entire anterior one-half of the body has undergone great changes in structure and size to support these great long whalebone blades and to accommodate this change in feeding habits.

One of the most amazing biological facts concerning the whalebone whales is the appearance for a time of small teeth in the jaws of the unborn fetus of these whales. These teeth appear in the developing jaws of the fetus and then slowly dissolve away and disappear, to be replaced at a later time by the permanent whalebone. This is an astonishing bit of evolutionary evidence that the whalebone whales are descended from very ancient ancestors which were equipped with teeth. .

A TABLE OF WHALEBONE

The Species of Whalebone Whales	The Whalebone Blades	
	Number (on one side)	Length

Suborder MYSTICETI—The Whalebone Whales

Family ESCHRICHTIIDAE

Eschrichtius robustus (Lilljeborg, 1861)
The Gray Whale . . . . 130 to 180   To 40 to 50 cm. (16 to 20 in.)

Family BALAENOPTERIDAE

Balaenoptera acutorostrata Lacepede, 1804
The Lesser Rorqual . . . . . 280 to 325   To 35 cm. (13.8 in.)

Balaenoptera borealis Lesson, 1828
The Sei Whale . . . . 220 to 400   To 80 cm. (31.5 in.)

Balaenoptera edeni Anderson, 1878
The Bryde's Whale . . . . . . 255 to 365   To 40 to 50 cm. (16 to 20 in.)

Balaenoptera musculus (Linnaeus, 1758)
The Blue Whale . . . . 270 to 395   To 1 m. (39-40 in.)

Balaenoptera physalus (Linnaeus, 1758)
The Fin Whale . . . . 260 to 473   To 70 to 90 cm. (27 to 35 in.)

Megaptera novaeangliae (Borowski, 1781)
The Hump-Backed Whale 270 to 400   To 85 cm. (33.5 in.)

Family BALAENIDAE

Balaena glacialis Muller, 1776
The Right Whale . . . . 206 to 268   To 2.8 m. (9 ft.)

Balaena mysticetus Linnaeus, 1758
The Bowhead Whale . . . . 325 to 360   To 4.5 m. (14.76 ft.) Usually 2 to 3 m. (6.5 to 9.8 ft.)

Caperea marginata (Gray, 1846)
The Pigmy Right Whale 230 to 250   To 70 cm. (27.5 in.)

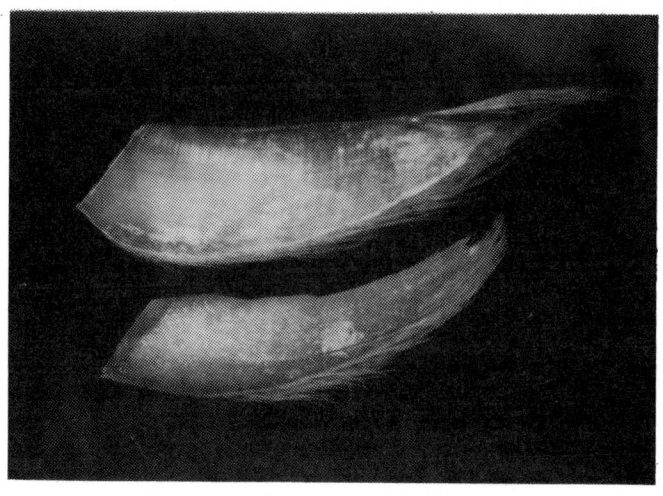

Photo of whalebone blades (baleen) of a whalebone whale *(Mysticeti)* showing their tapering outline and frayed inner margin.

All organisms which cannot pass between the baleen plates remain in the mouth and are swallowed.

A photo of the dried whalebone blades or baleen of the gray whale, *Eschrichtius robustus,* in external view.

Photo by Graybill.

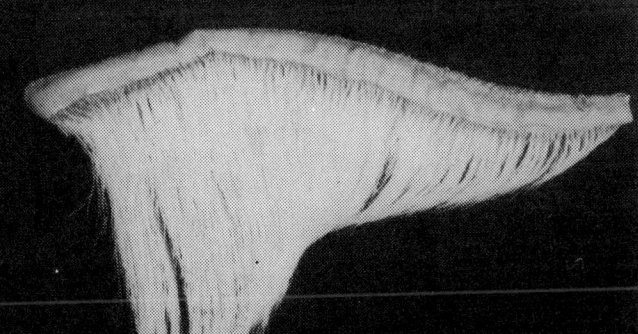

Photo of the whalebone blades of the left side of the gray whale, *Eschrichtius robustus,* in medial view.

Photo of the whalebone blades (baleen) of the left side of the gray whale, *Eschrichtius robustus,* in lateral view.

Ore. Inst. Mar. Biol.

Division 2
THE PHARYNX

Among the mammals, the pharynx is a chamber located posterior to the mouth, where the passage for air and the passage for food cross enroute to the lungs and to the stomach, respectively. In the head, the air passages (nasal cavities) lie above the food passage (mouth), while posterior to the pharynx, the food passage (esophagus) now lies above and dorsal to the air passage (larynx and trachea). The pharynx also contains the epiglottis, a somewhat leaf-like organ which is usually considered part of the respiratory system. It is attached ventrally and lies forward on the floor of the pharynx while the air is passing from the nasal chambers above across the pharynx into the larynx below. At such times as food is swallowed, the epiglottis drops in a hinged manner to cover the opening into the larynx posterior to it and the food, which is being swallowed, passes over and across it into the esophagus.

There are two slits located, one on each side, in the anterior area of the pharynx; each of these is the inner opening of the Eustachian tube which leads laterally on each side to connect the pharynx with the tympanic cavity of the middle ear.

In the toothed whales (*Odontoceti*), the pharynx is greatly complicated by the elongation and enlargement of the larynx and by its projection upward through the middle of the pharynx to connect with the nasal passage. As a result, the food passing through the pharynx passes to the right and/or left of the larynx enroute to the esophagus.

In the whalebone whales (*Mysticeti*), the pharynx is relatively simple and more closely resembles that of other mammals.

Division 3
THE ESOPHAGUS

The esophagus of whales is a simple, nearly-straight, thin-walled duct or tube leading from the pharynx backward to the first unit of the stomach. It is of simple structure, usually collapsed when not in use, and differs but little from that of other mammals.

Among the toothed whales (*Odontoceti*), its diameter is consistent with the size of the whale and the type of food which it consumes. A large esophagus is found in Killer Whales (*Delphinidae: Orcinus orca*), which are known to swallow a whole seal, and also in the Sperm Whales (*Physeteridae: Physeter macrocephalus*) which are known to swallow whole the very large, deep-water squids on which they feed.

Among the whalebone whales (*Mysticeti*), the esophagus is much smaller than in the *Odontoceti* and much smaller than the size of their bodies suggests. Large baleen whales have an esophagus which measures four, five, or six inches in diameter and which in large individuals might be distended or stretched to a diameter of eight or ten inches.

Division 4
THE STOMACH

The typical mammalian stomach is a single, curved, sac-shaped pouch which is the widest part of the alimentary tract. It is usually curved and somewhat pear-shaped with the largest (cardiac) end of this organ lying to the left and on the dorsal side of the abdomen; it then curves ventrally and to the right to form the pyloric end of the stomach. A sphincter muscle is located at the lower or pyloric end of the stomach where it joins the first portion (duodenum) of the small intestine. This sphincter muscle lies in the wall of the alimentary tract, completely encircles it, and is the point at which the passageway between the stomach and the intestine is opened and closed.

Many mammals have departed from the simple, single-chambered stomach described above and have developed various compartments to form a more complex stomach. Of these groups, the best known is the cattle or hollow-horned

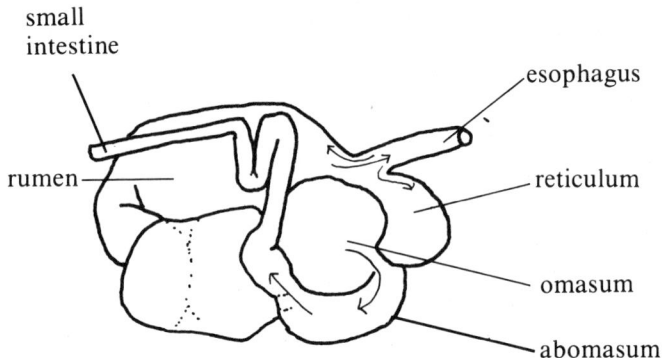

**A diagram of a bovine stomach showing four chambers.
Drawn from Gunderson.**

ruminant family (*Bovidae*) in which the stomach is divided into the following four chambers: rumen or paunch; reticulum or honeycomb bag; omasum, psalterum, or many-plies; and the abomasum. In addition, complex stomachs are found in the *Sirenia* (the three manatees and the dugong), in the anteaters, in some bats, and in the whales.

In general, the stomach of whales consists of three or more chambers plus the duodenal ampulla; this makes a total of four chambers. The first stomach or fore-stomach is a development of the lower end of the esophagus and is usually quite large, muscular, and sac-like. The second chamber or main stomach corresponds to the cardiac portion of the typical mammalian stomach, while the third chamber or pyloric stomach is simply the pyloric end of the mammalian stomach. The fourth chamber in this series is really not a part of the stomach, but rather an enlargment of the anterior region of the duodenum, known as the duodenal ampulla.

The main stomach lies somewhat to the left of the midline, is the largest of the chambers, and tapers toward its posterior end. The main stomach is in reality the cardiac portion of the stomach which has been separated by a constriction from the smaller pyloric portion of the stomach; it may lead into the pyloric stomach through a short tubular connection which is sometimes called the connecting channel; this connecting channel is known to have been developed from the pyloric

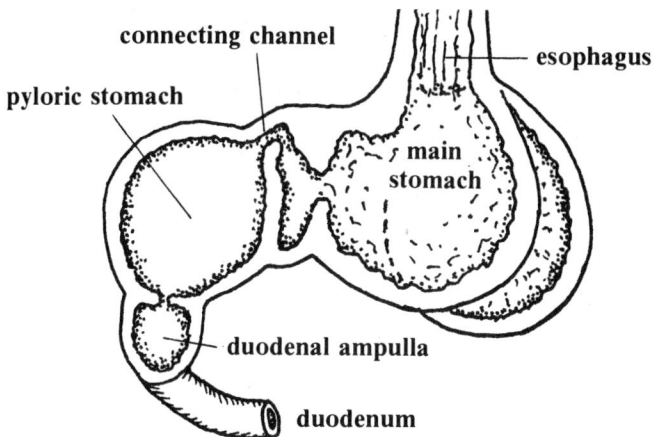

Diagram of the stomach of the Ganges River dolphin, *Platanista gangetica* (Odontoceti: Platanistidae). From Zhou Kaiya et alii.

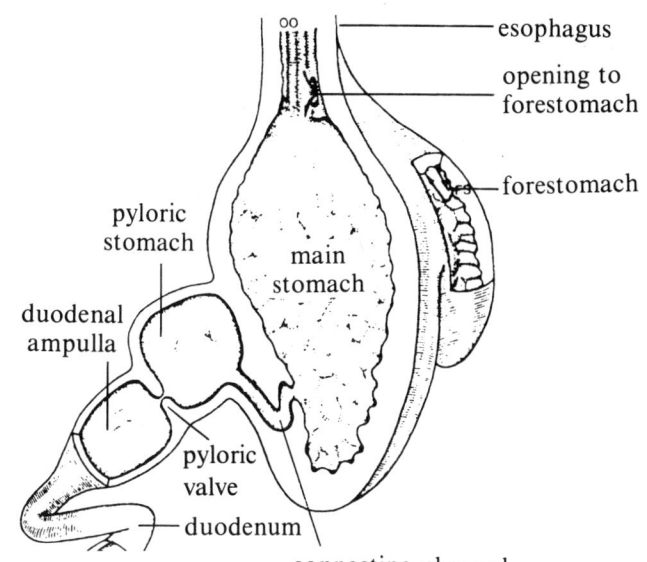

Diagram of the stomach of the Madeira River dolphin, *Inia geoffrensis boliviensis* (Odontoceti: Platanistidae). From Zhou Kaiya et alii.

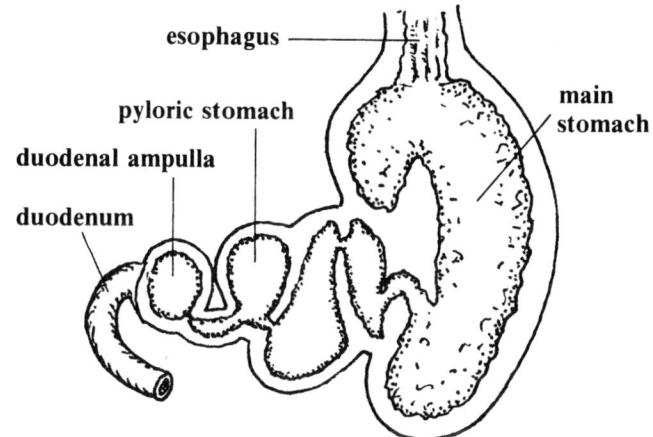

Diagram of the stomach of the Chinese River dolphin, *Lipotes vexillifer* (Odontoceti: Platanistidae). From Zhou Kaiya et alii.

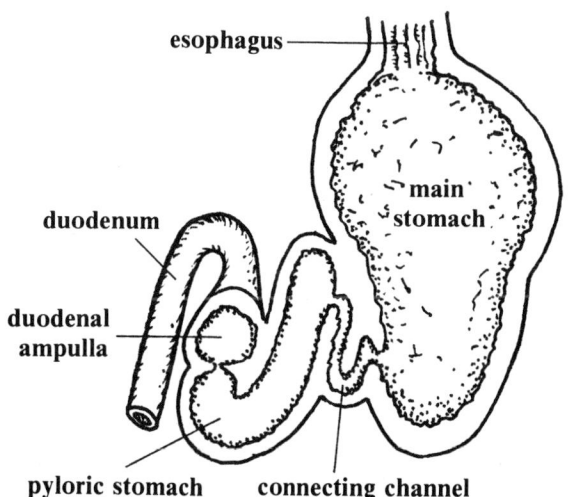

Diagram of the stomach of La Plata River dolphin, *Pontoporia blainvillei* (Odontoceti: Platanistidae). From Zhou Kaiya et alii.

stomach because the tissues which line them are similar. The connecting channel may be of various lengths and configurations; it is not present in all species. This is quite different from the stomachs of typical mammals where the cardiac and pyloric ends of the stomach form a single chamber.

The pyloric stomach usually lies to the right of the midline, is much smaller than the main or cardiac stomach, is often somewhat spherical in shape, and leads posteriorly into a small opening known as the pylorus. This opening is surrounded in all mammals by the pyloric muscles which, by contracting are able to close the opening leading from the pyloric stomach into the small intestine and thereby control the amount of food, fluids, etc., which pass onward into the small intestine. These muscles form the pyloric valve.

In most mammals the small intestine continues as a tubular structure of nearly uniform diameter. However, in the river dolphins (*Platanistidae*), the small intestine immediately expands into a spherical, balloon-like structure or ampulla for a short distance; this constitutes an additional chamber in this area, but it is really a part of the intestine rather than the stomach.

In the toothed whales (*Odontoceti*), the compartments within the stomach are usually three in number (forestomach, main stomach, and pyloric stomach), although in some of the beaked whales (*Ziphiidae*), the stomach may be composed of as many as 13 chambers or pockets. In most toothed whales, the first compartment or fore-stomach has a cellular structure similar to that of the esophagus and so is really the enlarged, expanded, and specialized posterior end of that tube or organ. However, in the beaked whales (*Ziphiidae*), the first chamber of the stomach is truly a part of the stomach and is not developed from the esophagus. The remaining compartments of most toothed whales are developments of the true stomach.

All three chambers of the stomach are separated from each other by constrictions which usually reduce the openings between these chambers to rather small orifices. Of these three chambers, the first chamber (fore-stomach) is often the largest, the second chamber (main stomach) is next in size, and the third chamber (pyloric stomach) is the smallest.

It is interesting to note at this point that in the young of the toothed whales, the first chamber of the stomach is smaller for a time than the second chamber, because the young are living upon milk and have not yet begun the digestion of harder and coarser foods. They need only the digestive juices

61

of the main stomach and as yet have no need to store food in the fore-stomach.

In the Amazon River dolphin, *Inia geoffrensis,* the typical mammalian stomach has been augmented by the creation of additional chambers. In the area where the esophagus empties into the main stomach, an aperture leads off from the posterior end of the esophagus into a chamber called the fore-stomach. It is a blind sack lying along the left, dorsal side of the main stomach and to which it is attached for a little more than one-half of its length. Since this fore-stomach connects with the alimentary tract by a single aperture, this opening must serve as both the entrance and the exit of the fore-stomach.

In the river dolphins (*Platanistidae*), a fore-stomach is present in *Platanista* and *Inia,* but it is absent in *Lipotes* and *Pontoporia.*

In the whalebone whales (*Mysticeti*), the stomach of all species is divided into three chambers (fore-stomach, main stomach, and pyloric stomach). Of these, the second chamber of the stomach is the largest and the first chamber is next in size.

Division 5
THE SMALL INTESTINE

The small intestine is divided into three regions: the duodenum, the jejunum, and the ileum. The duodenum, the shortest of the three, begins at the pylorus and extends posteriorly for a short distance, about 9 to 12 inches in man, out of a total intestine of 22 to 25 feet. The jejunum comprises about 2/5 of the remainder of the small intestine and the ileum comprises the other 3/5 of the small intestine. The ileum terminates at its junction with the large intestine; this junction is also the location of the caecum. In some whales, where the caecum is absent, it is very difficult to determine the end of the ileum and the beginning of the large intestine.

In general, whales have long intestines; this is particularly true as the size of the whale increases.

In the toothed whales (*Odontoceti*), the mesenteries supporting the small intestine are quite thick and the folds are fine in character. There is but a single hepatic or bile duct entering the duodenum from the liver; it is joined by two pancreatic ducts and all three enter the duodenum midway in its length.

In the baleen whales (*Mysticeti*), the intestines are long and the mesenteries supporting them are thin with large folds. In contrast to the *Odontoceti,* two bile ducts from the liver join a single pancreatic duct and together discharge into the duodenum near its midpoint.

Division 6
THE CAECUM

The caecum is a small blind sac located at the junction of the small intestine and the large intestine of which it is really a part. It varies greatly in size among the various species of mammals and is an organ of questionable value. It is reported that those mammals with small and/or simple stomachs possess a larger caecum than those mammals with larger and more complex stomachs.

In the toothed whales (*Odontoceti*), the caecum is usually absent, although the dolphins (*Delphinidae*) and the genus *Platanista* (*Platanistidae*) have a very small caecum.

In the whalebone whales (*Mysticeti*), the caecum is usually present as a very short organ, although the right whales (*Balaenidae: Balaena*) do not appear to possess this organ.

The vermiform appendix, which in man is a small, slender outpocket from the caecum, is absent in the whales.

Division 7
THE LARGE INTESTINE, RECTUM, AND ANUS

The large intestine extends from the end of the small intestine to the anus. It is often divided into two or more regions of which the commonest divisions are the colon and the rectum. In man, the combined length of the small and large intestine measures between 5 and 6.5 times the length of the body. The large intestine is much shorter than the small intestine and, in man, measures about 1/5 of the total length of the entire intestine or about 1/4 of the length of the small intestine.

Measuring an intestine is not an entirely scientific process. The length of the intestine when alive is reduced by the living muscular tissue which it contains; after death, these muscles relax and the intestine stretches to nearly double the length of the live intestine.

In the toothed whales (*Odontoceti*),... "the entire large intestine of adult toothed whales occupies no more than 10% of the length of the intestine; thus it is visibly shorter than in baleen whales" (Yablokov et alii).

Among the toothed whales (*Odontoceti*), the sperm whale (*Physeter macrocephalus*) has an exceedingly long intestine, probably due to its great size. Slijper estimates that a 55-foot sperm whale would have an intestine of about 500 feet (152 m.) in length and that this intestine would stretch to about 1200 feet (365 m.) after death.

In the baleen whales (*Mysticeti*), the large intestine is longer than in the *Odontoceti* and will exceed 10% of the length of the entire intestine. This is due in part to the larger size of the *Mysticeti* when compared with most *Odontoceti.*

The large intestine terminates at the anus. This is a simple organ consisting principally of one or two anal sphincter muscles which relax or constrict to open or close the anal opening. The whales differ little from other mammals in the structure and use of the anus. In all whales, the faecal discharge from the anus is a cloudy liquid.

Division 8
THE DIGESTIVE GLANDS

The digestive glands of mammals include the salivary glands, the liver, the pancreas, and various digestive glands associated with the stomach and the intestine. Of these, only the salivary glands, the liver, and the pancreas will be mentioned here.

Section a
THE SALIVARY GLANDS

The salivary glands in the mouth of whales are either missing or have atrophied and are no longer functional. In some species, the salivary ducts remain, while the glandular tissue formerly associated with them is missing. It is not difficult to understand why they would be of little use since the mouth of a whale is continually awash with water.

Digestive Gland Ducts in Whales

	Gall Bladder	Bile Ducts	Pancreatic Ducts
THE ODONTOCETI (The Toothed Whales)	0	1	1
THE MYSTICETI (The Whalebone Whales)	0	2	2

Section b
THE LIVER

In all mammals, the liver lies toward the right side of the body, at the anterior end of the abdominal cavity, just below the diaphragm, and adjoining the stomach and the duodenum. It is typically a bi-lobed organ with additional lobes developed in various animals.

In man, the liver is 5-lobed and weighs about 1/40 of the body weight.

In the whales, the liver is fundamentally bilobed and the gall bladder found in many mammals is absent in all whales. In some large whales, the liver is reported to consist of two large lateral lobes and one small median lobe. There are few differences between the livers of the various whales, although it should be noted that, in the toothed whales (Odontoceti), there is but a single bile duct, while in the baleen whales (Mysticeti) there are two bile ducts.

The livers, which were removed from five large whales at the whaling station at Fields Landing, California, in 1941, showed the following weights*:

THE WEIGHT OF THE LIVERS OF WHALES

Species	Total Weight Pounds	Kilograms	Weight of the Livers Pounds	Kilograms
Odontoceti				
Physeteridae				
Physeter macrocephalus				
The Sperm Whale				
Male: Length 43 ft.	86,000	39,000	925	420
Ziphiidae				
*Ziphius cavirostris****				
Cuvier's Goose-beaked Whale				
Female: 21.5 ft.	6,510	2,952.5	57.1	25.9
Mysticeti				
Balaenopteridae				
Balaenoptera physalus				
The Fin Whale				
Female: 71 ft.	130,942**	59,394	1,783	809
Megaptera novaeangliae				
The Hump-backed Whale				
Male: 41 ft.	82,000	37,195	1,050	476
Male: 44 ft.	88,000	39,916	800	363
Male: 45 ft.	90,000	40,823	1,400	635

*From the Jour. of Mammalogy 24:1, 1943, pp. 39-45.
**Includes an added 20% for blood and body fluids.
***Jour. of Mammalogy 42:1, Feb. 1961, pp. 71-76.

Section c
THE PANCREAS

The pancreas has a two-fold funtion. It produces digestive juices which enter the duodenum through a pancreatic duct and it also contains groups of glandular tissue cells, called the Isles of Langerhans, which are scattered through the pancreas; these are endocrine glands which produce insulin and other products which are transferred to the blood vessels passing through them.

The pancreas of mammals is an elongated organ lying against the back side of the stomach midway between the spleen and the duodenum. In man, it measures between 6 and 8 inches in length and about 1½ by 1 inches in width and thickness.

In the whales, the pancreas resembles that of most other mammals; there is very little difference in this organ between the whales and any typical mammal. It has been observed that the pancreas of adult female whales is larger than that of adult males.

In the toothed whales (Odontoceti), the pancreas has but a single pancreatic duct, while in the whalebone whales (Mysticeti), two pancreatic ducts are present.

The Weight of the Pancreas in Whales

Species	Weight of the Specimen		Weight of the Pancreas		Percent of Body Weight
	Kilograms (lbs.x.4536)	Pounds (kg.x2.205)	Kilograms (lbs.x.4536)	Pounds (kg.x2.205)	
ODONTOCETI					
Delphinidae					
Orcinus orca					
THE KILLER WHALE (Avg. Wt.)	—	—	3.5	7.72	—
Monodontidae					
Delphinapterus leucas					
THE WHITE WHALE (4 specimens)	—	—	2.30 to 5.61	5.07 to 12.37	.1 to .07
Physeteridae					
Physeter macrocephala					
THE SPERM WHALE (8 specimens)	26,251 to 51,695	57,883 to 113,987	4 to 14	8.82 to 30.87	.01 to .04
Ziphiidae					
Berardius bairdi					
THE NORTH PACIFIC, GIANT, FOUR-TOOTHED WHALE (Avg. Wt.)	—	—	5.0	11.025	—
MYSTICETI					
Balaenopteridae					
Balaenoptera acutorostrata					
THE LESSER RORQUAL (Avg. Wt.)	—	—	5.4	11.9	—
Balaenoptera musculus					
THE BLUE WHALE	109,930	242,396	40.	88.2	.036
Balaenoptera physalus					
THE FIN WHALE (3 specimens)	34,351 to 54,768	75,744 to 120,763	20 to 32	44.1 to 70.56	.04 to .08

From Quay et alii.

Chapter VI
THE RESPIRATORY SYSTEM

The respiratory system consists of those openings, passages, organs, etc. which bring the air which an animal requires from the atmosphere to the point where the oxygen contained in it can reach the blood stream. Actually, the process of respiration is not complete until the oxygen has been transferred to the blood and then delivered by the blood to the cells where it is finally used. Respiration likewise includes the reverse process in which carbon dioxide is transferred from the cells to the blood, then to the lungs, and finally passes out through the bronchi, the trachea, the larynx, the pharynx, and the nasal passages to the atmosphere.

In most mammals, the mouth is also used as an additional opening for the intake and discharge of air, but its use is not universal among them. The whales, for example, can neither inhale nor exhale through their mouth.

Among the mammals which live in the water, there have been many changes in their body structure during the millions of years since they gave up their terrestrial residence. Of these aquatic mammals, the whales have undergone the greatest and the most radical changes of which those involving the respiratory system are most amazing.

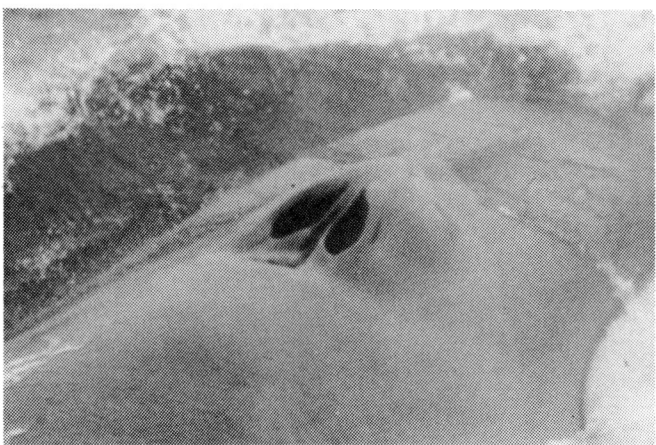

Photo of the blowholes of the fin whale, *Balaenoptera physalus.*
Photo by P. Ensor.

From: "Whales and Dolphins of New Zealand and Australia" by A.N. Baker. Victoria University Press, Wellington, 1983. Courtesy A.N. Baker.

Division 1
THE NASAL CAVITY
AND THE NASAL PASSAGES

The changes in the nasal cavity and the nasal passages to better adapt the whales to a life in water have been many and quite unusual. The anterior nasal opening (nares), better known as the blowhole, has moved from the front of the snout to the top of the head to make breathing more convenient. This has been accompanied by a change in the bones of the face. The nasal bones, which form the roof of the nasal cavity in most mammals, have been shortened, reduced in size, and pushed backward. These bones were simply pushed upward and backward by the slow backward migration of the blowhole and the nasal passage beneath it until the nasal bones have come to lie behind the blow hole in a vertical position upon the front slope of the cranium; they remain today as a greatly altered and reduced feature of the face.

The vomeronasal organ or Organ of Jacobson is absent in all modern whales. It is a small strange structure in the form of a diverticulum which has sensory functions and which is located in the front of the nose.

In the toothed whales (*Odontoceti*), the blowhole is a single opening which is usually a crescent-shaped slit with the two tips of the crescent pointing forward and located in the midline atop the head. A very few toothed whales have blowholes of other shapes and at other locations, thereby departing from a strict bilateral symmetry.

The sperm whales (*Physeteridae: Physeter*) have a blowhole which is an elongated S-shaped slit on the left, front corner of their head; the blowhole of the pigmy sperm whale (*Physeteridae: Kogia*) is placed atop the head, but to the left of the midline; and the blowhole of some of the river dolphins (*Platanistidae*) is a single, longitudinal slit atop the head.

The bones which surround the external narial aperture are not symmetrical; in these species, the bones of the left side of the head are smaller than the bones of the right side; this is especially true in the narwhal (*Monodontidae: Monodon*), the sperm whale (*Physeteridae: Physeter*), and in the bottle-nosed whales (*Ziphiidae: Hyperoodon*).

---

[1]It should also be noted that the *Sirenia,* which include three manatees and the dugong, have also shifted the nasal opening backward and upward to a position higher on the head; this is likewise due to their aquatic mode of life.

Photo of the blowholes of a hump-backed whale, *Megaptera novaeangliae,* **showing the fleshy "water guards" which surround the blowholes on the front and sides and help to keep the water out of the blowholes when the whale is breathing.**

Photo by Kewalo Basin Marine Mammal Laboratory.

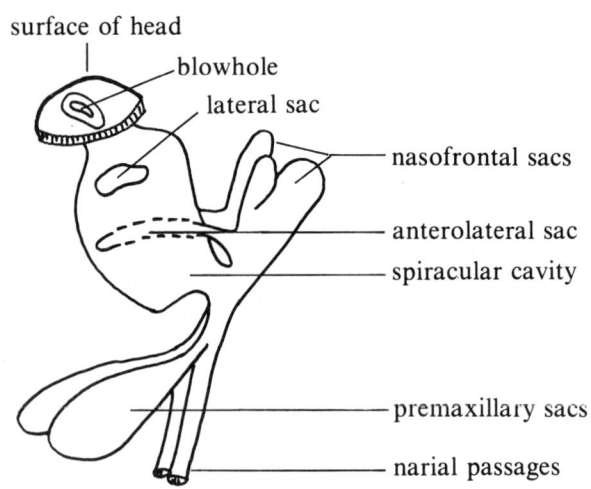

Diagram of the supracranial air passages and sacs of the narwhal, *Monodon monoceros,* **in lateral view.**

Drawn from Huber.

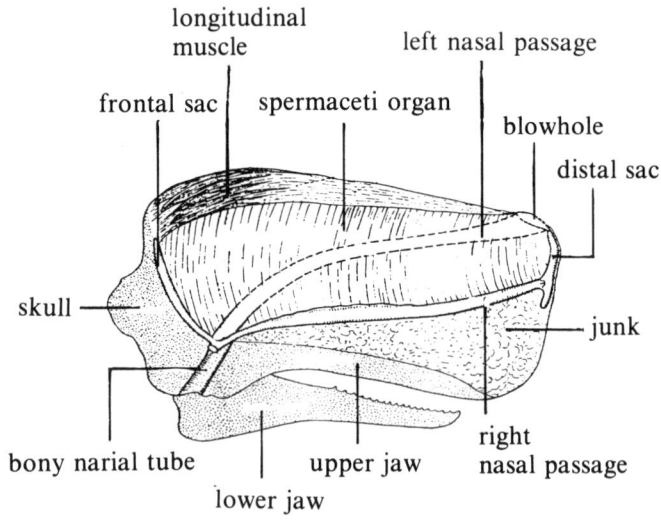

Diagram of the larger air passages in the head of the great sperm whale, *Physeter macrocephalus.*

From Raven and Gregory.

Although the nasal chamber leading upward to the blowhole in the toothed whales (*Odontoceti*) is divided medially by a bony septum, this septum is not continued to the surface; this allows the two parallel air passages to join above the skull and to become a single passage which then continues to the surface to discharge through a single blowhole.

In the toothed whales (*Odontoceti*), the air passages (supracranial) between the blowhole and the pharynx below show great variation and specialization. They include chambers, ducts, and valves, all of which are somehow associated with breathing, diving, and voice production.

A very unusual nasal passage is found in the sperm whale (*Physeteridae: Physeter*). Here the nasal passage ascends almost vertically and then turns and runs almost horizontally forward through the spermaceti case to the left, upper corner of the snout where it emerges through an S-shaped blowhole.

In the toothed whales (*Odontoceti*), there is a system of air sacs, folds, and plugs located at the place where the air passages change from a double duct to a single duct; these features separate the air passages into an upper and a lower portion. A pair of right and left premaxillary air sacs lie adjacent to the upper surface of the premaxilla and open into the lower part of this air passage. A pair of vestibular air sacs and other air sacs and tubes also open into the upper part of the air passage. The many and varied sounds of the toothed whales are generated in this region and emanate outward from it.

The epithelial tissue which lines the nasal cavity is more or less completely devoid of glands and cilia. The coiled, scroll-like turbinal bones with their olfactory epithelium, found in the nasal chambers of mammals, are reduced or absent in all whales. The sense of smell is believed to be completely absent in the toothed whales because the olfactory nerves and receptors are either absent or very rudimentary.

In the whalebone whales (*Mysticeti*), the blowholes are paired longitudinal slits which are located on the top of the head and which converge toward the front. They are separated by a longitudinal septum, are wider posteriorly, and are surrounded at the surface by a ridge of flesh which is higher in front and which helps to keep the water from entering the blowhole when the whale inhales air. These blowholes are closed and made water-tight by two plugs which are attached to the septum.

In the whalebone whales (*Mysticeti*), the nasal passages are directed upward and forward to the blowholes, while, in the toothed whales (*Odontoceti*), this air passage extends directly upward (with the exception of *Physeter*).

The nasal bones which formerly covered the nasal cavity have been "reduced to blunt wedge-shaped blocks" (Fraser) and now lie just posterior to the blowholes.

The supracranial air passages which are so complex in the toothed whales are not well developed in the whalebone whales and the sense of smell is very rudimentary or lacking. However, olfactory receptors are reported as being present over a very small area together with a few small conchae.

Division 2
THE PHARYNX

The pharynx is a part of both the digestive tract and the respiratory tract since the air enroute to the lungs and the food enroute to the stomach cross within this chamber. Both toothed whales and baleen whales pass the air from the nasal passages directly through the pharynx to the larynx. It is almost impossible for air or water to pass from the mouth into the larynx at this point as it does in land animals. Whales therefore cannot inhale or exhale air through their mouth, get water from the mouth into the lungs, belch through their nose, or get chyme from their stomachs into their larynx. By these arrangements, whales are able to open their mouth, to chew, and to swallow while under water without accidentally passing water into the lungs.

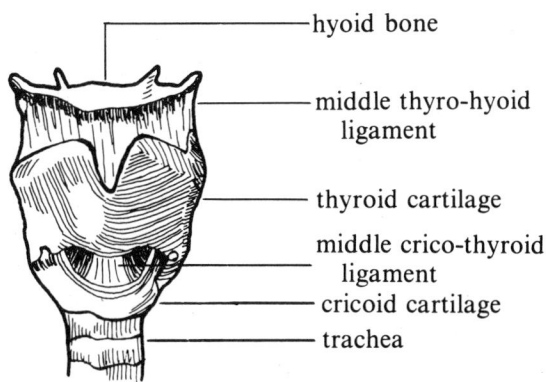

A diagram of the human larynx showing the thyroid and cricoid cartilages. The cartilages of the epiglottis and the two arytenoid cartilages are not shown.

Drawn from Pope.

Division 3
THE LARYNX

The larynx is a somewhat box-like chamber or organ which is composed of five principal muscles and cartilages (the epiglottis, the cricoid, the thyroid, and two arytenoid cartilages) which are located behind and/or below the pharynx and contain the vocal chords in most mammals; however, the vocal organs are either rudimentary or absent in all whales. The voice of whales consists of whistles, clicks, and moans which are produced by various muscles, valves, ducts, and chambers of the respiratory tract.

In the toothed whales (*Odontoceti*), the larynx has been elongated and contains a very unusual tubular structure projecting forward from it into and across the pharynx to the nasal passage. This is a tubular spout which has been developed from the arytenoid cartilages and the elongated epiglottis and which forms a very specialized air passage or "windpipe" between the larynx and the nasal passage; in it the forward projection of the glottis has been literally "enwrapped by the soft palate." This strange structure completely safeguards and separates the incoming air from both loss and contamination while enroute from the blowhole straight through to the lungs. The vocal chords are absent or very rudimentary in toothed whales and the rudiments of them are only occasionally visible in the adults.

In the whalebone whales (*Mysticeti*), the larynx differs but little from the basic pattern found in land animals; although the epiglottis is more elongated, cone-shaped, and pointed, it does not have the tubular larynx found in the *Odontoceti*. The vocal chords are absent in the whalebone whales and the rudiments of them are not visible in the adults.

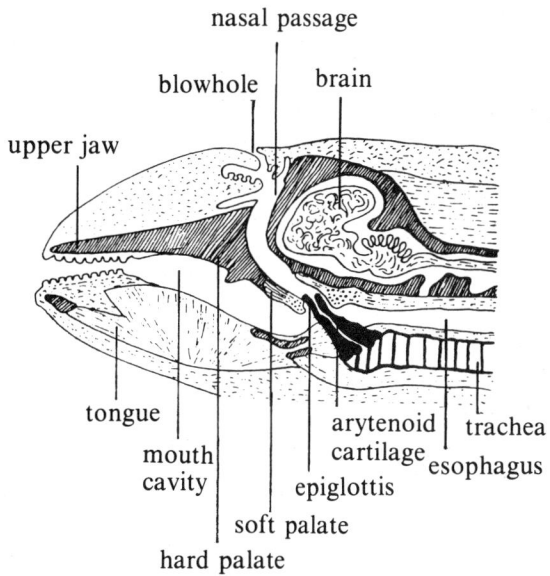

Diagram of the throat, larynx, and nasal passages of a porpoise, *Phocoena* species (Odontoceti: Delphinidae).

From Slijper.

Division 4
THE TRACHEA AND THE BRONCHI

The trachea in all mammals divides into two branches upon entering the thorax; the larger of these two branches supplies the right lung and the other branch supplies the left lung. However, in some whales, a third branch arises to supply the apical (anterior) part of the right lung. This third branch is also found in most of the even-toed ungulates (*Artiodactyla*) of which the cattle, deer, and pigs are the best known; however, it does not occur in the camels and the llamas. This is an additional bit of evidence that the whales might be distantly related to these animals.

The tracheae of whales are short because their necks are short, but their diameter will range from more than one inch in small whales to over twelve inches in very large whales. Tracheal rings and cartilages encircle and support the walls of these tubes and extend well into the lungs, thereby giving each air tube a firm, stable wall. These tracheal rings are made of hyaline cartilage and in most mammals, including man, are C-shaped and are incomplete and open on the dorsal side.

In the toothed whales (*Odontoceti*), the tracheal rings are complete (closed on the dorsal side) and form a complete and continuous ring around the trachea.

In the whalebone whales (*Mysticeti*), the tracheal rings are incomplete and are open upon the dorsal side, so that the ring which each forms does not completely encircle the trachea.

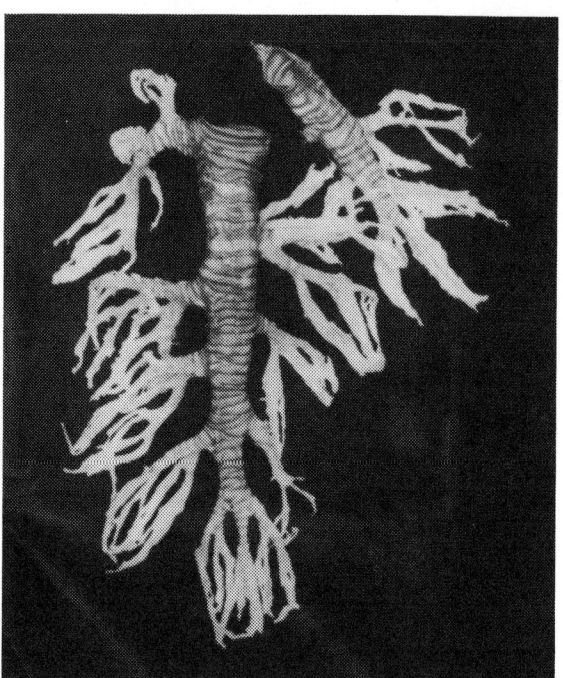

Photo of the trachea and bronchi of the arch-beaked whale, *Mesoplodon carlhubbsi.*

Ore. Inst. Mar. Biol.

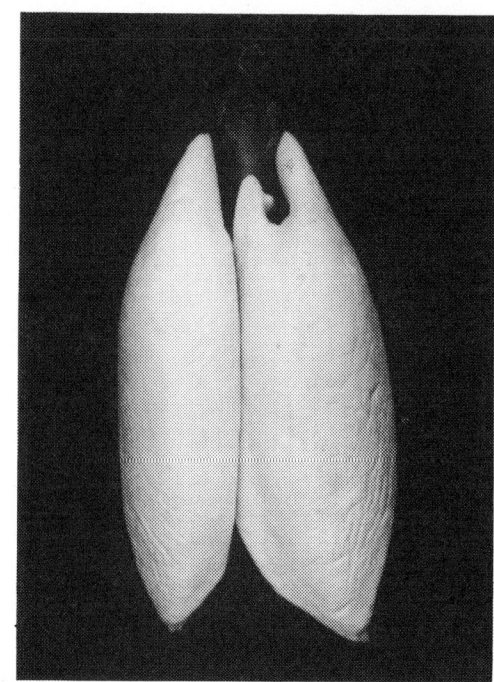

Photo of the lungs of the harbor porpoise, *Phocoena phocoena,* in dorsal view showing the contour of the lobes.

Ore. Inst. Mar. Biol.

Division 5
THE LUNGS

Among the mammals, the two lungs are variously divided into lobes; the left lung is usually divided into three lobes and the right lung, which is usually the larger of the two, is divided into four lobes. Lungs of a single lobe are found among the mammals in the rhinoceros, the hippopotamus, the elephant, the orangutan, and in the whales. In man, the right lung has three lobes and the left lung has but two lobes.

In all whales, however, the right and left lobes of the lungs usually remain undivided, but it should be noted here that in a very few of the toothed whales (*Odontoceti*), there are rudiments of an additional apical lobe in the lungs. It is interesting to note here also that those whales which are the deep divers have the smaller lung capacity. In general, the lungs of whales are placed farther back in the body than in most other mammals.

Within the lungs, the bronchi continue to divide as they penetrate the lungs until they end in the terminal pulmonary segments; of these, there are two types: acinous and tubular.

Within the toothed whales (*Odontoceti*), the terminal lung units are acinous (globular and clustered like grapes).

In the whalebone whales (*Mysticeti*), the terminal lung units are tubular or pipe-shaped.

The lungs of a fin whale (*Balaenoptera physalus*) were removed and weighed at the whaling station at Fields Landing, California, in 1941. This fin whale, a female, measured 21.6 m. (71 ft.) in length and weighed 59,394 kg. (130,942 lbs.); this weight included an added 20% for blood and body fluids which were lost in the processing. The lungs of this whale weighed 394 kg. (868 lbs.) and therefore made up about 0.66% (.0066) or about 1/151 part of the total body weight.

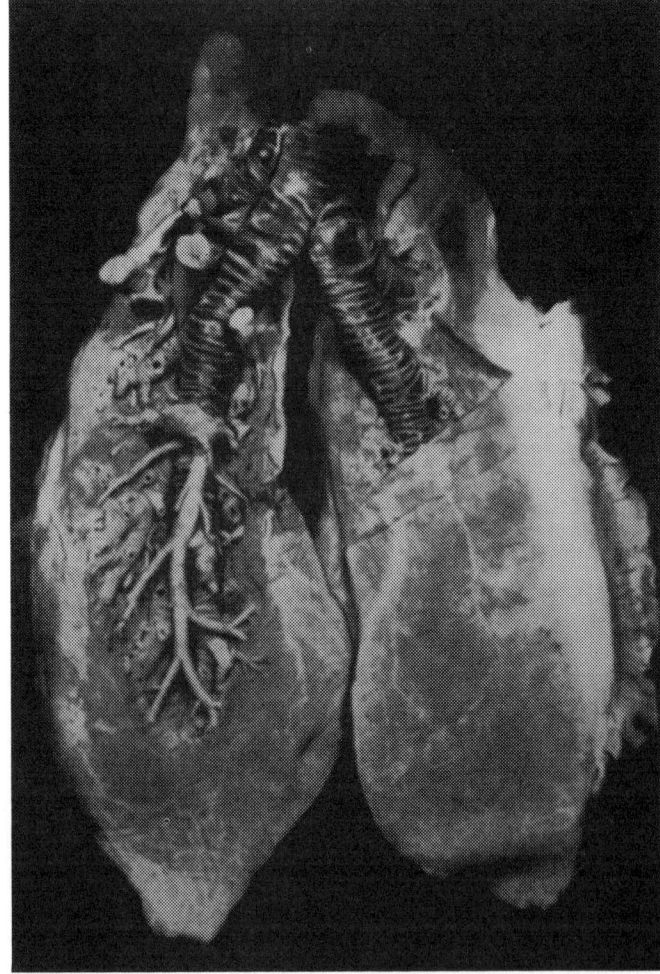

Photo of the lungs of the blue-white or striped dolphin, *Stenella coeruleoalba* (Odontoceti: Delphinidae).

From Fraser.

68

Chapter VII
THE CIRCULATORY SYSTEM

In general, the circulatory system of whales follows the basic pattern of the mammals. Like them, the heart is the central organ of this system and pumps the blood out to the body. This blood is first pumped by the left ventricle out the aorta to the body; it then returns from the body through veins which empty into the right auricle, passes through the tricuspid valves into the right ventricle, and is pumped out the pulmonary artery to the lungs. Blood returning from the lungs enters the left auricle, passes through the bicuspid (mitral) valves into the left ventricle and is again pumped out the aorta to the body.

Beyond this basic plan of circulation, there are a great many differences between the whales and the land mammals and also between the various species of whales. These differences are the result of evolutionary changes within their body and of the aquatic environment in which the whale lives, particularly as they relate to the habit of diving.

The Weight of the Heart in Whales

Species	Total Weight Lbs.	Kgs.	Weight of Heart Lbs.	Kgs.
Odontoceti				
Physeteridae				
Physeter macrocephalus				
THE SPERM WHALE				
Male: Length - 43 ft.	86,000	39,000	277	126
Ziphiidae				
Ziphius cavirostris				
CUVIER'S GOOSE-BEAKED WHALE				
Female: Length - 21.5 ft.	6,510	2,952.5	33.9	15.4
Mysticeti				
Balaenopteridae				
Balaenoptera physalus				
THE FIN WHALE				
Female: Length - 71 ft.	130,942**	59,394	842	382
Megaptera novaeangliae				
THE HUMP-BACKED WHALE				
Male: Length - 41 ft.	82,000	37,195	472	214
Male: Length - 44 ft.	88,000	39,916	400	181
Male: Length - 45 ft.	90,000	40,823	425	193

**Includes an added 20% for blood and body fluids.

Division 1
THE HEART

The heart of whales does not differ greatly from that of other mammals. Its size is in proportion to the size of the animal, but, in general, represents about 0.5% of the body weight; in large specimens, the heart will reach a weight of over 453.6 kg. (1,000 lbs.). It is slightly flattened dorsoventrally and is rounded at its apex. The heart is slightly smaller in female whales. In some large whales (*Physeter, Balaenoptera,* and *Megaptera*) the muscular wall of the ventricle measured from 7.6 to 12.7 cm. (3 to 5 in.) in thickness. In one specimen, the wall of the aorta measured 1.9 cm. (.75 in.) in thickness near its origin.

The pulse rate under normal surface activity ranges from about 60 to 140 beats per minute; it will drop while the whale is diving to between 4 and 15 beats per minute.

The hearts, which were removed from five large whales at the whaling station at Fields Landing, California, in 1941, showed the following weights*:

---

*From The Journal of Mammalogy 24:1, 1943, pp. 39-45.

Division 2
THE BLOOD VESSELS

In their blood vessels, the whales present some surprising departures from the arrangements found in other mammals. The most remarkable of these anatomical features is a network of blood vessels called a rete mirabile (L., net+wonderful; pl., retia mirabilia). These are complexes of blood vessels which consist of tangled, twisted, worm-like snarls of smaller blood vessels. These retia are found in all whales and other marine mammals, but in the whales are best developed in the bodies of the various species of the dolphin family (*Delphinidae*).

In the whales, there are no retia in the portal system (of veins). This is the system of veins which gathers the blood from the stomach, spleen, pancreas, and the small and large intestines and delivers it to the liver. It is also interesting to note that in whales the blood vessels which supply the brain pass through a retia before reaching the brain.

A very radical change has also taken place at the posterior end of the body; the absence of the hind legs and the development of the trunk and tail have greatly changed the circulatory pattern of the posterior part of the body.

PRINCIPLE NETWORKS OF BLOOD VESSELS (*Retia Mirabilia*)
IN THE BOTTLE-NOSED DOLPHIN (*Tursiops*)
(The following list from authors is incomplete)

Cranial Retia (rete basis cranii) are located below the cranium and adjoin the optic nerves and the ear (tympano-periotic) bones.

Cervical Retia (rete cervicale dorsale) are located above the vertebrae of the neck.

Thoracic Retia (rete thoracicum) are located in the thoracic cavity above the lungs and extend the entire length of the thoracic cavity and into the lumbar area.

Spinal Retia (rete spinale) are located in the spinal canal above and beside the spinal cord.

Lumbar Retia (rete lumbale) are an extension of the thoracic retia and are most obvious between the transverse processes of the lumbar vertebrae.

Pelvic Retia (rete pelvicum) are located above and between the two pelvic bones.

Ovarian Retia (rete genitale feminum) are located above the ovaries and uteri.

Testicular Retia (rete genitale masculinum) are located above and beside the testes.

Caudal Retia (rete caudale) are located in the haemal canal below the caudal vertebrae. These vessels are considered an extension of the spinal retia.

Division 3
THE BLOOD

In the whales, as in other mammals, the red blood cells, with the aid of their haemoglobin, transport oxygen from the lungs to the cells of the body. Whales are able to store more oxygen in their muscle cells than all other mammals, because they possess a muscle pigment called myo-haemoglobin which has a great affinity for oxygen. This feature accounts in part for their ability to remain under water for extended periods of time.

The blood of whales has some interesting features when compared with the blood of other mammals. The red blood corpuscles of whales are larger in size than those of land mammals and those of the sperm whale, which measure about .0105 mm. in diameter, are the largest in all mammals; in contrast, the red corpuscles of man measure about .0075 mm. in diameter. These red blood cells make up about 40% to 57% of the volume of the blood in whales and are therefore slightly more numerous than those of other mammals. In whales, the red blood cells number about 7 to 11,000,000 cells per cub. mm.; in man, they number about 5,000,000 cells per cub. mm. The blood of whales is estimated to comprise between 5% and 9% of the weight of the body.

Division 4
THE SPLEEN

The spleen of the mammals is located on the left side of the body just below the diaphragm and against the greater curvature of the stomach, where it is held in place by a fold of the peritoneum. The color of the spleen is usually of a purplish color, but it may appear to be grayish-blue, grayish-brown, or of a reddish-brown hue.

Among the whales, the size, shape, and the number of parts of this organ vary greatly; it may consist of one spleen, it may be lobulated, or it may in addition include several small accessory spleens. In general, the spleen of whales is much smaller and very much lighter in weight than the spleen of the land mammals. In whales, it usually represents about .02% (.0002 or 1/5,000) of the body weight, while in most terrestrial mammals, it is about 15 times larger and may represent about 0.3% (.003 or 1/333) of the body weight.

The spleens, which were removed from two large whales at the whaling station at Fields Landing, California, in 1941, showed the following weights*:

The Weight of the Spleen of Whales

Species	Total Weight		Weight of the Spleen		% of Body Wt.
	Lbs.	Kgs.	Lbs.	Kgs.	
Mysticeti					
Balaenopteridae					
Balaenoptera physalus					
The Fin Whale					
Female: 71-ft.	130,942**	59,394	15	6.800	.011%
Megaptera novaeangliae					
The Hump-backed Whale					
Male: 41 ft.	82,000	37,195	13.33	6.041	.016%

*From The Jour. of Mammalogy 24:1, 1943, pp. 39-45.
**Includes an added 20% for blood and body fluids.

Division 5
THE LYMPHATIC SYSTEM

The lymphatic system of mammals is an auxiliary circulatory system which consists of a network of ducts or vessels together with a system of lymphatic nodes or lymphatic glands and other accessory organs.

These lymphatic ducts gather a colorless fluid, called lymph, from the spaces within connective tissue and pass it through ever-enlarging vessels until it is emptied into the venous system by two lymphatic vessels. The largest vessel is the *thoracic duct* which drains the posterior one-half of the body and the left side of the anterior part of the body and empties into the left external jugular vein. The second vessel is the *right lymphatic duct* which collects fluid from the right anterior side of the body and empties it into the right external jugular vein.

The function and purpose of the lymphatic system is to collect the lymphatic fluids which have seeped from the capillaries and are "loose" in the tissues and to return them to the blood stream. In addition to water, these fluids contain various important blood proteins which cannot be lost without doing great harm to the metabolic processes of the body. The lymphatic system also removes harmful substances and bacteria from the lymphatic fluid and thereby performs an important function by helping to control infection within the body.

Associated with the lymph ducts are various organs including lymph nodes or lymph glands which are either scattered along the lymph vessels or are clustered in particular areas (neck, arm pit, groin, etc.). In addition, the spleen, the thymus gland, the tonsils, the adenoids, and other organs have lymphoid tissue and are associated with the lymphatic system.

The lymphatic system of the whales will not be discussed here, except to say that it has undergone great evolutionary changes associated with the loss of the hind legs, the development of a tail, and other anatomical changes which were caused by their change from a terrestrial habitat to an aquatic habitat.

Chapter VIII
THE ENDOCRINE SYSTEM
AND THE ENDOCRINE GLANDS

Among the mammals, there are several types of endocrine glands located in the head, neck, and trunk of the body. These glands do not have ducts for the discharge of their hormones, but instead discharge these hormones slowly through their cell membranes into the blood stream. These glands include the pituitary gland in the head, the thyroid and the parathyroid glands in the lower neck, the thymus gland in the upper chest, the adrenal glands above the kidneys, the pancreas below the stomach, the ovaries in the abdomen of the female, and the testes of the male usually located in the scrotum below the abdomen. The pineal gland and the tonsils are mentioned here but are omitted in the descriptions which follow.

Division 1
THE PANCREAS

The pancreas has two basic functions: it produces a digestive juice which empties through ducts into the duodenum of the small intestine, and it produces two hormones in special cells called the Islands of Langerhans which are scattered throughout the pancreas, but are most numerous in the "tail" end of the pancreas.

The hormones, insulin (from the beta cells) and glucagon (from the alpha cells) are complex hormones which aid in the absorption and management of carbohydrates within the body.

In man, the pancreas is located against the lower, back side of the stomach and measures about 15 to 20 cm. (6 to 8 in.) in length and about 3 cm. by 2.5 cm. (1.25 by 1 in.) in width and thickness.

In whales, the pancreas is very similar to those of other mammals. It is pinkish in color and is reported to comprise between 0.15% (1/666) and 0.20% (1/500) of the body weight. It is larger in older whales where it might weigh as much 35 kg. (77 lbs.) in an adult whale (*Balaenopteridae: Balaenoptera physalus*) (Slijper).

Division 2
THE ADRENAL GLANDS

The adrenal glands are located anterior to and/or above the kidneys and release their several hormones into the blood stream. These hormones, sometimes collectively called adrenaline or epinephrine, are very complex and affect a wide variety of physiological activities within the body including, in part, the management of salt and water, amino acids, glucose, blood vessels, muscular activity, and many others.

In the whales, the adrenal glands are described as "flattish, oval, (and) perceptibly lobed on the outside ..." (Slijper), although the adrenal glands of the smaller members of the dolphin and porpoise family (*Delphinidae*) are not lobed. The adrenal glands of whales are smaller than those of terrestrial mammals of equal size; in whales, they represent between 0.01% (.0001 or 1/10,000) and 0.08% (.0008 or 1/1250) of the body weight.

These glands from three large whales (sperm, fin, humpbacked) were weighed and measured (See table). They ranged in length from 6 to 9 inches and in width from 3.5 to 5.5 inches; their thickness varied from .375 to .8 inches.

The adrenal glands, which were removed from three large whales at the whaling station at Fields Landing, California, in 1941, showed the following weights*:

The Weight of the Adrenal Glands of Whales

Species	Total Weight		The Weight of Adrenal Glands	
	Lbs.	Kgs.	Lbs.	Kgs.
Odontoceti				
Physeteridae				
Physeter macrocephalus				
THE SPERM WHALE				
Male: Length - 43 ft.	86,000	39,000	0.77	0.350
Mysticeti				
Balaenopteridae				
Balaenoptera physalus				
THE FIN WHALE				
Female: Length - 71 ft.	130,942**	59,394	1.614	0.732
Megaptera novaeangliae				
THE HUMP-BACKED WHALE				
Male: Length - 45 ft.	90,000	40,823	2.6	1.210

*From Jour. of Mammalogy 24:1, 1943, pp. 39-45.
**Includes an added 20% for blood and body fluids.

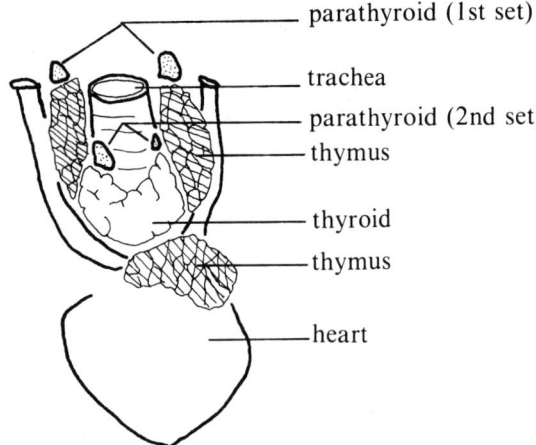

A composite diagram showing the approximate location of the endocrine glands of the throat and upper thorax in *Platanista gangetica*. The parathyroid glands are from two separate specimens.

Drawn from Kamiya et alii.

Division 3
THE THYROID GLAND

The thyroid gland is located in the lower part of the neck against the anterior end of the trachea (windpipe). This gland produces several complex hormones which have a wide variety of effects upon the metabolism of the body including the use of calcium by the body.

In man, the thyroid gland resembles a horseshoe in shape and consists of two lobes which lie against the trachea and which are connected in front by an isthmus.

In the whales, the thyroid gland is relatively larger (about twice) than in land mammals and represents between 0.01% (.0001 or 1/10,000) and 0.05% (.0005 or 1/2000) of the body weight. The thyroid gland is reported to weigh between 1/2 oz. (14 gr.) and 1 oz. (28 gr.) in an adult porpoise (Slijper); it is usually dark brown in color. In the larger whales, it is described as dark red in color, about 14 inches (35.56 cm.) in length, and weighing between 2½ and 9 pounds (1.134 and 4.08 kg.) (Slijper).

The thyroid glands, which were removed from four large whales at the whaling station at Fields Landing, California, in 1941, showed the following weights*:

The Weight of the Thyroid Gland of Whales

Species	Total Weight		The Weight of Thyroid Glands	
	Lbs.	Kgs.	Lbs.	Kgs.
Odontoceti				
Physeteridae				
Physeter macrocephalus				
THE SPERM WHALE				
Male: Length - 43 ft.	86,000	39,000	1.76	0.800
Mysticeti				
Balaenopteridae				
Balaenoptera physalus				
THE FIN WHALE				
Female: Length - 71 ft.	130,942**	59,394	1.614	0.732
Megaptera novaeangliae				
THE HUMP-BACKED WHALE				
Male: Length - 41 ft.	82,000	37,195	7.13	3.237
Male: Length - 45 ft.	90,000	40,823	6.52	2.960

*From Jour. of Mammalogy 24:1, 1943, pp. 39-45.
**Includes an added 20% for blood and body fluids.

Division 4
THE PARATHYROID GLAND

The parathyroid glands are extremely small glands which are associated with the thyroid gland and which produce a hormone, parathormone, which controls the metabolism of calcium within the body.

In man, the parathyroid glands are small, hemispherical bodies about the size of a pea. Normally, there are four separate glands; two are located in a vertical line a short distance apart on the lateral surface of the thyroid gland on each side of the trachea.

In whales, the parathyroid glands are small, irregularly egg-shaped bodies, which in the finwhales, are grayish or pinkish in color.

In very large whales, they will measure about 1.5 by 2.75 inches (3.8 cm. by 6.98 cm.) and weigh between about 0.33 and 4.5 oz. (9.35 and 127.57 gr.) (Slijper).

In the smaller whales, the parathyroid glands are variously located, but are usually anterior to the thyroid and thymus glands and usually on both sides of the trachea. They vary in size, shape, number, and location and, because of their small size, are usually very difficult to locate.

Division 5
THE THYMUS GLAND

The purpose of the thymus gland of mammals is not completely understood and its hormones and their effects are not fully known. This gland produces hormones which are associated with the production of white blood cells (lymphocytes) and with the growth of the body. It varies in size with the age and the state of nutrition of the body.

In man, the thymus is a bilobed gland which is located in the upper chest above the heart; it lies in the area between the neck and the thorax and close to the trachea and the aorta. It slowly disappears following puberty and appears to be of little importance thereafter.

In whales, the thymus has been described by Slijper as "a dark-red lobular organ found in the anterior thorax of fetuses and young animals."

In the Ganges dolphin *(Platanista gangetica),* the thymus consists of several, often separate, large, light-yellow lobes and is located in a ventral position just anterior to the heart.

Division 6
THE PITUITARY GLAND

The pituitary gland is a small, spherical organ consisting of two separate lobes or parts which are separated by a surface constriction. These two lobes have different origins and different functions and together produce at least eight separate hormones, nearly all of which are associated with growth and reproduction. The pituitary is a reddish brown color and rests at the base of the brain in a depression of the sphenoid bone. It is one of the most important glands in the bodies of mammals. In man, it is about the size of a pea and is located at the base of the brain directly behind the bridge of the nose.

In the whales, the pituitary gland differs in some anatomical details from that of typical mammals, but the hormones produced by this gland are the same as those of other mammals. In a very large whale, this gland will weigh about an ounce (28.35 gr.).

Division 7
THE TESTES

In the mammals, the testes are paired organs, usually oval in shape, and are variously located within the abdomen. In some mammals, they are retained within the abdomen throughout life; in others, they are placed outside the body in a scrotum, and in some animals they move in and out of the body with the breeding season. In addition to the production of sperm, these glands secrete hormones, of which testosterone is the most important. This hormone has an effect upon bone growth, red blood cell production, the use of amino acids by the body, and upon the level of body vitality.

In the whales, the testes differ somewhat from those of typical mammals, although there is very little difference in the hormones which they produce. They occupy a position high in the abdominal cavity next to the kidneys and are retained there within the body throughout life. The testes are elongated and oval in shape, whitish in color, and are unequal in size. They appear large in size when compared to land mammals; in the blue whale (*Balaenopteridae: Balaenoptera musculus*), they are reported to reach 30 inches (76.2 cm.) in length and to weigh as much as 100 pounds (45.36 kg.).

Division 8
THE OVARIES

The ovaries are paired organs which are located in the abdomen, one on each side of the uterus. They are glandular in structure and, in addition to producing the mammalian eggs, produce the hormones estrogen and progesterone, both of which are associated with the female sex characteristics and reproduction.

In humans, they are oval in shape, flattened, measure about 1.5 inches (3.8 cm.) in length, and somewhat resemble a large almond in size and shape.

In the whales, the ovaries are very little different from those of other mammals. In the toothed whales (*Odontoceti*), the ovaries are usually smooth externally, while in the whalebone whales (*Mysticeti*), they are plicate and ridged externally and somewhat resemble a bunch of grapes. In very large whales, the ovaries will reach a length of 12 inches (30.5 cm.) and a weight of over 20 pounds (9.07 kg.).

Division 9
OTHER GLANDS

Other endocrine glands found in the mammals include the pineal gland, the hypothalamus, the tonsils, the suprarenal glands, and others. These glands are all of importance to the health and well being of all mammals, although they are not as well known as those glands which have been mentioned on the previous pages. They are not discussed here.

Chapter IX
THE NERVOUS SYSTEM
AND THE SENSE ORGANS

In the study of the anatomy of the nervous system of mammals, scholars usually divide it into three parts:

1. *The central nervous system* consisting of the brain and the spinal cord;

2. *The peripheral nervous system* consisting of the cranial nerves, the spinal nerves, and the sympathetic nervous system; and

3. *The sense organs* which include the organs of touch (tactile), sight (visual), hearing (auditory), smell (olfactory) and taste (gustatory).

Division 1
THE CENTRAL NERVOUS SYSTEM

Of the three divisions of the nervous system, the brain and the spinal cord are by far the most important, for without them most organic functions would cease and the life of the organism would soon terminate.

The brain and the spinal cord are exceedingly complex organs and will be treated here in just enough detail to permit a basic understanding of these organs in the whales.

Section a
THE BRAIN

Of the many parts of the mammalian body, the brain is by far the most complex in its origin, structure, and functions. For this reason, the description of the typical mammalian brain and the brain of whales will be short and general in scope.

1) A General Description of the Brain

The brain is enclosed within the cranium of the skull and communicates with the exterior through various openings including a large opening in the base of the skull known as the *foramen magnum.* The brain is covered with three layers of tissue or membranes which are collectively known as the *meninges.* The outer layer, known as the *dura mater,* is composed of a smooth, very tough tissue; the middle layers, known as the *arachnoid membrane,* are delicate, transparent and web-like; and the inner layer, known as the *pia mater*, is thin, transparent, and abundantly supplied with blood vessels.

Within the skull, the brain is divided by scholars into five great divisions. Because the names of these divisions and their subdivisions are somewhat difficult to remember, they are set forth in the accompanying table. The short descriptions of the various divisions of the brain will follow this table.

THE DIVISIONS OF THE BRAIN

Divisions of the Primitive Brain	Five Major Divisions	Principal Units or Sub-divisions
prosencephalon (fore-brain)	1. *telencephalon* (end brain)	*rhinencephalon* (nose brain) olfactory lobes, tracts, bulbs
		cerebrum (great brain) two cerebral hemispheres
	2. *diencephalon* or *thalamencephalon* ('tween brain)	two *thalami*
		two *corpora striata*
		corpus pineale, *epiphysis cerebri*, or pineal body
mesencephalon (mid-brain)	3. *mesencephalon* (mid-brain)	*corpora quadrigemina*
		crura cerebri or *pedunculi cerebri*
rhombencephalon (hind-brain)	4. *metencephalon* (after-brain)	*pons Varolii* (bridge of Varolius)
		cerebellum (little brain)
	5. *myelencephalon* (spinal brain)	*medulla oblongata*

(1) The *telencephalon* or end-brain includes the cerebrum and its olfactory extensions. The *rhinencephalon* or olfactory lobes, located anteriorly in primitive vertebrates, are really an extension of the cerebrum and are concerned with the reception of the sensations of smell. They are large in the lower vertebrate animals, but they have declined in size and importance where the sense of smell is weak or absent.

The *cerebrum* (L. *cerebrum*, brain) is the largest part of the brain in mammals and occupies the entire upper portion of the skull. It is the center and seat of consciousness and all mental activity. It also receives and analyzes the many sensations received by the body and initiates voluntary acts and responses.

(2) The *diencephalon*, *thalamencephalon*, or 'tween-brain lies on the ventral surface of the brain just in front of the mid-brain. It contains a vast network of nerves and nerve tracts and acts as a relay station between various parts of the brain. Its principal units are listed below.

Two *thalami* (L. *thalamus*, chamber) lie directly below the cerebrum and are attached to it.

Two *corpora striata* (L. *corpus*, body + *striatus*, grooved) are two striped bodies, somewhat ridge-like, which are associated with the control of body temperature.

Corpus pineale, *epiphysis cerebri*, or the pineal body is a small body of glandular and connective tissue on the lower side of the brain.

(3) The *mesencephalon* or mid-brain lies on the lower side of the brain and consists of the principal parts listed below.

Corpora quadrigemina (L. *corpus*, body + *geminus*, twin) are four bodies of gray matter, which lie behind the crura cerebri; they include two superior colliculi and two inferior colliculi.

Crura cerebri (L. *crus*. leg + *cerebrum*, brain) or *pedunculi cerebri* are bundles of nerve fibers which connect with the cerebrum.

(4) The *metencephalon* or after-brain is located posterior to the mid-brain. It is associated with muscular activity and coordination and consists of the parts listed below.

Pons Varolii (L. *pons*, bridge + *Varoli**) is a small structure (about one inch in diameter in man) located between the mid-brain and the medulla. It consists chiefly of white fibers.

Cerebellum (L. *cerebellum*, little brain) is the second largest part of the brain and has functions relating to body and muscular coordination, movement, and balance.

(5) The *myelencephalon* or *medulla oblongata* (L. *medulla*, marrow + *oblongus*, oblong) lies at the lower, posterior area of the brain and extends from the pons at the base of the cerebellum downward and backward to merge imperceptibly into the spinal chord. In general, the medulla oblongata is roughly columnar in shape, tapering from front to back, longitudinally ribbed ventrally and containing a hollow space (the 4th ventricle) within, which is thinly covered on its dorsal side. It passes out of the skull through the *foramen magnum*, the large opening at the base of the skull, and extends posteriorly into the neural canal of the vertebral column where it is diminished in diameter and continues as the spinal cord. It is comparatively short (about 1.25 inches in man) and ends somewhere anterior to the origin of the roots of the 1st pair of cervical nerves; there are no external markings to indicate where the medulla ends and the spinal cord begins.

The medulla oblongata has many functions. It is the conduit or passageway for all impulses travelling in either direction between the brain and the spinal cord. The medulla oblongata contains the respiratory center which controls breathing; it regulates the tone and tension of the arteries and veins, and it exerts a controlling influence on the heart beat. In addition, it controls coughing and sneezing, the secretion of saliva and the gastric juices, mastication, swallowing (deglutition), vomiting, and the closing of the eyelids. The medulla oblongata is a very important and sensitive area in the brain of the vertebrates and any injury to it usually has profound consequences, including death.

2) Special Features of the Brain of Toothed Whales and Whalebone Whales

The brain of whales is one of the most unusual among the mammals; it is a typical mammalian brain which has undergone some very unusual modifications.

(1) It has departed from the typical elongated shape and has assumed a more globular or spherical shape, due perhaps to the compression resulting from the evolutionary changes in the shape of the whales' skull. As a result of this front-to-back compression, the cerebrum now overlies the cerebellum in most of the toothed whales.

---

*Constantio Varolius, born 1543, of Bologna, Italy.

(2) The cerebral hemispheres are more elaborately convoluted than would be expected in typical mammals.

(3) The cerebellum is well developed and is almost as highly convoluted as the cerebrum.

In general, the brain of whales is large and, in the great whales, achieves a greater total weight than the brain of any other mammal. The weight of the brain of the great whales, when compared to total body weight is less than that of many other mammals, including many of the smaller whales. Some comparisons of brain weights are listed in the accompanying table.

The convolutions (fissures, creases, etc.) of the brain of whales are also more numerous than in most mammals. Some scholars think that this means a greater mental capacity, while others think that the convolutions and fissures simply increase with the increase in size of the brain and are merely the result of an increase in volume.

The Relative Size of the Brains of Selected Whales

Species (Adult Specimens)	Weight of Brain (Adult Specimens) Lbs.	Kg.	Percent of Body Weight %	Rank
Sperm Whale	19.6	8.89	0.03	8
Fin Whale	18.3	8.30		
Blue Whale	15.25	6.91	0.007	10
Hump-backed Whale	15	6.80	0.02	9
Elephant	11	4.99	0.12	6
Bottle-nosed Whale	6.6	2.99	—	—
Pilot Whale	4.5	2.04	0.083	7
Beluga	4.2	1.90		
Bottle-nosed Dolphin	4	1.81	0.225	4
Narwhal	3.1	1.40		
Horse (Shire, 2,000 lbs.)	3.08*	1.39	0.154	5
Man	3	1.36	1.93	1
Common Dolphin	2.2	0.99	0.666	3
Porpoise	1.2	0.54	0.854	2

*Some scholars use 1/600 of body weight. Adapted from Slijper et alii.

The brains, which were removed from five large whales at the whaling station at Fields Landing, California, in 1941, showed the following weights*:

The Weight of the Brain of Whales

	Total Weight Lbs.	Kgs.	Weight of Brain Lbs.	Kgs.
Odontoceti				
Physeteridae				
Physeter macrocephalus				
THE SPERM WHALE				
Male: Length - 43 ft.	86,000	39,000	18.49	8.338
Mysticeti				
Balaenopteridae				
Balaenoptera physalus				
THE FIN WHALE				
Female: Length - 71 ft.	130,942**	59,394	18.353	8.325
Megaptera novaeangliae				
THE HUMP-BACKED WHALE				
Male: Length - 41 ft.	82,000	37,195	11.66	5.288
Male: Length - 44 ft.	88,000	39,916	15.	6.800
Male: Length - 45 ft.	90,000	40,823	15.94	7.229

*From The Jour. of Mammalogy 24:1, 1943, pp. 39-45.
**Includes an added 20% for blood and body fluids.

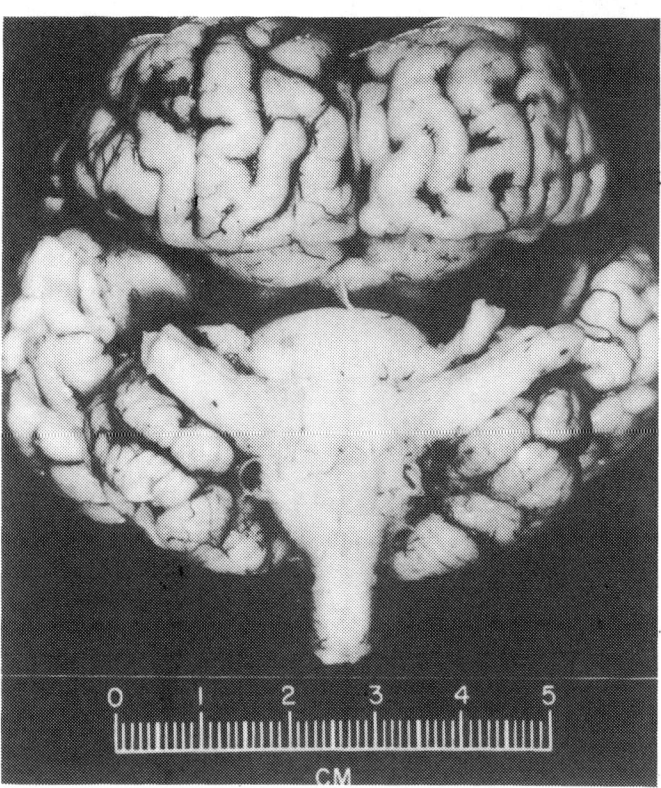

Photo of the brain of the Ganges River dolphin, *Platanista gangetica* (Odontoceti: Platanistidae), in ventral view showing the large auditory or 8th cranial nerve proceeding in a lateral direction.

From Herald.

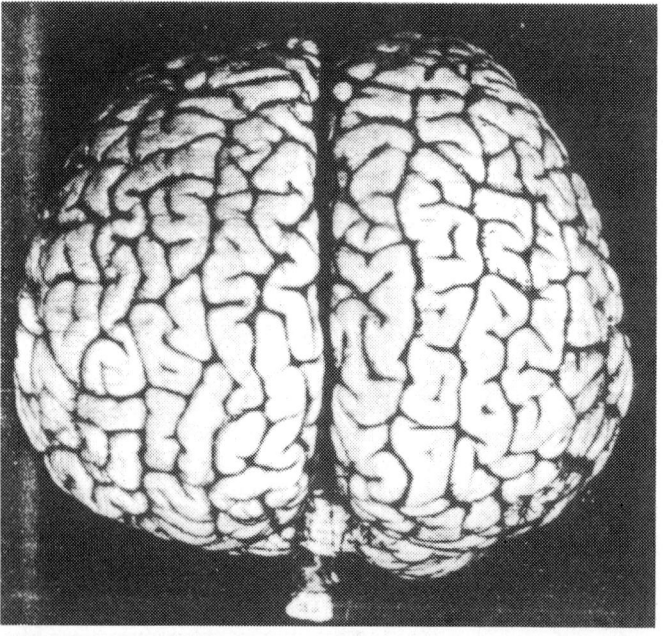

Photo of the brain of the Amazon River dolphin, *Inia geoffrensis* (Odontoceti: Platanistidae), in dorsal view.

From: Pilleri, Gregorio — Investigations On The Cetacea.

A Comparison of Some Features of the Brain

	Toothed Whales (*Odontoceti*)	Whalebone Whales (*Mysticeti*)
Relative Development of the Olfactory Areas	Olfactory structures are reduced or absent.	Olfactory areas are much reduced and very small for mammals.
	Sense of smell appears to be absent.	Sense of smell appears to be present, but very weak.
Relative Shape of the Cerebral Hemispheres	Width exceeds the length.	Length and width are nearly equal or length exceeds the width.
Relative Size of the Cranial Nerves	The auditory or 8th cranial nerve is the largest in most species, particularly those nerves which supply the cochlea of the ear.	The trigeminal or 5th cranial nerve is the largest.

The brains of all whales are in general the same as those of other mammals, and therefore differ very little superficially from them in their gross anatomy.

The olfactory lobes, which are forward extensions of the cerebrum, are very prominent in the lower vertebrates, but they decline in size in the higher groups of the vertebrates. In the whales, the olfactory lobes are greatly reduced and the olfactory areas which do remain are regarded as large in size, considering the fact that most whales appear to lack the sense of smell.

The cerebrum of whales is very well developed and in its complexity has been compared to the development of the brain in the *Primates* (man, apes, monkeys, etc.). In most mammals, the brain is longer than wide, but in most whales, it is typically wider than long due in part to its lengthwise compression by the bones of the skull. The brain is wider than long in nearly all toothed whales (*Odontoceti*) and in all but one whalebone whale (*Mysticeti*), the North Atlantic Right Whale (*Balaenidae: Balaena glacialis* Muller, 1776). The cerebrum is large and highly convoluted in all whales and overlies and covers the cerebellum in most species of toothed whales (*Odontoceti*).

Since animals with a high metabolic rate seem to have a large cerebrum, some scholars have suggested that this feature may be a factor which contributes to the large brain size of whales.

The *diencephalon* and the *mesencephalon* are regions including several components, each of which is composed of a multitude of nerve fibers of great complexity. In the whales, the gross anatomy of these areas will differ little from these structures in typical mammals.

The cerebellum has many functions including those that are associated with balance and body movement; because it is involved in these activities, the cerebellum is always larger in the more active species of animals. The cerebella of both the toothed whales (*Odontoceti*) and the whalebone whales (*Mysticeti*) are of similar appearance, although in the toothed whales, the cerebellum is usually almost entirely covered by the cerebrum, while in the whalebone whales the cerebellum is less completely covered. In the cerebellum of whales, the surface fissures, creases, and grooves of the brain are more pronounced than in land mammals, and those of the toothed whales are more numerous and deeper than those found in the whalebone whales. Because the cerebellum is large in whales, it comprises a considerable proportion of the weight of the brain. Some comparisons of the size of the cerebellum in various animals are given in the accompanying table.

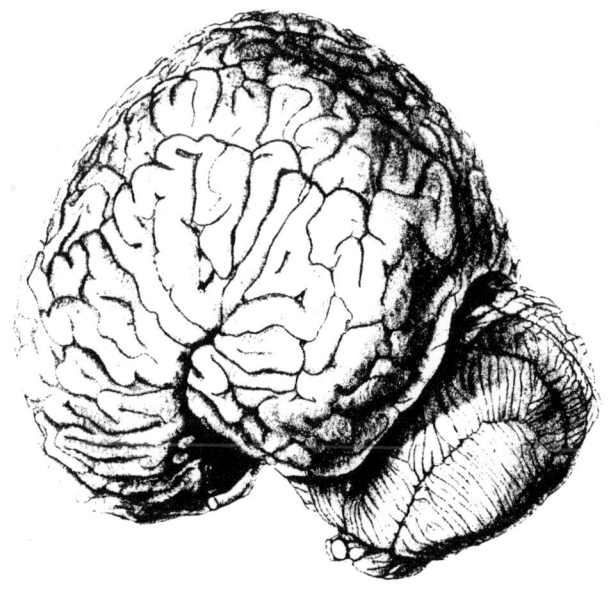

The brain of the bottle-nosed dolphin, *Tursiops truncatus* (Odontoceti: Delphinidae), in lateral view.

From Kruger.

From: K.S. Norris (ed.)—WHALES, DOLPHINS, AND PORPOISES. 1966. Pub. by the Univ. of California Press, Berkeley.

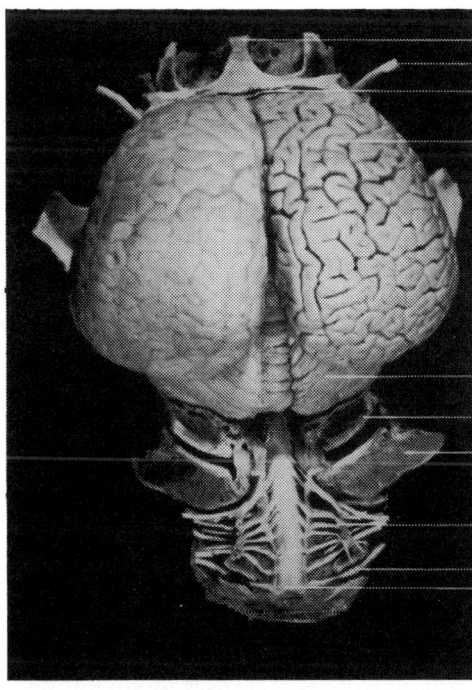

Bones of skull
Optic nerve
Dura mater
Cerebral hemisphere

Cerebellum
Occipital condyle
Atlas
Brachial plexus
Spinal nerve
Spinal cord

Photo of the brain and a portion of the spinal cord of the harbor porpoise, *Phocoena phocoena* (Odontoceti: Delphinidae), in dorsal view.

From Fraser.

**The Relative Size of the Cerebellum
Percent of the Total Brain
(By Weight)**

Group and/or Species	Percent of Total Brain (By Weight)
Baleen Whales In General	20%
Toothed Whales In General	15%
Inia, Platanista	6.7 to 11.8%
Other Species	15 to 19%
Land Mammals In General	10%

Adapted from Slijper.

The brains of five large whales were examined by Daniel P. Quiring, who reported* that the cerebellum of the four whalebone whales (*Balaenoptera physalus* and *Megaptera novaeangliae*) was larger than that of the single sperm whale (*Physeter*) examined.

He also noted that the cerebellum was covered dorsally by the cerebrum in the sperm whale, but in the fin and humpbacked whales, the cerebellum was comparatively larger than in the sperm whale and extended well behind the cerebrum.

The medulla oblongata is the intermediate or connecting link between the brain and the spinal chord and is the organ through which the messages and impulses pass in both directions. It carries out the control of the basic physiological functions including regulation of the heart beat, breathing, swallowing, circulation, etc. In the whales, it is a typical mammalian organ in both structure and function and offers very little which is different from the typical mammalian medulla.

Section b
THE SPINAL CORD

The spinal cord is a great trunk of nerve fibers which extends from the base of the brain (*medulla oblongata*) posteriorly down the spinal or vertebral canal to the tail. This cord leaves the skull through the large opening (*foramen magnum*) at the base of the skull and passes onward posteriorly, passing enroute through the spinal canal or spinal foramen of each vertebra. The spinal cord changes in diameter from front to back. It is largest where it emerges from the base of the brain (*medulla oblongata*) and is, of course, smallest at its posterior end.

In mammals, the spinal cord is slightly enlarged or swollen in the brachial area where it passes opposite the front legs and also in the lumbar region where it passes opposite the hind legs. In the whales, the enlargement of the spinal cord opposite these appendages is insignificant. The front feet have been transformed to flippers and have lost their specialized movements and, in addition, most of the flipper joints are now immobile. Meanwhile, the hind limbs are gone and only vestiges remain, so there is little need for a local enlargement of the spinal cord to coordinate the nerves

*Jour. of Mammalogy 24:1, 1943, pp. 39-45.

for these areas. Since the tail stock and the flukes of the whales are doubtless larger than the tail of their ancestors, we are obliged to assume that the nerves supplying these regions have increased in number, size, and scope over those of their ancestors.

Division 2
THE PERIPHERAL NERVOUS SYSTEM

The peripheral nervous system extends outward from the brain and spinal cord to the many organs, muscles, and surfaces of the body. It receives the stimuli from the various sense organs of the body and forwards them onward to the spinal cord and brain for analysis and instructions and then, in turn, receives the returning messages and transmits them to the appropriate parts of the body. The peripheral nerves are a major part of the communication system of the body of the vertebrates.

Section a
THE CRANIAL NERVES

The brains of vertebrate animals possess paired sets of nerves which emerge from the base of the brain and lead right and left to various organs and areas of the head, neck, and viscera. There are twelve pairs of these nerves in all mammals, including the whales; however, in the whales, some of these nerves have been modified as a result of changes within the whales' body, doubtless due in part to the environment in which they live. These cranial nerves are listed in the accompanying table on the following page.

Section b
THE SPINAL NERVES

The spinal nerves arise as branches from the spinal cord within the spinal or neural canal of the vertebral column. There are small openings (intervertebral foramen) between the vertebrae which open laterally and through which the spinal nerves pass outward from the spinal cord. At each vertebra, these spinal nerves are given off in pairs, one to the right side and another to the left side, and thereafter continue to the various organs, muscles, and other tissues which they supply.

Scholars often have difficulty in identifying the various spinal nerves in the back of the body of whales because they do not know for certain the identity of the nearby vertebrae from which these nerves have emerged.

The neck has seven vertebrae; they are easily identified because they include all of the vertebrae between the skull and that vertebra which bears the first rib.

The thoracic vertebrae include all of those vertebrae which bear ribs.

In most mammals, the lumbar vertebrae include all of those vertebrae between the last rib and the sacrum; and the caudal vertebrae include all of those vertebrae which lie posterior to the sacrum. However, in the whales, there is no sacrum and therefore the vertebrae beyond the last thoracic vertebra (with its ribs) are difficult to divide into groups; so, scholars usually lump the lumbar and sacral vertebrae together, but they are uncertain of the exact number of each. In whales, the last sacral vertebra is usually regarded as the last vertebra without chevron bones beneath it. The caudal vertebrae begin with the first vertebra to have chevron bones beneath it and extend backward from that point. Since the number of vertebrae in the lumbar-sacral area varies, it is difficult to know how many of each type are involved; and, since the spinal nerves are identified by the vertebrae from which they emerge, it is very difficult to identify the spinal nerves of this lumbar-sacral region.

So in the posterior part of the body, the spinal nerves are difficult to identify because of the reduction or disappearance of the posterior appendages and the adjoining sacrum and pelvis, and the concurrent development of a tail with its accompanying vertebrae and nerves. For these reasons it is difficult to match the vertebrae and the nerves in the area posterior to the neck and thorax and to accurately determine the number of spinal nerves in these areas.

Among the ocean dolphins (*Delphinidae*), the spinal nerves appear to range in number from 40 to 44; within this range, 44 is considered to be the usual (possibly correct) number.

The Cranial Nerves of Man and the Whales

The Cranial Nerves		Functions of the Cranial Nerves		
Number	Name	In Man	In Whales	Differences, Remarks, Etc.
I	Olfactory	Concerned with the sense of smell. Supplies nasal cavity and turbinal bones.	In *Odontoceti*—The olfactory nerve is present in embryo, but little remains in adult. In *Mysticeti*—The olfactory nerve is present, but reduced.	The sense of smell is practically absent in all whales. Authorities differ on the presence of the olfactory remnants.
II	Optic	Concerned with the sense of sight. Supplies the retina of the inner eye.	Same function.	Diameter of nerve varies with the species. In the blind Ganges dolphin, the optic nerve is thin and thread-like.
III	Occulomotor	Supplies the muscles of the eye including the sphincter muscle of the iris, the ciliary muscle, one oblique muscle, and three rectus muscles.	The occulomotor muscle is absent in the blind Ganges dolphin.	The size of the muscle varies with the visual activity of each species.
IV	Trochlear	Supplies the superior oblique muscle of the eye.	Absent in some species with small or weak eyes.	The size of the muscle varies with the visual activity of each species.
V	Trigeminal (or Trifacial)	Supplies various sensory and motor nerves to the face, scalp, mouth, pharynx, eyes, and teeth.	Same function, but greatly enlarged. Includes melon and air sacs, etc. of head.	In *Odontoceti*, it is the 2nd largest nerve. In *Mysticeti*, it is the largest cranial nerve. This nerve is enlarged because it supplies the surface of the head.
VI	Abducens	Supplies the external rectus muscle of the eye only.	Same function. Absent in some species with small or weak eyes.	The size of the muscle varies with the visual activity of each species.

The Cranial Nerves of Man and the Whales
(Continued)

The Cranial Nerves		Functions of the Cranial Nerves		
Number	Name	In Man	In Whales	Differences, Remarks, Etc.
VII	Facial	Supplies various sensory and motor nerves to the face, scalp, tongue, and salivary glands.	Same function.	This nerve is enlarged in all whales because it supplies the nerves for the blowhole.
VIII	Auditory	Concerned with the senses of hearing and balance. Supplies nerves to the inner ear including the cochlea, the vestibule, and semicircular canals.	Same function, but greatly enlarged.	In the *Odontoceti*, it is the largest of all cranial nerves. In the *Mysticeti*, it is the 2nd largest of the cranial nerves. The enlargment is due to the great development of the sense of hearing.
IX	Glossopharyngeal	Concerned with the sense of taste. Supplies various sensory and motor nerves to the pharynx, parotid glands, tongue, tonsils, Eustachian tubes, and tympanic cavities.	Same function. Supplies tastes buds on tongue.	Nerves are greatly reduced because taste is poorly developed. In *Odontoceti*, nerve is very small. In *Mysticeti* nerve is very small; it is smaller than in the *Odontoceti*.
X	Pneumogastric (or Vagus)	Supplies sensory, motor, secretory, and inhibitory nerves to nearly all organs in the thorax and abdomen.	Same function.	
XI	Spinal Accessory	Supplies motor nerves to the muscles of the neck; some of these nerve fibers join the vagus nerve.	Same function.	
XII	Hypoglossal	Supplies motor fibers to the muscles of the tongue.	Same function.	The size of this nerve is greatly reduced because the tongue is not active.

A Comparison of
The Number and Distribution of the Spinal Nerves

	Cervical	Dorsal or Thoracic	Lumbar	Sacral	Caudal	Total
Lagenorhynchus obliquidens THE PACIFIC STRIPED DOLPHIN	8	13	23±			
Phocoena phocoena THE HARBOR PORPOISE	8	11	25±			
Balaenoptera physalus THE FIN WHALE	8	12	24±			
Felis catus THE DOMESTIC CAT	8	13	7	3	7 (8)	38 (39)
Homo sapiens MAN	8	12	5	5	1 (coccygeal)	31

Section c
THE AUTONOMIC OR INVOLUNTARY NERVOUS SYSTEM

The autonomic or involuntary nervous system is a complex system of small, slender interconnected nerves and ganglia which are principally located within the body cavity. It consists of many parts including two parallel chains of ganglia which are connected by a series of nerve fibers. These chains lie within the body cavity on each side of the vertebral column and extend from the head to the tail. They are connected to the spinal nerves at each ganglion and also have many fibers extending out into the surrounding organs, muscles, and other tissues.

In whales, the functions of this system differ but little from that of other mammals and will not be discussed here.

Division 3
THE SENSE ORGANS

— Guide to Division 3 —

The sense organs of mammals are usually regarded as five in number. They include the senses of touch (tactile), sight (visual), hearing (auditory), smell (olfactory), and taste (gustatory). Although these senses are actively used by most mammals, the whales have lost nearly all perception of smell and taste and are therefore using but three of these five senses. Within these remaining three senses, the whales have developed some unusual and amazing modifications, particularly in the auditory sense. These five senses will be described briefly.

Section a
THE TACTILE SENSE ORGANS

The sense of touch is usually viewed as including several stimuli and the interpretation of them by the body; these include the stimuli of touch, pain, heat and cold, and also vibration. As in other mammals, the sensation of touch in whales is located in the skin. The skin of whales is thin, sensitive, and well supplied with nerves and blood vessels; it also contains various dermal receptors, the functions of which are not completely understood.

Whales do not have hair, but they do have vibrissae, which to the casual observer are often mistaken for hair. Vibrissae are most readily identified as the "whiskers" found upon the upper lip of the domestic cat. However, in whales, the vibrissae are much smaller and much shorter than the vibrissae found upon the bodies of terrestrial mammals.

Odontoceti. Among the toothed whales (*Odontoceti*), the sense of touch is located over the entire surface of the body and is well developed. The sensitivity is greatest in the areas of the head, flippers, belly, genital areas, and elsewhere. All toothed whales (*Odontoceti*) engage in communication by touching bodies and by stroking each other with their flippers during play, love making, and mating. They enjoy rubbing against objects and, in captivity, respond readily to trainers who rub or brush their bodies. The stimuli of touch from the surface of the head and surrounding areas is received and transmitted to the brain through the fifth cranial nerve (trigeminal), which in the toothed whales is the second largest of all the cranial nerves.

In the toothed whales (*Odontoceti*), the vibrissae are present in varying degrees of retention. On this basis, A.V. Yablokov has divided the toothed whales into four groups as follows:

1. In some species, the vibrissae do not appear in either the embryo or in the adult. These include the beluga (*Monodontidae: Delphinapterus*) and the narwhal (*Monodontidae: Monodon*).
2. In some species, the vibrissae are present only in the embryo. These include the great sperm whale (*Physeteridae: Physeter*), the pilot whales (*Delphinidae: Globicephala*), and the common dolphin (*Delphinidae: Delphinus*).
3. In some species, the vibrissae are retained throughout the nursing period and thereafter fall out. These include the bottle-nosed dolphin (*Delphinidae: Tursiops*), the rough-toothed dolphin (*Delphinidae: Steno*), and the long-beaked dolphins (*Delphinidae: Stenella*).
4. In some species, the vibrissae are retained in a limited number throughout life. These include the river dolphins (*Platanistidae: Platanista, Inia*).

Mysticeti. Among the whalebone whales *(Mysticeti),* the sense of touch is well developed. Sensations from the top of the head and surrounding areas are received by the fifth cranial nerve (trigeminal), which in the *Mysticeti* is the largest of all twelve cranial nerves.

The vibrissae of these whales are usually located on the head in the three areas listed below.

1. *on the end of the lower jaw* where there are usually two vertical rows of vibrissae;
2. *on the sides of the lower jaws* where there are usually one or more longitudinal rows of vibrissae; and
3. *on top of the head* where there are usually two rows of vibrissae on each side of the midline.

In all, these vibrissae range in number from a few to as many as 250 on the head of the right whale (*Balaenidae: Balaena glacialis glacialis*). In addition to the vibrissae, the bodies of these whales have minute (1 mm.) lumps or dermal receptors scattered over the head and snout with fewer distributed over the remainder of the body.

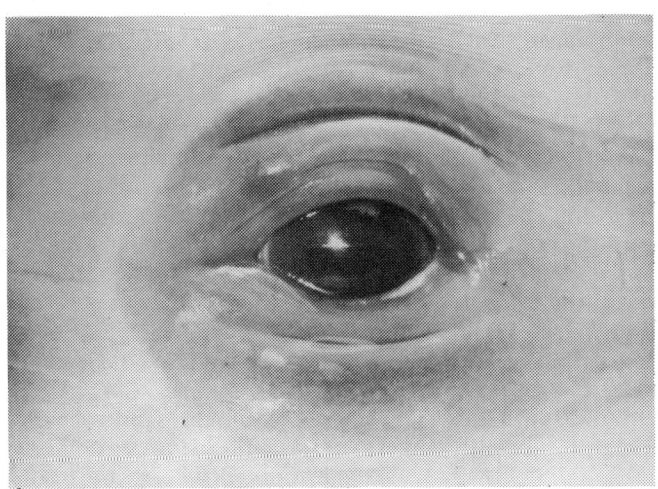

Photo of the left eye of the bottle-nosed dolphin, *Tursiops truncatus* (Odontoceti: Delphinidae).
**Kewalo Basin Marine Mammal Laboratory,
University of Hawaii.**

Section b
THE VISUAL SENSE ORGANS

The eyes of whales give an additional clue to the origin and ancestry of these animals. Their eyes most closely resemble the eyes of the ungulate mammals (cattle, etc.) in their asymmetrical eyeball, horizontal pupil, and other features, thereby suggesting an evolutionary descent from a group related to the modern ungulates.

The eyeballs of whales are set in orbits which are quite far back on the sides of the head. They are oval in shape, are somewhat flattened upon the back and top, are quite mobile, and possess elliptical pupils. The eyeballs are surrounded by muscular and connective tissue and are controlled, as in other mammals, by four rectus muscles, two oblique muscles, and one retractor muscle. They also possess the unusual feature of being able to move in and out of the orbit for a very, very short distance. The eye is bordered in front by a large, wide upper eyelid and a lower eyelid, both of which are functional and are opened and closed by muscles; only a small remnant remains of the third eyelid.

There are no tear (lacrimal) glands or tear ducts in whales; instead the eyes are protected and lubricated by secretions of the Harderian glands located in the inner corner of the orbit. Their secretion is an oily protein mucus which flows over the eyeball and is eventually washed away with the passing water.

The vision of whales varies with the species and ranges from those which appear to be completely blind (*Platanistidae: Platanista*) to some which possess rather good eyesight (*Delphinidae: Orcinus*). In general, their field of vision is quite large and, in those species in which the visual fields of the two eyes overlap, depth perception or stereoscopic vision is present. Because of their horizontal pupils, their field of vision is wider horizontally than vertically and is directed slightly downward.

The visibility of whales and other animals is restricted under water, because of the absence of adequate light. The eyes of all whales possess a reflective lining (*tapetum lucidum*) in the choroid layer which reflects light and intensi-

fies the image on the retina; this, of course, helps these animals to see in dim light. The species with the best vision appear to be those which are diurnal feeders and/or surface dwellers.

The eyeball of whales has been modified from those found in more typical mammals. In addition to its depressed shape and its elliptical cornea, iris, and pupil, the sclerotic coat, including the cornea and the conjunctiva, is greatly thickened and hardened (cornified) as a protective layer surrounding the eye. The lens of the eye is nearly spherical in shape. This tends to make the whale far-sighted (hyperopic) below the surface and near-sighted (myopic) above the surface. Although some whales stick their head out of the water to look about, it is doubtful if they receive as clear and sharp an image as do human beings.

The optic nerve, which enters the rear of the eyeball, is enclosed in an unusually heavy sheath of connective tissue and blood vessels, which is not found in other mammals. Other differences between the whales and land mammals include shorter eye chambers and more spherical lenses; in addition, the solutions of the eyeball have lower freezing points than those of land mammals and their refractive indexes are greater.

The differences between the eyes of the toothed whales (*Odontoceti*) and the whalebone whales (*Mysticeti*) are not as great as their similarities, but some differences do exist in both structure and function. Of all whales, the *Delphinidae* (dolphins and the porpoises) seem to have the best vision, but keen eye sight does not seem to be an attribute of whales.

In the toothed whales (*Odontoceti*), the sclerotic coat of the eyeball is thicker and heavier than in land mammals, but thinner than in whalebone whales. The ciliary muscle, which moves the lens into focus, is present in the eye, enabling the toothed whales to focus their eyes. The visual fields of the right and left eyes partially overlap in some species of toothed whales. This gives these animals a degree of depth perception or stereoscopic vision which is lacking in whalebone whales.

It should be noted that the Ganges River Dolphin (*Platanistidae: Platanista*) appears to be blind and that its eyes are very small and lack a lens. Sperm whales (*Physeteridae: Physeter*) also have small eyes, a feature which is doubtless associated with their feeding at great depths in the darkness of the sea.

In the whalebone whales (*Mysticeti*), the sclerotic coat of the eyeball is thicker than in the toothed whales (*Odontoceti*) and one of the very thickest of all mammals. The ciliary muscle found in the eyes of mammals appears to be absent in whalebone whales, thus depriving them of the ability to adjust the focus of their eyes by this method. The *tapetum lucidum*, the light-reflecting curtain behind the retina, covers a larger area of the interior of the eye in the whalebone whales than in the toothed whales; this means that whalebone whales have better night vision than the toothed whales. The eyes of the whalebone whales lie widely separated upon the sides of the head, making it impossible for their visual fields to overlap; they, therefore, lack the depth perception which is achieved through stereoscopic vision.

The eyes, which were removed from three large whales at the whaling station at Fields Landing, California, in 1941, showed the following weights*:

---

*From The Jour. of Mammalogy 24:1, 1943, pp. 39-45.

The Weight of the Eyes of Whales

Species	Total Weight Lbs.	Total Weight Kgs.	Weight of the Eyes Lbs.	Weight of the Eyes Kgs.
Odontoceti				
Physeteridae				
Physeter macrocephalus				
THE SPERM WHALE				
Male: Length — 43 ft.	86,000	39,000	0.64	0.290
Mysticeti				
Balaenopteridae				
Balaenoptera physalus				
THE FIN WHALE				
Female: Length — 71 ft.	130,942**	59,394	3.792	1.720
Megaptera novaeangliae				
THE HUMP-BACKED WHALE				
Male: Length — 45 ft.	90,000	40,823	2.16	0.980

Section c
THE AUDITORY SENSE ORGANS

A wide range exists in the development and specialization of the five common senses (touch, sight, hearing, smell, taste) found in mammals. In the whales, the sense of hearing is very important, is by far their most specialized sense, and is probably as well developed as in any other group of the mammals with the possible exception of the bats. Sound and hearing are very important and essential in the ocean because of the poor visibility; whales, therefore, find sound and hearing useful for locating their food, for noting the approach of enemies, for communication with each other, and for orientation with their surroundings. The sense of hearing in whales is similar to that of man and of other mammals, but the whales have developed some modifications and specializations of the hearing organs so that they now show some differences from typical mammals in the anatomy of their auditory apparatus.

The external ear (*pinna*) of whales has disappeared and the muscles which moved it have also atrophied. However, scholars have found remnants of ear (auricular) cartilage beneath the skin of some porpoises (*Delphinidae: Phocoena*); in addition, remnants of two external ear muscles linger beneath the skin of all whalebone whales.

In the absence of the external ear, the auditory canal begins as a simple opening on the surface of the head. These openings measure about 1 mm. in diameter in toothed whales (*Odontoceti*) and about 10 mm. in diameter in whalebone whales (*Mysticeti*) and are located somewhere about midway between the eye and the base of the flipper.

In the toothed whales (*Odontoceti*), the auditory canal passes rather directly in a gentle S-curve to the ear drum (tympanic membrane) which bulges outward slightly, but otherwise resembles the membrane of typical land mammals.

The structure of the external ear of whalebone whales (*Mysticeti*) is quite different. The external auditory canal of whalebone whales measures about 10 mm. in diameter at the surface of the head; it then becomes so small in diameter for a short distance as to be almost closed, and finally enlarges to include a long, slender, conical "plug" lying within it. This strange plug, together with a special cylindrical development of the tympanic membrane, occupies the inner part of the auditory canal. Here the tympanic membrane has developed an exceedingly strange, elongated, hollow, concave struc-

ture (tympanic core), which is bowed outward like the finger of a glove and which may reach a length of two to three inches in large whales; at this point, this finger-like core is in contact with the inner enlarged end of the ear plug. It is at this inner end that the ear plug continues to grow by the addition of its special horny material.

The middle ear, the space which is properly called the tympanum, lies on the inner side of the ear drum. It is a cavity or chamber surrounded by bone and into which there are five openings, as follows:

1. *The auditory canal* covered by the ear drum (tympanic membrane);
2. *The Eustachian tube* leading to the pharynx;
3. *The opening into the mastoid antrum* (cavity) in the mastoid process of the temporal bone;
4. *The oval window (fenestra ovalis),* covered by a membrane, leading to the vestibule (chamber) of the inner ear; and
5. *The round window (fenestra rotunda)* covered by a membrane, also leading to the inner ear.

The central chamber of this middle ear is spanned by a chain of three famous bones, the malleus (hammer), the incus (anvil), and the stapes (stirrup), which transmit sound vibrations from the ear drum across the tympanic cavity to the membrane of the oval window.

The inner ear occupies spaces within the temporal bone and consists of the cochlea for hearing, the semicircular canals for balance, and a double chamber called the vestibule which is partially divided into two incomplete chambers called the *sacculus* and the *utriculus*.

The cochlea is a tube of diminishing diameter which is coiled upon itself in approximately two turns in a snail-like fashion; it is closed at the smaller, upper end and open at the larger lower end through the oval window into the *sacculus* or front end of the vestibule. A thin, spiral, ribbon-like lamina extends spirally up the center of the cochlea and divides it into two halves. This cochlea is the organ of hearing which receives the sound vibrations from the outer and middle ears and transmits them to the nerves. In this coiled organ, the sounds of lower pitch are received in the area farthest from the oval window and the sounds of highest pitch are received nearest to the oval window. These sounds are received by the nerve fibers within the cochlea and transmitted by them through the auditory or 8th cranial nerve to the brain for interpretation.

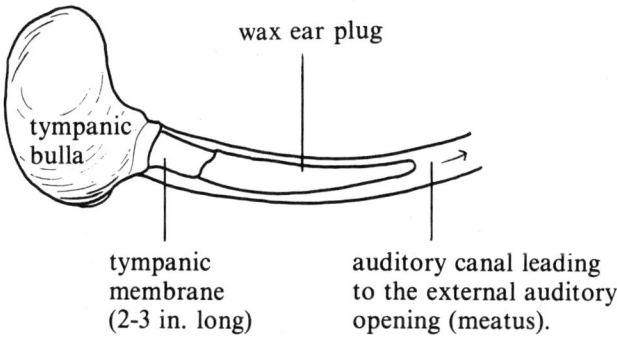

Diagram labels: wax ear plug; tympanic bulla; tympanic membrane (2-3 in. long); auditory canal leading to the external auditory opening (meatus).

Diagram of the external auditory canal of a fin whale, *Balaenoptera physalus* (Mysticeti: Balaenopteridae) showing the finger-shaped outpocket of the tympanic membrane into the external auditory canal and the hard wax plug which is located external to it.

Drawn from Fraser.

**Includes an added 20% for blood and body fluids.

Whales have tried to separate the hearing organs and related bones from their close attachment to the skull. In land mammals, the vibrations of sound are received through the air and their direction is easily determined. In water, it is difficult to determine the direction of sound if the ear bones are solidly attached to the skull because of the disturbing vibrations coming from the skull. The whales have attempted to solve this problem by partially separating the tympanic bullae (ear bones) from the skull, so that they are now loosely attached to the skull by one thin bone in the toothed whales (*Odontoceti*) and by two thin bones in the whalebone whales (*Mysticeti*). In addition, various bones of the ear, including the three little bones of the middle ear, have become thick and dense in structure and the tympanic bulla of the tympanic bone has developed into a very heavy, dense, hard, bean-shaped capsule; this increase in density is believed to be helpful in reducing the distracting vibrations which are transmitted from the skull and in improving the reception of sound. A foamy liquid fills the cavities in the bone surrounding the inner ear; this foam likewise helps to insulate the inner ear from unwanted outside vibrations. This partial separation of the tympanic bullae from the skull and their increase in density is believed to have greatly improved the hearing ability of whales and is most necessary for the improvement of directional hearing under water.

Whales produce a wide variety of sounds depending upon the species of the whale, the occasion, and their mood. These sounds may be either pulsating or continuous and have been described by many people as whistles, whines, squeals, screams, squeaks, clicks, moans, hums, growls, bellows, roars, etc. This skill of emitting sounds is much better developed in the toothed whales and their noise-making mechanism is likewise more complex than in the whalebone whales.

The sounds of whales are very complex and involved. They are most commonly measured in cycles or frequencies per second; these units are called "Hertz." These sounds will range from about 20 cycles per second in some whalebone whales to over 200,000 cycles per second in some toothed whales. Some of the sounds of whales are in the sonic or audio frequency range between 20 and 20,000 frequencies or cycles per second (20 to 20,000 Hertz); these are audible to human ears. A very few sounds of whales are in the sub-sonic or infra-sonic frequency range below 20 frequencies or cycles per second (20 Hertz); these are not audible to human ears. The remaining sounds of whales are in the ultra-sonic frequency range which is higher than 20,000 cycles per second (20,000 Hertz); these are inaudible to human ears.

In whales, the lower range of sound seems to be used for communication between individuals, while the higher frequencies are used in their echo-location and navigation.

The ability of whales to produce sound under water, to listen for its returning echo from objects in the water, and to determine the source of this echo, is known as echo-location. This skill is found only in toothed whales (*Odontoceti*). When sounds are emitted under water and then reflected back from nearby objects, these returning sounds are received by the "ears" of the whale and relayed to the brain for analysis. In echo-location, toothed whales show the ability to direct their sounds in selected directions and also to determine the direction and the distance from which the returning echo has come. This skill enables the toothed whales to detect the presence and shape of objects in cloudy water and in darkness, even though these objects remain unseen. This is a very special skill which is shared with bats and possibly a few other animals.

While the hearing mechanism of whales, including the cochlea, is very well developed and exceedingly efficient, the semicircular canals (for balance) are not. These canals consist of three separate arched tubes which lie in three separate geometric planes and which connect at both ends to the vestibule through five separate openings. These canals are exceedingly small in size although fully developed. In other particulars, they differ very little from those of typical terrestrial mammals.

**Comparison of Auditory Features
in Toothed Whales and Whalebone Whales**

Auditory Feature	Toothed Whales (*Odontoceti*)	Whalebone Whales (*Mysticeti*)
Ear bones connect to skull	Not directly connected	Directly connected
Ear plug present in external auditory meatus	Not present	Present
Cochlea coils	1.5+ coils	2 to 2.5 coils
Sounds generated in	Supra-cranial air sacs and larynx	Larynx and retro-laryngeal sac
Sounds emitted*	Of wide range including ultra-sonic, sonic, and sub-sonic	Primarily of low frequency (infra-sonic or sub-sonic)
Sound emission direction	Directional	Non-directional
Echo-location ability	Present	Absent

Adapted from A.V. Yablokov et alii.

Section d
THE OLFACTORY SENSE ORGANS

Evidence of the presence or absence of the olfactory organs in whales is difficult to obtain; however, the ethmoid bone of the skull does provide some interesting evidence on this subject. The ethmoid bone closes the front of the cranial cavity and also fills most of the nasal cavity. This ethmoid bone has a division known as the cribriform plate (L. *cribrum*, sieve + form) which separates the brain from the nasal cavity and which is perforated by holes through which the olfactory nerves pass between the ephithelium of the nose and the brain. Inspection of this plate and the nature of its perforations are used to determine the state of the evolutionary degeneration of the olfactory nerves.

The velocity of sound in water is nearly five times the velocity of sound in air. In air, sound travels at about 1128 feet (344 m.) per second; in water, its speed is about 4921 feet (1500 m. or 1.5 km.) per second.

*Ultra-sonic: 20,000 to 200,000 Hertz or cycles per second; not audible to humans.
Sonic: 20 to 20,000 Hertz or cycles per second; audible to humans.
Sub-sonic: below 20 Hertz or cycles per second; not audible to humans.

In the toothed whales (*Odontoceti*), scholars regard the sense of smell as entirely lacking, because there is no trace of an olfactory nerve or of an olfactory organ in the head of these whales. There is also very little evidence of any olfactory epithelium in the nasal passages. In some groups (*Delphinidae*), the cribriform plate of the ethmoid bone has no holes through which the olfactory nerves could pass, although it is reported that the beaked whales (*Ziphiidae: Hyperoodon*) retain a single pair of perforations in their cribriform plate for the passage of these olfactory nerves.

In the whalebone whales *(Mysticeti),* the sense of smell seems to be present, although it is very rudimentary, and a vestigial olfactory organ seems to be present in the nasal tissue. In addition, the cribriform plate of the ethmoid bone of these whales contains small perforations through which small nerves pass and terminate in the membranes of the nasal cavity.

Section e
THE GUSTATORY SENSE ORGANS

The sense of taste in mammals is associated with the tongue and the taste buds which occur upon it. The sensations of taste have been historically described as about four in number, namely, acid, sweet, bitter, and salt. These sensations are carried to the brain by the glossopharyngeal or 9th cranial nerve which supplies the tongue, pharynx, and related areas.

In the whales, the sensation of taste has atrophied and is either very weak or missing. The taste buds are lacking or occur only in an atrophied or degenerate form. Some reasons for this decline might be suggested: the mouth is continually awash with water with very little change in its quality; a wide variety of food is not available, so feeding is not particularly selective; and all available animal food which can be captured is suitable for consumption, so discrimination in the diet is not important.

In the toothed whales (*Odontoceti*), the quantity and quality of the taste which remains is uncertain. Some scholars think that a rudimentary sensation of taste may remain in some pits and papillae at the base of the tongue. However, the salivary glands which are associated with the sensation of taste are small or absent and the glossopharyngeal nerve (9th) which serves this area is small and not particularly well developed.

Toothed whales, however, do respond to substances in their surrounding water, indicating that they may have developed additional sensory organs. There are fossa or pits (*fovea*) at the base of the tongue in various toothed whales (*Odontoceti*) which are lined with a prismatic epithelium, while the surrounding surface of the tongue is covered with a squamous (flat) epithelium. They are obviously different from their surroundings and may prove to be chemoreceptors which are substituting for the sense of taste.

In the baleen whales (*Mysticeti*), there is some evidence that there are taste receptors near the tip of the snout, although the sensation of taste is not completely understood. Since the glossopharyngeal nerve of these whales is still relatively smaller than that found in the toothed whales, it is safe to assume that the whalebone whales have less ability to taste than the toothed whales.

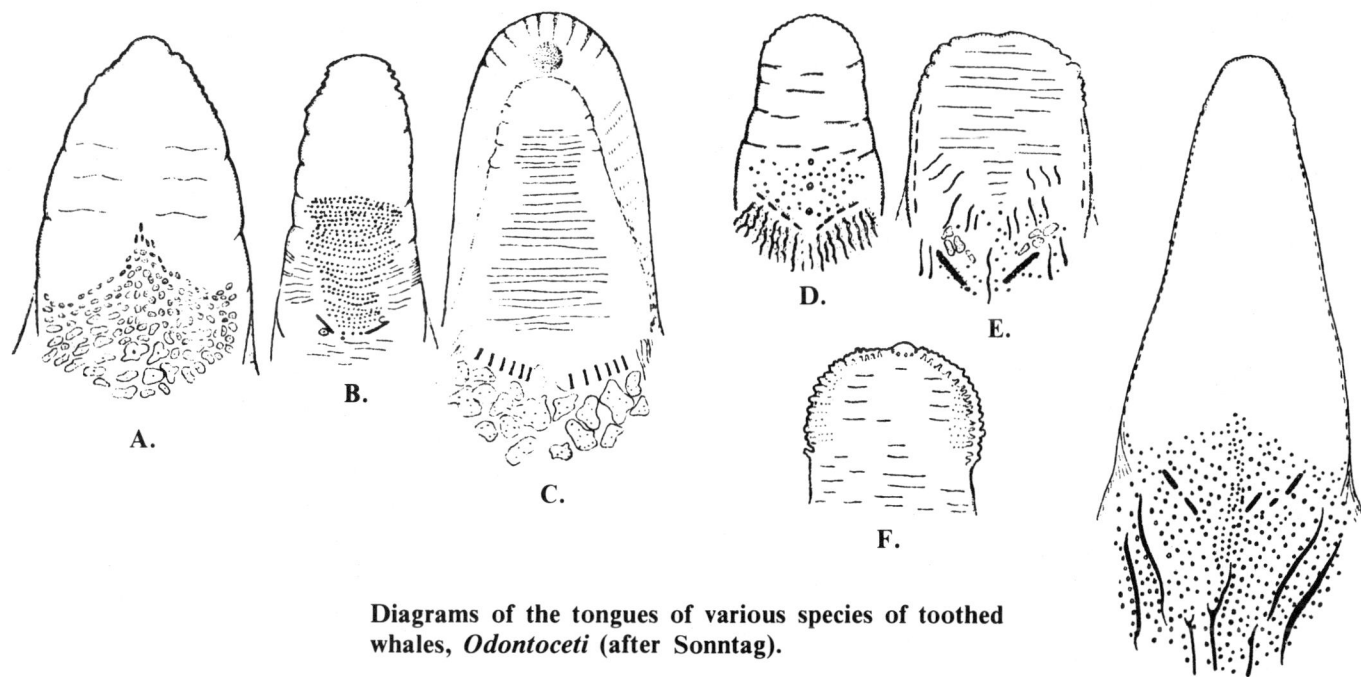

Diagrams of the tongues of various species of toothed whales, *Odontoceti* (after Sonntag).

A. **The White-beaked Dolphin, *Lagenorhynchus albirostris*.**
B. **The Common Dolphin, *Delphinus delphis*.**
C. **The White-headed or Gray Grampus, *Grampus griseus*.**
D. **The Harbor Porpoise, *Phocoena phocoena*.**
E. **The White Whale or Beluga, *Delphinapterus leucas*.**
F. **The Common Bottle-nosed Dolphin, *Tursiops truncatus*.**
G. **The Black Chilean Dolphin, *Cephalorhynchus eutropia*.**

From: Arvy, Lucie and Pilleri, Gregorio — Investigations On The Cetacea. 1970. 2:75-77 (fig. 2).

Chapter X
THE EXCRETORY SYSTEM

The principal function of the excretory system is to rid the body of the waste products resulting from the metabolism of food and from other biological processes; these waste products are then gathered up in solution by the blood and the blood, in turn, is passed through the kidneys. Within the kidneys, these waste products are withdrawn from the blood and transferred in liquid form (urine) to the ducts (ureters) which drain the urine from the kidneys into the bladder for later release from the body through the urethra. The principal organs of this excretory system, therefore, include the kidneys, the ureters, the urinary bladder (*vesica urinaria*), and the urethra.

Division 1
THE EXCRETORY GLANDS OF THE SKIN

While most of the terrestrial mammals have an abundance of sweat glands through which they are able to eliminate excess water and salt from their bodies, these sweat glands are absent in all whales. Mammals tend to accumulate a surplus of salt in their bodies and must eliminate it on a regular basis. This is especially true of whales which must live in a sea of salt and yet maintain a water balance with less salt than that which is found in the surrounding sea water. Lacking sweat glands and other facilities for the elimination of salt, the

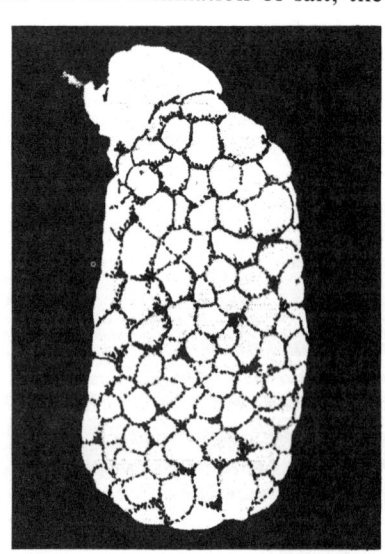

Photo of a kidney of the harbor porpoise, *Phocoena phocoena,* showing its divisions into lobules or renculi.

whales have solved the problem by passing the salt from their blood through their kidneys and outward with their urine. This requires a large amount of water which the whales must generate within their bodies by the oxidation of carbohydrates and fats. Since whales do not need to evaporate water from their skins to reduce their body temperature, they are much more economical than many other mammals in the use of water within their bodies.

Division 2
THE URINARY ORGANS

Section a
THE KIDNEYS

The kidneys of mammals are two in number and lie in the lumbar area attached to the dorsal side of the abdominal cavity; here they are placed nearly opposite each other on either side of the vertebral column. They are usually imbedded in fat and are held in position by this fat, by the tissue of the peritoneum, and by the arteries, veins, and ureters which are connected to them.

In man, the kidneys are "bean-shaped" with a depression (hilum or hilus) on their median surface; they measure about four inches in length, about two and one-half inches in width, and about one and one-half inches in thickness.

The surface of the kidney and its divisions vary greatly among the mammals. In man, the kidney has a smooth surface in the adult, although it is lobulated in the foetus; it is covered by a tough fibrous envelope called the capsule (*tunica fibrosa*), beneath which are the two functional layers, the cortex and the medulla, where the urine is extracted from the blood, collected, and discharged.

In many mammals, including the whales, the surface of the kidney is divided into lobes or lobules known as renculi (sing., renculus).* These divisions of the kidney are best observed in the kidneys of cattle (with 25-30 renculi) which are sold in the meat markets. Among the whales, the divisions of the kidney are very numerous. These divisions increase the surface area of the kidney and consequently the area of the cortex in which the salt and urine are removed from the blood.

The Divisions of the Kidney in Various Whales and Other Mammals

Species	Length of Species	Number of Lobes or Renculi
Delphinidae		
Neophocaena phocaenoides THE BLACK FINLESS PORPOISE	4½± feet	150±
Phocoena species THE COMMON PORPOISE	5-7 feet	250-300
Tursiops truncatus THE BOTTLE-NOSED DOLPHIN	10-12 feet	375±
Monodontidae		
Delphinapterus leucas THE BELUGA OR WHITE WHALE	15-18 feet	400±
Balaenopteridae		
Balaenoptera musculus THE BLUE WHALE	To 100 feet	3,000 ±
Man	—	Smooth, entire, compact
Dugong	To 9 feet	
Cat	—	
Horse	—	
Elephant	—	8±
Cattle	—	25-30±

Adapted from E.J. Slijper and A.V. Yablokov.

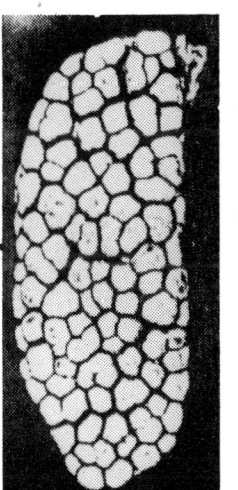 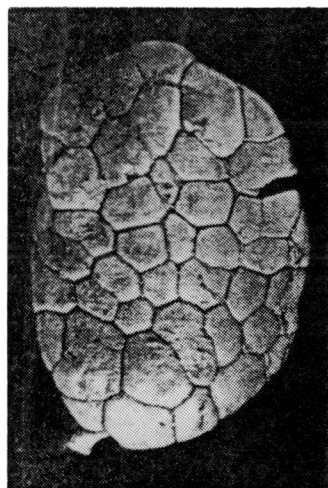

Left. **Photo of a kidney of the common dolphin,** *Delphinus delphis* **(Odontoceti: Delphinidae), in dorsal view, showing the lobules or renculi.**

From: Arvy, Lucie and Pilleri, Gregorio — Investigations On The Cetacea. 1973-4. 8:161-212 (pl. 2B).

Right. **Photo of a right kidney of the Indus River dolphin,** *Platanista minor* **(Odontoceti: Platanistidae), in dorsal view, showing the oval outline and the lobules or renculi.**

From: Cave, A.J.E. in Pilleri, Gregorio — Investigations On The Cetacea. 1973-4. 5:71-81 (pl. 1).

---

*Some scholars use a terminology in which a renculus is divided into several lobuli.

In superficial appearance, the kidneys of whales probably most closely resemble a bunch of grapes, although they do vary in general shape. The kidneys of the river dolphins (*Platanistidae*) tend to be smaller and more rounded or spherical than in other families of whales; the kidneys of the ocean dolphins (*Delphinidae*) are moderately elongated; and the kidneys of the beaked whales (*Ziphiidae*) and the rorquals (*Balaenopteridae*) are more elongated and slender (Yablokov).

Because the kidneys of whales are relatively larger than those of land mammals and because the surface divisions of

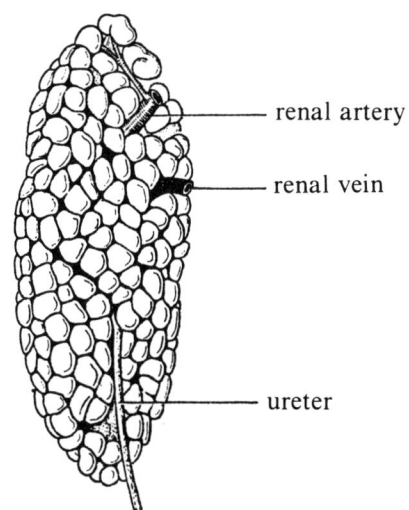

Diagram of the kidney of the common dolphin, *Delphinus delphis* **(Odontoceti: Delphinidae).**

From Anthony.

From: Arvy, Lucie and Pilleri, Gregorio — Investigations On The Cetacea. 1973-4. 5:231-310 (fig. 9).

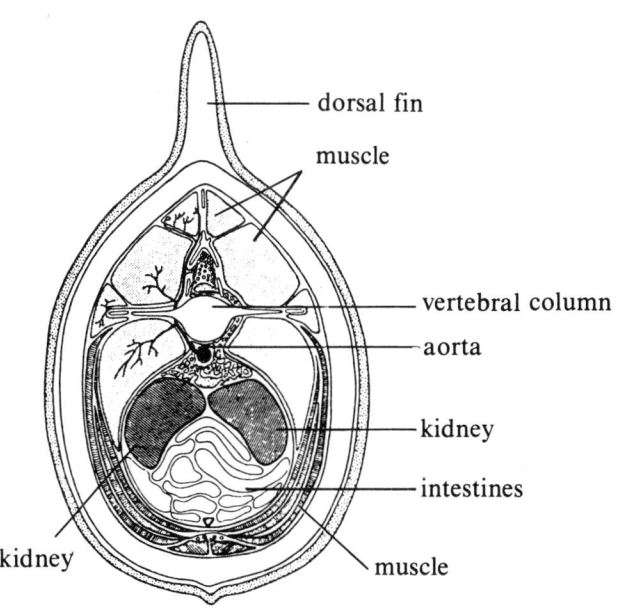

Diagram of a crosssection through the abdomen of the harbor porpoise, *Phocoena phocoena* **(Odontoceti: Delphinidae), showing the location of the kidneys.**

Drawn from Arvy.

From: Arvy, Lucie and Pilleri, Gregorio — Investigations On The Cetacea. 1973-4. 5:231-310 (fig. 5).

their kidneys are more numerous than in land mammals, it appears that the whales have made an adjustment to the special problem of keeping their salt content below that of the surrounding sea water. They have solved this problem by an increase in the size of the kidney and by an increase in the area of the cortex by developing a kidney of many lobules.

The kidneys, which were removed from two large whales at the whaling station at Fields Landing, California, in 1941, showed the following weights*:

The Weight of the Kidneys of Whales

Species	Weight of Whale Lbs.	Kgs.	Wt. of a Kidney Lbs.	Kgs.
Mysticeti				
Balaenopteridae				
Balaenoptera physalus				
THE FIN WHALE				
Female: Length — 71 ft. 130,942**	59,394		461	209
Megaptera novaeangliae				
THE HUMP-BACKED WHALE				
Male: Length — 41 ft.	82,000	37,195	424	192

*From The Jour. of Mammalogy 24:1, 1943, pp. 39-45.
**Includes an added 20% for blood and body fluids.

Section b
THE URETERS

The ureters of mammals are two in number and lead from each kidney to the urinary bladder. The urine, which is yellowish in color, and is being extracted continuously from the blood within the kidneys, collects in a cavity within the kidney known as the pelvis of the kidney. This pelvis, which is really the enlarged upper end of the ureter, soon narrows to become the ureter — a long, slender, flexible, muscular tube, which leads downward and backward to enter the bladder on its dorsal-posterior side.

In man, these ureters measure between 12 and 18 inches in length and about "the diameter of a goose quill" (3/8 inch).

In the whales, the ureters differ very little from those found in other mammals. They extend from the posterior end of the kidney and open into the bladder on its dorsal side at a position about one-third of its length from its posterior end.

Section c
THE URINARY BLADDER

The urinary bladder of mammals is a hollow, thin-walled, sac-like organ for the reception and temporary storage of urine. It has an inverted pear-like shape and lies in the lower-posterior end of the abdomen just inside (dorsal) of the pubic bones. It receives the urine from the kidneys through the ureters, stores it for a time, and then discharges it into the urethra. It contains two circular (sphincter) muscles at its lower-posterior end which control the release of the urine into the urethra.

In the whales, the bladder is much like those found in the terrestrial mammals. Like them, it is pear-shaped, but com-

paratively smaller than would be expected. In the smaller species of whales, the bladder's volume* measures from 100-200± cc (1/10-1/5± quart); while, in the larger whales, it may hold from 15-20± liters (4-5± gallons) (Yablokov).

Section d
THE URETHRA

The urethra in the mammals is a canal leading from the bladder to its exterior opening known as the *meatus urinarius*.

In the female mammals, the urethra is very short (1½± inches in a woman) so that the bladder, in reality, opens and/ or empties almost directly to the outside of the body. The urethra has no valves other than the two sphincter muscles at the base of the bladder which control the release of the urine.

In the male mammals, the urethra is much longer (8-9± inches in a man) than in the female mammals and is more complex because it is also used as the duct for the discharge of the semen of the male. It begins at the base of the bladder, extends through the pelvis, continues as the central duct within the penis, and terminates exteriorly as an external opening at the free end of the penis.

In the male, various ducts and glands of the male reproductive system open into the urethra. These include the following:

1. The two vas deferens (ducts) from the two testes join the two ducts from the two corresponding sac-like seminal vesicles and thereafter discharge their fluids together through their two newly-combined ejaculatory ducts into the urethra.
2. The duct of the single prostate gland, which is situated below and in front of the neck of the bladder, adds a portion of the seminal fluid into the urethra.
3. The two short ducts from the two diminutive Cowper's glands secrete a small amount of fluid into the urethra.

The whales do not differ much from the typical mammals in the structure, location, and function of the urethra. There are very few differences in the female whales, but, in the male whales, the small glands surrounding the urethra in other mammals are all missing except the prostate gland, which is diffuse in nature and which discharges its fluid through a series of openings along the urethra.

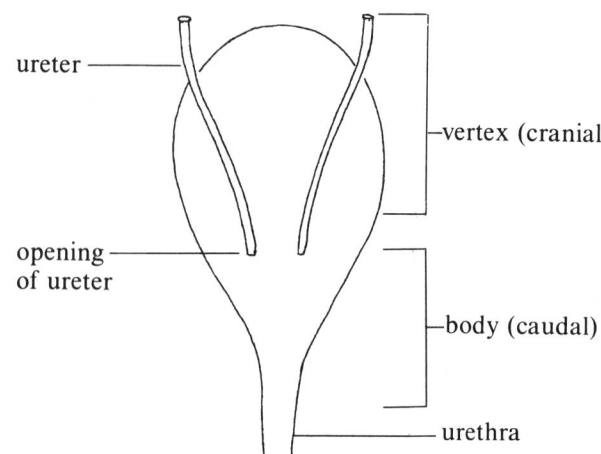

Diagram of the bladder of a typical whale.

From authors.

_____

*In man, the bladder holds about 10 oz. (1/3± quart).

Chapter XI
THE MALE REPRODUCTIVE SYSTEM

The basic purpose of the male reproductive system is to produce the sperm cells required for the fertilization of the egg and to see that these sperm cells are transported to the ovum or egg at its location within the female. To effect this creation and transportation of the sperm cells, the male mammals possess a series of organs, of which the two testes are the most important and essential. These male organs and accessories of the mammals are listed below.

—two testes (sing., testis)
—many spermatozoa
—one scrotum
—two spermatic cords
—two epididymes (sing., -mis)
—two vasa deferentia (sing., vas deferens)
—two ejaculatory ducts
—two seminal vesicles* (vesiculae seminales)
—one prostate gland
—two bulbo-urethral or Cowper's glands
—one urethra
—one penis

The reproductive organs of most mammals follow a similar pattern, although there are some variations between the different orders of the mammals. Although the above organs are all present in man, they are not all present in other mammals or in the whales.

Division 1
THE TESTES AND THE SCROTUM

The testes (testicles) are two comparatively small, glandular organs which produce the male sperm cells. These testes originate in the posterior area of the abdomen near the kidneys. In some mammals (armadillos, sea cows, sloths, elephants, whales, etc.) the testes remain in this area throughout life, while in most mammals they move during their development through the openings of the inguinal canals in the posterior body wall and come to lodge in the scrotum, a small, sac-like pouch at the rear of the body.

This scrotum, which contains the testes, is a pouch formed from skin, thin layers of muscle, and other tissues, and is divided into two chambers or pockets each of which contains a single testis. These testes retain their connection into the abdominal cavity through the spermatic cord.

The testes in the mammals are therefore found in one of three situations: either they are retained within the abdominal cavity throughout life as in the elephant and whales; or they are carried, as in most mammals, in the scrotum outside of the body; or they are held in a mobile condition, as in various rodents, in which the testes are kept within the body during quiescent times and pass outward through the inguinal canal into the scrotum during the breeding seasons.

The testes themselves assume various shapes and sizes in the various orders of the mammals. In man, they are oval in shape and measure about one and one-half inches in length; of the two testes, the left testis is usually larger than the right testis.

In the whales, we should expect some departures from the arrangement in typical mammals, and so we find that the testes are retained within the abdominal cavity of the body throughout the entire life of the whale. The testes in all whales are located in the dorsal-posterior part of the abdominal cavity just lateral to the kidneys and slightly farther to the rear. They enlarge by growth as the animal approaches maturity and finally diminish in size in old age. They are quite cylindrical in shape with tapering, rounded extremities and have been described as covered "with a white, smooth, and shiny surface" (Slijper). In a sample of 1,000 sperm whales captured by whaling ships, the left testis was found to be larger in 60% of the whales, the right testis was smaller in 30% of the whales, and both testes were about equal in size in 10% of these 1,000 sperm whales (Nishiwaki, 1955).

One investigator* after dissecting 5 fin whales (*B. physalus*) and 3 humpback whales (*M. novaeangliae*) concluded that "the testes do not lie in the abdominal cavity, as is commonly stated, but are situated in the pubic region in a pouch which appears to begin at the subcutaneous inguinal ring. From this they may readily be drawn into the abdominal cavity."

---

*Absent in the whales.

*Engle, Earl Theron, Jour. of Mamm. 8:1, 1927, pp. 48-51.

The Weight of the Testes of Some Large Whales

Species	Length (Slijper)	Weight of a Testis	
		Kilograms (Yablokov)	Pounds (Slijper)
Odontoceti			
Physeteridae			
Physeter macrocephalus			
THE SPERM WHALE—		10 kg. (22.05 lbs.)	25± lbs. (11.34± kg.)
Mysticeti			
Balaenopteridae			
Balaenoptera borealis			
THE SEI WHALE	—		15± lbs. (6.804± kg.)
Balaenoptera physalus			
THE FIN WHALE	—	15-20 kg. (33.075-44.1 lbs.)	60± lbs. (27.216± kg.)
Balaenoptera musculus			
THE BLUE WHALE	2'6" long (76.2± cm)	25-30 kg. (55.125-66.15 lbs.)	100± lbs. (45.36± kg.)

Division 2
THE SPERMATOZOA

The male germ cells, called sperm or spermatozoa (sing., *-zoon*), vary greatly among the mammals and other groups of animals. In general, they possess a head or body and a tail. The head contains the chromosomes, while the tail, by its vibration, supplies the motive power to swim in search of the ovum with which it aspires to unite.

The spermatozoa of whales resemble quite closely those of land mammals, particularly the Artiodactyla (even-toed mammals) of which the cow is an example. This is additional evidence indicating ancestral relationships with these mammals.

The Length of Spermatozoa of Various Whales

Species	Total Length (Microns)*	Length of Head (Microns)*	Remarks
Odontoceti			
Delphinidae			
Phocoena species			
THE PORPOISE	73.8	5.9	
Physeteridae			
Physeter macrocephalus			
THE SPERM WHALE	40.6	3.5	Elongated head with sharp tip.
Mysticeti			
Balaenopteridae			
Megaptera novaeangliae			
THE HUMP-BACKED WHALE	52.5	4.5	Head rounded; tail is very long.

*A micron is 1/1,000 of a millimeter.   From A.V. Yablokov et alii.

The Chromosome Numbers of Various Whales

Full Set

Order Cetacea — The Whales
  Suborder Odontoceti—The Toothed Whales
    Family Platanistidae—The River Dolphins 44

    Family Delphinidae—The Ocean Dolphins
      and Porpoises 44

    Family Monodontidae—The Narwhal
      and The White Whale 44

    Family Physeteridae—The Sperm Whales 42

    Family Ziphiidae—The Beaked Whales 42

  Suborder Mysticeti—The Whalebone Whales
    Family Eschrichtiidae—The Gray Whales 44

    Family Balaenopteridae—The Rorquals
      or True Fin-backed Whales 44

    Family Balaenidae—The Right Whales .... 42?

Chromosome Numbers of Selected Mammals

Full Set Diploid Number*

DOMESTIC CAT	38
HORSE	64
DOMESTIC SWINE....................	40
CATTLE	60
DOMESTIC GOAT....................	60
DOMESTIC SHEEP...................	54
MAN	46

*From various authors.

The spermatozoa (male) and the ova (female) of mammals, including the whales, differ in the kind of sex-determining chromosomes which they contain or carry; these sex chromosomes are in addition to the many other chromosomes contained in the germ cells of each species. These sex-determining chromosomes, called the X and Y chromosomes, determine the sex of the newly fertilized ovum or egg. While all ova or female germ cells carry only an X chromosome, the sperm or male germ cells are divided in their formation into two kinds: those sperm which carry or contain either a single X or a single Y chromosome. In the union of the sperm with the ovum or egg, the sex of the offspring is determined by which chromosome (either X or Y) is being carried by the one particular sperm which unites with the ovum or egg. An ovum with an X chromosome plus a sperm with an X chromosome produces a female offspring; while an ovum with an X chromosome plus a sperm with a Y chromosome produces a male offspring.

HOW SEX IS DETERMINED
By The Sex Chromosomes
(Greatly Abbreviated and Condensed)

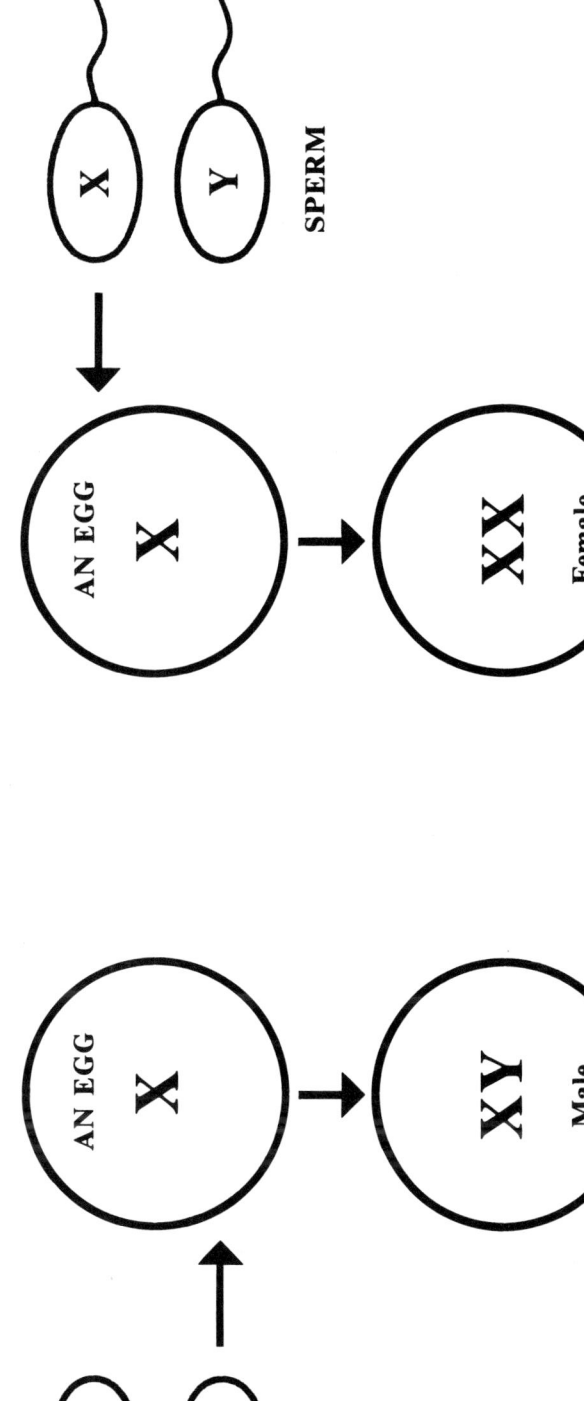

MALES

Males produce sperm.
50 percent of male sperm carry one X chromosome.
50 percent of male sperm carry one Y chromosome.

SPERM

FEMALES

Females produce eggs.
All viable eggs carry one X chromosome.

AN EGG

X

AN EGG

X

XX

Female

XY

Male

MALES

Males produce sperm.
50 percent of male sperm carry one X chromosome.
50 percent of male sperm carry one Y chromosome.

SPERM

OFFSPRING

Usually 50 percent are male.
Usually 50 percent are female.

— SYMBOLS —

X — Designates a female chromosome.
Y — Designates a male chromosome.

Division 3
THE VARIOUS DUCTS OF THE MALE REPRODUCTIVE SYSTEM

In passing from the testes to the outside of the body, the sperm cells of mammals are obliged to traverse a series of ducts; these include the seminiferous tubules where the sperm were formed, the vasa efferentia (sing., vas efferens), the epididymes (sing., -mis), the vasa deferentia (sing., vas deferens), the ejaculatory ducts, and finally, the urethra. The sperm pass from the seminiferous tubules, are gathered from them into many ducts called rete testis, and then pass into from 15 to 20 vasa efferentia which combine to form and to empty into the corresponding epididymis. Each epididymis then leads from the area of the testis to the corresponding vas deferens. This epididymis measures about 20 feet (6 m.) in length in man, is densely coiled, and lies in the scrotum behind each testis. The duct of the epididymis continues as the duct of the vas deferens which is at first coiled and thereafter straightens as it ascends to enter the body through the inguinal canal. It is joined enroute by arteries, veins, nerves, lymphatic vessels, etc., which are then collectively known as the spermatic cord. They then pass inward together through the inguinal canal (about 1½ inches in length) and thereafter separate. Each vas deferens, measuring about 12 to 18 inches, after separating from the other organs, is joined by the duct from the corresponding seminal vesicle to form the ejaculatory duct; this duct then passes between the lobes of the prostate gland and empties separately into the urethra. The urethra, in turn, carries the seminal fluid outward through the penis.

Within the whales, the various ducts leading from the testes to the exterior of the body differ but little from those of typical mammals. It should be noted that the testes lie within the body rather than in a scrotum outside the body; since this entire organ system lies within the abdominal cavity, the vasa deferentia do not pass from outside the body to the inside of the body through an inguinal canal.

Division 4
THE GLANDS OF THE MALE REPRODUCTIVE SYSTEM

In the mammals, a series of glands lies along the route taken by the sperm on their way from their origin in the testes to their discharge from the penis. The common, central duct into which and through which these glandular secretions pass is known as the urethra.

In man, the male urethra has a diameter of about three-eighths of an inch and a total length of about eight inches. It is divided into three portions, a prostatic portion, a membranous portion, and a spongy portion. The urethra begins at the base of the bladder and passes through the prostate gland (the prostatic portion); it then continues (the membranous portion) through the muscular floor of the pelvis known as the perineum to the base of the penis; and it finally passes through the penis (the spongy portion) to terminate in the opening at the distal end of the penis.

The fluids, which are secreted from these glands and ducts are known collectively as the seminal fluid, and serve to float the sperm along their course. The fluids from each testis and the corresponding epididymis flow into and through the vas deferens, which, at its end, is joined by the duct from the corresponding seminal vesicle to form the ejaculatory duct.

In man, the two seminal vesicles, which measure about two inches in length, are small sac-like organs with a mucous lining, and lie in the area between the bladder and the rectum; here they act as a reservoir for the seminal fluid and, in addition, add their secretion to it. The duct from each seminal vesicle joins the corresponding vas deferens to form the ejaculatory duct which then passes between the lobes of the prostate gland and empties into the urethra.

The single prostate gland is a firm, muscular, glandular organ, about the size of a walnut in man, which is located below and in front of the neck of the bladder. It discharges its fluids into the urethra through a series of about 20 to 30 small ducts. In man, both the upper end of the urethra and the two ejaculatory ducts pass through the lobes of the prostate gland.

In man, the two bulbo-urethral or Cowper's glands are about the size of a pea, lie one on each side of the prostate gland, and empty separately into the urethra through a duct about one inch in length. They secrete a thick, mucous-like fluid which is discharged into the urethra to join the seminal fluid.

In the whales, the accessory glands of the male reproductive system are fewer than in other mammals and are not conspicuous or well defined.

The prostate gland is the only male gland which can be identified in the whales. This gland is not present as a single, definitive, unified organ, but consists of glandular tissue which is scattered along the upper portion of the urethra and which opens into the urethra through many small, short ducts.

The two bulbo-urethral or Cowper's glands do not occur in the whales and the two seminal vesicles are likewise not present as distinct organs in whales.

The two ejaculatory ducts (formed by the union of the two vasa deferentia and the two ducts from the two seminal vesicles) are actually present, but are not well defined in whales because the whales lack definite seminal vesicles and also because these ducts do not pass through the prostate gland. In the absence of these two landmarks (the two seminal vesicles and the prostate gland), it should be remembered that the ejaculatory ducts are simply the last few inches of the seminal ducts or canals just before they discharge into the urethra.

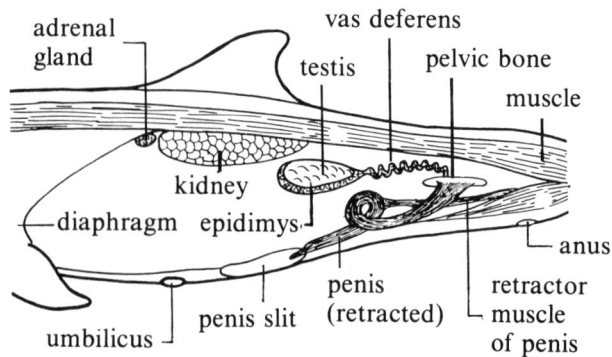

Diagram of the male reproductive system of the harbor porpoise, *Phocoena phocoena* (Odontoceti: Delphinidae).
From Slijper.

From: K.S. Norris (ed.)—WHALES, DOLPHINS, AND PORPOISES. 1966. Pub. by the Univ. of California Press, Berkeley.

Division 5
THE PENIS

The penis of mammals consists of three slender cylindrical bodies of spongy tissue which lie united together in a longitudinal, parallel position to form the body of the penis. The two *corpora cavernosa* are paired bodies which are placed side by side to form the upper portion of the penis. The single *corpus spongiosum* comprises the lower part of the penis and extends distally to expand into a terminal body called the *glans penis*. The urethra or uno-genital duct extends through the entire length of the *corpus spongiosum* and terminates in an external opening (meatus) in the *glans penis*. At the base of the penis, the two *corpora cavernosa* separate, their structures become more fibrous, and each attaches on its corresponding side to a ramus (extension) of the ischium.

In some mammals, the penis incorporates a slender cylindrical element of cartilage and/or bone. This feature, known as the penis bone, os penis, os priapi, or baculum, is found in various *Carnivora* (bears, dogs, etc.), in various *Pinnipedia* (walrus, sea lions, seals, etc.), and in some other mammals.

Among the whales, the penis lies in a genital slit or groove (sulcus) on the posterior portion of the belly in the midline behind the umbilicus and forward of the anus. The penis, when withdrawn, is carried folded in an S-shape and is completely concealed within this slit so that the surface contours of the body are continuous and present no interruptions to the flow of water over the stream-lined surface of the body.

The penis itself is best described as a slender, hard, rope-like organ which is covered in part by skin, and which tapers from its base to its extremity where it ends in a pointed glans. The penis bone or os penis is normally absent in whales. Among the larger whales, the penis may be of astonishing size. It has been reported to reach a length of ten feet and a diameter of over one foot in the large rorquals (Slijper).

Among the whales, the two *corpora cavernosa* of the penis are fused into a single unit to form the body of the penis. However, at the base of the penis, this single fused

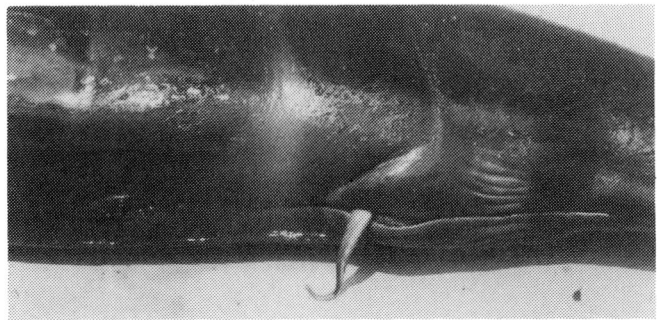

Photo of the uro-genital area of a newly born false killer whale, *Pseudorca crassidens*, showing the penis.
Sea Life Park, Hawaii.

corpus cavernosum separates into two bodies and from there continue inward to attach to the remnants of the two ischia which now lie buried deep in the body tissue. It is somewhat interesting to note that although most of the pelvic bones of the whales have disappeared, those bones to which the base of the penis is attached have remained in spite of the extreme evolutionary changes which have surrounded them.

The penis may be everted or extended during erection by both blood pressure and the action of adjoining muscles, but it does not undergo as much inflation due to blood pressure as is the case in many other mammals. The S-shape of the penis in whales has resulted in a sort of "joint," so that this organ is more flexible and mobile than in many other mammals. The enlarged glans at the terminal end of the penis is absent in all whales.

A penis bone (os priapi) or baculum has been reported from the flesh of a Right Whale (*Balaenidae: Balaena glacialis*) which was cylindrical in shape and measured 32 cm. (12.6 in.) in length and 13 to 20 cm. (5 to 7.8 in.) in circumference.

The anatomy of the whale penis resembles most closely that of the *Artiodactyla* (even-toed ungulates) of which the cattle, etc., are best known; this is further evidence that the ancestors of these two groups of mammals were closely related in ancient times.

Chapter XII
THE FEMALE REPRODUCTIVE SYSTEM

The basic purpose of the female reproductive system in mammals is to produce the egg cells or ova which, when fertilized, will develop into additional newly-created individuals. The female reproductive system also has the additional burden of caring for the developing embryo, foetus, etc., until it is liberated by birth from its mother and thereafter to feed it and otherwise care for it until it is able to live independently of its parents.

The ovaries of the female mammal are the most important organs of the female reproductive system because they produce the ova or egg cells which are the most important element in the formation of new individuals.

In addition to the two ovaries which female mammals possess, several additional reproductive organs are included in the female reproductive system; most of these are listed below.

Principal Organs and Structures

—two ovaries
—many ova
—two oviducts
    (or Fallopian tubes)
—one uterus (or womb)
—one vagina
—one clitoris and prepuce
—two or more mammary glands

Additional Organs and Structures

—the mons veneris
—the labia majora
—the labia minora
—the hymen
—the perineum
—two vulvo-vaginal glands
    (or glands of Bartholin)
—the urethral glands
—three pairs of ligaments:
    —the broad ligament of the
      uterus
    —the round ligament of
      the uterus
    —the utero-sacral ligament

The miscellaneous additional organs and structures listed above will not be included in the descriptions which follow, although two glands will be mentioned here. The two vulvo-urethral glands are small in size, are located one on either side of the vaginal opening, and secrete a mucus which lubricates the vagina. These urethral glands are not actually a part of the female reproductive system.

Differing somewhat from most mammals, the external genitalia of female whales are located and enclosed within a long, longitudinal groove or slit located on the median line on the posterior-ventral surface of the abdomen. Four organs or structures are located within this groove. The clitoris and prepuce are located at the anterior end of the groove; they are followed by the urethral opening *(meatus urinarius)* from the bladder, and finally by the genital aperture *(orificium vaginae)* leading inward to the vagina. The last organ in this area is the anus at the end of the alimentary canal; it, however, is not in the urogenital groove, but lies a short distance posterior to it. This groove or sulcus is bordered on each side by a lip or labium (sing., *labium;* pl., *labia*) which, together with its opposite, covers the four structures mentioned above and thereby retains the streamlined contours of the body surface. The hymen is absent in all toothed whales *(Odontoceti)* and is either absent or altered beyond recognition in the whalebone whales *(Mysticeti)*.

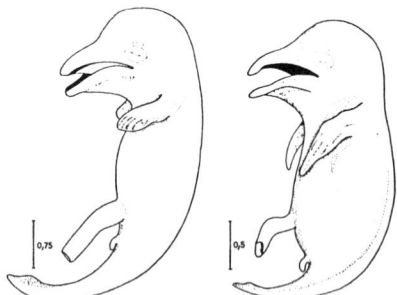

Diagram of the embryos of two whalebone whales. *Left.* The fin whale, *Balaenoptera physalus.* Length: 9 cm. (3.54 in.). *Right.* The hump-backed whale, *Megaptera novaeangliae.* Length: 10.5 cm. (4.1 in.).

From: Pilleri, Gregorio and Kukenthal, W.G. — Investigations On The Cetacea.

Twin male fetuses of the blue-white or striped dolphin *(Stenella coeruleoalba)* were obtained from a school of about 2,000 dolphins off Japan in 1966. The upper fetus measured 39.7 cm. (15.6 in.) in length. The lower fetus measured 43.5 cm. (17 in.) in length.

Photo by Toboyama et alii.

Division 1
THE OVARIES

The ovaries of all mammals lie in the abdomen, usually near the kidneys. They consist basically of a large number of follicles, each containing a single ovum. These follicles lie dormant in juvenile animals and develop, one at a time, after the animal reaches maturity. The ovaries of whales appear in immature females as a somewhat compressed, grooved, "bean-like body." They enlarge as the whale matures and have been reported in large whales to weigh as much as 35 pounds (16 kg.), although in one case, in an 83-foot blue whale (*Balaenopteridae: Balaenoptera*), the ovary weighed 65 pounds (29.4 kg.) (Slijper); in other rorquals (*Balaenoptera*), the ovaries are known to measure one foot in length and to weigh 22 pounds (10 kg.) (Slijper).

In the toothed whales (*Odontoceti*), the ovaries are somewhat spherical in shape and are not as elongated as in the *Mysticeti*. They are enclosed in an ovarian pouch (*bursa ovarica*), which gives them a somewhat smoother appearance.

In the whalebone whales (*Mysticeti*), the ovaries are more elongated than in the *Odontoceti*. They are usually described as resembling a huge cluster of grapes with surface grooves and ridges; they have also been described by some scholars as somewhat resembling the ovaries of birds.

Division 2
THE OVA OR EGGS

The ova or eggs of whales will measure between about .1 mm. and .2 mm. in diameter. They are produced within the ovaries and are enclosed within a spherical follicle (Graafian follicle), which, when mature, may measure 1½ to 2 inches in diameter. These follicles move slowly to the surface, usually toward the anterior end of the ovary, swell in size[1], and then burst or ovulate, thereby liberating the ovum from within the follicle into the funnel at the upper or anterior end of the oviduct. This ovum will be fertilized as it slides along the oviduct into a "horn" of the uterus and there will attach to the wall of the uterus to develop into an embryonic whale or fetus. In whales, the ova or eggs are released singly or one at a time, although occasionally two ova are released simultaneously, often resulting in twin young. The usual cycle of ovulation is once (or occasionally twice) per season in both the *Odontoceti* and the *Mysticeti*.

After the follicle has ruptured and the ovum liberated, the remnants of the follicle develop into an enlarged body of glandular and connective tissue known as the *corpus luteum* (pl., *corpora lutea*). It produces hormones during the period of pregnancy and then degenerates into a whitish mass of connective tissue known as the *corpus albicans* (pl., *corpora albicantia*). These *corpora lutea*[2] usually persist throughout life in the whales, although in land animals they usually disappear after a time, possibly to reduce their weight.

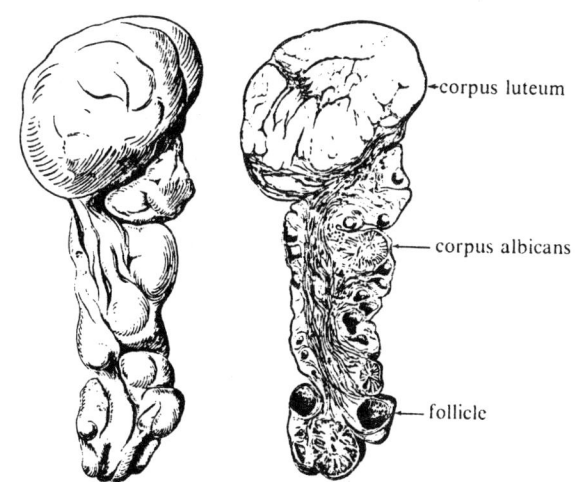

Diagram of the ovary of a pregnant fin whale, *Balaenoptera physalus* (Mysticeti: Balaenopteridae), in external view and in longitudinal section.

From Slijper.

From: K.S. Norris (ed.) — WHALES, DOLPHINS, AND PORPOISES. 1966. Pub. by the Univ. of California Press, Berkeley.

Division 3
THE OVIDUCTS OR FALLOPIAN TUBES

The oviducts are the two tubes which lead from the two ovaries to the two uteri and serve to transport the ova between these organs. The anterior end of each of the two oviducts is greatly enlarged into a wide thin, funnel-shaped organ, the Fallopian funnel, which is fitted against and partially surrounds its respective ovary. The funnel shape of the anterior end of each oviduct changes as it proceeds posteriorly to a slender, often-convoluted tube, then finally straightens to lead more directly to the corresponding upper corner of the uterus.

The oviducts of the whales vary in structure. Some are quite simple and straight, while others are strongly twisted and convoluted at their anterior end.

Division 4
THE UTERUS

The uteri of mammals show considerable variety in their shape. In some mammals, including man, the uterus is somewhat triangular in shape, while in most others, the two upper corners of the uterus which receive the oviducts are drawn out into tubular elongations known as "horns" or *cornua (sing., cornu; pl., cornua)*. The uterus of all mammals terminates posteriorly in a narrow, somewhat muscular, nipple-like, nozzle-shaped structure known as the cervix, which acts as the opening from the lower or posterior end of the uterus into the inner end of the vagina.

---

[2]These *corpora lutea* sometimes exceed the remainder of the ovary in size, particularly in the smaller toothed whales *(Odontoceti);* they have been reported to have an average weight of about 1.5+ pounds in sperm whales *(Physeter),* 1.5+ pounds in humpbacked whales *(Eschrichtius),* 2+ pounds in finback whales *(Balaenoptera),* and 5+ pounds in blue whales *(Balaenoptera)* (Slijper).

---

[1]Reported to reach three inches in diameter in rorquals (*Balaenopteridae*) (Slijper).

95

The uterus of all whales is divided at its anterior end into two "horns" or branches (*uterus bicornis*); these branches or horns, usually unequal in size, join posteriorly to form a single chamber (*corpus uteri*), which in turn opens through the muscular cervix into the anterior or upper end of the vagina. The two oviducts, descending posteriorly from the ovaries, open into the anterior ends of the right and left branches (horns) of the uterus. These horns of the uterus are comparatively large and are bent posteriorly at their anterior ends. The embryonic whales pass through their development in these horns and are always lying with their heads forward so that they are always born tail first.

It is interesting to note that in the toothed whales (*Odontoceti*), the fetus usually develops in the left horn of the uterus, while in the whalebone whales (*Mysticeti*), the fetus may develop in either horn of the uterus.

Division 5
THE VAGINA

The vagina of female mammals is a tubular-shaped, duct-like organ of varying dimensions which leads outward from the lower or posterior opening (cervix) of the uterus to the exterior surface of the body. During copulation, the vagina receives the penis of the male and the spermatic fluid which the penis deposits there. At the time of birth, the emerging young pass outward from the uterus through the cervix into the vagina and onward through it to the exterior of their mother's body. The vagina is largely muscular in construction, is usually longitudinally grooved, ribbed, or folded within and is usually without any special development.

In the whales, the posterior or lower part of the vagina is lined with longitudinal folds, while the upper part of the vagina has a "series of muscular, valve-like folds" which encircle the wall of the vagina in this region, and which have been described as resembling a series of funnels with their small openings pointing inward toward the cervix.

A very unusual structure called the vaginal "plug" is found in the vagina of some toothed whales (*Odontoceti*), but does not occur in any known species of whalebone whales (*Mysticeti*). This puzzling structure is formed by secretions from the wall of the vagina and is composed in part of hard, calcareous substances. The purpose of this "plug" is doubtless related to reproduction, possibly copulation.

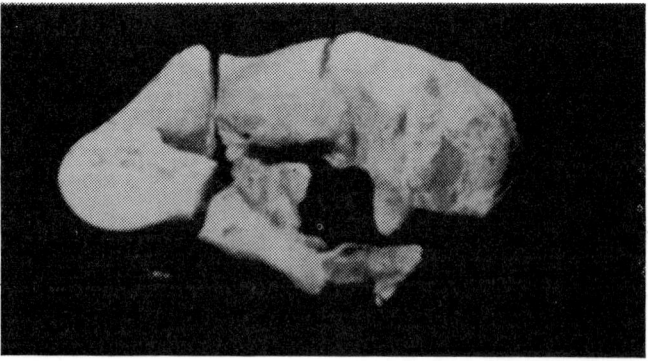

Photo of a vaginal plug from a common dolphin, *Delphinus delphis* (Odontoceti: Delphinidae). Plugs in this species are reported to range in length from about 1.1 to 6.7 cm. (.4 to 2.6 in.) and to be composed of about 55% mineral material (mostly sulphates) and about 45% organic material (Essapian).

Photo by Essapian.

Division 6
THE CLITORIS AND PREPUCE

The clitoris of female mammals is homologous (corresponds anatomically) to the glans penis of male mammals. Both are areas of great sexual sensitivity and stimulation. In the mammals, the clitoris assumes the form of a ridge or nubbin of various shapes and is accompanied by a surrounding fold of skin, the prepuce, which is homologous to the prepuce or foreskin of the penis of male mammals.

In the whales, the clitoris varies in size, shape, and development in the different species and, as in other mammals, is surrounded by the folds of skin which form the prepuce. The central body of the clitoris, the single *corpus cavernosum*, is prominantly developed in whales and, in the case of the sperm whale, is somewhat "hook-shaped" in form; in other species it is more ridge-like in its contours.

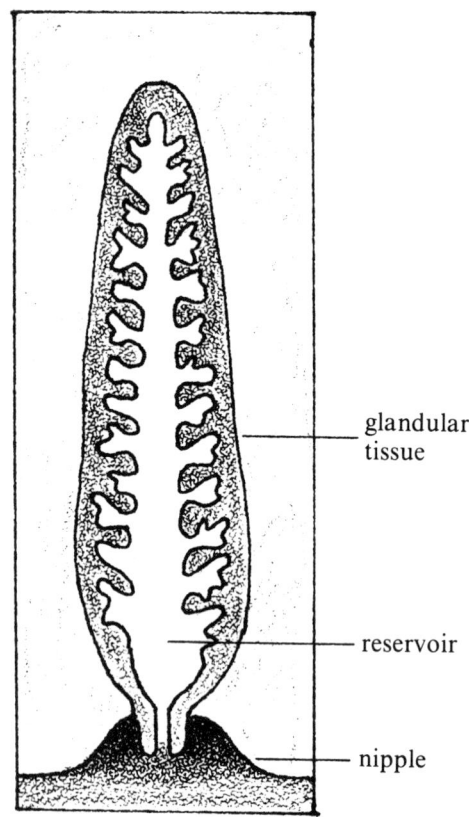

glandular tissue

reservoir

nipple

A diagram of the mammary gland of a fin-backed whale.

Division 7
THE MAMMARY GLANDS

Mammary glands are found in all female mammals, although the teats or nipples associated with these structures are not found in the five species of echidnas or in the platypus. These glands, which produce the milk for the young, are located in pairs along the ventral side of the body in the area between the front and the hind limbs. They range in number from a single pair in those animals which normally produce a single offspring to several pairs in those mammals which give birth to litters of several individuals.

The mammary glands of all whales are two in number and lie embedded in the wall of the abdomen on the right and left side of the uro-genital groove. These glands lie beneath the skin and on the outside of the muscles which form the abdominal wall. Each mammary gland bears a single nipple which lies recessed in a short longitudinal groove and which is protruded whenever the young whale is nursing. The nipples are set in "pockets" into which the young are reported to put their snout in an attempt to receive their quota of milk without swallowing much sea water. The mammary glands are oval in outline, lie forward of the nipples, and discharge their milk backward through a series of sinuses, reservoirs, and ducts to the nipples.

A female blue whale (*Balaenoptera musculus*) will produce between 500 and 600 liters (132.1 to 158.5 gals.) of concentrated, rich, fatty milk.

The sex of whales is most easily determined by inspecting the longitudinal grooves or slits on the belly.

Female whales have three grooves. The large groove in the midline is the uro-genital groove; it is bordered on each side by a single mammary groove, making a total of three grooves in all. In the females, the anus lies in the midline just posterior to the urogenital slit.

Male whales have a single median uro-genital slit which is followed at some distance by the anus. The males may have two rudimentary mammary grooves which may confuse the identification of their sex. However, the position of the anus, which is some distance behind the urogenital slit, is helpful in this identification.

Comparison of Some Ingredients in Milk

	Approximate Percent of Albumin	Approximate Percent of Fat	Aproximate Percent of Milk Sugar	Approx. Percent of Ash
Dolphin	7.6	43.8		0.5
Cow	3.5	3.7	4.9	0.7
Man	1.6	3.4	6.1	0.2

The Ventral Surface Of Whalebone Whales *(Mysticeti)*

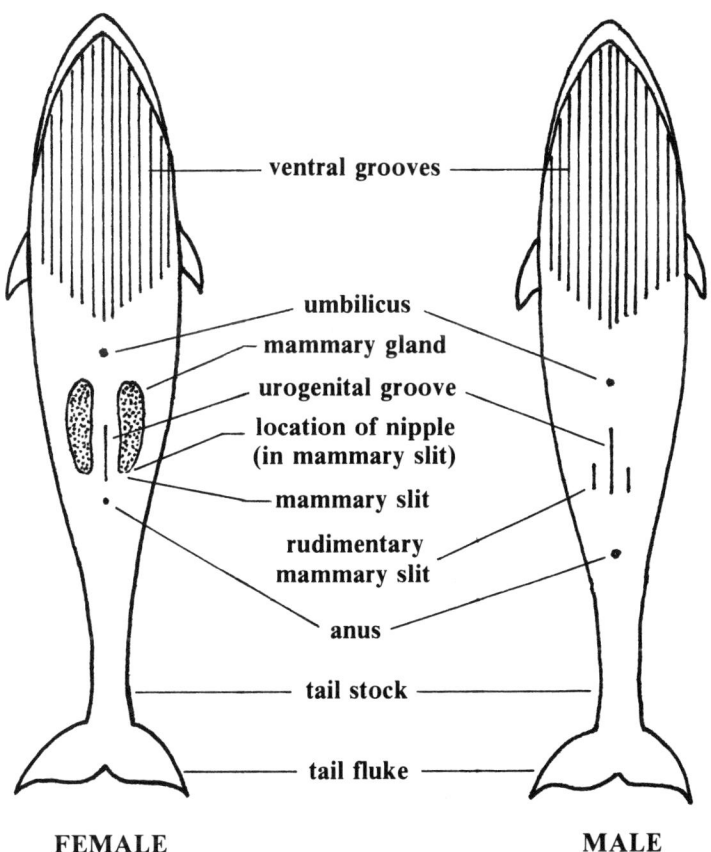

ventral grooves

umbilicus
mammary gland
urogenital groove
location of nipple
(in mammary slit)
mammary slit
rudimentary
mammary slit
anus
tail stock
tail fluke

FEMALE   **MALE**

—PART THREE—

The Living Whales

— PART THREE —
The Living Whales

Chapter I

THE POSITION OF THE WHALES IN THE ANIMAL KINGDOM

The students of the natural world have found it helpful to organize the animals, plants, and other creations of nature into groups. These groups are further subdivided into smaller and smaller groups, each of which is assigned a name (from Greek or Latin) which is usually descriptive of the group. This science of classification, known as taxonomy, is based solely upon the structure or morphology of these groups. Classification is a very useful tool and makes possible the precise identification of species and/or objects; it is also absolutely essential in organizing the information relating to each group or species.

The classification scheme given below begins with the largest group, the Animal Kingdom, and then lists the descending series of subdivisions to which the whales belong. Some of these subdivisions show two or more groups, of which only the last leads downward to the whales (Order Cetacea).

Kingdom Animalia—The Animal Kingdom
　Phylum Chordata—The Chordates or Vertebrate-like Animals and Related Groups
　　Subphylum Acrania—Vertebrate-like Animals without a Cranium
　　Subphylum Craniata—Vertebrate Animals with a Cranium
　　　Superclass Agnatha—Vertebrate Animals Without Jaws
　　　Superclass Gnathostomata—Vertebrate Animals with Jaws
　　　　Class Chondrichthyes—The Cartilaginous Fishes
　　　　Class Osteichthyes (Pisces)—The Bony Fishes
　　　　Class Amphibia—The Amphibians
　　　　Class Reptilia—The Reptiles
　　　　Class Aves—The Birds
　　　　Class Mammalia—The Mammals
　　　　　Subclass Prototheria—The Egg-laying Mammals
　　　　　Subclass Theria—The Viviparous Mammals
　　　　　　Infraclass Metatheria—The Viviparous Mammals with a Pouch
　　　　　　Infraclass Eutheria—The Viviparous Mammals with a Placenta
　　　　　　　Order Cetacea — The Whales
　　　　　　　　Suborder Archaeoceti — The Ancient Whales
　　　　　　　　Suborder Odontoceti — The Toothed Whales
　　　　　　　　Suborder Mysticeti — The Whalebone Whales

Chapter II
THE CLASSIFICATION OF THE WHALES
Arranged by Suborders, Families, Genera, and Species
THE LIVING WHALES
Order *CETACEA* Brisson, 1762

Chapter III
THE LIVING WHALES
Order *CETACEA* Brisson, 1762

The whales are one of the most interesting groups of the mammals because of their great size, their unusual body structure, their many adaptations to life in the water, and the legends and mystery which surround them.

The bodies of all whales are spindle-shaped (fusiform) and are streamlined to accommodate them to their aquatic life. The heads of whales are most unusual. In some species, including the giant sperm whale and the baleen or whalebone whales, the head is very large and comprises from one-fourth to one-third of the body length. In all whales, the nose and its nostrils, which appear in most mammals at the front of the head, have moved from the front of the head to the top of the head and there remain as the blowholes through which these animals breathe. In the whales, the bones of the skull are greatly modified from those which are found in more typical mammals. The skull is elongated in front and the brain case (cranium) is shortened or "telescoped"; this deformation is not apparent in the ancient, extinct whales *(Archaeoceti)*. The skulls of whalebone whales are quite symmetrical in shape, but those of the toothed whales are asymmetrical.

The jaws of most whales are greatly elongated and bear either simplified teeth or teeth which are greatly reduced in number; however, the baleen or whalebone whales, with their great, long jaws, are completely without teeth in their adult form, although teeth appear briefly in their embryos prior to the development of the whalebone or baleen plates.

Whales appear to have no neck because this region is not visibly constricted when viewed from the surface of the body. However, a neck is present and, although greatly shortened, contains the full complement of the seven bones found in all mammals. The necks of whales are very short, because the bones which comprise them are exceedingly flat and in some species are fused together in various combinations so that movement of the neck is reduced to a minimum.

The anterior limbs of the body are paddle-shaped for swimming and enclose within them the bones of the upper arm, forearm, wrist, and hand, all of which are flattened for swimming; these divisions of the anterior limb are not visible externally as they are in most mammals. The collar bone (clavicle), found in many mammals, is missing in all whales.

104

The hind limbs of whales have entirely disappeared and the pelvis to which they were once attached is small and rudimentary and is no longer attached to the sacral region of the vertebral column. This rudimentary pelvis often appears as a pair of small, slender bones buried in the flesh and lying high up on each side of the body near the vertebral column. There is no sacrum or sacral vertebrae, and the vertebrae of this region now resemble the vertebrae of the trunk (lumbar) region and the tail (caudal) region which adjoin them. These vertebrae continue in a diminishing series to the tail region, which is flattened dorso-ventrally and extended laterally into two pointed flukes; these flukes are supported from within by fibrous, partially-ossified tissue.

The skin of whales is smooth and bears a thick, subcutaneous layer of blubber beneath it. The skin bears no hair or fur as in most other mammals, but a few whiskers do occur around the mouth and upon the head of some species. Female whales possess a single pair of mammae which are located on the ventral surface on each side of the genital opening (vulva).

The internal organs of whales are the same as those found in other mammals, but they differ in many details from those of most mammals.

The living whales are divided into two great groups (suborders) on the basis of their teeth, blowholes, and other anatomical features.

Suborder ODONTOCETI (The Toothed Whales)
The Toothed Whales are mostly of smaller or medium size, although they do include the great sperm whale. They have teeth in their mouth and all have but a single blowhole on the top of the head ..... See page 106

Suborder MYSTICETI (The Whalebone Whales)
The Whalebone Whales are all large species with sheets of whalebone or baleen hanging from the roof of their mouth and through which they strain out their food. They have a double blowhole on the top of the head
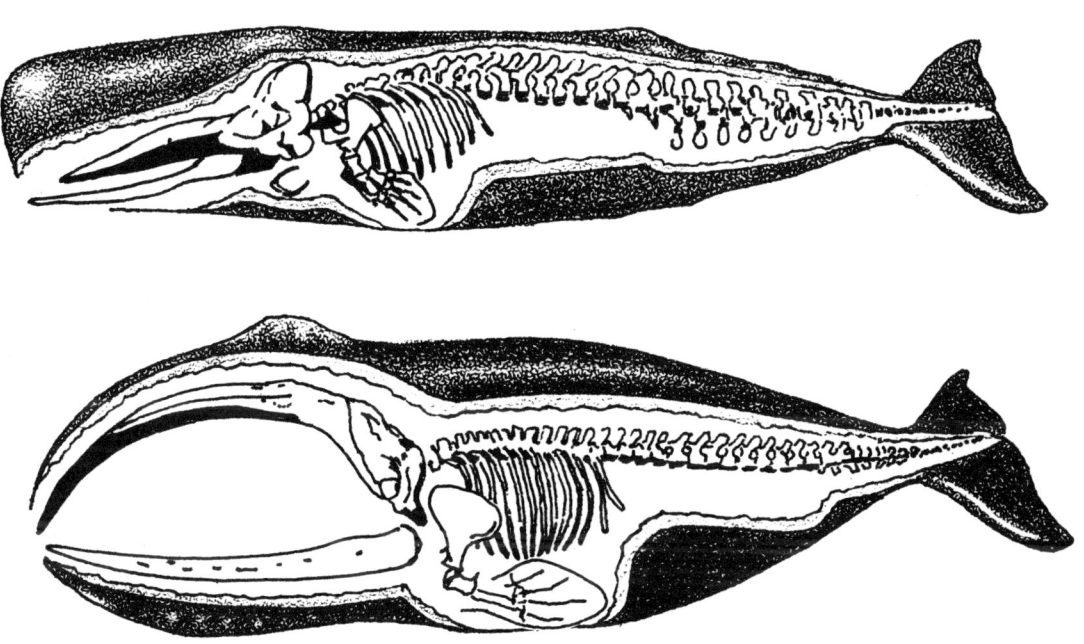

.... See page 263

Diagrams comparing the body outlines and skeletons of the two great suborders of whales.

Above: The toothed whales, suborder Odontoceti, are represented by the great sperm whale, *Physeter macrocephalus* (Physeteridae).

Below: The whalebone whales, suborder Mysticeti, are represented by the right whale, *Balaena* species (Balaenidae).

105

THE TOOTHED WHALES
Suborder *ODONTOCETI* Flower, 1867

These toothed whales include more than 85 percent of the whales which are living today. They are easily recognized by the presence of teeth in their jaws and also by the single opening of the blowhole upon the top of the head. In contrast, the whalebone whales have a double blowhole and a long series of whalebone or baleen plates hanging downward into the mouth from each of the upper jaw bones. In addition, these two great groups of whales differ in many other ways, most of which do not show from the surface of their bodies. The skulls of the baleen or whalebone whales are symmetrical, while those of the toothed whales are asymmetrical. The lower jaw bones of the whalebone whales are long and curved and do not touch or fuse together at the tip of the jaw, while those of the toothed whales are shorter, straighter, and are fused at their front tip. Most whalebone whales (except *Balaena*) have four fingers in their "hand" (manus) which lies buried within their flipper, while the toothed whales all have a full five fingers concealed within their flippers. There are many other anatomical differences between these two groups of whales, including the bones of the head, the thorax, the ribs, the trachea, various parts of the alimentary tract, the relative size of the males and females, and many other differences.

The number of different kinds of toothed whales is usually believed to be between about 65 and 70 species, but the exact number of species is very difficult to determine. Some species vary greatly in color and also vary in their anatomical features making it difficult to decide if they represent a single species or more than one species. Some species are rare and specimens of them are scarce, so that they have not been completely studied, and some others which have been captured were from distant places where facilities for their proper preservation were not available. In addition, the color patterns of many toothed whales deteriorate rapidly after death, thereby increasing the difficulties of their identification.

The toothed whales are a large group which most scientists have usually divided into the five family* groups listed below. However, some scholars feel that certain species do not resemble the members of these five families and suggest that additional families be described and named to accommodate these few species; three of these suggestions for additional families are listed below:

1. Some scholars think that the species of the Genus *Steno* and the Genus *Sotalia* should be removed from the Family Delphinidae and placed in an additional family to be known as the Family Stenidae.

2. Some scholars think that the true porpoises of the Genera *Phocoena*, *Neophocaena*, and *Phocoenoides* should be removed from the Family Delphinidae and placed in an additional family to be known as the Family Phocoenidae.

3. Some scholars think that the two species of the Genus *Kogia* should be removed from the Family Physeteridae and placed in an additional family to be known as the Family Kogiidae.

The living toothed whales are usually divided into the following five families:

1. The River Dolphin Family (5 species), Family Platanistidae (Susuidae) .... See page 107

2. The Ocean Dolphin and Porpoise Family (39+ species), Family Delphinidae ...... See page 119

3. The Narwhal and White Whale Family (2 species), Family Monodontidae .... See page 207

4. The Sperm Whale Family (18 species), Family Physeteridae .... See page 214

5. The Beaked Whale Family (18 species), Family Ziphiidae (Hyperoodontidae)...... See page 224

These families and the species which they include will be described in the above sequence on the pages which follow.

*All family names in Zoology end in *-idae*.

THE RIVER DOLPHIN FAMILY
Family *PLATANISTIDAE* Gray, 1863

The river dolphins are a small family of five species which occupy rather isolated areas of the world. They are an ancient family and some genera within it were once much more widely distributed in ages past. They show features which are more primitive than those of many other whales; for example, the brain is not compressed, the skull has not undergone the same strange transformation of the ocean dolphin family (Delphinidae) and other whales, and their neck vertebrae are relatively large and are not fused together as in many other species.

In general, these dolphins are of small size, rarely exceeding nine feet in length. Their most unusual feature is a long, slender beak which emerges from a small, blunt, rounded head. The jaws composing these beaks are long and slender and of equal length; the lower jaws are fused for much of their length. The jaws contain many, small, sharp teeth which are reported to number from about 100 to about 144 in *Platanista, Inia,* and *Lipotes,* and from about 200 to about 242 in *Pontoporia.* The vertebrae usually number between 41 and 45, there are 10 pairs of ribs of which 8 pairs articulate by two heads with the vertebrae, and the sternum is well developed.

In this family, the flippers are short and broad with square ends. The dorsal fins of the four genera are low and long, but differ in size; this fin is smaller in *Platanista* and *Inia* and larger in *Lipotes* and *Pontoporia.*

The eyes of the dolphins in this family are small and their vision is the poorest of all whales; this may be related to their habitat on the bottoms of dirty rivers and lakes where adequate light for normal sight is practically absent.

The river dolphins are more primitive than other whales in their anatomical features and somewhat resemble more ancient forms, particularly *Squalodon,* an extinct dolphin. Fossils of this family are known from the Lower Miocene Epoch to the Holocene (Recent) Epoch in South America and from the Middle Miocene and Lower Pliocene Epochs in North America; a few fossil forms are known from So. Asia. Of the living genera, only *Pontoporia* is known from fossils.

·The present day members of this family are limited to large rivers and other large bodies of fresh water, although one South American species (*Pontoporia*) does occur along the Atlantic shoreline during cooler seasons.

Some scholars believe that the Amazon River Dolphin, *Inia geoffrensis* (de Blainville, 1817), and the Chinese Freshwater Dolphin, *Lipotes vexillifer* Miller, 1918, are sufficiently different from *Platanista* and *Pontoporia* to merit the creation of a separate family; these two species would then be placed in a new and separate family to be known as the Family Iniidae. Still other scholars would remove the Genus *Pontoporia* with its single species (*P. blainvillei*) from this family and place it within the Delphinidae where it would then be known as *Stenodelphis blainvillei* (Gervais and d'Orbigny, 1844).

This family is usually divided into the four living genera listed below.

THE INDIAN RIVER DOLPHINS
Genus *PLATANISTA* Wagler, 1830

This genus contains two very closely related species from the rivers of southern Asia. They possess a head which is somewhat wedge-shaped and a long, somewhat flattish beak extending forward from it. This beak is clearly marked off from the head and bears within it many closely-set teeth which number from 27 to 30 in each of the four jaw bones.

The dorsal fin is small, low, and ridge-like and continues backward as a keel which ends on the top of the tail; this tail, in turn, is wide and has a concave posterior margin with a notch at its center. Another keel is present on the lower side of the body beginning behind the anus and extending backward. The flippers are large and broad with square ends.

The neck is slender and moveable and a constriction is visible on the outside of the body; the seven vertebrae within the neck are somewhat enlarged and are separated from each other.

Mature animals may reach a length of over 2.5 m. (8 ft.). The color of the body in adult animals is a dark lead gray on the dorsal surface.

The blow hole of these dolphins is very unusual in shape and location. It consists of a single, lengthwise, longitudinal slit located atop the head and placed a little to the left of the midline of the back.

The eyes of *Platanista* are very small and degenerate and are reported to lack the crystalline lens of functional mammalian eyes; as a result, these dolphins are doubtless almost blind. It should be noted that the optic nerve in these dolphins is very thin and thread-like, a consequence of its faulty eyesight. The external ear openings of this group are likewise very small.

The dolphins of this genus possess a strange, bony outgrowth of the skull known as the maxillary crests. They are flat, paired, oval bones which grow upward and forward from the maxillae and occupy a horizontal position on the skull above and forward of the external nares (blowholes). These crests differ in *Platanista gangetica* and *P. minor* and are therefor useful in distinguishing the skulls of these two species. These maxillary crests are more elongated in *P. gangetica* and more oval in *P. minor*.

In this genus, the vertebral formula is about C 7 + D 10 + L 9 + Ca 26 = 52. The formula for the finger bones is about I (2), II (6), III (6), IV (5), V (5).

This genus is known only from the Holocene Epoch (Recent).

The Genus *Platanista* is limited to the fresh waters of the Ganges, the Indus, and the Bramaputra Rivers of southern Asia.

Studies of these dolphins by various scholars indicate that several names of species appearing in older books are really duplicate names or synonyms of other previously named species. The following list indicates the older names and the more correct and current names of these species.

Old Names		Names Currently In Use
Genus *Susu*	is now	Genus *Platanista*
Platanista indi	is now	*Platanista minor*
Susu platanista	is now	*Platanista gangetica*

This genus includes the two living species listed below.

Platanista gangetica (Roxburgh, 1801)
   THE GANGES RIVER DOLPHIN ... See page 109
Platanista minor Owen, 1853
   THE INDUS RIVER DOLPHIN ..... See page 111

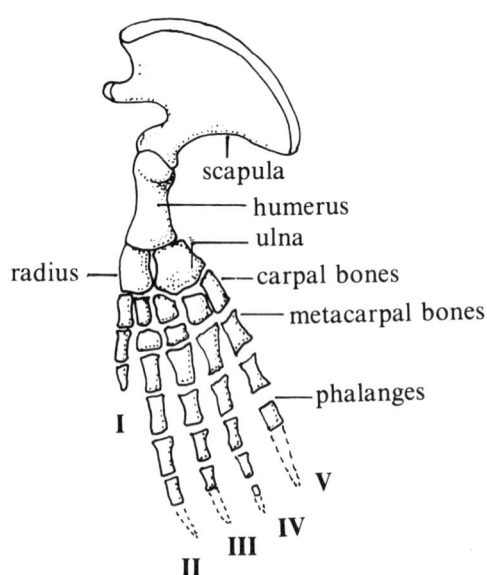

Diagram of the left pectoral girdle and appendage of the Ganges River dolphin, *Platanista* sp. (Odontoceti: Platanistidae).

Drawn from Howell.

From: Alfred Brazier Howell — AQUATIC MAMMALS. 1931. Courtesy of Charles E. Thomas, Publishers. Springfield, Ill.

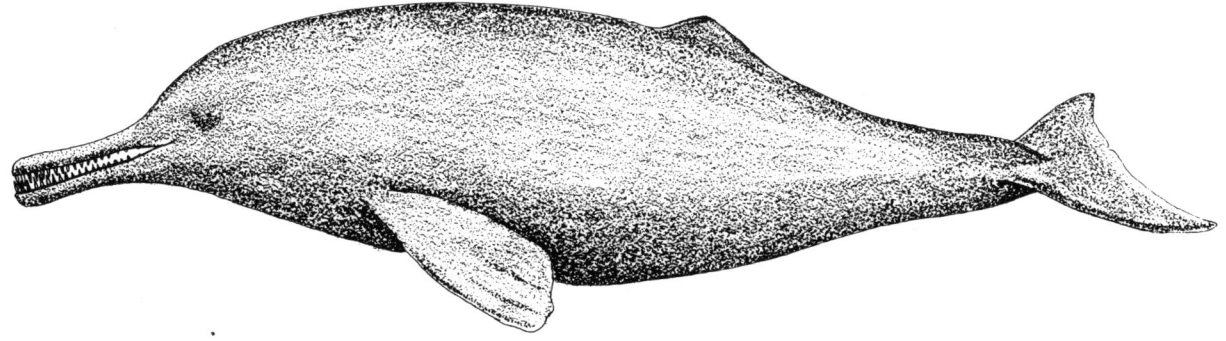

THE GANGES RIVER DOLPHIN OR SU-SU
Platanista gangetica (Roxburgh, 1801)

Identifying Features. This is a small river dolphin from India with a very long beak, square-ended flippers, and a longitudinal, slit-like blowhole located slightly to the left of the midline.

Size and Shape. The body is fat and chunky and usually reaches a length of less than 2 meters (78.7 in.). A very large specimen measured 240 cm. (8 ft. 10 in.), but most are much smaller. In general, the males will weigh between about 30 to 40 kg. (66 to 88 lbs.) and the females between about 80 to 85 kg. (176 to 187 lbs.). The head is plump and rounded and the forehead descends quite abruptly to a long slender beak which may reach as much as 40 cm. (16 in.) or more in length.

Color. The body color is a dark lead-gray to brownish gray; it is lighter below, becoming pinkish ventrally.

Distribution. This dolphin is found widely distributed within the fresh water river systems of the Ganges, Brahmaputra, and Meghna Rivers of India, Bangladesh, and Nepal from tidewater to the upland foothills. It does not enter the sea. It formerly occurred in the Karnaphuli River of Chittagong in southern Bangladesh.

Migration. Little is known of its migration. In prehistoric times, these dolphins used to move during the rainy season from the larger rivers into the tributaries. However, the large dams erected across these rivers will restrict their movements and divide the population into restricted geographical groups.

Fins and Flippers. The dorsal fin is small, low, and ridge-like and is located just behind the midpoint of the body. A low upper keel extends from the dorsal fin to the tail; a similar lower keel extends from the anus to the tail. The tail is wide and has a concave rear margin with a notch at the center; the flukes are pointed.

Teeth. The teeth number from 27 to 32 in each of the four jaws, about 108 to 120 in all. In young animals, the teeth are sharp, pointed, closely set, and more numerous (31-37), but they become worn, and are more compressed with age. The lower teeth are longer than the upper teeth and show when the mouth is closed.

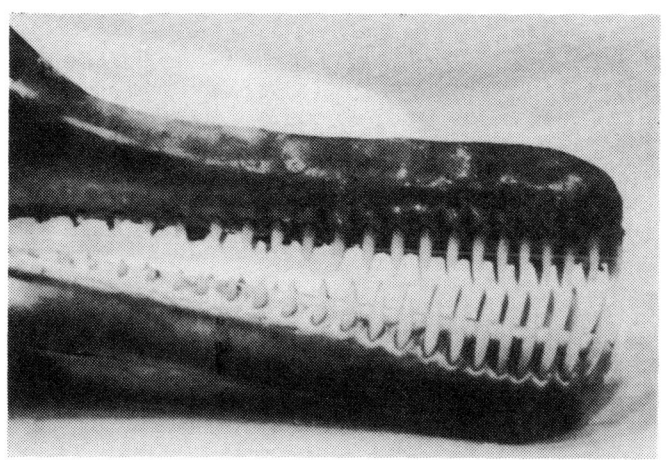
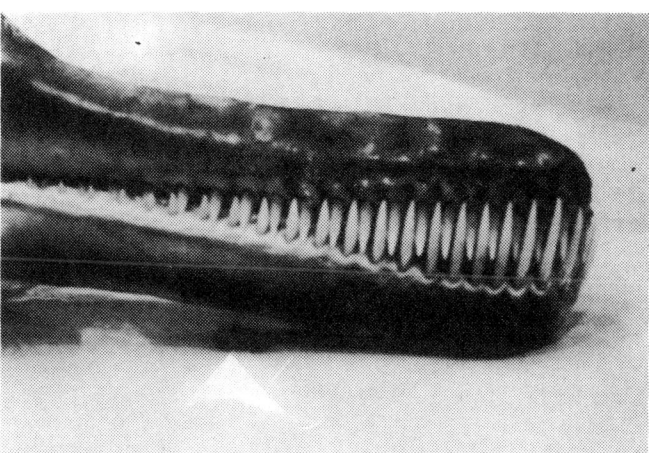

Photos of the beak and teeth of the Ganges River Dolphin, *Platanista gangetica* (Odontoceti: Platanistidae), in lateral view showing the exceedingly slender beak and sharp teeth.
From Herald.

109

Skeletal Notes. The bones of the neck are large in size, completely separated, and freely moveable. An external constriction of the neck is visible. There are 10 pairs of ribs, five pairs of which are two headed and four pairs of which articulate directly with the sternum; the sternum has three transverse segments. The temporal fossa of the skull is open. The maxillary crests of the skull are mentioned in the description of the Genus *Platanista*. The lower jaw bones are long and slender and are united by fusion for over one-half of their length to form a very long, narrow lower jaw. The jaws of the females are longer than those of the males. The vertebrae are all moveable and distributed about as follows: C 7 + D 11 + L 8 + Ca 25 = 51. The bones of the flippers are distributed about as follows: I(2), II(6), III(6), IV(5), V(5).

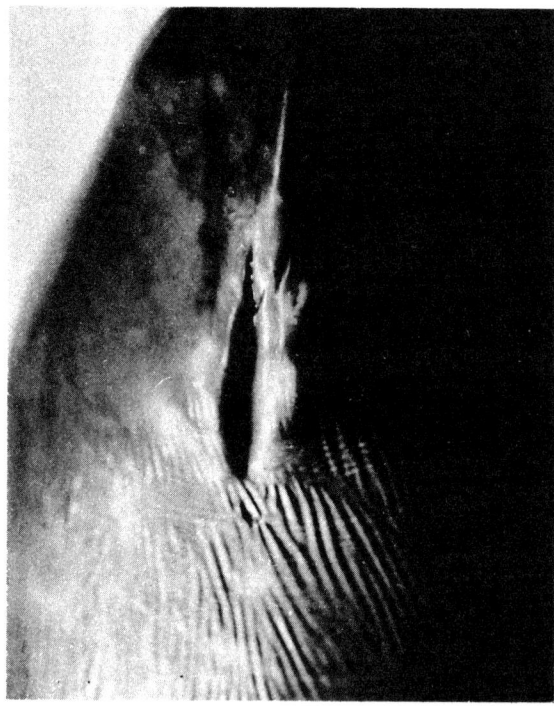

Photo of the blowhole of the Ganges River Dolphin, *Platanista gangetica* (Odontoceti: Platanistidae), in dorsal view, showing its longitudinal direction and slit-like opening.

From Herald.

Other Anatomical Notes. The eyes are small, degenerate, without a lens, and are probably almost blind. The optic nerve is reduced to the size of a thread. The ear openings are small, less than .5 cm. in diameter, but hearing is acute. Echo-location is employed for guidance in swimming and in the search for food. The blowhole is a longitudinal slit measuring between 4 and 5 cm. in length and is located slightly to the left of the midline of the body.

The stomach consists of four divisions: the fore-stomach, the main stomach which is divided into anterior and posterior portions, the connecting channel, and the pyloric stomach. The esophagus discharges directly and about equally into the fore-stomach and the anterior portion of the main stomach. The fore-stomach is an out-pocket from the esophagus, is not completely separated from the main

stomach, and does not contain any digestive glands; it is a storage organ in which some mechanical digestion takes place. The posterior portion of the main stomach is followed by a very short connecting channel which in turn leads into a spherical pyloric stomach. The pyloric stomach is followed by the muscular pyloric sphincter valve which controls the passage of food onward into the duodenal ampulla. A caecum is present in this species.

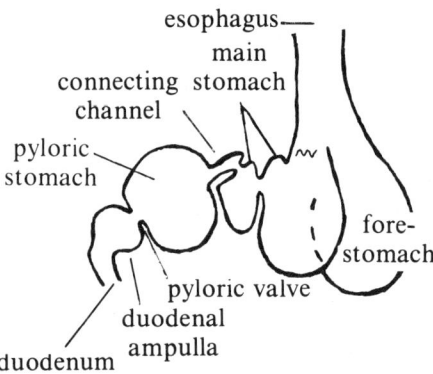

Diagram of the stomach of *Platanista gangetica* of the Ganges River.

From authors.

Food. Food consists of a wide variety of free-swimming and bottom-living fishes including catfish and carp, and also shrimp and crustaceans, etc. which they locate with their sonar skills.

Swimming and Diving. This species is a slow swimmer, often swimming on its right side. It usually surfaces every half minute when near the surface; it may leap from the water, breathe, and thereafter submerge again. It is occasionally observed floating at the surface with its head and beak visible. It usually travels in groups of two.

Reproduction. This species is reported to breed in the late spring (April to July) or later summer. The females are reported to mature at about 185 cm. (6 ft.) and the males at about 165 cm. (65 in.). The males and females copulate in a vertical position during which event their bodies are one-half above the water for a few seconds. They then fall back into the water where they remain motionless for a couple of minutes. The gestation period is uncertain, but has been reported as 9 to 12 months. The young are born about May and are reported to measure about 50 to 75 cm. (20 to 30 in.) in length and to be dark gray to pinkish red in color. The young remain close to the mother and, like other dolphins, are often captured with the mother.

Abundance. It is an uncommon species which is slowly being exterminated.

Economic Importance. This dolphin is hunted, killed, and eaten. Oil is extracted from its flesh for use in lamps and as an oil to rub upon the skin.

Miscellaneous. It is named "su-su" (Urdu) after the noise which it makes when exhaling.

THE INDUS RIVER DOLPHIN
Also known as "bhulan" (Sindhi) in the lower Indus valley
Platanista minor Owen, 1853

Identifying Features. This dolphin* has long been a confusing species. It resembles *P. gangetica* very closely and is regarded by some scholars as simply a variety of that species. It is a small river dolphin with a very long beak, square-ended flippers, and a slit-like blowhole located a small distance to the left side of the midline of the back. It differs from *P. gangetica* only in minute details and also in some features of the skull. See the description of the maxillary crests under the Genus *Platanista*. It is probably most easily identified by the fact that it is the only dolphin in the Indus River and its tributaries.

The Indus River Dolphin resembles the Ganges River Dolphin so closely that they are almost impossible to distinguish except by comparison of their skulls. See the description of *Platanista gangetica* for details.

Distribution. This dolphin is found in the Indus River of Pakistan and India from tidewater to the upland foothills. It does not enter the sea.

Teeth. The number of teeth in each of the four jaws is about 29 or 30, although the number may vary from 29 to 32.

Skeletal Notes. The vertebrae are distributed about as follows: C 7 + D 11 + L 8 + Ca 25 = 51.

Abundance. This dolphin is in imminent danger of becoming extinct. Its waterways are interrupted by dams, the government agencies which might protect it are useless, and an array of ignorant peasants are slowly killing them off for food. The population has been reduced to a few hundred. Scientists are predicting that this will be the first of the

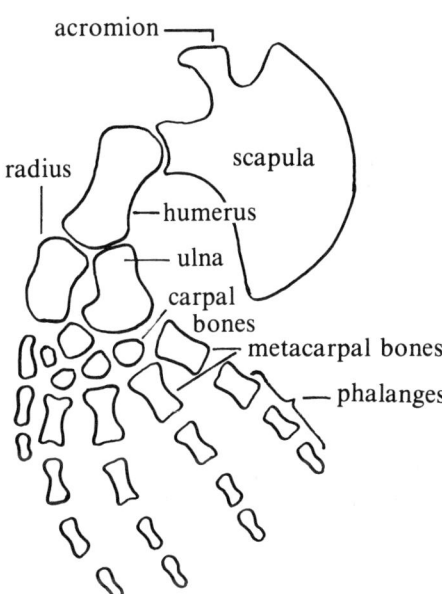

A diagram of the left appendage of the Indus River dolphin, *Platanista minor,* in lateral view.

From: Pilleri, Gregorio — Investigations On The Cetacea.

Cetacea (whales) to become extinct in historic times. It is a sad recommendation for the people of Pakistan.

Economic Importance. This little dolphin has no economic importance or value.

---

*Some authors prefer to use the name of *Platanista indi* Blyth, 1859, for this species.

THE AMAZON RIVER DOLPHINS
Genus *INIA* d'Orbigny, 1834

In the Amazon River dolphins, the head is rounded and the forehead is low and slopes quite steeply to the base of the beak. This beak tapers from its base into a long, slender, cylindrical snout which is curved very slightly downward (decurved) toward its end. The forward end of this snout contains a few, short, stout hairs or bristles. Each of the four jaw bones of the snout bears from about 25 to 34 teeth; these teeth therefor total between about 100 and 136 in all.

The dorsal fin is small, long, low, and ridge-like and continues backward as a low keel to the upper side of the tail flukes. The tail flukes are large, broad, and triangular and together form a tail with a posterior margin which is concave and which is marked with a notch at its center.

A constriction of the neck is visible from outside in all genera of the Platanistidae and the seven vertebrae within this neck are also separate as in all other members of this family. The blowhole is located atop the head and is nearly semi-circular in outline. The eyes are small and the ear openings are large.

The body color is variable and may be related to age and the amount of exposure to sunlight; young individuals are darker and get lighter with age. In mature adults, the body length may reach from about 2 to 2.75 meters (7 to 9 ft.).

The Amazon River dolphins are restricted to the fresh water rivers and lakes of the Amazon and Orinoco Rivers and their tributaries in northern South America.

The dolphins of the Orinoco and Amazon Rivers are not completely identical; those of the Orinoco River may be a sub-species of *Inia geoffrensis*. The dolphins of the upper Madeira River in western Brazil are also different from those dolphins in the remainder of the Amazon River Basin and may be a separate species or at least a subspecies of the Amazon River Dolphin. If they are regarded as a sub-species, these dolphins would then be named as shown below.

Inia geoffrensis geoffrensis (de Blainville, 1817)
THE AMAZON RIVER DOLPHIN

Inia geoffrensis boliviensis d'Orbigny, 1834
THE MADEIRA RIVER DOLPHIN

Inia geoffrensis humboldtiana Pilleri and Gihr, 1977
THE ORINOCO RIVER DOLPHIN

In this book we will assume that there is a single, widely-distributed species.

Studies of these dolphins by various scholars indicate that several names of species appearing in older books are really duplicate names or synonyms of other previously named species. The following list indicates an older name and the more correct and current name of this species.

Old Name		Name Currently In Use
Inia boliviensis	is now	*Inia geoffrensis*

This genus includes the single living species listed below.

Inia geoffrensis (de Blainville, 1817)
THE AMAZON RIVER DOLPHIN
OR BOUTU .... See page 113

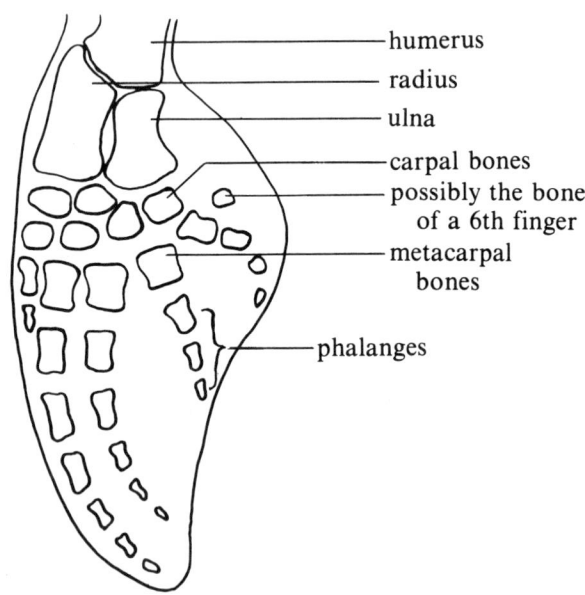

Diagram of the bones of the left flipper of the Amazon River dolphin, *Inia geoffrensis* (Odontoceti: Platanistidae).
Drawn from radiograph in Brit. Mus. (Nat. Hist.).

(labels on diagram:) humerus — radius — ulna — carpal bones — possibly the bone of a 6th finger — metacarpal bones — phalanges

Class Mammalia — The Mammals
   Order Cetacea — The Whales
      Suborder Odontoceti — The Toothed Whales
         Family Platanistidae — The River Dolphins

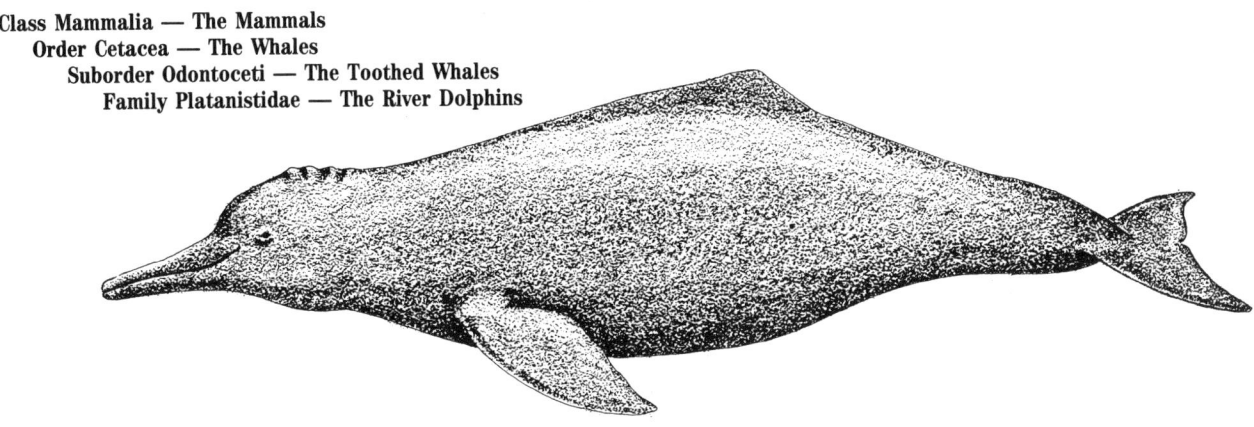

THE AMAZON RIVER DOLPHIN OR BOUTU*
Inia geoffrensis (de Blainville, 1817)

Identifying Features. This dolphin is a small species with a soft, light-colored skin and a long beak which is curved very slightly downward (decurved). The conical teeth have rough crowns.

Size and Shape. The body of this dolphin is thickset and plump, the head is rounded, the jaws are greatly elongated, the skin is soft, and the tail is large and wide. Its maximum size is reported to measure between 2 and 3 meters (6.5 to 9.5+ feet) in length and to weigh a maximum of about 300+ pounds (135+ kg), but most are considerably smaller.

Color. The color of the body is usually a bluish gray, although there is considerable variation. The young individuals are darker in color; they are dark gray or blackish above and shade to light gray below. The older dolphins become lighter in color, usually a pale pinkish or flesh color. They are darkest in color on the back near the blow hole, perhaps because this area receives the most sunlight.

Distribution. This dolphin is distributed throughout the basins of the Amazon and Orinoco Rivers. It ascends upstream 2500 km. (1553.5 mi.) into the interiors of Brazil, Bolivia, Peru, Equador, Columbia, and Venezuela.

*Boutu vermelho (Port.), red dolphin.

Migration. This is a fresh-water species which occupies the entire river basins, but which does not enter the sea.

Fins and Flippers. The dorsal fin is small, low, long, and ridge-like and has a long base which continues as a dorsal keel to the tail. The flippers are large and triangular in shape. The flukes of the tail are large, triangular in shape and bear a notch on their posterior margin where they meet at the midline.

Teeth. The teeth number from about 25 to 34 in each of the four jaw bones (total 100-136) and, in the upper jaw bones, occur only in the maxillae. The front teeth are sharp and pointed and have a ridged surface; the rear teeth are adapted for chewing.

Skeletal Notes. The beak or snout is long, slender, and cylindrical and is curved slightly downward (decurved). The two lower jaw bones are long and slender and are fused together for much of their length. The neck is visible externally and produces folds of skin as it is moved in various directions. The neck bones are all separate and movable. The vertebrae are distributed about as follows: C 7 + D 13 + L 5 + Ca 17 = 42. Three pairs of ribs articulate directly with the sternum. A very unusual feature of this species is the presence of the bones of a 6th finger imbedded in the flipper.

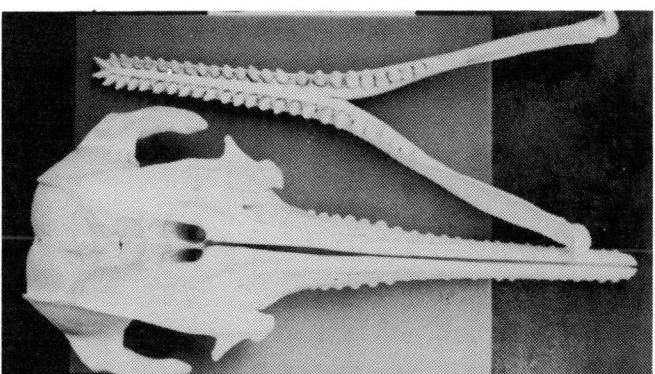

The skull and jaws of the Amazon River dolphin, *Inia geoffrensis,* in dorsal view.
Photo by Michael Graybill at Humboldt State Univ.

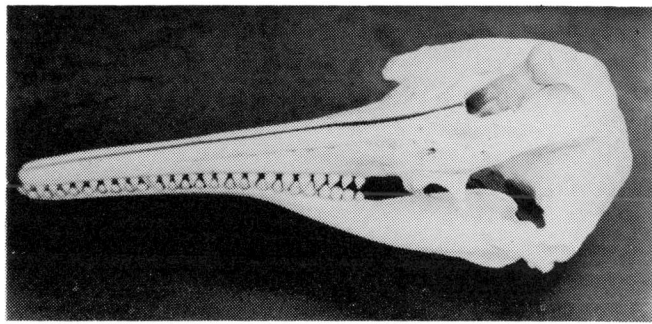

The skull and jaws of the Amazon River dolphin, *Inia geoffrensis.*
Photo by Michael Graybill at Humboldt State Univ.

Other Anatomical Notes. The eyes are small, the ear openings are large, and there are a few short bristles on the proboscis. The blowhole, located atop the head, extends across the head as a gentle arc with the ends pointing forward; it is located very slightly to the left of the midline. The caecum is absent. In dolphins, weighing between about 55 and 60 kg., the brain will weigh between about 550 and 650 grams.

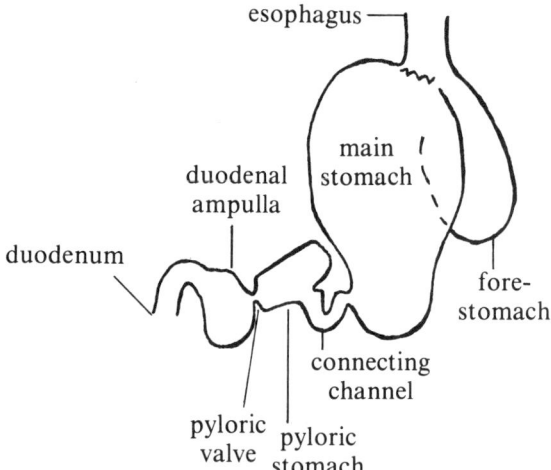

Diagram of the stomach of *Inia geoffrensis* of the Amazon River.
From authors.

The stomach consists of four parts: the fore-stomach, the main stomach, the connecting channel, and the pyloric stomach. The fore-stomach is developed as an out-pocket of the esophagus and therefor has no digestive glands in its lining; like the esophagus, it is quite muscular in construction. The esophagus discharges about equally into the fore-stomach and the main stomach. The fore-stomach is somewhat pear-shaped and is located above the main stomach and slightly to the left. The main stomach, which is large, quite muscular, and pear-shaped, opens into the pyloric stomach through the small, curved connecting channel. The pyloric stomach is small and somewhat elongated in this species; it discharges through the muscular pyloric sphincter valve into the duodenal ampulla.

Food. The food of this species consists of fishes which live near the bottom; stomach contents have included fishes, clams, snails, feathers, and plants. In captivity, this dolphin

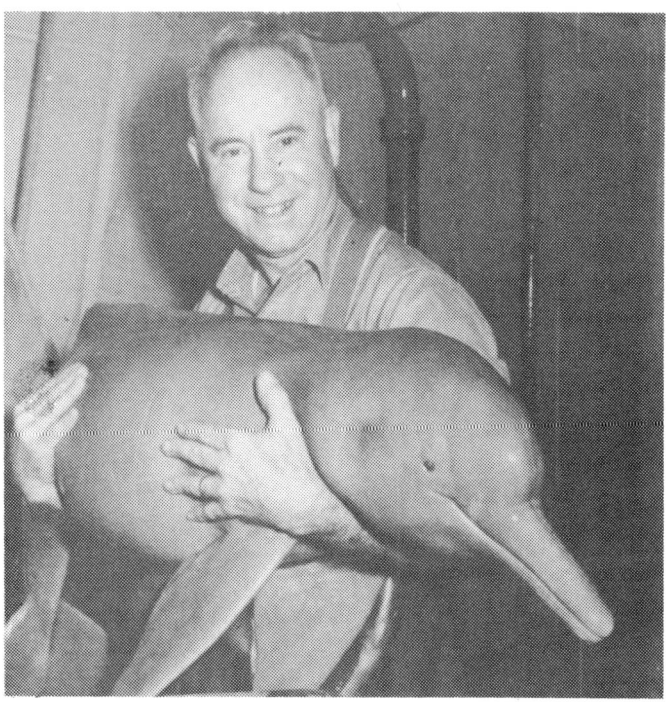

Photo of the Amazon River dolphin, *Inia geoffrensis* (Odontoceti: Platanistidae), with Robert Dempster, 1965.
Photo by Fred Jenne at Steinhart Aquarium,
San Francisco, California.

has eaten catfish and American smelt *(Osmerus mordax)*.

Swimming and Diving. On the average, this dolphin breathes every 30 to 45 seconds. It usually travels in pairs and likes to swim upside down. It is sometimes observed in the company of the other Amazon River dolphin (Tucuxi or Tookashee), *Sotalia fluviatilis* (Delphinidae).

Reproduction. The young, which are born from July to September, measure about 76 to 80 cm. (30 to 31+ in.) at birth. They are pink in color, but soon assume shades which more nearly resemble the adult coloration.

Abundance. This is an uncommon species.

Economic Importance. It is currently of no economic value to man.

Miscellaneous. This dolphin is an alert, inquisitive, intelligent species which lives singly or in small groups of six or less.

Photos of the Amazon River dolphin, *Inia geoffrensis* (Odontoceti: Platanistidae).

Photos by Fred Jenne at Steinhart Aquarium,
San Francisco, California.

THE CHINESE RIVER DOLPHINS
Genus *LIPOTES* Miller, 1918

The bodies of these dolphins are somewhat more robust than those of other fresh-water forms. The head is deep and rounded and the forehead, which is low, slopes uniformly to the base of the beak. This beak, which is long, slender, narrow, and cylindrical, is curved slightly upward (recurved), and contains between about 124 and 144 teeth; these teeth number from 31 to 36 in each of the four jaw bones.

The dorsal fin is of moderate size and is followed by a low keel of skin which continues backward without interruption to the tail. A constriction of the body at the neck is visible externally and the seven cervical vertebrae within are not fused together. The blowhole is located atop the head but to the left of the midline of the back. The eyes are small and degenerate and the eyesight is poor. The ear openings are large.

The color of the body is reported to be "bluish gray or grayish brown" on the back and then shades to lighter hues on the sides and belly. Adults will reach a length of 2.25 to 2.75 meters (7.5 to 9 ft.).

The distribution of this genus is limited to the fresh waters of Dungtinghu (Tungt'ing Hu Lake), located about 600 miles up the Chang Jiang (Yangtze River) in Hunan Province in China.

This genus is known only from the Holocene Epoch (Recent).

This genus includes the single living species listed below.

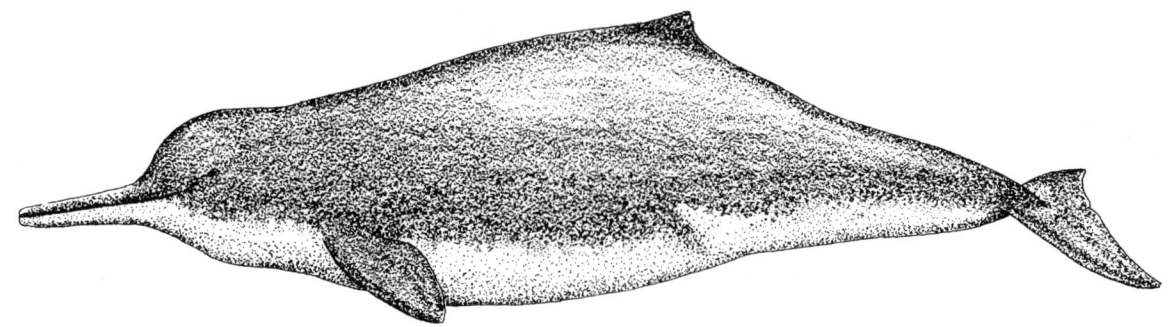

THE CHINESE RIVER DOLPHIN
Also known as the Yangtse River Dolphin and Pei C'hi
Lipotes vexillifer Miller, 1918

Identifying Features. This fresh-water dolphin lacks positive identification features other than its blowhole which is located atop the head in a crosswise position and a little to the left of the midline of the body. The beak is slender and is curved slightly upward.

Size and Shape. This dolphin is a small species which measures from about 2 to 2.5 meters (6.5 to 8+ feet) and will weigh from about 80 kg. (176 lbs.) to well over 125 kg. (275 lbs.).

Color. The color of the body is a blue-gray or grayish brown above, lighter on the sides, and whitish below.

Distribution. This species is limited to Dungtinghu (Tung-t'ing Hu Lake) in Hunan Province, China, which is located about 1,000 km. (621 mi.) upstream from the mouth of the Chang Jiang (Yangtse) River. It also occurs in nearby river waters; it does not enter the East China Sea.

Migration. It is reported to go upstream in the spring to clear water to breed.

Fins and Flippers. The dorsal fin is small and is located just behind the center of the body. It is triangular in shape, slightly convex on its front margin, and slightly concave on its posterior margin. The tip is slightly pointed; it continues posteriorly as a low dorsal keel. In this species, the dorsal fin is the highest of all of the fresh-water dolphins.

Teeth. The teeth number from about 31 to 36 in each of the four jaw bones. They are slender, sharp, and pointed and have grooves in their enamel somewhat like *Steno*.

Skeletal Notes. The proboscis or snout is long, narrow, and curved slightly upward; it measures about 30 cm. (12 in.) in length. The seven vertebrae of the neck are not fused together. The vertebrae are distributed about as follows: C 7 + D 11 + L 8 + Ca 19 = 45.

Other Anatomical Notes. The blowhole of this dolphin is located on top of the head in a crosswise position and is situated a very small distance to the left of the midline. A small bone or bit of ossified tissue lies on each side of the blowhole. The eyes are small, degenerate, and of limited use; they are located high on the head. The openings of the ears are visible. The tail is very wide, measuring about one-fourth of the body length, and is concave on its posterior margin.

Food. The food of this dolphin consists of fresh water fishes, including catfish, and other bottom-living species.

Swimming and Diving. It lives in muddy water where it employs echo-location for communication and for locating food. It is sometimes observed swimming in groups of 3 to 12 individuals. It is often seen swimming with the finless porpoise (*Neophocaena phocaenoides*).

Reproduction. Little is known of the habits of this species. The young are born in the spring (March and April), at which time they will measure about 1 meter (3.281 ft.) in length.

Abundance. This dolphin is one of the rare and uncommon species of the world. It is currently protected by law.

Economic Importance. The Chinese people value the blubber of this dolphin for its medicinal value and apply it both externally and internally for colds and other ailments.

Miscellaneous. Chinese legends contain a story describing how this dolphin is descended from a princess who jumped into this lake and was transformed into a dolphin. Each spring this dolphin-princess returns to the bank of the lake to search in the mud for her lover.

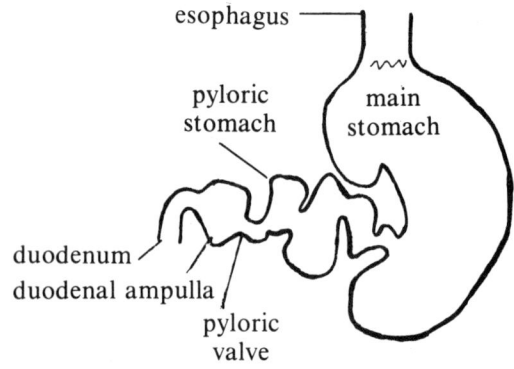

Diagram of the stomach of *Lipotes vexillifer* of China. From authors.

THE LA PLATA RIVER DOLPHINS
Genus *PONTOPORIA* Gray, 1846

The La Plata River dolphins are proportionally more slender than other fresh-water species. The head is rounded and the forehead is low and slopes gradually to the base of the beak. The snout or beak is slender and proportionally longer than in all other whales. The teeth in this genus are very numerous and total between about 200 and 240; they are fine, slender, pointed, and sharp and vary from about 50 to 60 or more in each of the four jaw bones.

The dorsal fin is well-developed, triangular, and pointed. The base of this fin is long and low and extends backward as a low keel from this fin to the tail. The flippers and the tail are both large in size and broadly triangular in outline.

A constriction of the body at the neck is visible externally and a few wrinkles and furrows are also present where the neck and the body join. The seven vertebrae of the neck are not fused into one or more solid units.

The color of the body is brownish in young individuals and changes in older individuals to grayish above and paler shades below. This species is of small size; both the males and the females will measure about 1.7 meters (5.5 ft.) in length when fully grown.

The distribution of this genus is confined to the La Plata River, its estuaries and tributaries, and to the nearby coastal waters of the western Atlantic Ocean. These dolphins are reported by some to migrate northward along the eastern coast of Uruguay during the winter season.

This genus is known from the Pleistocene Epoch in North America.

Studies of these dolphins by various scholars indicate that some names of species appearing in older books are really duplicate names or synonyms of other previously named species. The following list indicates older names and the more correct and current names of these species.

Old Name		Name Currently In Use
Delphinus blainvillei	is now	*Pontoporia blainvillei*
Pontoporia tenuirostris	is now	*Pontoporia blainvillei*
Stenodelphis blainvillei	is now	*Pontoporia blainvillei*

This genus includes the single living species listed below.

Pontoporia blainvillei (Gervais and d'Orbigny, 1844),
THE LA PLATA RIVER DOLPHIN ... See page 117

Class Mammalia — The Mammals
  Order Cetacea — The Whales
    Suborder Odontoceti — The Toothed Whales
      Family Platanistidae — The River Dolphins

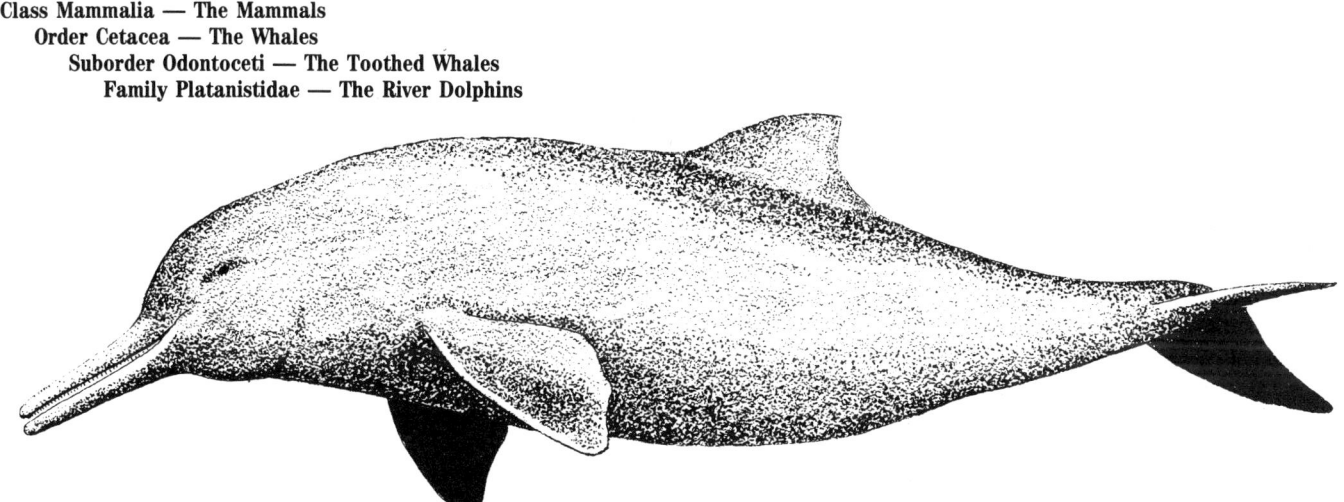

THE LA PLATA RIVER DOLPHIN
Also known as the Franciscana Dolphin
Pontoporia blainvillei (Gervais and d'Orbigny, 1844)

Identifying Features. Of all the whales, the La Plata dolphin has the distinction of having the longest snout in proportion to its length.

Size and Shape. This river dolphin is a small species with a slender body, a round head, and a very long proboscis. It measures 1.5 to 1.75 meters (60+ to 69+ in.) in length. A male specimen which measured about 157 cm. (62 in.) weighed about 32 kg. (70 lbs.); a female specimen which measured about 172 cm. (68 in.) weighed about 40 kg. (88 lbs.). It is one of the smallest of the fresh-water dolphins.

Color. The color of the body is a dull grayish white above and gradually shades to a paler color on the belly. The young individuals are more brownish in color. It has been reported that the dolphins from the east side of the river are nearly white in color.

Distribution. This species occurs in the estuary of the Rio de la Plata and the coastal waters of the Atlantic coast of South America from Baia de Santos (24° S.L.) in Brazil southward to Golfo San Matias (42° S.L.) and the Valdes Peninsula in Argentina. It does not inhabit rivers.

Migration. This dolphin leaves the estuaries during the winter months and moves northward along the coasts of Uruguay and Brazil.

Fins and Flippers. The dorsal fin is low, triangular in shape, and has a long base which continues posteriorly as a low keel to the tail. The flippers are medium-sized and triangular and the area between the fingers is concave, suggesting that these flippers may have developed from a webbed foot. The tail is likewise large and its posterior margin is concave with a notch at its center.

Teeth. The teeth are small, slender, and sharp and number between about 50 to 60 in each of the four jaw bones; their total number may range from about 200 to 240.

Skeletal Notes. The proboscis is very long and slender, and the neck vertebrae are all separate and independent. The vertebrae are distributed about as follows: C 7 + D 10 + L 7 + Ca 16 = 40. Four pairs of ribs articulate directly with the sternum; of these, the first four pairs of ribs have two heads.

Other Anatomical Notes. The blowhole is set crosswise atop the head and in this respect is similar to *Inia* and *Lipotes*. The neck is visible externally and exhibits wrinkles whenever the head is turned. The eyes are small and weak.

The stomach consists of three divisions: the main stomach, the connecting channel, and the pyloric stomach. Since the fore-stomach is practically absent, the esophagus discharges directly into the main stomach. The connecting channel is quite long and leads by a crooked passageway into the pyloric stomach, which in turn is followed by the muscular pyloric sphincter valve which controls the passage of food onward into the duodenal ampulla. There is no caecum in this species.

Food. This species eats mullet, croaker-like types of fishes, shrimp, and squid.

Swimming and Diving. Not much information is available concerning its swimming habits. They are a curious species and will approach small ships. They swim at a speed of about 5 to 7 km./hour and will blow about every 25 to 40 seconds. They are known to ride the bow waves of ships.

Reproduction. The young are born between October and January; they are small at birth, measuring about 45 to 50 cm. (18 to 20 in.) in length and weighing about 6 to 7 kg. (15 lbs.).

Abundance. This species is reasonably abundant along the coastal waters of its range.

Economic Importance. It is of no great importance although many are captured in coastal waters.

Miscellaneous. This is a gentle, curious, inoffensive dolphin which often appears near fishing boats, thereby allowing itself to be captured.

This species was originally described from a skull obtained in Uruguay and now in the Museum National d'Historie Naturelle, Paris.

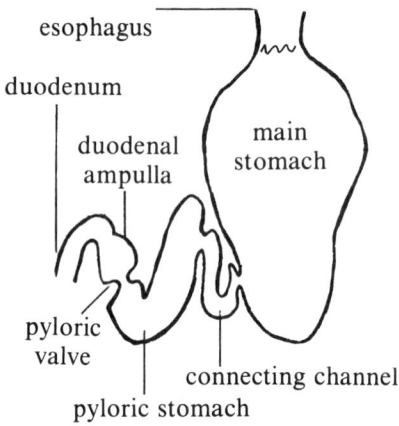

Diagram of the stomach of *Pontoporia blainvillei* of the Rio de la Plata.

From authors.

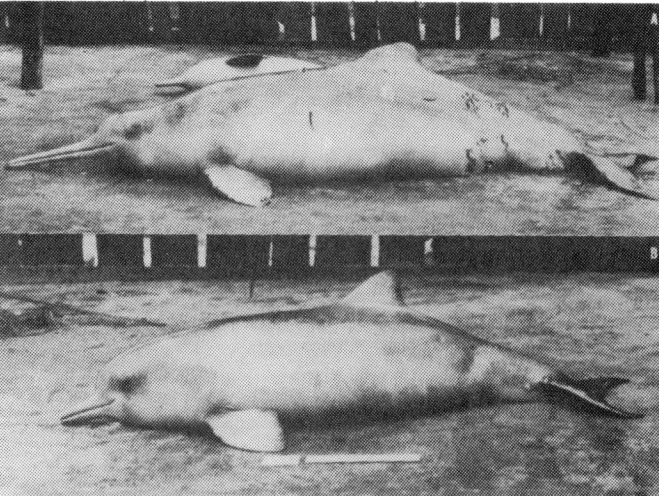

Photos of the La Plata River dolphin, *Pontoporia blainvillei*, taken in Uruguay. Above: adult. Below: juvenile.

From Brownell.

Reproduced by permission of the Dept. of Fisheries and Oceans, Dominion of Canada, from the Jour. Fish. Res. Bd. of Canada 32:7, July, 1975.

THE OCEAN DOLPHIN AND PORPOISE FAMILY
Family *DELPHINIDAE* Gray, 1821

The ocean dolphins, porpoises, and a few related species comprise the Family *Delphinidae,* the largest of the five families of the toothed whales. This family includes more than three dozen species of great diversity. They vary in size from small species about four feet in length to the killer whale which will reach a length of over 30 feet. They vary from species with a long snout or beak and more than 250 teeth to species without an extended beak and which may contain less than a dozen teeth.

In general, the members of this family are slender-bodied animals with stream-lined contours. They all possess a well-developed dorsal fin (except for the two species of *Lissodelphis* and possibly the single species of *Neophocaena*), which is usually located near the middle of the back. The two tail flukes are concave on their rear margins and a notch is present at the middle of this margin where the flukes join. There are no grooves on either the throat or the belly. The flippers are usually slender, pointed, sickle-shaped, and triangular or broadly rounded in outline. The family includes some genera *(Steno)* in which the beak is exceedingly long and narrow; in other genera *(Globicephala),* the jaws are short, a beak is not well developed, and a large, inflated forehead or melon is present; in addition, there are many species in which the jaws and rostrum are intermediate between these two extremes. Like most other toothed whales, there is a single, crescent-shaped or moon-shaped blowhole which is located atop the head with the points of the crescent directed forward.

In the skeleton of whales, the seven vertebral bones of the neck are often fused in various combinations. In this family, the first two vertebrae (the atlas and the axis) are fused in all genera, and additional vertebrae may become increasingly ossified and fused in older individuals. The double-headed ribs of the delphinids do not exceed about 7 or 8 in number.

The teeth of the *Delphinidae* are usually conical, pointed, and of various proportions. However, in the three genera of the true porpoises *(Phocoena, Neophocaena,* and *Phocoenoides),* the teeth are spade-shaped. This suggests that the porpoises may not be closely related to the dolphins and, for this reason, some scholars have placed these three genera in a separate family, the *Phocoenidae.* In the true dolphins, the teeth are small, slender, and numerous (reaching about 260 in some species), while in the larger species of this family, the teeth are larger, fewer in number, and more robust. *Grampus,* for example, has only from 4 to 14 teeth in the front of the two lower jaw bones combined; there are no functional teeth in the upper jaw bones of *Grampus.*

In this family, the esophagus leads directly into the fore-stomach. Because one of the functions of the fore-stomach is food storage, this chamber tends to be larger and more muscular than the main stomach. Another function of the fore-stomach is "mechanical digestion"; this accounts for its muscular walls and also for the sand and stones which occasionally occur there. The pyloric stomach in the *Delphinidae* is often quite tubular in shape and is preceded by a connecting channel in some genera including *Tursiops, Stenella,* and *Delphinus.*

The habits of the *Delphinidae* are very interesting. They are social animals and are rarely found alone. They are known to gather into schools or gams of as many as 1,500 individuals, although the usual gam numbers much less than 100 individuals. More commonly, they are seen in groups of less than a dozen and pairs and single individuals are sometimes seen.

They exhibit a playful personality and may be best observed swimming and playing about the bows of ships or in the tanks of the large public aquaria. They are agile, speedy swimmers and, when pressed, might reach a speed in excess of 25 miles per hour. When swimming leisurely, they often form into groups which surface and dive in regular, precise formations much like the close-order drill of soldiers.

They are all carnivorous and feed principally upon fishes and squids. Some of the larger species are predators and will attack, kill, and eat birds, otters, seals, sea lions, and other whales. They will also kill sharks.

The delphinid whales are world-wide in their distribution. They inhabit all oceans and the estuaries of some large rivers; a few species also occur in some lowland rivers. They prefer to live in the warmer waters of the globe; they are uncommon in the polar regions and are much more abundant in temperate and tropical seas. Most species are non-migratory, although they will follow their food supply.

Fossil specimens of over 40 different genera of the *Delphinidae* have been found in various places, extending from the early Miocene Epoch of the Tertiary Period down to the Holocene Epoch (Recent). This means that these whales have been swimming in the seas of this earth for at least 25,000,000 years.

Scholars differ in their opinions concerning which genera and species should be included within the Family *Delphinidae.* Some zoologists believe that the Family *Delphinidae* should be large and include all 20 genera and their 39+ species. (This is the pattern of this book.) Other scholars believe that some genera and their species within the Family *Delphinidae* are sufficiently different in their anatomical structure to warrant the creation of additional families for them. So the Family *Delphinidae* is often divided and various genera (with their species) are withdrawn and placed in separate families in various ways by different scholars. In some of these arrangements, the Family *Delphinidae* may even be reduced to as few as the following nine (9) genera:

Sousa (2 species)	*Lagenodelphis* (1 species)
Sotalia (2 species)	*Lagenorhynchus* (6 species)
Tursiops (1 species)	*Cephalorhynchus* (4 species)
Stenella (5± species)	*Lissodelphis* (2 species)
Delphinus (1 species)	

Some or all of the remaining eleven (11) genera and their species are sometimes distributed into the following new families:

Family *Stenidae* with the single genus *Steno* (1 species), and occasionally including the genus *Sousa* (2 species) and the genus *Sotalia* (2 species).

Family *Globicephalidae* with the five genera of *Peponocephala* (1 species), *Feresa* (1 species), *Pseudorca* (1 species), *Globicephala* (2 species), and *Orcinus* (1 species).

Family *Orcaellidae* with the single genus *Orcaella* (1 species).

Family *Phocoenidae* with the three genera of *Phocoena* (4 species), *Neophocaena* (1 species), and *Phocoenoides* (1 species).

Students of this family therefore should not be disturbed if they find that the arrangement of these genera and species varies widely in different books.

The dolphin family *(Delphinidae)* is usually divided into the 20 living genera which are listed below.

THE GENERA OF THE DELPHINIDAE

The above genera will be discussed on the following pages in the above sequence.

The Jaws and Teeth of the Larger Dolphins

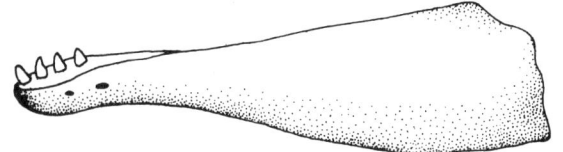

The teeth and jaw bone of *Grampus griseus.*

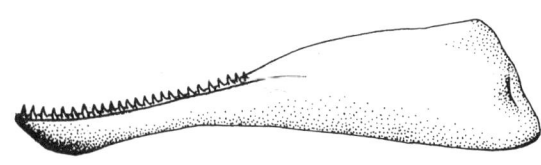

The teeth and jaw bone of *Peponocephala electra.*

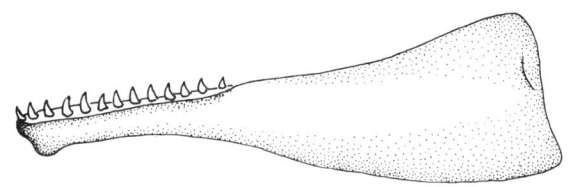

The teeth and jaw bone of *Feresa attenuata.*

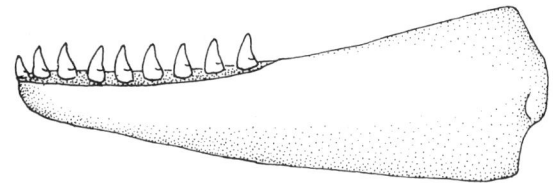

The teeth and jaw bone of *Pseudorca crassidens.*

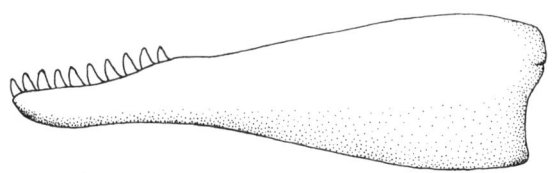

The teeth and jaw bone of *Globicephala melaena.*

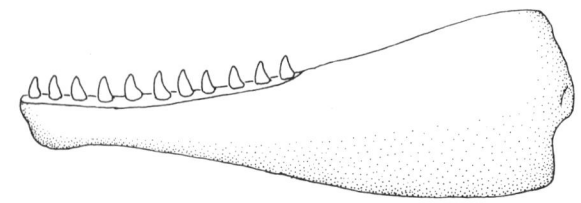

The teeth and jaw bone of *Orcinus orca.*

Guide for Separating the Medium-sized Whales with Inflated Heads
The beaked whales (*Ziphiidae*) are not included here.

Delphinidae The Ocean Dolphins	Shape of Head Length of Body	Teeth	Dorsal Fin	Flippers	Markings On Back	Color of Ventral Side	Remarks
Grampus griseus The Grampus	Plump; head with V-shaped mark on front. To 4.3 m. (14 ft.).	4 teeth on each side in front of lower jaw; varies 2-7. None visible in upper jaws.	Large, high, curved, w/pointed tip.		None.	Usually lighter below.	Identify by V-mark on head; also by few teeth.
Peponocephala electra The Small, Melon-headed Blackfish	Sloping. To 3 m. (9¾ ft.).	21 to 25 in each of 4 jaws.			None.	With an elongated, white area.	Identify by numerous teeth.
Feresa attenuata The Pigmy Killer Whale	Sloping. To 2.7 m. (8¾ ft.).	8 to 13 in each of 4 jaws.		Narrow and straight.	None.	With light area on belly.	Separate from *Pseudorca* by flipper.
Pseudorca crassidens The False Killer Whale	Sloping. To 6 m. (19¾ ft.).	7 to 12 in each of 4 jaws.		With obtuse angle or hump on leading edge.	None.	With white or light areas on belly.	Identify by hump or elbow on leading edge of flipper.
Globicephala macrorhynchus The Short-finned Pilot Whale	Fat and bulbous. To 6 m. (19¾).	7 to 12 in each of 4 jaws; set in front of mouth.		Long and slender; 1/6 of body length.	Gray area in some; spot behind eye in some.	Grayish, indistinct, or dark.	Identify by large head; look at color pattern; measure flipper.
Globicephala melaena The Long-finned Pilot Whale	Fat and bulbous. To 5 m. (16½ ft.).	8 to 13 in each of 4 jaws; set in front of mouth.		Long and slender; 1/5 of body length.	None. All black.	Pure white.	Identify by large head; look at color pattern; measure flipper.
Orcinus orca The Killer Whale	Sloping. To 9.5 m. (31 ft.).	10 to 13 in each of 4 jaws; large, heavy, thick.	2½ to 6 feet in height.	Large, broad, rounded, paddle-like.	Light saddle on back; spot behind eye.	Large white areas.	Identify by tall dorsal fin.

THE ROUGH-TOOTHED DOLPHINS
Genus *STENO* Gray, 1846

This genus contains a single species which has been set apart from all other dolphins by its snout and its teeth. The teeth, which number from about 20 to 27 in each of the four jaw bones, are large in size and are rough upon their crowns. The beak or snout of this genus is slightly compressed, slender, and exceedingly long; in proportion to its length, the snout of this dolphin is among the longest of all whales. The forehead is quite low, grades gradually downward to the base of the beak, and lacks the transverse groove between it and the beak. The union (mandibular symphysis) at the front of the lower jaw, where the two lower jaw bones join, is about one-fourth the length of the lower jaw bones. The vertebrae number about 65 or 66 in all.

This genus is known from the Lower and Middle Pliocene Epoch in Europe.

This genus was named for Nicolaus Steno (1631-1686), a Danish naturalist and physician, who was born in Copenhagen, but spent much of his adult life in Italy.

Studies of these dolphins by various scholars indicate that several names of species appearing in older books are really duplicate names or synonyms of other previously named species. The following list indicates the older names and the more correct and current names of these species.

Old Name		Name Currently In Use
Genus *Stenodelphis*	is now	Genus *Pontoporia*
Steno attenuata	is now	*Steno bredanensis*
Steno compressus	is now	*Steno bredanensis*
Steno perniger	is now	*Steno bredanensis*
Steno rostratus	is now	*Steno bredanensis*
Steno tucuxi	is now	*Sotalia fluviatilis*
Stenopontistes zambezicus	is now	*Steno bredanensis*

This genus contains the single living species listed below.

Steno bredanensis (Lesson, 1828)
THE ROUGH-TOOTHED DOLPHIN
. . . . See page 123

The rough-toothed dolphin, *Steno bredanensis*.
Sea Life Park, Hawaii.

THE ROUGH-TOOTHED DOLPHIN
Steno bredanensis (Lesson, 1828)

Identifying Features. The rostrum of this dolphin is unusually long and laterally compressed and the teeth are rough with fine, vertical ridges at their crowns. It lacks the transverse crease which separates the forehead from the proboscis. The eyes are large and brown.

Size and Shape. The body of this dolphin is both robust and stream-lined. It is largest in the area just in front of the dorsal fin and from this point tapers uniformly toward both the head and tail. This is a medium-sized dolphin which is reported to measure between about 1.8 to 2.4 meters (6 to 8 ft.) or more in length.

Color. The color of the body is slate colored to purplish black above and shades to a whitish color on the belly often with pinkish hues. The sides are marked with scattered yellowish white spots and the white of the belly is often spotted with black. The beak is whitish in color and the lips are white; the interior of the mouth is white at the back and is marked with small, dark-red spots. The surface of the body is often marked with lighter scratches and scars and by round, light, pinkish spots an inch or more in diameter.

Distribution. The distribution of this species is world-wide in tropical and warmer temperate seas. It occurs in the Atlantic, Pacific, and Indian Oceans and in the Caribbean Sea, the Mediterranean Sea, the Red Sea, the Bay of Bengal, and the Hawaiian Islands. In the western Atlantic it occurs as far north as Virginia (37° N.L.). It is pelagic and lives outside of the continental shelf where it avoids cold seas and cold currents. In the North Pacific Ocean, it does not go north of about 40° N.L.

Migration. This is not a migratory species.

Fins and Flippers. The dorsal fin is quite high and somewhat triangular in shape. The anterior margin is slightly convex and the posterior margin is concave. The fin terminates in a point which is directed backward. A low keel is present both above and below on the caudal peduncle.

The flippers are quite large, are nearly triangular in shape, and terminate in a blunt point. They are black in color.

The flukes of the tail are quite wide with tips which are pointed and directed backward. Their posterior margins are concave in outline and exhibit a deep notch where they join at the midline of the body.

Teeth. The teeth are quite stout and pointed and are rather large when compared with other dolphins. They number from about 20 to 27 in each of the four jaw bones and have

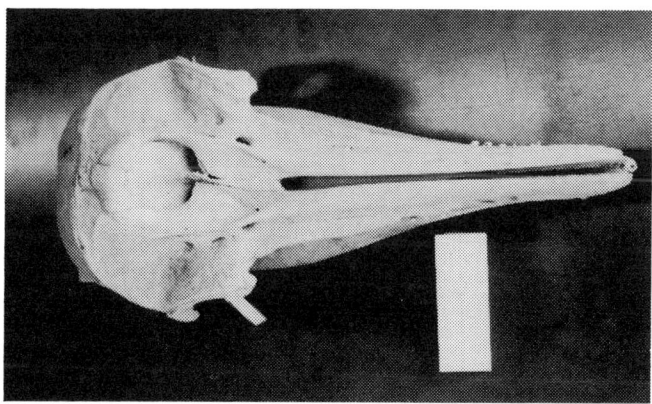

The skull of the rough-toothed dolphin, *Steno bredanensis,* in dorsal view.
Photo by Michael Graybill at Cal. Acad. of Sci.

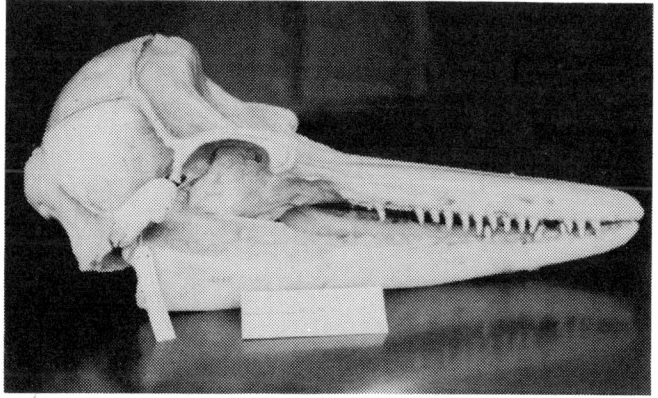

The skull and jaws of the rough-toothed dolphin, *Steno bredanensis,* in lateral view.
Photo by Michael Graybill at Cal. Acad. of Sci.

123

rough crowns which are marked with very fine, vertical ridges and furrows.

Skeletal Notes. The vertebrae number about 65 or 66 and are distributed as follows: C 7, D 13, L 15-16, Ca 30-31 = 65-66. The 1st and 2nd neck vertebrae are fused. The chevron bones number about 21 or 22. Of the ribs, 4 or 5 pairs have two heads and 5 pairs* connect with the sternum, which in turn is composed of 4 parts. The bones of the fingers are distributed as follows: I (3), II (8-9), III (6-7), IV (3), V (2).

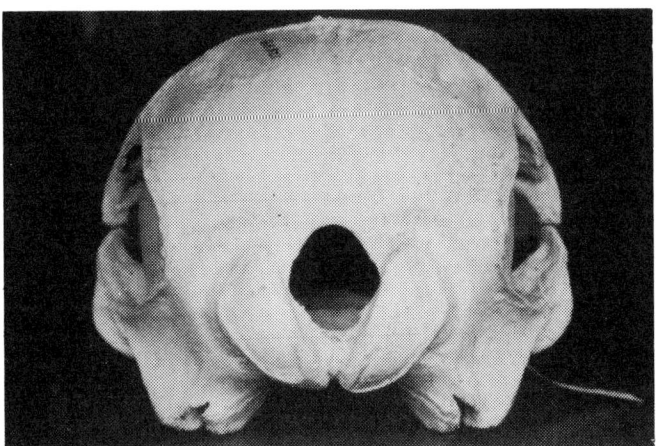

The skull of the rough-toothed dolphin, *Steno bredanensis,* **in posterior view.**
Photo by Michael Graybill at Cal. Acad. of Sci.

Other Anatomical Notes. Although the snout is very long, its length is obscured by the fact that it lacks the transverse crease which separates the forehead from the beak; the outline of the head therefore tapers gradually and uniformly to the snout. When viewed from above, this snout looks very narrow. The ear openings are small; hearing is acute.

Food. Its food consists of pelagic fishes, squid, etc.

Swimming and Diving. This species is a good swimmer and can achieve speeds of 15 or more knots (17 mi./hr.). It will blow every 8 to 10 seconds when actively swimming. This dolphin is often found with schools of bottle-nosed dolphins *(Tursiops)* and with schools of tuna fishes. It is known to travel in schools which may reach 50 individuals. It will ride the bow waves of ships.

---

*Some authors state that four pairs of ribs articulate directly with the sternum.

Reproduction. Very little is known of the reproductive habits of this dolphin. A female of this species *(Steno bredanensis)* gave birth in 1971 at Sea Life Park in Honolulu to a hybrid female which was reported to have been fathered by a bottle-nosed dolphin *(Tursiops* sp.).

Abundance. Because it does not frequent coast lines, this species is rarely seen.

Economic Importance. The rough-toothed dolphin has no economic importance.

Miscellaneous. A school of 17 individuals ran aground near Maalaea on Maui, Hawaii, on Sunday, 27 June 1976. The name *bredanensis* is derived from the name of a Mr. Van Breda, who painted a picture of this species from a carcass cast ashore at Brest in France.

The rough-toothed dolphin, *Steno bredanensis.*
Sea Life Park, Hawaii.

THE HUMP-BACKED DOLPHINS
Genus *SOUSA* Gray, 1866

This genus is not well defined and the number of species within it is still uncertain. It is not well separated from the genus *Sotalia,* although these two genera are reported to differ in their ear bones (tympanic bullae). This genus superficially resembles *Steno* and *Tursiops,* although it has about 15 to 20 fewer vertebrae and more teeth. It includes only Old World forms of which one is Asiatic and one is African; some of these species were formerly placed in the genus *Sotalia.* The species include both marine and fresh water forms and inhabit coastal seas, river mouths, and large river estuaries. Further studies of this genus will redefine and reaffirm the existing species and might possibly identify and define additional species and/or subspecies.

Many books and scholars will tentatively and with uncertainty list the following five provisional species as belonging in this genus:

1. *Sousa borneensis* Lydekker, 1901, The Malayan Dolphin. It occurs along the coasts of Borneo.
2. *Sousa chinensis* (Osbeck, 1765), The Chinese Humpbacked Dolphin or Indo-Pacific White Dolphin. It occurs along the southern coast of China.
3. *Sousa lentiginosus* Owen, 1866, The Speckled Dolphin. It occurs along the southern coast of India and Sri Lanka (Ceylon).
4. *Sousa plumbea* (G. Cuvier, 1829), The Lead-colored Dolphin. It occurs from the Indian Ocean eastward to the Malay Peninsula.
5. *Sousa teuszii* (Kukenthal, 1892). The Atlantic Humpbacked Dolphin. It occurs along the western coast of Africa from Senegal southward to Cameroon.

Studies of these dolphins by various scholars indicate that several names of species appearing in older books are really duplicate names or synonyms of other previously named species. The following list indicates the older names and the more correct and current names of these species.

Old Name		Name Currently In Use
Sousa borneensis	is now	*Sousa chinensis*
Sousa lentiginosa	is now	*Sousa chinensis*
Sousa plumbea	is now	*Sousa chinensis*
Sousa queenslandensis	is now	*Sousa chinensis*

At present, scholars are uncertain about the exact number of species in this genus. Some scholars believe that there are only two species: an Asiatic species (*S. chinensis*) and an African species *(S. teuszii).* This arrangement is followed in this book. Under this arrangement, *S. chinensis* would include *S. plumbea, S. borneensis,* and *S. lentiginosus.*

This genus contains the two living species listed below.

THE INDO-PACIFIC
HUMP-BACKED DOLPHIN
Also known as the White Dolphin
Sousa chinensis (Osbeck, 1765)

Identifying Features. The back of this dolphin is very high in the area below the dorsal fin. The tail stock is laterally compressed and has high dorsal and ventral ridges. They breathe with the head and beak on or above the water.

Size and Shape. The body is spindle-shaped and tapers from the center in both directions, the forehead is not high, and the proboscis is long. It will measure about 1.8 to 2.5 meters (70 to 98 in.) in length.

Color. The color of the body is variable. It may include ivory, ivory-gray, yellowish-white, silvery-white, or a lead color above, while the belly is usually somewhat pinkish. Some individuals are marked with gray spots over the entire body and some will have vertical lines on the sides of the body. Some scholars have reported that they find gray specimens off Africa, speckled specimens off India, and white specimens off Borneo. The eyes are black.

Distribution. This species is distributed over a vast area of warm water within the Indo-Western Pacific Faunal Area.

Its range extends from the Red Sea and South Africa eastward across the Indian Ocean to the islands of the East Indies, New Guinea, northward to Shanghai, China (32° N.L.), and eastward to northern and eastern Australia, including shorelines, estuaries, and occasionally rivers. This is a shoreline species which prefers to live in the calmer waters of estuaries and lagoons.

Migration. The southern populations migrate northward during the winter seasons.

Fins and Flippers. The dorsal fin is located near the center of the body; it is long, low, somewhat triangular in shape, and continues toward the tail as a large keel. In mature individuals, a large, narrow, prominent hump will develop on the back below the dorsal fin. The flipper has a front edge which is rounded and the tip is directed backward.

Teeth. The teeth number from about 31 to 37 or 38 in each of the four jaw bones. The teeth in *S. teuszii* number from about 26 to 30 in each of the four jaw bones.

Photo of the Indo-Pacific hump-backed dolphin, *Sousa chinensis,* at Marineland of Australia.

J. Reynolds.

From: "Whales and Dolphins of New Zealand and Australia" by A.N. Baker. Victoria University Press, Wellington, 1983. Courtesy A.N. Baker.

Photo of the Indo-Pacific hump-backed dolphin, *Sousa chinensis.*

Alan N. Baker.

From: "Whales and Dolphins of New Zealand and Australia" by A.N. Baker. Victoria University Press, Wellington, 1983. Courtesy A.N. Baker.

Skeletal Notes. The beak or proboscis is well developed in this species. The vertebrae are distributed approximately as follows: C 7 + D 12 + L 10 + Ca 22 = 51. Five ribs articulate directly with the sternum. The bones of the fingers are distributed approximately as follows: I (1), II (7), III (5), IV (3), V (2).

Other Anatomical Notes. There is variation in the color patterns of this species due to the fact that it appears to have sub-populations within the vast area which it occupies.

Food. It feeds upon a wide variety of fishes including mullet.

Swimming and Diving. Very little information is known. They do not ride the bow wave of ships.

Reproduction. Very little information is known. It copulates vertically in the water. The young are born in March and April in the northern hemisphere.

Abundance. It is moderately abundant in some areas; it is not a common species.

Economic Importance. Fishermen catch this dolphin in the eastern part of its range. It is of very little commercial value.

Miscellaneous. This is not a well known species.

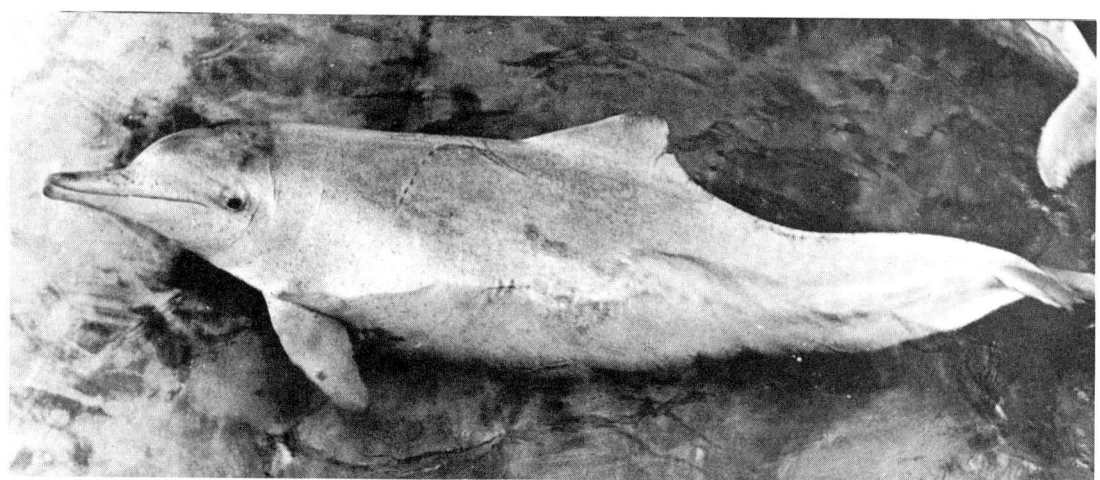

The Indo-Pacific hump-backed dolphin, *Sousa chinensis*, is a widely distributed species. It occurs from the Red Sea and the Cape of Good Hope eastward to the Canton River in China and the eastern coast of Australia. Note the hump beneath the dorsal fin.   **Photo by W.H. Dawbin.**

Reproduced by permission of the Dept. of Fisheries and Oceans, Dominion of Canada, from the Jour. Fish. Res. Bd. of Canada 32:7, July, 1975.

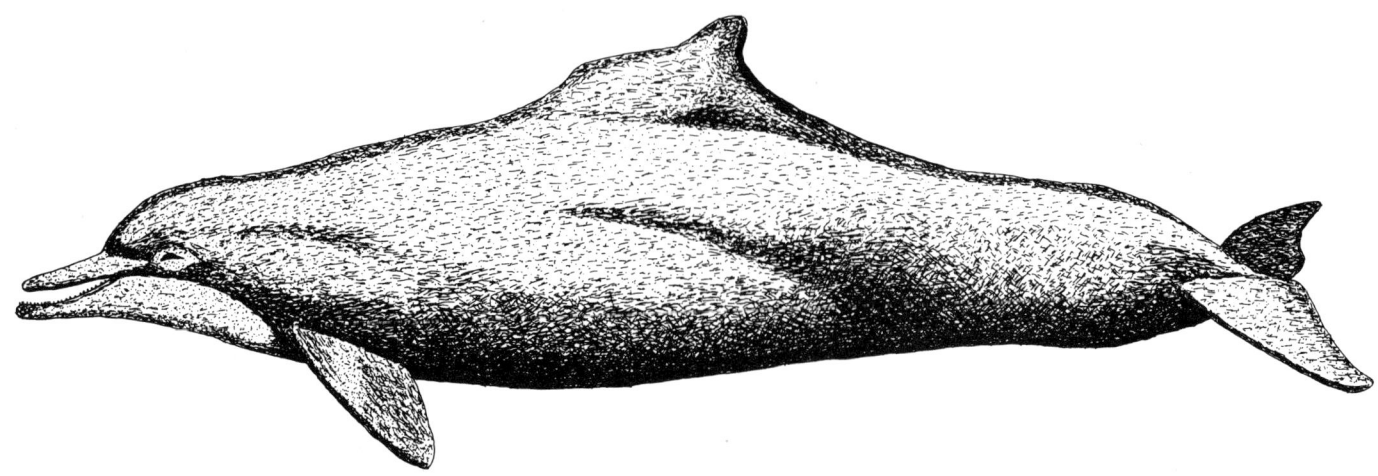

THE ATLANTIC HUMP-BACKED DOLPHIN
Also known as the West African Hump-backed Dolphin
Sousa teuszii (Kukenthal, 1892)

Identifying Features. The back of this dolphin is very high in the area below the dorsal fin. Like *Sousa chinensis,* the tail stock is laterally compressed with high dorsal and ventral ridges. It is separated from *S. chinensis* by its teeth. See below.

Size and Shape. This is a small dolphin with a spindle-shaped body which tapers in both directions from the middle of the body. The head presents a low, rounded profile and is separated by a constriction from the base of the beak, which in turn is long and narrow. It measures about 190 to 250 cm. (75 to 98 in.) in length.

Color. Information is uncertain.

Distribution. This dolphin is a warm water species which occurs along the western coast of Africa. It extends from Mauritania (20° N.L.) and Senegal southward to Angola (15° S.L.).

Fins and Flippers. The dorsal fin is located very near to the center of the back; it is low and continues as a dorsal keel toward the tail. The flippers are quite small, have curved anterior and posterior margins, and terminate in a rounded point. The flukes of the tail are wide, are pointed at their extremities with the tips directed backward, are somewhat concave on their posterior margin, and contain a notch where they meet at the midline of the body.

Teeth. The teeth are useful in separating this species from *S. chinensis.* In this dolphin, the teeth number from about 26 to 30 in each of the four jaw bones; *S. chinensis* has about 31 to 37 or 38 teeth.

Skeletal Notes. The beak is well developed. The vertebrae are distributed approximately as follows: C 7 + D 12 + L 10 + Ca 24 = 53. There are about 2 more vertebrae in this species than in *S. chinensis.*

Food. Its food consists of fishes, including mullet and herring. Very little is known concerning its habits.

Abundance. This is not a common species.

Economic Importance. This dolphin has very little economic importance.

Miscellaneous. This species was named for Edouard Teusz, who caught the first known specimen in 1892 in the harbor at Douala (4° N.L.) in the nation of Cameroon in western equatorial Africa.

THE RIDGE-BACKED OR
SOUTH AMERICAN DOLPHINS
Genus *SOTALIA* Gray, 1866

This genus contains species from the rivers and coastal waters of the northern and eastern coasts of South America. Students will find that books and various scholars have listed the following five species as belonging in this genus.

1. *Sotalia brasiliensis* E. van Beneden, 1875, The Brasilian Dolphin. It occurs in the coastal waters of eastern South America.
2. *Sotalia fluviatilis* (Gervais, 1853), The Amazon Tookashee Dolphin. It occurs in the Amazon River and its branches and in the Tocantins River.
3. *Sotalia guianensis* (P. J. van Beneden, 1864), The Guiana Dolphin. It occurs in the coastal waters of the Guianas and adjoining coastal areas.
4. *Sotalia pallida* (Gervais, 1855), The Amazon White Dolphin. It occurs in the Amazon River and its branches and in the Tocantins River.
5. *Sotalia tucuxi* (Gray, 1856), The Amazon Tucuxi Dolphin. It occurs in the Amazon River and its branches and in the Tocantins River.

At present, scholars are uncertain about the exact number of species in this genus. Some scholars believe that there is but a single species with two varieties as follows:

Sotalia fluviatilis fluviatilis (Gervais, 1853)
Sotalia fluviatilis guianensis (van Beneden, 1864)

Other students believe that there are two species as follows:

Sotalia fluviatilis (Gervais, 1853)
Sotalia guianensis (van Beneden, 1864)

Under this arrangement of but two species, *S. fluviatilis* would include *S. pallida* and *S. tucuxi; S. guianensis* would include *S. brasiliensis.* This book will accept this genus as having two species and describe them accordingly.

Studies of these dolphins by various scholars indicate that several names of species appearing in older books are really duplicate names or synonyms of other previously named species. The following list indicates the older names and the more correct and current names of these species.

Old Name		Name Currently In Use
Sotalia borneensis	is now	*Sousa chinensis*
Sotalia brasiliensis	is now	*Sotalia guianensis*
Sotalia chinensis	is now	*Sousa chinensis*
Sotalia gadamu	is now	*Tursiops truncatus*
Sotalia lentiginosa	is now	*Sousa chinensis*
Sotalia pallida	is now	*Sotalia fluviatilis*
Sotalia plumbea	is now	*Sousa chinensis*
Sotalia sinensis	is now	*Sousa chinensis*
Sotalia teuszii	is now	*Sousa teuszii*
Sotalia tucuxi	is now	*Sotalia fluviatilis*

This genus contains the two living species listed below.

Sotalia fluviatilis (Gervais, 1853)
THE AMAZON RIVER TOOKASHEE
DOLPHIN .... See page 130
Sotalia guianensis (van Beneden, 1864)
THE GUIANA COASTAL DOLPHIN
.... See page 131

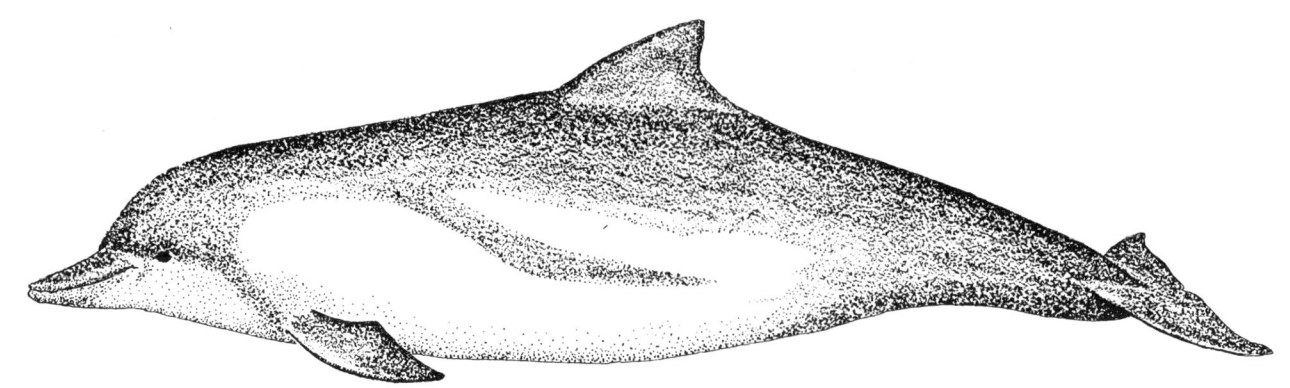

THE AMAZON RIVER
TOOKASHEE DOLPHIN
Also known as "Tucuxi" (Amazon Indian)
Sotalia fluviatilis (Gervais, 1853)

Identifying Features. This fresh-water dolphin occupies the Amazon River together with the Amazon River Dolphin or "Boutu" (*Inia geoffrensis*), where they often mingle together to form a single school. It may be separated from *I. geoffrensis* by size, since *S. fluviatilis* is one of the very smallest of dolphins. The dorsal fin of *S. fluviatilis* is much larger than that of *I. geoffrensis*.

Size and Shape. This little dolphin has a body which is typical of the smaller members of this family. It is spindle-shaped, being thickest in the area just anterior to the dorsal fin and then tapering uniformly toward both the head and tail. The head is low and the forehead slopes gradually toward the base of the beak; there is no severe transverse constriction present to mark the boundary between the head and the beak. In this species, the beak is quite long and, like the body, is dark colored above and light below. This species is one of the smaller dolphins. It will reach a length of about 1.7 meters (5 ft. 7 in.). They will weigh between about 30 to 40 kg. (66 to 88 lbs.) and may reach a maximum weight of about 50 kg. (110 lbs.).

Color. The color of the body above is charcoal gray to brownish; this includes the back, the dorsal fin, and the tail. The body is a yellowish white or ivory color below; this includes the lower jaw, the throat, the breast, the belly, and the area surrounding the anus. The color of the belly also extends upward toward the dorsal fin and toward the head. This is a light colored species of variable coloration. The flippers are the same color as the back.

Distribution. This dolphin lives in the Amazon River and its tributaries as far inland as the Andes Mountains, a distance of about 2,000 km. (1243 mi.); it also lives in the Orinoco and other rivers of Venezuela. Its range extends along the sea coast, including bays and rivers, from Venezuela westward to Panama.

Migration. Information is not readily available on their seasonal movements.

Fins and Flippers. The dorsal fin is situated at the center of the body. It is nearly triangular in shape and does not rest upon an elevated base. Both the anterior and posterior margins are only very slightly curved and the tip is not inclined backward to any degree. It is dark in color.

The flippers are curved on their anterior margin, nearly straight on their posterior margin, and terminate in a pointed tip.

The flukes of the tail are quite wide, are concave on their posterior margin, and exhibit a notch on their posterior border where they join at the midline.

Teeth. The teeth are irregular in position; they number from about 28 to 34 in each of the two upper jaw bones and from about 26 to 35 in each of the two lower jaws.

Skeletal Notes. The first two bones of the neck are united. The first 5 pairs of ribs have two heads and articulate with the sternum. The vertebrae are distributed approximately as follows: C 7 + D 12 + L 11 + Ca 26 = 56. The bones of the fingers are distributed approximately as follows: I (1), II (8), III (5), IV (4), V (2).

Food. These dolphins feed upon fishes, crabs, prawns, etc.

Swimming and Diving. Very little is known about this species in the wild. It is a leisurely swimmer and lives in small groups of 8 to 12 or more.

Reproduction. The young animals have been observed in February and March. They are nearly black above and pink below; they get lighter with age.

Abundance. This is not an abundant species.

Economic Importance. These dolphins have no economic importance.

Miscellaneous. The dolphins living in the Amazon River are somewhat smaller and lighter in color than *S. guianensis* which lives in the marine coastal regions.

130

THE GUIANA COASTAL DOLPHIN
Also known as the White Dolphin
Sotalia guianensis (van Beneden, 1864)

Identifying Features. This is a very small dolphin, which differs very little from *S. fluviatilis.* Its size, lighter color, teeth, and locality should help to distinguish it.

Size and Shape. The Guiana Coastal Dolphin is a small species which is only slightly larger and darker than *S. fluviatilis* of the Amazon river. It grows to a length of about 1.7 meters (67 in.).

Color. It is a bluish gray to brownish hue on the back and shades gradually to white on the belly.

Distribution. This dolphin is a South American species which lives in the marine coastal waters and brackish estuaries from Lake Maracaibo, Venezuela, southward along the Atlantic coast as far as Santos (24° S.L.) in Brazil; it also occurs along the eastern coast of Central America.

Fins and Flippers. The dorsal fin is quite prominent in size, triangular in shape, and curved very slightly backward at the tip. The flippers are of moderate size; they are convex on their leading edge and nearly straight on their trailing edge; they terminate in a pointed tip. The tail flukes are wide, possess pointed tips, are slightly concave on their posterior margins, and exhibit a notch where they meet at the midline.

Teeth. The teeth are reported to number from about 26 to 35 in each of the four jaws. Some scholars (Nishiwaki) have reported the teeth to number from 32 to 35 in the upper jaw and from 31 to 33 in the lower jaw. They are irregularly arranged.

Skeletal Notes. See *S. fluviatilis* for the number of vertebrae and finger bones. Five pairs of ribs articulate directly with the sternum.

Habits. Not much is known of the habits of this species. It feeds upon shoreline fishes. It is reported to live in small groups of less than 10 individuals.

Swimming and Diving. Very little is known about this species in the wild. It is a leisurely swimmer and lives in quiet shoreline waters.

Reproduction. The young animals have been observed in February and March. They are nearly black above and pink below; they get lighter with age.

Abundance. This is not an abundant species.

Economic Importance. These dolphins have no economic importance.

Miscellaneous. The dolphins living in the Amazon River are somewhat smaller and lighter in color than *S. guianensis* which lives in the marine coastal regions.

The Guiana Coastal Dolphin, *Sotalia guianensis,* **is an uncommon species which was discovered by A.B. Van Beneden in the last century. Although it resembles** *Tursiops,* **it may be separated from this species by its teeth, which are more numerous than those of** *Tursiops.*

THE BOTTLE-NOSED DOLPHINS
Genus *TURSIOPS* Gervais, 1855

The bottle-nosed dolphins are sturdy, robust whales of moderate size. Their forehead descends quite gently to the snout or proboscis, but is separated from it by a transverse groove or constriction. This proboscis is prominent, tapering, and quite long, and is wider than in many other species. The teeth are relatively large with smooth, conical crowns and number from about 18 or 19 to about 26 in each of the four jaw bones. The dorsal fin is high and concave on its posterior border. The vertebrae, which number from 61 to 65 in this genus, are usually distributed approximately as follows: C 7 + D 14 + L 15 + Ca 29 = 65. The bones of the flippers are distributed approximately as follows: I (1-2), II (7-9), III (5-8), IV (2-3), V (1-2).

Although several species have been described, it is very doubtful if there is more than one species which exhibits considerable variation and is of wide range. A bottle-nosed dolphin from the North Pacific Ocean, sometimes called the Pacific Bottle-nosed Dolphin (*Tursiops gilli* Dall, 1873), is usually regarded as a geographical variety of *T. truncatus* and is sometimes listed as *T. truncatus gilli* Dall, 1873. It is somewhat darker in color and more slender than *T. truncatus* and is marked with a pink area surrounding the anus; in addition, the teeth are more robust than those of *T. truncatus*. In this book, it is listed as a synonym of *T. truncatus*.

Studies of these dolphins by various scholars indicate that several names of species appearing in older books are really duplicate names or synonyms of other previously named species. The following list indicates the older names and the more correct and current names of these species.

Old Name		Name Currently In Use
Tursiops abusalum	is now	*Tursiops truncatus*
Tursiops aduncus	is now	*Tursiops truncatus*
Tursiops catalania	is now	*Tursiops truncatus*
Tursiops dawsoni	is now	*Tursiops truncatus*
Tursiops fergusoni	is now	*Tursiops truncatus*
Tursiops gadamu	is now	*Tursiops truncatus*
Tursiops gephyreus	is now	*Tursiops truncatus*
Tursiops gilli	is now	*Tursiops truncatus*
Tursiops hamatus	is now	*Tursiops truncatus*
Tursiops nesarnack	is now	*Tursiops truncatus*
Tursiops nuuanu	is now	*Tursiops truncatus*
Tursiops parvimanus	is now	*Tursiops truncatus*
Tursiops perniger	is now	*Tursiops truncatus*
Tursiops tursio	is now	*Tursiops truncatus*

This genus is known from the Upper Pliocene Epoch in Europe.

The distribution of this genus is world-wide in temperate and tropical seas; it does not occur in polar regions.

This genus contains the single living species listed below.

Tursiops truncatus (Montagu, 1821)
THE COMMON BOTTLE-NOSED
DOLPHIN.................. See page 133

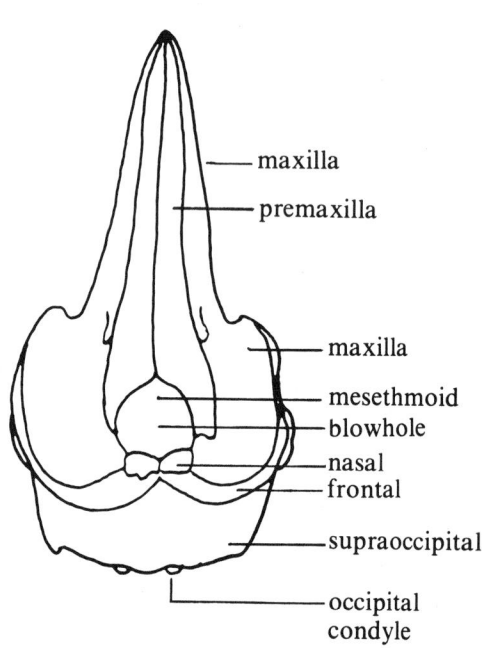

A diagram of the skull of the common bottle-nosed dolphin, *Tursiops truncatus*, in dorsal view.

Reprinted by permission of Louisiana State University Press from *The Mammals of Louisiana and Its Adjacent Waters* by George H. Lowery, Jr. Copyright © 1974 by George H. Lowery, Jr.

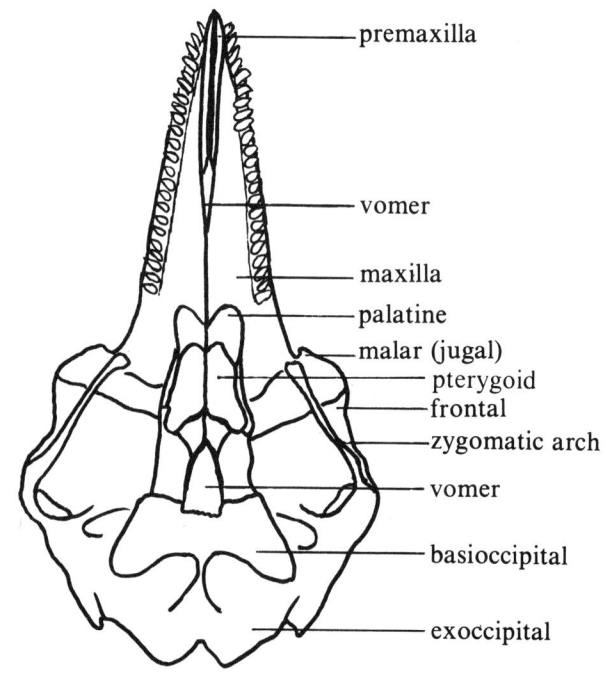

A diagram of the skull of the common bottle-nosed dolphin, *Tursiops truncatus*, in ventral view.

Reprinted by permission of Louisiana State University Press from *The Mammals of Louisiana and Its Adjacent Waters* by George H. Lowery, Jr. Copyright © 1974 by George H. Lowery, Jr.

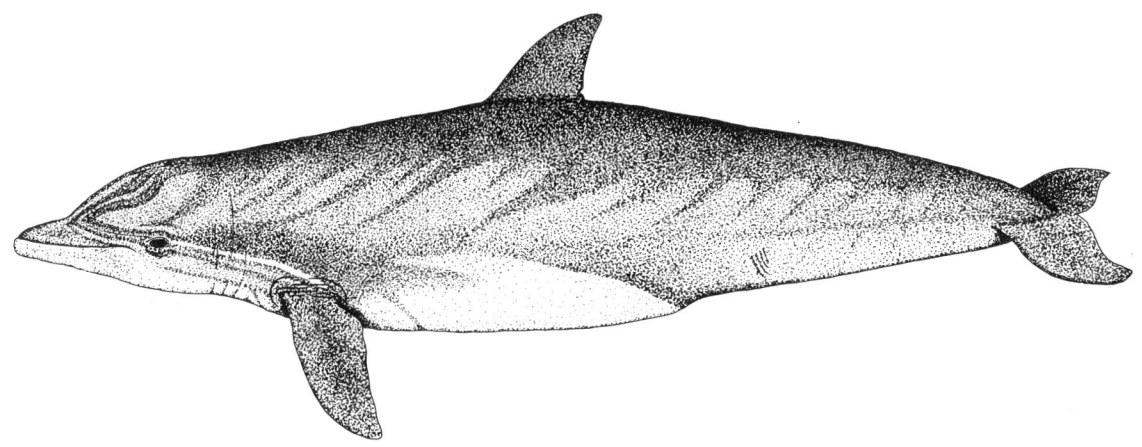

THE COMMON BOTTLE-NOSED DOLPHIN
Tursiops truncatus (Montagu, 1821)

Identifying Features. This dolphin may be identified by a combination of features. It is of medium size, is gray to brown in color, has a groove between the forehead and the beak, has a stout, robust proboscis, and has the lower jaw slightly longer than the upper jaw.

Size and Shape. The bottle-nosed dolphin is a medium-sized species, with a robust, spindle-shaped body. The head is likewise robust, the snout is cylindrical and short, and the lower jaw protrudes a short distance beyond the upper jaw. A transverse groove separates the forehead from the snout. They usually measure less than 3 m. (10 ft.) in length, although some are known which measured more than 3.5 m. (11½ ft.) or more. Adults will weigh from about 150 to 250 kg. (330 to 551 lbs.) or more. The males are slightly larger than the females.

Color. The body color of the back is uniformly a silvery-slate gray or brownish; the sides are lighter and shade gradually to a pinkish or white color on the throat and belly. A long, horizontal line often separates the upper and lower color fields. A faint, narrow line extends from the corner of the eye to the base of the flipper. An occasional specimen, perhaps old females, may be lightly spotted beneath; sometimes a wide darker band extends the length of the back. The flippers and tail flukes are darker in color. The eye is encircled by a black ring; the iris is brown. A few albino individuals have been known.

Distribution. This dolphin is world-wide in temperate and tropical seas. They are principally a coastwise species and usually frequent areas within the continental shelf where they are often seen in bays and harbors. In the Pacific Ocean, they extend from Japan and California southward to southern Australia and Chile; they occur in Hawaii and in the East China Sea. In the Atlantic Ocean, they extend from Norway and Nova Scotia southward to southern Argentina and southern Africa. In the Indian Ocean, this species extends from the Red Sea to the Cape of Good Hope and eastward across the Indian Ocean to western Australia, New Guinea, eastern Australia, and northward to Taiwan; it occurs throughout the tropical Pacific Ocean. It also occurs in the Mediterranean and Black Seas.

Some scholars believe tentatively that there may be two forms within this species:

1. a larger form which lives in cooler water and prefers the offshore areas, and
2. a smaller form which lives in warmer seas and which prefers shallower water.

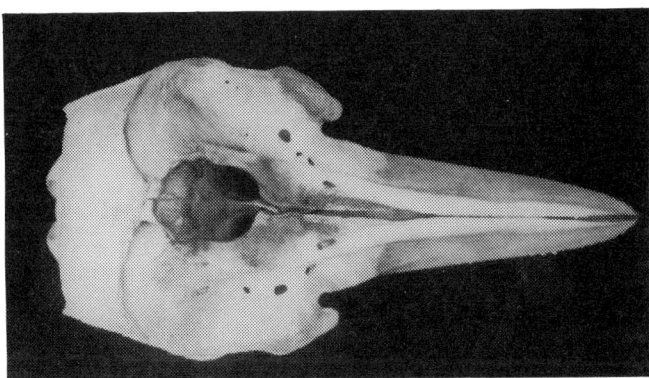

Photo of the skull of the bottle-nosed dolphin, *Tursiops truncatus,* in dorsal view.

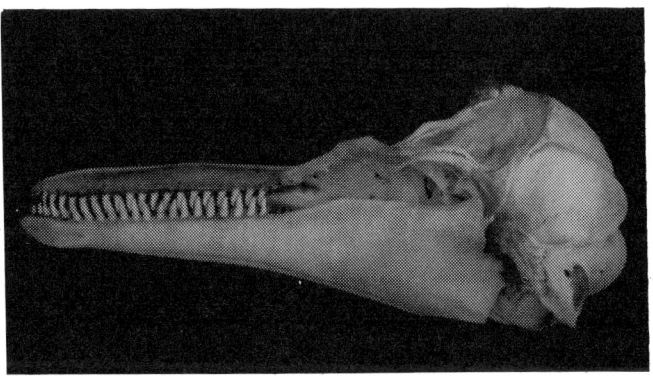

Photo of the skull and lower jaw of the bottle-nosed dolphin, *Tursiops truncatus,* in lateral view.

133

An albino common bottle-nosed dolphin *(Tursiops truncatus)* together with an animal of normal coloration.
Photo by Essapian.

A photo of the common bottle-nosed dolphin, *Tursiops truncatus.* Note the groove or crease which separates the forehead from the snout.

Migration. This is not a migratory species, although it may make small shifts of latitudes with the seasons.

Fins and Flippers. The dorsal fin is quite large and falcate in shape (convex in front, concave in the back) and is pointed somewhat backward at the tip. The flippers are curved on both edges and terminate in a rounded point. The flukes of the tail are wide, gently concave on their posterior margins, and exhibit a deep notch where they meet at the midline.

Teeth. The teeth are large, sharp, although often worn, measure about 10 to 13 mm. in diameter, and number between about 18 and 26 in each of the four jaw bones. Some scholars report the teeth to number about 20 to 26 in the upper jaws and about 18 to 24 in the lower jaws.

Skeletal Notes. In the neck, the 1st and 2nd vertebrae are united. The vertebrae are distributed about as follows: C 7 + D 12-14 + L 17 + Ca 26-27 = 61-64. Five pairs of ribs articulate with the vertebrae by two heads. Six pairs of ribs articulate directly with the sternum. The sternum has four parts. The bones of the fingers are distributed about as follows: I (1-2), II (7-9), III (5-8), IV (2-4), V (1-2).

Other Anatomical Notes. In a specimen which might weigh between about 150 and 200 kg., the brain might weigh between about 1300 and 1600 grams.

Food. The food of this species includes a wide variety of smaller shoreline fishes, including mullet; other foods will include squid and shrimp.

Swimming and Diving. These are sociable animals and will gather into schools of several hundred individuals. They often accompany pilot whales, hump-backed whales, and right whales. They will ride the bow waves of ships and have sometimes been observed swimming in the surf and riding breaking rollers along the beach. They will occasionally strand themselves on beaches. They are strong swimmers and have a maximum speed of about 15 knots (17 mi./h.). They can exceed this speed when riding the bow waves of ships. They are able to jump 6 meters (20 ft.) into the air and dive to a depth of about 300 meters (1,000 ft.).

Photo of bottle-nosed dolphins, *Tursiops* species, leaping within the enclosure at Sea Life Park. The two top dolphins are *Tursiops truncatus gilli* from the Pacific Ocean. The two dolphins at the extreme left and right are *Tursiops truncatus* from the Atlantic Ocean. The single dolphin in the middle and nearest to the camera is a hybrid resulting from a crossing of the other two species.
Sea Life Park, Hawaii.

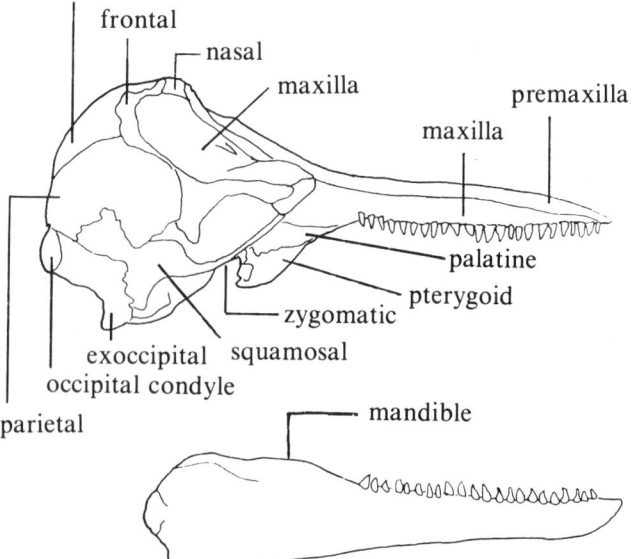

A diagram of the skull of *Tursiops truncatus* in lateral view.

Reprinted by permission of Louisiana State University Press from *The Mammals of Louisiana and Its Adjacent Waters* by George H. Lowery, Jr. Copyright © 1974 by George H. Lowery, Jr.

The above photo is of a young hybrid dolphin and its mother. The light-colored dolphin in the foreground is a female Atlantic bottle-nosed dolphin, *Tursiops truncatus,* and the mother of the smaller, darker dolphin in the background. The young, darker dolphin, a female, was fathered by a false killer whale, *Pseudorca crassidens,* and is therefore a hybrid individual. The young dolphin was born at Sea Life Park, Hawaii, on Wednesday, May 15, 1985, and weighed about 35 pounds (15.8 kg.) at birth. This photo was taken on May 17th when the hybrid was two days old.

Photo by Monte Costa.
Sea Life Park, Hawaii.

Reproduction. This dolphin mates in the spring (February to May in Florida) every two or three years. The gestation period lasts about 12 to 13 months and the young are nourished by the mother for 12 to 18 months. At birth, the young will measure from about 98 to 126 cm. (38 to 50 in.) or more and will weigh about 30 to 35 kg. (66 to 77 lbs.) at birth. It has been estimated that a dolphin which lives about 25 years will give birth to about 8 young individuals in that lifetime.

Abundance. The bottle-nosed dolphin is probably the most abundant species in the entire family of the *Delphinidae.*

Economic Importance. This dolphin does not have any economic value today, although it was once the basis of a small whaling industry off the eastern coast of the United States and elsewhere.

It is easily captured and easily trained and has therefore become an exhibit animal in various zoos and aquaria. These institutions consequently spend large sums of money to capture, buy, and maintain these animals for their exhibits.

Miscellaneous. Although the adult dolphins have no visible hair, there are a few sensory hairs in the embryo located on both sides of the upper jaw; they disappear after birth.

Various species of remora or sucker fishes (*Echeneiformes: Echeneidae*) are occasionally observed attached to this dolphin.

Photo of a female bottle-nosed dolphin, *Tursiops truncatus,* giving birth to a young individual.

Photo by Essapian.

From: K.S. Norris (ed.)—WHALES, DOLPHINS, AND PORPOISES. 1966. Pub. by the Univ. of California Press, Berkeley.

The common bottle-nosed dolphin, *Tursiops truncatus.*
Sea Life Park, Hawaii.

THE LONG-BEAKED DOLPHINS
Genus *STENELLA* Gray, 1866

This genus has been a very difficult group for scholars to study because most of the species within it are not clearly defined. In general, they are slender animals, of small to moderate size, and are marked with a color pattern of spots or bands upon the body. The forehead of these dolphins slopes gradually downward toward the base of the beak but is separated from this beak by a transverse groove; the beak itself is quite long and narrow. The teeth, which are small, pointed, and numerous, number from about 28 to 65 in each of the four jaw bones. The union (mandibular symphysis), where the two lower jaw bones meet in the front of the jaw, measures less than one-fifth of the length of the jaw bones. The vertebrae number between about 68 and 81 in the various species of this genus. The species of this genus also vary greatly in color; each species has its particular pattern and markings and these patterns in turn vary between individuals and also between geographical areas of the same species. Most have a dark band running from the base of the flipper to the eye.

The long-beaked dolphins are sociable and playful animals, rarely travel alone, and are most often seen in small groups.

In general, the long-beaked dolphins are found only in the tropical, sub-tropical, and warmer temperate seas of the globe.

This genus is known from the Holocene Epoch (Recent).

The Many Species of Stenella

More than two dozen species have been described and assigned to this genus, but many of these have proven to be identical to other species and are therefore regarded as synonyms. Of this number, possibly as few as *five species* may be valid, while the remainder are simply synonyms of these five species. This is a terrible tangle and will not be straightened out for several years to come. The following names form a partial list of some of the many species of *Stenella* which may appear in various books.

S. alope (Gray, 1846). Originally described from specimens of unknown origin, possibly Ceylon, now in the British Museum (Natural History). This is usually regarded as a synonym of *S. longirostris.*

S. asthenops (Cope, 1865). Originally described from two skulls of unknown origin now in the Academy of Natural Sciences of Philadelphia.

S. attenuata (Gray, 1846). Originally described from Pacific specimens of unknown origin. *This is a good species.* See description on the following pages.

S. clymene (Gray, 1850). Originally described as *Delphinus metis* Gray, 1846, from a single skull of unknown origin in the British Museum (Natural History) and later redescribed by Gray in 1850 as *Delphinus clymene* Gray, 1850. *This is a good species.* See description on the following pages.

S. coeruleoalba (Meyen, 1833). Originally described from a skeleton from off a beach on the eastern coast of South Africa and now in the Zoological Museum of Berlin. *This is a good species.* See description on the following pages.

S. crotophiscus (Cope, 1865). Originally described from a single skull of unknown origin now in the Museum, Peabody Academy of Science in Salem, Massachusetts.

S. dubia (G. Cuvier, 1812). Originally described from one or more skulls in the Museum National d'Histoire Naturelle in Paris. It is probably a synonym of *S. attenuata.*

S. euphrosyne (Gray, 1846). Originally described from a single skull in the Museum of the College of Surgeons in London. It is usually regarded as a synonym of *S. coeruleoalba.*

S. froenatus (Cuvier, 1836). Originally described from a specimen from the Cape Verde Islands. Some regard it as related to *S. frontalis.*

S. frontalis (G. Curvier, 1829). Originally described from the skull of a specimen taken near the Cape Verde Islands and now in the Museum National d'Histoire Naturelle in Paris. It is currently regarded as a form of *S. attenuata.*

S. graffmani (Lonnberg, 1934). Originally described from a skull and skin from the coast north of Acupulco, Mexico, and now in the Natural History State Museum, Stockholm. Some scholars regard this as a form of *S. attenuata.*

S. lateralis (Peale, 1848). This species was collected in the North Pacific Ocean by the U.S. Exploring Expedition. The type specimen was not preserved. It is a synonym of *S. coeruleoalba.*

S. longirostris (Gray, 1828). Originally described from a skull obtained off the west coast of Mexico and now in the Leiden Museum. *This is a good species.* See description on the following pages.

S. malayana (Lesson, 1826). Originally described from an East Indian specimen. This dolphin is probably *Sousa chinensis.*

S. marginata (Desmarest, 1855 ±). This is a synonym of *S. coeruleoalba.*

S. microps (Gray, 1846). Originally described from a Pacific Ocean specimen captured off Mexico. It appears to be a synonym of *S. longirostris.*

S. pernettensis (Blainville in Desmarest, 1817). This is the same as *S. pernettyi.*

S. pernettyi (Blainville, 1817). Originally described from a specimen obtained off the coast of Brazil. It resembles *S. plagiodon.*

S. plagiodon (Cope, 1866). Originally described from an Atlantic specimen of unknown origin. *This is a good species.* See description on the following pages.

S. roseiventris (Wagner, 1853). Originally described from a specimen from the Banda Sea in Indonesia. It was named for its pink belly. This appears to be a synonym of *S. longirostris.*

S. styx (Gray, 1846). Originally described from specimens from the west coast of Africa. This is regarded as a synonym of *S. coeruleoalba.*

It should be mentioned that the names of *Stenella dubia* (G. Cuvier, 1812) and *Stenella frontalis* (G. Cuvier, 1829), both first described from skulls, may yet appear as "full-blown" species, particularly *S. frontalis.*

Studies of these dolphins by various scholars indicate that several names of species appearing in older books are really duplicate names or synonyms of other previously named species. The following list indicates the older names and the more correct and current names of these species.

Old Name		Name Currently In Use
Prodelphinus	is now	*Stenella*
Stenella alope	is now	*Stenella longirostris*
Stenella asthenops	is now	*Identity is uncertain*
Stenella crotophiscus	is now	*Identity is uncertain*
Stenella dubia	is now	*Stenella attenuata*
Stenella euphrosyne	is now	*Stenella coeruleoalba*
Stenella froenatus	is now	*Stenella attenuata*
Stenella frontalis	is now	*Stenella attenuata*
Stenella graffmani	is now	*Stenella attenuata*
Stenella lateralis	is now	*Stenella coeruleoalba*
Stenella malayana	is now	*Sousa chinensis*
Stenella marginata	is now	*Stenella coeruleoalba*
Stenella microps	is now	*Stenella longirostris*
Stenella pernettensis	is now	*Stenella plagiodon*
Stenella pernettyi	is now	*Stenella plagiodon*
Stenella roseiventris	is now	*Stenella longirostris*
Stenella styx	is now	*Stenella coeruleoalba*

This genus is presumed to contain the five living species listed below.

A photo of the Pan-tropical Spotted Dolphin, *Stenella attenuata,* taken in the eastern tropical Pacific.
Photo by K. Sexton.
Reproduced by permission of the Dept. of Fisheries and Oceans, Dominion of Canada, from the Jour. Fish. Res. Bd. of Canada 32:7, July, 1975.

THE PAN-TROPICAL SPOTTED DOLPHIN
Also known as the White-Spotted or Bridled Dolphin
Stenella attenuata (Gray, 1846)

Identifying Features. This dolphin is best identified by its white lips and its spotted body; however, these body spots vary in size and number with age and with geographical location.

Size and Shape. In this species the body is small and spindle-shaped and usually measures between about 1.8 to 2.1 meters (71 to 83 in.) or more. As in most toothed whales, the males are very slightly larger than the females. They will weigh from about 90 kg. (198 lbs.) to 130 kg. (286 lbs.) or more. The beak is slender and is marked off from the forehead by a transverse constriction.

Color. The body of this species varies in color. They are usually iron bluish on the front upper part of the back and shade to a charcoal gray posterior to the dorsal fin. The beak is black with white lips and there is a white or lighter area on the center of the abdomen. The body is covered in the upper darker areas with small, light, grayish spots except along the midlines of the back and belly; on the belly, these spots often show up as darker spots against a lighter background. Some animals are almost a solid gray color. The young dolphins are born without spots and acquire them as they grow older, beginning with the belly and moving upward; they also have a very wide dark stripe or "cape" extending along the back.

Special mention should be made of the color forms and geographical races of *Stenella attenuata* which are listed below because they are especially complex. Dr. William F. Perrin has studied this difficult species with great success and has concluded that there are several geographical races represented here. *Stenella attenuata* (the spotted dolphin) appears to have the following four geographical races in the eastern Pacific Ocean:

a. *Eastern Tropical Pacific* (coastal form). This race of dolphins has been described as "relatively large, robust, (and) heavily spotted".

b. *Eastern Tropical Pacific* (offshore form). This race of dolphins is described as "smaller and more slender, spotted to a varying degree".

c. *Hawaiian Form.* This race of dolphins is described as "smaller yet, and less spotted" than the above two forms.

d. *Southern Form* (south of the Galapagos Islands). This race of dolphins is described as "less heavily spotted and smaller than their northern counterparts."

The dolphins of the Atlantic, Indian, and Pacific Oceans appear to be the same as those of the Eastern Tropical Pacific Ocean. (See "b." above.)

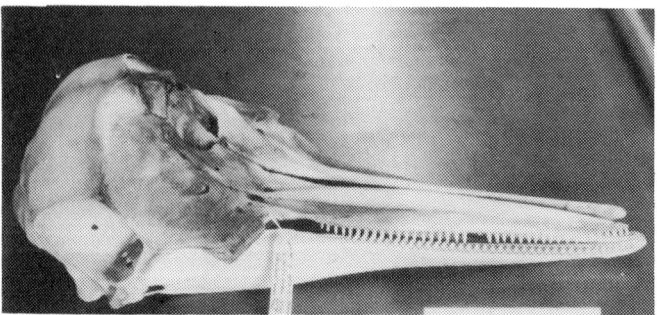

The skull of the pan-tropical spotted dolphin, *Stenella attenuata,* in dorsal view.
Photo by Michael Graybill at Cal. Acad. of Sci.

The skull and jaws of the pan-tropical spotted dolphin, *Stenella attenuata,* in lateral view.
Photo by Michael Graybill at Cal. Acad. of Sci.

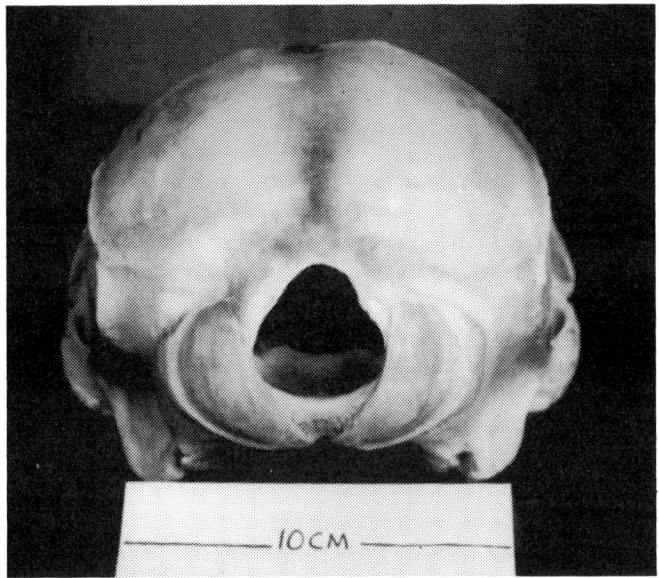

The skull of the pan-tropical spotted dolphin, *Stenella attenuata,* in posterior view.

Photo by Michael Graybill at Cal. Acad. of Sci.

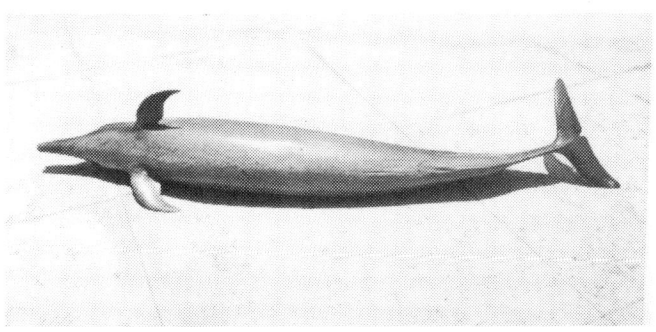

Photos of the pan-tropical, spotted dolphin, *Stenella attenuata.* **The lateral view shows the location and shape of the dorsal fin. The ventral view shows the shape of the head, flippers, and tail.**

Photos by Tinker.

Distribution. This dolphin is a warm-water species which is found world-wide in tropical and warm temperate seas. It occurs in the warmer areas of the Atlantic, Pacific, and Indian Oceans.

Migration. This is not a migratory species.

Fins and Flippers. The dorsal fin is of medium size, slightly convex on its anterior margin, and concave on its posterior margin; the tip is pointed backward. The flippers are convex on their leading edge and concave on their trailing edge; they terminate in a pointed tip. The flukes of the tail are quite wide; their posterior border is feebly concave in shape and exhibits a notch where they meet at the midline.

Teeth. The teeth are reported to number from about 35 to 45 in each of the four jaw bones. Nishiwaki reports the teeth as numbering from 41 to 45 in each of the upper jaws and 40 to 43 in each of the lower jaws.

Skeletal Notes. The vertebrae have been reported to number from about 77 or 78 to about 81. In the neck, the 1st and 2nd vertebrae are fused. The vertebrae are distributed approximately as follows: C 7 + D 15-16 + L 18-19 + Ca 37 = 78±. The chevron bones number about 24-25. The anterior pairs of ribs have two heads. Eleven pairs of ribs have a "middle rib bone." Five pairs of ribs connect to the sternum. The sternum has four parts. The digits of the fingers are distributed approximately as follows: I (2), II (9), III (7), IV (3), V (1-2).

Food. This species feeds principally upon squid, but it is known to eat surface fishes and also shoreline species, including herring, anchovies, and occasional carangid species. It feeds during the daytime.

Swimming and Diving. This species is a rapid swimmer; it has been timed at 21.5 knots (24.75 mi./hr.). It is known to occasionally ride the bow waves of ships.

Reproduction. The young are born in May and June in the northern hemisphere after a gestation period of about 11½ months; at birth they will measure about 90 cm. (35 in.) in length. The young are a uniform dark gray at birth, are white beneath, and are without spots until they approach maturity. This species will live to be at least 25 to 30 years of age.

Abundance. This is an abundant species. Schools of 2,500 dolphins have been observed following the schools of tuna fishes.

Economic Importance. This dolphin and other species of *Stenella* are associated with schools of tuna fishes and are therefore captured in the seine nets along with the tuna. In addition, these dolphins are hunted for their flesh by systematic drives by the natives of some areas; they have also been hunted on a commercial basis in some areas in Japan.

Miscellaneous. Included within this species are the forms of *S. dubia, S. frontalis,* and *S. graffmani.*

139

Class Mammalia — The Mammals
   Order Cetacea — The Whales
      Suborder Odontoceti — The Toothed Whales
         Family Delphinidae — The Ocean Dolphins and Porpoises

THE CLYMENE DOLPHIN
Also known as the Helmet Dolphin
Stenella clymene (Gray 1846, 1850)

Identifying Features. This dolphin is difficult to identify at a glance unless the viewer is trained or skillful in recognizing this species, because it has a strong resemblance to *S. longirostris* and *S. coeruleoalba* and is readily confused with them. However, a careful study of its color pattern may indicate its identity.

Size and Shape. The clymene dolphin is a small, slender species with a spindle-shaped body which tapers quite uniformly from its midpoint toward both the head and tail. Six adults which were measured ranged in length from 183 to 196 cm. (6 ft. to 6 ft. 5 in.). The beak is relatively short; it is neither as long nor as slender as the beaks of *S. longirostris* and *S. coeruleoalba*. Mature adults will weigh between about 70 to 80 kg. (154 to 180 lbs.).

Color. The color pattern of this species very closely resembles that of *S. longirostris*. The color pattern of both species consists of three color tones and three areas:
1. *a dark gray to black "cape"* covers the back of the body from the head three-fourths of the distance to the tail;
2. *a grayish lateral band* of varying width extends from the eye along the side of the body to the tail stock where it widens vertically to include the entire body and tail; and
3. *a white area* extends along the ventral surface of the body from the lower jaw to the anal area. This belly has a pinkish cast.

A distinctive feature of *S. clymene* is found on the side of the body beneath the dorsal fin; here the lower margin of the "cape" dips down in a gentle curve to nearly squeeze out the lateral band and to nearly touch the white area below. In *S. longirostris*, the upper and lower borders of this grayish lateral band are nearly parallel in the area below the dorsal fin. A narrow, dark stripe extends from the area of the anus along the lower border of the grayish area toward the eye. Another distinctive feature of *S. clymene* relates to the color band extending from the base of the flipper to the eye. In *S. clymene*, the borders of this band tend to converge slightly

as they approach the eye, while in *S. longirostris,* the borders of this band are parallel. The beak is dark at its tip and is marked above with a dark, longitudinal stripe which extends from the tip to the base of the beak. A light band, the width of the blowhole, extends from the blowhole forward to the base of the beak.

Distribution. The clymene dolphin is known from the temperate and tropical areas of the Atlantic Ocean. It is known from New Jersey to Florida, the Caribbean Sea, the Gulf of Mexico, Texas, the mid-Atlantic Ocean, Senegal (Africa), and the Gulf of Guinea (Western Africa).

Migration. Very little is known about the habits of this dolphin. It probably does not have a pronounced migratory pattern.

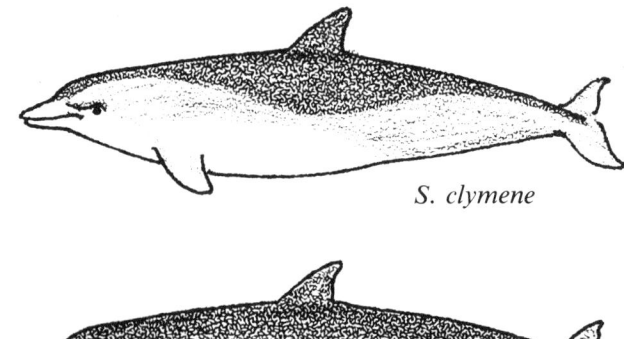

S. clymene

S. longirostris

Stenella clymene and *S. longirostris* are very difficult to distinguish. They differ in the width of the middle band below the dorsal fin.

From Wm. F. Perrin et al.—"Stenella Clymene, A Rediscovered Tropical Dolphin of the Atlantic." JOUR. OF MAMMALOGY 62:3, pages 583-598. 1981. Redrawn. By courtesy of Wm. F. Perrin.

Fins and Flippers. The dorsal fin is located at the mid-point of the back; it is somewhat triangular in shape with a very slightly rounded anterior margin and a concave posterior margin; the tip is somewhat acutely pointed. The flippers are slender, curved on both margins, and terminate in a pointed tip. The tail flukes are slightly concave on their posterior margin and are separated where they meet at the midline by a small median notch.

Teeth. The teeth are small, slender, tapering, and numerous; they number from about 39 to 49 in each upper jaw bone and from about 38 to 47 in each lower jaw bone.

Skeletal Notes. The skull of this dolphin is relatively short and broad when compared with the other species of *Stenella* and the beak is also quite short and broad. The vertebrae of this species are distributed as follows: C 7 + D 14-15 + L 17-21 + Ca 31-35 = 73-75.

Other Anatomical Notes. The bodies of some individuals show circular scars which are probably due to the bites of the small Brazilian Shark, *Isistius brasiliensis* (Quoy and Gaimard, 1824) in the family Dalatiidae.

Food. The food of this dolphin consists of squid, lantern fishes (Myctophidae), and doubtless other species. The remains of the many lantern fishes found in its stomach suggests that it feeds at night when these fishes come nearer to the surface.

Swimming and Diving. This species will leap and spin, but it does not leap as high or duplicate the involved spinning of *S. longirostris*. They will approach boats and will ride the bow waves. They are known to associate with *Delphinus delphis* and are often observed in schools of that species.

Reproduction. Information on the reproduction and life history of this species is not available; its habits doubtless very closely resemble those of the other species of *Stenella*.

Abundance. This is an uncommon species.

Economic Importance. This dolphin has no economic importance.

Miscellaneous. This species was originally described by J.E. Gray in 1846 as *Delphinus metis* based upon a single skull from an unknown locality. In 1850, Mr. Gray renamed the species *Delphinus clymene*. Thereafter scholars puzzled over this skull for about 125 years until a team of six scientists was able to identify living specimens and to better define its characteristics. This new redescription of *S. clymene* is in the Jour. of Mammalogy 62:3, August, 1981, pp. 583-598 (figs., photos, tables, biblio.).

The three species of *S. clymene, S. longirostris* and *S. coeruleoalba* are very closely related, similar in appearance, and are very difficult to distinguish. Scholars, who have studied these three species, believe that *S. clymene* is probably most closely related to *S. longirostris*.

A Table of the Teeth and Vertebrae of Three Species of Dolphins of the Genus Stenella

	Stenella clymene	Stenella longirostris	Stenella coeruleoalba
Number of Teeth			
In The Upper Jaw	39 to 49	48 to 64	39 to 51
In The Lower Jaw	38 to 47	47 to 62	39 to 55
Number of Vertebrae			
Cervical	7	7	7
Thoracic	14 to 15	13 to 16	13 to 15
Lumbar	17 to 21	16 to 21	22 to 23
Caudal	31 to 35	31 to 34	32 to 35
Total Number	73 to 75	69 to 75	71 to 79

From The Journal of Mammalogy 62:2, August, 1981

THE BLUE-WHITE OR STRIPED DOLPHIN
Also known as the Euphrosyne* Dolphin
Stenella coeruleoalba (Meyen, 1833)

Identifying Features. This dolphin may be recognized by a combination of features. It has a dark streak on the side of the body, but it has no criss-cross, hour-glass patterns, or yellow areas on the sides of the body. The teeth number between about 39 and 55 in each of the four jaw bones.

Size and Shape. The body of this dolphin is spindle-shaped and tapers uniformly from its center toward both the head and tail. It will reach a maximum length of about 2.7 meters (9 ft.) or more, but most are smaller and measure between about 220 to 235 cm. The forehead is low, rounded, and conical in shape and is separated from a rather prominent beak by a transverse constriction.

Color. In life, the body is a brownish color above and becomes a dark bluish color after death. It shades gradually to white on the belly; this white area extends forward to include the lower side of the proboscis. The side of the body is variously marked with stripes; usually, a short stripe extends forward and upward from the eye to the forehead; another stripe extends from the eye to the base of the flipper; and a long stripe extends from the eye backward to the area of the anus. This last stripe may give off one or two, short, black stripes which point toward the flipper. The eye is black, the proboscis is a blue-black color above, and there are no small spots on the body.

———————
*Euphrosyne (u-fros'-i-ne). One of the Three Graces in Greek mythology.

Distribution. This dolphin is distributed world-wide in tropical, sub-tropical, and warmer temperate seas; it is common in Japan, Hawaii, and the Mediterranean Sea. It has been reported as far north as Greenland and the Bering Sea.

Migration. In the North Pacific Ocean, they migrate with the changing seasons.

Fins and Flippers. The dorsal fin is roughly triangular in shape, has a concave rear margin with the tip pointing backward, and is located at the center of the body. The flippers are of moderate size and quite slender; they are convex on their leading edge, concave on their trailing edge, and terminate in a point. A low keel is present on the back at the tail and the notch on the margin of the tail is quite deep.

Teeth. The teeth of this dolphin are relatively small (3 mm. in diameter and 14-15 mm. long), sharp and pointed, and are inclined slightly inward. They number from about 39 to 55 in each of the four jaws. Among the dolphins, this species is exceeded in the number of teeth only by *S. longirostris* which has between about 46 to 65 teeth in each jaw bones.

Skeletal Notes. The vertebrae are distributed approximately as follows: C 7 + D 13-15 + L 22-23 + Ca 32-35 = 71-79. The first 5 pairs of ribs have double heads. The bones of the fingers are distributed approximately as follows: I (1), II (9-10), III (7), IV (4), V (2).

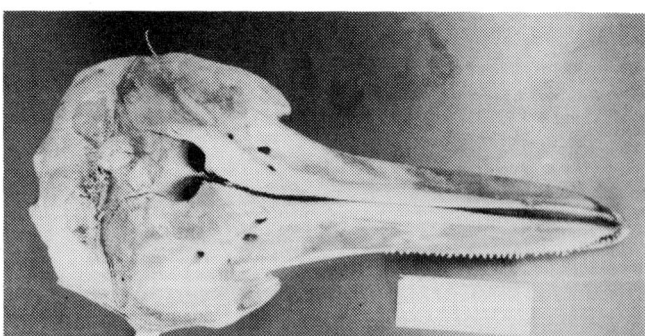

The skull of the blue-white or striped dolphin, *Stenella coeruleoalba,* **in dorsal view.**
Photo by Michael Graybill at Cal. Acad. of Sci.

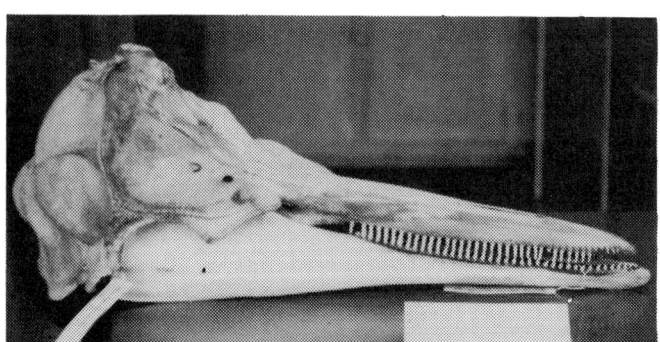

The skull and jaws of the blue-white or striped dolphin, *Stenella coeruleoalba,* **in lateral view.**
Photo by Michael Graybill at Cal. Acad. of Sci.

The blue-white or striped dolphin, *Stenella coeruleoalba.*
Photo by W.E. Schevill.

Food. The food of this species consists of squid, mackerel, sardines, etc.

Swimming and Diving. This is a sociable species which may gather into great groups led by one or more leaders. These groups may number from about 500 to 1,000 individuals, but some groups have been seen which exceeded 3,000 dolphins. Although a timid and mild-mannered species, they will approach ships and there ride the bow waves. They are reported to dive to depths of 100 meters, but never as deep as 200 meters; these dives last between 5 and 10 minutes.

Reproduction. In this species, the mating season is reported to be in May and June and again in November and December. The calves, which are born about every three years, will measure about 1 meter (40 in.) or more at birth. The gestation period is about 12 months and the young are nursed for about 18 months. The male dolphins are slightly larger than the females.

Abundance. This is one of the commonest species of dolphins in the warmer regions of the world.

Economic Importance. This species has long been hunted, captured, killed, and eaten in Japan. Because these dolphins associate with schools of tuna fishes, they are often captured in the purse seines along with the tuna; in this situation, the

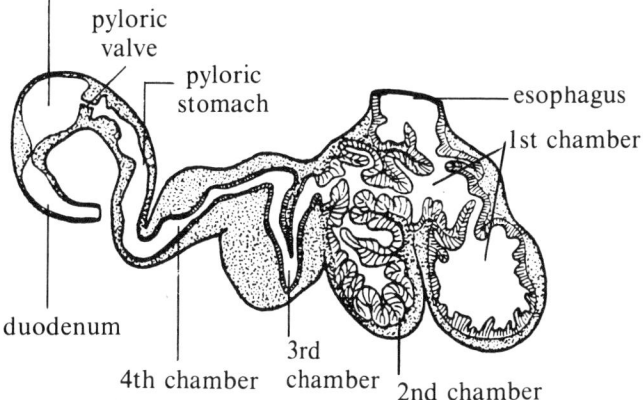

Diagram of the stomach of the blue-white or striped dolphin, *Stenella coeruleoalba* (Odontoceti: Delphinidae), in longitudinal section.

From: Gihr, M. and Pilleri, Gregorio — Investigations On The Cetacea. 1969. 1:15-65 (fig. 22C).

dolphins either drown, are killed, die upon deck, are freed from the net, or are thrown overboard from the vessel. These great catches of dolphins are the result of the ignorance, unwillingness, or inability of the dolphins to simply jump over the top of the nets which surround them.

Miscellaneous. On Sunday, March 2, 1958, a dolphin of this species appeared in the Ala Wai Canal, a drainage ditch in the Waikiki district in Honolulu, Hawaii. It was swimming slowly, not alert, and obviously sick and approaching its demise. It was captured in a large dip net by the author of this book, taken to the Waikiki Aquarium, photographed, and a skeleton prepared.

This species includes the color forms known as *S. euphrosyne, S. marginata,* and *S. styx.*

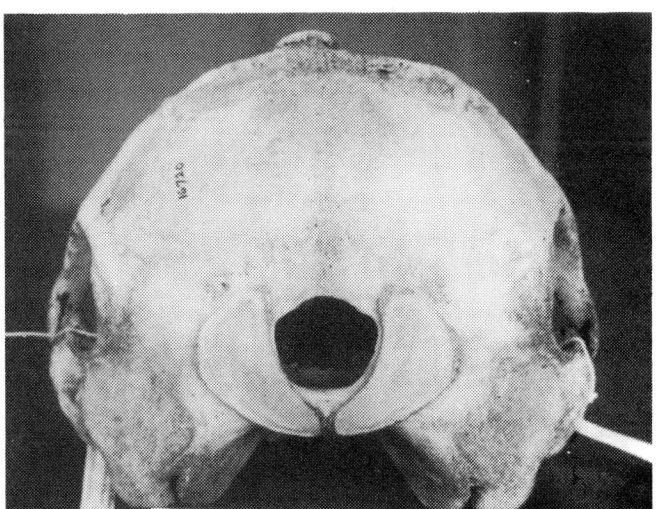

The skull of the blue-white or striped dolphin, *Stenella coeruleoalba,* in posterior view.

Photo by Michael Graybill at Cal. Acad. of Sci.

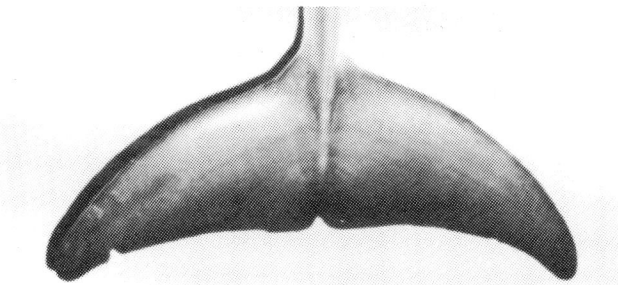

Photo of the tail flukes of the blue-white or striped dolphin, *Stenella coeruleoalba,* in ventral view.

Note the notch in the midline of the rear margin; this is a distinctive feature of the ocean dolphin and porpoise family *(Delphinidae).*

Photo by Tinker.

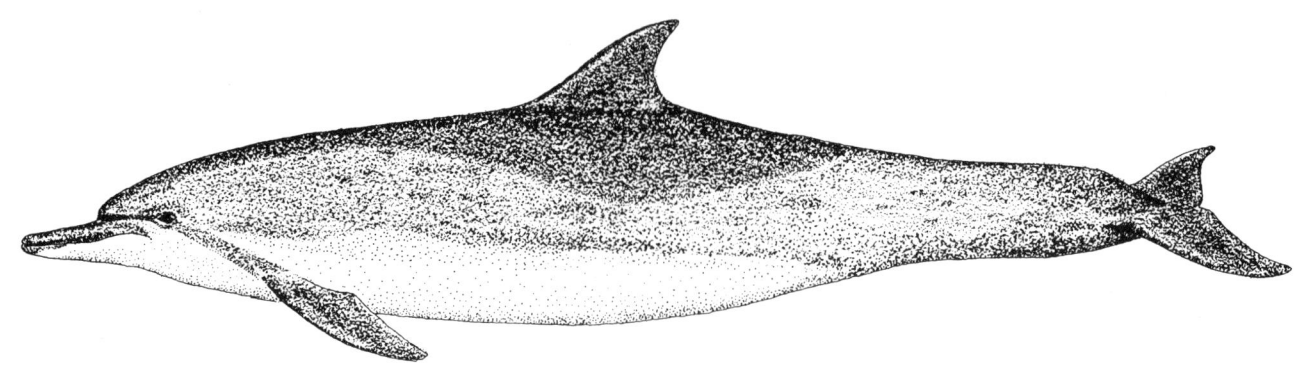

THE SPINNING DOLPHIN
Also known as the Long-snouted Dolphin
Stenella longirostris (Gray, 1828)

Identifying Features. Because this dolphin shows considerable variation in its color patterns, it is often a bit puzzling to identify. The slender body, the numerous teeth (46-65), the black lips, and the snout which is black above and white below, should identify this species. If it leaps from the water and rotates rapidly on the long axis of its body, it is this species. In some forms, the dorsal fin presents a nearly vertical anterior margin.

Size and Shape. This is a beautiful animal with a slender, streamlined body which is thickest just anterior to the dorsal fin and which then tapers uniformly toward the head and tail. The body of this dolphin will measure a maximum of about 2.1 meters (7 ft.) in length; most are smaller. Adults will weigh between about 70 and 80 kg. (154 to 176 lbs.). The proboscis is long and slender.

Stenella longirostris (the spinning dolphin) appears to have four geographical races in the eastern Pacific Ocean, according to Dr. W.F. Perrin.

a. The *"Costa Rican spinner"* from the coast of Central America. This is the longest and the most slender of these groups; it is gray in color.

Photo of spinning dolphins, *Stenella longirostris* (Odontoceti: Delphinidae). The mother is accompanied by its young which is only eight days old.

Photo by Nicki Clancey.

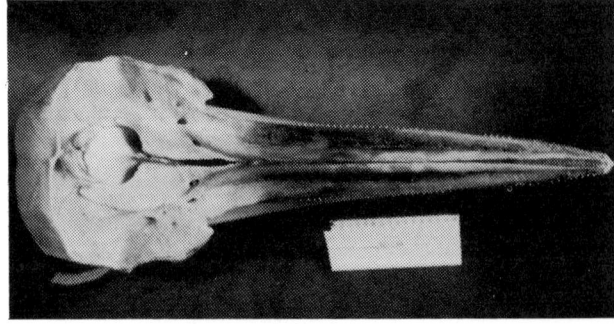

The skull of the spinning dolphin, *Stenella longirostris,* in dorsal view.

Photo by Michael Graybill at Cal. Acad. of Sci.

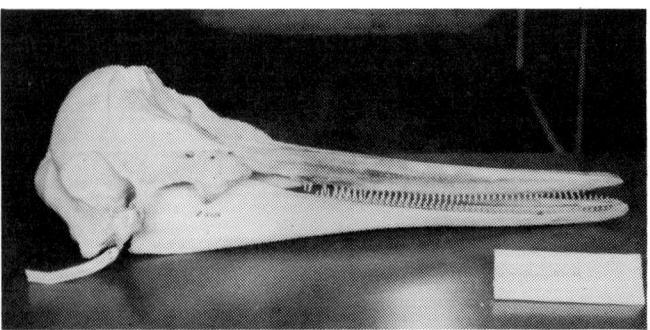

The skull and jaws of the spinning dolphin, *Stenella longirostris,* in lateral view.

Photo by Michael Graybill at Cal. Acad. of Sci.

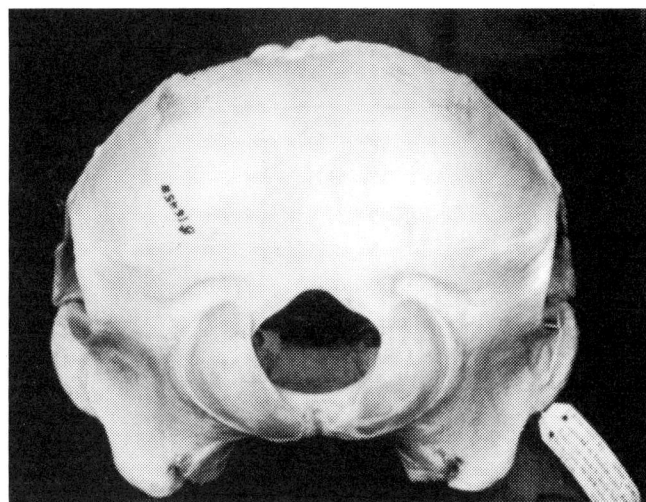

The skull of the spinning dolphin, *Stenella longirostris,* in posterior view.

Photo by Michael Graybill at Cal. Acad. of Sci.

b. The *"eastern spinner"* from the coast of North America seaward to about 800 km. (500 miles). This is an intermediate form between "a" and "c"; it is relatively short, slender, and gray in color.

c. The *"white belly spinner"* which lives in the offshore waters from about 145° W.L. eastward to a line about 500 miles off the coast. This form is relatively short, robust, and white in color below.

d. The *"Hawaiian spinner"* from the Hawaiian Archipelago. This form is relatively long and robust; it resembles the "white belly" form, but is larger. It is white below.

Forms "a", "b" and "c" above have a dorsal fin which is quite triangular in shape and which in "b" may have the tip of the dorsal fin directed slightly forward. Forms "a", "b", and "c" may show an enlarged region on the ventral side of the tail stock just posterior to the anus.

Color. In general, the color of the body is dark gray to black on the back, tan to yellowish brown on the sides, and white or light charcoal gray on the belly. The dark area of the back (cape) gets narrower anteriorly and extends to the base of the proboscis. The snout is black above and white beneath and the lips are black. In some individuals, the entire body is covered with fine gray spots. Large, old individuals are almost entirely black and are marked with light, faint speckles. Black lines extend from the eye to the base of the flipper and also from the upper lip backward above the corner of the mouth. There are no dark lines from the eye to the anus or to the tail. When viewed from the side of the body, the following areas are observed: a *dark area* on the back forward of the dorsal fin; a *dark area* in front of the tail which narrows anteriorly; and a *light area* which begins on the back and extends forward between the two darker areas. A few individuals have been reported which were pure white in color.

Distribution. This is a warm water dolphin which is worldwide in distribution. It inhabits the tropical, sub-tropical, and warmer temperate waters of the Atlantic, Pacific, and Indian Oceans. In the western Atlantic Ocean, it extends from Cape Hatteras, No. Carolina (35° N.L.) southward to Rio de Janeiro, Brazil (23° S.L.) It occurs in shoreline waters and also offshore areas.

Fins and Flippers. The dorsal fin is small and triangular in shape; its anterior and posterior margins are nearly straight and its tip is pointed and only very slightly inclined backward. The flippers are small in size and rather slender; their anterior and posterior margins are curved and the tip is pointed. The flukes of the tail are of medium size, are only slightly concave on their posterior margin, and exhibit a notch where they join at the midline.

Teeth. The teeth usually number about 55, although they may range in number from about 46 to 65 in each of the four jaw bones. They are more numerous than in any other species of whales.

Skeletal Notes. The vertebrae usually number between about 72 to 78. They are distributed approximately as follows: C 7 + D 15 + L 20 + Ca 36 = 78. Five ribs articulate directly with the sternum.

Food. It feeds upon squid and various small fishes which are captured and consumed at night.

Swimming and Diving. The spinning dolphin is a sociable species and gathers into small groups along the shoreline. It is also known to assemble into great herds of several hundred individuals. It approaches boats, will ride the bow waves, and will play in the waves about the boat.

Reproduction. The reproductive habits of this species do not differ much from those of the other species of *Stenella.* The gestation period approaches a year in length (possibly 10.5+ mo.) and the young, which are born singly, measure about 80 cm. (31-31.5 in.) at birth.

Abundance. The spinning dolphin is a very common species.

Economic Importance. This dolphin is associated with schools of tuna fishes and is captured with these fishes in the huge purse seine nets which are employed. The dolphins, unable to comprehend their danger, fail to jump over the net and often tangle in it, drown, or are pulled struggling or dead upon the boat with the tuna. This species is also caught by organized drives in some other areas of the world.

Miscellaneous. This species includes the forms known as *S. alope, S. microps,* and *S. roseiventris.*

Photo of spinning dolphins, *Stenella longirostris* (Odontoceti: Delphinidae), at Sea Life Park, Hawaii.

Class Mammalia — The Mammals
    Order Cetacea — The Whales
        Suborder Odontoceti — The Toothed Whales
            Family Delphinidae — The Ocean Dolphins and Porpoises

THE ATLANTIC SPOTTED DOLPHIN
Also known as the Gulf Stream Spotted Dolphin
Stenella plagiodon (Cope, 1866)

Identifying Features. This species resembles *S. attenuata* and is one of the several varieties or species about which there is considerable uncertainty. It is spotted over the body, except for the dorsal fin, flippers, and tail, and has a light streak along the midline of the back. The dorsal fin is rather acutely pointed and the beak is white-tipped.

Size and Shape. The body of this dolphin is spindle-shaped and tapers quite uniformly from the center of the body toward both the head and tail. The head is low and slopes gradually downward to the base of the beak where it ends in a transverse crease. The beak is quite long and slender and resembles those of the other species of *Stenella. The body* will measure about 2.2 to 2.4 meters (87 to 94 in.) or more in length and weigh between about 100 to 120 kg. (220 to 265 lbs.) or more.

Color. This is one of the many spotted dolphins. The back is a steel bluish color which shades to gray on the sides and finally to white or whitish on the belly. The upper part of the body is covered with lighter spots, while the lower surfaces are covered with darker spots; there are no spots upon the dorsal fin, the tail, or the flippers. A wide and broad band or cape covers the back of the body in young individuals and disappears as they grow older; the young are also unspotted. The beak or snout is tipped with white and the lips may be margined with white.

Distribution. This is an Atlantic Ocean species which occupies the offshore tropical and warmer temperate waters on both sides of this ocean including the Gulf of Mexico. They become less abundant north of Cape Hatteras, North Carolina (35° N.L.). Its distribution off South America is not well known.

Migration. This species has been reported to move into shallower inshore waters in the late spring and summer. This is an oceanic species and usually remains a short distance offshore (reported to be more than 5 miles) where the depth exceeds 100 fathoms (182+ m.).

Fins and Flippers. The dorsal fin is of moderate size, is curved backward, and is pointed at the tip. The flippers are quite large, are curved on both margins, and are bent backward. The flukes of the tail are quite wide, are concave on

their posterior margins, and exhibit a notch where they meet at the midline. Neither the fins, flippers, nor the tail is spotted.

Outline of the dorsal fins of two live *Stenella plagiodon* showing variation in form.

Drawn from Leatherwood.

Teeth. The teeth number from about 28 to 37 in each of the four jaw bones. They have also been reported to number from 30 to 36 in each of the upper jaw bones and from 28 to 35 in each of the lower jaw bones.

Skeletal Notes. The vertebrae are reported to be distributed approximately as follows: C 7 + D 15 + L 19 + Ca 36 = 77.

Food. The principal food of this species is squid; in addition, it eats herring, anchovies, and other species.

Swimming and Diving. This is a sociable dolphin and will occasionally gather into large herds which number in excess of 100 individuals; however, most herds number less than a dozen individuals. It is a curious species and will approach ships to ride the bow waves.

Reproduction. The adults mate vertically in the water in the summer season and the resulting young are born a bit less than a year later. The young are without spots when born and acquire them as they approach maturity.

Abundance. This is a fairly common species in the western Atlantic Ocean, particularly in warm water.

Economic Importance. This dolphin has no economic importance.

Miscellaneous. Various remora fishes (Echeneidae) attach to dolphins including this species and also to other dolphins, porpoises, and the larger whales.

THE SADDLE-BACKED DOLPHINS
Genus *DELPHINUS* Linnaeus, 1758

The saddle-backed dolphins are small, slender species which are streamlined in their·bodily contours. Their forehead slopes gently downward to the base of the beak, but is separated from the beak by a transverse groove or constriction. The beak is quite slender and contains many, small, acutely-pointed teeth; these usually number between about 40 and 58 in each of the four jaw bones. The palate of the upper jaw contains a deep, longitudinal groove on each side of the upper jaw. In this genus, the union (mandibular symphysis) of the jaw bones at the front of the lower jaw is less than one-fifth of the length of the jaw bones. The vertebrae of the backbone are reported to number between about 73 and 76. Of the seven vertebrae in the neck, the 1st and 2nd are fused together to form a single unit. Members of this genus rarely exceed 8 feet in length, although most individuals are 7 feet or less.

Within this genus, the color of the body is variable, but it is always darker above than below. The head is usually marked with a black ring which encircles the eye and also by a black line which extends forward from the eye to the groove which separates the forehead from the beak.

The distribution of this genus is world-wide in warmer temperate and tropical seas.

The exact number of species in this genus has not been clearly determined; this number ranges from one species to five or more. Some scholars recognize only a single species, *Delphinus delphis* Linnaeus, 1758, and then proceed to divide it into the three sub-species listed below.

1. *Delphinus delphis delphis* Linnaeus, 1758. The Common Saddle-backed Dolphin. This dolphin is world-wide in temperate and tropical seas; it sometimes enters fresh water.
2. *Delphinus delphis bairdi* Dall, 1873. The North Pacific Saddle-backed Dolphin. This dolphin inhabits the North Pacific Ocean.
3. *Delphinus delphis ponticus* Barabash-Nikiforov, 1935. The Black Sea Saddle-backed Dolphin. This dolphin is limited to the waters of the Black Sea. It is smaller in size.

Studies of these dolphins by various scholars indicate that several names of species appearing in older books are really duplicate names or synonyms of other previously named species. The following list indicates the older names and the more correct and current names of these species.

Old Names		Name Currently In Use
Delphinus acutus	is now	*Lagenorhynchus acutus*
Delphinus albimanus	is now	*Delphinus delphis*
Delphinus albirostris	is now	*Lagenorhynchus albirostris*
Delphinus algeriensis	is now	*Delphinus delphis*
Delphinus amazonicus	is now	*Inia geoffrensis*
Delphinus aries	is now	*Grampus griseus*
Delphinus attenuata	is now	*Stenella attenuata*
Delphinus bairdi	is now	*Delphinus delphis*
Delphinus bivittatus	is now	*Lagenorhynchus cruciger*
Delphinus blainvillei	is now	*Pontoporia blainvillei*
Delphinus bredanensis	is now	*Steno bredanensis*
Delphinus capensis	is now	*Delphinus delphis*
Delphinus cephalorhynchus	is now	*Cephalorhynchus commersonii*
Delphinus chinensis	is now	*Sousa chinensis*
Delphinus clymene	is now	*Stenella clymene*

Delphinus coeruleoalbus	is now	*Stenella coeruleoalba*
Delphinus commersonii	is now	*Cephalorhynchus commersonii*
Delphinus cruciger	is now	*Lagenorhynchus cruciger*
Delphinus cymodoce	is now	*Tursiops truncatus*
Delphinus densirostris	is now	*Mesoplodon densirostris*
Delphinus desmaresti	is now	*Ziphius cavirostris*
Delphinus didelphis	is now	*Delphinus delphis*
Delphinus dussumieri	is now	*Delphinus delphis*
Delphinus eschrichtius	is now	*Lagenorhynchus acutus*
Delphinus eutropia	is now	*Cephalorhynchus eutropia*
Delphinus fitzroyi	is now	*Lagenorhynchus obscurus*
Delphinus fluviatilis	is now	*Sotalia fluviatilis*
Delphinus fosteri	is now	*Delphinus delphis*
Delphinus frontatus	is now	*Steno bredanensis*
Delphinus fulvofasciatus	is now	*Delphinus delphis*
Delphinus gangetica	is now	*Platanista gangetica*
Delphinus geoffrensis	is now	*Inia geoffrensis*
Delphinus griseus	is now	*Grampus griseus*
Delphinus guianensis	is now	*Sotalia guianensis*
Delphinus heavisidii	is now	*Cephalorhynchus heavisidii*
Delphinus intermedius	is now	*Feresa attenuata*
Delphinus janina	is now	*Delphinus delphis*
Delphinus kingi	is now	Identity is uncertain
Delphinus longirostris	is now	*Stenella longirostris*
Delphinus major	is now	*Delphinus delphis*
Delphinus melas	is now	*Globicephalus melaena*
Delphinus moorei	is now	*Delphinus delphis*
Delphinus nesarnack	is now	*Tursiops truncatus*
Delphinus obscurus	is now	*Lagenorhynchus obscurus*
Delphinus orca	is now	*Orcinus orca*
Delphinus pallidus	is now	*Sotalia fluviatilis*
Delphinus pernettensis	is now	*Stenella plagiodon*
Delphinus peronii	is now	*Lissodelphis peronii*
Delphinus phocaenoides	is now	*Neophocaena phocaenoides*
Delphinus phocoena	is now	*Phocoena phocoena*
Delphinus plagiodon	is now	*Stenella plagiodon*
Delphinus plumbeus	is now	*Sousa chinensis*
Delphinus pomeegra	is now	*Delphinus delphis*
Delphinus ponticus	is now	*Delphinus delphis*
Delphinus rissoanus	is now	*Grampus griseus*
Delphinus roseiventris	is now	*Stenella longirostris*
Delphinus rostrata	is now	*Inia geoffrensis*
Delphinus sowerbensis	is now	*Mesopolodon bidens*
Delphinus tropicalis	is now	*Delphinus delphis*
Delphinus tursio	is now	*Tursiops truncatus*

In addition to the above species, the exact identity of the following dolphins is not entirely settled.

Delphinus capensis Gray, 1828. The Cape Dolphin.
   This dolphin, from the South Atlantic Ocean, South Africa, Japan, and elsewhere, is most often regarded as a synonym of *Delphinus delphis*.

Delphinus tropicalis van Bree, 1971. The Arabian Sea Saddle-backed Dolphin.
   The exact name and status of this dolphin is uncertain. It is regarded by some scholars as a variety of *Delphinus delphis*, while others regard it as a distinct species.

Delphinus roseiventris Wagner, 1853. The Red-bellied Dolphin.
   This species from eastern Indonesia has been transferred to the genus *Stenella* and may prove to be a variety or synonym of another species, possibly *Stenella longirostris*.

This genus is known from the Lower and Middle Pliocene Epoch in Europe.

This genus contains the single living species listed below.

Delphinus delphis Linnaeus, 1758
   THE COMMON DOLPHIN . . . . See page 148

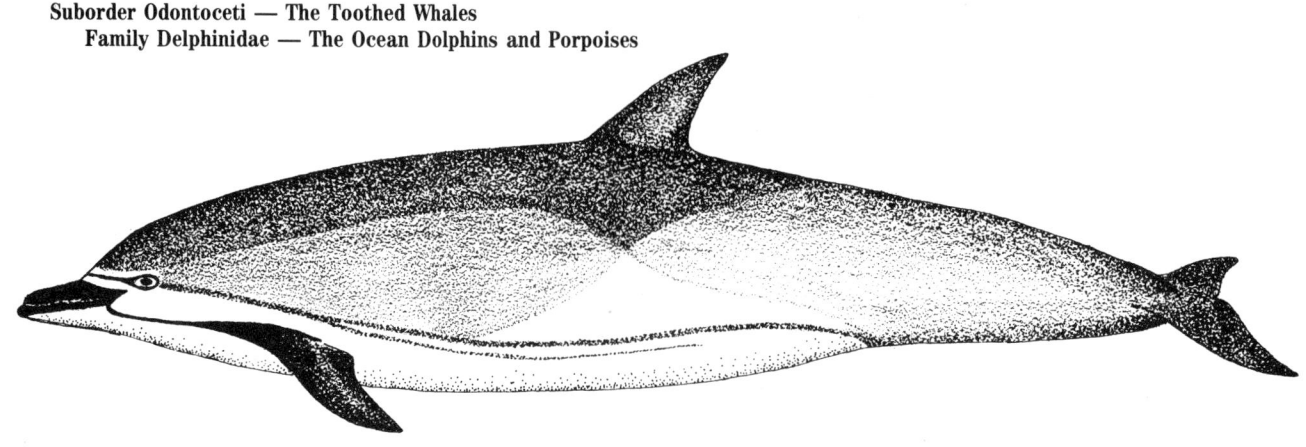

THE COMMON DOLPHIN
Also known as the Crisscross Dolphin
and the Saddle-backed Dolphin
Delphinus delphis Linnaeus, 1758

Identifying Features. This dolphin can be identified by a crisscross color pattern on the side of the body. It has a yellow patch on the side, a black line from the flipper to the lower jaw, and a black line from the eye forward to the junction of the forehead and the base of the beak. A black ring encircles the eye.

Size and Shape. The body of this dolphin is medium-sized, spindle-shaped, and very slender. The males, which are slightly larger than the females, will reach a length of about 2.6 meters (8½ ft.), but most are smaller. They will weigh between about 75 and 125 kg. (165 and 275 lbs.) or more. The tail stock is narrow, but it lacks the keels which are often found on its upper and lower edges. The proboscis is quite long and slender and is separated from the forehead by a V-shaped, transverse constriction.

Color. The typical color pattern of this species is a crisscross or hourglass design on the side of the body; this pattern varies considerably in both design and color in different geographical areas and in different population groups. The body is usually black to brownish above from head to tail and yellowish brown and gray on the sides. A dark line extends from the eye forward to the base of the forehead, and another dark line extends forward from the base of the flip-per to the corner of the mouth. The eye is encircled by a black ring and the snout may be white-tipped. This species resembles *Stenella coeruleoalba,* but exhibits a different pattern of stripes. Occasionally, a dolphin will be observed which is pure white in color. The color of this dolphin changes after death.

Distribution. This dolphin is a pelagic species which inhabits both coastal and offshore waters of the tropical, subtropical, and warmer temperate seas of the world including the Mediterranean Sea, the Black Sea, and the Gulf of Mexico; it enters bays and even occasionally enters rivers.

Migration. This is a non-migratory species.

Fins and Flippers. The dorsal fin is high, nearly triangular in shape, and has a pointed tip which is inclined slightly toward the rear. It is usually dark around its edges and lighter in color near its center, although it varies in both color and shape. The flippers are roughly triangular in shape and bear a pointed tip. The tail flukes are of the usual delphinid design and are black in color above and below.

Photos of the common dolphin, *Delphinus delphis,* at sea off the coast of Oregon.

Photos by Graybill.

148

Photo of the common dolphin, *Delphinus delphis,* **leaping in the southern ocean.**
R. Stewart.

From: "Whales and Dolphins of New Zealand and Australia" by A.N. Baker. Victoria University Press, Wellington, 1983. Courtesy A.N. Baker.

Teeth. The teeth of this species are small, pointed, and measure about 3 mm. in diameter. They usually number from about 40 to 58 in each of the four jaw bones; however, some dolphins have more teeth above than below and others are the reverse.

Skeletal Notes. The first two vertebrae of the neck are united. The vertebrae are distributed about as follows: C 7 + D 14 + L 21 + Ca 31-32 = 73-74. The chevron bones number from about 22 to 27. There are 14 pairs of ribs of which 4 or 5 pairs have intercostal ribs which connect to the sternum. The bones of the fingers are distributed about as follows: I (2), II (9), III (6-7), IV (3-4), V (1-2). A deep, longitudinal groove occurs in the roof of the mouth just inside each row of teeth.

Other Anatomical Notes. There is no caecum. In a specimen which might weigh between about 40 and 60 kg., the brain might weigh between about 650 and 800 grams.

Food. The food of this dolphin includes squid, herring, pilchard, anchovies, hake, etc.; in captivity it will eat sardines and mackerel.

Swimming and Diving. The common dolphin usually travels in schools, some of which have been observed to number more than 1,000 individuals, and schools exceeding 100,000 individuals have been reported. It will approach ships and follow them; here it usually spends its time riding the bow waves and frolicking nearby. It has been observed to pass ships which are doing from 15 to 18 knots. They have been measured in dives as deep as 243 m. (800 ft.). This species has been recorded in vertical jumps as high as about 6.6 meters (21½ ft.).

Reproduction. The adult dolphins mate in the spring and fall, the gestation period is estimated at 10 to 12 months, and the young are born in the early summer months of the following year. The young measure about 75 to 85 cm. (30 to 34 in.) at birth and contain a few sensory hairs upon their proboscis; these disappear in due time.

Abundance. The common dolphin is one of the most numerous and abundant of all whales.

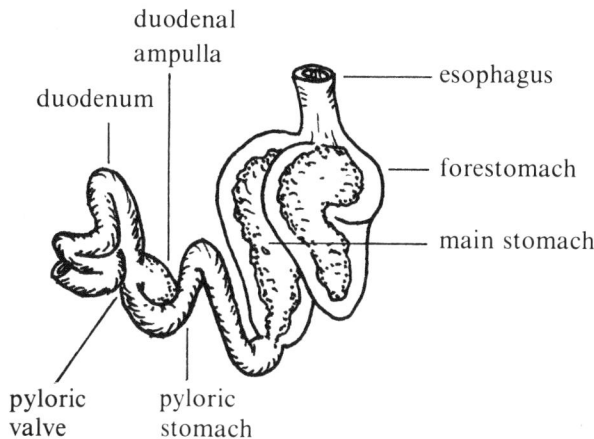

Diagram of the stomach of a fetus of the common dolphin, *Delphinus delphis* **(Odontoceti: Delphinidae).**

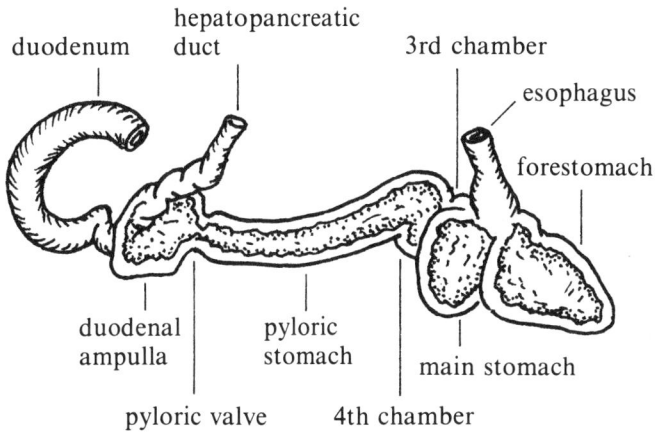

Diagram of the stomach of the common dolphin, *Delphinus delphis* **(Odontoceti: Delphinidae).**

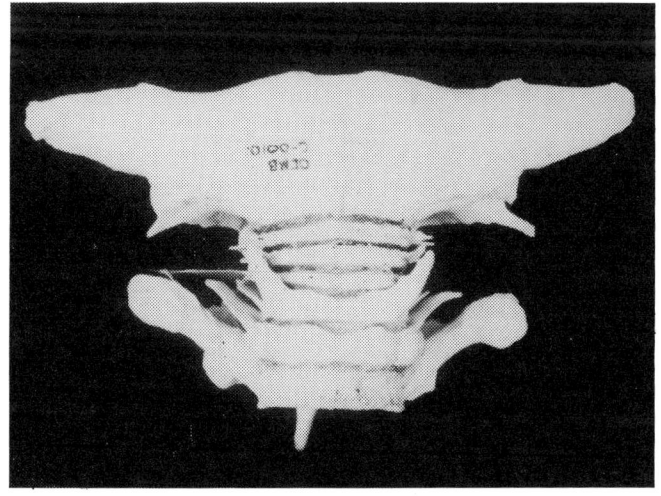

Photo of the cervical vertebrae of the common dolphin, *Delphinus delphis,* **in ventral view, showing the seven vertebrae fused into a single unit.**
Ore. Inst. Mar. Biol.

Economic Importance. This dolphin is often associated with tuna fishes and is therefore surrounded, captured, entangled, drowned, killed, etc., in large numbers in these fishing operations. In some area, including the Black Sea, these mammals have been systematically hunted for their flesh.

Miscellaneous. This species is occasionally captured and placed on exhibit, but it is not as easily trained as other species of small whales.

Scholars have decided that there are three or more groups or races of *Delphinus delphis* in the northeastern Pacific Ocean.

1. *a northern group, both coastal and offshore.* This group extends from central California southward into the Gulf of California.

2. *a southern coastal group.* This group extends from southern California into the Gulf of California along the eastern coast of Baja California.

3. *a warm water group.* This group is found seaward from Central America and extends southward and seaward for an unknown distance.

Other forms or geographical races within this species are known from several areas including the Mediterranean Sea, the Black Sea, the Atlantic Coast of Europe, and Japan. In addition, a form from near Arabia, known as *Delphinus delphis tropicalis* van Bree, 1971, which has a very long beak, may, after additional study, emerge as an additional species distinct from *Delphinus delphis*.

Photo of two common dolphins, *Delphinus delphis,* taken off the western coast of Mexico.

Photo by R.S. Wells.

Photo of a common dolphin, *Delphinus delphis,* taken off Baja, California.

Photo by R.L. Pitman.

Photo of a stranded common dolphin, *Delphinus delphis,* showing the hour-glass color pattern which is typical of this species.

Photo by L. Ullberg.

THE SHORT-SNOUTED, WHITE-BELLIED
DOLPHINS
Genus *LAGENODELPHIS* Fraser, 1956

Since these dolphins resemble the species of both *Delphinus* and *Lagenorhynchus,* they are usually considered as intermediate in form between these two genera. The body of these dolphins is quite robust, particularly forward of the dorsal fin, and measures about 2.5 meters when fully grown. The dorsal fin is described as triangular and pointed at the tip; the flippers are small, and the beak is short. The skull is reported to resemble those of the species of *Lagenorhyncus.* However, "the premaxillary bones are fused dorsally in the midline" and a pair of deep, longitudinal grooves is present on the palate; these features resemble the species of *Delphinus.* The teeth in this genus number from about 39 to 44 in each of the four jaw bones.

This genus was originally based on a single specimen from "the mouth of the Lutong River, Baram, Borneo." The species was named "after Dr. Charles Hose, a former resident of the Baram district," who collected a skeleton in 1895.

This genus contains the single living species listed below.

Lagenodelphis hosei Fraser, 1956
THE SHORT-SNOUTED, WHITE-BELLIED
DOLPHIN . . . . See page 152

THE SHORT-SNOUTED, WHITE-BELLIED DOLPHIN

Also known as Fraser's Dolphin, the Sarawak Dolphin,
and the Bornean Dolphin
Lagenodelphis hosei Fraser, 1956

Identifying Features. The stout, robust body together with the very short beak, a small, dark fin, very short flippers, and the three longitudinal stripes on the body should help to identify this species.

Size and Shape. The body of this species is plump and robust, particularly in the area in front of the dorsal fin. The body is of medium size and will reach a length of about 2.5 meters (98 in.). It will weigh from about 80 to 100 kg. (176 to 220 lbs.). The beak is short, but distinct and plainly visible.

Color. The back of the body is gray to black in color from the head to the tail. The belly is white in color with a pinkish tinge from the lower jaw to the area of the anus. Between these areas are three, parallel, longitudinal stripes: (1) an upper light stripe which begins above the eye and extends to a point midway between the anus and the tail; (2) a dark middle stripe which begins above the eye and extends backward to an area behind the anus; and (3) a light stripe which begins both above and below the eye and which extends backward and downward to end posterior to the anus. The eye is surrounded by a dark area which extends forward a short distance as a narrow band. The snout and lips are dark and a dark band extends from the lower jaw to the base of the flipper. The dorsal fin, flippers, and tail flukes are dark grayish to black in color.

Distribution. This is a tropical species which is widely distributed in the warmer waters of the world. It occurs in the Atlantic, Pacific, and Indian Oceans from the coast of Africa eastward across the Indian Ocean to the East Indies, Australia, and Japan, and then across the entire tropical Pacific Ocean to the Americas. It occurs in the tropical Atlantic Ocean including the West Indies. It appears to be an oceanic species which ranges between 40° N.L. and 40° S.L.

Migration. This is not a migratory species.

Fins and Flippers. The dorsal fin is small, triangular in outline, only slightly falcate in shape, and pointed at the tip. Dorsal and ventral keels occur on the tail stock. The flippers are very small, are dark colored above and below, and are attached to the light colored area on the side of the body. The flukes of the tail are dark in color above and below.

Teeth. The teeth number between about 39 to 44 in each of the four jaw bones.

Skeletal Notes. The vertebrae are distributed about as follows: C 7 + D 14 + L 21 + Ca 39 = 81.

Other Anatomical Notes. The blowhole is located very slightly to the left of the midline.

Food. It subsists upon squid and various surface and subsurface fishes.

Photo of the short-snouted, white-bellied dolphin, *Lagenodelphis hosei,* captured in Fiji in 1930. L. Turley.

From: "Whales and Dolphins of New Zealand and Australia" by A.N. Baker. Victoria University Press, Wellington, 1983. Courtesy A.N. Baker.

Swimming and Diving. This dolphin is a sociable animal and has been observed in small groups and also in large herds which exceeded 500 individuals. They have been described as "aggressive swimmers" and are believed by some scholars to be deep divers. They do not follow ships. They often associate in herds with *Stenella attenuata, S. longirostris, S. plagiodon,* and *Peponocephala electra.*

Reproduction. Very little is known of the habits of this species.

Abundance. This species appears to be quite common within its range.

Economic Importance. This dolphin associates with tuna fishes and in these situation is often captured in the huge purse seines of the tuna boats; here it is usually entangled, drowned, or killed, but rarely liberated.

Miscellaneous. This species was first known from a skull and skeleton found sometime before 1895 on a beach in Sarawak. It was first described by F.C. Fraser in the Sarawak Museum Journal, December, 1956.

Photo of *Lagenodelphis hosei* aboard the deck of a tuna boat following its capture in a tuna purse seine.
Photo by J. La Grange.

Photo of *Lagenodelphis hosei* showing some of the details of the head.
Photo by J. La Grange.

Photo of a young, immature specimen of *Lagenodelphis hosei* captured in a tuna purse seine. The color pattern of this juvenile differs from that of the adult during the first few months of life.
Photo by L. Ford.

Photo of a group of three *Lagenodelphis hosei* taken about 500 miles west of southern Equador showing the dark lateral stripe and the blunt beak.
Photo by J.F. Lambert.

THE WHITE-SIDED DOLPHINS
Genus *LAGENORHYNCHUS* Gray, 1846

The bodies of these dolphins are small and spindle-shaped and taper quite uniformly toward both extremities. The beak is short and broad at its base and is separated from the head by the usual transverse constriction. The caudal peduncle at the end of the trunk is deep vertically and is laterally compressed; a distinct dorsal and ventral crest or keel extends along the upper and lower margins of this peduncle. The dorsal fin is large, tall, and pointed at its tip and the flippers are curved and pointed. The vertebrae usually number about 80 in all, but their number may vary from as few as 74 to as many as 92. The union (mandibular symphysis) of the jaw bones at the front of the jaw usually measures about one-fifth or less of the length of the jaw bones. The teeth are small and number from about 22 to 40 or more in each of the four jaw bones. Some species may reach a length of 3 meters (9.8 ft.), but most are much smaller.

Studies of these dolphins by various scholars indicate that several names of species appearing in older books are really duplicate names or synonyms of other previously named species. The following list indicates the older names and the more correct and current names of these dolphins.

Older Names		Names Currently In Use
Lagenorhynchus coeruleoalba	is now	*Stenella coeruleoalba*
Lagenorhynchus electra	is now	*Peponocephala electra*
Lagenorhynchus fitzroyi	is now	*Lagenorhynchus obscurus*
Lagenorhynchus floweri	is now	*Cephalorhynchus commersonii*
Lagenorhynchus ognevi	is now	*Lagenorhynchus obliquidens*
Lagenorhynchus superciliosus	is now	*Lagenorhynchus obscurus*
Lagenorhynchus thicolea	is now	Of uncertain identity
Lagenorhynchus wilsoni	is now	*Lagenorhynchus cruciger*
Sagmatius amblodon	is now	*Lagenorhynchus australis*

This genus includes six species of which three species inhabit the northern hemisphere and three species inhabit the southern hemisphere.

The species, *Lagenorhynchus electra* Gray, 1846, has been removed from this genus and is now known as *Peponocephala electra* (Gray, 1846).

This genus is known only from the Holocene Epoch (Recent).

This genus contains the six living species listed below.

Northern Species

Southern Species

A photo of six Pacific white-sided dolphins, *Lagenorhynchus obliquidens*, taken off northern California. Note that the shape of the dorsal fin is strongly convex on its anterior margin and strongly concave on its posterior margin.

Photo by W.C. Flerx.

THE ATLANTIC WHITE-SIDED DOLPHIN
Lagenorhynchus acutus (Gray, 1828)

Identifying Features. A combination of characters will help identify this species: (1) a robust body, (2) a very short beak, (3) a black back and white belly, and (4) a band of white or yellowish white on the side of the body which begins below the dorsal fin and extends backward. It may also be recognized by a yellowish flash as it surfaces.

Size and Shape. This is a medium-sized dolphin with a spindle-shaped body which will reach a length of about 3 meters (9 ft. 10 in.) and weigh about 180 to 200 kg. (396 to 441 lbs.) or more. The tail stock is deep and wide and narrows laterally just in front of the tail flukes; this is a distinctive feature of this species. The snout is very short and will measure about 5 cm. (2 in.) from its tip to the deep, transverse groove which separates it from the forehead. The forehead is low in front and slopes very gradually upward.

Color. The back is black, the belly is white, and the sides are marked with gray, tan, and yellowish-white colors of which the most prominent is a large, oval, white to yellowish area which begins below the dorsal fin and extends backward to above the anus. The beak is all black and the edges of the lower jaw may be either black or white. The dorsal fin may be both black and gray; the eye is not encircled by black; and a line of varying intensity may extend from the mouth and/or eye to the base of the flipper. The area surrounding the anus is black. The color of this species varies; some individuals are almost white in color.

Distribution. This dolphin is a species of the North Atlantic Ocean where it is distributed from Davis Straits and southern Greenland eastward to Norway and southward to the latitude of New York City and the British Isles.

Migration. Little is known of its migratory habits, although it is sometimes stranded in great numbers.

Fins and Flippers. The dorsal fin is located just forward of the center of the body and is tall, curved backward, and pointed. The dorsal fin is followed by a keel which extends toward the tail; a ventral keel is also present. The flippers are small, triangular in shape, curved backward, and pointed; the flippers are black but are attached in a white area. The flukes of the tail connect at their midline with very high dorsal and ventral keels from the tail stock. The flukes are notched where they join at the midline.

Teeth. The teeth are pointed, are relatively small (5± mm. in diameter), and number between about 30 and 40 in each of the four jaw bones.

Skeletal Notes. The vertebrae are distributed approximately as follows: C 7 + D 15 + L 18-22 + Ca 38± = 78-82. The two front vertebrae of the neck are united. There are 15 pairs of ribs of which 6 have two heads. The bones of the fingers are distributed approximately as follows: I (1-2), II (10), III (6), IV (2-3), V (2).

Food. The food of this animal includes squid, herring, and other species.

Swimming and Diving. These dolphins are sociable animals and gather into herds usually of 40 to 50 individuals, but occasionally are seen in great groups which number more than 1,000 individuals. They do not regularly follow ships or often play in their bow waves. They are often seen in the company of pilot whales.

Reproduction. The gestation period is about 10 months and the young, which measure about 95 cm. (37 in.) or more at birth, are born in the spring and early summer. Its life span may approach 30 years.

Abundance. This is an abundant species in the areas of its range.

Economic Importance. Occasionally, this species is captured with pilot whales, but it does not support an organized fishery.

THE WHITE-BEAKED DOLPHIN
Lagenorhynchus albirostris (Gray, 1846)

Identifying Features. A tentative identification may be made on the basis of the color of the body. The dorsal fin is black; this black color also extends down onto the side of the back and body. This black area on the side of the body is bordered in both front and back by large white areas. The beak is usually white-tipped.

Size and Shape. The body of this dolphin is quite robust in shape and will reach a length of about 3+ meters (9 ft. 10 in.) or more; most, however, are smaller. The beak is broad, short, and distinct and is marked off from a low forehead by the usual transverse crease.

Color. The body of this dolphin is black above and white beneath. The black area surrounding the dorsal fin extends downward onto the back and sides and in this area is bordered anteriorly and posteriorly by large white areas; of these white areas, the most obvious is the large area on the back behind the dorsal fin. Black also covers the flippers, the tail stock, and the tail flukes. The white area of the belly extends forward to the lower jaw but does not extend above the flippers. The beak varies in color from white to gray, both above and below, and the snout is usually white-tipped. The eye is surrounded by black and a speckled area sometimes occurs just behind it. The area behind the blowhole is marked with white. A narrow, black line extends from the corner of the mouth to the base of the flipper. Specimens from the eastern Atlantic Ocean are reported to have beaks which are lighter in color than those from the western Atlantic Ocean.

Distribution. This is a cold-water species which is commonest in the western North Atlantic Ocean. It occurs from Labrador, the Davis Strait, and Greenland eastward to Norway and the Barents Sea and southward to Massachusetts and France.

Migration. This dolphin travels north and south with the seasons. In the spring and summer, they are found in the Davis Strait west of Greenland, but they move southward from autumn to the end of November. They winter in the latitudes north of Cape Cod (42° N.L.) and remain there until April to June, or even July, when they again begin their northward journey.

Fins and Flippers. The dorsal fin of this dolphin is quite large and tall and its concave posterior margin gives it a sickle-shaped appearance. It is usually dark gray in color. The flippers are triangular in shape and are pointed at the tip; they are black in color. The flukes of the tail are dark in color above and below and are notched at their midline.

Teeth. The teeth measure about 6 mm. in diameter and number between about 22 to 28 in each of the four jaw bones; they are usually more numerous in the upper jaws.

Skeletal Notes. The vertebrae are distributed approximately as follows: C 7 + D 14-16 + L 24-27 + Ca 43-45 = 88-93. The usual number is about 93 vertebrae. There are usually 15 pairs of ribs of which the anterior 5, 6, or 7 pairs may have 2 heads. The digits of the fingers are distributed as follows: I (3), II (7), III (5), IV (2), V (1).

Other Anatomical Notes. The tail stock bears keels both above and below. Because this is a cold-water species, it has a thick layer of fat enclosing the body.

Food. This dolphin eats squid and octopus, herring, sardines, cod, capelin, etc., and sometimes bottom-living crustacea.

Swimming and Diving. This animal is a sociable species and is usually seen in very small herds, however, some herds will occasionally exceed 1,500 individuals. It does not usually follow ships and is rarely observed riding the bow waves or lingering nearby.

Reproduction. The young, which are born in the summertime, measure between about 1 meter (39 in.) and 1.2 meters (48 in.) at birth.

Abundance. This is an abundant species.

Economic Importance. There are no large fisheries for this dolphin. It is captured in small numbers in scattered locations throughout its range.

THE PACIFIC WHITE-SIDED DOLPHIN
Lagenorhynchus obliquidens Gill, 1865

Identifying Features. The beak of this species is so short that it is scarcely visible in front of the forehead. The dorsal fin is large, curved, and marked with two colors; it is black along its anterior margin and gray along its posterior border. A diagonal white stripe on the side of the back is also helpful in identification.

Size and Shape. The body of this dolphin is spindle-shaped, stocky, and thick-set. It will reach a length of about 2.0 to 2.3 meters (78 to 90 in.), but most are smaller. Large individuals which measure as much as 2.13 meters (7 ft.) in length might weigh 114 kg. (250 lbs.) or more. A pregnant female dolphin was recorded as weighing 95 kg. (209 lbs.).

Color. The back of the body is a greenish black color and the belly is white. The sides of the body are light grayish and shade gradually to black above and white below. A white stripe begins on the side of the body forward of the dorsal fin and continues diagonally downward toward the anus. It is interesting to note that the dorsal fin is black on its anterior margin and gray on its posterior margin. The lips and the eyes are usually in the dark areas. The edges of the white areas are well defined. A few pure white dolphins of this species have been reported from areas offshore from California.

Distribution. This is a temperate-water species which is limited to the North Pacific Ocean. On the east, it ranges from south-eastern Alaska southward to Baja California and on the west from Kamchatka southward to Taiwan (Formosa). It occurs in the Sea of Japan, but it does not occur in the Bering Sea.

Migration. Along the seacoast of California, this dolphin appears to spend the winter and spring seasons along the coastline and to then move seaward during the summer and fall months. In the winter and spring these dolphins feed upon the anchovies, *Engraulis mordax,* which are abundant in large schools in fairly deep water close to shore; in the summer, the dolpins move offshore to feed upon the saury, *Cololabis saira,* which is abundant there in large schools.

Fins and Flippers. The dorsal fin is large, convex on its front margin, and strongly concave on its rear margin. The flippers are of medium size, triangular in shape, and widest at their base. Both the flippers and the tail are black in color above and below. The flukes of the tail bear a notch where they meet at the midline.

Teeth. The teeth measure from about 3 to 5 mm. in diameter and number from about 23 to about 34 (usually 30) in each of the four jaw bones.

Skeletal Notes. The vertebrae usually number about 74 in all and are distributed about as follows: C 7 + D13-14 + L 20-24 + Ca 30-34 = 73-78. The 1st and 2nd vertebrae of the neck are united. The 1st 6 pairs of ribs have 2 heads. The bones of the fingers are distributed approximately as follows: I (1-2), II (6-8), III (6), IV (2-3), V (1-2).

Photo of a female Pacific white-sided dolphin, *Lagenorhynchus obliquidens,* leaping in the pool at the Vancouver Public Aquarium in Vancouver, British Columbia.
Photo by The Vancouver Public Aquarium.

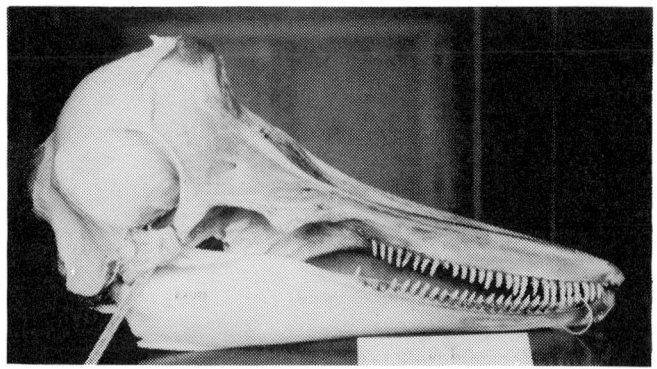

The skull and jaws of the Pacific white-sided dolphin, *Lagenorhynchus obliquidens,* in lateral view.
Photo by Michael Graybill at Cal. Acad. of Sci.

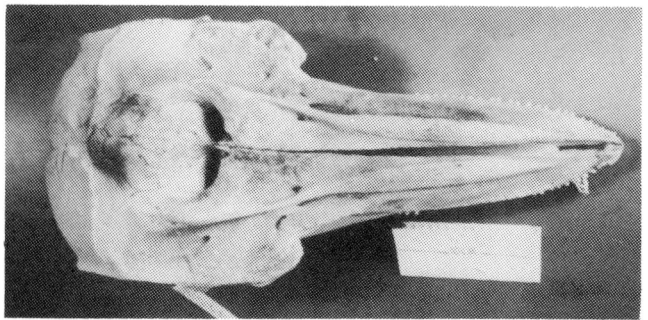

The skull of the Pacific white-sided dolphin, *Lagenorhynchus obliquidens,* in dorsal view.
Photo by Michael Graybill at Cal. Acad. of Sci.

Other Anatomical Notes. The tail stock is without significant keels.

Food. Anchovies, squid, and a wide variety of fishes make up the diet of this dolphin.

Swimming and Diving. This dolphin is an active, energetic swimmer. It is a sociable animal and usually gathers into small herds of 20 or more individuals, although some herds are observed which include several hundred dolphins. They will join groups of other whales, including *Stenella coeruleoalba* and *Grampus griseus.* It will approach ships where it may ride the bow waves or frolic in the waves nearby. When caught in nets it often escapes through holes or by jumping over the top. It will jump from the water and may occasionally perform a somersault. It has been timed while swimming at a speed of 15 knots (17 m.p.h.).

Reproduction. This dolphin mates during the summer months and the young are born the following spring or summer after a gestation period of about 10 months.

Abundance. The Pacific White-sided Dolphin is an abundant species.

Economic Importance. This dolphin is captured in small numbers in a few areas, but there is no organized fishery for it. It is often captured and placed on exhibit in zoos and public aquaria.

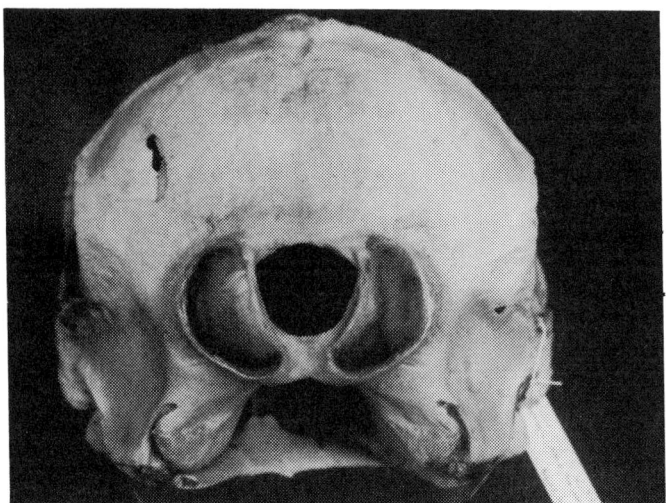

The skull of the Pacific white-sided dolphin, *Lagenorhynchus obliquidens,* in posterior view.
Photo by Michael Graybill at Cal. Acad. of Sci.

Photo of a Pacific white-sided dolphin, *Lagenorhynchus obliquidens* which beached at La Jolle, California, showing its short, blunt beak and large, curved dorsal fin.
Photo by W.F. Perrin.

Class Mammalia — The Mammals
   Order Cetacea — The Whales
      Suborder Odontoceti — The Toothed Whales
         Family Delphinidae — The Ocean Dolphins and Porpoises

PEALE'S BLACK-CHINNED DOLPHIN
Also known as Peale's Dolphin, the Southern Dolphin,
and Delfin Austral
Lagenorhynchus australis (Peale, 1848)

Identifying Features. This dolphin is not well known because of its southern habitat. It can best be identified by the black area which covers the head and which also extends to include the jaws and the eyes. There is an oval, white patch in the axilla of the flipper.

Size and Shape. The body is of moderate size and is known to reach a length of over 2 meters. The largest known specimen was reported to measure 216 cm. (85 in.) It will weigh between about 110 to 120 kg. (243 to 265 lbs.) or more. It has a very short, broad beak which is separated from a low, gradually-sloping forehead by a transverse crease.

Color. In general, the back is charcoal gray to black and the belly is white in color. The eyes and jaws are black; the black area of the head extends backward to surround the eyes. A narrow black line extends from the corner of the mouth to the base of the flipper. A long, narrow black line often extends backward from the base of the flipper and borders a lighter area above it. There is also a white patch in the axilla (arm pit) of the flipper.

Distribution. This is primarily a coastal species which is restricted to the southern end of South America and the Falkland Islands. It is reported as common in the bays and channels of Tierra del Fuego. On the Atlantic Ocean side of South America, it extends northward to about the Gulf of San Matias (about 42° S.L.) It is also known from the cooler waters south of Africa. On the Pacific Ocean side of South America, it occurs as far north as Valparaiso (33° S.L.).

Migration. Although little has been recorded, one is led to suppose that this species makes limited northward and southward movements with the seasons.

Fins and Flippers. The dorsal fin is of medium size, has a long base, and is not sharply pointed; it is inclined backward and is sickle-shaped in appearance. A rather prominent dorsal keel extends backward from this fin; a similar keel is also present on the midventral line of the tail stock. The flippers are not very large, are black in color, and are arched backward; they terminate in a blunt point. The rear margin of the tail has a distinct central notch.

Teeth. The teeth measure about 3 mm. in diameter and number about 30 in each of the four jaw bones.

Skeletal Notes. The vertebrae are distributed approximately as follows: C 7 + D 15 + L 24 + Ca 35 = 81.

Food. The food of this dolphin is undoubtedly squid and fishes, however, one specimen from the Falkland Islands had a part of an octopus in its stomach.

Swimming and Diving. This is a sociable species and travels in small groups of 2 to 5 or more, although larger groups of 3 or 4 dozen have been observed. It is known to ride the bow waves of ships within its area.

Reproduction. It probably differs very little from other closely related species.

Abundance. This is a species which is fairly common in the restricted area which it occupies.

Economic Importance. It is probably of little economic value.

Class Mammalia — The Mammals
  Order Cetacea — The Whales
    Suborder Odontoceti — The Toothed Whales
      Family Delphinidae — The Ocean Dolphins and Porpoises

THE HOUR-GLASS DOLPHIN

Also known as the Southern White-sided Dolphin

Lagenorhynchus cruciger (Quoy and Gaimard, 1824)

Identifying Features. The color pattern of the body must serve as the basis for the identification of this dolphin. A black stripe begins with the black snout and jaws and continues backward along the midline of the back to the tail. See the notes on color below.

Size and Shape. This species is one of small size which seems to measure about 152 to 183 cm. (5 to 6 ft.) in length. Males have been reported to measure 163 cm. (64 in.) and females are known which have measured 183 cm. (72 in.) in length. They will weigh between about 90 to 110 kg. (198 to 243 lbs.) or more. The forehead is low and slopes very gradually forward and downward to a beak which is wide and very short. An upper and lower keel is present on the tailstock. This species resembles *L. acutus* rather closely.

Color. The color of the body is arranged in a longitudinal pattern. A wide, black stripe with wavy borders extends dorsally from the mouth and beak backward along the midline of the back to the tail. This stripe is bordered below by a wavy, white band of varying width which extends along the side of the body from the head to the tail. Below these two stripes, a black band of widely varying width begins with the eye and extends backward to the tail; it widens to include the flippers, then narrows slightly, then widens again to one-half the body height just below the dorsal fin, and finally extends onward to the tail as a narrow stripe. The jaws, dorsal fin, flippers, and tail are always black. The entire belly is white, except for the lips and the end of the tail stock and tail flukes.

Distribution. This dolphin is a pelagic species which is circumpolar in the southern hemisphere from about 25° S.L. southward to the ice pack. It is found on both sides of the Antarctic Convergence,* although it is more common on the northern side.

Migration. This is not a migratory species, although it may make limited shifts in latitude with the changing seasons and currents.

Fins and Flippers. The dorsal fin is large, high, concave on its rear margin, and black in color. The flippers are of comparatively large size, somewhat triangular in shape, and possess gently curving margins. They are black in color. The flukes of the tail are black in color and bear a notch where they meet at the midline.

Teeth. The teeth are conical in shape and number about 28 in each of the four jaw bones.

Skeletal Notes. The vertebrae are distributed approximately as follows: C 7 + D 15 + L 22 + Ca 34 = 78.

Food. It is presumed that this species feeds upon squid and fishes.

Swimming and Diving. This dolphin is known to approach ships and to ride the bow waves for short lengths of time. It has also been observed to jump from the water and to spin before falling back into the sea.

Reproduction. Little is known of the reproductive habits of this dolphin, however, it probably differs little from the other members of its genus.

Abundance. Little is known regarding the abundance of this dolphin.

Economic Importance. This species is of very little economic importance.

---

*The Antarctic Convergence is an area which stretches around the earth as an irregular band of water just north of the Antarctic continent; here the colder, northward flowing waters from the Antarctic meet and sink beneath the warmer sub-Antarctic waters; it is an area of abundnt marine life.

GRAY'S DUSKY DOLPHIN
Lagenorhynchus obscurus (Gray, 1828)

Identifying Features. This species is identified by a combination of features. It is less than 213 cm. (7 ft.) in length, has a short beak, a high dorsal fin, and is generally black above and white below. White of varying patterns occurs on the sides of the body below and behind the dorsal fin. The dorsal fin is often darker on its front half and lighter on its posterior half. The snout is black-tipped.

Size and Shape. The dusky dolphin is a small to medium-sized species with a robust, spindle-shaped body, and a short, broad beak. It will measure as much as 2.1 meters (82+ in.) in length, although most individuals are smaller. It will usually weigh between about 110 and 120 kg. (243 and 265 lbs.) when mature.

Color. The basic colors of the body are black-to-gray and white. The black areas include the jaws, the top of the head and back, the dorsal fin, the flippers, and the tail. The white areas include the throat and belly and irregular, widely-varying patterns on the side of the body below and behind the dorsal fin. The lips are black. A black streak extends from the eye to the base of the flipper. Occasionally, dolphins are seen which are entirely white in color; these are doubtless albino forms.

Distribution. This dolphin is a circumpolar species which lives in the temperate waters of the southern hemisphere from about 30° S.L. southward to about 58° S.L. or more. It appears to be a coastal species. In the western South Atlantic Ocean, it occurs in the Falkland Islands and off Argentina; it occurs off South Africa and at the Kerguelen Islands in the southern Indian Ocean; and it occurs off southern Australia and New Zealand and along the Pacific coast of South America as far north as Peru.

Migration. This is not a migratory species, although it may be expected to shift its latitude with the changing currents and seasons. It appears to travel in larger groups in the summer months.

Fins and Flippers. The dorsal fin is large and concave on its posterior margin; it is darker in color along its front margin and lighter in color along its rear margin. The flippers are quite large and are black above and below. The flukes of the tail are dark in color above and below and are notched where they join at the midline.

Teeth. The teeth are conical and pointed and number about 28 to 36 in each of the four jaw bones.

Skeletal Notes. The vertebrae are distributed as follows: C 7 + D 15 + L 23 + Ca 36 = 81.

Food. This dolphin is presumed to subsist upon squid, anchovies, and various fishes which occur within its area.

Swimming and Diving. The habits of this species are not unlike those of other members of its genus. It will approach ships, ride the bow waves, and frolic nearby for a time. It is reported to turn somersaults. It is a sociable species and is usually seen in small groups; however, it will gather into great herds which number several hundred individuals.

Reproduction. The adults mate in the late summer and the young are born nearly a year later. They are small at birth and will measure about 60 cm. (24 in.) in length and weigh about 5 kg. (11 lbs.).

Abundance. This is a fairly common species in some areas within its range. Huge schools are occasionally seen off New Zealand.

Economic Importance. This species is not hunted commercially and no organized fishery for it exists, although it may be captured occasionally. It has been exhibited in various public aquaria in the southern hemisphere.

THE SOUTHERN DOLPHINS
Genus *CEPHALORHYNCHUS* Gray, 1846

The southern dolphins, which comprise this genus, are all small in size compared to other oceanic species. Their rostrum or snout does not form a distinct beak and there is no transverse constriction at the base of the forehead. The dorsal fin is rather small, low, and rounded and the flippers are likewise small. The teeth are small and pointed and number between 24 and 32 in each of the four jaw bones. The color is usually black and white with some brownish shades, but each species has its own distinct color pattern.

The distribution of this genus is limited to the southern hemisphere; all four species occupy temperate and cooler seas in four separate areas.

C. commersonii inhabits the waters off Argentina and areas to the eastward;

C. eutropia occurs off the coast of Chile;

C. heavisidii is distributed along the southwestern coast of Africa; and

C. hectori is restricted to the waters surrounding New Zealand.

This genus is known only from the Holocene Epoch (Recent).

Studies of these dolphins by various scholars indicate that several names of species appearing in older books are really duplicate names or synonyms of other previously named species. The following list indicates the older names and the more correct and current names of these dolphins.

Old Names		Names Currently In Use
Cephalorhynchus albifrons	is now	*Cephalorhynchus hectori*
Cephalorhynchus albiventris	is now	*Cephalorhynchus eutropia*
Electra clancula	is now	*Cephalorhynchus hectori*
Electra hectori	is now	*Cephalorhynchus hectori*

This genus contains the four living species listed below.

THE PIEBALD OR BLACK AND WHITE DOLPHIN
Also known as Commerson's Dolphin and Tonina Overa
Cephalorhynchus commersonii (Lacepede, 1804)

Identifying Features. The body is largely white in color; this white area encircles the body including the back forward of the dorsal fin and also including most of the sides and the belly. The dorsal fin is low.

Size and Shape. This dolphin is a small species which measures less than 182 cm. (6 ft.) in length. A specimen which measured 160 cm. (62.9 in.) is regarded as large for this species. The beak is short and broad and almost indistinguishable from the head; it leads to a forehead which rises gradually upward. There is no transverse crease separating the beak from the forehead.

Color. The color pattern is quite astonishing because the black and white areas are sharply separated. The white area is large and encircles the entire body forward of the dorsal fin; it includes the back forward of the fin, the sides, the entire belly, and an oval spot on the throat. The black (or dark gray) areas include the head and flippers, the dorsal fin, the top and sides of the tail stock, an area at the anus, and the entire tail. A wide, black band extends from the head to the base of the flipper.

Distribution. The range of this dolphin includes the Atlantic coast of southern South America and a few scattered islands. It extends from the Golfo San Matias and Peninsula Valdes (42-43° S.L.) in southern Argentina southward to Cape Horn (55° S.L.) and eastward to the Falkland Islands (52° S.L.) and South Georgia in the south Atlantic Ocean; it also occurs at the Kerguelen Islands (49° S.L.) in the Indian Ocean. It occurs in Chilean waters south of about 50° S.L. It is primarily a coastal species.

Migration. This is a non-migratory species.

Fins and Flippers. The dorsal fin is very low and is rounded at the tip. The flippers are small, rather short, and broadly rounded at their tips. The flukes of the tail are black in color and exhibit a notch on their posterior margin where they meet at the midline.

Teeth. The teeth are small and pointed and usually number about 29 or 30 (occasionally 31 or 32) in each of the four jaw bones.

Skeletal Notes. The vertebrae are distributed approximately as follows: C 7 + D 12 + L 24 + Ca 20 = 63. Four pairs of ribs articulate directly with the sternum.

Other Anatomical Notes. Some scholars have reported that the leading edge of the flippers exhibits small serrations; others have not mentioned it.

Food. The food of this dolphin consists of a wide variety of schooling fishes including silversides, sardines, and anchovies; it also is known to eat squid, shrimp, and krill.

Swimming and Diving. This shoreline species usually travels in small groups of from two to four individuals, but occasionally will be observed in groups as large as 20 individuals. Its usual swimming speed is about 6 to 7 knots. When it surfaces, it breathes two or three times, then submerges for 15 to 20 seconds to reappear at most unpredictable locations. It is an active species and will leap in various patterns and will also approach ships, where it will ride in the bow waves. It may be captured and, when surrounded by a net, will not attempt to jump over it to freedom, but will usually look for an escape exit somewhere below the surface. It is attracted to captured or wounded individuals and will linger in their area for a time. It frequents kelp beds.

Reproduction. The young are born in early summer, usually between December and February. They are brown in color at birth, after which they slowly change to a grayish color, and finally to their black and white pattern.

Abundance. This species is reported to be fairly abundant in the southwestern Atlantic Ocean south of about 42° S.L. Its shoreline distribution together with its curiosity about ships may in time lead to its reduction in numbers.

Economic Importance. Although occasionally captured, this dolphin has no economic value.

Miscellaneous. This dolphin is attacked by killer whales (*Orcinus orca*). Its white coloration may possibly be useful in hiding near the ice floes.

This species was named for Philibert Commerson, the naturalist who accompanied Louis Antoine de Bougainville, the French navigator and explorer, on his trip around the world between 1766 and 1769.

Class Mammalia — The Mammals
  Order Cetacea — The Whales
    Suborder Odontoceti — The Toothed Whales
      Family Delphinidae — The Ocean Dolphins and Porpoises

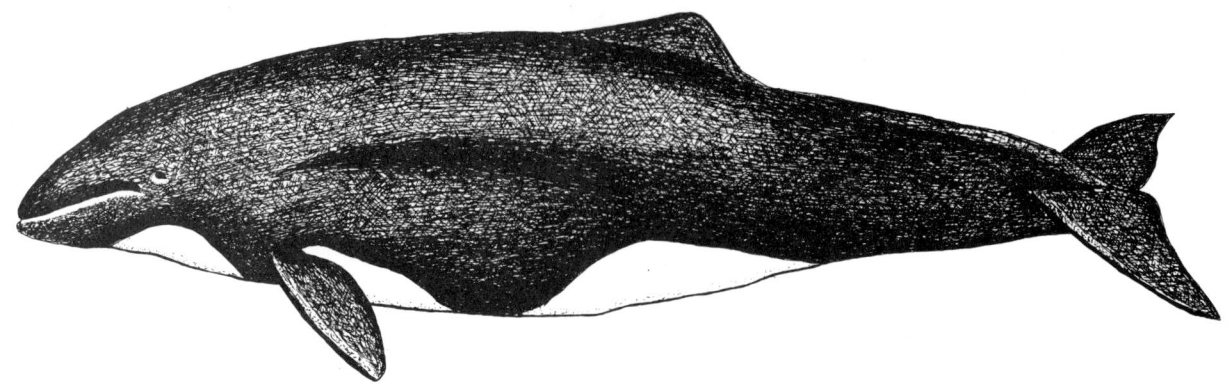

THE BLACK CHILEAN DOLPHIN
Also known as the White-bellied Dolphin
Cephalorhynchus eutropia (Gray, 1846)

Identifying Features. The identity of this species may be established by its color. The body is entirely dark gray except for white areas on the belly. The dorsal fin is very low.

Size and Shape. This species is one of the very smallest of dolphins and probably does not exceed 152 cm. (5 ft.) in length; most will measure about 120 cm. (47 in.) and weigh about 45 kg. (99 lbs.). One record showed a length of 1.4 m. (55 in.). The beak is very short and leads upward to a gradually sloping forehead. There is no transverse crease separating the head from the beak. Dorsal and ventral keels are present on the tail stock.

Color. The body is almost completely enveloped in a coat of a dark gray hue, except for three white areas on the ventral side; they are (1) an area on the throat, (2) an area on the chest between the flippers, and (3) an area on the belly. A thin, thread-like, white line borders the lips.

Distribution. The range of this dolphin extends along the western coast of Chile from near Conception, Chile, (37° S.L.) southward to Isla Navarino (55° S.L.) near Cape Horn.

Migration. This is a non-migratory species, but it probably shifts position somewhat with the changing seasons.

Fins and Flippers. The dorsal fin is very low and triangular in outline and has a rounded tip; its anterior and posterior margins are quite straight. The flippers are small and short, are not greatly curved, and have rounded tips. The flukes of the tail are turned strongly backward at their ends, the rear margin of the tail is deeply concave, and a notch is present in the center.

Teeth. The teeth number between about 28 and 31 in each of the four jaw bones.

Skeletal Notes. The vertebrae are distributed approximately as follows: C 7 + D 12 + L 24 + Ca 20 = 63.

Food. The food of this dolphin consists of squid, shrimp, and miscellaneous fishes.

Swimming and Diving. Very little has been recorded about this dolphin. It does not follow ships and is rarely observed at sea.

Reproduction. The habits of this species are not well known; they probably differ very little from those of other members of this genus.

Abundance. This is a rare and uncommon species.

Economic Importance. There are no fishing activities based upon this little dolphin, although some are caught in Chile and used as cheap bait for crab traps.

THE SOUTH AFRICAN DOLPHIN
Also known as Haviside's Dolphin or the Benguela Dolphin
Cephalorhynchus heavisidii (Gray, 1828)

Identifying Features. This dolphin is a small species which is best identified by its very dark gray color above and the three oval extensions of white which extend upward from the white of the belly. The dorsal fin is small, low, triangular, and pointed.

Size and Shape. This dolphin is a very small species which measures from about 1.2 to 1.3 meters (47 to 51 in.) in length. Its weight is estimated at 45 kg. (100 lbs.) or more. The body is spindle-shaped with its greatest depth occurring between the dorsal fin and the flippers. The beak is very small, rounded, and wide and the forehead slopes gradually upward. There is no transverse crease separating the head from the beak.

Color. The body is a uniform, dark gray over its entire upper surface, including the head, lower jaw, tail stock, and tail. Areas of white cover the chest and belly as far back as the anus. Three oval pockets of white extend upward against the gray-black of the sides; one is forward of the flippers, a second is behind and above the flippers, and a third projects backward on the sides above the anus. The boundary between the white and dark areas is very definite.

Distribution. The range of this species is limited to the cooler waters of the southern hemisphere. It occurs south and southwest of Africa from the Cape of Good Hope northward along the Atlantic coast to Cape Cross (22° S.L.) on the Skeleton Coast of Namibia (South-west Africa); this is in the area of the northward-flowing Benguela Current.

Migration. Since this is a coastal species which lives in a northward flowing current, it doubtless shifts its latitude with the changing seasons.

Fins and Flippers. The dorsal fin is small, low, triangular in shape, and has a pointed tip; it is located just behind the center of the body. Keels are not well developed on the tail stock. The flippers are rather short, narrow, curved somewhat in front, and pointed at their tips. The tail is small, quite narrow front-to-back, and is strongly curved backward at its ends; the rear margin bears a notch at its center.

Teeth. The teeth are small, slender, and pointed and number about 25 to 30 in each of the four jaw bones.

Skeletal Notes. The lower jaw is slightly longer than the upper jaw. The vertebrae are distributed about as follows: C 7 + D 12 + L 23 + Ca 22 = 64.

Food. This dolphin feeds upon squid and a variety of small fishes.

Reproduction. It is presumed that the reproductive habits of this species differ but little from those of other members of this genus.

Abundance. This dolphin is a rare and uncommon species.

Economic Importance. No economic value attaches to this species. It is occasionally caught in the purse seines of commercial fishermen.

Miscellaneous. This species was named for Captain Haviside, a native of England, who was an employee of the British East India Company and who brought the original specimen from southwestern Africa to England in 1827. His name was originally misspelled in the original description and remains that way.

THE NEW ZEALAND WHITE-FRONT DOLPHIN
Also known as Hector's Dolphin
Cephalorynchus hectori (van Beneden, 1881)

Identifying Features. Significant diagnostic features of this species include a deep body, a small rounded dorsal fin, and a large white or gray area on the forehead.

Size and Shape. The body of this species is robust and deep in the area above the flippers. The beak is short and wide and leads upward to a forehead which rises rapidly to a point above the flippers. There is no transverse crease between the head and the base of the beak. The dorsal fin is low, rounded posteriorly, and located just behind the high point of the back. This is a small species in which the body length will range between about 1.3 to 1.6 meters (51 to 53 in.) or more and weigh between about 35 to 55 kg. (77 to 121 lbs.) or more.

Color. The color of the back and sides is black and/or dark gray of varying intensity. The forehead is marked by a large white or light gray area and the throat and lower jaw are also white in color. The entire belly is white, but it is separated from the white of the throat by a black band which crosses the throat ventrally to connect the bases of the flippers; this band is somewhat V-shaped and points posteriorly at the midline. A black or gray spear of color projects forward into a white area just above the anus. Black areas cover the sides of the head, the eyes, the flippers, the dorsal fin, and the tail. A thin, black line crosses over the top of the head behind the blowhole. An oval white spot is present in the axilla of the flippers.

Distribution. This dolphin is restricted in its distribution to the waters of New Zealand. It is reported to extend from the South Island to the Bay of Islands at the extreme northern end of the North Island. It is a shoreline species and does not venture much beyond 5 miles from shore. It is occasionally seen in the estuaries of rivers.

Migration. This is a non-migratory species, although it may shift its latitude with the changing seasons and currents.

Fins and Flippers. The dorsal fin is small and has a distinctly rounded, convex, posterior margin. The flippers are small, have somewhat parallel front and rear borders, and possess rounded tips. The tail fin is curved backward at its extremities and bears a notch at the center of its rear margin. A low keel extends from the dorsal fin toward the tail.

Teeth. The teeth may number from about 24 to 32 in each of the four jaw bones; 28 to 30 seems to be the usual number.

Skeletal Notes. The vertebrae of this species are distributed approximately as follows: C 7 + D 12 + L 23 + Ca 23 = 65.

Food. Although little is known of its food habits, it is known to feed upon squid, shrimp, and small marine fishes.

Swimming and Diving. Very little information has been recorded on its habits. It appears to prefer the shallow waters of the coastline. It has been observed in small groups which approach a dozen in number. It is curious about ships and will sometimes linger in their area, where it often rides the bow waves.

Reproduction. Little has been recorded on the reproductive habits of this species; however, its habits may be presumed to resemble those of the other members of this genus. The young are born in the summer months and bear the same color pattern as the adults.

Abundance. Various reports indicate that this is a fairly common species along the northern shores of the South Island of New Zealand.

Economic Importance. No economic importance attaches to this species; it is not hunted commercially and does not normally appear in the catch of other fisheries.

Miscellaneous. This dolphin is reported to frequent the mouths of river including those in which the water is discolored or muddy.

Photo of a New Zealand white-front dolphin, *Cephalorhynchus hectori*, stranded at Pallister Bay, North Island, New Zealand.
N. Crewe.

From: "Whales and Dolphins of New Zealand and Australia" by A.N. Baker. Victoria University Press, Wellington, 1983. Courtesy A.N. Baker.

THE RIGHT-WHALE DOLPHINS
Genus *LISSODELPHIS* Gloger, 1841

The right-whale dolphins are small, slender, streamlined animals which have their greatest diameter in the area of the flippers. The beak is quite long and tapers forward from a broad base; the transverse constriction which separates the forehead from the base of the beak is less severe than in most dolphins. The dorsal fin is absent in this genus, a feature which separates it from most other dolphins;* however, a median caudal ridge is present and the flukes of the tail bear a notch at the middle of their posterior margin. The flippers are curved, pointed, and comparatively small. The teeth are small, numerous, and number between about 40 and 53 in each of the four jaw bones. The vertebrae are distributed approximately as follows: C 7 + D 14-15 + L 29-30 + Ca 37-39 = 88-90. These are small dolphins which will measure less than eight feet in length.

---

*The common name of Right-whale Dolphin refers to the right whales (*Balaena*) which also lack the dorsal fin. Other toothed whales which lack a distinct dorsal fin include the sperm whale *(Physeter)*, the narwhal *(Monodon)*, the white whale *(Delphinapterus)*, and the finless porpoise *(Neophocaena)*.

The color of the body in both species is black above and white below, but the patterns are quite different. It is interesting to note that the border line between the colors is sharply defined. The two species of this genus are so similar that they may prove to be simply two color varieties of a single species.

These dolphins inhabit cooler, temperate seas.

This genus is known only from the Holocene Epoch (Recent).

This genus contains the two living species listed below.

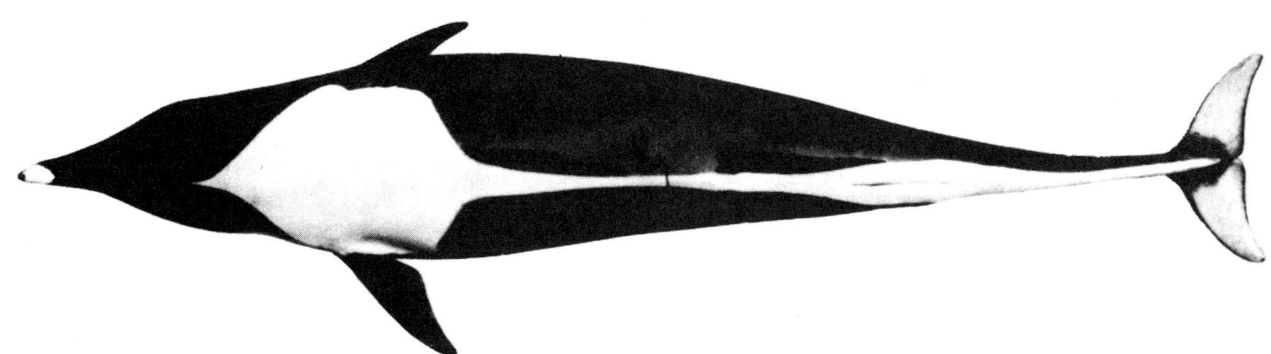

Photos of the northern right-whale dolphin, *Lissodelphis borealis*, showing the slender body and white ventral area characteristic of this species. Note that the dorsal fin is absent in this species.

Photos by F.G. Wood.

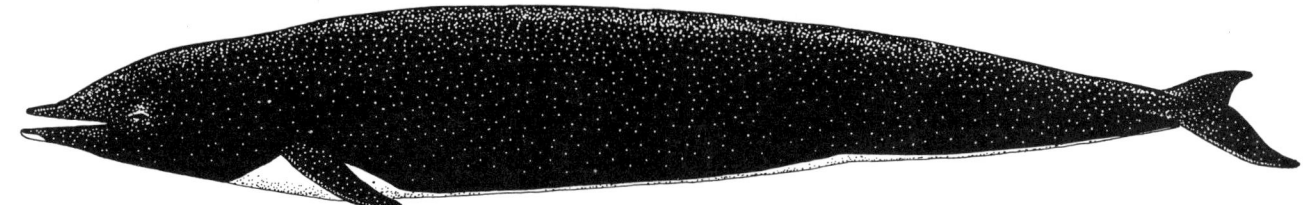

THE NORTHERN RIGHT-WHALE DOLPHIN
Lissodelphis borealis (Peale, 1848)

Identifying Features. The back of the body is entirely black and lacks the dorsal fin; the white of the belly narrows to a long, thin stripe toward the tail.

Size and Shape. This is a very slender and very beautiful dolphin which will reach an average length of about 2 to 2.5 meters (79 to 98 in.) and an average weight of about 75 kg. (165 lbs.). The beak is short and distinct and continues imperceptibly into the forehead which in turn rises very gradually to the head and back. The body is spindle-shaped and has its greatest diameter well forward of its midpoint. The body of this dolphin is wider than it is deep.

Color. The color of the body is black above and white below. The white areas consists of (1) a small oval spot below the tip of the chin, (2) a large oval area on the chest, (3) a very long slender white stripe extending from the white patch on the chest to the tail, and (4) the lower surface of the tail flukes. All other surfaces are black. Those dolphins of this species which inhabit the waters of Japan vary in color from the typical color pattern described here. This Japanese color variety has been described and named *Lissodelphis borealis albiventris* Nishiwaki, 1972.

Distribution. This is a North Pacific Ocean species which extends from about latitude 50° N.L. (Vancouver Island) southward to Baja California on the east and from Japan southward in the western Pacific Ocean. This seems to be an oceanic species, since it is rarely seen near shore; however, it does not seem to be present in the central North Pacific Ocean. It is reported to prefer a water temperature of about 15° C (59° F).

Migration. Their migration pattern is not well known, however, they are known to migrate into cooler waters during the summer months. They often gather into groups of 200 to 300 individuals or more and some groups have been seen which appeared to have over 3,000 individuals; these large groups may somehow be associated with their migration pattern. They are more abundant in both California and Japan during the winter season from September to June.

Fins and Flippers. The dorsal fin is absent, the flippers are small, slender, and pointed, and are black in color above and below. The tail flukes are quite deeply notched at the center of their posterior margin; they are black above and white below. Keels extend along the upper and lower midline of the tail stock.

Teeth. The teeth are small, slender, and pointed. They vary in number from about 40 to 53 in each of the four jaw bones. They are usually more numerous in the lower jaw.

Skeletal Notes. The first two neck vertebrae are united. The vertebrae are distributed approximately as follows: C 7 + D 14-15 + L 29-30 + Ca 37-39 = 88-90. The chevron bones number from 27 to 30. The ribs number 14-15 pairs; of these, the first 5 or 6 pairs have 2 heads. The sternum has 4 parts. The bones of the fingers are distributed approximately as follows: I (1-2), II (8), III (9), IV (3), V (2-3).

Other Anatomical Notes. The jaws are narrow and slender and the lower jaw is slightly longer than the upper jaw. There

Photos of the northern right-whale dolphin, *Lissodelphis borealis,* **leaping in formation at the surface off the coast of Oregon.**

Photo by Graybill.

is no evidence of a dorsal ridge along the posterior portion of the back.

Food. A variety of fishes are consumed including lantern fishes and, in addition, a sizeable component of squid.

Swimming and Diving. This is a lively animal which is active and quick and which will frequently leap from the water. It is a speedy swimmer and is reported as capable of swimming 35 km/hour (21.7 mph). It travels in small groups of a few individuals; however, schools of 3,000 have been observed in the North Pacific Ocean. They will occasionally approach boats, but they are cautious about riding the bow waves of vessels.

Titian R. Peale, the naturalist aboard the United States Exploring Expedition (1838-42), first described this dolphin in 1848. He said,

> "While in the water it appears to be entirely black, the white lines being invisible. It is remarkably quick and lively in its motions, frequently leaping entirely out of the water, and from its not having a dorsal fin, is sometimes mistaken for a seal."

They have occasionally been observed swimming in schools with other small whales including the common dolphin *(Delphinus delphis)*, the Pacific white-sided dolphin *(Lagenorhynchus obliquidens)*, pilot whales *(Globicephala sp.)* and Dall's porpoise *(Phocoenoides dalli)*.

Reproduction. Very little information has been recorded on their reproduction. The young are born in April and May and appear to be rather small at birth; some young specimens have been observed which were between 61 to 71 cm. (24 to 28 in.) in length. The young are reported to be "cream-colored to grayish" at birth and achieved their black and white color pattern after a year or more.

Abundance. Although the total population of this species is unknown, it appears to be one of the more abundant species.

Economic Importance. Very little value attaches to this species. It was formerly hunted on a very limited basis in Japan and is occasionally captured during other fishing operations.

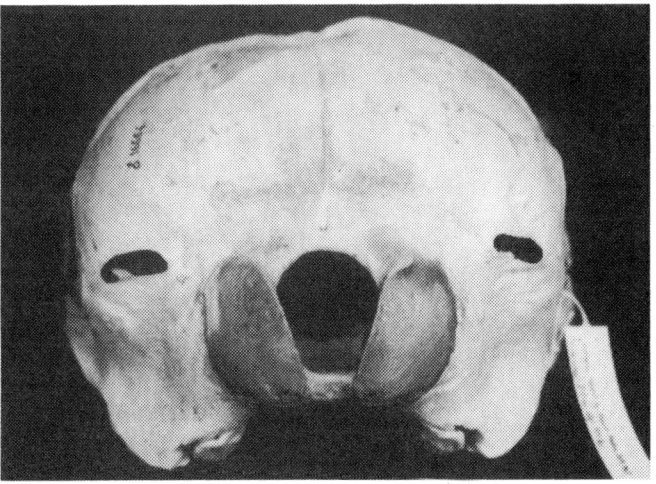

The skull of the northern right-whale dolphin *Lissodelphis borealis,* in posterior view.
Photo by Michael Graybill at Humboldt State Univ.

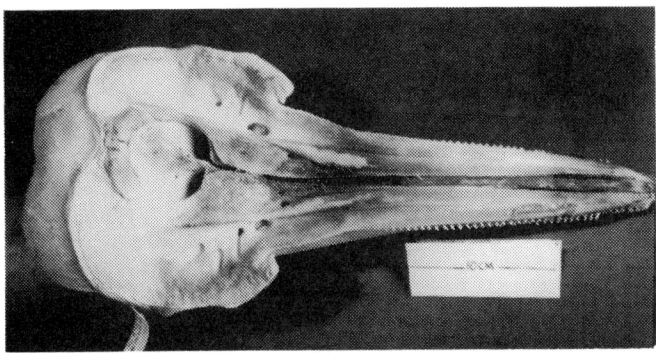

The skull of the northern right-whale dolphin, *Lissodelphis borealis,* in dorsal view.
Photo by Michael Graybill at Humboldt State Univ.

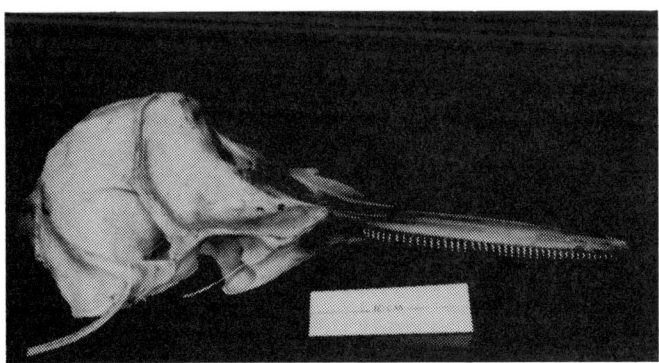

The skull of the northern right-whale dolphin, *Lissodelphis borealis,* in lateral view.
Photo by Michael Graybill at Cal. Acad. of Sci.

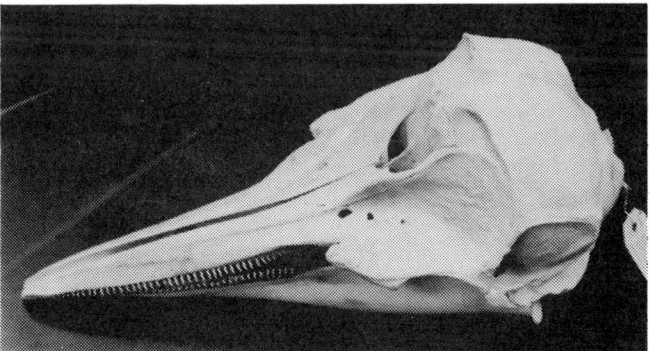

The skull of the northern right-whale dolphin, *Lissodelphis borealis,* in lateral view.
Photo by Michael Graybill at Humbolt State Univ.

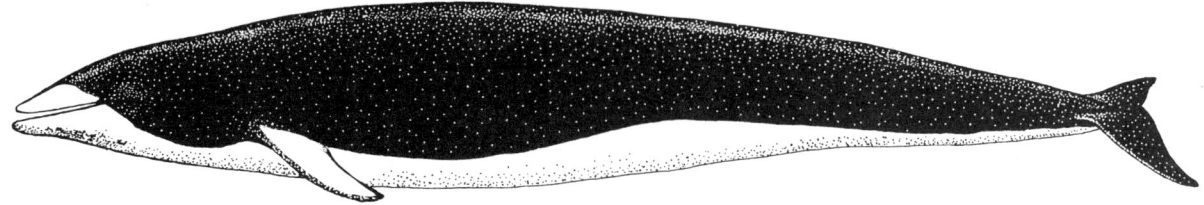

THE SOUTHERN RIGHT-WHALE DOLPHIN
Also known as Delfin liso
Lissodelphis peronii (Lacepede, 1804)

Identifying Features. A white or gray beak and forehead together with the missing dorsal fin will identify this species.

Size and Shape. This dolphin is a small, slender, beautiful species which will reach a length somewhere between 183 to 244 cm. (72 to 96 in.) and will weigh between about 55 and 65 kg. (121 to 143 lbs.). The body is long, particularly in the area of the tail stock, and is wider than it is deep. The beak is small and merges imperceptibly into the profile of the forehead.

Color. The color pattern is a simple black and white, although the black color is often lighter and has been described by some as purplish brown or bluish black. The black areas include (1) the entire top of the back except for the forehead, (2) the upper, outer surface of the tail flukes, and (3) occasionally, a small dark area at the tip of the flipper or a narrow border along the leading edge of the flipper. The dividing line between black and white is usually very sharp and there is usually no gradation from one color area to another. The dividing line begins on the forehead and passes vertically between the eyes and the mouth, then posteriorly above the base of the flippers, and finally rather directly backward to end at the tail.

Distribution. This dolphin is a circumpolar species of the southern hemisphere. It is an oceanic species and lives principally north of the Antarctic Convergence* where it is circumpolar in the West Wind Drift. It occurs in the northward-flowing Humbolt Current to the west of Chile, in the northward-flowing Falkland Current east of Argentina, in the northward flowing Benguela Current west of southern Africa, and in the seas which lie to the south of Africa, Australia, and New Zealand.

Migration. This dolphin is not a migratory species, although it may shift its latitude with the changing seasons and currents.

*The Antarctic Convergence is an area which stretches around the earth as an irregular band of water just north of the Antarctic continent; here the colder, northward flowing waters from the Antarctic meet and sink beneath the warmer sub-Antarctic waters; it is an area of abundant marine life.

Fins and Flippers. The dorsal fin is absent, although a keel is present on the caudal peduncle. The flippers are small, gently curved on both margins, and terminate in pointed tips. They are white above and below except for an occasional dark border on their leading edge. The tail is small, notched medially on the posterior margin, and variously shaded above with black, gray, and white.

Teeth. The teeth are small and sharp and have their tips inclined slightly inward; they number from 37 to 49 in each of the four jaw bones.

Skeletal Notes. The vertebrae are distributed approximately as follows: C 7 + D 14 + L 29 + Ca 38 = 88. The skull is elongated and likewise the jaws. There are 14 pairs of ribs of which 5 pairs have 2 heads.

Food. The diet of this dolphin consists of squid and fishes.

Swimming and Diving. Various reports indicate that this dolphin is an active species and quick in its movements; it will leap from the water and frolic in the waves, but it will not approach vessels or often ride the bow waves, although it may follow vessels at some distance. It usually travels in small groups numbering from 4 to 20; however, groups of over 200 are occasionally sighted, and a few groups exceeding 1,000 individuals have been seen. They are occasionally seen in the company of Gray's dusky dolphin (*Lagenorhynchus obscurus*).

Reproduction. Very little has been recorded concerning this species.

Abundance. This is not an abundant species; its exact numbers are unknown.

Economic Importance. This dolphin has no economic importance, although it may be captured occasionally by fishermen.

Miscellaneous. This species is named for Mr. Francois Peron, a naturalist aboard the French vessel *Geographe*, who discovered this species south of Tasmania.

The Northern Right-whale Dolphin
Lissodelphis borealis (Peale, 1848)

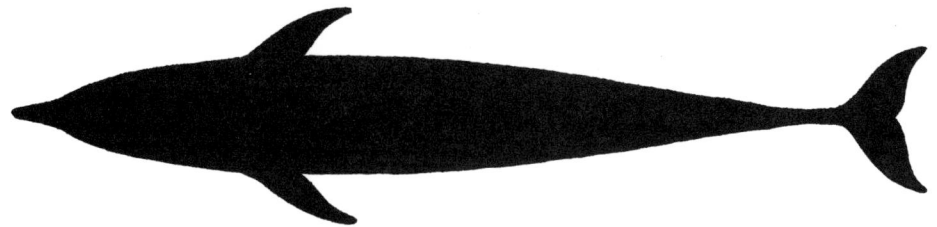

The Dorsal Color Pattern

The Ventral Color Pattern

Drawn from Nishiwaki.

The Southern Right-whale Dolphin
Lissodelphis peronii (Lacepede, 1804)

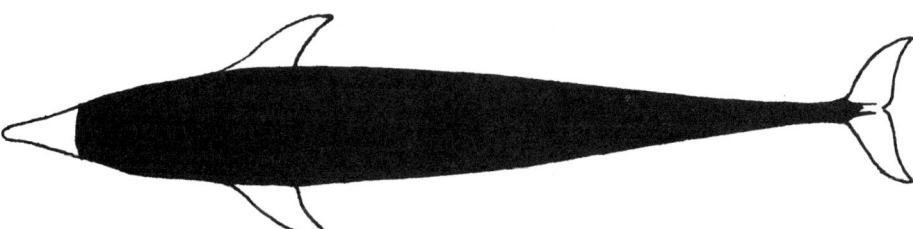

The Dorsal Color Pattern

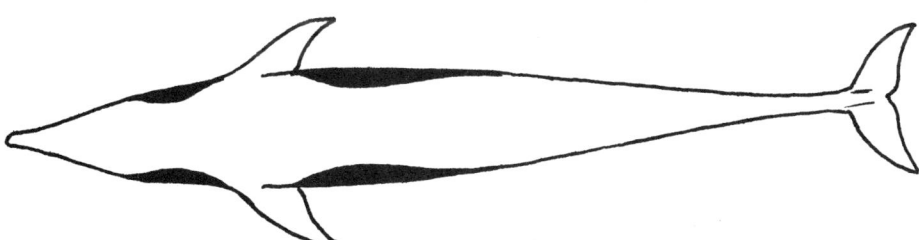

The Ventral Color Pattern

The Color Pattern In Lateral View

Drawn from Nishiwaki.

THE GRAMPUS DOLPHINS
Genus *GRAMPUS* Gray, 1828

The body of these dolphins is quite long and is somewhat cylindrical and robust in shape in the half of the body forward of the dorsal fin. The beak appears to be lacking, but in reality is very short and is not separated from the forehead by a transverse groove. The forehead is bulged and is nearly vertical in front. The dorsal fin is very high and is strongly curved and pointed at its tip; it is located just forward of the midpoint of the body. The flippers are long, narrow, curved, and pointed and the tail contains a distinct notch between the flukes. The teeth are large, are located in the front of the mouth, and number from 2 to 7 in each of the lower jaw bones. The teeth of the two upper jaw bones are usually not visible and lie buried in the gums; however, occasionally 1 or 2 pairs of vestigial teeth are visible. The vertebrae are distributed approximately as follows: C 7 + D 12-13 + L 18-19 + Ca 30-31 = 68-69. There are 12 or 13 pairs of ribs of which 6 or 7 pairs have two heads.

The color of these animals is usually grayish above and lighter below; the tail and the flippers are black above and likewise lighter below. The young individuals are lighter in color than the adults and older individuals become lighter with age. The body surface is usually covered with various marks, spots, scars, and streaks, probably due to conflicts.

This genus resembles *Globicephala,* but in reality is more closely related to the beaked dolphins, such as *Tursiops.*

Studies of these dolphins by various scholars indicate that several names of species appearing in older books are really duplicate names or synonyms of other previously named species. The following list indicates the older names and the more correct and current names of these species.

Old Name		Name Currently In Use
Genus Grampidelphis	is now	*Genus Grampus*
Grampus orca	is now	*Orcinus orca*
Grampus rectipinna	is now	*Orcinus orca*
Grampus stearnsi	is now	*Grampus griseus*

This genus is known only from the Holocene Epoch (Recent).

This genus contains the single living species listed below.
Grampus griseus (Cuvier, 1812)
THE WHITE-HEADED OR GRAY GRAMPUS..........See page 173

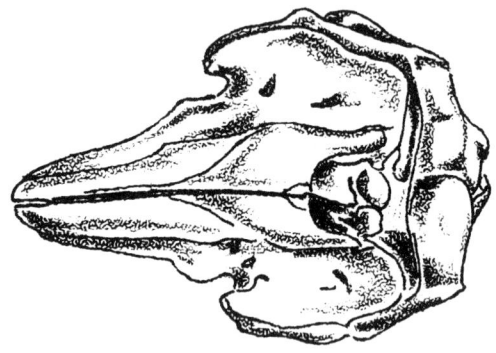

Drawing of the skull of the grampus, *Grampus griseus,* in dorsal view.

Photo of a group of the white-headed grampus, *Grampus griseus,* taken at sea in the Pacific Ocean off the state of Washington, U.S.A. Their blunt heads, light color, and scratched bodies help to identify them at sea.

Photo by C. Fiscus.

Class Mammalia — The Mammals
  Order Cetacea — The Whales
    Suborder Odontoceti — The Toothed Whales
      Family Delphinidae — The Ocean Dolphins and Porpoises

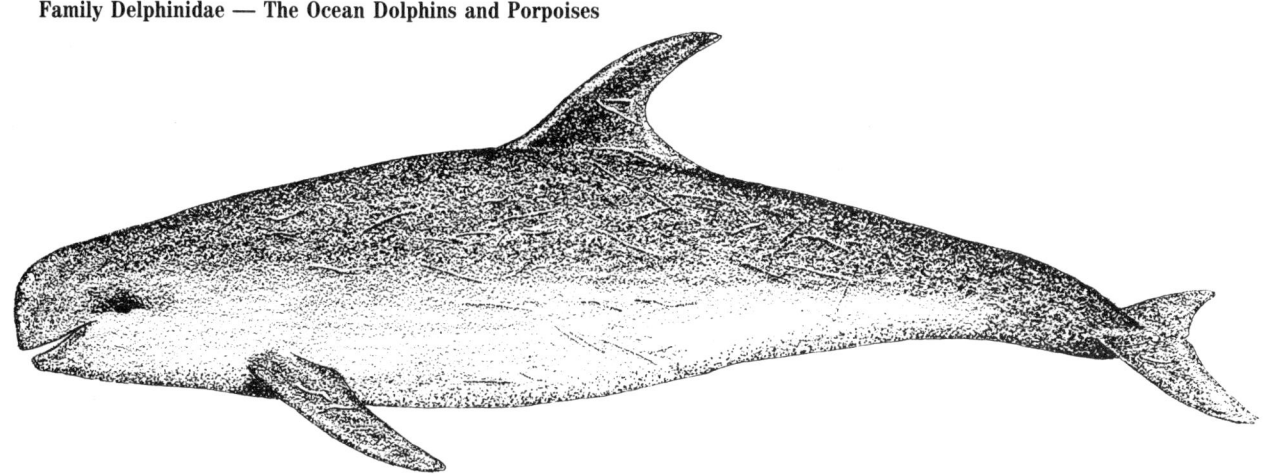

THE WHITE-HEADED OR GRAY GRAMPUS
Also known as Risso's Dolphin
Grampus griseus (Cuvier, 1812)

Identifying Features. The most important clue to the identity of this species is the dentition; there are from 2 to 7 (usually 3 or 4) pairs of teeth in the lower jaw; the upper jaw is without visible teeth. It also exhibits a V-shaped groove on the front of its head which points downward. In addition, this species has a small melon (bulbous forehead), a tall, slender dorsal fin, and numerous scratches on the body.

Size and Shape. The body of this species is robust in front and slender posteriorly. The front of the head is bulbous and nearly vertical and is marked in front with a V-shaped crease which points downward. A beak is not visible. The body will reach a maximum length of over 4.3 meters (14+ feet), although most individuals are smaller. Most will measure from about 2.75 to 3.5 meters (9.0 to 11.5 ft.) in length and will weigh about 300 kg. (662 lbs.). This dolphin bears a superficial resemblance to the pilot whales.

Color. The color of the body varies considerably. The males are usually gray or a bluish white above with dark brown patches and are lighter below; this light area may be anchor-shaped and extend to the tail; the females are a more uniform brown color. Other adults are almost black or white in color. Young individuals are light in color particularly about the head; some individuals will approach a white color. The body gets lighter in old dolphins. The entire body is usually covered with many scars.

Distribution. This dolphin is widely distributed in the warmer temperate and tropical seas of the world. In the Pacific Ocean, it occurs from British Columbia to Chile and from the Kurile Islands southward to New Zealand. In the Atlantic Ocean, it occurs from Newfoundland and the North Sea southward to Argentina, Cape Horn, and South Africa. It occurs in the Baltic Sea, the Mediterranean Sea, the Caribbean Sea, the Gulf of Mexico, and the Indian Ocean. It does not seem to occur in waters of less than 100 fathoms (183 m.) in depth.

Migration. These dolphins move with the seasons, but their times and routes are not well known.

Fins and Flippers. The dorsal fin is large, high, curved, quite narrow, pointed at the tip, and is located at the center of the body. The flippers are long and narrow and have pointed tips; they are dark in color both above and below. The flukes of the tail are quite wide and the notch between them is deep.

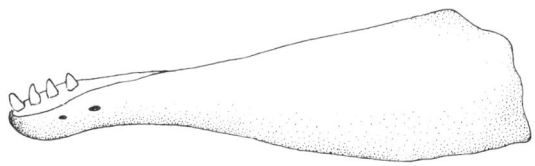

The teeth and jaw bone of *Grampus griseus*.

Teeth. There are usually 4 teeth on each side at the front of the lower jaw, although in some individuals these teeth may number anywhere from 2 to 7 pairs. These teeth are relatively large and usually measure 3.5 to 4.0 cm. (1.38 to 1.58 in.) in length; about half this length protrudes above the gums. There are usually no functional teeth in the upper jaw.

Skeletal Notes. The vertebrae are distributed as follows: C 7 + D 13-14 + L 18-19 + Ca 30-31 = 68-69. Of the 7 neck vertebrae, 6 are united and the 7th is very thin. There are 12-13 pairs of ribs of which the first 6 pairs have 2 heads; the 13th rib is a floating rib. Five pairs of ribs articulate directly with the sternum. The bones of the fingers are distributed approximately as follows: I (2), II (8-10), III (5-8), IV (3-5), V (1-2).

Other Anatomical Notes. The keels on the midline of the tail stock are not prominent. The front margin of the head is slightly concave. The mouth is able to open very wide. In a male specimen which measured 3.25 meters (10 ft. 7 in.) in length, the right testis weighed 14 lbs. and the left testis weighed 7 lbs.

Food. This dolphin feeds upon cuttlefish and various fishes. It is interesting to note that in captivity, it will cease to eat when the water temperature is lowered to 10°C (50° F).

Swimming and Diving. This is a sociable species and gathers into small groups from a few to 20 or more and, on rare occasions, groups as large as 100 have been seen. They are slow swimmers, but can develop speeds of 20 knots when urged. They play in the water, jump and splash, and beat the water with their tail. They do not approach boats and only occasionally will be near enough for good observation. They rarely ride the bow waves of ships.

Reproduction. The adults copulate in June and give birth 12 to 14 months later. The young, at birth, will usually measure between about 1.5 to 1.8 meters (59 to 71 in.) in length; this is often about one-half the length of the mother. At birth and for sometime thereafter, the young exhibit a series of about 7 vertical, gray stripes upon the side of the body.

Abundance. Although this species is widely distributed, it seems to be nowhere abundant.

Economic Importance. A few of these whales are captured in the small fisheries in various countries, but their number is not significant.

Photo of *Grampus griseus* in a tank at Marineland of Florida. Note the gape of the mouth and the many scratches which cover the body.

Photo by Marineland of Florida.

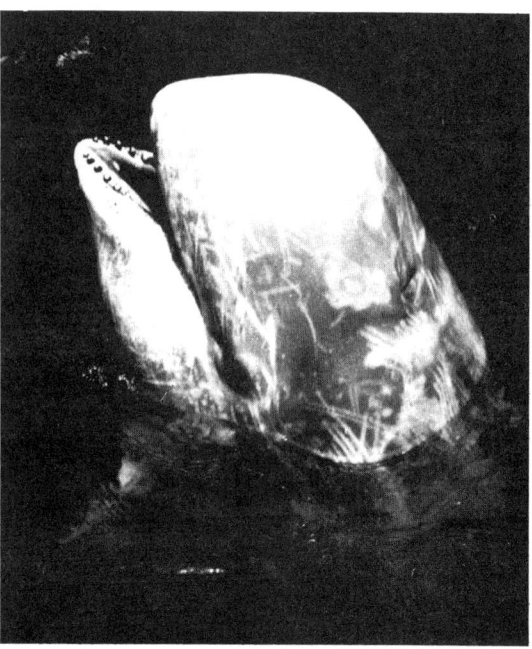

Photo of the head of *Grampus griseus* taken in the Enoshima Aquarium in Japan. Note the teeth and the many scratches which cover the head.

Photo by W.J. Houck.

A photo of two free-swimming specimens of *Grampus griseus* taken off San Clemente Island, California. Note the size and shape of the dorsal fin. The darker specimen on the right is believed to be a young individual.

Photo by L. Hobbs.

Photo of a young *Grampus griseus* in a tank at Marineland of Florida. Note the color pattern on the chest and belly.

Photo by Marineland of Florida.

THE SMALL, MELON-HEADED BLACKFISHES
Genus *PEPONOCEPHALA* Nishiwaki and Norris, 1966

The bodies of these dolphins are quite slender and elongated and terminate in a slender caudal peduncle and a notched tail. The head is somewhat pointed and wedge-shaped when viewed from above and the forehead slopes gently downward to the snout and upper jaw, but there is no elongated rostrum or beak in this genus. The dorsal fin is quite large, nearly straight in front, concave in the rear, and bears a blunt tip which is curved slightly backward. The teeth number between 21 and 25 in each of the four jaw bones; these teeth enable the observer to separate this genus from *Grampus, Feresa, Pseudorca, Globicephala,* and *Orcinus,* all of which have fewer than 15 teeth in each of their jaw bones.

The color of the body is black above and lighter below and there is a large whitish patch enclosing the anal region; the lips are also whitish in color. Within this genus, large individuals may reach a length of nine feet.

These dolphins (*Peponocephala*) resemble the pigmy killer whales (*Feresa*), but have pointed tips on their flippers, while those of *Feresa* have rounded tips. These dolphins also resemble the false killer whales (*Pseudorca*), but may be separated from them by their flippers. *Peponocephala* has

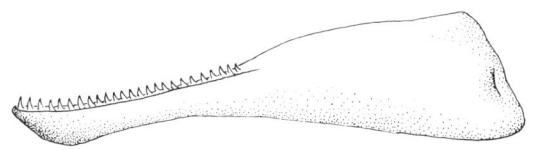

The teeth and jaw bone of *Peponocephala electra.*

a uniformly curving outer margin on its flippers, while the flippers of *Pseudorca* have an obtuse angle or hump upon the outer curvature of their flippers.

This genus was created by Dr. Masaharu Nishiwaki and Dr. Kenneth S. Norris in 1966 to receive *Lagenorhynchus electra,* which did not fit comfortably in the Genus *Lagenorhynchus.*

This genus contains the single living species listed below.

Peponocephala electra (Gray, 1846)

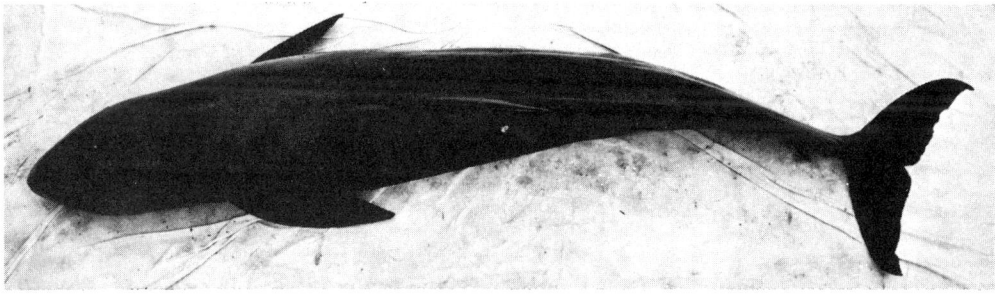

Photos of the small, melon-headed blackfish, *Peponocephala electra.*
Photos by D. Au, W. Perryman, and R.L. Pitman

175

THE SMALL, MELON-HEADED BLACKFISH
Also known as the Melon-headed Whale
Peponocephala electra (Gray, 1846)

Identifying Features. This blackfish is identified by the following features: dark color above, small size (to 9 ft.), inflated head, flippers with pointed tips, from 21 to 25 teeth in each of the four jaw bones, and white lips.

Size and Shape. This blackfish is the smallest of the dolphins with inflated heads and will usually reach a length of about 2 to 2.5 meters (6.6 to 8.2 ft.) or more. The body is long and slender and terminates in a long tail stock. The forehead is gently rounded, the upper jaw overhangs the lower jaw, and a beak is not visible. It resembles the false killer whale (*Pseudorca*), but the head is more pointed than *Pseudorca*, the body is smaller, and the flipper does not have a hump on its outer margin. It resembles the pigmy killer whale, *Feresa attenuata,* more than any of the other members of the Delphinidae.

Color. In general, the color of the body is a very dark gray to black above and lighter below. An elongated white area marks the belly and encloses the anus. Lighter areas occur in some individuals around the eye, along the lower lip, between the jaw and the flippers, and at the tip of the chin.

Distribution. This dolphin is a warm-water species which is world-wide in the tropical and warmer temperate seas of the world.

Migration. Very little information is available on its seasonal movements.

Fins and Flippers. The dorsal fin has a rather long base, is nearly straight on its front margin, is curved at the top, and is very slightly concave on its rear margin. It measures about 23 cm. (10 in.) in height. The flippers are of moderate size with pointed tips. The flukes of the tail bear a notch where they meet at the midline; they are dark in color above and below.

Teeth. The teeth number from about 21 to 25 in each of the four jaw bones and are usually more numerous in the upper jaws. This feature separates this species from similar dolphins.

Skeletal Notes. The vertebrae are distributed approximately as follows: C 7 + D 14 + L 17 + Ca 44 = 82. Of the 14 pairs of ribs, 7 possess two heads (capitulum and tubercle). In the neck vertebrae, the first 3 are fused together and the remaining 4 are separated. The bones (phalanges) of the fingers are distributed as follows: I (2-3), II (8-9), III (6-7), IV (3-4), V (2-3).

Food. The diet of this dolphin consists of squid and small surface fishes.

Swimming and Diving. This is a sociable species which has been known to gather into groups of 100 to 200 individuals; some schools have been reported which consisted of 500 to 1500 individuals. It has the happy habit of standing vertically in the water with its head above the surface. This is not a rapid swimmer. It can be trained to jump and at these times will leap 5 meters (16.4 ft.) above the water.

Reproduction. The adults are reported to mate during the spring and summer and the young are born a year later. The young dolphins measure about 1.2 meters (47 in.) at birth and will nurse for 9 to 12 or more months.

Abundance. This dolphin is not well known, but it appears to be more numerous than formerly estimated.

Economic Importance. There are no organized fisheries for this species. They are occasionally captured, driven ashore, or stranded; at these times, their flesh will be used for human food, animal food, bait for crab traps, etc.

Miscellaneous. At birth, the young have sensory hairs on the sides of their snout; these disappear in due time.

THE PIGMY KILLER WHALES
Genus *FERESA* Gray, 1871

This genus includes a single living species of one of the rarest and least-known of the small whales and about which almost nothing was known until recent times. In general, they have a long, slender, tapering body and a head which is inflated and which slopes quite rapidly downward from the forehead to the snout. This head is much less inflated and bulbous than that of *Globicephala* and most closely resembles the head of *Pseudorca*. The beak is absent and the snout, which is a bit longer than the lower jaw, imparts an underslung, shark-like aspect to the profile of the head. The dorsal fin is high and has an almost straight front border, a concave posterior border, and a straight, slender tip. The flippers are rounded and of moderate length. The teeth are large, conical in shape, and number from 8 to 13 in each of the four jaw bones. The vertebrae are reported to number about 68 to 70 in all. Large individuals reach a length of 2.75 meters (9 ft.), but most are smaller.

The color of the body is dark gray throughout with some markings. The lips have a narrow white band along their edges which in some individuals may extend to a large white patch which covers the chin and lower jaw. A large white area surrounds the vent and may even extend up the sides of the body; it may also extend posteriorly toward the tail as a slender, irregular stripe.

This genus and its species resembles the False Killer Whale (*Pseudorca*), but they are smaller and are marked with white areas, whereas *Pseudorca* is entirely black except for a grayish area between the flippers.

Studies of these whales by various scholars indicate that several names of species appearing in older books are really duplicate names or synonyms of other previously named species. The following list indicates the older names and the more correct and current names of these species.

Old Name		Name Currently In Use
Feresa intermedia	is now	*Feresa attenuata*
Feresa occulta	is now	*Feresa attenuata*
Orca intermedia	is now	*Feresa attenuata*

F. intermedia Gray, 1871, was based upon a skull which has since been lost.

This genus includes the single living species listed below.
Feresa attenuata Gray, 1875
THE PIGMY KILLER WHALE .... See page 178

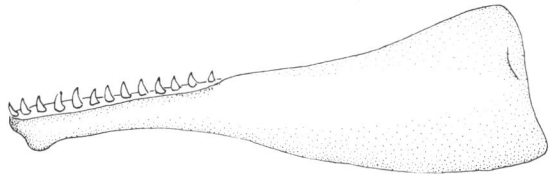

The teeth and jaw bone of *Feresa attenuata*.

Photos of the pigmy killer whale, *Feresa attenuata*. Note the white margin of the lips, the large white area on the belly, the notch on the tail, and the large dorsal fin.

Photos by P.B. Best.

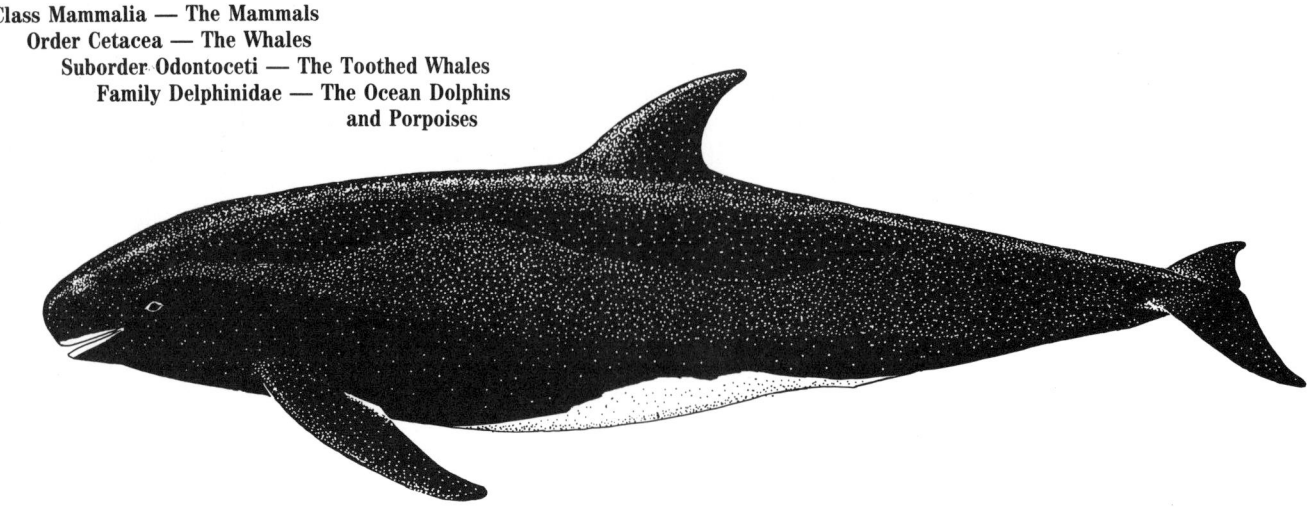

THE PIGMY KILLER WHALE
Also known as The Slender Pilot Whale and The Slender Blackfish
Feresa attenuata Gray, 1875

Identifying Features. The slender body, the rounded head, the white lips and underslung jaw, the absence of a beak, and the large, sub-triangular, long-based dorsal fin should help to identify this species. The white chin spot is also a feature of this species. The teeth number about 8 to 11 in each upper jaw and 12 or 13 in each lower jaw. There is a distinctive groove on the skin of the belly which begins anterior to the umbilicus and ends at the anus.

Size and Shape. This little-known whale resembles the False Killer Whale (*Pseudorca crassidens*), but is a smaller species. The body is very long and slender, particularly behind the anus, and will measure from about 2.2 to 2.7 meters (86 to 106 in.) in length. The head is rounded and narrowed at the front, is without a beak, and has an underslung jaw.

Color. The body is a dark gray to black color on the back and sides and is marked with lighter areas below. There are white areas on the lips and chin and a faint, whitish, anchor-shaped area on the chest between the flippers; there is a white area on the belly and lighter areas on the sides of the body. A white patch usually marks the tip of the lower jaw. These light areas change following death. The flippers and flukes are black in color above and below.

Distribution. The distribution of this species is undoubtedly world-wide in tropical, sub-tropical, and warmer temperate seas. In the North Pacific Ocean, it is known from Japan, Hawaii, and the warmer eastern areas. In the tropical Atlantic Ocean, it is known from the West Indian area and from tropical western Africa. It is also recorded from the Indian Ocean.

Migration. Very little information is available on this subject. It is doubtless a non-migratory species.

Fins and Flippers. The dorsal fin is large and slightly triangular in shape; it has a straight anterior margin and a concave posterior margin. The tip is backward-pointing, lacks ridigity, and may incline toward the side. This fin is located very near the center of the body. The flippers are narrow, rather straight, and are uniformly rounded on their outer margins and tips; this feature will separate this species from the false killer whale *(Pseudorca crassidens),* in which the flipper has a hump or "elbow" on its outer margin.

Teeth. The teeth are conical in shape, larger than in most dolphins, and number from 8 to 13 in each of the four jaw bones. The skull is asymmetrical, including the jaw bones. The right jaw is the smaller of the two and curiously usually has about one tooth less than the larger left side. The teeth are usually more numerous in the lower jaw bones.

Skeletal Notes. The anterior 3 or 4 neck vertebrae are united. The vertebrae are distributed approximately as follows: C 7 + D 12-13 + L 16-17 + Ca 31-34 = 68-70. The chevron bones number about 23 to 25. The ribs number 12 or 13 of which 6 pairs have two heads. The first 4 or 5 ribs are attached directly to the sternum, the next 4 or 5 ribs connect indirectly to the sternum, and the remainder are floating ribs.

Other Anatomical Notes. The skin is thin and easily scratched and the flippers are often notched from the bites of other creatures. A very unusual groove, 1 to 3 cm. in depth, extends along the midline of the belly from the anus forward to the chest. In the males, this groove includes the umbilicus, the rudimentary nipples, the penis, and the anus. In the females, the groove contains the umbilicus, the female urogenital organs, and the anus; the nipples lie outside and lateral to this median groove.

Food. It is presumed to feed upon squid and small fishes.

Swimming and Diving. This little whale is associated with tuna fishes and is sometimes captured in the large seines of this fishery. Dr. Masaharu Nishiwaki reports (1964) that a group of 14 whales, when captured in a net in Sagami Bay (Japan), stood vertically with their heads above the water and were not easily frightened. This is an aggressive animal and will attack and kill other dolphins and porpoises in tuna nets and when confined by captivity; other dolphins seem to be afraid of this species.

Reproduction. Very little information is available on the reproduction of this species.

Abundance. This is a rare and uncommon species.

Economic Importance. The false killer whale is of no economic importance, although a few individuals are captured in tuna nets and beach seines, or driven ashore in small bays.

THE FALSE KILLER WHALES
Also known as The False Pilot Whales
Genus *PSEUDORCA* Reinhardt, 1862

Some scholars think that these small whales are misnamed and that they should probably be called "The False Pilot Whales," because they resemble the pilot whales (*Globicephala*) much more closely than they resemble the true Killer Whales (*Orcinus*). Like the pilot whales, their bodies are long and slender and taper gradually toward the tail. Unlike the inflated, bulbous head of the pilot whales (*Globicephala*), the head of *Pseudorca* is relatively small and rounded, but not inflated, and tapers quite uniformly to the snout. The beak appears to be absent, but in reality exists as an exceedingly short and broad beak.

The flippers are quite long, slender, narrow, curved, and pointed, although they are shorter and wider than those of the pilot whales (*Globicephala*). These flippers bear an obtuse angle or hump along their outer margin which will positively identify these whales, since this hump does not occur in any other whale.

The dorsal fin, although relatively small, is variable in size and is located just behind the mid-point of the body. It is concave on its posterior margin and bears a bluntly pointed tip which is directed backward.

The teeth are large and are clearly visible. They are sharp, circular in cross section, and number from 7 to 12 in all four jaw bones. This genus (*Pseudorca*) may be separated from *Globicephala* and *Grampus* by the teeth. In *Pseudorca* the teeth are scattered along most of the length of the jaw bones, while in *Globicephala* and *Grampus* these teeth are fewer in number and are confined to the front of the mouth.

The vertebrae are distributed approximately as follows: C 7 + D 10 + L 9-11 + Ca 22-24 = 50-51. The 7 cervical (neck) vertebrae are fused in various combinations; the anterior 5 or 6 vertebrae are always fused, while the 7th vertebra may also be fused to the other 6 in older animals. The bones of the fingers are distributed approximately as follows: I (1), II (6), III (5), IV (2), V (1).

Photo of the tail of the false killer whale, *Pseudorca crassidens*, showing the deep notch on its posterior margin. This notch is a characteristic of the Family Delphinidae.
Sea Life Park, Hawaii.

Large individuals may reach a length of 6 meters (20 ft.), although most are much smaller. The females are usually one or two feet shorter than the males.

The color of the body is blackish with lighter areas between the flippers, particularly in younger individuals.

This genus is known from the Upper Pliocene Epoch in Europe and Japan.

This genus includes the single living species listed below.

Pseudorca crassidens (Owen, 1846)
THE FALSE KILLER WHALE .... See page 180

Photo of three false killer whales, *Pseudorca crassidens*, in Arikawa Bay, Japan. This species is usually uniformly black over the entire upper surface. This feature is often helpful in separating them from the species of *Globicephala*, some of which exhibit somewhat lighter color patches on their upper surface.
Photo by T. Kasuya.

THE FALSE KILLER WHALE
Also known as The False Pilot Whale
Pseudorca crassidens (Owen, 1846)

Identifying Features. This little whale may be separated from all other whales by the presence of a hump or elbow-like prominence on the curved outer margin of its flippers. The large teeth are also distinctive.

Size and Shape. The body of this whale is long and slender and in males will reach a maximum length of about 6 meters (19.7 ft.). The females will reach a maximum of about 5 meters (16.4 ft.). The head is bulbous and flattened and tapers forward from the blowhole to the snout. The upper jaw is longer than the lower jaw and overhangs it a short distance. The mouth opening is large and long. The skull has a flat, broad rostrum, but the beak is not visible externally. The males will measure from 2 to 3 feet longer than the females.

Color. Black is the predominant color of the body and covers its entire surface except for a gray area on the belly between the flippers and occasional whitish dapplings on the leading edge of the flippers. The body is often marked with scars.

Distribution. The false killer whale is a warm water species which is distributed world-wide in the open oceans of the tropics, the sub-tropics, and the warmer waters of the temperate zones. It is an oceanic species and does not frequent coastal waters. In the North Pacific it is distributed from Alaska to Panama; it occurs in the Sea of Japan and in the South China Sea; it is also widely distributed in the South Pacific, Indian, and Atlantic Oceans and in the Mediterranean Sea.

Migration. This is a non-migratory species, although it may shifts its position a few degrees with the changing seasons and currents.

Fins and Flippers. The dorsal fin is tall, curved, sickle-shaped, and pointed at the tip. It is located forward of the center of the body. The flippers are exceedingly long and narrow and exhibit an angular hump near the middle of their outer margin; this hump is found in no other whale. The flukes of the tail possess the median notch which is characteristic of this family.

The false killer whale, *Pseudorca crassidens.*
Sea Life Park, Hawaii.

The false killer whale, *Pseudorca crassidens.*
Sea Life Park, Hawaii.

Photo of the head of a newly born false killer whale, *Pseudorca crassidens.*   **Sea Life Park, Hawaii.**

Photo of a portion of a herd of 253 false killer whales, *Pseudorca crassidens,* which stranded in 1978 at Manukai Harbor, North Island, N.Z.

New Zealand Herald, Auckland.

Teeth. In this little whale, the teeth are large, strong, and pointed and are located in the front of the mouth. They are about 1.5 to 2 cm. (½ to ¾ in.) in diameter, about 8 cm. (3 in.) in length, and number from 7 to 12 in each of the four jaw bones. They are circular in cross-section and in this feature differ from the teeth of the killer whale (*Orcinus orca*) which are elliptical in cross section. There are always more teeth in the lower jaw bones. The usual number is about 9 to 12 teeth in each lower jaw bone and about 7 to 10 in each upper jaw bone.

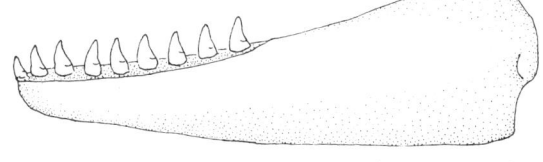

The teeth and jaw bone of *Pseudorca crassidens.*

Skeletal Notes. In this species, the usual number of vertebrae is 50, although they vary in number from 47 to 52. These vertebrae are usually distributed approximately as follows: C 7 + D 10 + L 10 + Ca 23 = 50. In the 7 cervical vertebrae, the first 6 are usually united into a single unit and the 7th vertebra is free. The thoracic vertebrae are usually 10 in number and are determined by the number of ribs. The lumbar vertebrae vary from 9 to 11 in number, although 10 is the usual number. The caudal vertebrae may vary from 18 to 26, although the usual range is from about 20 to 23.

The ribs vary in number from 9 to 12 pairs, although the usual number is 10 pairs. These ribs are not always in pairs; occasionally a specimen may appear which lacks a single rib on either side. Ribs 1 through 5 are true ribs and attach to the sternum. The first 6 pairs of ribs articulate by 2 heads with two adjoining vertebrae; the tubercle of the rib touches the vertebrae to which it belongs, and the head of the rib extends forward to meet the centrum of the vertebrae anterior to it. Ribs 7 to 10 have lost their head and therefore articulate through their tubercle with the transverse process of their corresponding vertebrae.

The sternum consists of four parts in various stages of ossification beginning anteriorly; of these, the 1st 3 parts are usually fused into a single unit. The sternum articulates with

4 pairs of ribs.

The bones of the fingers are distributed approximately as follows: I (2), II (8), III (6), IV (4), V (2).

Other Anatomical Notes. In a specimen which measured 2.93 meters (9 ft. 7 in.) in length, the heart weighed 1.743 kg. (3 lbs. 13.5 oz.).

Food. The diet of this whale consists of squid and various fishes. It is known to eat tuna and to steal fish from the lines of fishermen. It is also known to catch and eat the "mahi-mahi" fish, *Coryphaena hippurus,* and to catch, kill, and eat other smaller dolphins and porpoises.

Swimming and Diving. This whale is a sociable species and travels in small groups; however, it is not uncommon to see groups of 100 individuals and, in a few instances, large groups have been observed which included an estimated 1,000 individuals. These whales have been observed to leap above the water and to approach ships, where they will ride the bow waves. They occasionally associate with schools of tuna fishes and are captured in the seines of the tuna fishermen. There are records in which these whales were known to dive to a depth of 1,000 feet. The most amazing habit of these whales is that of beaching themselves in great groups of as many as 100 to 300 individuals and to resist any attempts to return them to the sea. These whales set an all-time record for swimming ashore and beaching themselves. It is reported that in 1946, 835 of these whales beached themselves near the city of Mar del Plata in Argentina.

Reproduction. Mating in this species is presumed to occur the year around, because embryos of various sizes are found at the same time and the young are born around the year. The length of pregnancy is long, possibly 12 to 14 months, and the young measure from about 1.5 to 2.1 meters (59 to 83 in.) at birth.

Abundance. The size of their population is not well known, but they seem to be quite common.

Economic Importance. This dolphin is not hunted regularly. A few are captured in the nets of tuna fishermen and those which are stranded on beaches usually decay before they can be utilized. A few are killed each year in Japan and elsewhere.

THE PILOT WHALES
Genus *GLOBICEPHALA* Lesson, 1828

The pilot whales have long, slender bodies which are quite robust in front and are more slender and tapering posteriorly; almost the posterior one-third of the body is composed of a long, deep caudal peduncle or tail stock which supplies the power to drive the tail flukes. The head is large, inflated and bulbous, and contains a small oil case; the profile of the forehead is steep and rounded. The skull bears a very short, broad rostrum which is practically invisible as a beak in an exterior view. The cleft of the mouth is inclined downward and the lips exhibit rounded protuberances.

The dorsal fin is thick, has a long base, and is inclined backward at its tip, particularly in the males. The front border of this fin has a long, gently-curving slope, while the rear margin is concave. It is placed quite far forward on the back at a point almost one-third of the length of the body from the head. The flippers are long, slender, narrow, curved, and pointed, and are placed low on the sides of the body.

The teeth are large, quite slender, occasionally curved, and number from 7 to 13 in each of the four jaw bones. These teeth are found only in the front one-half of the mouth. The location of the teeth within the mouth is very helpful in separating the three genera of *Globicephala, Grampus,* and *Pseudorca.* In *Pseudorca,* the 7 to 12 teeth are distributed along the length of the jaw bones, while in *Globicephala* and *Grampus,* the teeth are confined to the front of the mouth.

The vertebrae are distributed approximately as follows: C 7 + D 11 + L 12-14 + Ca 28-29 = 58-59. Of the 7 cervical (neck) vertebrae, the first 5 or 6 are fused into a single, immobile unit; this is also the condition in *Pseudorca.* The skeleton contains 11 pairs of ribs of which 6 pairs have double heads and 5 pairs articulate with the sternum. The bones of the fingers are distributed approximately as follows: I (3-4), II (9-14), III (9-11), IV (2-3), V (1-2).

In color, these whales are almost completely black, although some have gray areas on the back just behind the dorsal fin and others are marked with grayish or whitish areas on the chin, throat, and belly.

Large individuals are reported to reach a length of 28 feet, although most animals will measure less than 20 feet in length.

The distribution of this genus is world-wide in tropical and temperate seas.

Most scholars are uncertain about the number of species in the Genus *Globicephala.* Some believe that there is only one species (*G. melaena*) with various sub-species. Others believe that there are two or three species and sub-species; these scholars might arrange their species as follows:

1. *Globicephala macrorhynchus* Gray, 1846. The Short-finned Pilot Whale.

This is a warm water species of wide range; it occurs in the tropical and warmer temperate seas of the Atlantic Ocean from Virginia (38° N.L.) southward and across the warmer waters of the entire Pacific and Indian Oceans.

2. *Globicephala melaena* (Traill, 1809). The Long-finned Pilot Whale.

a. *Globicephala melaena melaena* (Traill, 1809).
This sub-species occurs in the cooler waters of the Atlantic Ocean from Virginia (38° N.L.) northward.

b. *Globicephala melaena edwardii* A. Smith, 1834.
This sub-species occurs in the entire southern hemisphere in cooler temperate seas.

3. *Globicephala scammoni* Cope, 1869. The North Pacific Pilot Whale or Blackfish.

This species occurs on both sides of the North Pacific Ocean and along the Kurile and Aleutian Islands. Some scholars regard *G. scammoni* as a sub-species or even a synonym of *G. macrorhynchus.*

In this book, this genus will be regarded as having but two species: *G. macrorhynchus* and *G. melaena.*

Studies of these pilot whales by various scholars indicate that several names of species appearing in older books are really duplicate names or synonyms of other previously named species. The following list indicates the older names and the more correct and current names of these species.

Old Name		Name Currently In Use
Globicephala brachyptera	is now	*Globicephala macrorhynchus*
Globicephala edwardii	is now	*Globicephala melaena*
Globicephala guadaloupensis	is now	*Globicephala macrorhynchus*
Globicephala indica	is now	*Globicephala macrorhynchus*
Globicephala intermedius	is now	*Globicephala macrorhynchus*
Globicephala leucosagmaphora	is now	*Globicephala melaena*
Globicephala melas	is now	*Globicephala melaena*
Globicephala scammonii	is now	*Globicephala macrorhynchus*
Globicephala siebold	is now	*Globicephala macrorhnychus*
Globicephalus	is now	*Globicephala*
Globicephalus rissii	is now	*Grampus griseus*

This genus is known from the Pleistocene Epoch in North America. Fossils of *G. melaena* have been found in Japan which indicate that this species may have lived there as recently as the 10th century A.D.

This genus contains the two living species listed below.

Globicephala macrorhynchus Gray, 1846
THE SHORT-FINNED PILOT WHALE . . . .
. . . . See page 183
Globicephala melaena (Traill, 1809)
THE LONG-FINNED PILOT WHALE . . . .
. . . . See page 185

Class Mammalia — The Mammals
  Order Cetacea — The Whales
    Suborder Odontoceti — The Toothed Whales
      Family Delphinidae — The Ocean Dolphins and Porpoises

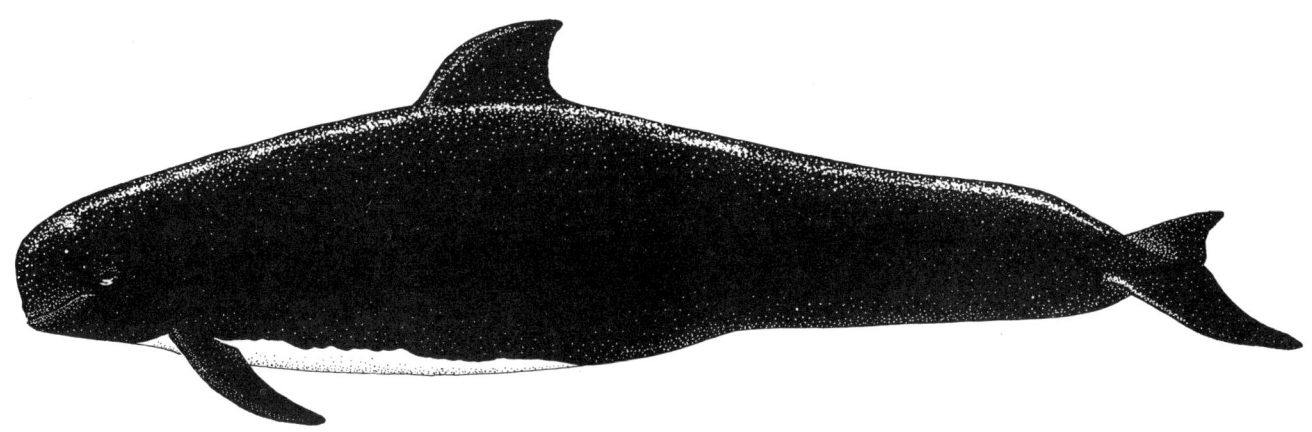

THE SHORT-FINNED PILOT WHALE
Also known as the Blackfish
Globicephala macrorhynchus Gray, 1846

Identifying Features. The bulbous and inflated head will identify the two species of the pilot whales. This species may be separated from *G. melaena* by its teeth and flippers. *G. macrorhynchus* has from 7 to 12 teeth in each of the four jaw bones and a flipper which is 1/6 of the body length; *G. melaena* has from 8 to 13 teeth and a longer flipper which is 1/5 of the body length. In this species, the dorsal profile of the head and neck has a dip or notch in it at the blowhole. They may also be separated on the basis of distribution; *G. macrorhynchus* is the warm water species.

Size and Shape. The body of this whale is robust in front and greatly elongated posteriorly. The head is inflated, bulbous, thick, and squarish; it becomes enlarged with age and somewhat flattened in front and will eventually overhang the mouth. Individuals will reach a maximum length of about 6 meters (20 ft.), although a few are known to exceed this length; the males are more robust and about 50 cm. (1.5 ft.) longer than the females. The trunk is very slender, laterally compressed, and bears keels above and below.

Color. These whales are black or blackish above and gray or whitish below. The gray areas, which vary in size and color, are located beneath the chin and on the belly. These light ventral areas are anchor-shaped on the chest, extend backward as a slender band, and enlarge posteriorly into an elongated, oval-shaped area surrounding the anus. Some individuals present as many as three lighter grayish areas on the upper surface: (1) a patch behind the eye; (2) a chevron-shaped, backward-pointing marking on the back behind the blowhole; and (3) a saddle-shaped area on the back posterior to the dorsal fin. All individuals do not show these markings. The young whales are lighter in color than the adults.

Distribution. Of the two species of *Globicephala,* this whale (*G. macrorhynchus*) is the warm-water species and *G. melaena* lives in cooler water. This species is widely distributed in the tropical and warmer temperate seas of the world. In the Atlantic Ocean, it occurs from about 35° N.L.

southward to about 15° S.L. It occurs across the entire Indian Ocean, and in the Pacific Ocean from the Gulf of Alaska and Japan southward to about the latitude of Peru. It occurs in northern Australia, but it does not occur in New Zealand.

Because the species of *Globicephala* are exceedingly hard to distinguish and to classify, there is still uncertainty regarding the occurrence of *G. melaena* in the North Pacific Ocean.

Migration. Very little information is available regarding their seasonal movements. Off California, they come nearer shore in the spring when the squid are spawning.

Fins and Flippers. The dorsal fin is large, is supported by a long base, and is located forward of the body center; it is long, inclined backward, and is concave on its posterior margin. The flippers are very long, slender, and pointed at their tips. The flukes of the tail exhibit a notch on their posterior margin where they meet at the midline of the body.

Teeth. The teeth number between 7 to 12 in each of the four jaw bones; this is fewer than *G. meleana* which has from 8 to 13 teeth. These teeth are located at the very front of the jaw bones and usually number 8 or 9.

A photo of a short-finned pilot whale, *Globicephala macrorhynchus,* at sea showing the rounded head, open blowhole, and the outline of the dorsal fin.
Photo by Graybill

183

Fetus of a short-finned pilot whale *(Globicephala macrorhynchus)* **procured from a beached specimen on Lanai Island on October 3, 1958. Length about 51 cm. (20 in.)**
Photo by Tinker.

Skeletal Notes. The vertebrae of this whale are distributed as follows: C 7 + D 11 + L 12 + Ca 27 = 57. The first 6 vertebrae of the neck are fused into a single, immobile unit. The bones of the fingers are distributed as follows: I (3), II (9-14), II (9-11), IV (2), V (1).

Other Anatomical Notes. The external nostril (blowhole) is short (front to back).

Food. The diet of this whale consists mostly of squid and various fishes.

Swimming and Diving. These whales are social animals with a strong herding instinct. They usually travel in small groups of a few individuals or in larger groups approaching 100 or more. They prefer to live at sea and do not frequent shorelines unless they are driven ashore by fishermen or, having lost their instinct of self-preservation, come streaming ashore to beach themselves, to struggle, and to die on the seashore. They are known to dive to depths of 600 meters (1967 ft.) or more during tests and also pursuing squid. They do not ride the bow waves of ships. The large oceanaria usually exhibit pilot whales because of their willingness to learn and to perform.

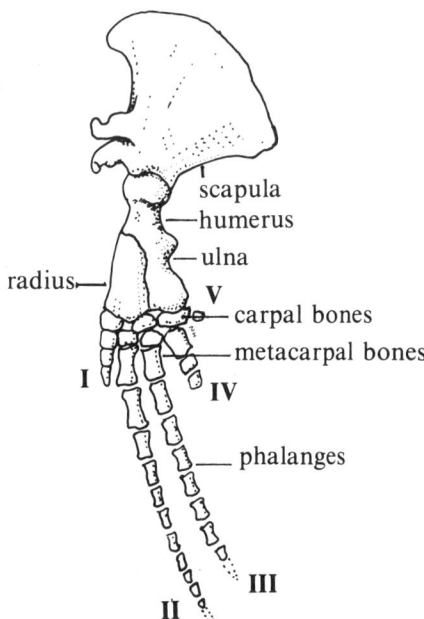

Diagram of the left pectoral girdle and appendage of a pilot whale, *Globicephala* **sp. (Odontoceti: Delphinidae).**
Drawn from Howell.

From: Alfred Brazier Howell — AQUATIC MAMMALS. 1931. Courtesy of Charles E. Thomas, Publishers. Springfield, Ill.

Photo of the short-finned pilot whale, *Globicephala macrorhynchus.* **Note the long, slender trunk and the long, slender, curved flipper. This genus lacks the elbow-like hump on the curved, outer edge of the flipper—a feature found in the false killer whale,** *Pseudorca crassidens.*
Photo by Marineland of the Pacific.

Photo of a scene at Ruakaka, New Zealand, where 68 pilot whales, *Globicephala* **species, beached themselves in August, 1923.**
Art Studios.

From: "Whales and Dolphins of New Zealand and Australia" by A.N. Baker. Victoria University Press, Wellington, 1983. Courtesy A.N. Baker.

Reproduction. The young appear to be born throughout the year at about 3 year intervals and, at birth, will measure about 140 cm. (55 in.). Their life span is thought to approach fifty years.

Abundance. The pilot whales are among the more numerous of the medium-sized whales. They are still quite common in spite of limited hunting extending over many years.

Economic Importance. These whales have been hunted from prehistoric times and are still harvested in small numbers in scattered localities including the West Indian islands and Japan. In these operations, it is customary procedure to drive these groups of whales ashore.

Miscellaneous. Some scholars believe that there are two forms of these whales in the North Pacific Ocean.

THE LONG-FINNED PILOT WHALE
Also known as the Atlantic Pilot Whale, Northern Pilot
Whale, Blackfish, Pothead, Caa'ing Whale, Piloto,
Calderon, etc.
Globicephala melaena (Traill, 1809)

Identifying Features. The inflated, spherical head and the robust body with the long tapering trunk will help to identify the pilot whales. The dorsal fin has a long base; it is low, directed backward, and is set quite far forward on the body. This species has 8 to 13 teeth in each of the four jaw bones and a flipper which is 1/5 of the body length. (See this section in the preceding description of *G. macrorhynchus.*)

Size and Shape. The body of all pilot whales has a rounded, bulbous head in front, followed by a robust body and an elongated, tapering tail. There is no constriction at the neck and the body is quite cylindrical from the head backward to the region of the dorsal fin; thereafter it tapers gradually to the tail. This tail stock is long, high, laterally compressed, and bears a keel on both its upper and lower ridges. The males are a little larger than the females. The males of this species will reach an average length in excess of 6 meters (19.7 ft.) and a maximum of possibly 8 meters (26 ft.) or more. The females will measure from 5 to 6 meters (16.4 to 19.7 ft.) or more.

Color. The body is colored a dark chocolate-gray hue to black and is marked below with white or light gray in varying patterns. These light areas extend from the lower jaw to the chest, bases of the flippers, belly, and anus. Some animals are reported to have a gray area behind the dorsal fin and an oval patch behind the eye. This gray area is also a characteristic of *G. macrorhynchus* and should be so noted. Some will exhibit a short, diagonal, upward, grayish streak just above and behind the eye, and an occasional animal will show a white patch on the chin. A few individuals have been seen which are completely white.

Distribution. The distribution of this species is limited to the cooler waters of the globe.

In the Atlantic Ocean, it occurs from the latitude of about Virginia (38° N.L.), northwestern Africa, and the Mediterranean Sea northward to Greenland, Iceland, and the Barents Sea.

In the North Pacific Ocean, the occurrence of this species is clouded in uncertainty, because the species and their varieties are very difficult to identify. Most scholars seem to think that it does not occur in this area, although it has been reported from this region.

In the southern hemisphere, it is world-wide and encircles the globe in the area of the West Wind Drift; here it also occurs in the Humbolt, Falkland, and Benguela Currents. These northern and southern populations do not seem to meet, mix, or interbreed. They are separated in the equatorial Atlantic Ocean by a wide band of warm, tropical water.

Migration. This whale is a migratory species and moves northward and southward with the seasons on both sides of the North Atlantic Ocean. In the western Atlantic Ocean, they go north to Greenland in the summertime to feed upon the squid (*Illex* sp.).

Fins and Flippers. The dorsal fin has a long base and is located anterior to the middle of the body; it is high, long, bent backward, and roundly pointed at the tip. Dorsal and ventral keels are present. The flippers are long, very narrow, and curved and measure about 1/5 or more of the body length. The flukes of the tail bear a notch on their posterior margin where they join at the midline.

Teeth. Each of the 4 jaw bones contains about 8 to 13 conical teeth which are set in the front of the mouth. The teeth are quite large and measure about 1.5 cm. (9/16 in.) in diameter and about 5 cm. (2 in.) in length.

Skeletal Notes. The vertebrae are distributed about as follows: C 7 + D 11 + L 12-13 + Ca 28-29 = 58-60. Six pairs of ribs have two heads, and five pairs of ribs articulate directly with the sternum. The first 5 or 6 vertebrae of the neck are fused together into a single unit. The bones of the fingers are distributed about as follows: I (3-4), II (9-14), III (9-11), IV (2-3), V (1-2).

Other Anatomical Notes. The blowhole is placed slightly off center to the left.

Food. The diet of this whale consists mostly of squid and a wide variety of fish.

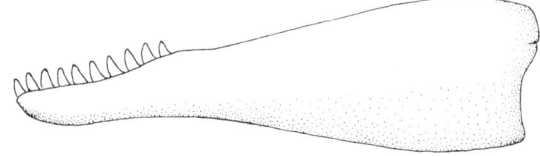

The teeth and jaw bone of *Globicephala melaena.*

Swimming and Diving. This pilot whale is a gregarious species and usually travels in small groups of 4 to 6 individuals. They are occasionally seen in herds of 50 or more and, on some occasions, they will gather by the hundreds. They are not particularly friendly with ships and do not ride the bow waves of vessels. In the North Atlantic Ocean, they are often seen with the Atlantic White-sided Dolphin (*Lagenorhynchus acutus*). They have an inborn fear of the killer whale (*Orcinus*) and will come into shallow water and beach themselves if other escape routes are not available.

Reproduction. The age of these whales can now be determined since scholars discovered that two layers of dentine are deposited in their teeth each year. Young female whales reach sexual maturity at approximately six years of age,

while in the males, maturity and mating are delayed until about the 12th year. The adults mate in February and March in warm water and the young are born in July to October, 15 to 16 months later, in cooler water; thereafter the young are nursed for about 20 months. Each adult female probably raises one calf about every three years. The young, when born, are reported as a brownish to tan-gray color, and will measure about 1.4 meters (55 in.) or more in length. They are toothless and will remain with their mother for the most of the next two years.

Abundance. It is presumed that this is a fairly abundant species; however, information on their numbers is lacking. Reduction in the number of whales being captured each year suggests that this fishery may be over-exploited and fishing should be restrained.

Economic Importance. This small whale has supported a fishery from very ancient times. When herds have appeared along a coastline, the inhabitants have gone to sea in small boats and have successfully driven the whales ashore. This fishery was carried on in Newfoundland, western Greenland, Iceland, the many islands north of England (Faroe, Shetland, and Orkney Islands), and on the coasts of Peru and Chile. These catches have declined in size and are now of less importance.

Each whale would yield 40 gallons of blubber oil and 2 gallons of head and jaw oil.

Miscellaneous. In olden times, this whale was used in Europe to locate schools of herring and was therefore called the "pilot" whale.

Photo of the long-finned pilot whale, *Globicephala melaena,* lying upon the deck of a whaling station in Newfoundland. Note the long flippers of this species and the gray and white color pattern of the ventral side. **Photo by J.C. Mead.**

THE KILLER WHALES
Genus *ORCINUS* Fitzinger, 1860

The killer whales are the largest of the dolphin-like whales and are probably the most widely known. They possess large, strong, robust bodies which are known to reach a length of 9+ meters (30 ft.). Their head is relatively small for their body size, the snout is rounded and broad, and the rostrum proceeding forward from the skull is not readily visible externally as a beak at the front of the head.

The dorsal fin of killer whales is most astonishing for its height. In large males, it projects steeply upward from a comparatively short base to a height of as much as 1.8 meters (6 ft.); in these males, this fin is vertical on its rear margin. In the females, the fin is shorter, usually about three feet or less in height and is slightly concave and recurved on its posterior border. The flippers of killer whales are likewise different from those of other whales. They are thick, massive, strong, and are oval-shaped with rounded ends; they may measure as much as six feet in length and four feet in width. These flippers are black above and white below.

The teeth of this genus are massive and strong and (unlike *Grampus* and *Globicephala*) are distributed along the full length of each jaw bone. These teeth number between 10 and 13, in each of the 4 jaw bones, are oval in cross-section, are about two inches in diameter, have curved tips, and have large, antero-posteriorly flattened roots.

The vertebrae are distributed about as follows: C 7 + D 11-12 + L 10 + Ca 21-24 = 50-52. Of the 7 cervical (neck) vertebrae, the first two, three, or more are usually fused together into a single unit and the last two or more vertebrae are usually free. There are 11 or 12 pairs of ribs of which 6 or 7 pairs usually have double heads and 5 or more pairs articulate with the sternum. The bones of the fingers are distributed as follows: I (2), II (6-7), III (4-5), IV (3-4), V (2-3).

The color of the body is black with large white areas. There is usually a large white spot on the temple above and behind the eye; a large light area (usually white) occurs behind the dorsal fin and extends downward and forward onto the upper back. The white area on the belly extends backward from the chin to beyond the vent and usually continues as a narrow stripe almost to the tail. The white area of the belly gives off a wide, white branch on each side which extends upward and backward onto the flank of the body. In these whales, the color boundaries are quite sharp and distinct.

The distribution of this genus is world-wide, particularly in cooler waters.

The name of *Orcinus rectipinna* is a synonym and should be replaced by *Orcinus orca*.

This genus is known from the Middle Pliocene Epoch in Europe.

This genus contains the single living species listed below.

Orcinus orca (Linnaeus, 1758)
THE KILLER WHALE . . . . See page 188

Photo by K.C. Balcomb.

Photo by K.C. Balcomb.

Photo by W.F. Samaras.

Photo by K.C. Balcomb.

Photos of killer whales, *Orcinus orca,* in various poses taken in Puget Sound, Washington, U.S.A., and at San Benitos Islands (top right) off Baja, Mexico, showing the color pattern of this species. The configuration of the dorsal fin is different in the males and females. In the males, the rear margin of the dorsal fin is nearly straight, while in the females, the rear margin is curved.

Class Mammalia — The Mammals
Order Cetacea — The Whales
Suborder Odontoceti — The Toothed Whales
Family Delphinidae — The Ocean Dolphins and Porpoises

THE KILLER WHALE
Orcinus orca (Linnaeus, 1758)

Identifying Features. The killer whale is the largest of the ocean dolphins and probably the best known of all whales. It is easily recognized by its great, tall dorsal fin and its black and white colors.

Size and Shape. The body of the killer whale is very broad, robust, and spindle-shaped. Large adult males will reach a length of 9.5 meters (31 ft.), but most are much smaller. Large adult females will reach a length of 7 to 8.2 meters (23 to 27 ft.), but most will measure nearer 6 meters (20 ft.).

Color. In this species, the body color is black with a large white area extending along the lower side from the chin to the anus; this white area gives off a lateral, upward, posteriorly-directed extension on each side just anterior to the anus. A large, distinctive white spot is located just behind the eye. The flippers and tail flukes are black above and white below. In addition, a light saddle-shaped area of various shapes and colors is often present on the back just posterior to the dorsal fin. In Antarctic Seas, the white areas are yellowish in color. In newborn calves, these light colored areas are of a yellowish hue; they become white as they grow older. Some whales of this species have been seen in the wild which were completely black or completely white.

Distribution. The killer whale has been described as the most widely distributed mammal on earth because it inhabits the polar, temperate, and tropical seas of the globe. It is commonest in the eastern and western Pacific Ocean, the northeastern Atlantic Ocean, and the Antarctic Seas. It appears to stay within 800 km. (500 mi.) of the shoreline and will enter inland seas, bays, and estuaries. Its preference for coastlines is doubtless due to the presence of more food in these areas.

Migration. These whales move northward and southward with the seasons, possibly following the migrations of their various sources of food.

Fins and Flippers. The dorsal fin of killer whales is the tallest of all whales. In an adult male, it may reach a height of 1.8 meters (6 ft.) and its posterior margin may be nearly vertical. In female whales, the fin may measure as much as .9 meters

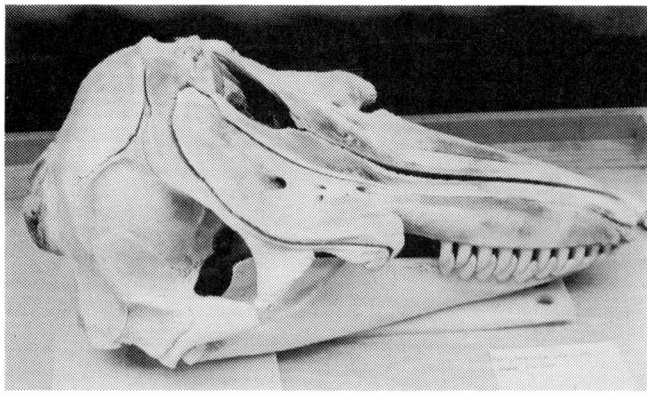

The skull of the killer whale, *Orcinus orca,* showing the right side in lateral view.
Photo by Michael Graybill at Humboldt State Univ.

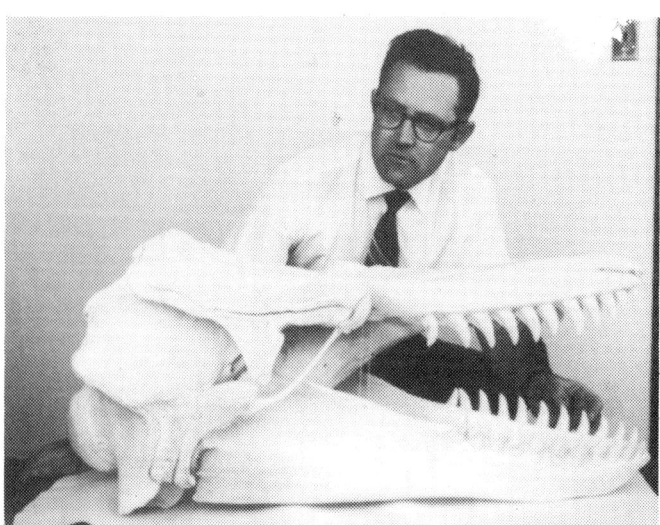

Photo of the skull and jaws of the killer whale, *Orcinus orca,* in lateral view. Photo taken with Mr. Vincent F. Penfold at the Vancouver Public Aquarium.

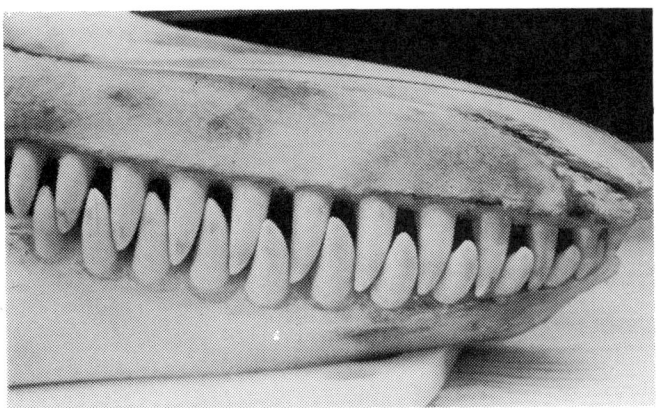

**The jaws and teeth of the killer whale, *Orcinus orca*.
Photo by Michael Graybill at Humboldt State Univ.**

(3 ft.) in height, but its posterior margin will be concave and its tip pointed toward the rear. The young of both sexes have smaller fins with sloping margins on the front and rear borders.

The flippers of this whale are quite unlike those of other whales for they are large, broad, rounded, and paddle-shaped. The tail is large, thick, notched at its center, and measures about 1/4 of the body length.

Teeth. The teeth are large, heavy, and thick and number between about 10 to 13 or 14 (usually 12) in each of the jaw bones. They are curved at the tip, point slightly inward, and interlock with those of the opposite jaw when the mouth is closed. The teeth are oval in cross-section, pointed, and measure about 10 to 13 cm. (4 to 5 in.) in length of which about 5 cm. (2 in.) protrudes above the gums.

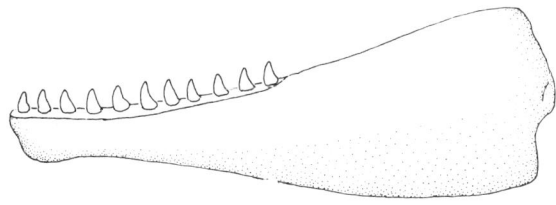

The teeth and jaw bone of *Orcinus orca*.

Photo of a killer whale, *Orcinus orca* (Odontoceti: Delphinidae), taken in Alaska between St. Paul and St. Matthew Islands, showing the light gray area just behind the dorsal fin.
Photo by Scheffer.

**Killer whales, *Orcinus orca*, leaping in the pool at the Vancouver Public Aquarium in Vancouver, British Columbia. "Bjossa," a female, is on the left; "Hyak," a male, is on the right. Note the paddle-like flippers, the difference in the outlines of the heads, and the difference in the dorsal fins.
Photo by The Vancouver Public Aquarium.**

Skeletal Notes. The vertebrae are distributed approximately as follows: C 7 + D 11-12 + L 10 + Ca 21-24 = 50-52; the usual number is 52. The first 3 or 4 vertebrae of the neck are usually fused into an immobile unit. There are 11 or 12 pairs of ribs of which 6 or 7 pairs have 2 heads. About 5 pairs of ribs articulate directly with the sternum. The bones of the fingers are usually distributed approximately as follows: I (2), II (6-7), III (4-5), IV (3-4), V (2-3).

Other Anatomical Notes. The flippers of the male grow proportionately larger with age. In young males, they measure about 1/9 of the body length, while in old males they may measure 1/5 of the body length.

Food. The diet of this species includes a wide variety of large animals; these are known to include all large whales, all available species of dolphins and other smaller cetaceans, all available seals and sea lions, walruses, sea otters, sea birds, sea turtles including the great leatherback turtle, squids, a wide array of fishes including various sharks, Pacific halibut, salmon, ling cod, the pelagic opah fish, and doubtless a great many more. The killer whale is reported to eat 4% of its body weight daily.

Swimming and Diving. This whale is a very good swimmer and is reported to be able to swim at a speed of 25 knots (28.8 mph). It travels in groups of 2 or 3, sometimes as many as 20 to 30, and is occasionally seen in great groups which might include as many as 150 or more individuals.

Photo of a herd of 17 killer whales, *Orcinus orca*, which were stranded in May, 1955, on the beach at Paraparaumu, North Island, New Zealand.
Evening Post Newspaper.

From: "Whales and Dolphins of New Zealand and Australia" by A.N. Baker. Victoria University Press, Wellington, 1983. Courtesy A.N. Baker.

Reproduction. The males and females are believed to mate between about December to February and to give birth to the young about 11 or 12 months later. At birth, the young will measure about 2.5 meters (8+ ft.) or more in length and will weigh between 350 and 400 pounds; it will remain with its mother for about 2 years. It is presumed that an adult female will give birth to a calf about every three or more years. These whales are often divided into social groups of which one group will consist of both young and old males and the other group will consist of the females and the calves.

Abundance. The population of this species is probably not very large. Because they live near coastlines and are easily observed, their numbers may be overestimated.

Economic Importance. Killer whales do considerable damage to other animal populations. They also do damage to fishing gear and interrupt these activities. They have been hunted commercially in Norway, Japan, and elsewhere, but the catch has not been large. They are occasionally captured for exhibit in large oceanaria.

Photo of a killer whale, *Orcinus orca* (Odontoceti: Delphinidae), in ventral view showing the location of the umbilicus, the penis, and the anus.

Photo by Ernest Walker.

Photo of a male killer whale, *Orcinus orca,* (Odontoceti: Delphinidae), in lateral view showing the enormous dorsal fin with its nearly straight and vertical margins.

Photo by Ernest P. Walker.

THE IRRAWADDY RIVER DOLPHINS
Genus *ORCAELLA* Gray, 1866

The Irrawaddy River dolphins are small cetaceans which may reach a length of about 7 feet (2.13 m.). Their head is inflated and bulbous with a bulging forehead; this has led some observers to remark that these whales seem to resemble a miniature Beluga in most aspects except color. There is a very short, pointed beak present and the mouth below it is encircled by lips. It is interesting to note that the blowhole atop the head is placed somewhat to the left of the midline of the body. The head is followed by a slight constriction of the body indicating the presence of a functional neck; this is most apparent in thin animals.

The dorsal fin is small, concave on the rear margin, and pointed; it is located just behind the mid-point of the body. A low ridge of skin extends from this fin backward along the midline of the back. The flippers are small, broadly triangular, and pointed.

The teeth, which are small and conical, occur in all 4 jaw bones. The upper jaws have from about 12 to 19 teeth on each side, while the lower jaw bones have from about 12 to 17 teeth in each jaw bone.

The vertebrae are distributed approximately as follows: C 7 + D 14 + L 14+ Ca 28 = 63. Of the cervical (neck) vertebrae, the 1st and 2nd vertebrae are fused and the remaining 5 are separate. There are 14 pairs of ribs; of these, the first 8 pairs have two heads and only the first 5 pairs articulate with the sternum. The last two pairs of ribs are floating and do not articulate with the backbone. The bones of the fingers are distributed approximately as follows: I (2), II (8), III (6), IV (3), V (1). The 5th finger is not ossified in most individuals.

The color of the body is a dark slate-blue or gray, except for the lower surfaces of the body which are a lighter shade.

The distribution of this genus is limited to the rivers and shorelines of southeastern Asia and the islands of the East Indies.

Some scholars have divided these dolphins into the following two subspecies:

Orcaella brevirostris brevirostris (Gray, 1866)
Orcaella brevirostris fluminalis Anderson, 1871

Most students of these dolphins believe that there is only one species which varies somewhat in some of its external features.

Studies of these dolphins by various scholars indicate that several names of species appearing in older books are really duplicate names or synonyms of other previously named species. The following list indicates the older names and the more correct and current names of these species.

Old Name		Name Currently In Use
Genus *Orcella*	is now	Genus *Orcaella*
Orcaella fluminalis	is now	*Orcaella brevirostris*

This genus is known only from the Holocene Epoch (Recent).

This genus contains the single living species listed below.

Orcaella brevirostris (Gray, 1866)
THE IRRAWADDY RIVER DOLPHIN
. . . . See page 192

THE IRRAWADDY RIVER DOLPHIN
Also known as the Irrawaddy Dolphin and
Snub-fin Dolphin
Orcaella brevirostris (Gray, 1866)

Identifying Features. This is a small species with an inflated head, a dark body, and a blowhole situated slightly to the left of the midline. The dorsal fin is very small.

Size and Shape. In size and shape, some scholars have described this dolphin as a miniature Beluga (*Monodontidae: Delphinapterus leucas*), but they differ widely in color. The body is largest in front of the dorsal fin, the head is spherical and bulging, the beak is very short, and the eyes are large. The mouth is surrounded by a lip and slopes upward toward the eyes. The neck is moveable and a slight constriction may be observed in the profile of this region. Adult males will reach a length of about 2 to 2.5 meters (6.5 to 8.2 ft.). and a weight of 90 to 100 kg. (198 to 220 lbs.).

Color. The body is a slaty-bluish gray to blackish color over the back and sides, including the dorsal fin, the flippers, and the tail. The belly is a paler color and may often approach white.

Distribution. This is a tropical species which once extended from East Africa eastward to northern Australia. It is known from East Africa, the Arabian Sea, the Bay of Bengal, the Malay Peninsula, Vietnam, Borneo, Java, New Guinea, and northern Australia. It can live permanently in either fresh or salt water and has been recorded from the Ganges (India), the Brahmaputra (Bangladesh), the Irrawaddy (Burma), and the Mekong (Vietnam) Rivers. This dolphin is seldom seen in the sea; it has been recorded 1,440 km. (900 mi.) inland in rivers.

Migration. This dolphin is presumed to be a non-migratory species. Very little information is available on its migratory habits.

Fins and Flippers. The dorsal fin is small, low, and sickle-shaped; it is placed slightly to the rear of the center of the body. Dorsal and ventral ridges or keels extend from the fin backward toward the tail. The flippers are quite large, broad, triangular in shape, and end in a tip which points slightly backward. The tail is small and bears a notch at its center.

Teeth. The teeth number from about 12 to 19 in each of the 4 jaw bones. They are small and measure about 6 mm. (¼ in.) in diameter. It is interesting to note that the upper teeth are slightly smaller than the lower teeth and occasionally are 2 or 3 more in number. The usual number is 12 to 19 in each upper jaw and 12 to 17 in each lower jaw.

Skeletal Notes. The vertebrae are distributed as follows: C 7 + D 14 + L 14 + Ca 28 = 63. The 1st two neck vertebrae are united. There are 14 pairs of ribs of which the 1st 8 pairs have 2 heads. The last 1 or 2 pairs of ribs do not articulate with the backbone and are therefore floating. The 1st 5 pairs* of ribs articulate with the sternum via a middle bone. The bones of the fingers are distributed as follows: I (2), II (8), III (6), IV (3), V (1). The 5th finger is not ossified in some flippers.

Other Anatomical Notes. The blowhole is located atop the head just a little to the left of the midline of the body. The liver is bilobed, the uterus has two horns, and the stomach has a special digestive gland. Sensory hairs are present in young dolphins on each side of the upper jaw; there are 5 pairs in a row 3 cm. long, located 2 cm. above the mouth and 5 cm. back from the midline of the rostrum.

Food. The diet of this dolphin consists of fish, although some think it may eat an occasional crustacean.

Swimming and Diving. This dolphin is a slow, leisurely swimmer. It is rarely found alone and usually travels in small groups of 2 or 3 individuals. It is reported to breathe every 70 to 150 seconds with a loud noise. As it emerges from the water, the head is visible first and then the back; the tail also usually breaks the surface. It is reported to follow the river steamers.

Reproduction. Very little information is available on the reproductive habits of this species. The gestation period is probably about one year; the young appear to be born around August each year. At birth, the young measure about 65 cm. (25 in.) in length.

---

*Some scholars say that 4 pairs articulate directly with the sternum.

Abundance. From ancient times, this species has been distributed over a very wide area, but it appears to be less abundant than formerly, probably due to the pressure of the growing human population.

Economic Importance. This dolphin has no economic importance and there are no fisheries based upon it. It is regarded and treated differently in each of the many countries which it borders. In India, it is reported that it is captured in some areas and its oil used for rheumatism. The Burmese people in some areas think that this dolphin has the power to attract fishes to their nets and therefore do not harm it. They have even refused to capture specimens for scientists. In most countries, it enjoys the protection of law.

Miscellaneous. This dolphin is reported to squirt water from the mouth.

**Photo of a female Irrawaddy River Dolphin, *Orcaella brevirostris,* taken at Townsville, Queensland, Australia.
Photo by G.E. Heinsohn.**

Reproduced by permission of the Dept. of Fisheries and Oceans, Dominion of Canada, from the Jour. Fish. Res. Bd. of Canada 32:7, July, 1975.

THE TRUE PORPOISES
Genus *PHOCOENA* G. Cuvier, 1817

The true porpoises are usually confused with the various genera of dolphins and, as a consequence, the name of "porpoise" is often carelessly and erroneously applied to the various species of the dolphins. The name of "porpoise" should be reserved for the 6 species which are described on the following pages.

The true purpoises are a small group of three genera and six species as follows:

1. Genus *Phocoena* G. Cuvier, 1817.
   The True Porpoises (4 species)
2. Genus *Neophocaena* Palmer, 1899.
   The Finless Porpoises (1 species)
3. Genus *Phocoenoides* Andrews, 1911.
   The Dall's White-flanked Porpoises (1 species)

These three genera of porpoises are occasionally separated from the dolphin family (*Delphinidae*) by some scholars and placed in a separate family called the *Phocoenidae*. In this book, these porpoises will be regarded as a part of the great family of the *Delphinidae* (the ocean dolphins, porpoises, and related species).

The porpoises of the Genus *Phocoena* are small species which seldom exceed 1.8 meters (6 ft.) in length. They have spindle-shaped bodies which are largest in the area just anterior to the dorsal fin; from this point their bodies taper quite rapidly toward their head and tail. The head is small, short, and wide and is somewhat flattened on the forehead. The skull bears a short, broad rostrum, but it is not visible externally as a beak.

The dorsal fin is located just behind the middle of the back; it is triangular in shape, has a longer front margin than rear margin, and is only very slightly concave on its rear border.

The flippers are quite small, have a narrow base, and are pointed at their tips. It is interesting to note that horny spots or areas occur on the front margins of the dorsal fin, the flippers, and the tail flukes.

The teeth are the principal anatomical feature used to separate the porpoises from the true dolphins. The dolphins all have conical teeth, while the teeth of the porpoises are flattened and spade-like in appearance. In this genus, the teeth number from about 14 to 28 or 30 in each of the upper jaw bones, and from about 16 to 28 in each of the lower jaw bones. The front teeth are small and conical in shape, while those of the sides are small, laterally compressed, and somewhat spade-like in appearance; these lateral teeth may have either one, two, or three crowns.

The vertebrae are distributed approximately as follows: C 7 + D 12-14 + L 14-17 + Ca 27-32 = 62-66. The ribs number from 12 to 14 pairs; of these, only 5 pairs articulate with the sternum. The 7 cervical (neck) vertebrae may be fused together in various combinations from 2 to all 7 vertebrae. The bones of the fingers are distributed approximately as follows: I (1-3), II (5-10), III (5-8), IV (2-6), V (1-3).

The color of the body in this genus is usually slate gray or black above, the flanks are usually grayish, and the lower surfaces are white or whitish in color; some species are entirely black.

The distribution of this genus is nearly world-wide, but the species occupy more restricted areas.

Studies of these porpoises by various scholars indicate that several names of species appearing in older books are really duplicate names or synonyms of other previously named species. The following list indicates the older names and the more correct and current names of these species.

Old Name		Name Currently In Use
Genus *Phocaena*	is now	Genus *Phocoena*
Phocoena albiventris	is now	*Cephalorhynchus eutropia*
Phocoena albus	is now	*Delphinapterus leucas*
Phocoena brachycium	is now	*Phocoena phocoena*
Phocoena brevirostris	is now	*Orcaella brevirostris*
Phocoena crassidens	is now	*Pseudorca crassidens*
Phocoena cruciger	is now	*Phocoena phocoena*
Phocoena dalli	is now	*Phocoenoides dalli*
Phocoena d'orbigny	is now	*Lagenorhynchus cruciger*
Phocoena lineata	is now	*Phocoena phocoena*
Phocoena lunata	is now	*Phocoena phocoena*
Phocoena obtusata	is now	*Cephalorhynchus eutropia*
Phocoena pectoralis	is now	*Cephalorhynchus heavisidii*
Phocoena philippi	is now	*Phocoena spinnipinnis*
Phocoena relicta	is now	*Phocoena phocoena*
Phocoena rissonis	is now	*Grampus griseus*
Phocoena storni	is now	*Phocoena dioptrica*
Phocoena tubercilifera	is now	*Phocoena phocoena*
Phocoena vomerina	is now	*Phocoena phocoena*

This genus is known from the Middle Miocene Epoch to the Holocene Epoch (Recent).

This genus contains the four living species listed below.

Phocoena dioptrica Lahille, 1912
   THE SPECTACLED PORPOISE .. See page 195
Phocoena phocoena (Linnaeus, 1758)
   THE HARBOR PORPOISE .... See page 196
Phocoena sinus Norris and McFarland, 1958
   THE GULF OF CALIFORNIA PORPOISE.....
   .... See page 199
Phocoena spinipinnis Burmeister, 1865
   THE BLACK PORPOISE .... See page 200

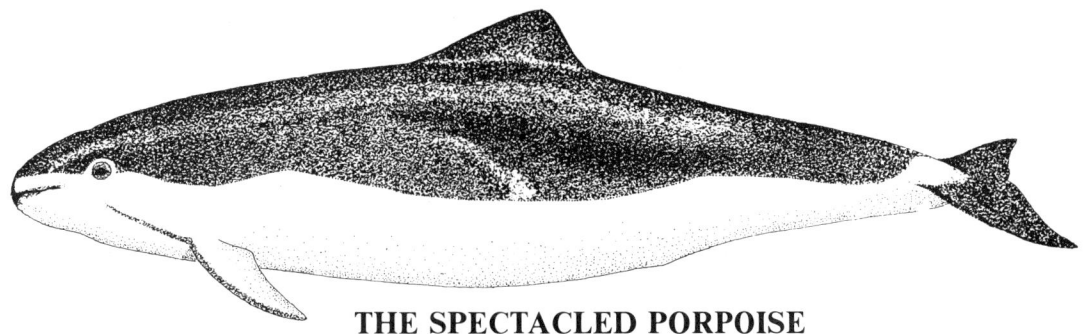

THE SPECTACLED PORPOISE
Also known as Marsopa de anteojos
Phocoena dioptrica Lahille, 1912

Identifying Features. The most significant feature of this little porpoise is a black circle around the eye. In addition, it is black above and white below with a sharp line dividing these color areas. The trailing edge of the dorsal fin is straight.

Size and Shape. The body of this porpoise is plump in the center and tapers quite uniformly from the middle of the body to the head and tail. The head is tapering and the mouth is located at the terminal end of the head. A beak is not apparent or obvious. This is a small species. Most specimens measure about 1.7 meters (6 ft. 6 in.), but some may be larger.

Color. The entire upper half of the body is a shining black color and the entire lower surface is white. These colors meet on the sides of the body on a line extending from the head to the tail. The black eye is encircled by a white area which makes the eye more prominent. The flippers are entirely white, although a few scholars have described the upper side of the flippers as being dark in color, and some flippers are known to be dark on both surfaces. The tail flukes are black above and white below. A dark line runs from the base of the flippers to the corner of the mouth.

Distribution. This species is limited to a small area in the western South Atlantic Ocean. It occurs along the coastline of eastern South America from Uruguay in the north southward to Cape Horn. It also occurs in the Falkland Islands and around South Georgia to the east. It also occurs on the western side of Tierra del Fuego in Chile. It has also been reported from New Zealand in the South Pacific Ocean.

Migration. This is a non-migratory species.

Fins and Flippers. The dorsal fin has a rather long base, is low in height, and has rather straight margins on its anterior and posterior borders. It is triangular in shape and is located at the center of the body. The flippers are somewhat triangular in shape, have rounded tips, and arise in the white area of the body. The flukes of the tail are black above and white below and are notched at the midline.

Teeth. The teeth are very small in this species and number from about 17 to 23 above and 16 to 20 below on each side of the mouth. The usual number seems to be 21 in each upper jaw and 17 in each lower jaw bone.

Skeletal Notes. The vertebrae of this species are distributed approximately as follows: C 7 + D 13 + L 16 + Ca 32 = 68. The chevron bones are 15 in number. In the neck, the 1st 5 vertebrae are fused and the 6th and 7th are free. There are 13 pairs of ribs, of which 9 pairs have two heads. There are 8 pairs of middle rib bones. The last 4 pairs of ribs are flat in lateral view. The sternum has 4 parts which unite in young animals.

Habits. Very little is known of the habits of this rare porpoise.

Reproduction. The young appear to be born in the early spring.

Abundance. This is a very rare species with a restricted range.

Economic Importance. This porpoise has no economic importance.

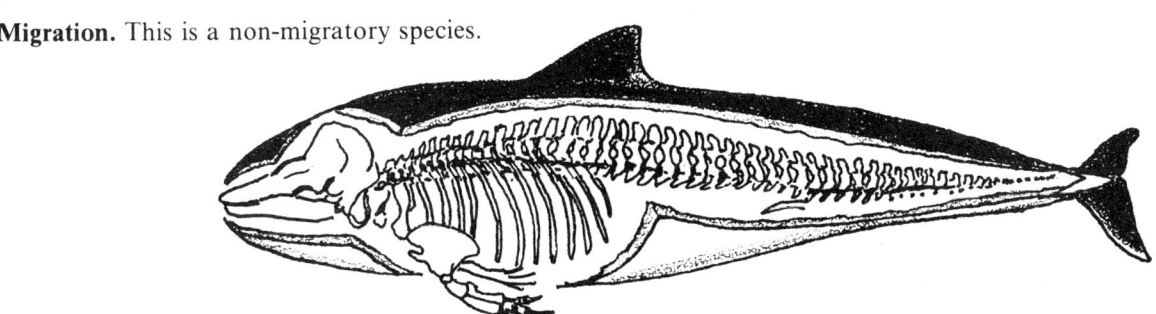

Diagram of the outline of the body and the skeleton of a porpoise, *Phocoena* species (Odontoceti: Delphinidae).

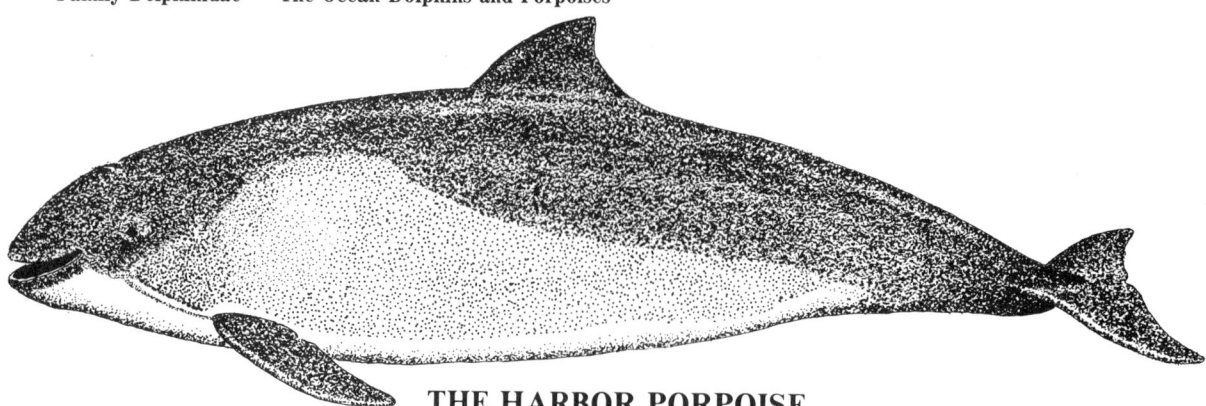

THE HARBOR PORPOISE
Also known as The Common Harbor Porpoise
Phocoena phocoena (Linnaeus, 1758)

Identifying Features. This little porpoise lacks positive characters for quick identification. It is of small size and measures from 1.4 to 1.8 meters (55 to 71 in.). It has a small, triangular dorsal fin, and possesses a small, sloping, rounded head without a distinct beak. It is grayish above and has white extending up the sides of the body just forward of the dorsal fin. All porpoises have small spade-shaped teeth.

Size and Shape. This porpoise is one of the smallest of the whales and reaches a maximum size of about 150 cm. (5 ft.) to 180 cm. (71 in.) and a weight from about 45 kg. (99 lbs.) to 55 kg. (121 lbs.). The body is truly spindle-shaped and is thickest just forward of the dorsal fin from which point it tapers gradually toward both extremities. The head is rounded and tapers forward to the mouth which is located at the very front of the head (terminal); the beak is small and scarcely visible.

Color. The color areas of the body are not sharply defined. The back is a bluish gray to black color and the belly is white. The sides are gray and the borders between these areas are very indistinct. White extends from the belly up the sides in the area just forward of the dorsal fin. There is a dark line running from the base of the flipper to the corner of the mouth. A few porpoises of this species have been reported which were pure white in color.

Distribution. This is a cooler water, shoreline porpoise of the northern hemisphere and is uncommon in the tropics. It seems to prefer water which is cooler than about 15° C. (59° F.). In the Atlantic Ocean, it extends from the Davis Strait and Greenland, Iceland, the Barents Sea, the White Sea

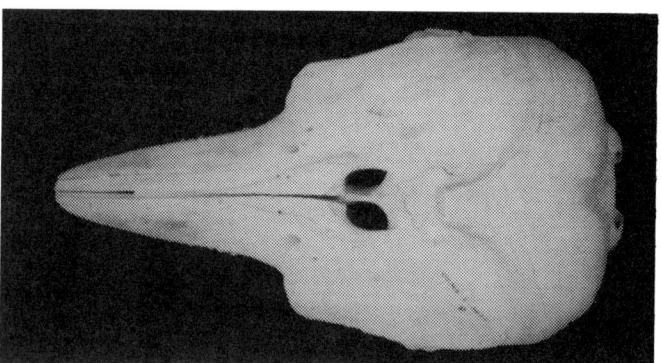

Photo of the skull of the harbor porpoise, *Phocoena phocoena,* in dorsal view.
Photo by Michael Graybill at Ore. Inst. Mar. Biol.

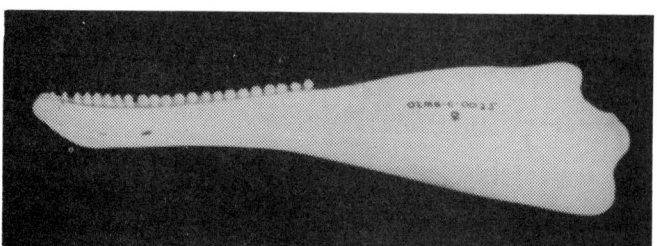

Photo of the left jaw bone (mandible) of the harbor porpoise, *Phocoena phocoena,* in lateral view.
Photo by Michael Graybill at Ore. Inst. Mar. Biol.

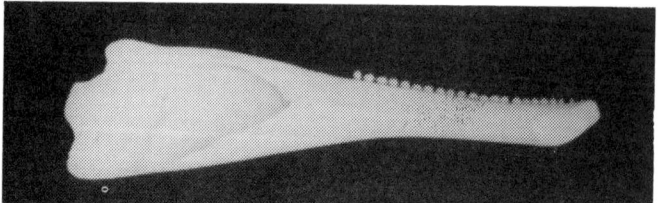

Photo of the left jaw bone (mandible) of the harbor porpoise, *Phocoena phocoena,* in medial view.
Photo by Michael Graybill at Ore. Inst. Mar. Biol.

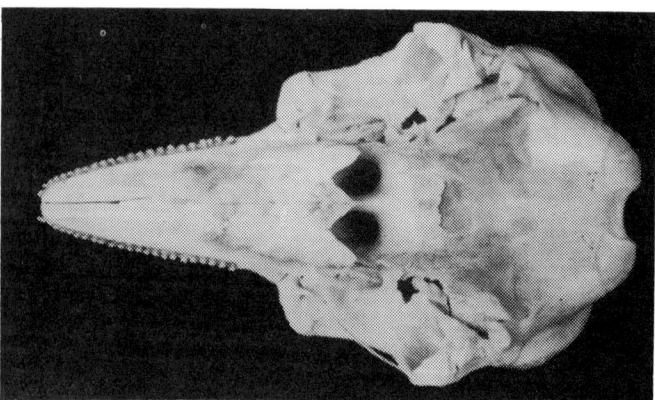

Photo of the skull of the harbor porpoise, *Phocoena phocoena,* in ventral view.
Photo by Michael Graybill at Ore. Inst. Mar. Biol.

(Beloye More in No. Russia), the Norwegian Sea, and the Baltic Sea in the north southward to the latitude of Delaware (38° N.L.) and Senegal (15° N.L.). It occurs in the Mediterranean Sea, the Black Sea, and the Sea of Azov nearby. In the Pacific Ocean, it ranges from Point Barrow, Alaska, southward to Los Angeles, California (34° N.L.), and to Japan on the west. It also occurs in the Sea of Okhotsk.

Migration. This porpoise travels with the seasons. They leave the Baltic Sea between November and February to escape the winter freeze; they return in the following summer. They move northward into the North Sea in July and August. It is a shoreline species and will ascend rivers for many miles. In the Bay of Fundy (between New Brunswick and Nova Scotia in eastern Canada), these porpoises migrate into the Bay in June and July and out again in September and October.

Fins and Flippers. The dorsal fin is small, low, triangular in shape, inclined backward, and located in the center of the body. The flippers are small, nearly oval in shape, and arise in the white area about 1/5 of the body length from the front. The flukes of the tail possess a notch at the center of their posterior margin.

Teeth. The three genera of porpoises all have teeth in which the crowns are spade-like in appearance when viewed from the side. These teeth are small and measure about 2.5 to 3 mm. in diameter at the crown. In *P. phocoena*, they number from about 19 to 28 in each of the four jaw bones, are slightly flattened, and are very slightly bent backward.

Skeletal Notes. In this species, the neck is not allowed much freedom of movement, because the 1st 6 vertebrae are fused into an immobile unit; the 7th vertebra is free. The vertebrae are distributed approximately as follows: C 7 + D 12-14 + L 14-17 + Ca 27-32 = 62-66. There are 12 pairs of ribs of which 5 pairs* articulate with the sternum. The bones of the fingers are distributed approximately as follows: I (2-3), II (12-14), III (6-8), IV (3-5), V (1-3).

---

*Some scholars say that 4 pairs of ribs articulate directly with the sternum.

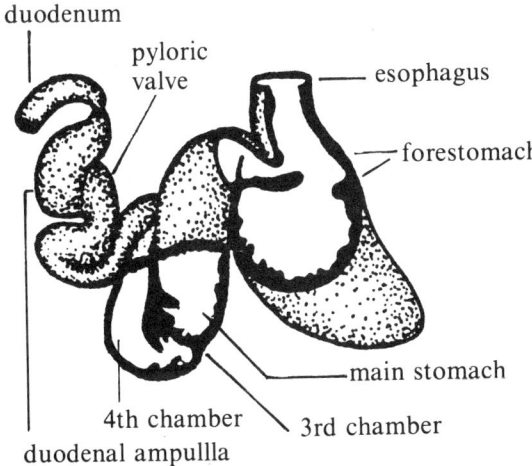

Diagram of the stomach of the harbor porpoise, *Phocoena phocoena* (Odontoceti: Delphinidae).

From Jungklaus.

Other Anatomical Notes. An unusual feature of this species is a series of tubercles along the anterior margin of the dorsal fin. This feature is found in only one other member of the Delphinidae, the Black Porpoise, *Phocoena spinnipinnis*.

Food. The diet of this porpoise consists almost entirely of fish; in the North Pacific Ocean, they are reported to eat any fish less than 30 cm. (12 in.) in length and an unknown component of squid.

Swimming and Diving. It is common for this porpoise to travel in small groups of 2 to 10 individuals, but it may gather into schools of 100 or more porpoises. This species swims by a series of short dives about 15 seconds apart. It is timid and wary in disposition and does not often approach ships and will only occasionally ride upon their bow waves.

Reproduction. The adults mate in the summer from June to October and the young are born in the spring (May-June) or summer after a gestation period of about 9 to 11 months. The young are large at birth, often measuring 75 to 90 cm. (30 to 35 in.), which is nearly one-half the length of the mother. They are nursed from the summer onward for a period of about 8 months.

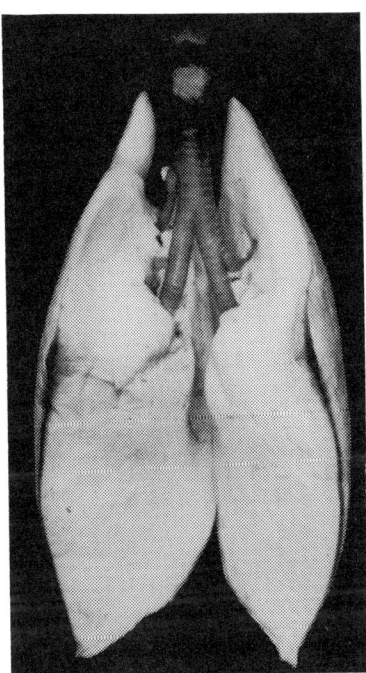

Photo of the lungs of *Phocoena phocoena* in ventral view showing the lobes, the larynx, the trachea, and the bronchi.
Ore. Inst. Mar. Biol.

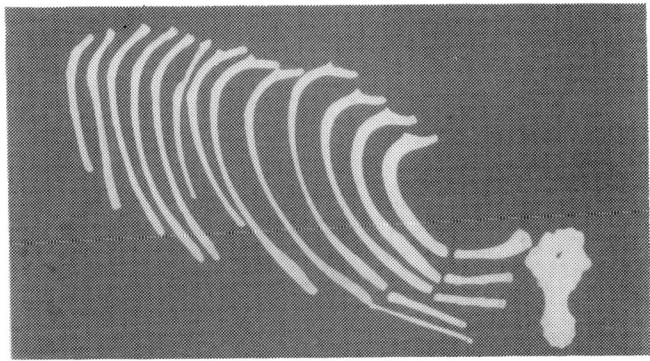

Photo of the sternum and thirteen ribs of the left side of the harbor porpoise, *Phocoena phocoena*, in medial view.
Ore. Inst. Mar. Biol.

Abundance. On the coast of Norway, this species is the most abundant of the small whales; next in abundance is the Atlantic White-sided Dolphin (*Lagenorhynchus acutus*). This porpoise is less abundant today than formerly due to its habits of frequenting the coastlines of the world.

Economic Importance. This little porpoise has no real economic value today. During the 11th and 12th centuries, this porpoise was caught in large numbers off the coast of Normandy where its flesh was used for food and its oil for lamps. Today, it is occasionally captured in the nets of fishermen from villages on Newfoundland and Greenland.

Miscellaneous. Some scholars have regarded those animals of this species which live in the Black Sea as a separate species and have named them *Phocoena relicta* Abel, 1905, or *Phocoena phocoena relicta* Abel, 1905. Their differences are not of sufficient importance to separate them from *P. phocoena* (Linnaeus, 1758).

P. phocoena is the type species of this genus.

This porpoise does not adjust to captivity and has been described as "prone to go into terminal nervous shock." It is therefore not exhibited in the large oceanaria.

Photo by W. Webber.

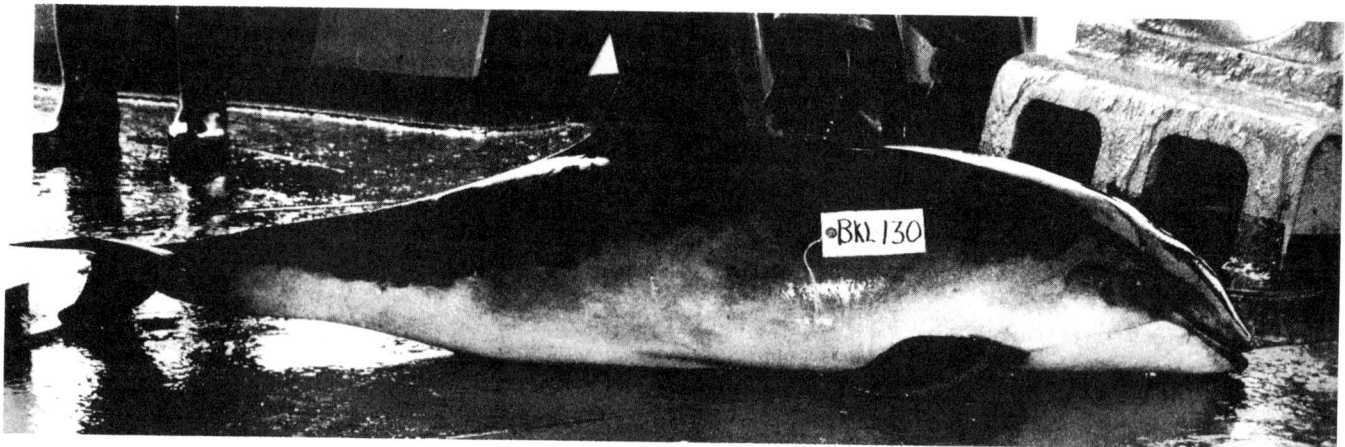

Photo by B. Long.

Photos of the carcasses of two harbor porpoises, *Phocoena phocoena.* Note the spindle-shaped body, the low dorsal fin, the black lips, and the dark line extending from the corner of the mouth to the base of the flipper. The color of the upper and lower surfaces of the body merge in a very irregular manner along the side of the body.

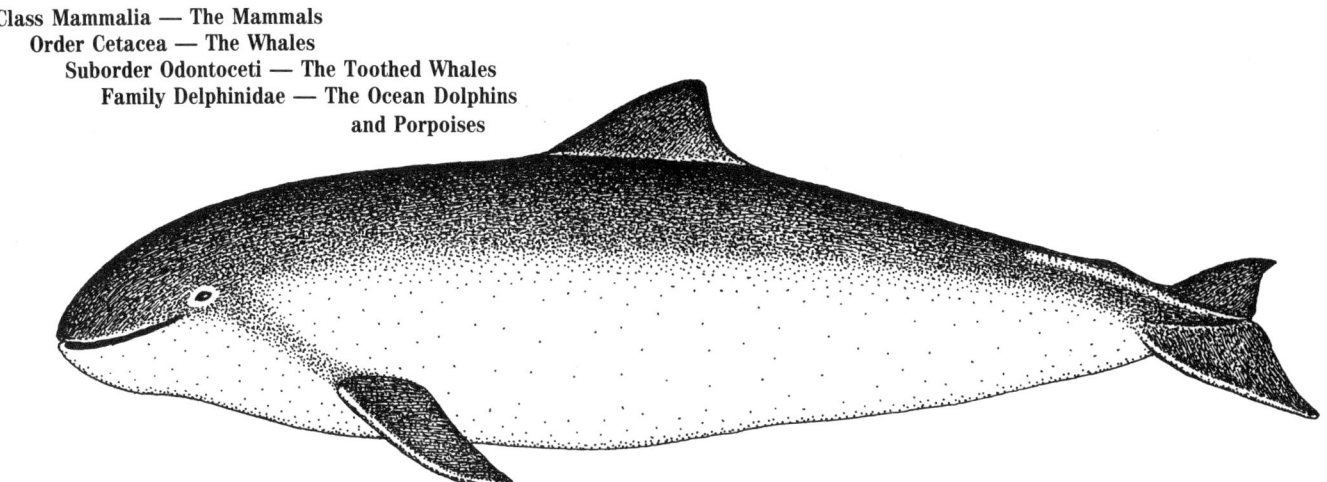

THE GULF OF CALIFORNIA PORPOISE
Also known as Chochito or Vaquita* Gulf Porpoise
Phocoena sinus Norris and McFarland, 1958

Identifying Features. In this species, the limited distribution along western Mexico and in the Gulf of California, together with its small size, dark color, and small dorsal fin, should be sufficient to identify this small porpoise. However, it is very difficult to distinguish from *Phocoena phocoena.*

Size and Shape. The Gulf of California porpoise is the smallest member of the Genus *Phocoena* and one of the very smallest of the whales. It will reach a maximum length of nearly 1.5 meters (5+ feet.) and will weigh about 50 kg. (110 lbs.) when fully grown. The body is robust in shape, the head its rounded, and a beak is practically nonexistant. For the original description, see Jour. of Mammalogy 39:1, February, 1958, pp. 22-39.

Color. The body is a uniformly "dull lead gray" to a dark brownish color above and shades gradually through lighter hues on the sides to nearly white on the chin, throat, and belly. A darker stripe extends from the eye backward and downward to the base of the flipper.

Distribution. This species has a restricted distribution on the western coast of Mexico. It occurs in the Gulf of California from its northern end southward to the Tres Marias Islands (21-22° N.L.) and nearby along the western coast of the State of Jalisco. This is a distance of about 1500 km. (932 mi.).

Migration. Very little is known of the migratory habits of this species.

Fins and Flippers. The dorsal fin is small in size and triangular in shape, and the flippers are small, short, and rounded at their extremities. The flukes of the tail bear a notch on their posterior margin where they join at the midline.

Teeth. The teeth, as in the other members of the Genus *Phocoena,* are spade-like at their extremities and number about 20-21 in each upper jaw and about 18 in each lower jaw. The mandible (lower jaw) bones are short and heavy as a consequence of the short skull of this species.

Skeletal Notes. The bones (osteology) of the skull of this porpoise are very well described in the original description of this unusual species. The vertebrae are distributed ap-

proximately as follows: C 7 + D 12 + L 11 + Ca 32 = 62. Of the 7 neck vertebrae, the first 3 are fused into a single immobile unit.

Food. The food of this porpoise is known to include squid, a croaker (*Bairdiella icistius*), a grunt (*Orthopristis reddingi*), and doubtless a small component of crustacea.

Swimming and Diving. The favored habitat of this porpoise is in the shallower shoreline waters where it gathers into small groups of 2 to 5 individuals and swims and feeds in a leisurely fashion. Groups have been observed which included 40 individuals. It is a very shy and timid species and will not approach boats or allow boats to approach it. It seems to prefer warmer waters with temperatures approaching 20° C. (68° F.).

Reproduction. Very little is known of the reproductive habits of this species, but they probably do not differ much from those of related species. It is believed that the young are born in the months of May and June, at which time they are reported to measure about 60 cm. (23.6 in.) in length.

Abundance. This is an uncommon species with a restricted distribution and a small population. Although it was known to the local fishermen of the area and occasionally captured by them, it was unknown to scientists prior to the discovery of a single skull on March 18, 1950, by Dr. Kenneth S. Norris of California. Since that time, additional skulls have been found and a few live animals have been captured and studied. It will doubtless remain an uncommon species and may even be facing extinction.

Economic Importance. The Gulf of California Porpoise has no economic importance, although it is occasionally entangled and captured in the gill nets of local fishermen.

Miscellaneous. Scholars have speculated about the origin and ancestry of this strange porpoise and why its geographical distribution is so restricted. It is usually regarded as derived from a South American species, possibly *Phocoena spinnipinnis* or *Phocoena dioptrica.* Dr. Masaharu Nishiwaki regards it as possibly anatomically midway between *Phocoena phocoena* and *Phocoena dioptrica.*

---

*Lit., Small cow (Spanish).

Class Mammalia — The Mammals
  Order Cetacea — The Whales
    Suborder Odontoceti — The Toothed Whales
      Family Delphinidae — The Ocean Dolphins and Porpoises

THE BLACK PORPOISE
Also known as Burmeister's Porpoise and Marsopa espinosa
Phocoena spinipinnis Burmeister, 1865

Identifying Features. This porpoise is a small species which is entirely dark in color. The spiny denticles on the leading edge of the dorsal fin occur only in this species and in *P. phocoena.*

Size and Shape. The body of this little porpoise is robust and spindle-shaped and tapers quite uniformly toward the head and tail. The head is quite small and the mouth is located at the very front (terminal) of the head. The head of this species is smaller and more pointed than *P. phocoena* and resembles somewhat the head of *Phocoenoides dalli.* The body ranges from about 1.5 meters to possibly 2 meters (59 to 79 in.) in length.

Color. The exact color of this species when alive is not well documented because it turns very dark in color very soon after death. The entire body is described as light brown, grayish, and blackish. A photo of a dead specimen showed a faint lighter stripe or area extending from near the tip of the lower jaw backward toward the base of the flipper.

Distribution. This species inhabits the coastal waters of southern South America. On the Atlantic Ocean side, it is found from Uruguay southward to Cape Horn and then northward on the Pacific Ocean side to Peru.

Fins and Flippers. The dorsal fin is triangular in shape, is located just posterior to the center of the body, and rises at a very low angle. The anterior margin is straight or slightly concave and the posterior margin is straight or possibly slightly convex. The tip is pointed. The anterior border of the dorsal fin bears a series of spiny denticles; this is unusual among whales; it also occurs in *P. phocoena.* There is a keel on the midline of the back between the dorsal fin and the tail; a similar keel occurs on the ventral side posterior to the anus. The flippers are small, have gently curving convex margins, and end in a rounded tip. The flukes of the tail bear a notch where they meet at the midline.

Teeth. The teeth, as in other members of the Genus *Phocoena,* are somewhat spade-shaped at their crowns. They are very small and number from about 14 to 19 in each of the 4 jaw bones. The usual number is 14 to 18 in each upper jaw and 17 to 19 in each lower jaw. This is the only porpoise in which the teeth are more numerous in the lower jaw.

Skeletal Notes. The vertebrae are distributed approximately as follows: C 7 + D 13 + L 16 + Ca 32 = 68. The first 3 vertebrae of the neck are fused into a single, immobile unit. Four pairs of ribs are reported to articulate directly with the sternum.

Habits. Very little has been recorded concerning the habits of this porpoise. They are reported to live in small groups numbering from 2 to 8 individuals. This species is known to feed upon both squid and fishes.

Abundance. The number of porpoises of this uncommon species which inhabit the waters of South America is unknown. Continued fishing may affects it future numbers.

Economic Importance. This porpoise is hunted and captured in quite large numbers by seines and gill nets off the coasts of both Uruguay and Peru.

Miscellaneous. The black porpoise was first observed and described by Herman Karl Conrad Burmeister, a German zoologist, who was Director of the Argentina Museum of Natural Sciences in Buenos Aires.

THE FINLESS PORPOISES
Genus *NEOPHOCAENA* Palmer, 1899

The finless porpoises are small animals which grow to a length of about five feet. Their head is larger than *Phocoena* and is rounded and bulbous with a convex forehead which covers the beak. The skull bears a short, broad rostrum, but it is not apparent externally as a beak. The distinguishing feature of this genus is the absence of a dorsal fin. In its place upon the back is a long, linear series of horny, wart-like tubercles which extend from near the neck backward to the area above the anus. The flippers are of rather large size with small bases and pointed tips.

The teeth, although larger than those of *Phocoena,* are small and numerous and bear the spade-shaped crowns which are characteristic of the three genera of porpoises. These teeth number between about 13 and 21 in each of the two upper jaw bones and from about 14 to 21 in each of the two lower jaw bones. The vertebrae are distributed approximately as follows: C 7 + D 13-14 + L 12-14 + Ca 25-31 = 58-63. The bones of the fingers are distributed approximately as follows: I (2), II (5-7), III (5-6), IV (3-4), V (2).

The color of these animals is grayish above and lighter below.

The distribution of this genus extends from Korea southward along the Pacific coast of Asia, through the East Indies, and westward along the southern coast of Asia, possibly as far as the Cape of Good Hope.

This genus is known only from the Holocene Epoch (Recent).

Studies of these porpoises by various scholars indicate that several names of species appearing in older books are really duplicate names or synonyms of other previously named species. The following list indicates the older names and the more correct and current names of these species.

Old Name		Name Currently In Use
Genus *Meomeris*	is now	Genus *Neophocaena*
Genus *Neomeris*	is now	Genus *Neophocaena*
Neophocaena asiaeorientalis	is now	*Neophocaena phocaenoides*
Neophocaena phocoenoides	is now	*Neophocaena phocaenoides*
Neophocaena sunameri	is now	*Neophocaena phocaenoides*

The number of species within this genus has not been completely determined. Some scholars believe that there is only a single, variable, widely-distributed species(with possible subspecies) which they call—

Neophocaena phocaenoides (G. Cuvier, 1829)
> A species distributed from Korea southward and westward to possibly the Cape of Good Hope, Africa.

Other scholars believe that there may be as many as three species in this genus and name them as follows:

1. *Neophocaena phocaenoides* (G. Cuvier, 1829)
   A species distributed from Borneo to Pakistan.
2. *Neophocaena asiaeorientalis* (Pilleri and Gihr, 1972)
   A species distributed along the coast of China.
3. *Neophocaena sunameri* Pilleri and Gihr, 1975
   A species distributed from Korea to Japan.

In this book, this genus will be treated as having only one, variable, widely-distributed species listed below.

Neophocaena phocaenoides (G. Cuvier, 1829)
THE FINLESS PORPOISE ....See page 202

THE FINLESS PORPOISE
Formerly and erroneously known as the Black Finless Porpoise
Neophocaena phocaenoides (G. Cuvier, 1829)

Identifying Features. The most prominent feature of this porpoise is the absence of the dorsal fin.

Size and Shape. The body of this porpoise is largest at the center and is nearly circular. The head is comparatively small and spherical and the forehead is quite steep. The rostrum of the skull does not extend forward beyond the "lips" as a visible beak. A small constriction is visible at the "neck." This is one of the smallest whales in the world and will measure from about 1.2 meters to 1.83 meters (47 to 72 in.) in length.

Color. The color of the body is a light bluish gray above and lighter beneath. It turns black on death. In *N. phocaenoides,* the lower surface is lighter in color and there may be white, gray, or purplish red patches on the lips, throat, and belly; in the form known as *N. asiaeorientalis,* the entire body is darker and there are no light areas on the throat and chest. Some individuals are reported to have a dark crosswise band under the lower lips. Although occasionally known as the black finless porpoise," it is not black.

Distribution. The range of this porpoise extends along the seacosts of Asia from Japan and Korea southward and eastward to the Cape of Good Hope in Africa. It enters rivers and has been reported to ascend the Changjiang (Yangtse) River as far as the Ich'ang Gorge in Hupeh Province, a distance of 1600 km. (1,000 mi.) from the sea. It is also known from Sumatra and Borneo.

Migration. These porpoises are known to migrate with the seasons along the coasts of Japan. Very little information is available on their migrations.

Fins and Flippers. The dorsal fin is absent. The flippers are quite large, triangular in shape, and pointed at the tips; they are "dusky" above and lighter beneath. The midline of the back has a ridge of skin which bears a series of numerous, small, round, scale-like tubercles. The tail bears a notch on its rear margin at the midline.

Teeth. The teeth are small, laterally compressed, and number from 13 to 21 or 22 (usually 15) in each of the four jaw bones.

Skeletal Notes. The vertebrae are distributed approximately as follows: C 7 + D 13-14 + L 11-14 + Ca 25-31 = 58-63. The neck bones are variously united; the 1st through the 3rd, 4th, or 5th are united; the remainder are free. The lumbar bones

are usually about 13 in number, but depend somewhat upon the chevron bones and the caudal count. When the chevron bones are small, lost, or are not ossified, they are sometimes not counted; this makes the lumbar bones more numerous. There are usually 14 pairs of ribs of which 11 pairs have 2 heads. Three pairs of ribs articulate directly with the sternum. The bones of the fingers are distributed approximately as follows: I (2), II (5-7), III (5-6), IV (3-4), V (2).

Photo of the finless porpoise, *Neophocaena phocaenoides,* playing in the Ujina Aquarium in Hiroshima.
Photo by Nishiwaki and Kasuya.

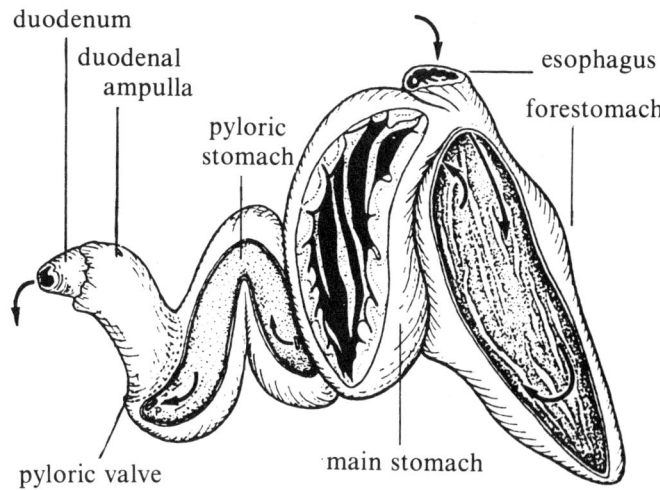

duodenum
duodenal ampulla
pyloric stomach
esophagus
forestomach
pyloric valve
main stomach

Diagram of the stomach of the finless porpoise, *Neophocaena phocaenoides* (Odontoceti: Delphinidae).

From: Pilleri, Gregorio and Gihr, M. — Investigations On The Cetacea. 1972. 4:107-162 (fig. 3).

Food. The diet of this porpoise includes squid and a variety of fishes; it has also been reported to eat prawns. They have a small mouth and eat slowly.

Swimming and Diving. This porpoise lives at the surface. When swimming, it will dive for 3 minutes and then return to the surface; they roll as they surface to breathe and the tail does not leave the water. They usually live together in small groups of any number up to a dozen and occasionally gather into herds of 50 or more individuals. Although sluggish swimmers, they are active in captivity and can be trained to perform.

Reproduction. The adults mate in the spring from February to summer, but the length of gestation, possibly 10 to 12 months, and the season at which the young are born are uncertain. The males and females of this species have the unusual habit of rubbing their backs together. The young of this species are carried upon the backs of their mothers, where they rest upon the bed of tubercles which occurs on the middle of the back. In both sexes of this species, the back possesses a flat area which is covered with rough skin. This gives the young porpoise an area on which to rest which is not slippery. The young will measure about 100 cm. (3¼ ft.) at birth and will weigh about 7 kg. (15 lbs.).

Abundance. The total number of animals of this species is unknown, but it is not an abundant species.

Economic Importance. This porpoise does not support a fishery; however, individual animals are continually being caught in various fishing operations by individual fishermen.

The young of the finless porpoise, *Neophocaena phocaenoides*, riding upon the back of its mother.

THE WHITE-FLANKED PORPOISES
Genus *PHOCOENOIDES* Andrews, 1911

The porpoises of this genus are small animals which may grow to a length of nearly seven feet. Their bodies are quite deep and narrow and appear as if they had been laterally compressed. The head is quite small and the lower jaw is slightly longer than the upper jaw. The skull bears a short, wide rostrum, but it is not visible externally as a beak.

The dorsal fin is triangular in shape with the front and back margins of almost equal length and slope. This fin is situated slightly forward of the mid-point of the back and is usually predominantly black in color with a white tip of varying size. The flippers are quite small, have pointed tips, and are placed quite far forward on the body. The caudal peduncle in these porpoises is very deep and narrow and bears both dorsal and ventral ridges.

The teeth are very small and are only slightly expanded and flattened; they are surrounded by very strange, hard tubercles which cover the adjoining gums. These teeth number from about 19 to 28 on each side of the upper and lower jaws.

The vertebrae of the backbone are more numerous in this genus than in the backbone of any other whale. The vertebrae in this genus are distributed approximately as follows: C 7 + D 14-18 + L 24-27 + Ca 44-49 = 92-98. The bones of the fingers are usually distributed approximately as follows: I (1-2), II (6-7), III (4-6), IV (1-3), V (1).

The color of the body is black or dusky above and white below. This white color of the belly extends upward onto the lower sides of the body as a great white area. This white area is larger on the porpoises around Japan than it is on the porpoises of the eastern Pacific Ocean. These Japanese porpoises were believed by some scholars to be a different species and were therefore described and named True's Porpoise (*Phocoenoides truei* Andrews, 1911). Later studies have shown that this Japanese porpoise is really a color phase of *P. dalli* of the North Pacific Ocean; it could be referred to as a variety of *P. dalli* and called *Phocoenoides dalli truei* Andrews, 1911.

The distribution of this genus is limited to the North Pacific Ocean. This genus is known only from the Holocene Epoch (Recent).

This genus contains the single living species listed below.

Phocoenoides dalli (True, 1885)
DALL'S WHITE-FLANKED
PORPOISE . . . . See page 205

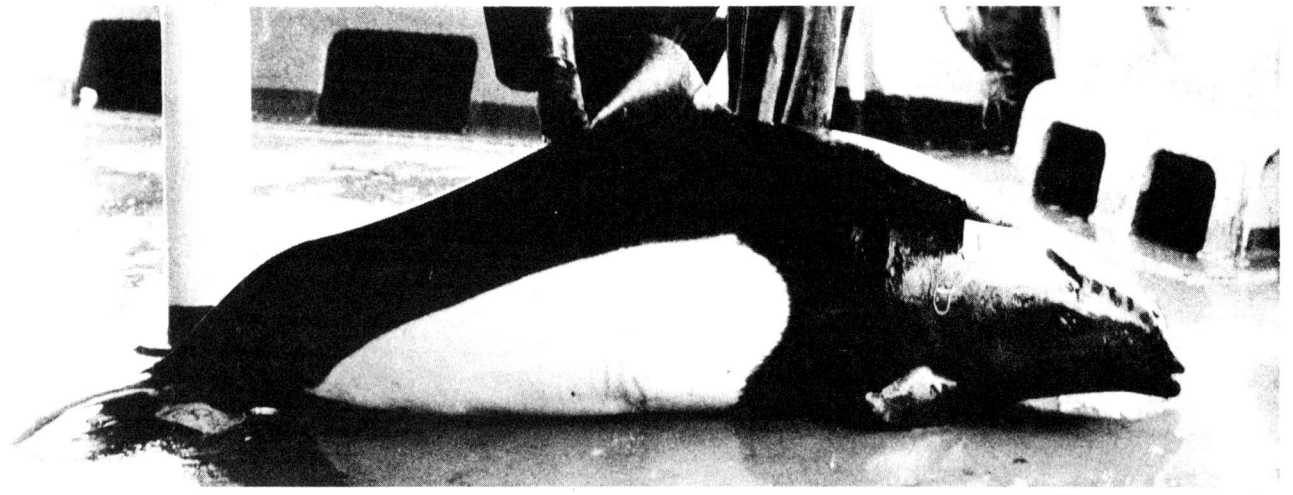

Photo by R. Beach.

Dall's white-flanked porpoise, *Phocoenoides dalli,* is a deep-bodied species from the North Pacific Ocean. The typical color pattern is shown above. A color variety, shown at the left, is found in Japan; it has a larger white area on the side of the body.

Photo by W.J. Houck.

DALL'S WHITE-FLANKED PORPOISE
Also known as Dall's Porpoise
Phocoenoides dalli (True, 1885)

Identifying Features. Preliminary identification of this species may be made from its color. The entire back is black in color except for a white tip on the top of the dorsal fin. There is a great white area on the posterior half of the belly which extends up onto the sides in the area below and behind the dorsal fin; this white area is visible from a ship at sea.

Size and Shape. The body of this porpoise is very thick and deep vertically below the dorsal fin. The body is laterally compressed so that it is much higher than wide. The head is comparatively small, the beak is flat and very short, and the lower jaw is slightly longer than the upper jaw. It will reach a length of about 2.0 meters (78 in.) and a weight of about 110 to 130 kg. (243-287 lbs.). A rare California specimen was reported to measure 93 inches (236.22 cm.), but most specimens are considerably smaller.

Color. The entire back of the body is black except for a white area on the tip of the dorsal fin. On the belly, a great white area extends from a point below the dorsal fin backward to the region of the anus and halfway upward upon the flank of the body. There is a narrow white margin on the upper side of the trailing edge of the tail flukes. The border lines which divide the color areas are sharply defined. A few of these porpoises have been seen which were entirely black and entirely white.

Distribution. This porpoise is a North Pacific Ocean species which extends on the eastern side from the southern Bering Sea southward to the middle of Baja California (27-28° N.L.); on the western side of the Pacific Ocean, it extends from the southern Bering Sea and the southern part of the Sea of Okhotsk southward to central Honshu, Japan (36° N.L.). It stays within about 800 km. (500 mi.) of the shoreline. A color phase of *P. dalli*, sometimes known as *P. dalli truei*, is found in Japanese waters; both color varieties are known from around the island of Honshu.

Migration. These animals shift their position with the seasons. During the winter months, they move southward and toward shore. In the summer months, they will move offshore and toward the Aleutian Islands and beyond.

Fins and Flippers. The dorsal fin is triangular in shape and is located forward of the body center. It is moderately high

and its tip is inclined slightly backward. Well developed dorsal and ventral keels are present on the tail stock. The flukes of the tail are notched at the midline, are quite large in size, and are usually marked with a white border. The flippers are rather small and terminate in a pointed tip.

Teeth. The teeth are very small and pointed and, like other porpoises, have somewhat spade-shaped crowns. The number of teeth varies widely, but will number from about 19 to 28 in each of the four jaw bones. All teeth are poorly rooted and are easily lost. The mouth contains some very strange horny structures on the gums between the teeth; here they form a tough, hard dental ridge which replaces somewhat the function of the teeth.

Skeletal Notes. The vertebrae of the backbone are distributed approximately as follows: C 7 + D 14-18 + L 24-27 + Ca 44-49 = 92-98; the usual number is about 96. The chevron or V-bones range in number from about 25 to 35; the usual number is about 34. The neck vertebrae are usually all united, but occasionally the 7th may be free. There are usually 15 to 18 pairs of ribs of which 12 pairs have two heads. The bones of the fingers are usually distributed approximately as follows: I (1-2), II (6-7), III (4-6), IV (2-3), V (1). The 5th finger is usually soft and not ossified. The rudimentary pelvic bones measure from about 4 to 6 cm. (1.5 to 2.5 in.) in length.

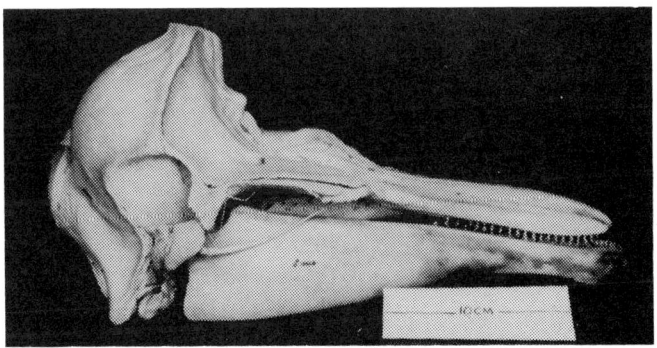

The skull and jaws of Dall's white-flanked porpoise, *Phocoenoides dalli,* in lateral view.
Photo by Michael Graybill at Humboldt State Univ.

Other Anatomical Notes. In a specimen which might weigh between about 75 and 100 kg., the brain might weigh between about 800 and 900 grams. The penis measures about 15 cm. (6 in.) in length.

Food. The diet of this porpoise includes squid, herring, sardines, and other surface fishes. They also eat fishes from deeper water which rise to the surface during the night.

Swimming and Diving. This porpoise is a sociable species and usually travels in small groups of 2 to 30 individuals; occasionally, however, it will gather into great groups numbering from 500 to a 1,000 or more animals. This is a rapid swimmer and a very rapid breather. Each exhalation is accompanied by a whistle. To breathe, it jumps from the water for an instant and then submerges with a small splash. They do not engage in jumping activities. It will approach ships and ride the bow waves. It is most commonly observed in the passages between the islands of British Columbia and Alaska.

Reproduction. Information on the life history of this species is limited. The young are usually born in the spring and summer (July to August or September) after a gestation period of about 10 or 11 months. They will measure about 100 cm. (39 in.) at birth and weigh about 25 kg. (55 lbs.) or more. The young are marked with slate-gray or brownish-gray colors which slowly disappear as they mature.

Abundance. This species was once abundant and visible over its entire range. Its numbers are declining to the point where it will soon need complete protection.

Economic Importance. A small fishery based upon this species has existed in Japan for many years. The carcasses are used for human food. These porpoises are also caught in the great nets of commercial fishermen and by occasional fishermen; in these cases, the killing is unnecessary and the carcass is wasted.

Miscellaneous. This porpoise was named to honor Dr. Willian Healy Dall (1845-1927), a zoologist long associated with the U.S. National Museum. For additional information see Jour. Mammalogy 23:1, 1942, pp. 41-51.

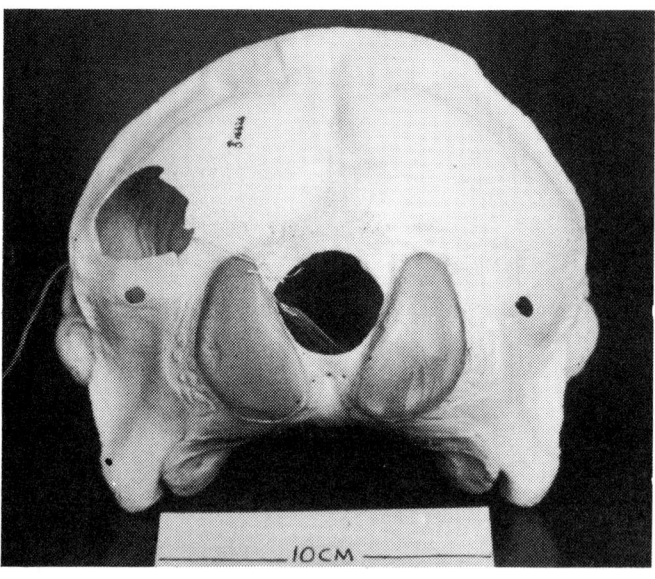

The skull of Dall's white-flanked porpoise, *Phocoenoides dalli,* in posterior view.
Photo by Michael Graybill at Humboldt State Univ.

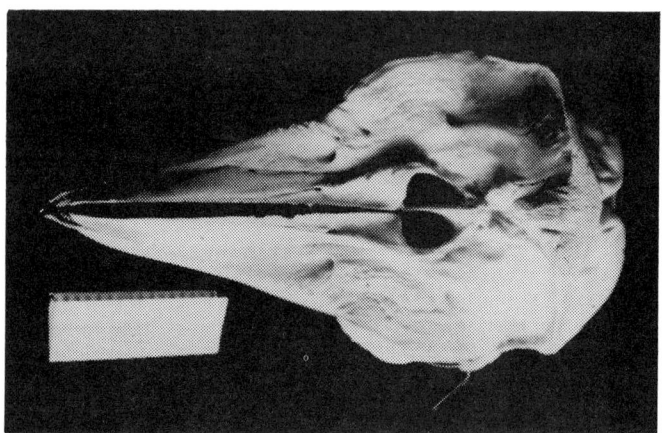

The skull of Dall's white-flanked porpoise, *Phocoenoides dalli,* in dorsal view.
Photo by Michael Graybill at Humboldt State Univ.

THE NARWHAL AND WHITE WHALE FAMILY
Family *MONODONTIDAE* Gray, 1821

This family includes but two species, the beluga and the narwhal, both of colder northern seas. Their bodies are generally spindle-shaped with quite uniform upper and lower contours and with a slight constriction at the neck. The head is small, blunt, and rounded in outline; there is no great extension of the jaws to form a prominent beak; and the cleft of the mouth is short. In these whales, the head is movable in all directions, due in part to the fact that the bones of the neck are not fused.

The flippers are short, broad, and rounded; the tail flukes are large and are separated by a conspicuous notch; the dorsal fin is absent; and, in addition, there are no external grooves on the throat as in the beaked whales (*Ziphiidae*).

Fossils of this family are known from the Pleistocene (Glacial) Epoch in No. America and Europe and from the Holocene (Recent) Epoch in the Arctic. No extinct genera are known.

The two species in this family are placed in two separate genera which may be separated on the basis of their color and their teeth. The beluga is yellowish or white in color, while the narwhal is marked with many gray to brown spots upon a lighter background. The differences in the teeth are discussed below.

Some scholars have included these two whales within the Family *Delphinidae*.

This family includes the two living genera listed below.

Delphinapterus Lacepede, 1804 (1 species)
Monodon Linnaeus, 1758 (1 species)

A photo of the carcass of a white whale or beluga, *Delphinapterus leucas,* in ventral view, which was harpooned by the Inuit (Eskimo) people in northeastern Canada.
Photo by P.F. Brodie.

THE WHITE WHALES OR BELUGAS
Genus *DELPHINAPTERUS* Lacepede, 1804

This genus contains a single species, the white whale or beluga of colder northern seas. This whale is of only moderate size and will reach a maximum length of about 5.5 meters (18 ft.), although a few specimens have been recorded which exceded 6 meters (20 ft.) in length. Although the males and females are of the same general bodily proportions, the males are usually one or two feet longer than the females. The head is blunt and rounded and the jaws do not extend forward to form a visible beak. The dorsal fin is missing, but its place is occupied by a very low ridge of skin. The flukes of the tail are separated by a deep median notch.

The teeth of the beluga number from 8 to 10 or 11 in each of the two upper and two lower jaws in both males and females. The usual number is 9 or 10 teeth above and 8 or 9 teeth below, and the upper jaw bones always have one more tooth each than the two lower jaw bones; the total number of teeth is always 32 or more. These teeth are somewhat irregular in position, are widely spaced, and are directed obliquely forward in the upper jaws and in the front of the lower jaws.

Studies of these whales by various scholars indicate that several names of species appearing in older books are really duplicate names or synonyms of other previously named species. The following list indicates the older names and the more correct and current names of these species.

Old Name		Name Currently In Use
Catodon candicans	is now	*Delphinapterus leucas*
Delphinapterus borealis	is now	*Lissodelphis borealis*
Delphinapterus dorofeevi	is now	*Delphinapterus leucas*
Delphinapterus friemani	is now	*Delphinapterus leucas*
Delphinapterus marisalbi	is now	*Delphinapterus leucas*
Delphinapterus peronii	is now	*Lissodelphis peronii*

This genus is known only from the Holocene (Recent) Epoch.

This genus includes the single living species listed below.

Delphinapterus leucas (Pallas, 1776)
THE WHITE WHALE or BELUGA See page 209

Photo of the white whale or beluga, *Delphinapterus leucas*, in the Vancouver Public Aquarium in Vancouver, British Columbia. Note the flexibility of the neck due to the fact that the cervical vertebrae are not fused together.

Photo by K.C. Balcomb.

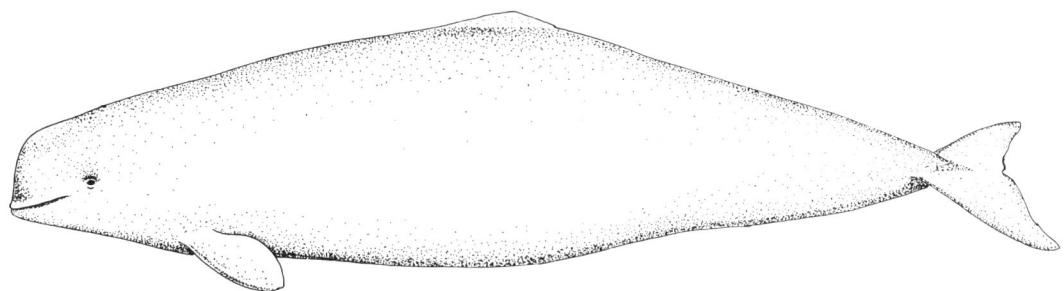

THE WHITE WHALE OR BELUGA
Delphinapterus leucas (Pallas, 1776)

Identifying Features. The absence of the dorsal fin and the uniform color of the body (white in adults; gray in the young) should identify this species.

Size and Shape. The body of the beluga is spindle shaped; it is deepest at its center and tapers quite uniformly toward both the head and tail. The head is rounded and swollen and the mouth is quite large; a small beak is present, although it is not very obvious. A constriction is apparent in the neck region indicating the ability to move the head. Large males may reach a maximum length of about 5.5 to 6 meters (18 to 19 ft. 8 in.); most, however, measure 5 meters (16 ft. 5 in.) or less. The females are about two feet shorter than the males.

Color. The adult animals are an ivory white color over the entire body. The young are light brown at birth and later change in their 2nd year to a bluish gray which is marked with small blackish spots; this color slowly fades until they are from 4 or 5 to 6 or 7 years of age; at this time they have achieved the adult coloration.

Distribution. The beluga is circumpolar in arctic and subarctic seas. It will come south to Sakhalin Island, the Aleutian Islands, the St. Lawrence River, and other areas to about 50° N.L. It is common in Hudson Bay. It is occasionally found as far south as Massachusetts and the Bay of Biscay (Spain). Their northern limit is determined by the presence of ice. Their southward limit seems to be bounded by warmer water; they do not seem to enter water which is warmer than about 15° C (59° F).

Migration. They migrate northward and southward with the seasons to avoid the cold winter. In these seasonal migrations, they often gather into groups of 100 to 200 individuals. In Norway, they come south into the Baltic Sea when it is cold. They are known to ascend the Yukon River for 1120 km. (696 mi.).

Fins and Flippers. The dorsal fin is absent, but there are projections of skin at this point and a ridge of skin extends along the midline toward the tail. The flippers are quite small, are somewhat oval in outline, have a rounded tip, and are curved upward at the end. The tail is without a notch at the midline on its posterior margin.

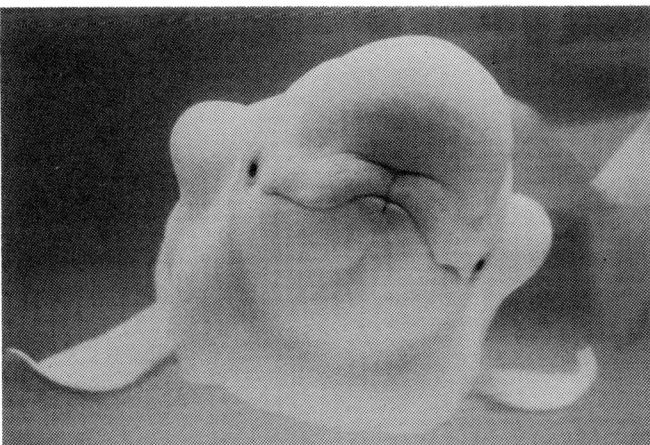

A remarkable picture of the head of the white whale or Beluga, *Delphinapterus leucas.*
**Photo by Stefani I. Hewlett
Vancouver Public Aquarium.**

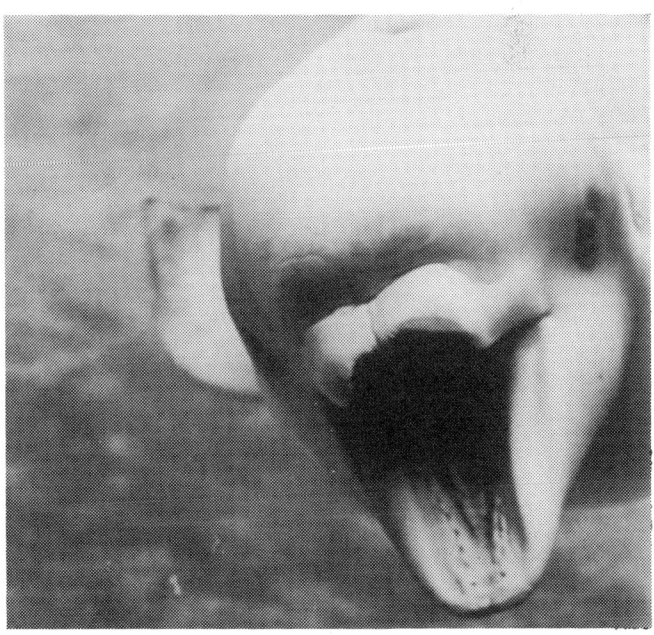

Photo of the head of the white whale or beluga, *Delphinapterus leucas,* with mouth agape showing the teeth of the lower jaw.
Photo by Vancouver Public Aquarium.

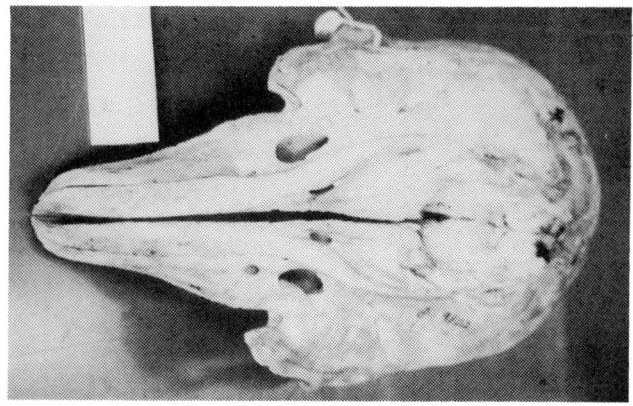

The skull of the white whale or beluga, *Delphinapterus leucas,* in dorsal view.
Photo by Michael Graybill at Cal. Acad. of Sci.

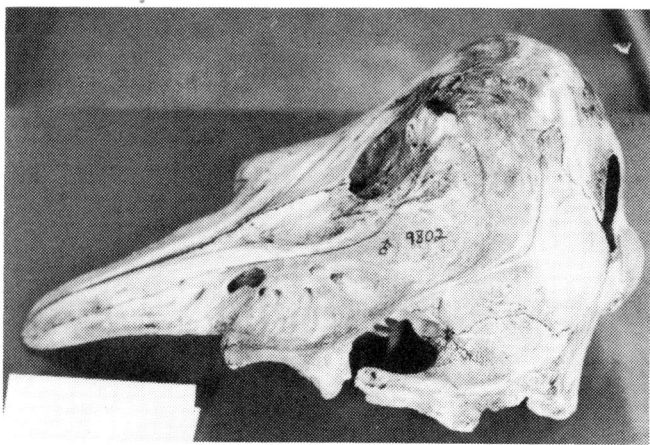

The skull of the white whale or beluga, *Delphinapterus leucas,* in lateral view.
Photo by Michael Graybill at Cal. Acad. of Sci.

Teeth. The teeth number from 8 to 10 or 11 in each of the four jaw bones. The usual number is 9 or 10 teeth above and 8 or 9 teeth below. These teeth measure about 10 to 16 mm. in diameter and are set in an irregular manner facing slightly forward.

Skeletal Notes. The skull is symmetrical and the 7 neck vertebrae are all separate. The vertebrae are distributed approximately as follows: C 7 + D 11-12 + L 6-9 + Ca 23-26 = 50-51. The usual number is probably nearer C 7 + D 12 + L 7 + Ca 25 = 51. The chevron bones are very difficult to count. There are 11-12 pairs of ribs of which 7-8 pairs have two heads; of these about 7 pairs* articulate with the sternum. The dorsal ribs are not completely ossified and the last rib in particular is difficult to locate and count. The sternum has 5 parts. The bones of the fingers are distributed approximately as follows: I (1-2), II (6-7), III (4-5), IV (2-4), V (2-4).

Other Anatomical Notes. The eyes are brown in color. The lips are movable and strong and are useful in feeding off the bottom. The blowhole is located just slightly to the left of the midline of the body. In some individuals the two flukes of the tail are slightly unequal in size. In a specimen which weighs between about 300 and 500 kg. the brain will weigh between about 2100 to 2300 grams.

Food. This whale is a bottom feeder and eats squid and various fishes including flounders, herring, smelt, and cod; it also eats prawns and other crustacea.

Swimming and Diving. The beluga travels in small groups of 5 to 10 individuals, although groups numbering 100 or 200 have been observed, and in some instances groups of 1,000 individuals have been observed. It lives in the surface waters of shallow areas.

Reproduction. The adults mate in April-May and the young are born in the summer (June-July) about 12 to 14 months

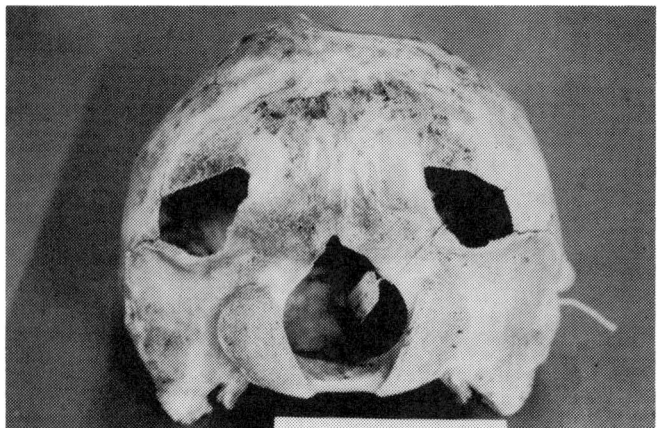

The skull of the white whale or beluga, *Delphinapterus leucas,* in posterior view.
Photo by Michael Graybill at Cal. Acad. of Sci.

later. They measure about 1.5 meters (59 in.) at birth and may weigh about 45 kg. (99 lbs.) or more. The young are born every 2nd or 3rd year. The males mature in about 8 years, while the females are mature at about 5 years of age. Their life span is at least 25 years.

Abundance. They are becoming less abundant and are in need of legal protection.

Economic Importance. The beluga has been hunted for centuries for its skin, flesh, and oil by the natives of its areas. There are no fisheries based upon this whale except for those of individual fishermen. Killer whales (*Orcinus orca*) prey upon them.

Miscellaneous. The beluga has a voice and can make a call which is quite strong when compared to other whales.

---

*Some authors report that 5 pairs of ribs articulate directly with the sternum.

THE NARWHALS
Genus *MONODON* Linnaeus, 1758

This genus contains a single species, the narwhal or tusked whale of northern polar seas. It resembles the white whale and, like it, is of moderate size. It will reach a maximum length of about 5.5 to 6 meters (18 to 19 ft. 8 in.), but most individuals are much smaller in size. The body is spindle-shaped, the flippers are small and rounded, and the dorsal fin is absent. The head is rounded, the cleft of the mouth is small, and the vertebrae of the neck are not fused.

In the narwhal, the lower jaws are without any teeth, while in the upper jaws, the young are reported to begin with a total of about four teeth of which only two remain. In the females, these two upper teeth usually remain embedded and undeveloped in their nearly horizontal position. In the males, the right tooth remains in the right upper jaw undeveloped and embedded in bones as in the females, while the single remaining tooth of the upper left jaw begins an amazing forward growth to form a great, long tusk. This tusk spirals from right to left (counter clockwise) as it grows and may eventually reach a length of about 2.74 meters (9 ft.).

This genus is known from the Pleistocene (Glacial) Epoch in Europe and North America.

This genus includes the single living species listed below.

Monodon monoceros Linnaeus, 1758
THE NARWHAL .... See page 212

Photos of an adult male narwhal, *Monodon monoceros,* killed by the Inuit people in eastern arctic Canada, showing the long tusk which develops from the upper left canine tooth of the male and the mottled color pattern of the adult.

Photos by D. Lusby.

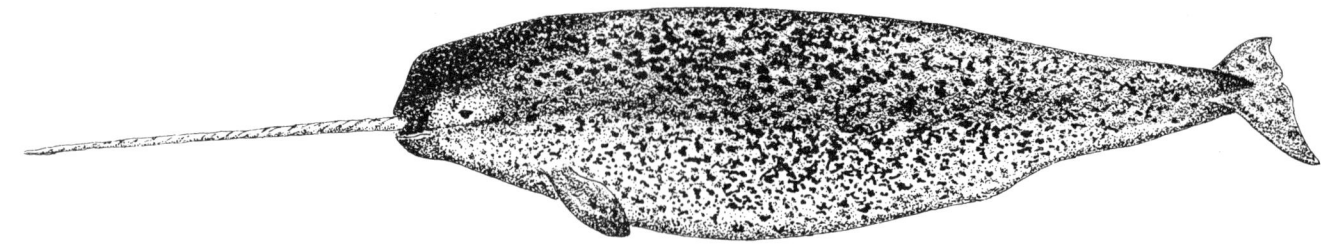

THE NARWHAL
Also known as the Unicorn Whale
Monodon monoceros Linnaeus, 1758

Identifying Features. The adult male narwhal may be recognized immediately by its great long tusk. Since the female and the young lack the tusk, they can be recognized by a combination of characters including the absence of the dorsal fin, the small, round head, and the bluish gray body color marked with brownish spots.

Size and Shape. The narwhal is a medium-sized whale with a plump, cylindrical body, a small spherical head, and a small mouth. The males (without the tusk) measure from about 4 to 5.5 meters (13 ft. 1 in. to 18 ft.) in length; the females are smaller than the males and usually measure about 4 meters (13 ft. 1 in.) in length. To get the total length of the male, the length of the tusk should be added to the length of the body.

Color. The body of the adult narwhal is a mottled bluish gray color above and whitish below. The young are bluish gray and develop the steel gray and brownish spots on the back as they grow older; there are no spots on the belly. The color of the body gets lighter with age and becomes a whitish color in old individuals.

Distribution. The narwhal is circumpolar in Arctic seas southward to about 70° N.L. It occurs in the open waters of Canada's arctic islands, between Baffin Land and Greenland, and occasionally in European waters. It is rare in northern Alaska and not abundant in the seas north of Siberia. Occasionally, stragglers will wander south as far as England.

In the Bering Sea, the narwhal is known from a 1957 stranding at Kiwalik Bay on the south side of Kotzebue Sound and in the same year a live specimen was beached at Nelson Lagoon just west of Port Moller on the northwestern shore of the Alaska Peninsula.

Migration. This species migrates with the seasons, sometimes traveling in great groups numbering as many as 1,000 to 2,000 animals. Migrations are observed along the eastern side of Baffin Land during the 2nd week of August. In the northward spring migrations, the males often precede the female herds.

Fins and Flippers. The dorsal fin is absent and has been replaced along the posterior midline of the back by a low fold of skin which measures 2 to 3 feet in length and thereafter continues to the tail as a small ridge. The flippers are small, roughly oval in outline, and have rounded tips. The two flukes of the tail are convex on their posterior margins and exhibit a median notch where they join at the midline.

Teeth. The young narwhal has 4 teeth on each side in the upper jaw; they include 2 incisors, 1 canine, and 1 molar. Of these 4 teeth, 2 will drop out; in the male, the single left canine will develop into the horizontal tusk, while the 4th tooth on the right side remains undeveloped. This tusk (when viewed from back to front) will spiral in a counter-clockwise direction, perforate the upper lip, and eventually reach a maximum length of about 2.7 meters (8 ft. 10 in.) or nearly 9 feet. There is considerable variation in the growth of these tusks. Sometimes, the right tooth will grow into a tusk, sometimes two tusks will develop, and sometimes neither tooth will develop into a tusk.

Females also have a single pair of teeth in the front of the mouth, but they usually both remain undeveloped. There are also cases in which females have developed one or two tusks.

The purpose of these tusks is unknown. They are not used in fighting since the males are peaceful. It has been suggested that they are used to poke airholes in the ice overhead. Some scholars have suggested that the tusk is an "accidental

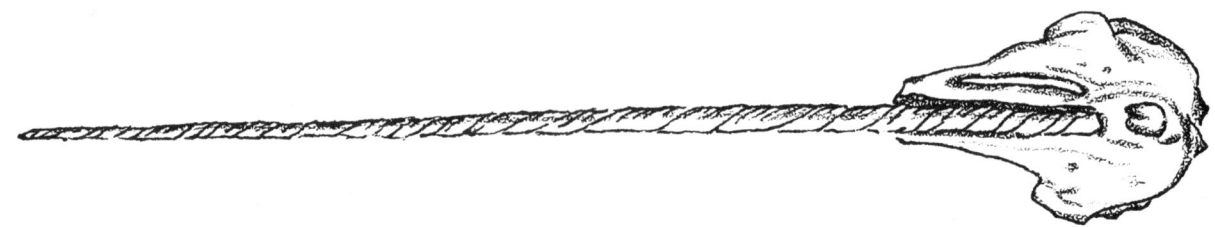

Diagram of the skull and tusk of a male narwhal, *Monodon monoceros* **(Odontoceti: Monodontidae).**

adornment" which is "specialized beyond usefulness" and that the species has survived in spite of it; similar specialization has often led to extinction.

Skeletal Notes. The skull is asymmetrical in the males due to the tusk. The vertebrae of the neck are all separate leaving the neck freely movable; a constriction is visible at the neck on the outside surface of the body. The vertebrae are distributed approximately as follows: C 7 + D 11-12 + L 6-10 + Ca 26-27 = 50-55. Six pairs of ribs articulate directly with the sternum. The bones of the fingers are distributed approximately as follows: I (1-2), II (5-8), III (4-6), IV (2-4), V (2-3).

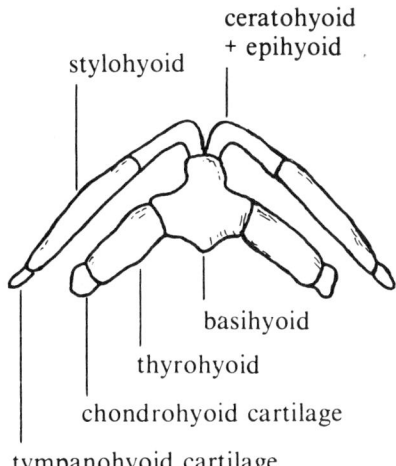

The hyoid bones of the Narwhal *(Monodon monoceros).*

Other Anatomical Notes. The mouth is small and the beak is very small and not readily apparent. The uterus is bihorned and the caecum is absent.

Food. The diet of the narwhal includes squid, bottom fishes including halibut, flounders, miscellaneous fishes, and occasional prawns and other crustacea.

Swimming and Diving. The narwhal usually travels in small groups composed of males, females, and the young; these groups number less than a dozen. They are good swimmers and live much of their time in open water. When they arrive at the surface, they exhale with a whistle, lie motionless for a few moments, and then submerge.

Reproduction. The narwhals mate in about mid-April and the female bears a calf about mid-July after a gestation period of about 14 or 15 months; the calf will then nurse for about the following 20 months. The females will sometimes bear two young. At birth the young will measure about 1.5 meters (59 in.) and will weigh about 75 to 80 kg. (165.3 to 176.4 lbs.). It appears that the interval between calves is 3 years or longer.

Abundance. This species is common in a few areas, but it is uncommon over the greater part of its range. It has probably been over-hunted. It is in need of stringent legal protection.

Economic Importance. The narwhal has very little economic importance other than for its flesh, skin, ivory, blubber, etc., which are used by the Inuit people which border its range. Various superstitions may have assisted in its decline, including the belief in Oriental medicine that the powdered tusk would reduce fever, etc.

THE SPERM WHALE FAMILY
Family *PHYSETERIDAE* Gray, 1821

The great sperm whale is without question the most famous and the best known of all the larger toothed whales. It is so radically different from all other whales that it and two smaller relatives have been placed in a separate family called the *Physeteridae*. It is also the largest species in the entire group of about 67+ toothed whales. In addition, the body of the sperm whale is one of the most amazing among the mammals. The head is massive, cylindrical, and barrel-shaped, comprises about one-third of the length of the body, and is occupied by the giant spermaceti oil reservoir. The snout on the front of the head is high and blunt and bears the single, S-shaped nostril upon its front left corner; the location of this nostril, far to the left of the midline of the body, is a very interesting example of asymmetry among the mammals.

The fossil members of this family are known from the Lower Miocene Epoch to the Holocene (Recent) Epoch.

This family contains two living genera, *Physeter* and *Kogia,* which are very different, both in size and form. These genera are similar in their nostril, their spermaceti reservoir in the head, and a few other features, but their differences are far more numerous than their similarities. For this reason, some scholars believe that the Genus *Kogia* should be removed from this family and placed in a separate family to be known as the *Kogiidae.*

This family usually includes the two living genera listed below.

An aerial photo of a group of sperm whales taken off Japan.
Note the calves swimming to the right of their mothers.
Photo by T. Kasuya.

THE GREAT SPERM WHALES
Genus *PHYSETER* Linnaeus, 1758

The great sperm whale is very unusual among the world's mammals, because its skull has been changed and distorted by evolution more than that of any other mammal, living or extinct.

The body of the great sperm whale bears a gigantic head comprising about one-third of the body; this head is followed by a cylindrical trunk of equal size which merges imperceptibly into the posterior third of the body, which in turn tapers quite uniformly to the tail. The flippers of the great sperm whale are small, broad, and rounded; the dorsal fin appears to be absent, but in its place there is a long, low ruffle of skin along the posterior third of the back. The tail is wide and its two flukes, which are nearly triangular in shape, exhibit a notch at the center of their rear margin.

The throat of the great sperm whale is marked by a few, irregular, longitudinal grooves. The vertebrae of the neck are partly fused; the atlas or 1st cervical vertebra is separate from the rest, but the remaining vertebrae of the neck from numbers 2 through 7 are usually fused into a single, immobile unit. In all, the total number of vertebrae in the backbone is about 50 or 51.

The two lower jaw bones are small, long, and slender and contain from 16 to 30 teeth in each of these lower jaw bones;

these teeth are large, may measure as much as eight inches in length, and fit into pits or sockets in the upper jaws. The teeth of the upper jaws are non-functonal and include from 10 to 16 vestigial teeth on each side which remain buried in the gums.

Fossils of this genus are known from the Middle and Upper Miocene Epoch to the Pleistocene (Glacial) Epoch in North America and from the Lower and Middle Miocene Epoch in Europe.

Studies of these whales by various scholars indicate that several names of species appearing in older books are really duplicate names or synonyms of other previously named species. The following list indicates the older names and the more correct and current names of these species.

Old Name		Name Currently In Use
Physeter bidens	is now	*Mesoplodon bidens*
Physeter catodon	is now	*Physeter macrocephalus*
Physeter breviceps	is now	*Kogia breviceps*
Physeter microps	is now	*Physeter macrocephalus*
Physeter simus	is now	*Kogia simus*
Physeter tursio	is now	*Physeter macrocephalus*

This genus includes the single living species listed below.

Physeter macrocephalus Linnaeus, 1758
THE GREAT SPERM WHALE .... See page 216

Photo of a female sperm whale, *Physeter macrocephalus,* and calf taken off Baja, California.
Photo by K.C. Balcomb.

Photo of the tail flukes of two sperm whales, *Physeter macrocephalus,* which are thrown into the air as these two whales begin a deep dive.

Note the triangular shape of each fluke, their nearly straight posterior margin, and the median notch which separates them.
Photo by K.C. Balcomb.

Class Mammalia — The Mammals
   Order Cetacea — The Whales
      Suborder Odontoceti — The Toothed Whales
         Family Physeteridae — The Sperm Whales

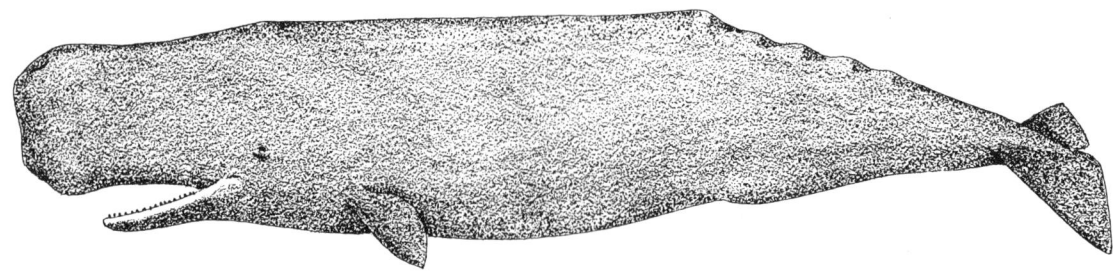

THE GREAT SPERM WHALE
Also known as the Cachalot
Physeter macrocephalus Linnaeus, 1758

Identifying Features. Of all the whales, this species may be identified by its mammoth head. In the water, it exhales by a blow which is directed forward and to the left due to the fact that its blowhole is near the left front corner of the head.

Size and Shape. The great sperm whale is by far the largest of the toothed whales and, in the case of the males, will reach a length of about 15 to 20 meters (49 ft. 2 in. to 65 ft. 1 in.); most, however, are smaller. The females will reach a length of 11 to 17 meters (36 ft. to 55 ft. 9 in.); most of these will **measure nearer 11 meters in length. However, most individuals do not achieve this length and are more apt to meas**ure 50 feet and 40 feet, respectively, or even less. The body is most unusual because it is composed of a great barrel-shaped head which may measure between 1/4 and 1/3 of the body length. The skin appears loose and wrinkled and there is a series of small, irregular, longitudinal creases beneath the jaw and the throat. The skin is exceedingly thick on the back and sides and has been reported to measure as much as 36 cm. (14 in.) in thickness in this area.

Color. The great sperm whale is a bluish or brownish gray to black over most of its body. Whitish areas occur on the belly around the naval and there are a few whitish splashes on the front of the head. The lips, both upper and lower, are irregularly margined with white and the interior of the mouth is white. The young are light at birth, get darker as they mature, and then get lighter again in old age. Albino great sperm whales have been observed in the sea.

Distribution. Great sperm whales are found worldwide in the deeper waters of the tropical and warmer temperate seas. They inhabit both hemispheres as far north and south as about 70°; the females do not normally go beyond 40° or 50° or where the water is cooler than 10° C. (50° F.), while the males will enter cooler water during the summer season. They also enter the Mediterranean Sea.

Migration. These whales migrate with the seasons. In the northern hemisphere, the older males go north in the spring first, but no farther than about 70° N.L.; later, they are followed part way by nursing females and many other males. In going north, these whales tend to stay near the shoreline and when going southward, they stay farther offshore. They always seem to stay in water which is at least 182.8 meters (600 ft.) in depth.

The accompanying photos are of a group of sperm whales which swam ashore and beached at Florence, Oregon (44° N.L.) in June, 1979. The whales all died on the beach and were burned and/or buried there.

Photos by Graybill.

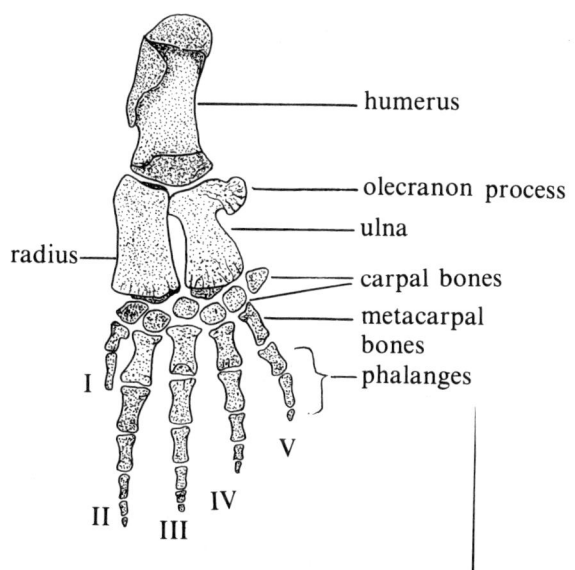

Diagram of the left anterior appendage of the great sperm whale, *Physeter macrocephalus* (Odontoceti: Physeteridae), in lateral view. Note the shortened bones of the upper arm and forearm.

Drawn from Flower.

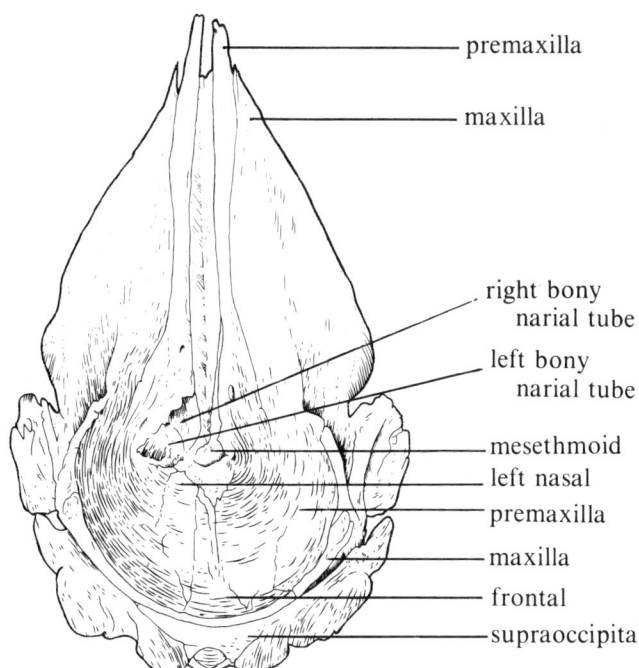

Diagram of the skull of a juvenile sperm whale, *Physeter macrocephalus*, in dorsal view.

Drawn from Raven and Gregory.

Fins and Flippers. The dorsal fin is absent in this species, but there is an angular hump on the back about 2/3 of the distance from the front at the point where the back begins to taper toward the tail; this hump is followed by a series of large, low ruffles of skin. The tail stock also bears a keel on its ventral midline which extends from the anus to the flukes.

The flippers are oval in shape and are comparatively small; they terminate in a rounded tip. They may reach a maximum size of as much as 1.8 meters (6 ft.) in length and 91 cm. (3 ft.) in width.

The tail is thick, broad, triangular in shape, and has a notch in the center of the rear margin. In a large whale, the width of the two flukes may measure over 4 meters (13 ft.) from tip to tip.

Teeth. The teeth in the great sperm whale are found in both the upper and lower jaws, but the upper teeth do not develop and remain buried in the gums; these upper teeth vary from about 10 to 16 in each of the two upper jaw bones. The teeth of the lower jaw bones number between about 16 and 30 in each of the two lower jaw bones and fit into sockets in the upper jaw when the mouth is closed. These lower teeth are of huge size and in some instances may reach a length of about 20 cm. (8 in.) and a diameter of 10 cm. (4 in.). These teeth apparently do not erupt above the gums until the whale is about 10 years old.

Skeletal Notes. The skull of great sperm whales has been deformed by evolution more than the skull of any other mammal. It is asymmetrical and compressed, with an upper jaw which is flattened, widened, and extended to hold the "greatly enlarged nose" which is known as "the case" and which contains a large quantity of spermaceti oil. The two lower jaw bones come together in front to form a single, long, narrow, cylindrical lower jaw in which most of the teeth are set.

The vertebrae are distributed approximately as follows: C 7 + D 11 + L 8 + Ca 24 = 50. In the neck vertebrae, the 1st

vertebra (atlas) is free, but the remaining 6 vertebrae are fused into a single unit. Most of the vertebrae are large and round except toward the tail where they become smaller, including the terminal 9 or 10 within the tail. There are 11 pairs of ribs of which the first 8 pairs have 2 heads, the 9th and 10th have one head, and the 11th rib has one head and is short and small. The 1st 3 ribs* articulate with the sternum. These ribs, together with the sternum, form a chest cage which is stronger than that of any other whale. The sternum is large and strong and is divided down the midline into a right and left side, each of which has 2 or 3 bones. The bones of the fingers are distributed approximately as follows: I (1-2), II (5-8), III (4-8), IV (4-5), V (2-7). Some scholars think that they are usually distributed as follows: 1-5-5-4-3.

---

*Some authors report that four ribs articulate with the sternum.

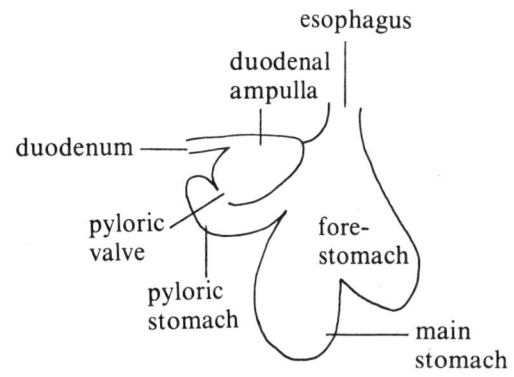

Diagram of the stomach of *Physeter macrocephalus*.
Drawn from Rice.

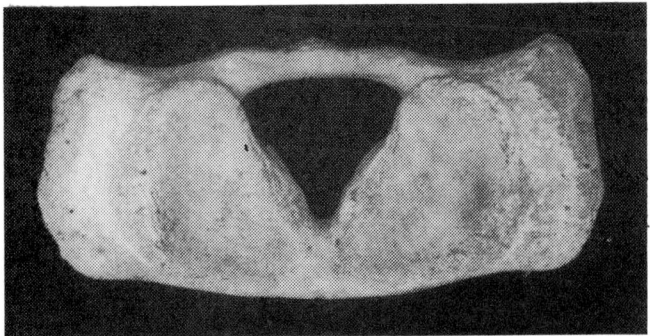

Photo of the first cervical vertebra (atlas) of the sperm whale, *Physeter macrocephalus*, in anterior view.
Photo by Michael Graybill at Ore. Inst. Mar. Biol.

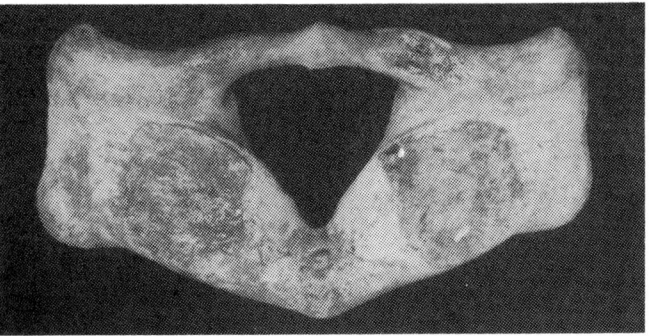

Photo of the first cervical vertebrae (atlas) of the sperm whale, *Physeter macrocephalus*, in posterior view.
Photo by Michael Graybill at Ore. Inst. Mar. Biol.

Although the bones which originally constituted the pelvic girdle and the hind legs of whales have about disappeared except for the two pelvic bones, an occasional ossified thigh bone (femur) may occur buried in the flesh, and a few rare whales have been captured in which a rudimentary stump of the hind leg was found projecting from the surface of the body.

Other Anatomical Notes. The head is proportionately smaller in young whales and in females. The layer of blubber is about 6 inches thick. The anus is located in a depression in the body outline or profile. The single external nostril is S-shaped and the left nasal bone is missing. The gullet is sufficiently large to swallow a man. There is no hair visible on either the embryo or the adult. The 1st stomach holds about 300 liters. The uterus has two horns. The caecum is not present. Rudimentary nipples are located behind the penis in the male. A single great sperm whale, which was captured off California and processed in the whaling station at Fields Landing, California, in 1941, showed the following weights:

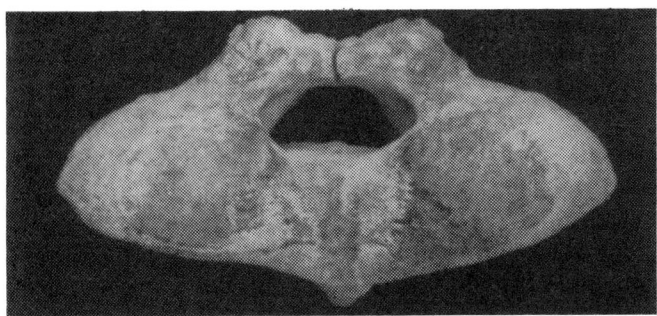

The second cervical vertebra (axis) of the sperm whale, *Physeter macrocephalus*, in anterior view. The five cervical vertebra which follow are all fused together with the axis, but are not visible.

The Weight of A Great Sperm Whale*

Sex and Length	Male — 43 feet	
	Weight	
	Pounds	Kilograms
Total Body Weight	86,000	39,000
Adrenal Gland	0.77	0.350
Thyroid Gland	1.76	0.800
Brain	18.49	8.338
Liver	925.	420.
Heart	277.	126.
Eye (one)	0.64	0.290

From the Jour. of Mammalogy 24:1, 1943, pp. 39-45.
In a specimen which might weigh between about 35,000 to 40,000 kg. (77,175 to 88,200 lbs.), the brain might weigh between about 7,000 to 9,000 grams (15.4 to 19.8 lbs.).

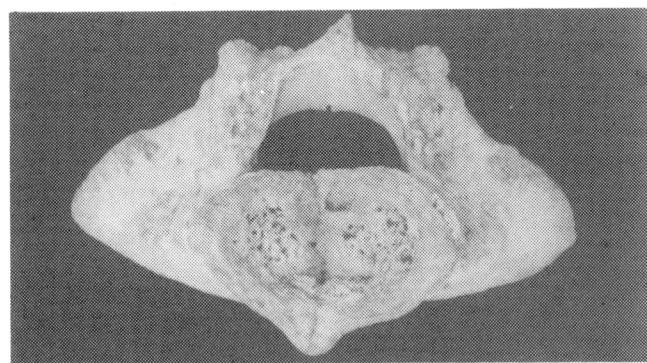

The seventh cervical vertebra of the sperm whale, *Physeter macrocephalus*, in posterior view. The other cervical vertebrae which precede it are all fused together into a single unit of six vertebrae; only the atlas is separate.

Food. The principal foods of great sperm whales are squids, both large and small, and an array of miscellaneous animals including skates and small sharks. They often swallow unusual things; some whales have stones in their stomach and a few have swallowed a coconut and a glass ball.

Swimming and Diving. Great sperm whales live in groups of from 2 to 50 individuals. They are slow swimmers, do not jump, and rest and sleep at the surface. They make deep dives in search of large squid; one such dive was recorded at 996.7 meters (3,270 ft.). Dives are usually of 30 to 40 minutes duration, but they may last nearly one hour. On returning to the surface, they will rest for about 10 minutes and make about 50 blows before again attempting another dive. These deep dives may be expected whenever the whale lifts its tail above the water as it begins its dive. The young whales wait at the surface while the mother is diving. The blow or spout is about 3 to 4 meters (10 to 13 ft.) in height and is directed diagonally forward and to the left.

Reproduction. The adult whales mate during the months from January to June in the warmer waters below 40° N.L. At the mating season, the whales gather into harems, consisting of 2 to 3 males, 20 to 40 females, and a few other males and calves. Mating is most active in April and is accompanied by a great deal of fighting among the males.

Pregnancy lasts about 16-17 months and the young are born from about July to August in the northern hemisphere. The young measure about 4 to 4.5 meters (13 to 15 ft.) at birth and are nursed by their mother for about 13 or more months. Mating by females seems to occur only once every 3 to 4 years.

Abundance. The great sperm whale was once a very abundant species. Groups of 500 to 600 were occasionally encountered and there is one report in 1912/13 of a group off Patagonia which numbered between 3,000 and 4,000 whales. Today, the population is greatly reduced, but it is still probably the most abundant of the large whales.

Economic Importance. This whale once supported a great worldwide industry based upon the value of its oil, ivory, and ambergris. More recently, the bones and flesh have been added to the above products and are being processed for food, fertilizer, etc. The use of mineral oil together with political pressure and the complaints of environmentalists are slowly bringing an end to this industry.

The flesh of the great sperm whale has not found favor as a food for humans. It is reported to be a very dark purplish-black color, probably due to the myoglobin contained in it, and also to be of a greasy texture.

Ambergris has long been a prize which was sought by whalers and others because of its high market value as a fixing agent for perfumes. When fresh, ambergris is a moist, waxy substance of a grayish color, often with a marbled pattern and with its substance and color laid down in concentric layers; as it gets older, it will become dry and somewhat brittle. It is generated in the alimentary tract of the sperm whale and occasionally found there at the time the whale is being "processed." Usually the ambergris is voided by the whale, in which case, it floats away on the waves to be washed ashore on some distant beach. Ambergris is described as having an "earthy" smell and as usually having the beaks of squids scattered through it. It gets soft at about 60° C. (140° F.) and melts between about 63 to 65.5° C. (145-150° F.) into a dark, oily liquid. It is soluble in ether, absolute alcohol, and some volatile oils and fats. The standard test for ambergris has been to immerse a heated wire into the substance, at which time, it will melt into a dark pool and give off a white vapor.

Photo of a young male sperm whale, _Physeter macro-cephalus,_ stranded at Melbourne Beach, Florida.
Photo by P. Winfield

THE PIGMY AND DWARF SPERM WHALES
Genus *KOGIA* Gray, 1864

This genus contains two very rare and unusual species of smaller whales (listed below), but some scholars doubt that they should be placed together with the great sperm whale in the Family *Physeteridae*. Many scholars believe that the genus *Kogia* should be removed from this family and placed in a separate family to be known as the Family Kogiidae.

The bodies of both the pigmy sperm whale (*Kogia breviceps*) and the dwarf sperm whale (*Kogia simus*) are somewhat cylindrical in front and then taper symmetrically toward the tail. In this genus, the head is heavy, blunt, and somewhat rounded, and contains a spermaceti oil reservoir within. The snout is somewhat conical, the beak is very short, and the lower jaw bones are small, narrow, and shorter than the upper jaws, thereby imparting a somewhat shark-like aspect to the front of the head.

The flippers are small, broad, and oval in outline; the dorsal fin is falcate or sickle-shaped in both species and is located either near the middle of the back (*K. simus*) or posterior to the middle (*K. breviceps*); and the tail flukes are notched at the center of their posterior margin.

The teeth of the lower jaws are slender, pointed, and curved backward and inward; they number between 8 and 16 in each of the two lower jaw bones. The vertebrae of the neck are usually united from 2 through 7 and occasionally the 1st vertebra or atlas is included.

The blowhole of the two whales in this genus, like that of the great sperm whale, lies atop the head to the left of the midline of the body and farther forward than in the other toothed whales. The males are larger than the females and may reach about 4 meters (13 ft.) in length.

The color of the members of this genus is blackish or dark gray above, becomes lighter on the sides and belly, and in some instances may approach white on the belly.

These two species may be separated by the grooves on the throat. In *Kogia breviceps* (de Blainville, 1838), the throat is smooth and without grooves. In *Kogia simus* Owen, 1866, the throat has a few, short, irregular wrinkles or grooves. In addition, *K. simus* has a smaller body, smaller and shorter teeth, a larger dorsal fin placed farther forward, and a shorter union (mandibular symphysis) between the lower jaw bones.

This genus is known only from the Holocene (Recent) Epoch.

This genus includes the two living species listed below.

Kogia breviceps (de Blainville, 1838)
     THE PIGMY SPERM WHALE . . . . . See page 221
Kogia simus Owen, 1866
     THE DWARF SPERM WHALE . . . . See page 223

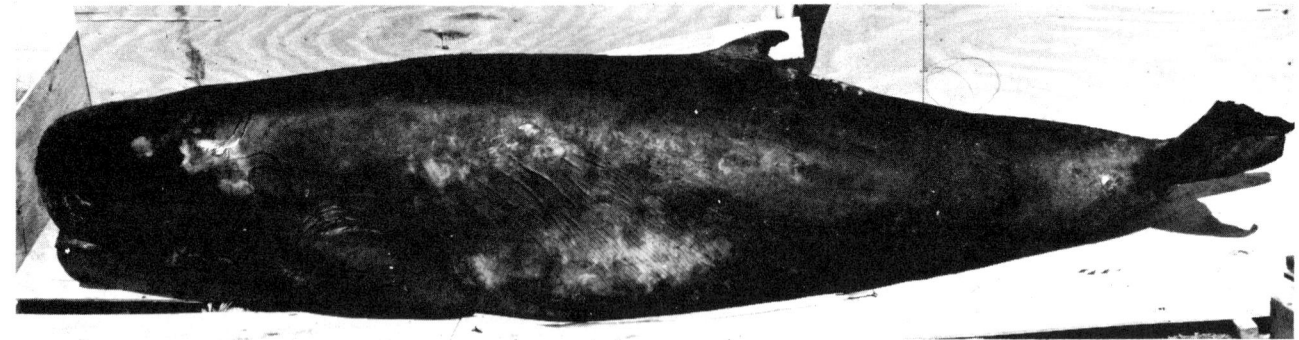

Photo by D.K. Caldwell.

The pigmy sperm whale, *Kogia breviceps*, may reach a length of 4 m. (13 ft.). In this species, the dorsal fin is small and is located posterior to the center of the body.

From Leatherwood et alii.

Photo by D.K. Caldwell.

The dwarf sperm whale, *Kogia simus*, may reach a length of 2.8 m. (9 ft.). In this species, the dorsal fin is larger than in *K. breviceps* and is located near the middle of the body. The irregular, light-colored areas on the body are due to decomposition.

From Leatherwood et alii.

Class Mammalia — The Mammals
Order Cetacea — The Whales
Suborder Odontoceti — The Toothed Whales
Family Physeteridae — The Sperm Whales

THE PIGMY SPERM WHALE
Also known as The Lesser Cachalot
Kogia breviceps (de Blainville, 1838)

Identifying Features. This species is best recognized by its short length (to 3.4 meters or 11 ft.); a small dorsal fin; a spherical head; an underslung jaw; sharp, slender, curved teeth in the lower jaw bones; a crescent-shaped "bracket" mark on the side of the head; a round white spot in front of the eye; and its dark steel-grey color. The spout is directed slightly to the left.

Size and Shape. The body of this rare whale is spindle-shaped, very robust, and has a spherical head which is conical in front. This head overhangs the lower jaw and gives it an underslung appearance. The mouth is small and narrow. It lacks the grooves on the throat which are found in *K. simus.* Specimens are known to reach a length of 3.4 meters (11 ft.) and may measure as much as 4 meters (13 ft.) in length; however, most specimens will measure about 3 meters or less. The blowhole is located slightly to the left of the midline.

A very unusual bracket-shaped mark is located on the side of the head between the eye and the base of the flipper. The upper arm of the bracket extends forward and slightly upward, while the lower arm extends downward and slightly forward. It is L-shaped on the right side of the head.

Color. The body is dull in color. It is a dark steel grayish, bluish, or blackish above and shades gradually to grayish white on the belly; the appendages are likewise gray. A round white spot is often present just in front of the eye. Older animals are reported to be speckled beneath.

Distribution. This species is widely distributed in the tropical and temperate seas of the world. It does not often enter cooler water and seems to avoid the mid-ocean areas. It has a wider north-and-south range than *K. simus.* It inhabits the water off both coasts of the United States, the Gulf of Mexico, and the Gulf of California.

Migration. Very little is known of its migration habits.

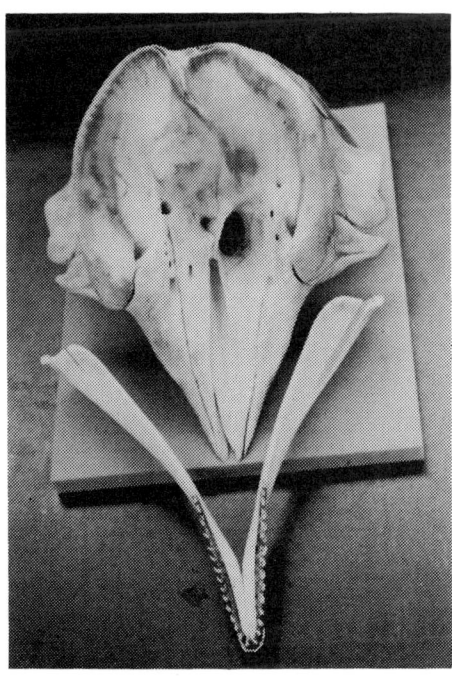

Photo of a pigmy sperm whale, *Kogia breviceps,* stranded near Wellington, North Island, New Zealand.

F. O'Leary.

From: "Whales and Dolphins of New Zealand and Australia" by A.N. Baker. Victoria University Press, Wellington, 1983. Courtesy A.N. Baker.

The skull and jaw bones of the pigmy sperm whale, *Kogia breviceps,* in dorsal view.
Photo by Michael Graybill at Humboldt State Univ.

221

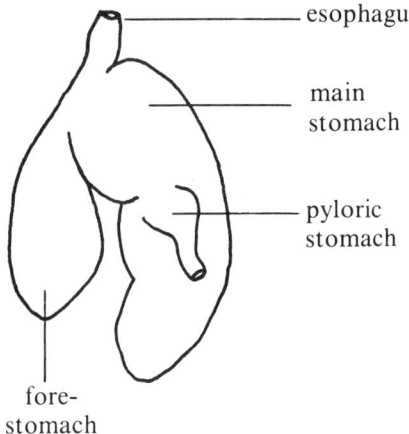

A diagram of the stomach (possibly incomplete) of *Kogia breviceps*.

Drawn from Benham.

Fins and Flippers. The dorsal fin is located behind the center of the back. It is small and deeply concave on its posterior border. The flippers are located quite far forward on the body, are of medium size, and are somewhat pointed. The posterior margin of the tail is concave and bears a notch at its midpoint.

Teeth. The teeth of the lower jaw number from 9 to 16 on each side; they are sharp and slender, are curved backward and inward, and fit into sockets in the upper jaw. The upper teeth number from 3 to 7 on each side and are small and almost vestigial.

Skeletal Notes. The vertebrae are distributed approximately as follows: C 7 + D 13 + L 9 + Ca 27 = 56. The neck bones are usually all united; this renders the head nearly immobile.

The tail has about 27 vertebrae and the chevron bones number about 17. There are 13 pairs of ribs of which 8 pairs have 2 heads. Six pairs of ribs articulate directly with the sternum. There are 4 pairs of costal cartilages which articulate with the sternum, plus 4 additional pairs. The sternum has 3 parts. The bones of the fingers vary in number and are hard to count; they are distributed approximately as follows: I (2), II (8), III (8), IV (7), V (5).

Other Anatomical Notes. The external nostril is farther forward than in most small whales. Only the left nostril opens to the exterior. The caecum and the gall bladder are absent. The liver discharges the bile through a bile duct which empties directly into the duodenum. In a young adult specimen measuring 2.49 meters (8.16 ft.), each testis measured about 1 by 4 in. in size. The penis measured about 45.72 cm. (18 in.) in length.

Food. The diet of the pigmy sperm whales consist of squid and miscellaneous fishes.

Swimming and Diving. Very little information is known about their habits. They seem to gather into small groups of 3 to 6 individuals, although only single individuals seem to be stranded. They are reported to swim with their flippers held against the body. They are not known to follow ships or to ride on their bow waves.

Reproduction. Very little information is available regarding its reproductive habits. The young will measure about 120 cm. (47 in.) at birth after a gestation period approaching about 11 months.

Abundance. This is one of the more uncommon species of whales in spite of its wide distribution.

Economic Importance. There is no economic importance attached to this species.

Miscellaneous. This species is sometimes identified at sea by its red, watery fecal discharge which it releases as it dives.

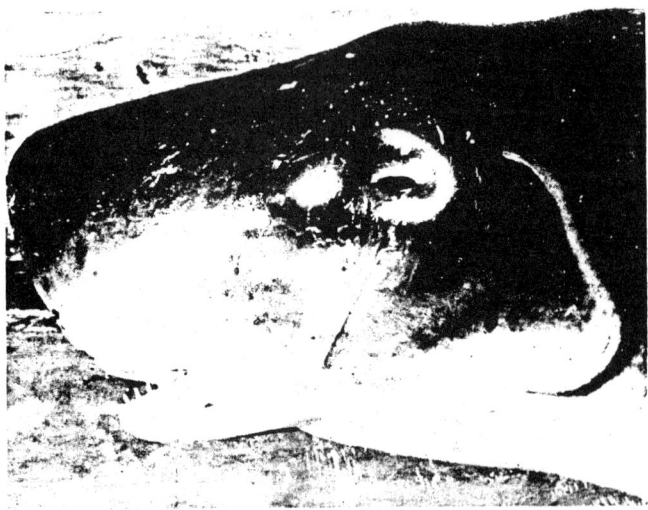

Photo by D.K. Caldwell.

Photo of the side of the head and lower jaw with teeth of the pigmy sperm whale, *Kogia breviceps*.

Photo by D.K. Caldwell.

THE DWARF SPERM WHALE
Kogia simus Owen, 1866

Identifying Features. The dwarf sperm whale resembles the pigmy sperm whale (*K. breviceps*), but is smaller, has a larger dorsal fin, has fewer teeth, lacks the round white spot in front of the eye, and has a few gular grooves on the throat which are not present in *K. breviceps*.

Size and Shape. The body is robust and tapers toward both extremities. This tapering or narrowing is very pronounced where the tail stock joins the tail. The head is spherical and squarish with a somewhat conical shape to the snout. The lower jaw is set beneath the snout giving it an underslung, shark-like aspect. A crescent-shaped bracket mark is present on the side of the head. Most specimens will measure between 2 and 2.7 meters (79 in. to 8 ft. 10 in.) in length.

Color. The entire upper surface of the body is a dull, dark, steel-gray hue; this color shades gradually to light gray on the sides and to a dull white on the belly.

Distribution. The dwarf sperm whale is a warm water species which is widely distributed in the tropical and warmer temperate seas of the world. It is known from the Caribbean area, the Gulf of Mexico, and along both coasts of the United States.

Migration. It is possible that this species shifts with the seasons, but not much is known about its habits.

Fins and Flippers. The dorsal fin is much like that of the dolphins and is located quite near the midpoint of the back; it is much larger than the dorsal fin of *K. breviceps*. A mid-dorsal keel extends from the dorsal fin backward and ends upon the upper surface of the tail. The flippers are short, broad, convexly curved on both margins, and pointed. The tail bears a median notch on its posterior margin.

Teeth. The teeth are small, slender, and sharp. They usually number about 11 on each lower jaw bone, although they may number from about 8 to 13; *K. breviceps* usually has 12 or more teeth in each lower jaw. The teeth of the upper jaw, when present, are 3 in number on each side and are small and inconspicuous.

Skeletal Notes. The vertebrae are distributed approximately as follows: C 7 + D 13 + L 9 + Ca 27 = 56. The vertebrae of the neck region are usually united from 2 through 7 and sometimes include the 1st vertebra or atlas.

Other Anatomical Notes. The single blowhole is located off center to the left. Only the left nostril opens to the surface; this is a feature of all three species in the Family Physeteridae.

Food. Very little is known of the habits of this species. The diet of this whale includes squid and miscellaneous fishes, many of which are captured at depths reported to be beyond 250 to 300 meters (820 to 984 ft.).

Swimming and Diving. These are sluggish swimmers and do not seem to follow ships or to leap from the water. The spout of this species is directed to the left. They seem to live in small groups of 2 or 3 to 6 or 7 individuals.

Reproduction. The young will measure about 1 meter (3.3 ft.) in length at birth and will weigh about 45 kg. (99 lbs.).

Abundance. The dwarf sperm whale is one of the uncommon species of whales.

Economic Importance. This species is of no economic importance.

Miscellaneous. This little whale has not been extensively studied.

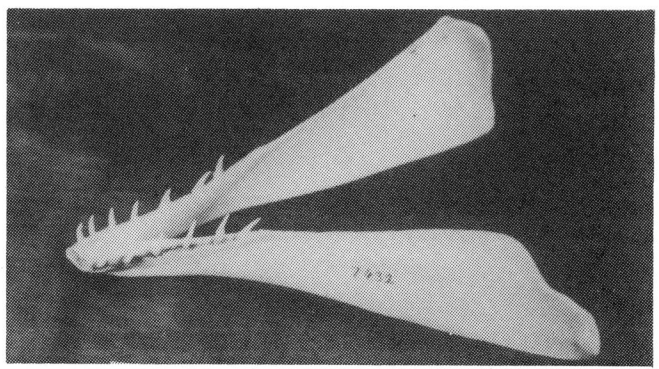

The lower jaw bones and teeth of the dwarf sperm whale (*Kogia simus*).
Photo by Univ. of British Columbia.

THE BEAKED WHALE FAMILY
Family *ZIPHIIDAE (Hyperoodontidae)* Gray, 1865

The ziphiid whales are the second largest family of whales, but they are the rarest and the most poorly known of all groups. They include in all about 18 species which are distributed through 6 genera. They are of medium size, although some are known to reach as much as 12.8 meters (42 ft.) in length.

Several features separate the members of this family from other groups and help to identify them. *First,* most ziphiid whales do not have a notch at the center of the rear margin of the tail flukes similar to that found in the *Delphinidae,* although a few species and/or specimens of *Berardius* and *Ziphius* may possess such a notch. *Second,* longitudinal gular grooves are found beneath the throat; these grooves are V-shaped, converge anteriorly, but are open at the pointed front end of the V; these grooves number from two to six and occur only in this family of toothed whales.

The bodies of beaked whales are more robust than those of most toothed whales; the dorsal fin is small, sickle-shaped, and is located on the posterior half of the body; and the flippers are small, ovate in shape, and shorter than in most whales. The head is not marked off externally from the beak by a groove as in the *Delphinidae;* in this family, the head merges gradually into a beak which is quite slender and tubular in shape.

The skulls of ziphiid whales are asymmetrical in all species except those of the genus *Berardius;* in this genus the skulls of the two species are nearly symmetrical. The nasal aperture or blowhole is median in position on the top of the head and is half-moon shaped with the tips of the crescent directed forward. Within this family, the vertebrae of the entire backbone number between about 43 and 49; the neck vertebrae tend to become partly fused in various combinations; these are usually the first 3 or 4 vertebrae.

The dorsal and lumbar vertebrae have tall, slender neural spines and the transverse processes are short.

Among the ziphiid whales, the teeth are reduced in number and, with the exception of the genus *Tasmacetus,* are limited to one or two pairs of functional teeth which are restricted to the lower jaw; all species, however, appear to have minute, vestigial teeth in all jaws. These functional teeth, although large, are often buried beneath the gums and do not emerge in the males until maturity is reached; in female whales, these large teeth usually remain buried in the gums throughout life.

Another astonishing feature of this family is the number of divisions or compartments within the stomach; these divisions are reported to vary from 9 to 14 within the various members of this family. Some species including *Hyperoodon* and *Ziphius* are reported to lack the fore-stomach.

The beaked whales are worldwide in all oceans, but are everywhere uncommon. They occur either singly or in schools which may reach as many as 40 individuals. Only one species, *Hyperoodon ampullatus,* of the North Atlantic is migratory.

There are fossil records of ziphiid whales from the Lower Miocene Epoch to the Holocene (Recent) Epoch; but, among the living genera, only *Mesoplodon* has been found as a fossil.

The Finger Bones Of Some Ziphiid Whales
(Phalanges plus Metacarpals)

Ziphiidae (6 genera)	I	II	III	IV	V	Total
Tasmacetus shepherdi	1	5	4	3	2	15
Berardius species	1	6	5	4	3	19
Indopacetus pacificus	—	—	—	—	—	—
Mesoplodon grayi	1	6	5	4	3	19
Ziphius cavirostris	2	6	6	5	3	22
Hyperoodon species	2	7	6	5	3	23

From Oliver

Note. The counts of the phalanges or finger bones may vary between authors because there is a lack of uniformity in what is to be included in the count. The terminal or end phalanx is often lost in the cleaning process and may have been overlooked because of its small size or because it is not completely ossified, particularly in young specimens.

A Key To The Genera[1] Of The Beaked Whales
(Choose either I or II; if II is chosen, then choose A or B. Continue in this manner.)

I. The teeth occur in both the upper and lower jaws, usually totalling between 80 and 108 in all, and usually with 19 to 22 pairs in the upper jaws and 25 to 27 pairs in the lower jaws. The two front teeth of the lower jaws are placed at the tips of the jaws, are larger and longer than the other teeth, and possess "bulbous bases and conical crowns." They are also separated from the smaller teeth which follow by a small space (diastema) of two or three centimeters (1 inch). The tail does not usually contain a notch[2] at the center of its rear margin . . . . Genus *TASMACETUS*. See page 229

II. The teeth occur only in the lower jaws and are limited to either two or four large teeth which may not project far above the gum line. (Choose either A or B below.)

A. The teeth of the lower jaws number four, none of which project very far above the gums. The first pair is located at the tips of the lower jaws and the second pair about 10 centimeters (4 in.) farther back . . . . Genus *BERARDIUS*. See page 231

B. The teeth of the lower jaws are limited to two large functional teeth which do not often erupt above the gums until adult status is reached; these teeth usually appear earlier in male individuals. Small non-functional teeth are occasionally present in all jaws. (Choose either 1 or 2 below.)

1. The beak is normal in size and length; the head is of usual proportions and does not have an enlarged, bulbous, inflated appearance. (Choose either a or b below.)

a. The teeth of the lower jaws are two in number; they may be of various sizes and shapes includ-

---
1. The Genus *Indopacetus* is omitted from this key because it contains but a single species, *I. pacificus* (Longman, 1926), which is exceedingly rare and is limited to the southern oceans.
2. If such a notch is present, your specimen probably belongs in the Family *Delphinidae.*

ing some which are very large and laterally flattened; they are located in various positions in the front half of the jaws. These teeth are not usually visible in females and may not be clearly visible in some males. The cleft of the mouth is large and reaches over halfway from the snout to the eye. The body length rarely exceeds 6 to 6.7 meters (20 to 22 ft.)........
..... Genus *MESOPLODON*. See page 237

b. The teeth of the lower jaw are two in number; they are located one each at the very tip of each lower jaw bone. They are not usually visible in females. A low, dorsal keel extends along the midline of the back from the dorsal fin to the tail. The cleft of the mouth is smaller and reaches about halfway from the snout to the eye. The body length may reach from 8.5 to 9 meters (28 to 30 ft.).....................
.... Genus *ZIPHIUS*. See page 256

2. The beak is comparatively short; the head has an enlarged, bulbous, inflated appearance and presents a high, nearly vertical forehead when viewed from the side. ....
.... Genus *HYPEROODON*. See page 259

This family includes the six genera of living beaked whales listed below.

The above genera are discussed on the following pages in the above sequence.

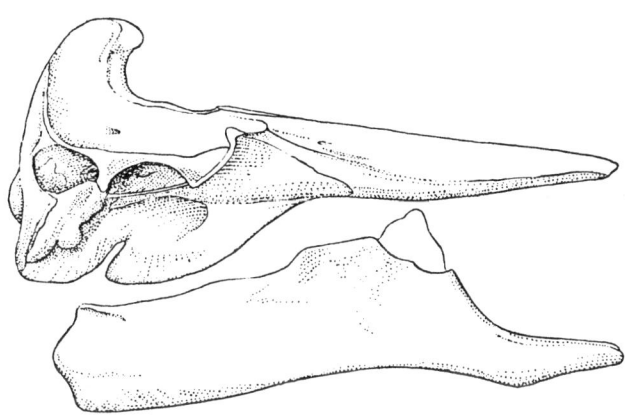

A drawing of the skull and lower jaw of a species of *Mesoplodon* (Ziphiidae) showing the single, immense tooth found in some species of this genus.

From MAMMOLOGY, 3rd Edit., 1986. By Dr. Terry A. Vaughan. Saunders College Pub. Co., New York. Courtesy of Dr. Terry A. Vaughan.

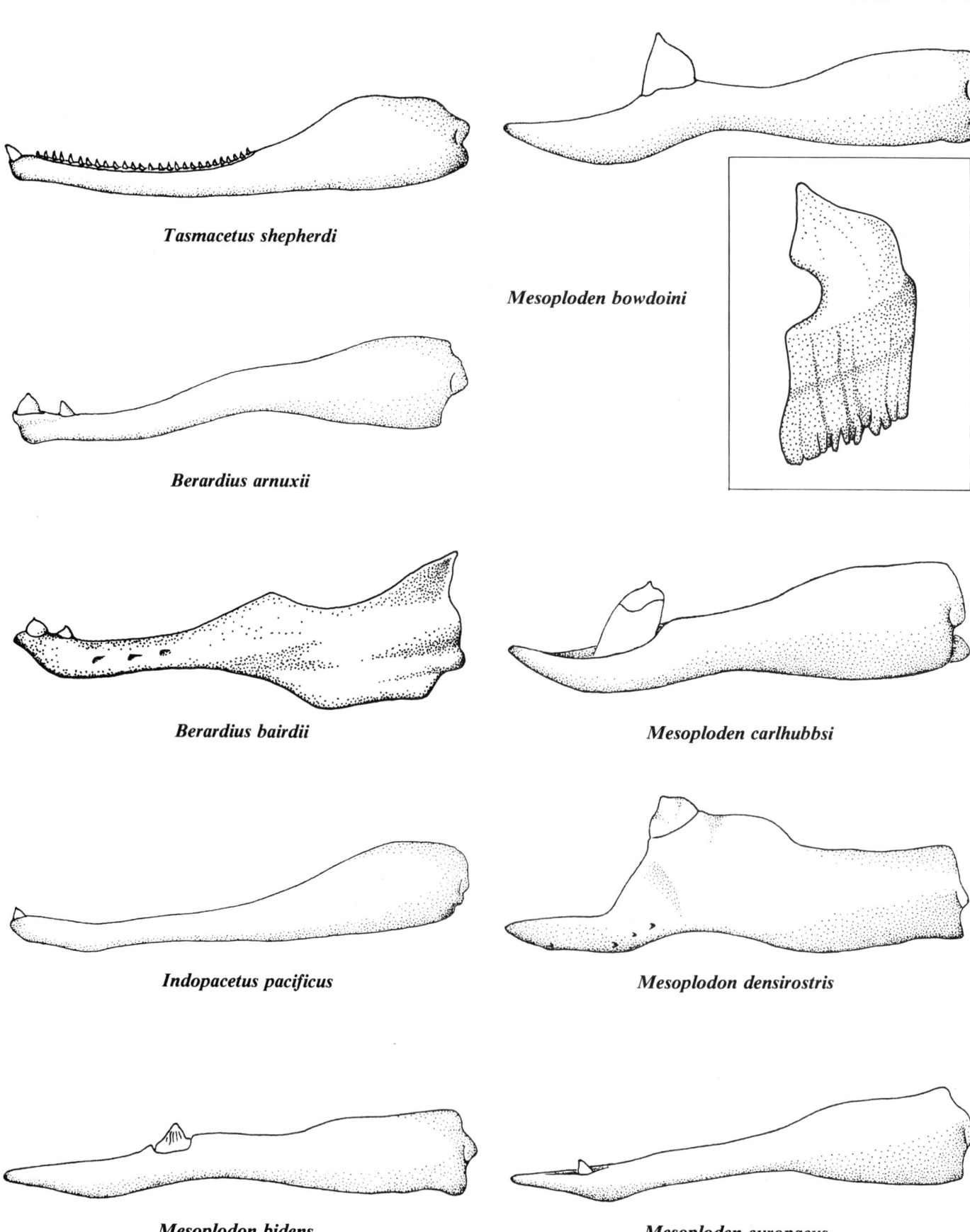

Tasmacetus shepherdi

Mesoploden bowdoini

Berardius arnuxii

Berardius bairdii

Mesoploden carlhubbsi

Indopacetus pacificus

Mesoplodon densirostris

Mesoplodon bidens

Mesoploden europaeus

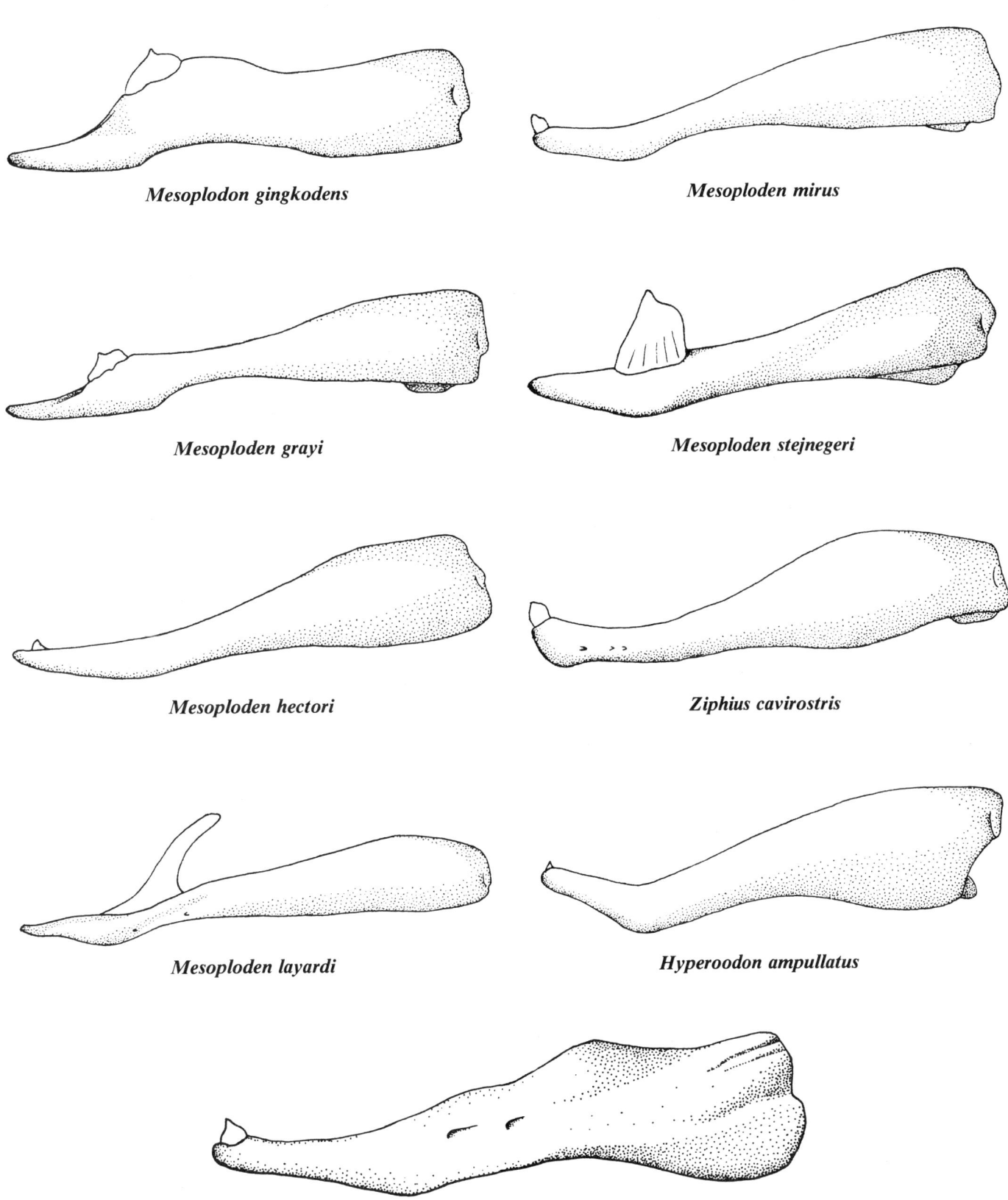

Mesoplodon gingkodens

Mesoploden mirus

Mesoploden grayi

Mesoploden stejnegeri

Mesoploden hectori

Ziphius cavirostris

Mesoploden layardi

Hyperoodon ampullatus

Hyperoodon planifrons

The Distribution of the Species of the Beaked Whales (Ziphiidae)

	Arctic Seas	Atlantic Ocean					Indian Ocean			Pacific Ocean					Antarctic Seas
		North Cool	North Temperate	Tropical	South Temperate	South Cool	Tropical	Temperate	Cool	North Cool	North Temperate	Tropical	South Temperate	South Cool	
Tasmacetus shepherdi					•			•					•		
Berardius arnuxii						•			•					•	•
bairdi										•	•				
Indopacetus pacificus							•	•			•	•	•		
Mesoplodon bidens		•	•												
bowdoini					•	•			•				•	•	•
carlhubbsi										•	•		•*	•*	
densirostris			•	•	•		•	•			•	•	•		
europaeus			•	•	•										
gingkodens							•				•	•	•*		
greyi			•*		•	•		•	•				•	•	
hectori					•			•			•*		•		
layardi					•	•		•	•				•	•	
mirus		•	•		•			•							
stejnegeri										•	•				
Ziphius cavirostris		•	•	•	•	•	•	•		•	•	•	•	•	
Hyperoodon ampullatus	•	•	•	•											
planifrons					•	•	•	•	•			•	•	•	•

*Uncertain, doubtful, or most unusual.

228

THE SHEPHERD'S BEAKED WHALES
Genus *TASMACETUS* Oliver, 1937

This genus contains but a single species and may be separated from all other beaked whales (Ziphiidae) by the teeth. It possesses functional teeth in all jaws, in addition to a single pair of large teeth which are located one each in the very front of each lower jaw. These teeth may number from 17 to 22 pairs in the upper jawbones and from 18 to 27 pairs in the lower jaws. The other five genera in this family do not have small functional teeth, but they do possess numerous, small, vestigial teeth buried in the flesh of all jaws, in addition to the one or two pairs of larger teeth in the lower jaws.

This genus is known only from the Holocene (Recent) Epoch.

This genus includes the single living species listed below.
Tasmacetus shepherdi Oliver, 1937

Class Mammalia — The Mammals
  Order Cetacea — The Whales
    Suborder Odontoceti — The Toothed Whales
      Family Ziphiidae — The Beaked Whales

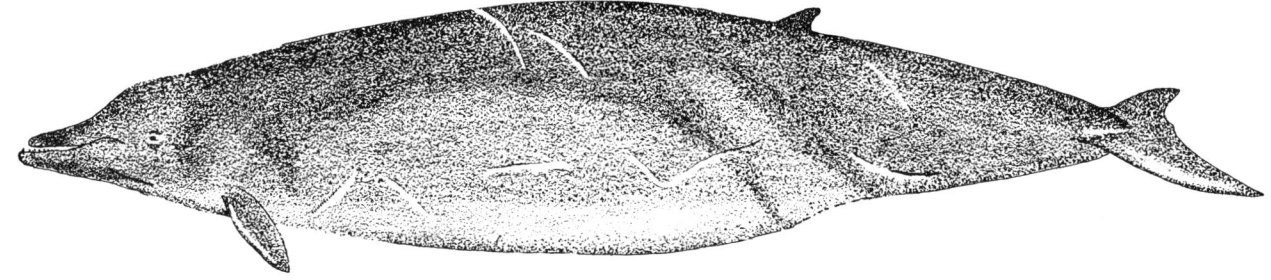

THE SHEPHERD'S BEAKED WHALE
Also known as the Tasman Whale
Tasmacetus shepherdi Oliver, 1937*

Identifying Features. This whale is an extremely uncommon species and is best known from skeletons. It reaches over 6 meters (20+ ft.) in length, lacks a notch on the tail, and has about 20 or more teeth in each of the four jaw bones.

Size and Shape. This beaked whale has a robust body, a rounded head with the usual proboscis projecting forward, and a tail without a notch. Known specimens have measured between 6 and 7 meters (19.7 to 23 ft.); these have included less than a dozen specimens, all of which were either beached carcasses or skeletons. The skull is symmetrical, and the eye is large and is located directly below the blowhole. There are two grooves on the throat.

Color. It is impossible at this time to know the exact color of this whale, because dead whales turn dark or black very shortly after death. It is presumed that the body is dark in color upon the back and shades to white on the belly. The side of the body is reported to have vague stripes and to contain scratches.

Distribution. This whale may eventually prove to be a circumpolar species in the southern hemisphere because all known specimens have come from the beaches of eastern Australia, New Zealand, the Tasman Sea, Chile, and Argentina. No living specimen has been seen to this date.

Fins and Flippers. The dorsal fin is small and is located about 2/3 of the body length from the head. The flippers, as in other members of the Ziphiidae, are small, oval in shape, and short.

Teeth. This genus and species has more teeth than any other beaked whale. In the males, there are 2 large teeth in the front of the lower jaw. A single tooth is placed on each side of the midline (mandibular symphysis) of the lower jaw; these 2 teeth are described as having "conical crowns and bulbous bases." In addition, there are between 18 to 27 teeth in each of the lower jaw bones and between 17 to 22 teeth in

*See original description in Proc. Zool. Soc. of London Vol. 107, Ser B., 1937, pp. 371-381 (19 figs.).

each side of the upper jaw. There is a space (diastema) of about 4 cm. (1.5 in.) between the large, front teeth of the lower jaw and the other teeth which follow.

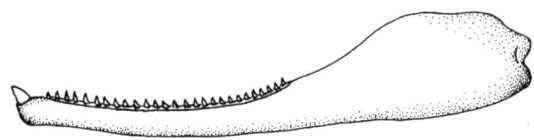

Jaw and teeth of *Tasmacetus shepherdi*.

Skeletal Notes. The first 5 vertebrae are fused together; the 6th vertebra is fused to the 5th by the neural spine and the upper part of the neural arch; and the 7th vertebra is separate and free. Two spines project upward from these fused cervical vertebrae; the 1st spine is composed of the united spines of the 1st 3 vertebrae; the 2nd spine is formed from the combined spines of the 4th, 5th, and 6th vertebrae. The vertebrae are distributed approximately as follows: C 7+ D 9-11 + L 11-14 + Ca 18 = 45-49. There are about 9 pairs of ribs of which 7 are 2-headed; the 8th and 9th ribs have a single head each. The cartilaginous sternal ribs include 6 pairs. The sternum is composed of 4 units. The vestigial pelvic bones are "sinuous" in shape and measure about 17.1 cm. (6.75 in.) in length and 1.6 cm. (5/8 in.) by 1 cm. (3/8 in.) in width and thickness, respectively. The chevron or V-bones beneath the caudal vertebrae number at least 10 pairs. In the flippers, the numbers of phalanges plus the metacarpal bones are approximately as follows: I (1), II (5), III (4), IV (3), V (2).

Other Anatomical Notes. The eye is located directly below the blowhole.

Food. The food is known to consist of squids and various fishes, some of which seem to indicate that this species feeds upon or near the bottom.

Photo of Shepherd's beaked whale, *Tasmacetus shepherdi*, stranded in September, 1966, at Onaero, New Zealand.
Taranaki Newspaper, Ltd.

From: "Whales and Dolphins of New Zealand and Australia" by A.N. Baker. Victoria University Press, Wellington, 1983. Courtesy A.N. Baker.

Swimming and Diving. At this time, all known specimens have been obtained from beaches. Very little is known of the habits of this whale.

Abundance. This ziphiid whale is one of the rarest of whales.

Economic Importance. This whale is of no economic importance.

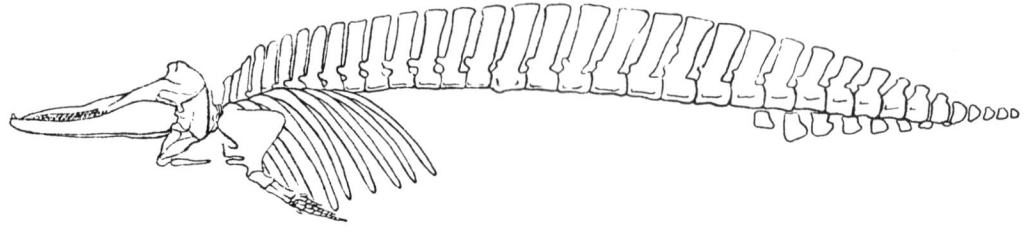

A drawing of the skeleton of Shepherd's Beaked Whale, *Tasmacetus shepherdi*.

From MAMMOLOGY, 3rd Edit., 1986. By Dr. Terry A. Vaughan. Saunders College Pub. Co., New York. Courtesy of Dr. Terry A. Vaughan.

THE GIANT, FOUR-TOOTHED WHALES
Genus *BERARDIUS* Duvernoy, 1851

This genus contains two species which are the largest of the beaked whales and which are known to reach a length of 12.8 meters (42 ft.). Their bodies are large, heavy, robust, solid, and generally spindle-shaped. As in other ziphiid whales, the flippers are short, the dorsal fin is small and is nearly straight on its posterior border, and the tail flukes may possess a notch at the center of their rear margin. The color of the body is a brownish black and is often marked below with white spots.

The forehead, although somewhat inflated, is not sharply marked off from the beak as in the *Delphinidae*. In this genus, the beak or rostrum tapers slightly and the tip of the lower jaw extends beyond the tip of the upper jaw. The skull is very nearly symmetrical and it should be noted that the first three vertebrae of the neck are usually fused together.

The functional teeth, usually two pairs, are confined to the lower jaws. The first pair is triangular in cross section and is located at the tips of the lower jaws. This pair is followed about four inches farther back by a smaller pair of teeth and occasionally by a third pair; the second pair may not be apparent in female individuals.

The giant bottle-nosed whales usually travel in small schools of about 20 individuals. They are alert and are not often captured. They feed upon squid and fishes for which they dive to considerable depths. They may be recognized by their habit of raising the flukes of the tail above the water as they begin their dive.

This genus was named for a Captain Berard who procured the type specimen of *B. arnuxii* for Mr. Georges-Louis Duvernoy.

This genus is known only from the Holocene (Recent) Epoch.

Studies of these whales by various scholars indicate that several names of species appearing in older books are really duplicate names or synonyms of other previously named species. The following list indicates the older names and the more correct and current names of these species.

Old Name		Name Currently In Use
Berardius arnouxi	is now	*Berardius arnuxii*
Berardius arnouxii	is now	*Berardius arnuxii*
Berardius arnuxi	is now	*Berardius arnuxii*
Berardius hectori	is now	*Mesoplodon hectori*

This genus includes the two living species listed below.

Berardius arnuxii Duvernoy, 1851
SOUTHERN, GIANT,
FOUR-TOOTHED WHALE...... See page 232

Berardius bairdii Stejneger, 1883
THE NORTH PACIFIC, GIANT,
FOUR-TOOTHED WHALE...... See page 233

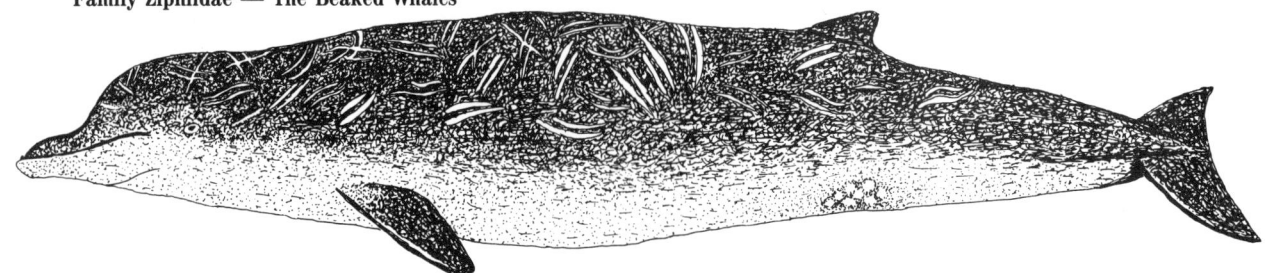

THE SOUTHERN, GIANT, FOUR-TOOTHED WHALE

Also known as Arnoux's Beaked Whale, The Southern Four-toothed Whale,
and The Southern, Giant, Four-toothed, Bottle-nosed Whale
Berardius arnuxii Duvernoy, 1851

Identifying Features. This ziphiid whale may be identified by a combination of characters including its large size, robust body, small dorsal fin, two grooves on the throat, and four triangular teeth in the front of the lower jaw; of these, the first two may be visible when the mouth is closed.

Size and Shape. The body of this whale is quite large, solid and robust. The females are larger than the males. A single female, which measured 9.75 meters (32 ft.), may be regarded as about the maximum length for this species. This species is smaller than *B. bairdii*. It has a bulging forehead and a pronounced tubular proboscis, the lower jaw of which is longer than the upper jaw. The throat contains two longitudinal grooves which converge anteriorly.

Color. The back of the body is covered with a bluish black or gray color which shades gradually to a lighter color below. The skin is marked by many scars and scratches.

Distribution. This ziphiid whale is found in all southern oceans. It enters the ice fields and is reported to sometimes be trapped within them. It ranges from about 33° S.L. southward to the ice fields and at this latitude encircles the globe.

Migration. Very little information is known about the migratory habits of this whale.

Fins and Flippers. The dorsal fin is small and is placed about 2/3 of the body length from the head. It is triangular in

shape and nearly straight on its posterior border. The flippers are small, short, and broad; they possess somewhat parallel borders and are rounded at the tips. The tail is larger and wider than that of *B. bairdii* and lacks a median notch, although a slight trace of it is visible.

Teeth. The teeth of this species are unique. There are only 4 teeth in the front of the lower jaw which are somewhat triangular in cross-section. These teeth are about 7.5 cm. (3 in.) in height and are separated from the tooth behind by about 10 to 20 cm. (4 to 8 in.). In the females, these teeth usually do not emerge but remain buried in the gums. There are no rudimentary teeth apparent in either the lower or upper jaws.

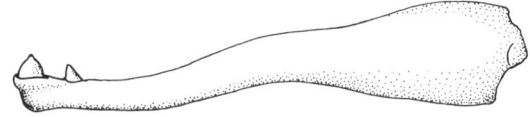

Jaw and tooth of *Berardius arnuxii*.

Skeletal Notes. The vertebrae are distributed approximately as follows: C 7 + D 10-11 + L 12 + Ca 17-19 = 47-48. The 1st 3 cervical vertebrae are fused into a single unit. Seven pairs of ribs articulate directly with the sternum.

Food. The diet of this species consists of squid and fishes.

Swimming and Diving. These animals gather into schools of up to 20 individuals. These whales are alert and very hard to approach or capture. They do not follow ships and are not known to approach them or to ride their bow waves.

Reproduction. The reproductive habits of this species are virtually unknown. It is estimated that the young measure about 4.6 meters (15 ft.) at birth and that the gestation period extends for about 14 months.

Abundance. This is an uncommon species even in the geographical area which it inhabits.

Economic Importance. There is no economic importance attached to this species. Its habit of avoiding ships indicates that it was probably rarely harpooned by whalers.

Miscellaneous. This species was named for two Frenchmen, Berard and Arnoux. Captain Berard commanded a corvette, the *Rhin,* and Arnoux was the surgeon aboard this vessel when they transported the first specimen from New Zealand to France.

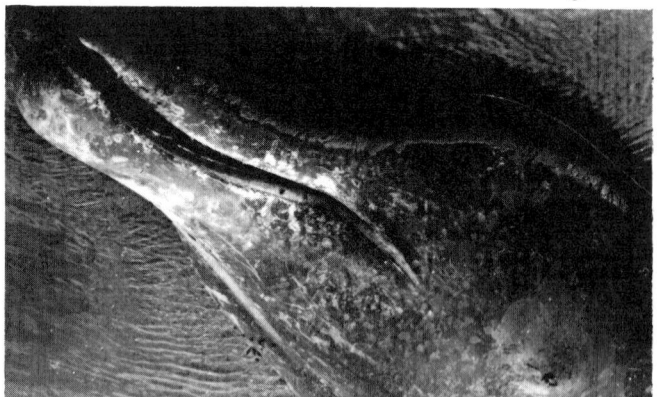

Photo of the head of the southern giant four-toothed whale, *Berardius arnuxii*, stranded December, 1974, at Te Horo, New Zealand.

J.M. Moreland.

From: "Whales and Dolphins of New Zealand and Australia" by A.N. Baker. Victoria University Press, Wellington, 1983. Courtesy A.N. Baker.

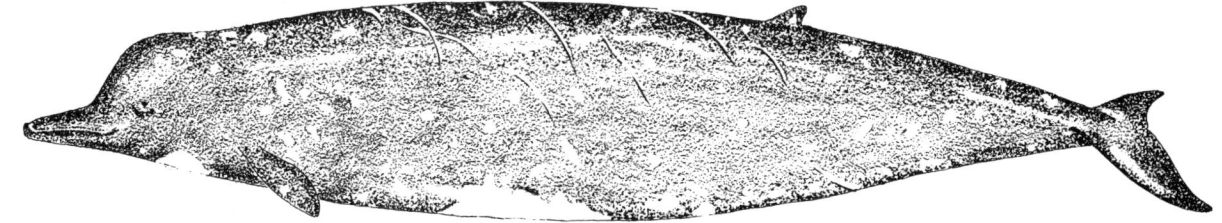

THE NORTH PACIFIC, GIANT, FOUR-TOOTHED WHALE
Also known as Baird's Beaked Whale, The Northern, Four-toothed Whale,
and the North Pacific, Giant, Four-toothed, Bottle-nosed Whale
Berardius bairdii Stejneger, 1883

Identifying Features. This is a large species which will reach a length of over 13 meters (40 ft.); the dorsal fin is small and is located 2/3 of the body length back from the head; and two grooves are present on the throat. There are 4 teeth in the lower jaw of which two are located at the front and two are placed farther back; the two front teeth are visible when the mouth is closed.

Size and Shape. Baird's beaked whale is the largest of the beaked whales. The largest recorded female measured 12.8 meters (42 ft.) and the largest male measured 11.8 meters (39 ft.) in length. Their bodies are large, long, cylindrical, solid, and robust and reach their greatest diameter at the center of the body. The head is rather short and inflated in front and leads into a long proboscis which looks much like that of the bottle-nosed dolphin (*Tursiops*). The lower jaw is longer than the upper jaw. Two longitudinal grooves measuring about 50 to 60 cm. (20 to 24 in.) are present on the throat.

Color. The body is a uniform brownish black or bluish gray color above and shades to a lighter hue on the sides and belly; the lower side is usually marked with white spots and larger white areas on the throat and belly. The back is always marked with many scars and scratches.

Distribution. The distribution of Baird's beaked whale is limited to the North Pacific Ocean. It ranges from the Bering Sea in the north to southern California and to southern Japan. It also occurs in the Sea of Okhotsk, but it does not go north of the Bering Sea. They do not seem to occur in waters which are shallower than 1,000 meters (3,281 ft.).

Migration. Yearly north and south migrations are made with the seasons. In these movements, they are reported to travel in groups of 10 to 20 which are led by old males.

Fins and Flippers. The dorsal fin is small and triangular in shape; it is located 2/3 of the body length back from the head. The flippers are small, have somewhat parallel sides, and end in a rounded tip; they are placed quite far forward on the body. The tail sometimes has a weak notch at the midline on its rear margin; most species in this family (Ziphiidae) do not have this notch on the tail.

Teeth. Two pairs of teeth (4 in all) are present in the lower jaws of both sexes, although those of the female may remain buried in the gums. The two front teeth are located at the front of the jaw bones, are somewhat triangular in cross section, and will measure about 9 cm. (3.5 in.) in length. The rear teeth (1 in each jaw bone) are set about 20 cm. (8 in.) farther back in each jaw bone; they are quite triangular in shape and are smaller in size than the front teeth. There are no functional teeth in the upper jaw and no other rudimentary teeth are visible. The lower jaw is longer than the upper jaw and extends about 10 cm. (4 in.) beyond it; as a result of this the two large front teeth are visible even though the mouth is closed.

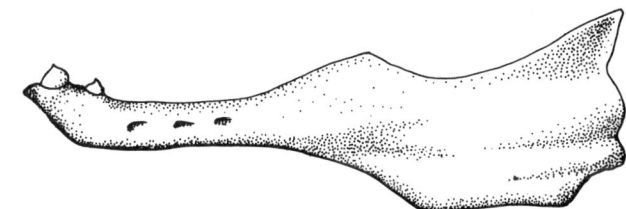

Jaw and tooth of *Berardius bairdii*.

Skeletal Notes. The vertebrae are distributed approximately as follows: C 7 + D 10-11 + L 12 + Ca 17-19 = 47-49. The 1st 3 neck vertebrae are fused into a single unit. The sternum is divided into 5 parts.

Other Anatomical Notes. Additional smaller grooves may be present on the midline of the throat outside the larger paired grooves.

Food. The diet of this beaked whale consists principally of squids and fishes, but it has been known to occasionally eat other animals including crustacea and sea cucumbers.

Swimming and Diving. This whale is rarely seen alone but usually gathers into groups of about 20 or less. They are very alert, avoid ships, and are very hard to capture. When preparing for a dive, they raise their tail into the air and, when returning to the surface, they exhale in a low, wide, "bushy" spout. When rising to the surface to breathe, they usually stick their snout and head far enough above the water to be recognized. They apparently dive to considerable depths for they remain submerged for as long as one hour.

233

Reproduction. Very little is known about their reproductive habits. They mate from December to May and are reported to be particularly active in February. The gestation period has been reported to be between 10 and 14 months. Two young whales, which were measured at the time of birth, had an overall length of 4.7 meters (15.4 ft.) and 4.57 meters (15 ft.).

Abundance. The abundance of this species is not well known, but it is nowhere common.

Economic Importance. A few of these whales are captured each year, but their numbers are not great and no organized fishery depends upon them.

Miscellaneous. This species is named for Spencer Fullerton Baird (1823-1887), founder of the U.S. National Museum of Natural History and long time Secretary of the Smithsonian Institution.

Photos of adult specimens of the North Pacific, Giant, Four-toothed Whale, *Berardius bairdii*, taken in Japan. (From U.S. Department of Commerce, National Oceanic and Atmospheric Administration, National Marine Fisheries Service, NOAA Technical Report: NMFS Circular 444, 1982. p. 90.)

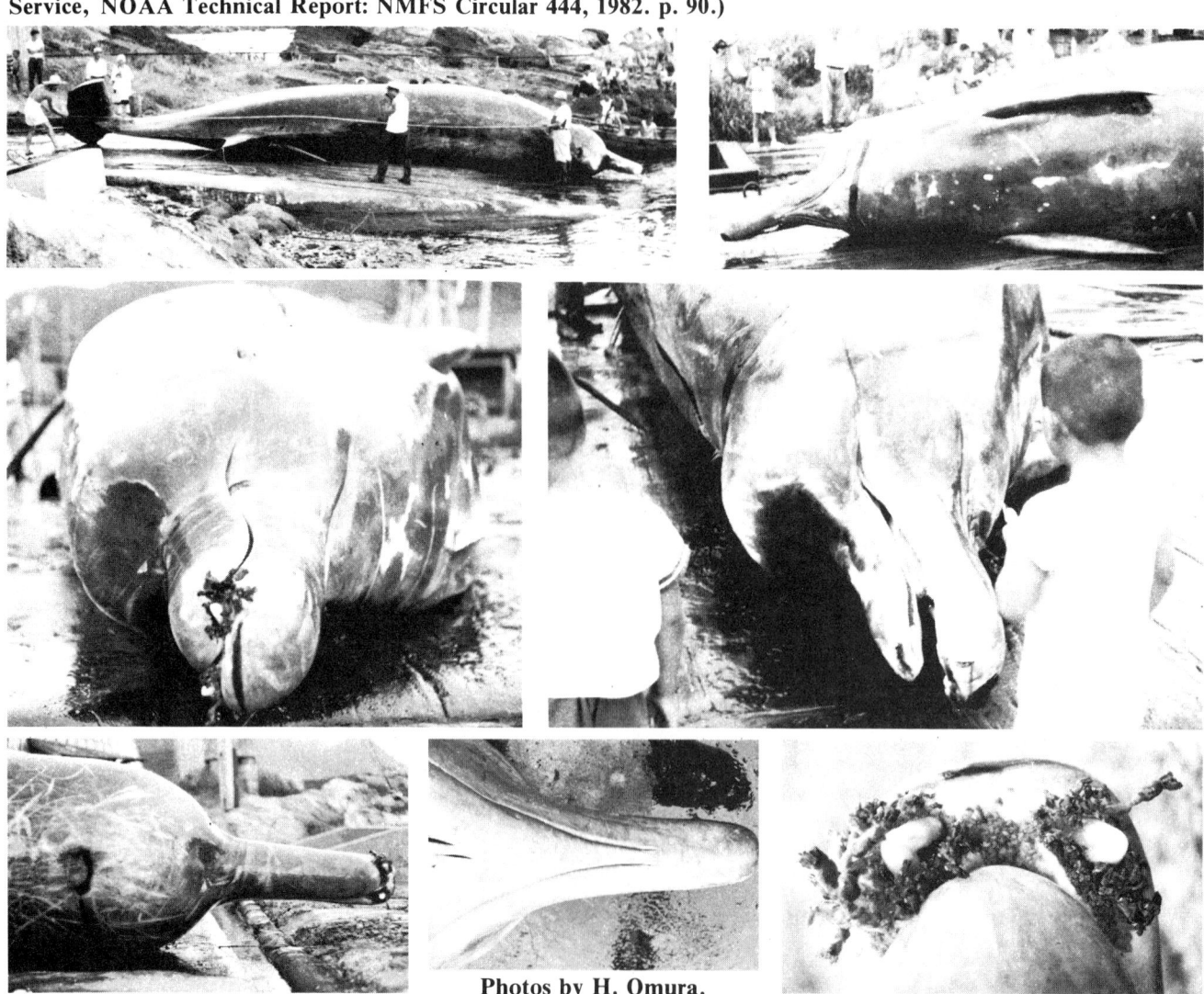

Photos by H. Omura.

Upper Left: Dorsal view. Note the location of the dorsal fin and the bottle-like shape of the proboscis.

Upper Right: Ventral view. Note the forward locaton of the flippers and their position against the body.

Middle Left: Anterior view of the head and proboscis. Note the teeth at the anterior end of the lower jaw.

Middle Right: Anterior view of the head and proboscis. Note the absence of visible teeth.

Lower Left: Dorsal view of the head. Note the shape and position of the blowhole, the bottle-shaped snout, and the teeth protruding from the exposed anterior end of the jaw.

Lower Center: Ventral view of the head and proboscis. Note the two converging grooves on the throat which are a characteristic of the *Family Ziphiidae.*

Lower Right: Dorsal view of the anterior tip of the proboscis. Note that the lower jaw extends beyond the upper jaw, thereby placing the two front teeth outside of the closed mouth. The dark material surrounding the teeth is a colony of goose-neck barnacles *(Lepadidae).*

THE INDO-PACIFIC BEAKED WHALES
Genus *INDOPACETUS* Moore, 1968

This genus contains but a single species which is known at this time from but two records: (1) a single skull and jaw found on a beach at McKay, Queensland, Australia; (2) a skull from Mogadishu on the eastern coast of Somalia, Africa, on the Indian Ocean. The characters which separate this genus from the other ziphiids are based upon these skulls and are set forth by Dr. Moore in the reference given below. Students interested in studying the ziphiid whales should consult the following reference: Moore, Joseph Curtis. "Relationships Among The Living Genera Of Beaked Whales With Classification, Diagnoses and Keys." *Fieldiana: Zoology* 53(4), December 13, 1968, pp. iv, 209-298 (24 illustrations).

Some scholars have regarded this species as identical to *Hyperoodon planifrons*.

The genus *Indopacetus* was created in 1968 by Dr. Joseph Curtis Moore to receive this single species which had previously been included in the genus *Mesoplodon*.

This genus includes the single living species listed below.

Class Mammalia — The Mammals
Order Cetacea — The Whales
Suborder Odontoceti — The Toothed Whales
Family Ziphiidae — The Beaked Whales

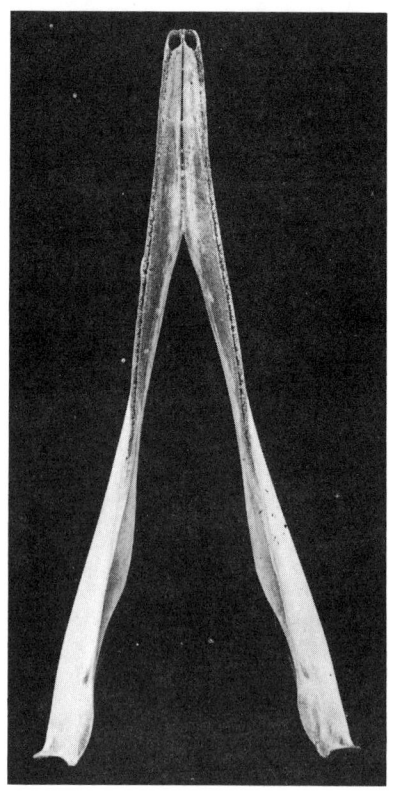

THE INDO-PACIFIC BEAKED WHALE
Indopacetus pacificus (Longman, 1926)

Identifying Features. Since very little information is available concerning this species, it is difficult to describe its appearance. At present, it is known only from two large skulls, which indicates that it is undoubtedly a large species.

Size and Shape. Since only two skulls of this species are known, a description of it must await the appearance of one or more specimens. The original skull from Queensland, Australia, measured approximately 118.6 cm. (46.7 in.) in length. This is a large skull for most beaked whales and probably belonged to a whale which measured over 7 meters (22.96 ft.) in length.

Color. The color of this whale is unknown but it is probably of a dark bluish or black hue.

Distribution. At present, this species is known from only two skulls from two widely separated localities: (1) MacKay (21° S.L.), Queensland, Australia, and (2) near Mogadishu (2° N.L.) on the eastern coast of the Somalia Republic, Africa.

Fins and Flippers. Without seeing this species, it is safe to assume that it has a small dorsal fin located somewhere behind the center of the body and a tail in which the two flukes are probably not separated by a median notch. The flippers are doubtless small and located quite low and at a point quite far forward on the body.

Jaw and tooth of *Indopacetus pacificus*.

Teeth. Two forward-pointing teeth are present at the very front of the lower jaw bones; each is located at the tip of its respective mandible.

Skeletal Notes. The skull of the Queensland specimen, from which this species was first described, measured 118.6 cm. (46.7 in.) in length. As in other whales of this family, the rostrum is very long. The mandible measured 106.6 cm. (41.9 in.) in length of which about one-fourth was occupied by the mandibular symphysis. It is interesting to note that the cribriform plate (of the ethmoid bone), which forms a part of the forward wall of the cranium, is not perforated, thus indicating that no olfactory nerves pass inward through it to the brain; the sense of smell is therefore entirely lacking in this species.

Habits. Nothing is known of the habits of this ziphiid whale.

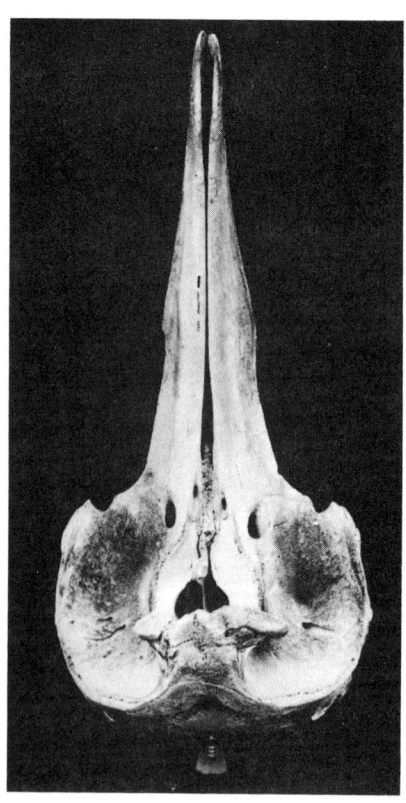

Photo of the skull and jaws of the Indo-Pacific beaked whale, *Indopacetus pacificus*. Living or freshly stranded whales of this species have not been seen to date.
Queensland Museum.

From: "Whales and Dolphins of New Zealand and Australia" by A.N. Baker. Victoria University Press, Wellington, 1983. Courtesy A.N. Baker.

THE GERVAIS' BEAKED WHALES
Genus *MESOPLODON* Gervais, 1850

Of the six genera of beaked whales, the Genus *Mesoplodon* includes the largest number of species. Like the other ziphiid whales, they have stout, spindle-shaped bodies, short flippers, a low dorsal fin located on the rear half of the body, and a tail without a notch at the center of its posterior margin. These whales are intermediate in size and usually do not exceed about 6 meters (19.7 ft.) in length. As in most toothed whales, the males are larger than the females. The head is not inflated and the beak tapers gradually from its base to its tip.

In this genus, the functional teeth are two in number and are confined to the lower jaws. These teeth show considerable variation in size, shape, and position along the jaw bone; they are much more prominent in the males, but they do not usually erupt through the gums until maturity is reached, and these teeth may then be lost in old age so that only one tooth or no teeth finally remain. In female individuals, the functional teeth rarely erupt above the gum line. In addition, small, non-functional, vestigial teeth may be present in all jaws of both sexes.

The color of these whales is generally grayish or blackish above and usually shades gradually to grayish or yellowish colors on the sides and white or yellowish white below.

The members of this genus appear to be more pelagic in their habits than the other beaked whales. They travel either singly or in small groups and feed upon squid and fishes.

The members of this genus occur in both the Atlantic and the Pacific Oceans.

Studies of these whales by various scholars indicate that several names of species appearing in older books are really duplicate names or synonyms of other previously named species. The following list indicates the older names and the more correct and current names of these species.

Old Name		Name Currently In Use
Mesoplodon australis	is now	*Mesoplodon grayi*
Mesoplodon floweri	is now	*Mesoplodon layardi*
Mesoplodon gervaisi	is now	*Mesoplodon europaeus*
Mesoplodon guntheri	is now	*Mesoplodon layardi*
Mesoplodon haasti	is now	*Mesoplodon grayi*
Mesoplodon hotaula	is now	*Mesoplodon ginkgodens*
Mesoplodon knoxi	is now	*Mesoplodon hectori*
Mesoplodon mirum	is now	*Mesoplodon mirus*
Mesoplodon pacificus	is now	*Indopacetus pacificus*
Mesoplodon sowerbensis	is now	*Mesoplodon bidens*
Mesoplodon thomsoni	is now	*Mesoplodon layardi*
Mesoplodon traversi	is now	*Mesoplodon layardi*

Mesoplodon bidens (Sowerby, 1804) is the type species of this genus.

This genus is known from the Middle and Upper Miocene Epoch in North America and from the Upper Miocene to the Middle Pliocene Epoch in Europe.

This genus includes the eleven living species listed below.

The above species are discussed in the above sequence on the following pages.

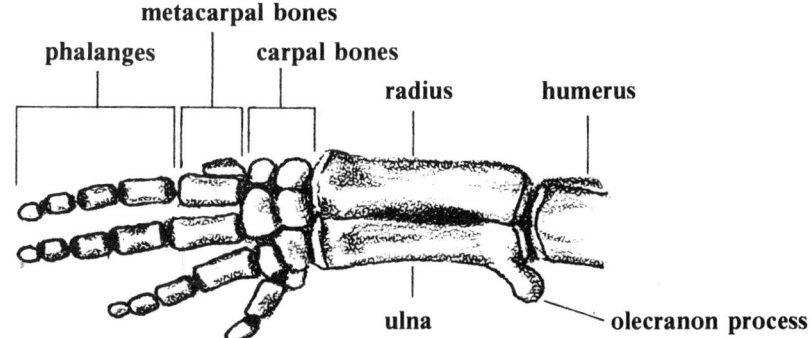

**The left flipper of *Mesoplodon densirostris* in dorsal view.
From Kasuya and Nishiwaki.**

Class Mammalia — The Mammals
  Order Cetacea — The Whales
    Suborder Odontoceti — The Toothed Whales
      Family Ziphiidae — The Beaked Whales

SOWERBY'S NORTH SEA BEAKED WHALE
Mesoplodon bidens (Sowerby, 1804)

Identifying Features. Identification may depend somewhat on its northern range, since it occurs farther north than any other species of the beaked whales. It has an elongated proboscis, two grooves on the throat, no median notch on the tail, and two large, sharp teeth (one on each side) which are located midway between the end of the snout and the angle of the mouth.

Size and Shape. The body of this species is rather slender and tapers quite uniformly toward the head and tail; in cross-section, it is slightly higher than wide. The head is small, has a low bulge in front of the blowhole, is slightly concave at the forehead, and terminates in a slender, pointed proboscis. They will reach a length of about 5.6 meters (18 ft. 4 in.).

Color. The upper surface of the body varies in color from a grayish or bluish black to a deep black hue. This color shades to a grayish or whitish color ventrally. The lower jaw is usually white in color. The young are lighter in color ventrally and the under surface of their flippers is lighter than in the adults; they are also without spots. The bodies of the males are marked with many scars and long scratches.

Distribution. This is a North Atlantic whale which has been described as the "most northerly of the beaked whale species." It ranges from below the pack ice southward to more temperate seas. It is described as inhabiting the waters from Newfoundland southward to Massachusetts in the west and from southern Norway southward to the Bay of Biscay (Spain). It appears to be most abundant in the North Sea. It is an oceanic form. It is not known from either the Pacific or Indian Oceans.

Migration. Very little is known of their migratory habits.

Fins and Flippers. The dorsal fin is of moderate size and is located behind the center of the body. It varies in shape from triangular to concave on its posterior margin. The flippers are located quite far forward on the body; they are quite long, have a straight forward margin, and rest against a shallow depression on the body wall known as a "flipper pocket." The posterior margin of the tail is not notched and is usually concave in outline.

Teeth. These animals possess two very large, pointed teeth (one on each side) located in the middle of each lower jaw. They measure about 10 cm. (4 in.) in length (vertically) and about 2.5 cm. (1 in.) in width (front to back). These teeth are visible on the outside of the mouth beside the upper lip. The upper teeth emerge and are functional in the adult males, but they remain buried in the gums of the females throughout life. In addition, both sexes possess small, vestigial teeth which, although sometimes visible, do not usually perforate the gums.

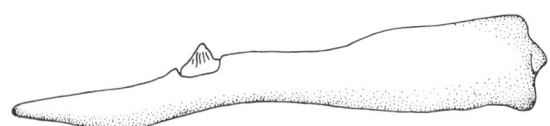

Jaw and tooth of *Mesoplodon bidens*.

Skeletal Notes. The vertebrae are distributed approximately as follows: C 7 + D 10 + L 9 + Ca 20 = 46. Seven pairs of ribs articulate directly with the sternum. The bones of the fingers are distributed approximately as follows: I (1), II (6), III (6), IV (3-4), V (2-3).

Other Anatomical Notes. The blowhole is situated slightly to one side of the midline of the body.

Food. The diet of this whale consists principally of squid.

Swimming and Diving. This ziphiid whale is a good swimmer, it avoids ships, and it does not ride in the bow waves of vessels.

Reproduction. The adults mate from February to April and the young are born in the spring after a pregnancy of about 12 months; lactation continues thereafter for about a year. The young will measure 2 meters (6½ ft.) at birth and will reach a length of 3 meters (9-10 ft.) within a year.

Abundance. This is an uncommon species.

Economic Importance. This small whale has very little economic importance. A few are captured in scattered areas, but there is no organized fishery for it.

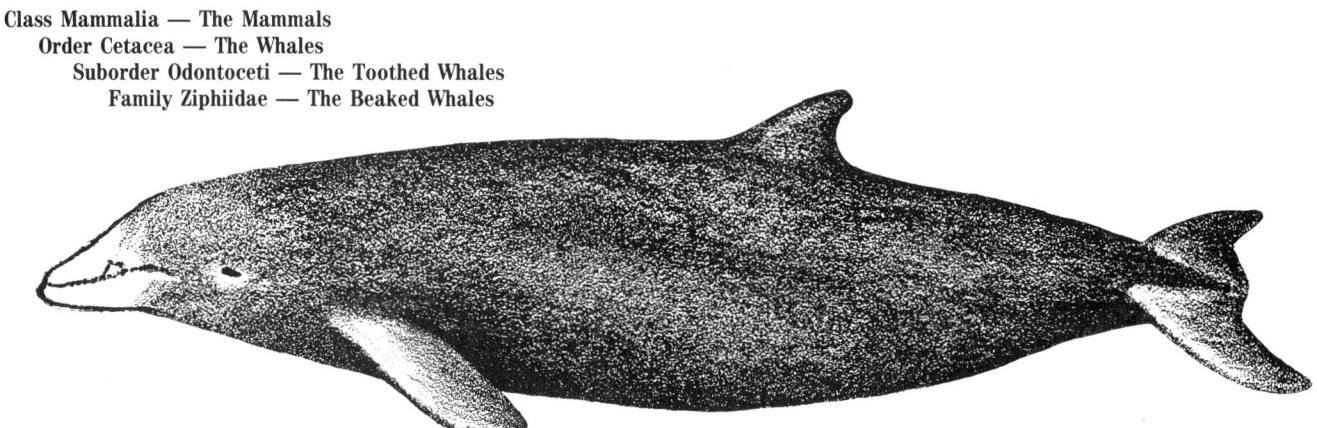

THE DEEP-CRESTED BEAKED WHALE
Also known as Andrew's Beaked Whale, Bowdoin's Beaked Whale,
and the Splay-toothed Beaked Whale
Mesoplodon bowdoini Andrews, 1908

Identifying Features. This species is most easily identified by its size and by its teeth. This whale is intermediate in size and will measure about 3 to 5 meters (9.8 to 16.4 ft.) in length. A single very large tooth is set in each jaw bone at a point just to the rear of where the two lower jaw bones fuse together; this is nearly midway along the jaw bone and back about 20 cm. (8 in.) from the tip of the jaw. The socket in which each tooth rests is raised somewhat above the surrounding surface of the jaw bone. The front margin of this tooth is nearly straight and is inclined backward; the rear margin is convexly curved and ends at its upper extremity in a small, pointed, pimple-like elevation. The beak and a small adjoining area of the skull are sometimes white in color.

Size and Shape. The body of this whale is spindle-shaped and tapers quite uniformly from a point forward of the center toward both extremities. The outline of the head rises quite abruptly, but smoothly, behind the beak and continues with the dorsal outline of the body. The lower jaw is large, thick, and strong and projects a short distance forward of the upper jaw. Two throat or gular grooves are present on the throat; they measure less than a foot (30 cm.) in length and, although they converge anteriorly, they do not meet in front. The tail stock is quite slender and is bordered above and below by rather sharp keels or ridges; these keels extend out onto the upper and lower surfaces of the flukes where they gradually terminate. The surface of the body is covered by a very thin epidermis, beneath which a 6 cm. (2.5 in.) layer of blubber blankets the body; the flesh beneath is a bright red color. Most of the specimens of this whale have measured 4.25 meters (14 ft.) or less in length, but some have measured just short of 5 meters (17 ft.) in length.

Photo of the left lower jaw bone of the deep-crested beaked whale, *Mesoplodon bowdoini*, in lateral view.
National Museum of New Zealand.

From: "Whales and Dolphins of New Zealand and Australia" by A.N. Baker. Victoria University Press, Wellington, 1983. Courtesy A.N. Baker.

Color. The color of the body is nearly jet black over its entire surface which in turn gives off shimmering bluish and/or brownish hues. The beak and the adjoining region of the head are whitish in color. The surface of the body is covered with whitish linear scratches and other scars, most of which are doubtless inflicted by other whales.

Distribution. This species seems to be most numerous in the cold waters of the southern hemisphere. Specimens have come most commonly from New Zealand, Tasmania, southern and western Australia, and the Kerguelen Islands which lie in the Antarctic Ocean south of India. It is still unknown or scarce in the North Pacific, Atlantic, and Indian Oceans. Specimens reported from the North Pacific Ocean have probably been *M. carlhubbsi* or *M. stejnegeri* which were misidentified.

Fins and Flippers. The dorsal fin is located behind the center of the body; it is small and concave on its posterior margin. The flippers of this species are quite large and, as in other members of this family, are placed well forward on the body; they rest against "flipper pockets," a shallow depression on the body wall. The tail flukes are bordered on their posterior edge by a crenulated or scalloped margin; they lack the median notch found in the dolphins (Delphinidae) and in a very few other ziphiid whales.

Teeth. The teeth of this species are among the largest and strangest among the toothed whales (Odontoceti). They are just two in number and are placed one in each lower jaw bone just posterior to the point of union (mandibular symphysis) of the two jaw bones. These teeth will measure as much as 15 cm. (6 in.) in height and 9 cm. (3.5 in.) in width (front to back). These teeth are inclined slightly backward and outward and bear a sharp denticle at their upper, forward corner. Although these large, flat lateral teeth are characteristic of this species, it should be remembered that in the young males, these teeth may not have erupted above the gums. In adult females, these teeth probably do not usually appear above the gum line. The large, lower teeth of this species are known to occasionally have a large eroded cavity on their lower, anterior margin; the cause of this depression is not known.

Other Anatomical Notes. The trachea of a 5.18 meter (17 ft.) specimen had an external diameter near its base of over 7.6 cm. (3 in.). The testes measure about 7.5 x 10 cm. (3 by 4 in.) in size and the penis measures about 91.4 cm. (3 ft.) in length.

Habits. Practically nothing is known concerning the habits of this whale except perhaps that it eats squids and avoids ships.

Abundance. This ziphiid whale is an uncommon species.

Economic Importance. No economic importance attaches to this small whale.

Miscellaneous. This species was named for Mr. George S. Bowdoin, a contributor to the American Museum of Natural History in New York City.

Photo of a beached carcass of a deep-crested beaked whale, *Mesoplodon bowdoini,* from Taurikura, New Zealand. The large tooth indicates that the specimen is an adult male.

Photo by D. Young.

From: "Whales and Dolphins of New Zealand and Australia" by A.N. Baker. Victoria University Press, Wellington, 1983. Courtesy A.N. Baker.

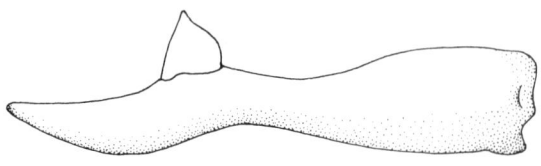

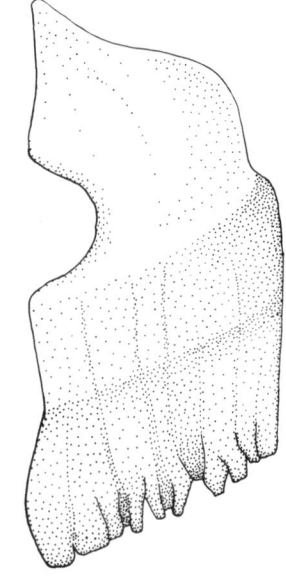

The jaw and tooth of *Mesoplodon bowdoini.*

THE ARCH-BEAKED WHALE
Also known as Hubbs' Beaked Whale
Mesoplodon carlhubbsi Moore, 1963

Identifying Features. The identification of this species must depend upon its teeth, since very few of these whales have been seen alive and only a very few have been studied. The lower jaws have one pair of very large teeth which are located, one on each side, at a point in each jaw bone just behind the place (mandibular symphysis) where the two jaws are fused together. See photo below. The end of the beak (both jaws) is white in color half way or more to the eyes. A white "beanie" patch marks the top of the head in adult males.

Size and Shape. The body of this whale is spindle-shaped and tapers quite uniformly toward the head and tail. The middle of the body is higher than wide and so gives the body an oval outline in cross-section. The head is low, slightly elevated in front of the blowhole, and tapers to a long, slender proboscis. Two horizontal grooves are present on the throat; the naval is located at the middle of the body. It will reach a length of at least 5.2 meters (17 ft.).

Color. The exact color of the body is not fully known until more specimens have been studied. The general coloration is of a dark hue. The rostrum is of a uniform white or pale color in adult animals. The males are reported to have a white "beanie" area on top of the head. One beached specimen was described as "reddish black in color dorsally and dark gray laterally."

Distribution. The exact distribution of this species is not fully known. It occurs in the temperate waters of the North Pacific Ocean including the latitudes from British Columbia and Japan to California. A skull has also been reported found on the North Island of New Zealand; this skull may prove to be misidentified.

Migration. Very little is known of its migratory habits.

Fins and Flippers. The dorsal fin is behind the middle of the body and is directly above the anus. The flippers are small and slender and rest against the shallow "flipper pockets" on the body. The tail fin does not have a notch on its posterior margin.

Teeth. The teeth are only two in all and are placed, one in each lower jaw bone, at a point back a few inches (15 cm. or 6 in.) from the front and at the posterior end of the fused union (mandibular symphysis) of the two lower jaw bones. These teeth are flattened laterally and measure about 16 to 17 cm. (6 to 7 in.) in total height, including that portion which is buried in the jaw bone; they measure about 9 cm. (3½ in.) from front to back and about 1.4 cm. (.55 in.) in width. These teeth stand vertically in the jaw and bear a small, pimple-like point projecting forward at their upper angle, somewhat like the teeth of *M. stejnegeri*. In the females, these teeth do not usually erupt through the gums.

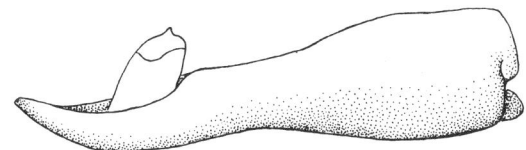

The jaw and tooth of an adult male.

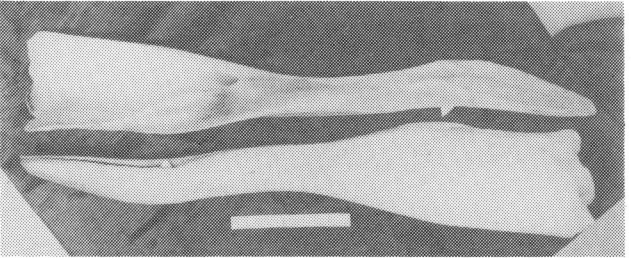

The lower jaws and teeth of the arch-beaked whale *(Mesoplodon carlhubbsi)* in dorsal view.
Photo by Univ. of British Columbia.

The lower jaws and emerging teeth of the arch-beaked whale *(Mesoplodon carlhubbsi).*
Photo by Univ. of British Columbia.

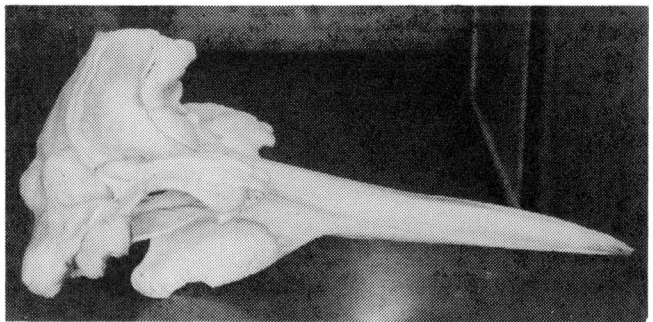

The skull of the arch-beaked whale, *Mesoplodon carlhubbsi,* in lateral view.
Photo by Michael Graybill at Cal. Acad. of Sci.

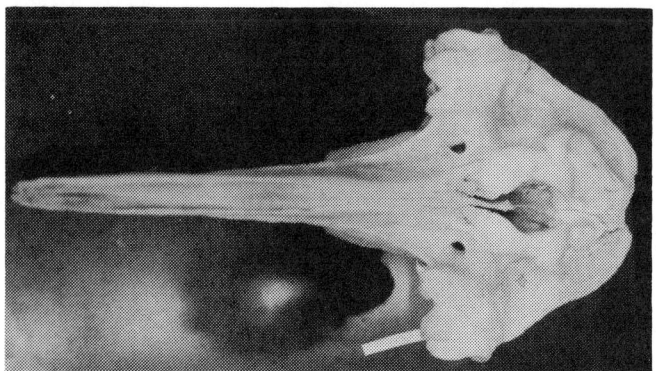

The skull of the arch-beaked whale, *Mesoplodon carlhubbsi,* in dorsal view.
Photo by Michael Graybill at Cal. Acad. of Sci.

Skeletal Notes. The vertebrae are distributed approximately as follows: C 7 + D 11 + L 9 + Ca 19 = 46. The 1st 2 or more neck vertebrae are united and the last 3 to 5 neck vertebrae are free. The ribs number 11 pairs of which the 1st 7 pairs have 2 heads and the last 2 pairs (10th and 11th) are rather short. The chevron or V-bones number 8 or 9. The sternum has 5 parts. The bones of the fingers are distributed approximately as follows: I (1), II (5), III (5), IV (4), V (3).

Food. Relatively nothing is known of its eating habits except that it undoubtedly feeds upon squids and sub-surface fishes.

Swimming and Diving. It is an oceanic species which avoids ships.

Reproduction. Information on the reproductive habits of this species is very scanty.

Abundance. There is no information at present regarding its abundance; it appears to be very rare.

Economic Importance. This species has no economic importance.

Miscellaneous. This species was named for Dr. Carl Hubbs (1894-1979), an ichthyologist at The Scripps Institution of Oceanography, Univ. of California, LaJolle, California.

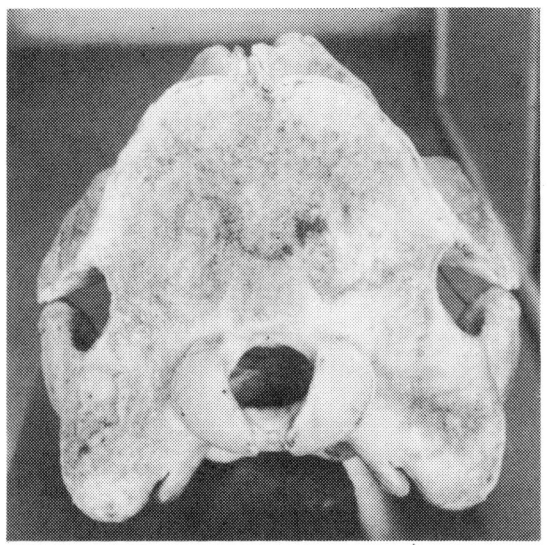

The skull of the arch-beaked whale, *Mesoplodon carlhubbsi,* in posterior view.
Photo by Michael Graybill at Cal. Acad. of Sci.

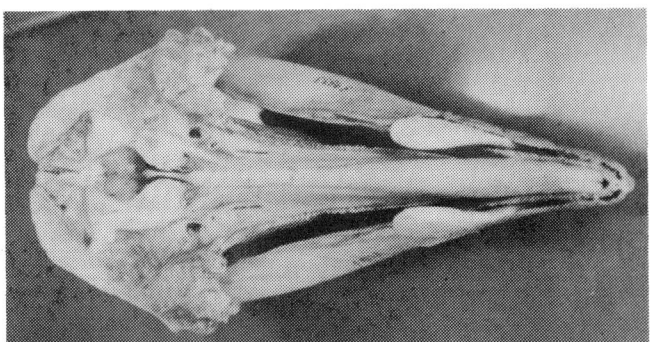

The skull and jaws of the arch-beaked whale, *Mesoplodon carlhubbsi,* in dorsal view.
Photo by Michael Graybill at Cal. Acad. of Sci.

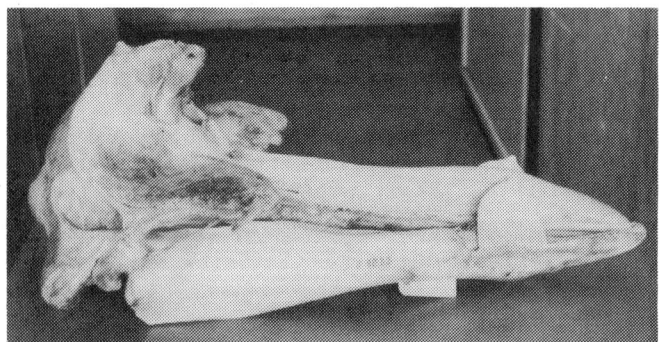

The skull and jaws of the arch-beaked whale, *Mesoplodon carlhubbsi,* in lateral view.
Photo by Michael Graybill at Cal. Acad. of Sci.

Class Mammalia — The Mammals
Order Cetacea — The Whales
Suborder Odontoceti — The Toothed Whales
Family Ziphiidae — The Beaked Whales

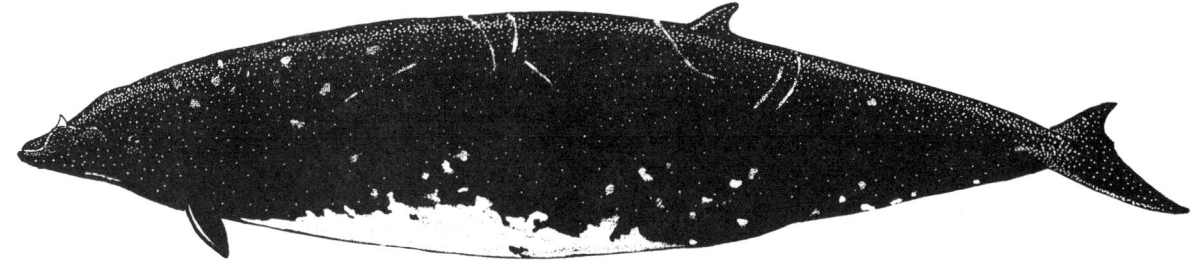

de BLAINVILLE'S DENSE-BEAKED WHALE
Also known as de Blainville's Atlantic Beaked Whale,
and the Dense-beaked Whale
Mesoplodon densirostris (de Blainville, 1817)

Identifying Features. The lips will immediately identify this species for, about halfway back from the snout, they curve upward and then downward to form a pronounced curve. This curve of the lips is due to the upward curve of the jaws beneath and the single, large projecting tooth.

Size and Shape. The body of this whale is robust and spindle-shaped. It slopes uniformly from the middle of the body toward the tail and the head. The body height is greatest near its middle and is higher at this point than it is wide. The head slopes downward near the angle of the mouth and continues as a slender proboscis. These whales will measure from about 4 meters (13 ft.) to about 5.2 meters (17 ft.) in length and will weigh about 100 pounds or more per linear foot. The lower jaw extends beyond the upper jaw. The front of the head is somewhat flat in its contours.

Color. The body is reported to be a dark gray to shining black color which shades to lighter hues and white on the ventral surface. The flippers are dark above and lighter below.

Distribution. This is an oceanic species which appears to occupy the tropical and warmer temperate seas of the world. It occurs in the North Atlantic Ocean including the Gulf of Mexico, the South Atlantic Ocean, and the Indian Ocean, but it appears to be rare in the Pacific Ocean, although it has been recorded from Midway Island (Hawaii), Taiwan (Formosa), Lord Howe Island (Tasman Sea), and Tasmania. Its range seems to be between 45° N.L. and 45° S.L.

Migration. Very little is known of the migrations of this species; it is presumed to be non-migratory.

Fins and Flippers. The dorsal fin is usually triangular in shape, but may be concave on its posterior margin with a tip which is somewhat pointed. It is located behind the center of the body. The flippers are quite small and narrow and terminate in a pointed tip; they rest against the body in shallow "flipper pockets." The tail is without a notch and is not deeply concave on its posterior margin.

Teeth. Each lower jaw bone possesses a single, large, flat, triangular tooth which is set about halfway back in the mouth and just behind the union (mandibular symphysis) of

Photo of the anterior view of the head of de Blainville's dense-beaked whale, *Mesoplodon densirostris,* from the Indian Ocean.   Y. Okada.

From: "Whales and Dolphins of New Zealand and Australia" by A.N. Baker. Victoria University Press, Wellington, 1983. Courtesy A.N. Baker.

A tooth from a lower jaw of *Mesoplodon densirostris.* This species has a single, large, flat tooth located near the middle of each lower jaw bone.
Photo by Tinker.

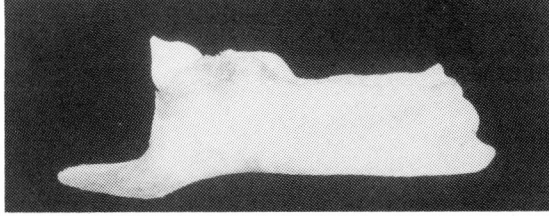

Lower left jaw of de Blaineville's dense-beaked whale *(Mesoplodon densirostris)* in lateral view showing the single tooth.

Photo by Tinker.

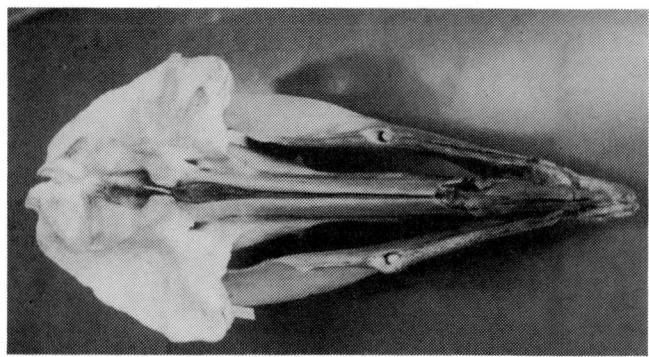

The skull and jaws of de Blaineville's dense-beaked whale, *Mesoplodon densirostris,* in dorsal view. Note the emerging tooth near the center of each lower jaw bone.
Photo by Michael Graybill at Cal. Acad. of Sci.

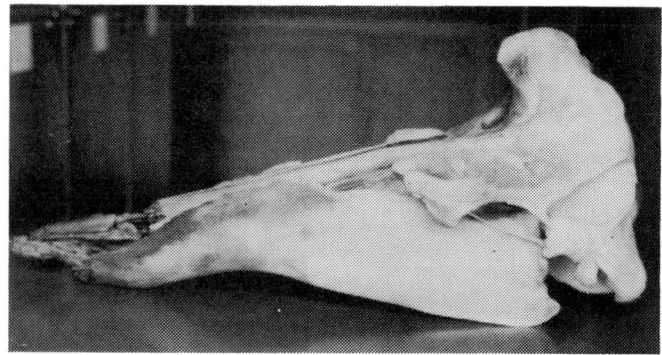

The skull and lower jaws of de Blaineville's dense-beaked whale, *Mesoplodon densirostris,* in lateral view.
Photo by Michael Graybill at Cal. Acad. of Sci.

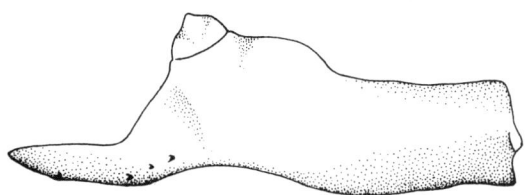

The lower jaw and single tooth of *Mesoplodon densirostris.*

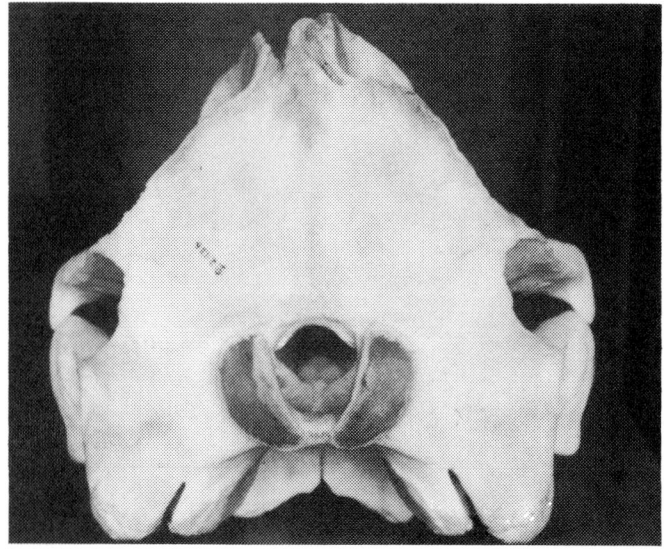

The skull of de Blaineville's dense-beaked whale, *Mesoplodon densirostris,* in posterior view.
Photo by Michael Graybill at Cal. Acad. of Sci.

the two jaw bones. This is about 30 cm. (12 in.) back from the tip of the jaw. These teeth are tilted and inclined slightly forward and are set in large sockets within the lower jaw bone. They will measure about 9 cm. (3.5 in.) in horizontal length and about twice that in vertical length, of which only 1 or 2 cm. extends above the gums and skin. In the females and in the younger individuals, these large teeth will not be visible above the gums. The jaw bone will exhibit the same shape as in the adult males.

Skeletal Notes. The vertebrae are distributed approximately as follows: C 7 + D 10-11 + L 8-11 + Ca 17-21 = 45-47. The most usual formula is as follows: C 7 + D 11 + L 9 + Ca 20 = 47. The 1st 3 cervical vertebrae are fused to form a single unit. Neck ribs are usually found on the 7th cervical vertebra. There are 11 pairs of ribs of which the 1st 7 pairs have 2 heads, and the 1st 5 pairs connect to the sternum. The 1st 10 pairs are normal, but the 11th pair is small and vestigial and measures only about 3 cm. in length. This 11th rib does not ossify, is difficult to locate, and, when omitted, effects the counting of the vertebrae. The sternum consists of 5 parts, although some scholars have found only 4 sternebrae. The finger bones (phalanges) are distributed approximately as follows: I (1), II (5), III (6), IV (4), V (2).

Other Anatomical Notes. In the females, the teeth are smaller than in the males and do not emerge as high above the gums as in the males. The lower jaw of the female does not project as far forward as in the male and the jaw bone (mandible) behind the tooth is not as heavy as in the male. The uterus is 2 horned.

Food. The diet of this whale appears to be almost exclusively squid.

Swimming and Diving. This whale is known to travel in small groups of 2 to 6 of which at least one is a male. When surfacing, the snout is lifted out of the water and the blow is directed forward at an angle. The dorsal fin is visible, but not the flukes of the tail. This species does not frequent shorelines and it avoids ships.

Abundance. This is an uncommon species and is not often seen or captured.

Economic Importance. This whale has no economic importance.

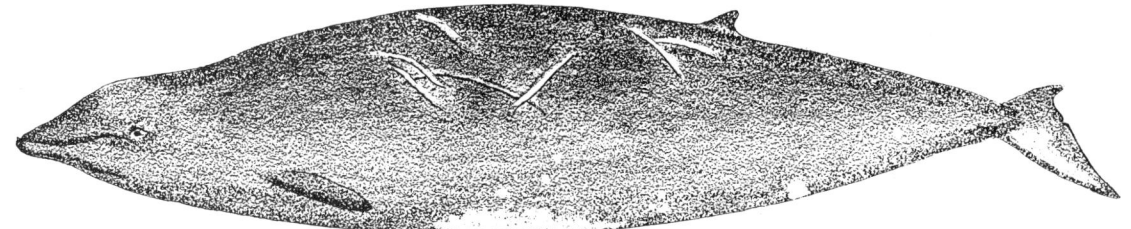

THE GULF STREAM BEAKED WHALE
Also known as the Antillean Beaked Whale and
Gervais' Beaked Whale
Mesoplodon europaeus (Gervais, 1855)
Often listed as *Mesoplodon gervaisi* (Deslongchamps, 1866)

Identifying Features. A few of the species of *Mesoplodon* are so similar in appearance that they do not present features which are distinct and different from closely related species. This species is difficult to identify; however, it is larger than all but *Berardius, Ziphius,* and *Hyperoodon,* is slender-bodied, and has its single tooth located farther forward than in the other species of *Mesoplodon.*

Size and Shape. The body of this whale is large, long, and slender; in cross-section, it is higher than wide, particularly in the middle of the body. The body has a spindle-shaped profile and tapers quite uniformly toward the head and tail. A slight constriction may be present at the neck. The head is small and grows gradually smaller to merge into a narrow beak. The lower jaw is longer than the upper jaw. The usual V-shaped grooves are present on the throat. They are reported to reach a length of at least 6.7 meters (22 ft.) and are believed to be the largest members of the Genus *Mesoplodon.*

Color. The entire back and sides are colored with a grayish black hue which gradually shades to a lighter color on the lower sides and belly. All of the appendages are dark in color. Some individuals have white areas on the belly around the anus. The body is usually covered with many scars and scratches.

Distribution. This whale inhabits the western North Atlantic Ocean from about the latitude of New York southward to the West Indies and into the Caribbean area. It has also been reported from England. It is unknown in the Pacific and Indian Oceans.

Migration. The migratory habits of this species have not been studied; they may move northward and southward with the seasons.

Fins and Flippers. The dorsal fin is small and varies in shape from triangular to falcate; it is placed well behind the middle of the body. Low dorsal and ventral keels are present on the upper and lower sides of the tail stock. The flippers are unusually small, have a blunt tip, are placed low on the body, and rest against it in their shallow "flipper pockets." The tail flukes are very wide and the tail is without a notch on its posterior margin.

Teeth. There is a single tooth on each side in the lower jaw. They are somewhat farther forward than in some species of *Mesoplodon* and are about 1/3 of the distance from the tip of the jaw to the corner of the mouth. These teeth are wide and pointed and are located at about the place (mandibular symphysis) where the two jaw bones come together. They are set back about 8 cm. (3 in.) from the end of the jaw, will measure about 10 cm. (4 in.) in height, and are flat and sharp. They fit into a depression on the outside of the upper lip. In the females, these teeth remain buried in the gums.

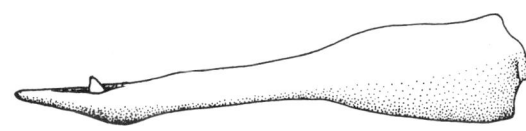

Jaw and tooth of *Mesoplodon europaeus.*

Skeletal Notes. The vertebrae are distributed approximately as follows: C 7 + D 10 + L 10-11 + Ca 20 = 47-48. The 1st 3 bones of the neck are united into a single unit. There are 10 pairs of ribs of which the first seven have two heads. The first 5 ribs are attached to the sternum. The sternum consists of four bones. The bones of the fingers vary but are distributed approximately as follows: I (2), II (5-6), III (5-6), IV (4), V (3).

Other Anatomical Notes. The testes weigh about 160 grams each.

Food. The food of this whale seems to consist almost entirely of squid.

Reproduction. Little is known of the reproductive habits of this whale. At birth, the young are estimated to measure about 2 to 2.2 meters (79 to 87 in.).

Abundance. This is an uncommon species and is rare within its known range.

Economic Importance. This species has no economic value.

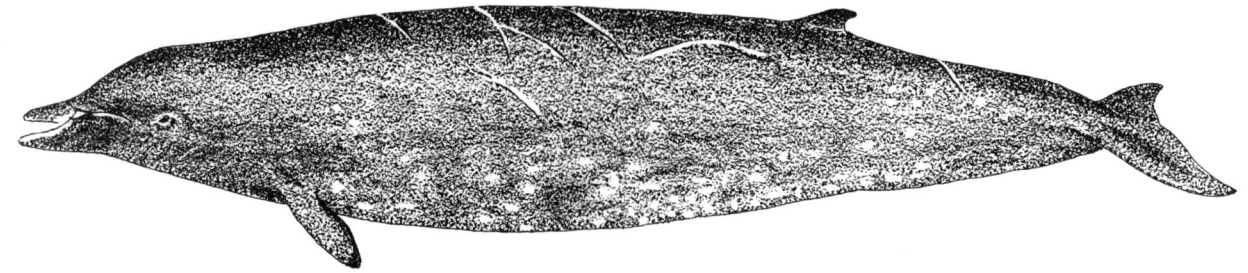

THE GINKGO-TOOTHED BEAKED WHALE
Mesoplodon ginkgodens Nishiwaki and Kamiya, 1958

Identifying Features. This species is very difficult to identify because it and the other species of *Mesoplodon* are very similar in appearance. After a determination of the genus has been made, the only reliable feature for the identification of this species is the single, large, flat tooth in each lower jaw. These teeth are flat and leaf-like and are placed just posterior to the fusion line of the jaw bones (mandibular symphysis). In an adult male, these teeth will measure about 9+ cm. (3.5+ in.) in height and about 10 cm. (4 in.) in width (front to back).

Size and Shape. The body of this whale is slender and spindle-shaped. The upper and lower profiles of the body curve uniformly toward both the head and tail. The head is slightly swollen aboves the eyes and slightly depressed at the base of the proboscis. The V-shaped grooves on the throat are very distinct and conspicuous. The upper jaw is narrow and pointed and rests between the flap-like lips of the lower jaw. It is known to reach a length of 5.2 meters (17 ft.).

Color. In beached animals, the entire upper part of the body is uniformly blackish in color above, including the head, the fin, the flippers, and the tail flukes. This blackish color shades gradually downward on the sides to a somewhat lighter grayish color on the belly. Some scholars believe that the color of the living animal is a "deep marine blue." The entire body is covered with spots, scars, and scratches.

Distribution. This whale is known from both sides of the North Pacific Ocean and from the Indian Ocean. It appears to inhabit tropical and temperate seas.

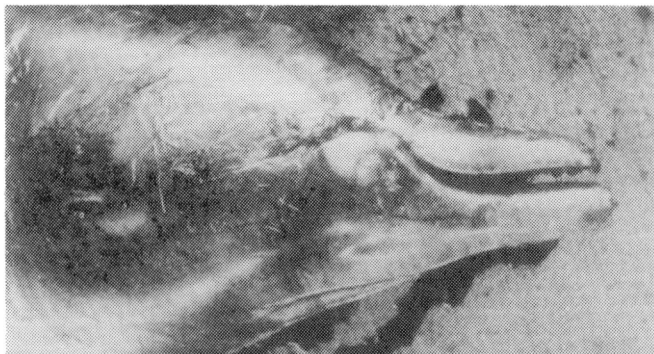

Photo of the head of the ginkgo-toothed beaked whale, *Mesoplodon ginkgodens,* from Japan.
Y. Okada

From: "Whales and Dolphins of New Zealand and Australia" by A.N. Baker. Victoria University Press, Wellington, 1983. Courtesy A.N. Baker.

Migration. Very little is known of its habits.

Fins and Flippers. The dorsal fin is small, slightly concave on its posterior margin and is situated posterior to the center of the body. The flippers are small, are placed low on the body, and terminate in rounded tips. The flukes are reported to be very wide and convex on their posterior margin and to have a minute suggestion of a notch at the midline.

Teeth. In this species, a single, large, flat tooth is located in each jaw bone just posterior to the fusion line (mandibular symphysis) of the two jaws. This tooth is very flat and is inclined slightly toward the front. These teeth are slightly wider than high and very flat. Their vertical length was 9.1 cm. (3.5 in.); the front-to-back length was 9.9 cm. (4 in.); and their thickness was 16 mm. (5/8 in.). In the females, these teeth will usually remain buried in the gums.

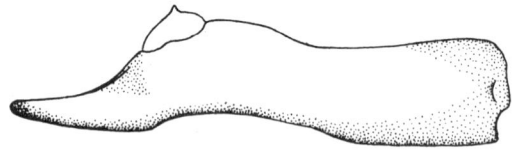

Jaw and tooth of *Mesoplodon ginkgodens*.

Skeletal Notes. The vertebrae are distributed approximately as follows: C 7 + D 10 + L 10 + Ca 21 = 48. Four neck vertebrae are united to form a single unit. The ribs number 10 pairs of which the 1st 7 pairs have 2 heads. The chevron or V-bones are about 11 or more in number. The bones of the fingers are distributed approximately as follows: I (1), II (6), III (5), IV (4-5), V (3).

Food. Its diet consists of squid and fishes.

Swimming and Diving. This seems to be an oceanic species which does not frequent the shorelines. It is not known to follow ships.

Reproduction. The reproductive habits of this whale are doubtless nearly identical to those of the other species of *Mesoplodon*.

Abundance. This is a rare and uncommon species.

Miscellaneous. The name of *ginkodens* was selected because the shape of the tooth resembles the leaf of the sacred ginkgo tree of Japan.

Class Mammalia — The Mammals
  Order Cetacea — The Whales
    Suborder Odontoceti — The Toothed Whales
      Family Ziphiidae — The Beaked Whales

von HAAST'S SCAMPERDOWN BEAKED WHALE
Also known as the Scamperdown Beaked Whale
and Gray's Beaked Whale
Mesoplodon grayi von Haast, 1876

Identifying Features. A combination of characters may help to identify this species. In addition to the two longitudinal grooves on the throat, this whale has a large triangular tooth in each lower jaw, from 10 to 22 very small teeth possibly buried at the back in each upper jaw, and a whitish color over the snout and part of the head.

Size and Shape. The body is of medium size, quite slender, spindle-shaped, and tapers quite uniformly from its middle toward the head and tail. It is laterally compressed and is reported to measure between about 3.5 meters (11.5 ft.) and 5 meters (16.4 ft.) in length. It is the smallest of the Genus *Mesoplodon*. The blowhole is located above the eyes, is very wide, and is placed slightly to the left of the midline. The head tapers to a very slender proboscis.

Color. The upper part of the body is a dark color, possibly a dark slate gray or olive drab, and gets lighter, possibly a brownish gray toward the abdomen which is light gray or whitish in color; the dorsal fin is dark in color and the

flippers and tail flukes are dark above and below. The flippers have a lighter border. Scattered white spots may be present over the body. The head and beak of adult animals vary in the amount of white coloration which they exhibit. It is not uncommon to find the lower jaw and throat white, and this white area has also been reported to sometimes extend onto the beak above.

Distribution. The distribution of this species is worldwide in the southern hemisphere south of 30° S.L. It prefers the open ocean and does not frequent coastlines. It is known from western and eastern Australia eastward across the southern ocean to New Zealand, onward to Chile, Argentina, and the Falkland Islands to both coasts of southern Africa. Of late, a single specimen has been recorded from The Netherlands.

Migration. At this time the migratory habits of this whale are unknown.

Fins and Flippers. The dorsal fin is pointed, is of medium size, and is situated well behind the middle of the body. It is usually hook-shaped with a pointed tip and a concave posterior margin. The flippers are short, quite wide, and terminates in a pointed tip. The tail is without a median notch on its posterior margin.

Teeth. There is a single, medium-sized, triangular, laterally-compressed tooth set in each lower jaw bone just opposite the posterior end of the line of fusion (mandibular symphysis) of the lower jaw bones. These large teeth are placed about 20 cm. (8 in.) back from the tip of the lower jaw. They

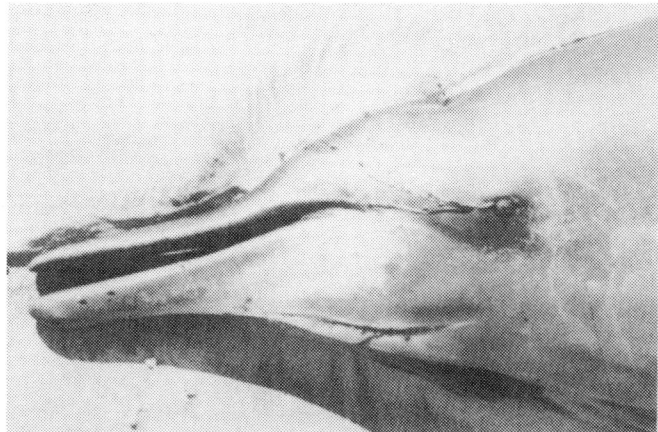

Photo of the head of a female von Haast's scamperdown beaked whale, *Mesoplodon grayi,* beached near Whakatane, North Island, New Zealand. **Photo by A. van Wouden.**

From: "Whales and Dolphins of New Zealand and Australia" by A.N. Baker. Victoria University Press, Wellington, 1983. Courtesy A.N. Baker.

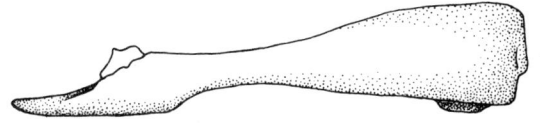

Jaw and tooth of *Mesoplodon grayi.*

measure about 10 cm. (4 in.) in height and about 7 to 8 cm. (3 in.) from front to back. These teeth are inclined forward, have a pointed denticle, and have serrated edges. In addition, there may be between 10 and 22 very small teeth in the back of each upper jaw; these teeth may be buried in the gums. These upper jaw teeth are located behind the single lower jaw tooth. In the females, all teeth, both large and small, do not usually appear above the gums.

Skeletal Notes. The vertebrae are distributed approximately as follows: C 7 + D 10 + L 11 + Ca 20 = 48. The 1st 3 bones of the neck are united to form a single unit. There are 10 ribs of which the 1st 5 have 2 heads; of these, 5 articulate with the sternum. There are at least 10 chevron bones. The bones of the fingers are distributed approximately as follows: I (1), II (5), III (5), IV (4), V (3).

Other Anatomical Notes. The umbilicus is located in the center of the body.

Food. The principal food of this whale is squid.

Swimming and Diving. This is an oceanic species which does not frequent shorelines. It appears to be a gregarious species and to travel in small groups. It does not follow ships and is therefore seldom seen at sea. Individuals in the Indian Ocean were reported by Dale W. Rice to have the "peculiar habit of sticking its long needle-like white snout out of the water as it breaks the surface to blow."

Reproduction. The young appear to be born in the spring of the year and will measure about 2 meters (79 in.) or more in length.

Abundance. This may be a fairly common species but is rarely seen except when stranded upon a beach.

Economic Importance: There is no economic importance attached to this whale.

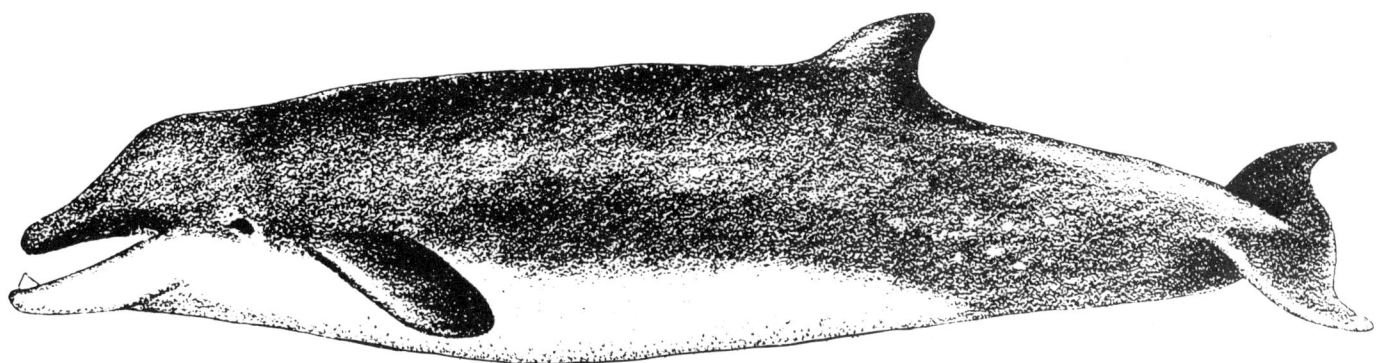

HECTOR'S BEAKED WHALE
Also known as the Skew-beaked Whale
Mesoplodon hectori (Gray, 1871)

Identifying Features. For many years this species was known only from skulls and skeletons and has therefore been hard to identify. However, it can still be best identified by its teeth. There are two, large, flat, triangular teeth located almost at the tip of the lower jaw. In other species of this family, these teeth are either not flat or are located farther away from the tip of the jaw.

Size and Shape. The bodies of these whales are large and robust. They are thickest near their center and taper quite uniformly toward the head and tail. They are known to reach a length of at least 4.43 meters (14 ft. 6 in.), although most of the specimens which have been measured were somewhat shorter. The beak of this species is relatively shorter than in other beaked whales and there is no transverse crease separating it from the forehead. Two longitudinal grooves are present on the throat.

Color. The color of the body is reported to be a dark brownish gray above and to become lighter and paler beneath. The underside of the head, belly, and the tail flukes are reported to be pale to white in color. These colors appear to have been reported from beached individuals and therefore may not represent the colors of the living animal.

Distribution. Hector's beaked whale was long believed to be an oceanic species which was widely distributed in the temperate waters of the southern oceans. For many years it was known from New Zealand, Tasmania, Tierra del Fuego (So. Argentina), the Falkland Islands, and South Africa. Specimens are now known from the eastern North Pacific, where carcasses have been found (1975) upon the beaches of southern California (U.S.A.) just above 33° N.L.; this stranding included a single female and a young individual.

Fins and Flippers. The dorsal fin is small and low and is located about 2/3 of the body length behind the head. It is somewhat triangular in shape with an anterior margin which is nearly straight and a posterior margin which is concave. The flippers are small, short, and rounded at their extremities. The flukes of the tail lack the notch at the midline on their posterior margin. This notch on the posterior margin of the flukes is always useful in separating the member of the Ziphiidae from the Delphinidae (the Ocean Dolphins and Porpoises), all of which possess the notch.

Teeth. In this species, the teeth are probably the most reliable clue to its identification. Two teeth are set together at the tip of the lower jaw, each of which is set in its own jaw bone about 2.3 cm. (1 in.) back from the tip of each jaw bone. These teeth are small, flat, and somewhat triangular in outline above the gum line. The anterior edge is very slightly concave. In one specimen, these teeth projected about 3.3 cm. (1.25 in.) above the gum line; their weight was recorded as 37 and 39 grams (1.3 and 1.37 oz. av.). It should be remembered that these teeth, although present in both sexes, do not usually erupt above the gum line in the females; in the males, they erupt only after they have reached maturity. The teeth of the females are smaller than those of the males and will need to be uncovered and exposed by dissection.

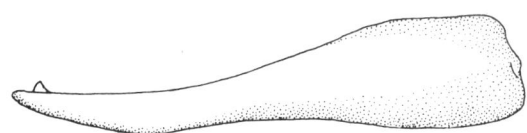

Jaw and tooth of *Mesoplodon hectori*.

Skeletal Notes. The existing skeletons of this species have been procured from carcasses lying on beaches; most of these have been incomplete. Complete skeletons may be found in the U.S. National Museum (USNM 504260) and in the Dominion Museum in Wellington, New Zealand (DM 1832). It is interesting to note that the two jaw bones or mandibles of the males are fused together in front at the point where they meet (mandibular symphysis), but in the females these bones do not fuse. The skull of this species is extremely asymmetrical.

Other Anatomical Notes. In a dissected beach specimen, the right and left testes measured 11.3 cm. and 12.6 cm. in length and weighed 84.5 grams and 115.5 grams, respectively.

Food. This species is known to feed upon squid and probably most available fishes.

Abundance. Hector's beaked whale is truly one of the rarest whales in the sea. Specimens are extremely scarce and have thus far come only from dead, beached carcasses. Its identification at sea is difficult because it does not have any anatomical features which are easily recognized.

Economic Importance. This species has no economic importance. It is of great interest and curiosity to students of whales.

Miscellaneous. This species was named in 1871 for Sir James Hector.

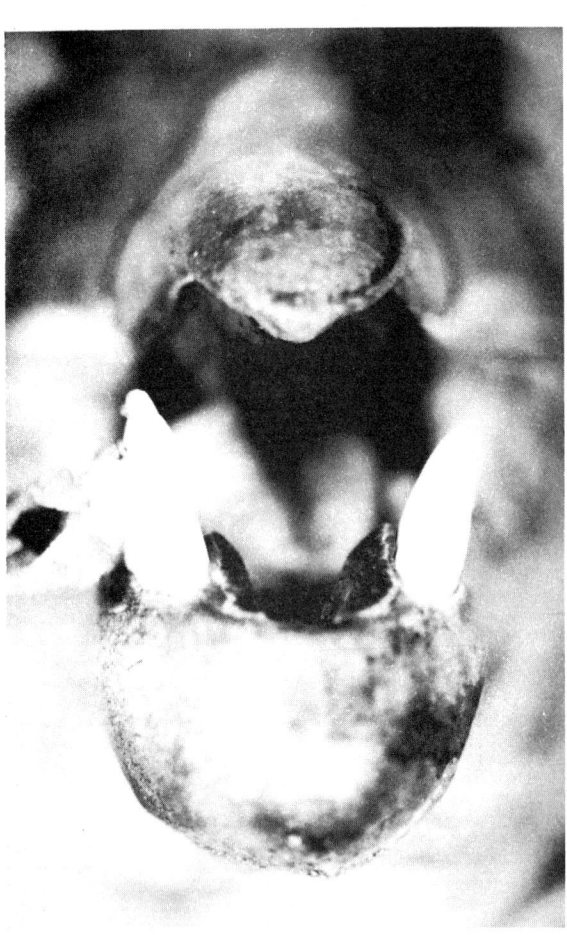

A photo of the anterior end of the proboscis of Hector's Beaked Whale, *Mesoplodon hectori,* showing an anterior view of the two teeth of this species which are set at the extreme ends of the two jaw bones.

Photo by J.G. Mead.

A photo of the dorsal fin of a male specimen of Hector's Beaked Whale, *Mesoplodon hectori,* showing the nearly-straight anterior margin and the concave posterior margin.

Photo by J.G. Mead.

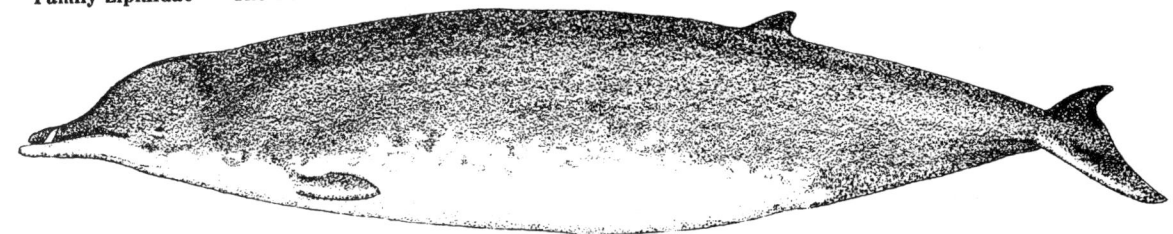

THE STRAP-TOOTHED BEAKED WHALE
Also known as Layard's Beaked Whale
Mesoplodon layardi (Gray, 1865)

Identifying Features. The most distinctive features of this whale is a pair of teeth in the adult males. A large, flat, elongated tooth is set in each jaw bone somewhat back from the tip and projects backward, outward and upward beside the upper lip. The females and the young lack these teeth and are therefore very difficult to identify.

Size and Shape. The body is robust and spindle-shaped and tapers uniformly from its midsection toward the head and tail; it is laterally compressed, so it is higher than it is wide. The descending dorsal profile exhibits a low depression just above the head and the forehead descends rapidly to the base of the proboscis. The head is small and the lips are straight but end in a curve as in many other members of this genus. The body will measure from about 5 to 6 meters (16.4 to 19.7 ft.) or more in length. This is one of the largest species of the Genus *Mesoplodon*.

Color. A dark, chocolate gray color covers the entire upper surface of the body and appendages. This color shades gradually downward to a lighter gray on the abdomen; yellow shades may also be present on the abdomen. White areas are reported on the throat, on the belly as far backward as the vent, and possibly on the top of the head in old males. Some scholars report lighter areas on the back and sides anterior to the dorsal fin. The body is usually marked with many scratches and scars. The color of this species in life is not firmly documented since many of the records are from beached carcasses.

Distribution. The distribution of this species is not well known. It appears to be worldwide in the temperate and cooler seas of the southern hemisphere. It is known from New Zealand, southern Australia, Tasmania, South Africa, the Falkland Islands, Uruguay, Argentina, and Chile. Scholars believe that the distribution of this species extends between 30° and 45° S.L., although this whale has been observed as far south as the Antarctic Convergence.

Migration. Very little is known of the migratory habits of this species.

Fins and Flippers. The dorsal fin is small and low and is placed about 2/3 of the body length behind the head. A dorsal keel extends backward to the flukes. The flippers are small, have convex margins, and terminate in a rounded tip. The flukes of the tail are wide and have pointed tips. The tail is not notched at the center of the posterior margin.

Teeth. A very unusual pair of teeth grows from the lower jaw of this whale. A single tooth is located in each lower jaw

bone about 30 cm. (12 in.) back from the tip of the jaw and at about the rear margin of the mandibular symphysis; it is large, long, slender, flat, pointed, sharp, without roots, and covered with enamel. It is pointed backward at an angle of about 45° and inclined outward so that it lies outside of the upper lip. As this tooth grows upward, it curves inward over the top of the proboscis and thereby restricts the opening and closing of the mouth. It has been reported that, in old males, these two opposite teeth will approach a meeting in the midline above the proboscis. In this situation, these teeth may approach 35 cm. (14 in.) in length. They terminate in a small, sharp denticle. In these whales, the teeth of the females do not develop as in the males and may be found beneath the gums of the lower jaws.

It should be remembered that the teeth of young specimens are flat and triangular and resemble the teeth of other species of *Mesoplodon*. The strap-like teeth occur only in adult male whales.

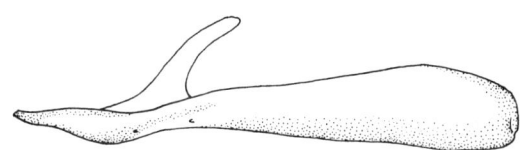

Jaw and tooth of *Mesoplodon layardi*.

Skeletal Notes. The vertebrae are distributed approximately as follows: C 7 + D 10 + L 10 + Ca 19 = 46.

Food. Almost nothing is known of the habits of this species. The basic food of this whale is squid plus a small component of miscellaneous fishes.

Swimming and Diving. This is an oceanic species which avoids coastlines and does not follow ships.

Reproduction. The young are born in the early spring (September) and will measure about 2.2 meters (86.6 in.) in length at birth.

Abundance. There is very little information on the abundance of this species, but it is believed to be reasonably common within its range.

Economic Importance. This whale has no economic value.

Miscellaneous. The name of this species honors Edgar Leopold Layard, Curator of the South African Museum in Cape Town, who in 1865 reported a skull of this whale in the collection of his museum.

TRUE'S NORTH ATLANTIC BEAKED WHALE
Also known as True's Beaked Whale
and The Wonderful Beaked Whale
Mesoplodon mirus True, 1913

Identifying Features. There are few positive clues to the identity of this species. The teeth, which are two in number, are placed at the very tip of the lower jaw bones and are visible in the adult males. The single tooth, which occupies the very tip of each jaw bone is somewhat triangular in cross section, laterally compressed, pointed, moderate in size, and is inclined forward. These teeth are the only teeth in the entire mouth and, in the case of the females, do not usually appear above the gums.

Size and Shape. The body of this species is robust and spindle-shaped and tapers uniformly toward the head and tail. Where the dorsal profile descends to the head, there is a depression at the blowhole which intensifies a very low, gentle curve over the top of the head; the forehead then descends rather abruptly to the base of the proboscis. These whales will reach a length of at least 5.18 meters (17 ft.).

Color. The upper surfaces of the head, back, tail, and flippers are a dull dark gray or blackish color; the lower side of the flippers and tail flukes is likewise dark. The color of the back shades gradually downward to lighter hues, often yellowish on the sides and belly; in some cases, the lower surface has been described as white or whitish. There is usually a gray area in front of the vent and a dark center line on the abdomen. In addition, the body may be dappled with dark spots. The body is reported to sometimes be covered with white spots and the skins of most animals are covered with long, parallel scratches.

Distribution. The distribution of this whale seems to be limited to the temperate waters of the North Atlantic Ocean. On the western side, it occurs from Nova Scotia (45° N.L.) southward to Florida (25° N.L.) and the West Indian Islands; on the European side it is known from Ireland and the English Channel (50° N.L.) and adjoining shores. A few stranded specimens are known from the southeastern coastline of South Africa and Australia.

Migration. Almost nothing is known of its migratory habits. Its distribution in the North Atlantic Ocean seems to suggest that it is associated with the Gulf Stream Current.

Fins and Flippers. The dorsal fin is very low, nearly triangular in shape, often slightly concave on its rear margin, and is located 2/3 of the body length back from the head. It is followed by a dorsal keel on the tail stock; a similar keel is present on the ventral side. Neither keel reaches to the tail. The flippers are quite small, slender, and with nearly parallel sides and a rounded tip; they are inserted low on the body and in the dark colored area. The tail is quite large, slightly concave posteriorly, and lacks the notch at the midline on the posterior border, although a weak nick has been observed at this point.

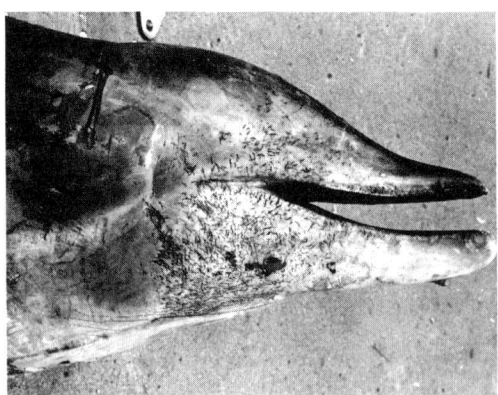

Photo of the head of True's North Atlantic beaked whale, *Mesoplodon mirus,* **from Port Fairy, Victoria, Australia.**
R. Warneke.

From: "Whales and Dolphins of New Zealand and Australia" by A.N. Baker. Victoria University Press, Wellington, 1983. Courtesy A.N. Baker.

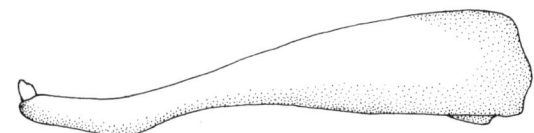

Jaw and tooth of *Mesoplodon mirus*.

Teeth. There are 2 large teeth, measuring about 5 cm. (2 in.) in length, located at the very tip of the lower jaw. They set back about 5 cm. (2 in.) from the tip of the jaw bone and are about 5 cm. (2 in.) apart. These teeth are visible when the mouth is closed. In addition, it should be noted that in the male, these teeth are somewhat oval in cross-section and, in one instance, measured 1/2 in. by 1 in. (in cross section). They are more compressed than the teeth of *Ziphius* and can be used to distinguish these species.

Skeletal Notes. The vertebrae are distributed approximately as follows: C 7 + D 10 + L 11 + Ca 18-19 = 46-47. The first 3 cervical vertebrae are fused into one unit. The atlas and axis are strongly fused while the 3rd vertebra is fused at the arch and also at the centrum. The remaining vertebrae are free. The 1st 7 ribs have 2 heads and the 1st 5 ribs are connected to the sternum. There are about 9 chevron bones. The sternum is composed of 4 parts. The scapula is wider than high and the upper edge is quite round. Some of the carpal (wrist) bones are combined with other carpals or metacarpals. The bones of the fingers are distributed approximately as follows: I (2), II (4), III (4), IV (3), V (2).

Other Anatomical Notes. The testes weigh from about 150 to 170 grams each.

Food. It feeds upon squid and fishes.

Swimming and Diving. It is an oceanic species and does not frequent shorelines or follow ships. Very little is known of its swimming habits. It travels in small groups. Its blow is low and scarcely visible.

Reproduction. A female specimen measuring 5.18 meters (17 ft.) in length contained a foetus which measured 2.6 meters (7 ft. 2 in.).

Abundance. This species appears to be an uncommon whale; however, it may be more numerous than observations indicate.

Economic Importance. There is no economic value attached to this species.

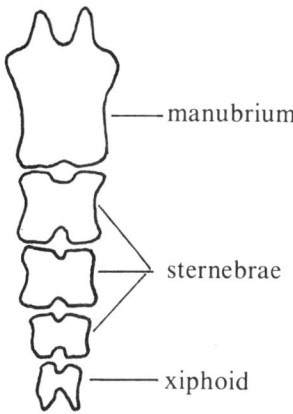

A diagram of the sternum of *Mesoplodon mirus.*
Drawn from Thorpe.

U.S.N.M.

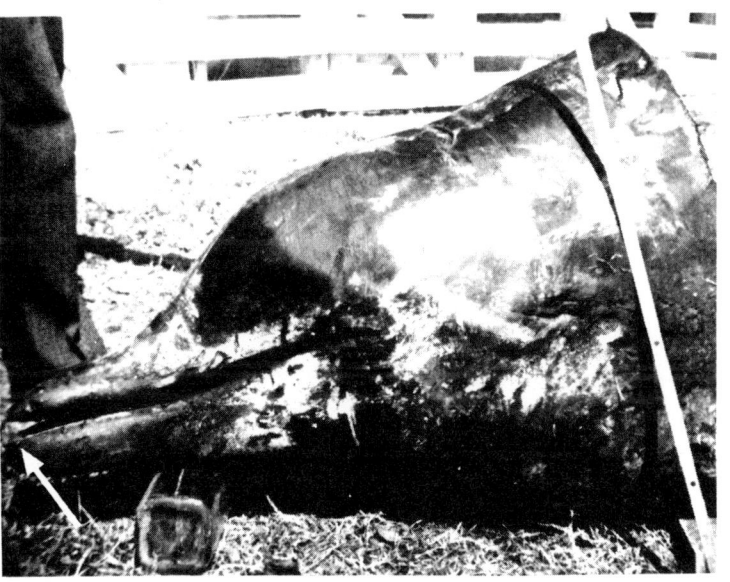

U.S.N.M.

Photos of the head of True's North Atlantic Beaked Whale, *Mesoplodon mirus,* showing the shape of the proboscis and the two long grooves on the throat.

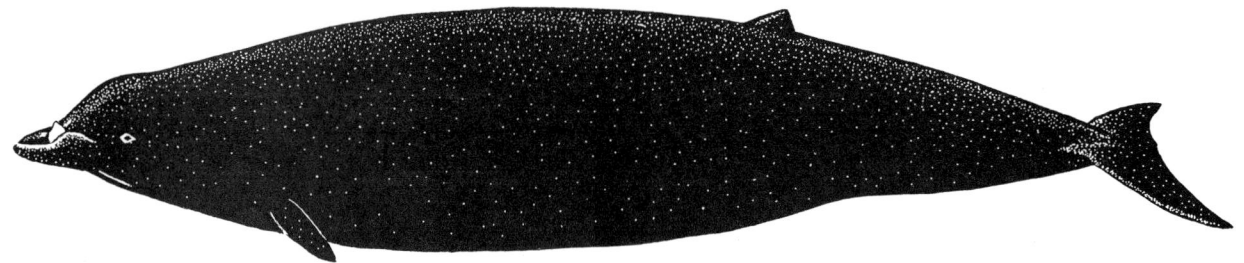

THE BERING SEA BEAKED WHALE
Also known as The North Pacific Beaked Whale,
The Saber-toothed Whale, and Stejneger's Bering Sea Beaked Whale
Mesoplodon stejnegeri True, 1885

Identifying Features. The easiest feature to observe in this whale is the great, flat tooth set half-way back in each lower jaw bone. Each tooth is laterally compressed, has a straight front edge and a convexly curved rear edge, and is marked by a small point (denticle) on top at the front. It is plainly visible in all adult males and can be used to identify them; the females are very difficult to identify. There are areas of whitish color spread over the entire front of the head.

Size and Shape. The body of this whale is spindle-shaped and tapers gradually and uniformly toward the head and tail. The head slopes gradually downward to join the base of the proboscis which is cylindrical in shape and pointed at its extremity. The body is laterally compressed and is therefore higher than it is wide. The descending anterior profile describes a shallow depression over the blowhole and then descends gradually to the base of the proboscis. Beginning at the corner of the mouth, the lips curve upward and down as they proceed forward. This is a large beaked whale and will reach a length of 5 to 6 meters (16.5 to 19.7 ft.).

Color. The entire body of this whale is brownish, grayish, or blackish above and lighter below. So few live specimens have been observed that the color pattern of the living animal is not well known. Lighter areas have been observed bordering the lips and a crosswise band of brownish color passes over the blowhole.

Distribution. The distribution of this whale is limited to the North Pacific Ocean. On the American side it extends from the Bering Sea and the Gulf of Alaska southward to San Diego, California (33° N.L.); on the Asiatic side, it extends southward to Japan (30° N.L.).

Food. It feeds upon squids and some fishes including salmon.

Migration. This is probably a non-migratory species, although it probably shifts its latitude with the seasons.

Fins and Flippers. The dorsal fin is small and triangular in shape; it is located behind the middle of the body about 2/3 of the body length toward the tail. It is followed by a dorsal keel which extends backward to the center of the tail. The flippers are small in size and measure about 1/10 of the body

length. They have nearly parallel sides, a rounded tip, and are placed low upon the body. The margin of the tail is only very slightly concave and the tips are pointed.

Diagram of the outline of the dorsal fin and tail flukes of *Mesoplodon stejnegeri*.

Drawn from Roest.

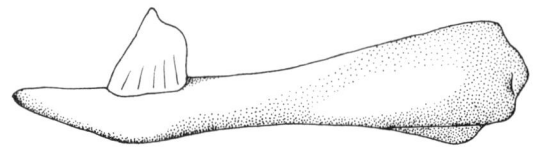

The lower jaw and single tooth of *Mesoplodon stejnegeri*.

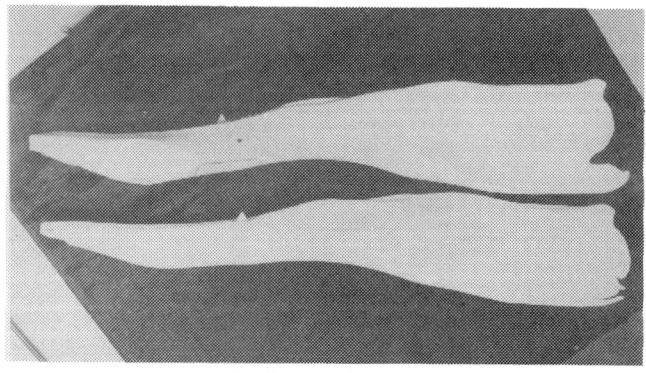

The jaws and emerging teeth of the Bering Sea beaked whale (*Mesoplodon stejnegeri*). These teeth were destined to grow much larger.
Photo by the Univ. of British Columbia.

254

Teeth. This whale possesses two very large teeth which will measure 30 cm. (8 in.) in height, 10 cm. (4 in.) from front to back, and 2.5 cm. (1 in.) in width (thickness). They are located well back from the front of the mouth and project upward along the outer side of the upper lip, where they are readily visible. These teeth are inclined backward and have a nearly straight anterior margin which ends in a small, sharp, pointed denticle. The teeth of the females usually remain buried in the gums. In addition to the above information, it should be noted that these large teeth do not fit too well and often tear the flesh of the upper lips and jaws.

Skeletal Notes. The vertebrae are distributed approximately as follows: C 7 + D 10 + L 10 + Ca 19 = 46. In the neck, the 1st 3 vertebrae are fused into a single unit. There are 10 ribs in all; of these, the 1st 7 have 2 heads. The V-bones are 10 in number. The sternum has 5 parts. The bones of the fingers are distributed approximately as follows: I (1), II (5), III (4), IV (4), V (3).

Food. It feeds upon squids and some fishes, including salmon.

Swimming and Diving. These whales are reported to travel in very small groups of 2, 3, or more. It is an oceanic species and does not frequent shorelines or follow ships.

Reproduction. The young will measure 155 cm. (5 ft. 1 in.) or more at birth; they are born in the spring.

Abundance. Very little information is available on the numbers of this species. It appears to be a very rare whale.

Economic Importance. This ziphiid whale has no economic value.

Miscellaneous. This species is named for Leonard Hess Stejneger (1851-1943) who was Curator, Department of Biology at the Smithsonian Institution, from 1911 to 1943.

Upper Left: A photo showing a dorsal view of the head of a specimen of the Bering Sea Beaked Whale, *Mesoplodon stejnegeri,* taken at Homer, Alaska. Note the two, large, white teeth projecting upward from the lower jaws.

Upper Right: A photo of the dorsal fin of the Bering Sea Beaked Whale, *Mesoplodon stejnegeri.*

Lower: A photo of a lateral view of the head of a Bering Sea Beaked Whale, *Mesoplodon stejnegeri.* Note the curved outline of the mouth and the enormous tusk-like tooth of this species.

All photos by F.H. Fay.

THE GOOSE-BEAKED WHALES
Genus *ZIPHIUS* G. Cuvier, 1823

This genus includes a single living species with a large, robust, spindle-shaped body. The head is relatively smaller than in other beaked whales and the cleft of the mouth is quite short and reaches only about halfway from the tip of the snout to the eye. The flippers are small and rounded, the dorsal fin is quite low and is curved on both the front and rear edges, and the tail lacks a distinct notch on its posterior margin between the flukes, although some individuals have a very small indentation at this point. A small ridge of skin extends along the midline of the back from the dorsal fin to the tail; this is a very distinctive feature and is almost certain identification of this genus and species. Individuals are known to have reached 8.5 meters (28 ft.) in length.

The functional teeth in this genus consist of a single pair of large, blunt, conical teeth, located one each at the tips of the two lower jaw bones; these large teeth erupt through the gums only in the males and then not until the whale is mature. In addition, small vestigial teeth may be present buried in the flesh of all jaws of both sexes.

This genus and species was created by Baron Georges Cuvier, the great French anatomist, following his study of a fossil specimen.

Studies of these whales by various scholars indicate that several names of species appearing in older books are really duplicate names or synonyms of other previously named species. The following list indicates the older names and the more correct and current names of these species.

Old Name		Name Currently In Use
Delphinorhynchus australis	is now	*Ziphius cavirostris*
Epiodon chathamensis	is now	*Ziphius cavirostris*
Hyperoodon desmaresti	is now	*Ziphius cavirostris*
Hyperoodon gervaisi	is now	*Ziphius cavirostris*
Petrorhynchus capensis	is now	*Ziphius cavirostris*
Ziphius grebnitzkii	is now	*Ziphius cavirostris*
Ziphius layardii	is now	*Mesoplodon layardii*
Ziphius novaezealandiae	is now	*Ziphius cavirostris*
Ziphius savii	is now	*Ziphius cavirostris*
Ziphius semijunctus	is now	*Ziphius cavirostris*
Ziphius seychellensis	is now	*Mesoplodon densirostris*

This genus is known only from the Holocene (Recent) Epoch.

This genus includes the single living species listed below.

Ziphius cavirostris G. Cuvier, 1823
CUVIER'S GOOSE-BEAKED WHALE . . . .
. . . . See page 257

Photo by W.J. Houck.

A photo of Cuvier's Goose-beaked Whale, *Ziphius cavirostris,* stranded on a beach in northern California.

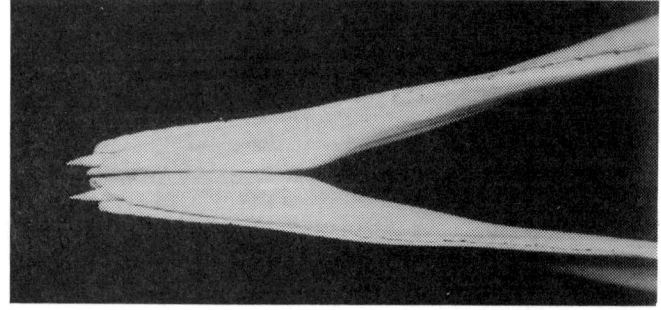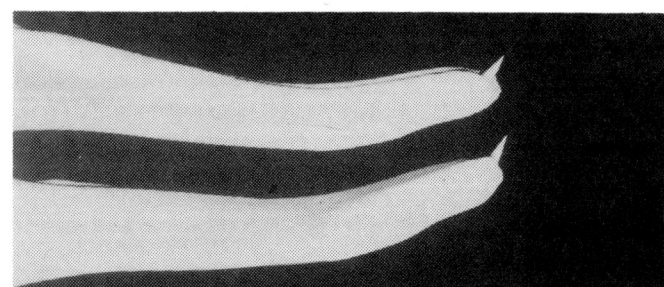

The jaws of an unidentified ziphiid whale, possibly of a young female *Ziphius cavirostris,* in dorsal and lateral views.

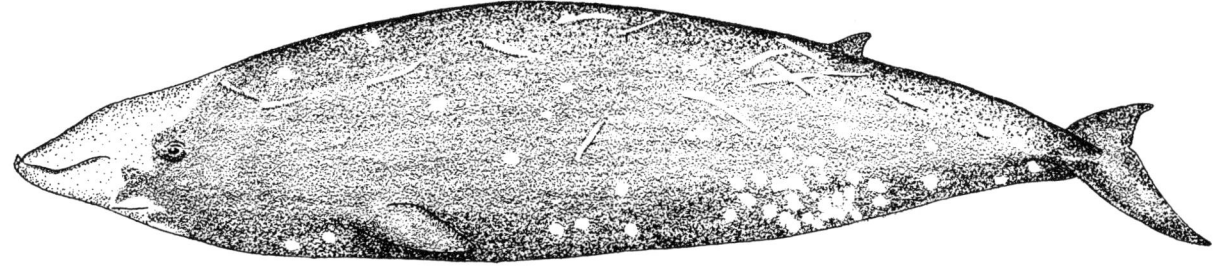

CUVIER'S GOOSE-BEAKED WHALE
Ziphius cavirostris G. Cuvier, 1823

Identifying Features. A combination of characters will help to identify this whale. It may reach or exceed 7 meters (23 ft.) in length. The dorsal fin is low and is placed in the last 1/3 of the body, the mouth is short and goes only a little more than half way to the eye, the head may be whitish, and the tail flukes are lighter beneath. A ridge of skin extends along the back from the dorsal fin to the tail. See teeth below.

Size and Shape. The goose-beaked whale is the 4th largest of the ziphiid whales and is exceeded in size only by Arnoux's Beaked Whale (*Berardius arnuxii*), Baird's Beaked Whale (*Berardius bairdii*), and the North Atlantic Bottle-nosed Whale (*Hyperoodon ampullatus*). It will reach a length of about 7 meters (23 ft.) although most specimens will measure less than 6 meters (19+ ft.) In this species, the females are larger than the males. The body is robust and spindle-shaped and tapers very uniformly from its mid-section toward the extremities. The head is rather small, the proboscis is short and not distinctly marked off from the head, the cleft of the mouth is short, reaching only about one-half the distance to the eye, and the lower jaw is about an inch longer than the upper jaw. There is a slight external constriction in the region of the neck.

Color. The body is usually darker above and lighter below. The color of the back varies from black to grey to brown, often with pinkish hues around the head and abdomen. A specimen freshly beached near Humboldt, California, was cream-colored over the front half of the head; this color extended along the back about half way to the tail. A young specimen was described as having an "egg-plant blue" back, brown sides and tail, and a white belly. The body is usually covered with scattered, oval, whitish spots and many scratches. Dead specimens lying on a beach change color soon after dying and are therefore a poor source for determining the color of living specimens.

Distribution. This is the most widely distributed of the beaked whales (*Ziphiidae*). It seems to occur worldwide in all tropical and temperate seas. It apparently does not enter polar regions, although it is found in some cold water areas including the Bering Sea and the Sea of Okhotsk. Beached specimens are known from both shores of North America, including the Gulf of California. They appear to prefer water which is warmer than 10° C. (50° F) and deeper than 1,000 meters (3,281 ft.).

Migration. Very little information is known about their migratory habits. They appear to migrate northward and southward with the seasons.

Fins and Flippers. The dorsal fin is quite large for a beaked whale, is triangular in shape, and is concave on its posterior margin; it may measure 25 cm. (9.8 in.) or more in height. It has a long base and is placed 2/3 of the body length back from the head. The flippers are small, have somewhat parallel sides, and end in a slightly rounded tip; they are held against the body in shallow "flipper pockets." The tail is concave on its posterior margin and, unlike most other ziphiid whales, may have a very shallow notch at the midline. The tail is light-colored beneath.

Teeth. In this beaked whale, there are two, large, blunt, conical, peg-shaped teeth in the front of the mouth. They are located, one each, at the very tip of each lower jaw bone, where they may be visible at the end of the snout. They are oval in cross-section and may measure as much as 8 cm. (3 in.) in length. These teeth are visible only in mature males; in the females, these teeth do not appear above the gums. In addition, there are small vestigial teeth in all jaws of both sexes. These teeth are small and slender, about "the size of a toothpick," and may be reabsorbed during growth; they number from about 4 or 5 to 28 or 30 in each of the 4 jaw bones.

The jaw and tooth of *Ziphius cavirostris*.

Skeletal Notes. The vertebrae are distributed approximately as follows: C 7 + D 9 + L 11 + Ca 20 = 47. The 1st 2 neck vertebrae are usually fused into a single unit. There are 9 pairs of ribs; of these, 7 pairs have 2 heads and 2 pairs have a single head. Five pairs of ribs articulate directly with the sternum. The bones of the fingers (without the metacarpals) are distributed approximately as follows: I (1), II (3-6), III (5-6), IV (4), V (1-2). The skull is asymmetrical; the bones of the right side are larger than those of the left side.

Other Anatomical Notes. A beached specimen measuring 5.59 meters (18 ft. 4 in.) had an exposed penis which measured 32 cm. (12.6 in.) in length. The eyes are large and dark. The blowhole atop the head is crescent-shaped and has the ends directed forward. The throat grooves are deeper than in most other ziphiid whales and are more widely separated; two throat grooves measured 30.5 cm. (12 in.) in length in a specimen measuring 6.57 meters (21.55 ft.) in length. The blubber is reported to be 6 cm. (2.5 in.) thick and white in color.

Food. The diet of this whale includes squids, some fishes, and an occasional sea cucumber, crab, or starfish.

Swimming and Diving. These whales travel in small groups of 3 to 5 and at times may number as many as 10 to 25 or even 40 in a group. They dive vertically and will remain below for one-half hour; as they begin these dives, they lift the tail vertically and then submerge. They have been observed to leap from the water and to fall back with the usual splash. Their spout or blow is low and directed slightly to the left. They are oceanic in their range and avoid shorelines and ships.

Reproduction. The males fight considerably and inflict scratches of 2 parallel lines upon each other, the females, and the calves. The breeding season is uncertain, but appears protracted. Pregnancy lasts from 10 months to a year and the young, when born, are about one-third the length of the mother, usually about 2 meters (6 ft. 7 in.) or more. In a female specimen measuring 6.57 meters (21.55 ft.), the genital opening measured 35 cm. (13.7 in.) in length and the mammary slits measured 12 cm. (4.75 in.) in length.

Abundance. Of the 18 species of beaked whales, this species is probably the most numerous and the most widely distributed. It is not facing extermination.

Economic Importance: A few localities, principally in Japan, used to hunt this whale with limited success.

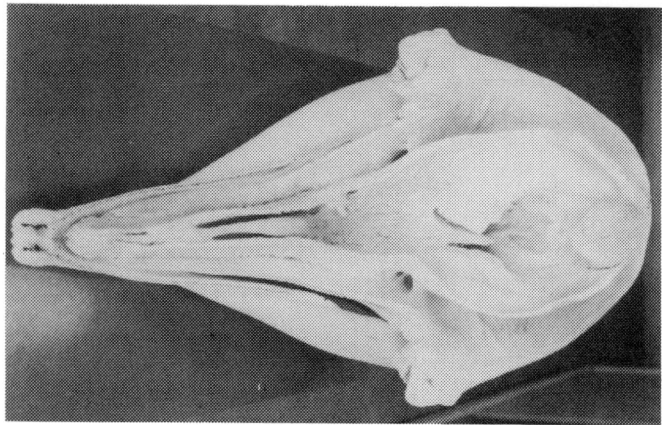

The skull and jaws of Cuvier's goose-beaked whale, *Ziphius cavirostris,* in dorsal view.
Photo by Michael Graybill at Cal. Acad. of Sci.

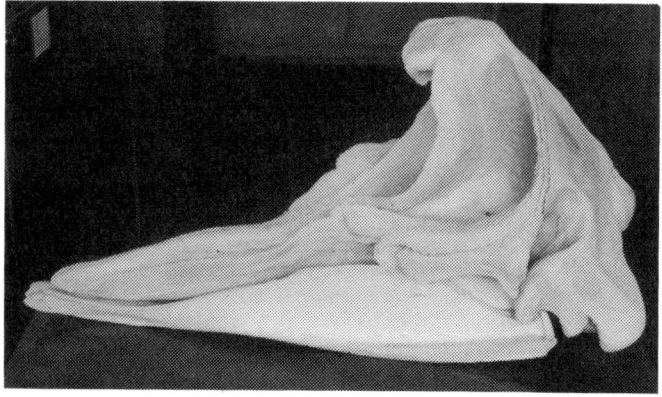

The skull and jaws of Cuvier's goose-beaked whale, *Ziphius cavirostris,* in lateral view.
Photo by Michael Graybill at Cal. Acad. of Sci.

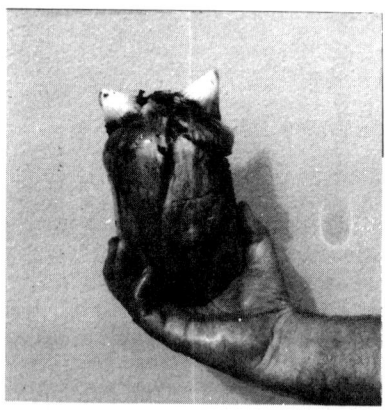

Photo of a ventral view of the two teeth located at the terminal end of the lower jaw of Cuvier's Goose-beaked Whale, *Ziphius cavirostris.*
Photo by W.A. Huck.

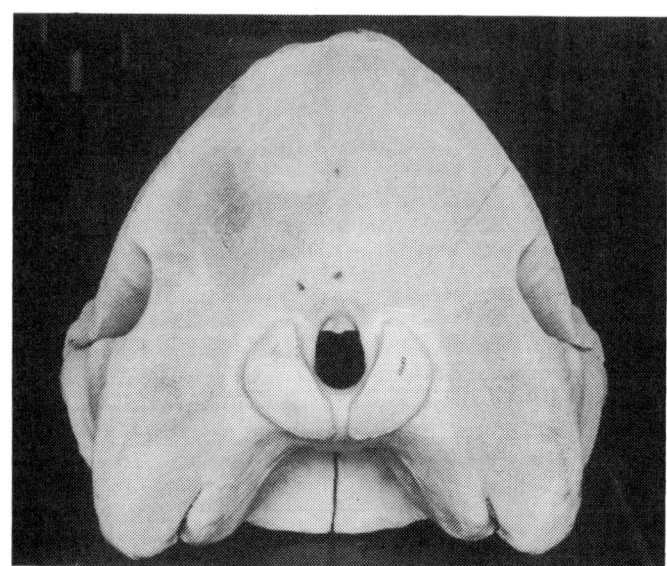

The skull of Cuvier's goose-beaked whale, *Ziphius cavirostris,* in posterior view.
Photo by Michael Graybill at Cal. Acad. of Sci.

THE BOTTLE-NOSED WHALES
Genus *HYPEROODON* Lacepede, 1804

The true bottle-nosed whales are most easily recognized by their large, inflated, bulbous forehead which is nearly vertical in front and which results from an elaborate upward growth and development of the maxillary bones. The beak appears small, distinct, and well-defined, although it is overshadowed by the forehead above it. The body is quite cylindrical in shape and, in adult males, may reach a length of 9.75 meters (32 ft.). The flippers are small, the dorsal fin is low and curved on both margins, and the tail lacks the notch at the middle of its posterior margin between the flukes. This notch is important because it helps to separate these whales from the members of the *Delphinidae*, which possess a notch on their tail.

The functional teeth of this genus include a single pair of teeth located at the very tips of the lower jaw bones; these teeth eventually emerge in the adult males, but usually only one tooth remains in old males. In addition, small, vestigial teeth are present in all jaws of both males and females. In this genus, all of the vertebrae of the neck are solidly fused together in adult individuals. The bodies of these whales are dark in color above and shade gradually to lighter hues on the sides and belly; they also become lighter in color with age.

This genus is known only from the Holocene (Recent) Epoch.

Studies of these whales by various scholars indicate that several names of species appearing in older books are really duplicate names or synonyms of other previously named species. The following list indicates the older names and the more correct and current names of these species.

Old Name		Name Currently In Use
Hyperoodon butskopf	is now	*Hyperoodon ampullatus*
Hyperoodon desmaresti	is now	*Ziphius cavirostris*
Hyperoodon rostratus	is now	*Hyperoodon ampullatus*

This genus includes the two living species listed below.

Hyperoodon ampullatus (Forster, 1770)
Hyperoodon planifrons Flower, 1882

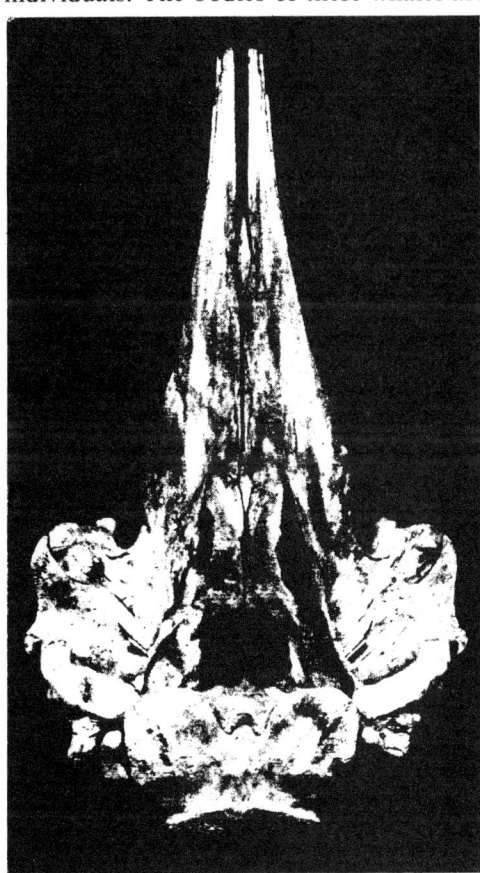

Ventral view.

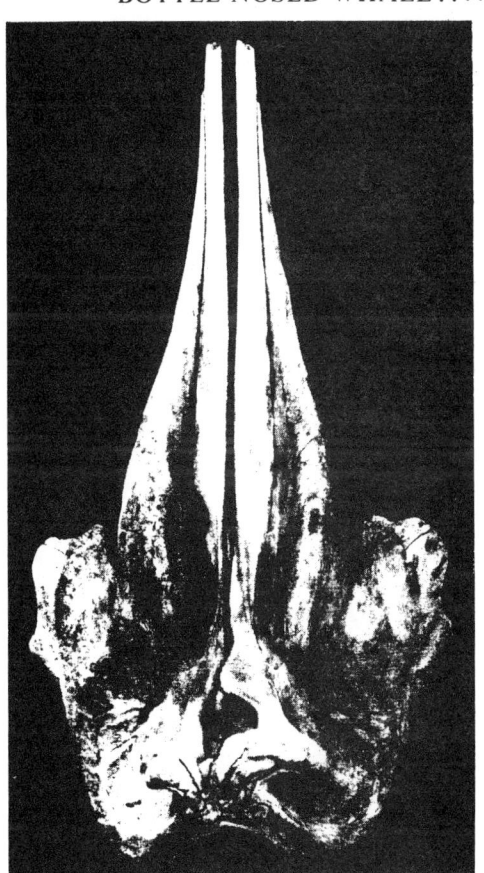

Dorsal view.

Photos of the skull of the North Atlantic Bottle-nosed Whale, *Hyperoodon ampullatus*.

Photos by Mitchell and Kozicki.

Reproduced by permission of the Dept. of Fisheries and Oceans, Dominion of Canada, from the Jour. Fish. Res. Bd. of Canada 32:7, July, 1975.

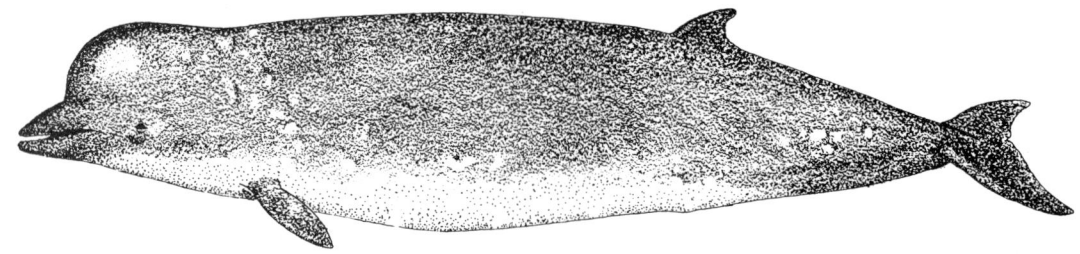

THE NORTH ATLANTIC BOTTLE-NOSED WHALE
Also known as the Northern Bottle-nosed Whale
Hyperoodon ampullatus (Forster, 1770)

Identifying Features. The identification of this species is not difficult. The males possess a fat, bulbous, spherical head including a forehead which is often nearly vertical in front in older animals. The beak is short and cylindrical in shape. In addition, the color of the body is usually brownish above and becomes lighter on the sides and belly. Old males are lighter in color than young ones and usually have a white or whitish head.

Size and Shape. The body is robust, quite cylindrical in shape, and tapers gradually toward the tail, but not especially toward the head. Adult specimens have been known to reach a maximum length of about 9.8 meters (32 ft.), although most specimens will be much shorter. The forehead is vertical in older animals and the beak is much like that of the dolphins. In the females, the bulge of the head is not as pronounced as in the males. The caudal peduncle is round and quite slender where it attaches to the tail. Two V-shaped grooves are present on the throat.

Color. The color of the back varies from very dark grayish hues to brown. The color of the back shades gradually to lighter hues of brown on the sides and belly; the body may also be marked with patches of a grayish color, placed at random. In the older males, the head becomes lighter or even white in color. The flippers and the tail flukes are brownish above and below. Occasionally, female whales are observed which exhibit a lighter band of color around the neck.

Distribution. This bottle-nosed whale is a pelagic, cold-water species which inhabits the North Atlantic Ocean from the latitude of the New England States (40-45° N.L.) and the Cape Verde Islands (15° N.L.) northward to the polar ice. They seem to prefer water which is 1,000 meters (3,281 ft.) or more in depth.

Migration. In the Atlantic summer, they go northward to the Arctic Ocean and return in the winter to the latitude of western Europe.

Fins and Flippers. The dorsal fin stands about 30 cm. (12 in.) in height and is located at a point about 2/3 of the distance to the tail; it is curved backward and pointed at the tip. The tail is without a median notch on its posterior margin.

Teeth. The front of the lower jaw bears 2 teeth (1 pair) in the adult males. The females usually develop similar teeth, but they are smaller in size and do not emerge above the gums.

These teeth, which are smaller than those of *Berardius* and *Ziphius,* are cone-shaped, being wider at their base, and narrower toward their pointed crowns; they will measure about 5 cm. (2 in.) in height and about 1.5 cm. in diameter. These teeth are not always clearly visible above the gums. In a few instances, a 2nd pair of teeth has been found embedded in the lower jaw at a point just behind the normal pair. Other small vestigial teeth numbering 5 or 6 or more are often found buried in the gums of all four jaws.

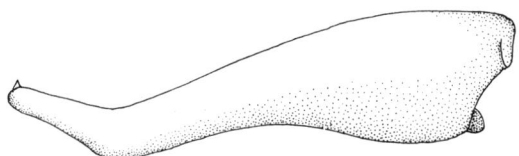

The jaw and tooth of *Hyperoodon ampullatus*.

Skeletal Notes. The skull of the male develops a pair of large bony crests or ridges on its upper side; these are known as maxillary crests and give the skull its unusual shape. These crests are absent in the females. The bones of the vertebral column are distributed approximately as follows: C7 + D9 + L 9-11 + Ca 18-20 = 43-46. The vertebrae of the neck are all fused to form a single unit. There are 9 pairs of ribs of which 6 pairs have 2 heads and 3 pairs have a single head. Five pairs of ribs articulate directly with the sternum. The sternum has 3 segments. The bones of the fingers (phalanges) are distributed approximately as follows: I (1), II (5), III (5), IV (4), V (2).

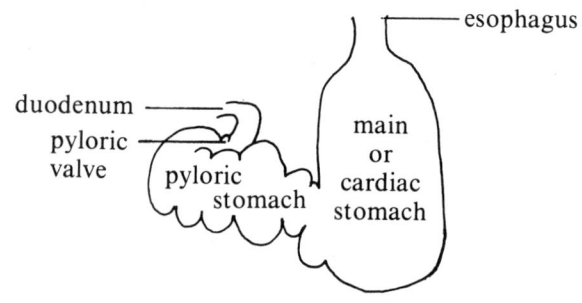

Diagram of the stomach of *Hyperoodon ampullatus*.
Drawn from Rice.

Other Anatomical Notes. These whales have an exceedingly complex set of stomachs. The jaws are equal in length, a feature which helps to separate this species from the many species of *Mesoplodon*. The dorsal profile of the neck is depressed somewhat in the area of the blowhole.

Food. The diet of this whale consists of squid and various fishes, including herring.

Swimming and Diving. This bottle-nosed whale travels in compact groups of 2 or 3 to 12 or more individuals and on a few occasions has been observed in schools of several hundred animals. They keep offshore and seem to prefer water which is beyond 100 fathoms (182.8 meters) in depth. They are good swimmers and divers and can remain submerged for at least 45 minutes. When beginning their deep dives, they will raise the tail aloft and go directly downward. Their spout is 1 or 2 meters high, shaped like an inverted tear drop, and is dense enough to be visible. They are curious about boats and will sometimes approach them.

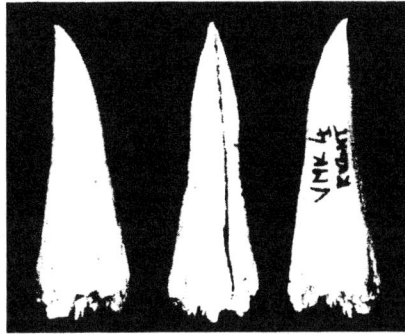

A photo of teeth of the North Atlantic Bottle-nosed Whale, *Hyperoodon ampullatus.*
From Edward Mitchess and V. Michael Kozicki.

Reproduced by permission of the Dept. of Fisheries and Oceans, Dominion of Canada, from the Jour. Fish. Res. Bd. of Canada 32:7, July, 1975.

Reproduction. The adults mate in the spring and the young are born a year later between March and June after a gestation period of about 12 months; they will measure about 3 meters (9.8 ft.) or more at birth.

Abundance. This whale was once one of the commoner species in the northern latitudes, but it has been over-hunted and is now scarce.

Economic Importance. During the 19th century, a small whaling industry existed in the Arctic Ocean for these whales. In addition to their flesh, they contain a small quantity of oil in their head which is quite similar to the spermaceti oil of the sperm whale. A few are still captured at scattered locations.

Miscellaneous. The bottle-nosed whales, like the pilot whales, will flee at the approach of the killer whale *(Orcinus).* They will help their wounded members, but they will abandon a dead whale.

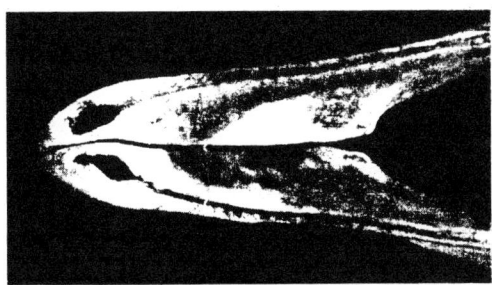

A photo in dorsal view of the anterior end of the lower jaw bones of the North Atlantic Bottle-nosed Whale, *Hyperoodon ampullatus.* **Note the mandibular symphysis and the location of the sockets for the teeth.**
From Edward Mitchess and V. Michael Kozicki.

Reproduced by permission of the Dept. of Fisheries and Oceans, Dominion of Canada, from the Jour. Fish. Res. Bd. of Canada 32:7, July, 1975.

THE SOUTHERN BOTTLE-NOSED WHALE
Also known as the Southern Flat-headed Bottle-nosed Whale
Hyperoodon planifrons Flower, 1882

Identifying Features. The bulbous head should help to identify this whale, since the only other species with a similar head is found in Arctic seas to the north. In addition, two conical teeth occur at the very tip of the lower jaw; these teeth erupt above the gums only in the adult males.

Size and Shape. The body is quite cylindrical in shape and tapers toward the tail in the last 1/3 of its length. The head is spherical and inflated in shape and increases in size with age to the point where the forehead is vertical or even overhangs the proboscis beneath. The beak is cylindrical in shape and resembles those of dolphins. The blowhole rests in a depression behind the swollen head. This is a smaller species than *H. ampullatus* of northern seas and will reach a maximum length of possibly 9 meters (29.5 ft.) in large males; most males, however, will measure about 7 to 8 meters (23 to 26.25 ft.). The females are smaller and will measure about 6 to 7 meters (19.7 to 23 ft.) in length.

Color. The back of the body has been described as gray, brownish black, and bluish black. This color becomes lighter on the sides, throat, and belly; here it has been described as creamy gray and grayish white. The dorsal fin, flippers, and tail are dark in color.

Distribution. The distribution of this whale includes the southern oceans of the world, including both Antarctic seas and cooler temperate waters. It has been recorded from Australia, Tasmania, New Zealand, Antarctica, Brazil, Chile, Argentina, the Falkland Islands, and South Africa. It has also been recorded from Sri Lanka (Ceylon), a record which indicates its tolerance for warmer water.

Migration. Very little is known of the migratory habits of this whale. It doubtless shifts its latitude with the seasons.

Fins and Flippers. The dorsal fin is located about 2/3 of the body length from the head; it is of medium size and will measure as much as 30 to 40 cm. (11.8 to 15.7 in.) in height. It is quite straight on its anterior margin and is concave on its posterior margin; its tip is pointed and directed to the rear. The flippers are quite small and short, have somewhat parallel sides, and terminate in a blunt tip. The tail is large and broad; it lacks the nick at the center of its posterior margin.

Teeth. The entire mouth has a single pair of prominent teeth located at the very tip of the lower jaw bones. Each tooth is conical in shape, has a small point (denticle) at its very end, and points slightly forward and outward. In addition, small, slender, vestigial teeth occur in all 4 jaws of both sexes. The two large teeth are developed in both sexes, but only those of the males push through the gums at maturity; the two front teeth of the females lie just below the gums and remain undeveloped throughout life.

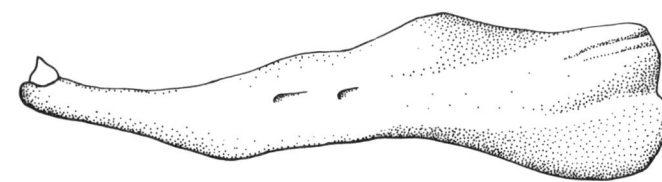

The jaw and tooth of *Hyperoodon planifrons*.

Skeletal Notes. The vertebrae are distributed approximately as follows: C 7 + D 9 + L 10 + Ca 20 = 46. All 7 of the neck vertebrae are fused to form a single unit. There are 9 pairs of ribs; of these, the 1st 7 have 2 heads and the 8th and 9th have a single head. There are about 10 or more chevron bones. The sternum is composed of 4 bones of which at least 3 are always united. The bones of the fingers (phalanges) are distributed approximately as follows: I (2), II (6), III (5), IV (4-5), V (3). A specimen 7.0 meters (22.9 ft.) long had a skull which measured 1.4 meters (4.59 ft.) in length.

Food. Very little is known of the habits of this southern species. Its diet consists of squid and doubtless any available fishes.

Swimming and Diving. The swimming and diving pattern of this species is not well known. They have not been reported to follow ships or to exhibit any curiosity regarding them.

Reproduction. The young will measure 2.7 meters (9 ft.) or more at birth. Their reproductive cycles are doubtless geared to the seasons of their environment and probably resemble those of *H. ampullatus* in the North Atlantic.

Abundance. This species does not appear to be common anywhere within the area it occupies. It appears to be a rare species.

Economic Importance. Very little economic importance attaches to this species.

262

THE WHALEBONE WHALES
Suborder *MYSTICETI* Flower, 1864

The whalebone whales are a group of less than a dozen species which most scientists have usually divided into the three family groups listed below.

These whales are a very unusual group of animals and differ radically in their body structure from the toothed whales. The most obvious differences are their great size, their large head and jaws, and the strange whalebone or baleen plates which hang downward into the mouth from their upper jaws. In addition, the whalebone whales have a blowhole with a double opening, whereas, the toothed whales have but a single blowhole. The whalebone whales (except *Balaena*) have only four fingers on the "hand" which is concealed within their flipper, while the toothed whales have the usual five fingers. It should be noted that the whalebone whales have rudimentary teeth in the embryos of their unborn young; these teeth soon disappear and are in turn followed by the development of the whalebone or baleen plates prior to their birth. Other differences between the whalebone whales and the toothed whales include differences in the cranium, the bones of the face, the thorax, the ribs, the trachea, the relative sizes of the males and females, and many other features including many differences in the alimentary canal.

The living whalebone whales are usually divided into the three families listed below.

1. Family *Eschrichtiidae* (1 species)
   THE GRAY WHALE FAMILY .... See page 271
2. Family *Balaenopteridae* (6 species)
   THE RORQUAL OR TRUE FIN-BACKED
   WHALE FAMILY .... See page 276
3. Family *Balaenidae* (3 species)
   THE RIGHT WHALE FAMILY ... See page 293

These families and the species which they include will be described in the above sequence on the pages which follow.

A Key to the Families of Whalebone Whales
(Choose A or B; if A is chosen, then choose 1 or 2.)

A. Longitudinal grooves are present on the throat, sometimes extending onto the belly; the dorsal fin on the back is either present or absent.
   1. Longitudinal grooves on the throat are from 2 to 4 in number; the dorsal fin is absent ....
      Family *Eschrichtiidae*
      THE GRAY WHALE FAMILY. See page 271
   2. Longitudinal grooves on the throat are numerous, usually between 14 and 100 in number; the dorsal fin is present ....
      Family *Balaenopteridae*
      THE RORQUAL or TRUE FIN-BACKED
      WHALE FAMILY .... See page 276

B. Longitudinal grooves are not present on the throat; the dorsal fin is absent on the back (except in *Caperea marginata*, which has a small, irregular fin)
   Family *Balaenidae*
   THE RIGHT WHALE FAMILY ....
   .... See page 293

The following table will help to compare and separate the three families of the whalebone whales.

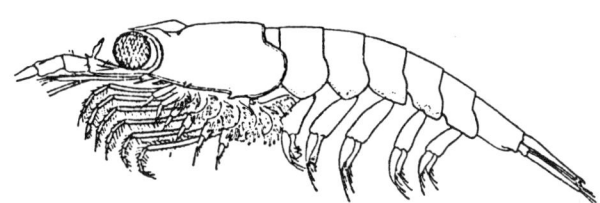

An example of krill, the pelagic euphausid crustaceans (*Euphausia* sp.), which furnish a large component of the diet of the whalebone whales (*Mysticeti*).

From Boden et alii.

A COMPARISON OF SOME EXTERNAL FEATURES OF THE WHALEBONE WHALES
(Order Cetacea: Suborder Mysticeti)

The Species Of The Whalebone Whales	A Dorsal Fin Present On The Back	The Number Of Longitudinal Grooves On Throat And Belly Counted Between The Flippers	The Length Of The Ventral Grooves	The Number Of Ridges On Top Of The Head
THE GRAY WHALE FAMILY (Family Eschrichtiidae)				
The Gray Whale (*Eschrichtius robustus*)	None	2, rarely 4	Short; 6 ft. long; only on throat.	None
THE RORQUAL OR TRUE FIN-BACKED WHALE FAMILY (Family Balaenopteridae)				
The Lesser Rorqual (*Balaenoptera acutorostrata*)...	Present	15 to 25	The grooves end well forward of the navel.	1 central ridge
The Sei Whale (*Balaenoptera borealis*)	Present	35 to 56	The grooves end well forward of the navel.	1 central ridge
The Bryde's Whale (*Balaenoptera edeni*)	Present	40 to 50	The grooves extend to the navel or beyond.	1 central ridge plus 1 smaller lateral ridge on each side.
The Blue Whale (*Balaenoptera musculus*)	Present	55 to 88	The grooves extend to the navel or beyond.	1 central ridge
The Fin Whale (*Balaenoptera physalus*)	Present	56 to 100	The grooves extend to the navel or beyond.	1 central ridge
The Hump-backed Whale (*Megaptera novaeangliae*)	Present	14 to 22	The grooves extend to the navel.	Ridges indistinct; replaced by 3 irregular rows of tubercles.
THE RIGHT WHALE FAMILY (Family Balaenidae) The Right Whale (*Balaena glacialis*)	None	None	The grooves are absent.	1 poorly-defined, central ridge covered with callosities.
The Bowhead Whale (*Balaena mysticetus*)	None	None	The grooves are absent.	None
The Pigmy Right Whale (*Caperea marginata*)	Present	None	The grooves are absent.	None

A COMPARISON OF SOME EXTERNAL FEATURES OF
THE WHALEBONE WHALES
(Order Cetacea: Suborder Mysticeti)

The Number Of Whalebone Plates On One Side	The Color Of The Whalebone Plates	The Color Of The Right Lower Lip	The Color Of The Lower Side Of The Flippers And Flukes	Gray Areas On Back Between Head And Dorsal Fin	Distribution
140 to 180	Yellowish white.	Mottled gray.	Gray	None	North Pacific Ocean only; near coastlines.
300 to 325	White to yellowish white; posterior plates may be brown or black.	Grayish or whitish	Flippers are whitish below with a white band across outer surface. Flukes are grayish or whitish below.	A chevron stripe on back is sometimes present; a whitish area on side may be present in the northern hemisphere.	In all oceans.
318 to 340	Ash black with blue tinge and fine, light bristles; often light in front.	Gray	Flippers and flukes are gray below.	None	In all oceans except polar and tropical seas.
250 to 350	Slate gray with dark bristles.	Dark gray	Flippers are gray below. Flukes are gray below.	Sometimes present.	In warm temperate and tropical waters of Atlantic, Pacific, and Indian Oceans.
270 to 395	All black with black bristles.	Gray	Flippers are grayish blue to white below.		In all oceans.
262 to 473 Usually 350 to 360	Dark gray to bluish-gray; 1/5 to 1/3 of right front is whitish.	White	Flippers are whitish below. Flukes are whitish below.	A faint, V-shaped mark is present on the back just behind the head.	In all oceans except polar and tropical seas.
270 to 400	Black to grayish black.	Black to grayish black.	Flippers are white below. Flukes are whitish below.	None	In most oceans. A migratory species.
250 to 390	Black	Black	Flukes are dark below.	None	In temperate waters of No. Atlantic, No. Pacific, and entire southern hemisphere.
325 to 360	Dark gray to black.	Black	Flukes are dark below.	None	In the Arctic Ocean and arctic seas.
About 230	Yellowish white	Blackish to brownish.	Flippers and flukes are dark below.	None	In temperate waters of southern oceans.

OUTLINES OF THE HEADS OF SOME VERY LARGE WHALES

TOOTHED WHALES — Odontoceti (67 species)

Physeter macrocephalus
THE GREAT SPERM WHALE

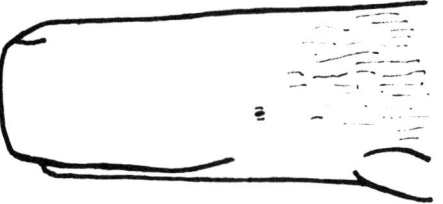 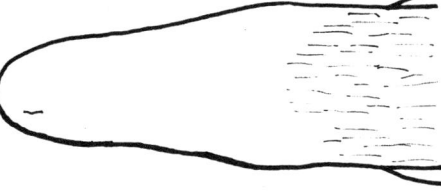

Berardius bairdii
**THE NORTH PACIFIC, GIANT,
FOUR-TOOTHED WHALE**

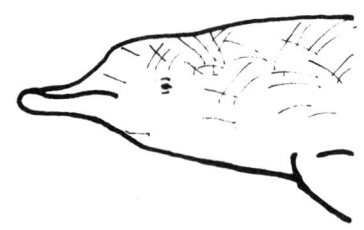 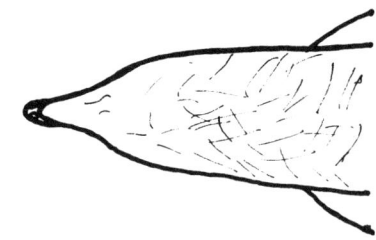

WHALEBONE WHALES — Mysticeti (10 species)

Eschrichtius robustus
THE GRAY WHALE

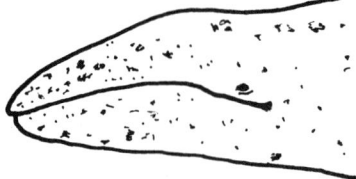 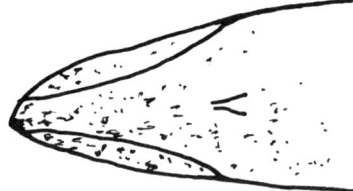

Balaenoptera acutorostrata
**THE LESSER RORQUAL
OR MINKE WHALE**

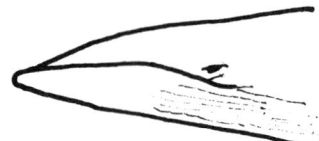 

Balaenoptera borealis
THE SEI WHALE

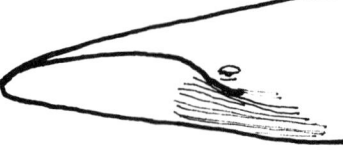 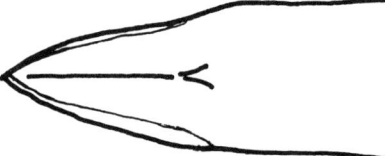

Balaenoptera edeni
THE BRYDE'S WHALE

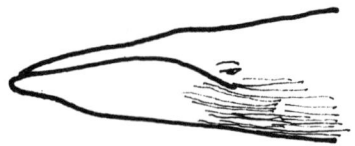 

Drawn from Leatherwood et alii.

WHALEBONE WHALES — Mysticeti (10 species)
(Continued)

Balaenoptera musculus
THE BLUE WHALE

Balaenoptera physalus
THE FIN WHALE

Megaptera novaeangliae
THE HUMP-BACKED WHALE

Balaena glacialis
THE RIGHT WHALE

Balaena mysticetus
THE BOWHEAD WHALE

Drawn from Leatherwood et alii.

THE SURFACING SEQUENCE OF SOME LARGE WHALES

Left to Right: The whale surfaces and "blows," glides slowly at the surface for a few moments, and finally submerges, often with the tail elevated.

Physeter macrocephalus
THE GREAT SPERM WHALE

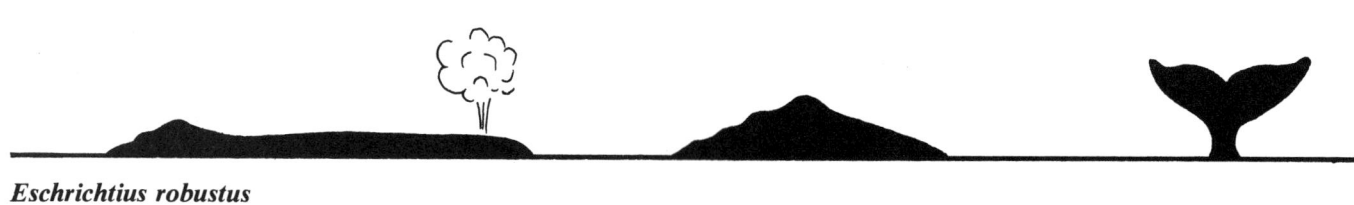

Eschrichtius robustus
THE GRAY WHALE

Balaenoptera borealis
THE SEI WHALE

Balaenoptera edeni
THE BRYDE'S WHALE

Drawn from Leatherwood et alii.

THE SURFACING SEQUENCE OF SOME LARGE WHALES
(Continued)

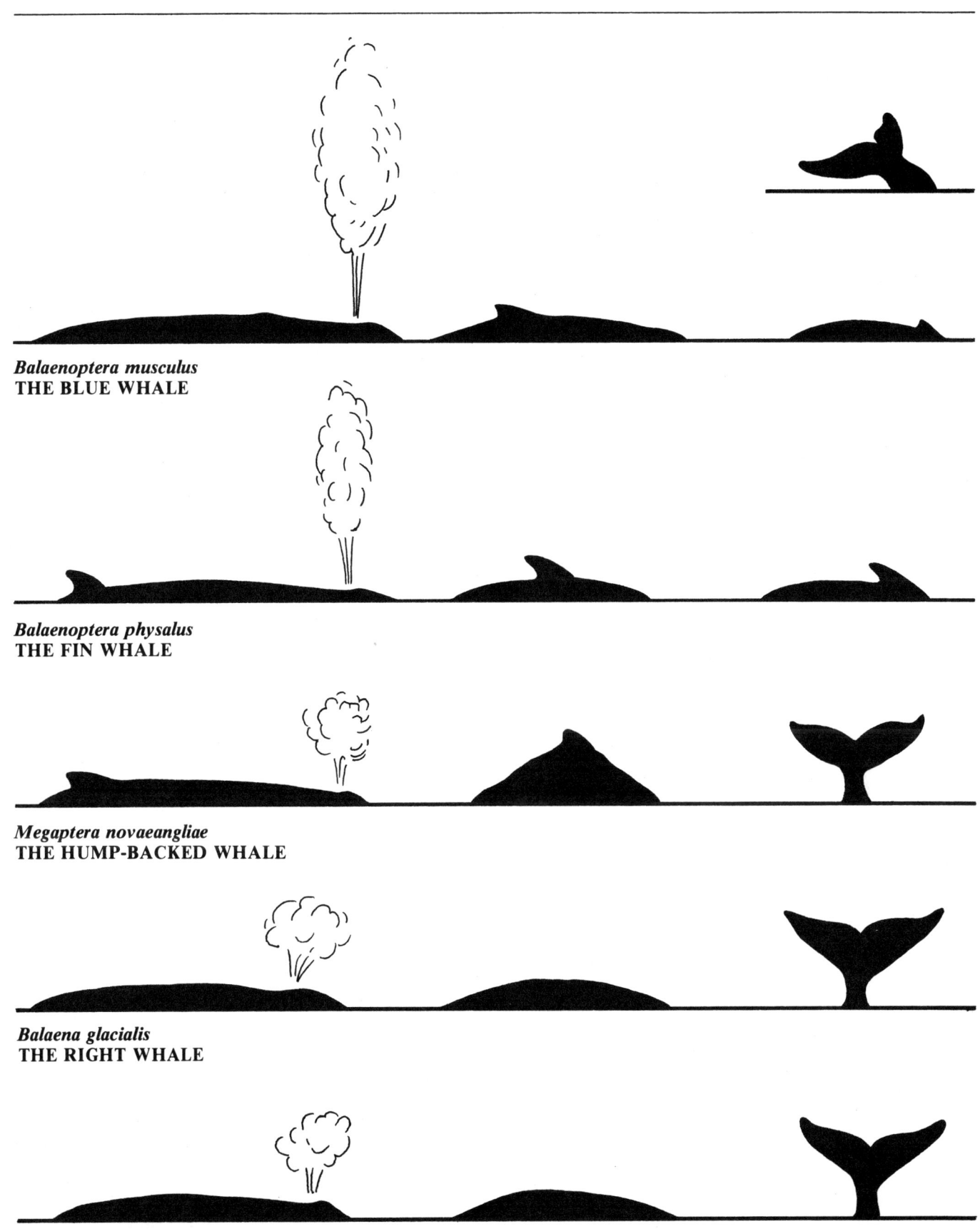

Balaenoptera musculus
THE BLUE WHALE

Balaenoptera physalus
THE FIN WHALE

Megaptera novaeangliae
THE HUMP-BACKED WHALE

Balaena glacialis
THE RIGHT WHALE

Balaena mysticetus
THE BOWHEAD WHALE

Drawn from Leatherwood et alii.

THREE TYPES OF LARGE WHALES

The following diagrams show the body outline and skeleton of three types of large whales.

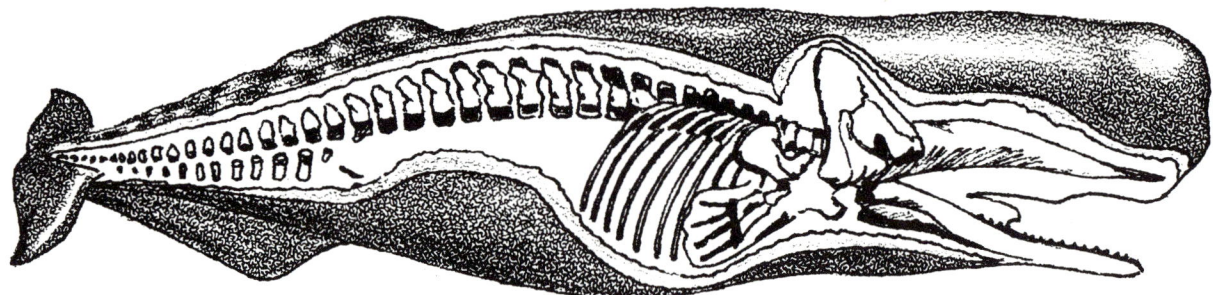

Diagram of the skeleton of the largest of the toothed whales, the great sperm whale, *Physeter macrocephalus* (Odontoceti: Physeteridae). The head is not typical of the other toothed whales, for it contains a great basin on the upper side of the skull which contains the famous "case" and its spermaceti oil.

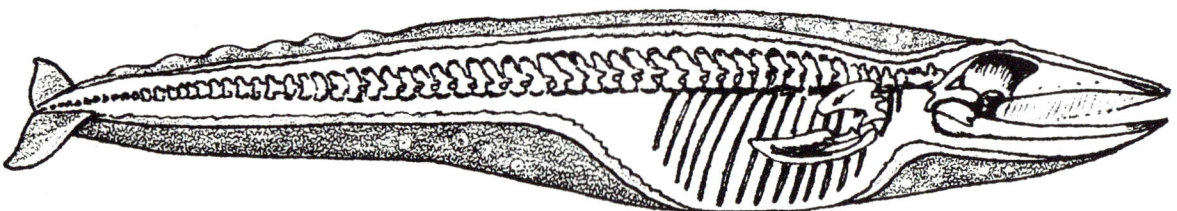

Diagram of the skeleton of the gray whale, *Eschrichtius robustus* (Mysticeti: Eschrichtiidae). The upper jaws of the these whales support the whalebone or baleen plates suspended beneath them. The upper jaws in this family are not arched as much as in the family of the Right Whales (Balaenidae).

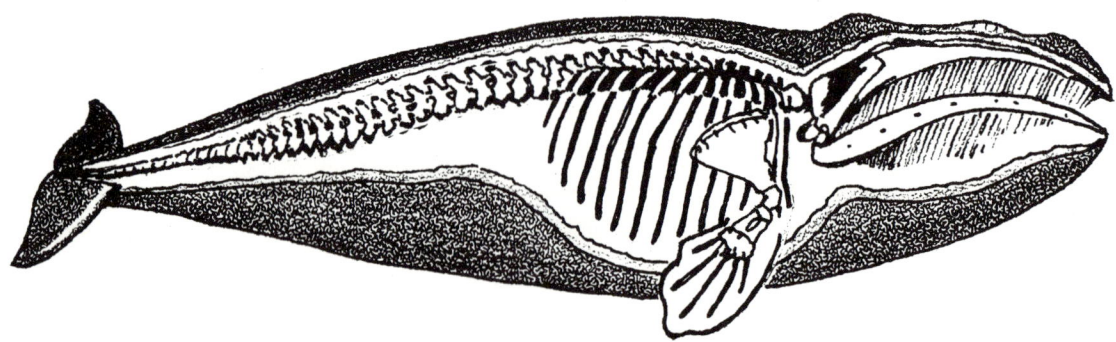

Diagram of the skeleton of a right whale, *Balaena* species (Mysticeti: Balaenidae). The arch of the upper jaws is higher than in the rorquals or fin-backed whales; this arching of the jaws provides space for the longer whalebone or baleen blades of the right whales.

THE GRAY WHALE FAMILY
Family *ESCHRICHTIIDAE* Ellerman and Morrison-Scott, 1951

The gray whale family contains a single species of moderate size which is limited to the North Pacific Ocean. This family has no fin on the back (although 8 or 10 low humps are present) and the longitudinal grooves on the throat usually number between two and four. The head is only moderately large for whalebone whales and the rostrum and snout are deeper than those of most other whalebone whales. The mouth is located midway between the top and the bottom of the head and the lips are arched with the curvature increasing toward the back. The mouth contains the usual two rows of baleen plates suspended from the upper jaw, but they are shorter and less numerous than in other whalebone whales. These baleen plates will usually number between 130 and 180 on each side and will reach a maximum length of about 20 inches (50.8 cm.).

Although there is only one living species in this family, there is evidence that similar whales inhabited the North Atlantic Ocean in fairly recent times.

The members of this family are known from the Pleistocene Epoch and the Holocene (Recent) Epoch.

This family includes the single living genus listed below.

Eschrichtius Gray, 1864 (1 species)

THE GRAY WHALES . . . . See page 271

THE GRAY WHALES
Genus *ESCHRICHTIUS* Gray, 1864

The characteristics of this genus are merged with those of the family and the species.

Most scholars regard the gray whales as the most primitive of the whalebone whales (*Mysticeti*). These opinions are based upon various anatomical peculiarities including freely-movable cervical vertebrae, large pelvic (innominate) bones, long nasal bones, more hair than in other species, and other features. The gray whales have but four fingers within their flipper. The first finger (pollex or thumb) disappeared in ancient times leaving only the four true fingers to support the flipper.

The name of this family and this genus honors Dr. Daniel Frederick Eschricht (1798-1863), a Danish biologist and physician of the 19th century and a professor of zoology at Copenhagen.

This genus is known from the Pleistocene (Glacial) Epoch to the Holocene (Recent) Epoch.

Studies of these whales by various scholars indicate that several names of species appearing in older books are really duplicate names or synonyms of other previously named species. The following list indicates the older names and the more correct and current names of these species.

Old Name		Name Currently In Use
Genus *Rhachianectes*	is now	Genus *Eschrichtius*
Eschrichtius gibbosus	is now	*Eschrichtius robustus*
Eschrichtius glaucus	is now	*Eschrichtius robustus*
Rhachianectes glaucus	is now	*Eschrichtius robustus*

This genus includes the single living species listed below.

Eschrichtius robustus (Lilljeborg, 1861)

THE GRAY WHALE . . . . See page 272

271

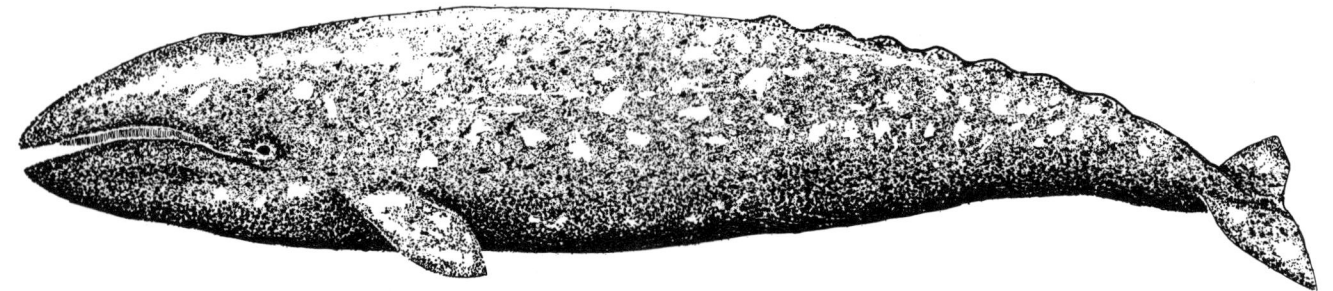

THE GRAY WHALE
Also known as the California Gray Whale
Eschrichtius robustus (Lilljeborg, 1861)

Identifying Features. This is a large whalebone whale, without a dorsal fin, with a curved rostrum, usually with two long grooves on the throat, and usually covered with many scars. The trailing edge of the tail is usually ragged.

Size and Shape. In its anatomical features, this species occupies a position midway between the right whales (*Balaenidae*) and the rorquals or fin-backed whales (*Balaenopteridae*).

This whalebone whale has a body which is largest at the flippers, is rather fat in contours, and tapers quite uniformly toward the tail. This is a large species and may measure as much as 15 meters (49.2 ft.) in length. The females are larger than the males and may occasionally reach about 15 meters (49.2 ft.); the males will usually measure about 13 meters (42.65 feet) or less in length. They will usually weigh between about 25 to 35 tons (22,679.6 to 31,751.4 kg.).

Color. The color of the body varies but is usually a dark gray or bluish gray above and lighter below. The surface of the body is covered with many scars from barnacles, bites, and scratches from various sources. The body is lighter beneath and is flecked with light gray or white spots, both above and below. Individuals of this species which were pure white in color have been reported from near St. Lawrence Island in the Bering Sea.

Distribution. The gray whales inhabit the shallow, coastal waters of the North Pacific Ocean only. However, its population is divided into two groups, one in the eastern Pacific Ocean and another in the western Pacific Ocean. The gray whales on the eastern or American side travel between the Chukchi Sea and the Beaufort Sea in the Arctic Ocean southward through the Bering Sea to the Gulf of California and the islands nearby.

The gray whales on the western or Asiatic side travel between the Sea of Okhotsk, the Kamchatka Peninsula and the Aleutian Islands southward to Korea and Japan. These whales are now very scarce.

It should be mentioned here that a population of gray whale formerly occurred in the North Atlantic Ocean. Fossils from Britain, Holland, and Sweden indicate that it was alive in historic times, possibly as late as 1725 A.D. This group was doubtless exterminated by over-hunting.

Migration. The gray whales on the eastern or American side of the North Pacific Ocean migrate each year between the Arctic Ocean and the sub-tropical waters of the western coast of Baja California. They start northward sometime between February and May, usually in late March or the beginning of April. They travel up the coastline of California, Oregon, and Washington to Vancouver Island, at which point some turn northwestward and cut across the Gulf of Alaska to the Aleutian Islands. It is interesting to note that they go through the western side of the Aleutian Islands near 180° W. Longitude and feed on the western or Siberian side of the Bering Sea; some whales proceed onward into the Arctic Ocean where they feed in the Chukchi Sea and the western side of the Beaufort Sea north of Alaska.

The southward migration usually begins in late September or October and extends as late as February. Going southward, many whales are known to leave the Bering Sea through Unimak Pass; they then turn eastward and usually pass southward along the coasts of Washington and Oregon in late autumn (late November, December and January) and reach the western coast of Baja California between January and March; they do not go south of 20° N.L. In this tropical latitude, they mate and give birth to their young, frequently in "Scammon's Lagoon" (28° N.L.). It should be remembered that these whales do not travel as a single group and that the migration, mating, and calving extends over many weeks.

In northern California, they have been observed going south as early as September and going northward as late as August.

Each northward or southward migration is a distance of about 8,000 kilometers (5,000 miles).

The gray whales on the western or Asiatic side of the North Pacific Ocean travel north and south from the Sea of Okhotsk, the Aleutian Islands, and the Bering Sea in the north to southern Japan and southern Korea in the south. From March to May they go northward in small groups along the western side of Japan following the Korean coastline. It is interesting to note at this point that these whales also used to travel along the eastern side of Japan, but were doubtless killed off in this area. They begin their northward migration from southern Korea about the middle of March and have all left this area by the middle of May; they arrive at their northern feeding ground in May and June.

They begin their southward journey from the Sea of Okhotsk, the Aleutian Islands, and the Bering Sea in October and pass southward along the coast of Korea between November and January. These whales have been observed to travel southward in three groups:

1. *the pregnant females* arrive in southern Korea between the end of November and the middle of January;
2. *other females plus many males,* usually in groups of several females plus 20 to 30 males, arrive between early December and the middle of January; and
3. *the immature males* linger on the feeding grounds, come south to avoid the cold, and return northward again between March and May to their feeding ground.

Fins and Flippers. Like the right whales (*Balaenidae*), the gray whale has no dorsal fin on its back, although there are usually 10 (occasionally 7 to 15) uneven folds of skin or "knuckles" along the midline of the posterior third of the back; other than these folds of skin, there are no other keels on the surface of the body.

The flippers are oval in shape and somewhat wider than in most whales. They measure about 17 or 18 per cent of the body length and in a 15 meter (49 ft.) whale would measure about 2.6 meters (8.5 ft.) in length. Most flippers will measure about .76 meters (2.5 ft.) in width and about 6.5 feet in length. Although paddle-shaped in outline, they terminate distally in a small, pointed tip.

The tail flukes of this whale are very large and from side to side measure almost one-fourth of the body length; typically they will measure about 3 meters (10 ft.) in length (left to right) and about .75 meters (30 in.) in width. The flukes are deeply scalloped, have a wavy, thick posterior margin and present a deep notch where they join at the midline. They are grayish in color both above and below.

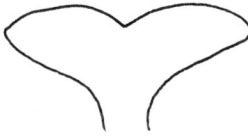

Diagram of the tail flukes of the gray whale, *Eschrichtius,* showing the deep medial notch.

Drawn from Andrews.

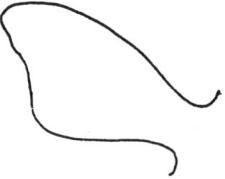

Diagram of the flipper of the gray whale, *Eschrichtius,* (left side, dorsal view).

Drawn from Andrews.

Baleen. The head of this whale is quite long and slender. The snout is high, rigid, narrow, and blunt in front. The profile of the head curves uniformly from the front to the nostrils atop the head; this curvature of the upper jaw is less than in the right whales (*Balaenidae*) and more than in the rorquals (*Balaenopteridae*). The width of the upper jaw is also wider

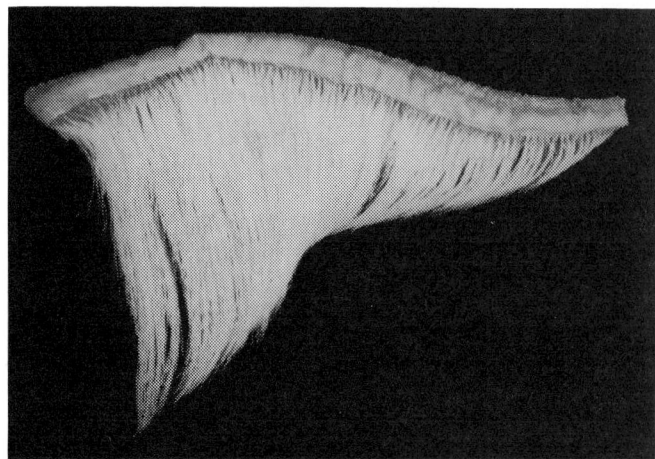

Photo of the whalebone blades (baleen) of the left side of the gray whale, *Eschrichtius robustus,* in medial view.

Photo of the whalebone blades (baleen) of the left side of the gray whale, *Eschrichtius robustus,* in lateral view.

Ore. Inst. Mar. Biol.

than in the *Balaenidae* and narrower than in the *Balaenopteridae*.

The arching upper jaw supports a series of yellowish-white baleen plates numbering from about 130 to 180 on each side of the upper jaw and measuring as much as 40 to 50 cm. (16 to 20 in.) in length and as much as 25 cm. in width. These baleen plates are very short at the front of the mouth, increase in length to a point just behind the midpoint of the jaws, and thereafter become gradually shorter toward the back of the jaws. They are thin and flat, and are widest where they attach to the upper jaws. They become narrower as they descend downward and finally terminate in a point at their lower extremity. Their outer edge is quite smooth and continuous, while their inner edge is frayed out into a fringe of coarse, rigid bristles which extends for its entire length. The plates on the right side of the mouth seem to wear faster than those on the left side.

Skeletal Notes. The skull of the gray whale has a curved dorsal profile when viewed from the side due to the great, long, narrow, curving rostrum which extends forward to support the whalebone blades.

The lower jaws are long, slender, and heavy and are bowed outward and slightly downward at their centers; they con-

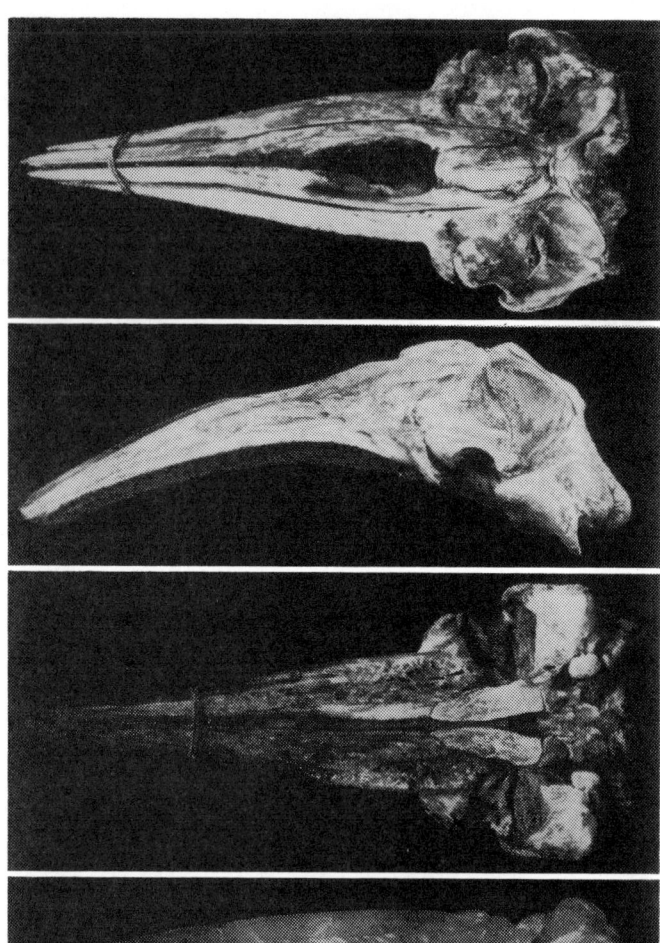

The skull and lower jaw of the Gray Whale, *Eschrichtius robustus*. Above photos from top to bottom: the skull in dorsal view; the skull in lateral view; the skull in ventral view; and the lower jaw bone.

Photos by Nishiwaki and Kasuya.

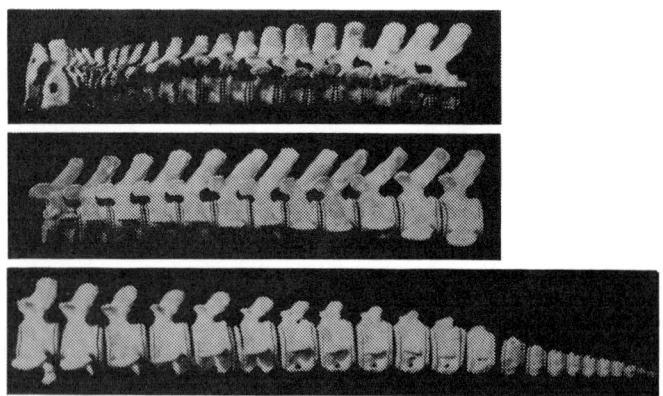

Photo of the vertebral column of a gray whale, *Eschrichtius robustus* (Mysticeti: Eschrichtiidae), in lateral view.

First row: 7 cervical and 14 thoracic or dorsal vertebrae.

Second row: 12 lumbar vertebrae (including the sacral vertebrae).

Third row: 23 caudal vertebrae with a few chevron bones showing below.

Photos by Nishiwaki and Kasuya.

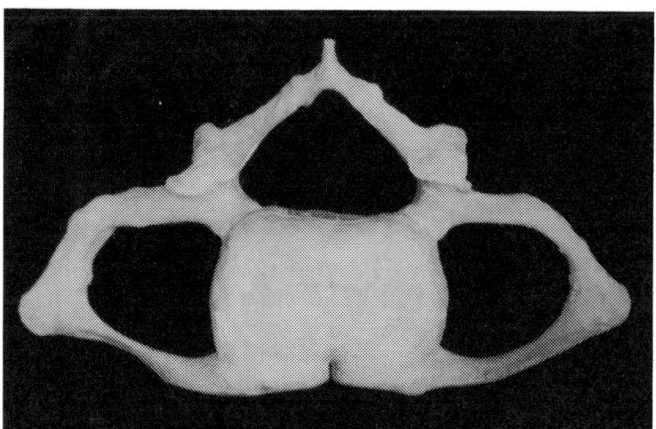

Photo of a cervical vertebra of the gray whale, *Eschrichtius robustus*.

Ore. Inst. Mar. Biol.

verge at the front of the mouth, but they are not fused where they meet at the mandibular symphysis in the front of the lower jaw. These lower jaw bones lack the coronoid process which extends upward at the proximal end of the mandible.

In the gray whales, all seven bones of the neck are separate and movable. The vertebrae are usually distributed approximately as follows: C 7 + D 14 + L 12 + Ca 23 = 56.

The neural spines on top of the dorsal vertebrae point in different directions; dorsal spines 1 to 6 usually incline forward, spines 7, 8, and 9 are directed vertically, and spines from 10 to 14 are inclined backward. The remaining spines of the lumbar and caudal vertebrae are all inclined backward. The ribs number 14 in all. Nos. 1 and 2 have single heads; nos. 3 through 7 have 2 heads each; nos. 8 through 14 have a single head; and the 14th rib is relatively larger than in other species. The sternum is strong in this species, but its form and shape vary widely. Two rudimentary pelvic or innominate bones, each composed of three bones (ilium, pubis, ischium) measure about 500 mm. (19.7 in.) in length; they represent the evolutionary remnants of the pelvis of their ancestors. The gray whales have but four fingers, since they lack the first digit. The bones of the fingers (phalanges) are distributed approximately as follows: II (3), III (3), IV (4), V (1).

The lower jaw extends very slightly beyond the upper jaw and bears within a narrow, thick tongue which is a gray color and salmon pink toward the rear. The palate in the roof of the mouth is white in color.

In a specimen which might weigh between about 10,000 to 20,000 kg., the brain might weigh between about 4,000 to 4,500 grams.

Other Anatomical Notes. When the head is viewed from the side, the mouth will be seen to bisect the head extending from the tip of the snout backward to the eye.

In this species, the eye is placed higher on the head than in other baleen whales. The iris is dark brown and is encircled by a narrow, white-colored ring. The upper eyelid is long and contains two wrinkles which, when joined with the wrinkles from the lower eyelid, form a circle around the eye.

The external opening of the ear (auditory meatus) has a diameter slightly smaller than a pencil and lies about 50 to 60 cm. (20 to 24 in.) behind the eye and slightly below it.

The nostrils or blowholes open in a shallow depression located on top of the head just behind the highest point and just anterior to the eyes. They are two in number, measure about 20 cm. (8 in.) in length, are widest in front, are contracted in the middle, and are narrower at the back. They lie side by side, but are closer in front than in the back; in front, they are separated by about 7 cm. (3 in.) and at the back by a distance of about 21 cm. (8 in.).

Among the whalebone whales, the gray whales have more sensory hairs scattered over their head than any other species. These hairs are always located forward of the blowhole and measure about 2 to 3 cm. (1 in.) in length. As many as 60 hairs have been counted on the head, distributed in a median row and three longitudinal rows on each side. About 120 hairs have been counted on the lower jaw in this species, distributed in three irregular rows on each side. They may reach as much as 40 mm. (1.5 in.) in length.

It is usual for the gray whales to have two longitudinal furrows on the throat; however, occasionally individuals will exhibit three or even four such grooves. These grooves begin about a meter behind the tip of the lower jaw and extend backward for a distance of 100 to 190 cm. (39 to 75 in.). They measure about 5 cm. (2 in.) in depth and about 5 cm. in width.

Food. The food of the gray whale comes from two areas. Like other baleen whales, they feed upon amphipods of various species in their northern habitat, together with sardines and other surface fishes, herring eggs, and other miscellaneous items in the plankton. In addition, gray whales are known to scoop up material from the bottom, particularly in the lower latitudes of their range. At these times, they ingest kelp and other algae, bottom forms of various sorts, mud, and small stones; of this lot, the stones are often found in their stomachs and the entire content of their alimentary tract is discolored by the algae. Feeding is carried on almost exclusively in Arctic waters and is normally suspended during their migrations and during their stay in the southern latitudes; some exceptions have been noted in which female whales have fed upon schooling fish off California by rising vertically beneath the school.

Swimming and Diving. Because the gray whale is a coastal species, its swimming and diving habits are suited to shallower water. It is a comparatively slow swimmer, usually travelling at a speed of 3 or 4 knots; however, when attempting to flee, it may attain a speed of 7 or 8 knots. Normally, this whale will take a series of 3 to 5 shallow dives to a depth of about 30 meters (98.4 ft.), each lasting about 3 to 4 minutes. Deep dives will often follow shallow dives; at these times the whale may descend about 100 meters (328 ft.) and remain beneath the surface for a period of 17 or 18 minutes. The lower limit to which this whale can descend is about 600 meters (1968.6 ft.). It is possible to predict the type of dive in which the whale is engaged by watching its tail flukes: preceeding deep dives, the tail will be raised above the surface of the water; while on shallow dives, the tail remains below the water's surface. These whales do not curve the back in diving as the rorquals do, but maintain a fairly straight body when swimming and diving. The spout of this whale is directed vertically upward and then spreads outward. It will rise to a height of 3 to 4 meters (9.8 to 13.1 ft.) or more and then slowly drift away with the wind. The top of the plume will often show a slight division indicating that the blow came from a double blowhole of two nostrils.

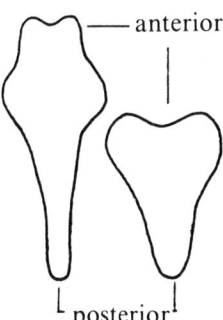

Diagram of two sterna of gray whales, *Eschrichtius,* showing variations in size and shape.

Drawn from Andrews.

Reproduction. The gray whales are presumed to mate once every two or three years in their southern breeding ground between late November or early December and February or March. Following the mating season, the females slowly increase their weight by about 25 per cent during a gestation period of about 12 to 13 months. The young, which are born in January and February, will measure between 3.6 and 5.5 meters (11.8 to 18 ft.) at birth. The young are nursed for 6 to 8 months and are weaned possibly in August at a length of about 7.5 meters (24.6 ft.). At the end of their first year, the young will measure about 9 meters (29.5 ft.) in length. They are reported to reach sexual maturity at possibly 8 years or less at which time they will measure more than 10 or 11 meters (33 to 36 ft.) in length. Their life span is judged to approach about 50 years.

Abundance. The gray whale was hunted to the verge of extinction, but fortunately did not disappear. The stock in the eastern North Pacific Ocean has increased to the point where it is no longer in danger. In the western North Pacific Ocean, these whales are very scarce and their future may still be in doubt.

Economic Importance. Native people who occupied the shoreline along the migration routes of the gray whales hunted this whale for its flesh. In addition to the Koreans and the Japanese, the Indians of the western coasts of North America have hunted this whale from very ancient times. Of these, the most vigorous, aggressive, and daring were doubtless the Makah Indians, who inhabited the Olympic Peninsula in northwestern Washington.

The blubber of the gray whales is a pinkish to reddish color and will measure between 15 and 40 cm. (6 and 15 in.) in thickness. The blubber and the carcass of this whale would produce between 25 and 40 barrels of oil; the female whale, being larger than the male, would usually produce about 40 barrels of oil.

Miscellaneous. Parasites infest the bodies of all large whales, including this species. These include most commonly an amphipod crustacean (*Cyamus scammoni* Dall) and a barnacle (*Cryptolepas rhachianecti* Dall). The barnacles are scattered over much of the body, particularly on the upper and lateral surfaces, and leave behind a circular scar which heals as a whitish spot. The amphipods cluster about the blowholes, the anus, the genital area, and along the trailing edges of the flippers and the flukes.

The gray whales are related to the extinct Cetotheridae of the Oligocene, Miocene, and Pliocene Epochs.

THE RORQUAL OR TRUE FIN-BACKED
WHALE FAMILY
Family *BALAENOPTERIDAE* Gray, 1864

The fin-backed whale family contains six species which are of medium or large size and which inhabit the cooler temperate and polar waters of both the northern and southern hemispheres.

This family is most easily recognized by the presence of a triangular dorsal fin located on the back toward the tail. Its members possess the baleen or whalebone plates within the mouth which may number as many as 300 plates hanging downward from each side of the upper jaw; these plates range in length from about six or eight inches to more than three feet. The flippers in this family are more slender and tapering than those of the right whales (*Balaenidae*) and are exceedingly long and slender in the hump-backed whales. All six species within this family have but four fingers within their flippers; the middle finger is missing. The 7 cervical vertebrae are all separate in all 6 members of this family. This family includes the great blue whale which is the world's largest animal.

Fossil members of this family have been found in North America from the Upper Miocene Epoch and the Holocene (Recent) Epoch; in Europe they are known from the Pliocene Epoch.

This family was formerly divided into three genera, however, most scholars today divide this family into the two genera listed below.

THE RORQUALS OR TRUE FIN-BACKED WHALES
Genus *BALAENOPTERA* Lacepede, 1804

Of the six living species of fin-backed whales, five species are included within this genus; the sixth species, the hump-backed whale (*Megaptera*) has been separated from the true fin-backed whales (*Balaenoptera*) because of its body shape and proportions and because of its great, long flippers. The fin-backed whales have pectoral fins which are shorter and smoother than those of the hump-backed whales. In addition, the pectoral fins of the five fin-backed species are quite slender in outline and taper at their extremities. The true fin-backed whales have comparatively slender bodies, while the hump-backed whale is more robust and stocky in form.

The fin-backed whales are cosmopolitan in distribution and, with the exception of Bryde's whale (*B. edeni*), are found in the cooler waters of all hemispheres.

The blue whale has often been listed as *Sibbaldus musculus* (Linnaeus, 1758), but, today, most scholars place it in the Genus *Balaenoptera* with the other fin-backed species.

This genus is known from the late Miocene Epoch and the Lower Pliocene Epoch to the Pleistocene (Glacial) Epoch in North America and from the Middle Pliocene Epoch in Europe.

Studies of these whales by various scholars indicate that several names of species appearing in older books are really duplicate names or synonyms of other previously named species. The following list indicates the older names and the more correct and current names of these species.

Old Name		Name Currently In Use
Genus *Sibbaldus*	is now	Genus *Balaenoptera*
Balaenoptera arctica	is now	*Balaenoptera borealis*
Balaenoptera australis	is now	*Balaenoptera physalus*
Balaenoptera bonaerensis	is now	*Balaenoptera acutorostrata*
Balaenoptera brydei	is now	*Balaenoptera edeni*
Balaenoptera davidsoni	is now	*Balaenoptera acutorostrata*
Balaenoptera huttoni	is now	*Balaenoptera acutorostrata*
Balaenoptera patachonica	is now	*Balaenoptera physalus*
Balaenoptera robusta	is now	*Eschrichtius robustus*
Balaenoptera rorqual	is now	*Balaenoptera physalus*
Rorqualis borealis	is now	*Balaenoptera musculus*

This genus is usually divided into the five living species listed below.

Chart to Help Identify
The Five Species of Fin-backed Whales or Rorquals
Genus _Balaenoptera_

The Species of _Balaenoptera_	Color	Head and Ridges on Head	Dorsal Fin	Blow or Spout	Diving	May Approach Ships
The Lesser Rorqual or Minke Whale _B. acutorostrata_	Back is dark. Flipper with white band above, white below. Right upper jaw sometimes whitish. Light chevron on back.	Head is flat, narrow, pointed, triangular; 1 ridge on top.	Fin is high and falcate; visible with blow.	Low, indistinct, inconspicuous.	Tail never visible. Tailstock arched when diving. Submerges quietly.	Occasionally
The Sei Whale _B. borealis_	Uniformly dark; shiny, metalic luster.	Head is flat, pointed; 1 ridge on top.	Fin is large, falcate and set 2/3 distance to tail; visible with blow. Fin and head are visible almost simultaneously. Front has 30° angle.	Inverted cone; 3 meters high.	Dives w/o a roll. Sinks quietly. Tail never visible.	No
The Bryde's Whale _B. edeni_	Back is dark. White below is sometimes visible.	Head is flat, pointed; 3 ridges on top.	Fin is small, sharply pointed, with ragged trailing edge. Front has 70° angle.	Single, tall, thin, vertical; 4 meters high.	Rolls body high in water when diving; arches tailstock.	Occasionally
The Blue Whale _B. musculus_	Back is mottled blue. No chevron on back.	Head is broad, flat, somewhat U-shaped; 1 ridge on top.	Fin is small, low, triangular to falcate; set 3/4 distance to tail; is visible long after blow; may be followed by a fleeting glimpse of tail.	Single, vertical, slender; 9 to 12 meters high (29.5 to 39.4 ft.).	Makes a low roll when diving; often raises tail before diving.	Not usually
The Fin Whale _B. physalus_	Back is gray w/o many scars. Chevron on back. Right lower lip is whitish. Upward stripes behind eye.	Head is flat, narrow, V-shaped; 1 ridge on top.	Fin is larger; set 2/3 distance to tail; visible after blow; front has 40-50° angle.	Single, vertical, narrow, inverted, cone-shaped; first feature to be seen; 4 to 6 meters high (13-19.7 ft.).	Rolls high out of water. Flukes rarely shown when diving.	Not usually

277

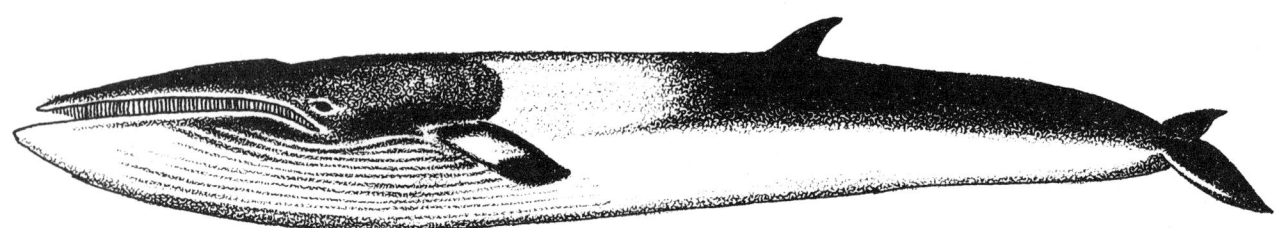

THE LESSER RORQUAL OR MINKE WHALE
Also known as The Little Piked Whale
and The Sharp-headed Finner Whale
Balaenoptera acutorostrata Lacepede, 1804

Identifying Features. The lesser rorqual is the smallest of the rorquals (*Balaenopteridae*) and always measures less than 10 meters (33 ft.) in length. It has a slender body, a pointed rostrum, a single ridge atop the head, and usually a white band across the top of each flipper.

Size and Shape. The body of this whale is slender and spindle-shaped and terminates anteriorly in a rostrum which is slender, tapering, and pointed. The snout is triangular in outline when viewed from above and is marked on its upper surface with a single median ridge. Most individuals when fully grown will measure between about 8 meters and 9.5 meters (26.2 and 31.1 ft.) in length. Large individuals are reported to weigh about 10,000 kilograms (11 tons). The throat contains from 50 to 70 longitudinal grooves which extend from the chin backward onto the chest, but they do not reach the region of the navel.

Color. The color of the body on the upper surface is variously described as bluish gray, brownish gray, and grayish black; the body is lighter on the sides and almost white on the belly and on the lower sides of the flippers and flukes. The whales in the North Pacific Ocean (northern minke whale) are marked with a wide, diagonal, white band across the middle of the upper side of the flippers; this band is usually absent in those whales (southern minke whale) which live in the southern hemisphere. The whales of this species have a lighter, chevron-shaped marking on the back and also a lighter area on the back just forward of the dorsal fin; these marks vary between individuals and also between geographical regions. Some individuals have the anterior half of the upper lip margined by white or whitish hues. On some whales there are "bracket marks" of a light gray color located in a vertical position just above and slightly to the rear of the base of the flipper; they look somewhat like large gill slits. Vague lighter color areas extend upward from the belly onto the sides in two areas, one above and behind the flipper and another below and forward of the dorsal fin.

Distribution. The lesser rorqual is worldwide in all oceans from the Arctic to the Antarctic. In the northern hemisphere, this species seems to prefer waters over the continental shelf. It will invade the polar regions and is often seen occupying areas of open water within the polar ice. It will enter harbors and rivers and will occasionally approach ships. It is occasionally stranded on both coasts of the United States including the Caribbean Sea and the Gulf of Mexico. It is uncommon in the tropics.

This whale is a variable species and has been described under several names. Some biologists recognize the following sub-species:

1. *B. acutorostrata acutorostrata* Lacepede, 1804.
   This is the form from the North Atlantic Ocean which is reported to be slightly larger than the other forms; the baleen plates are more numerous, and the white band on the flippers is narrower.
2. *B. acutorostrata bonaerensis* Burmeister, 1867.
   This sub-species inhabits the southern hemisphere. The flippers lack the white band and are gray in color.
3. *B. acutorostrata davidsoni* Scammon, 1872.
   This sub-species inhabits the North Pacific Ocean. In this form, the snout is reported to be shorter and the dorsal fin is reported to be higher and placed farther back on the body.
4. *B. acutorostrata thamaha* Deraniyagala, 1963.
   This sub-species is described from the area of Sri Lanka (Ceylon). It may not be sufficiently different to merit recognition.

Migration. These whales gather into groups and travel northward and southward with the seasons, but they do not all participate and may therefore be found in almost any latitude at any season of the year.

Fins and Flippers. The dorsal fin is located at a point two-thirds of the body length behind the head. It is falcate or sickle-shaped, convex on its anterior margin, and concave on its posterior margin. The flippers are small, narrow, and pointed; their margins are quite straight and give the flipper a slender, triangular aspect. The tail flukes are large, have a fairly straight posterior margin, are deeply notched where they meet at the midline, and are supported by dorsal and ventral median keels or crest which extend backward from the tail stock.

Photo of the head of the lesser rorqual or minke whale, *Balaenoptera acutorostrata,* **taken at Waikane, New Zealand.**

Alan N. Baker.

From: "Whales and Dolphins of New Zealand and Australia" by A.N. Baker. Victoria University Press, Wellington, 1983. Courtesy A.N. Baker.

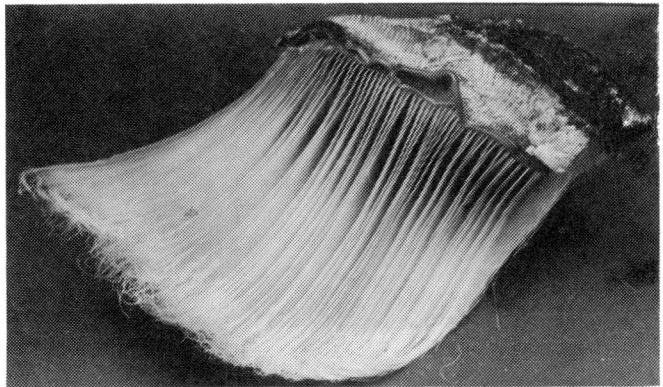

A photo of the dried whalebone blades or baleen of the lesser rorqual or Minke whale, *Balaenoptera acutorostrata,* **in external view.**

Photo by Graybill.

Baleen. The baleen plates number between 230 and 360 in each side of the upper jaw. They are small in size and reach a maximum length of about 35 cm. (13+ in.) and as much as 12 cm. (4.7 in.) in width. The plates in the back of the mouth are dark in color, while those at the front and center are usually yellowish white or pure white in color.

Skeletal Notes. The bones of the neck in this species are all separate and distinct. The vertebrae are distributed approximately as follows: C 7 + D 11 + L 12-13 + Ca 18-20 = 48-50. Some scholars place the count of the caudal vertebrae at 17 to 19. The sternum is cross-shaped and comparatively large. There are 11 pairs of ribs of which only the 1st pair articulates with the sternum; of these, the 1st rib is the shortest and the 4th or 5th rib is the longest, exceeding 66 cm. (26 in.) in length. The chevron bones below the caudal vertebrae are usually 9 or 10 (occasionally 8) in number. The bones of the fingers are distributed approximately as follows: I (3-5), II (6-9), IV (5-8), V (3-4). The third finger is missing.

Other Anatomical Notes. The eyes are located near the corner of the mouth and anterior to the blowhole. Sensory hairs occur on the front of the lower jaw and along the margins of the upper and lower lips. In small specimens, the blubber of the tail stock will measure about 2.5 inches in thickness. The uterus has two horns. The caecum is present.

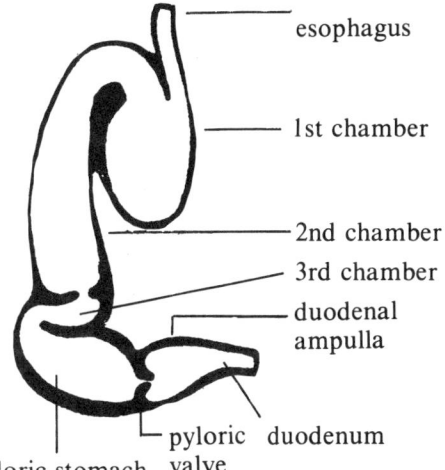

Diagram of the stomach of a rorqual or true fin-backed whale, *Balaenoptera* **species (Mysticeti: Balaenopteridae).**

From: Gihr, M. and Pilleri, Gregorio — Investigations On The Cetacea. 1969. 1:15-65 (fig. 22A).

Food. This small whale feeds upon a wide variety of animals, including fishes, squid, krill, and other forms in the plankton. In the North Atlantic Ocean, it feeds in part upon capelin (*Osmeridae: Mallotus villosus*); while in the North Pacific Ocean, its food includes anchovies (*Engraulidae*). The short baleen plates suggest that this whale is adapted to a greater variety of food than whales with longer baleen plates.

Swimming and Diving. These whales tend to be more solitary than other baleen species, although schools containing as many as 100 or more individuals are occasionally seen. It likes coastal waters and will also penetrate the ice pack farther than any other baleen whale. They swim at a speed of about 9 to 11 km. per hour (5.5 to 6.8 mi. per hr.); when fleeing, they will swim at a rate of 18.5 to 27 km. per hr. (10 to 15 knots). They take shallow dives lasting from 5 to 7 minutes and when surfacing will spout to a height of about 2 meters (6.5 ft.). This spout is too small to be of much use in the identification of this species. These whales will jump from the water and reenter it without splashing or they will fall flat upon the surface with an accompanying splash. They will stick their heads vertically above the water, both when surrounded by pack ice and when in open water. They show a curiosity about boats and will approach them at fairly close range.

Reproduction. Breeding in this species is less seasonal than in most whales. Although they breed throughout the year, they are most active between January and June (especially between February and April) in the northern hemisphere. The gestation period lasts from 10 to 10.5 months. The young at birth will measure between 2.8 and 3 meters (9.1 to 9.8 ft.) and will be nursed for a period of about 6 months. The young calf will follow its mother for about two years and will reach maturity at about four years of age. The life span of this species probably approaches 50 years.

Abundance. The lesser rorqual is the most common of all the baleen whales. It is being actively hunted and has experienced a reduction in numbers in some areas.

Economic Importance. Formerly, this whale was too small to be hunted, while the larger species were available. However, with the larger whales reduced in numbers and protected in part by various governments, whalers have turned their attention to the hunting of this species in increasing numbers.

Miscellaneous. The name of Minke seems to come from the name of a "whale gunner named Meincke, who misidentified these tiny whales as Blues!"

Above: Photo of the lesser rorqual or Minke whale, *Balaenoptera acutorostrata,* beached at Santa Barbara, California.
Photo by S. Anderson

From: "Whales and Dolphins of New Zealand and Australia" by A.N. Baker. Victoria University Press, Wellington, 1983. Courtesy A.N. Baker.

Right: Photo of the head of the lesser rorqual or Minke whale, *Balaenoptera acutorostrata,* taken at Santa Barbara, California.
Photo by S. Anderson.

From: "Whales and Dolphins of New Zealand and Australia" by A.N. Baker. Victoria University Press, Wellington, 1983. Courtesy A.N. Baker.

Left: Photo showing the open mouth of the lesser rorqual or Minke whale, *Balaenoptera acutorostrata.*
National Museum of New Zealand.

From: "Whales and Dolphins of New Zealand and Australia" by A.N. Baker. Victoria University Press, Wellington, 1983. Courtesy A.N. Baker.

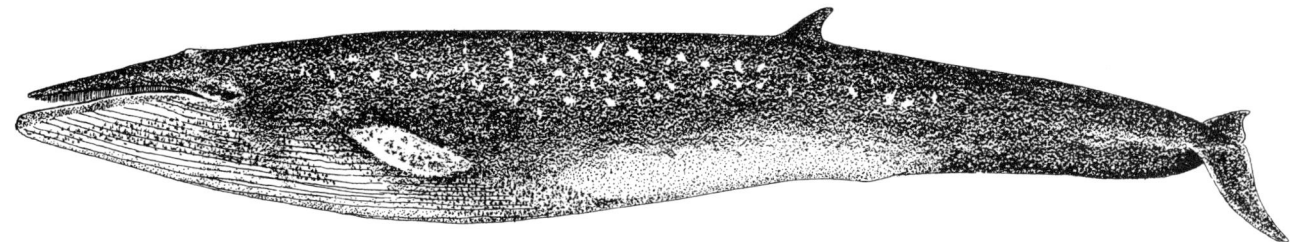

THE SEI WHALE
Also known as Rudolphi's Rorqual, The Pollock Whale,
and Sejhval (Norwegian)
Balaenoptera borealis Lesson, 1828

Identifying Features. This whale cannot be easily distinguished in the water from the Fin Whale (*B. physalus*) and Bryde's Whale (*B. edeni*). Next to the Lesser Rorqual (*B. acutorostrata*), this is the smallest of the rorquals. It has a very small flipper, a single central ridge on the top of a flat head and black whalebone plates with white fringes. *B. edeni* has 3 ridges on the head, one is median and two smaller ridges are lateral. The back side of the flippers and the lower side of the flukes or caudal fin are gray in color. Both of the lower lips are gray in color together with the interior of the mouth.

Size and Shape. The body of the sei whale is quite slender and spindle-shaped and, in many features, resembles a miniature fin whale (*B. physalus*). These whales usually measure about 17 to 18 meters (55.7 to 59.0 ft.) in length when fully grown; however, most will measure about 15 meters (49.2 ft.) in length.

The head is flat, slender, and pointed and the mouth is very large. The throat and part of the belly are occupied by a series of longitudinal grooves. These grooves vary in number from about 32 to 62, begin a short distance back from the chin, and terminate midway between the bases of the flippers and the navel.

Color. The color of the back is black, blue gray, or a "galvanized blue-gray," often with a brownish tint due to diatoms; it shades gradually to gray on the sides and finally to white on the belly. The sides are marked with an irregular pattern of spots and scars and the throat and chest display a large, white, arrow-shaped design. The color of the head is the same on both the right and left sides, so that it does not exhibit the asymmetrical patttterns of the Fin Whale or Common Rorqual (*B. physalus*). However, some of the baleen plates which border the right lip may be marked with white.

Distribution. The sei whale is an oceanic species which is worldwide in all temperate seas. It seems to prefer warmer water, to avoid the polar seas, and is not known to venture beyond the drift ice. It seems to avoid the tropical seas, possibly because food is less abundant there.

The Sei Whale varies noticeably between the northern and southern hemisphere; the principal difference is in their size.

Most biologists recognize the following two sub-species.
1. *Balaenoptera borealis borealis* Lesson, 1828.
   This is the smaller sub-species and occupies the northern hemisphere.
2. *Balaenoptera borealis schlegellii* Flower, 1865.
   This is the larger sub-species and occupies the southern hemisphere.

Migration. Sei whales migrate with the seasons from the temperate regions to the cooler sub-arctic feeding grounds. There are two groups or stocks of whales in the North Pacific Ocean, one in the western Pacific Ocean from Japan and Korea northward and the other in the eastern Pacific Ocean from Alaska southward to Mexico. These groups do not mix, although their migration period is similar.

Fins and Flippers. The dorsal fin is comparatively tall, varies in height from 25 to 65 cm. (10 to 25.5 in.), and is located just forward of the anus and the last third of the body; it is the largest fin among all of the rorquals. The dorsal fin is curved on both its anterior and posterior margins and its tip is directed backward.

The flippers are small in size, pointed, and are dark in color beneath.

The flukes of the tail are large and wide and, together from tip to tip, measure just less than one-fourth of the total body length. Their rear margin is nearly straight and they are separated at the midline by a deep notch on their posterior margin.

The tail stock is strongly compressed laterally and bears rather sharp ridges above and below.

Baleen. The baleen plates in this species number from about 220 to about 400 on each side of the upper jaw; they are black, bluish-black, or grayish-black in color and are bordered by a fringe of fine, soft, silky, whitish hair. These baleen blades when held at particular angles to the sunlight may appear first blue and then green; this occurs only in this species. Baleen blades lose some of their color after they have been dried. Some of these plates will reach a length of 80 cm. (31.5 in.); their width varies from one-third to one-half their length. The baleen plates which border the right lip are lighter in color; this is a very unusual departure from a bilateral color pattern.

Skeletal Notes. In an adult whale of this species, the skull will measure from about 2 meters (6.5 ft.) to 3.4 meters (11.15 ft.) or more in length and the mandible or lower jaw will measure almost as long as the skull. All of the cervical vertebrae (neck bones) are separate in this species. The vertebrae are distributed approximately as follows: C 7 + D 13-14 + L 13-15 + C 20-23 = 55-57. The chevron bones number about ten in this species. Of the 13 or more pairs of ribs, only the first pair has two heads. The sternum is somewhat star-shaped and measures about 45 cm. (17.7 in.) in width in a whale which measures about 15.3 meters (50.2 ft.) in length. The pelvic bones measure about 22 cm. (8 in.) in length. The bones of the fingers (phalanges) are distributed approximately as follows: I (3-4), II (5-7), IV (4-6), V (2-3). The third finger is missing.

Other Anatomical Notes. The eye is located just above the corner of the mouth. The eyeball is large, measuring about 30 cm. (12 in.) in circumference, and is bordered above and below by thin eyelids, and finally by 1, 2, or 3 longitudinal creases, grooves, or furrows. The pupil is elliptical in shape and measures about 1.5 cm. (5/8 in.) in length. The iris is a dark brown color.

The opening of the ear is located behind and below the eye at a distance of about 70 cm. (27+ in.). It is oval in shape and is reported to vary in diameter from 5 to 30 mm. (.2 to 1.2 in.).

The blowholes lie at the summit of the head where they extend in a longitudinal direction; they are long, slender, and somewhat slit-like and converge toward their anterior end. At their posterior ends they are separated by about 23 cm. (9 in.) and by about 4 cm. (1.5+ in.) at their anterior ends. The posterior part of the opening is wider than the anterior part. These openings close when the animal dies.

The female genital opening is a long slit lying in the midline of the ventral surface just anterior to the anus. Two mammary slits lie lateral to the opening of the vagina; they measure about 18 cm. (7 in.) in length and are separated by about 18 cm. (7 in.). The teats which lie within the mammary slits measure about 5 cm. (2 in.) in length. The uterus has two horns.

The penis is carried within the body and is located in a groove about 1 meter (3.3 ft.) anterior to the anal opening. Near the posterior end of this groove are a pair of smaller slits which contain the rudimentary mammae of the male.

There are a few sensory hairs around the nostrils, on the upper part of the upper jaw, and on both sides and front of the lower jaws. On the lower jaw, there may be 2 or 3 rows of hairs at the mandibular symphysis. These hairs are whitish in color, are about 7 to 10 mm. in length, and are aligned in vertical rows which are about 4 or 5 cm. apart. The caecum is present.

Food. This whale is a plankton feeder and consumes various crustaceans including copepods and euphausids; in addition, they will eat sardines, squid, and a wide variety of available small schooling fishes.

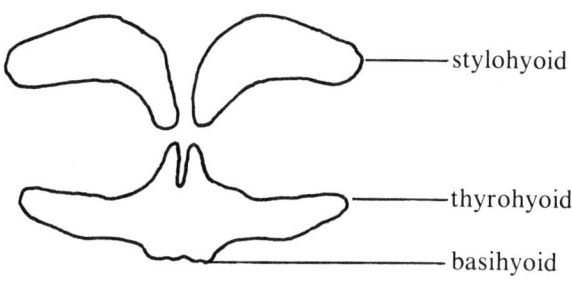

A diagram of the hyoid bones of the sei whale, *B. borealis*. Drawn from Nishiwaki et alii.

Swimming and Diving. The sei whale travels in small groups of less than 5 or 6 individuals and is reported to be the fastest swimmer of the five rorquals. It can apparently reach a speed of about 20 knots for short periods of time. This is a surface dwelling whale and does not dive deeply. When this whale comes to the surface, the snout is first observed followed by the top of the head and then the spout. This spout is a low, cone-shaped column which rises to a height of 3 to 5 meters (9.8 to 16 ft.).

Reproduction. The sei whales mate in warmer latitudes during the autumn and winter months, possibly from September to March, although sporadic mating is reported to take place throughout the year. The gestation period lasts a year or more so that the young are born in the warmer latitudes. The young will measure about 4.5 to 5 meters (15 to 16.5 ft.) at birth, will be nursed for 5 or 6 months, and weaned at a length of about 8 or 9 meters (26.24 to 29.5 ft.).

Abundance. Next to the lesser rorqual (*B. acutorostrata*), the sei whale was probably the most abundant of the baleen whales prior to the reduction in numbers of the larger whales and the subsequent shift in whaling to this species. It has been over-exploited and requires continued and complete protection.

Economic Importance. This whale has the most palatable flesh of the large whales; it is therefore hunted for human food and canned or frozen for use as food in Japan, Norway, and neighboring countries. It yields little oil, but possesses real economic value as a source of protein.

Miscellaneous. The length of life of this species is not well known, but is presumed to be less than other baleen whales. It is difficult to determine the age of these whales because the ear plugs are small. This whale was named "Sei" by the Norwegians after a fish of the same name, because both migrate into Norwegian waters at the same time of the year.

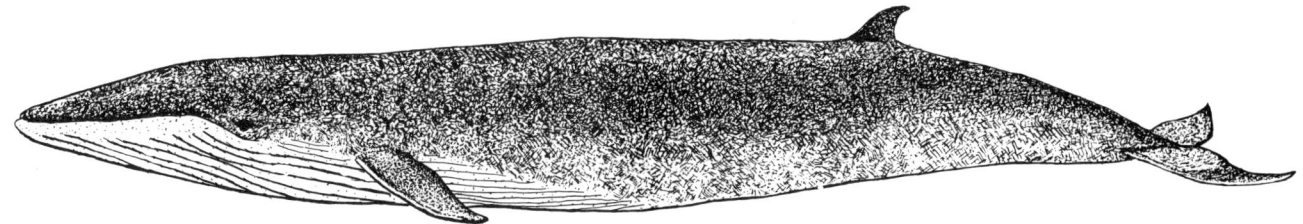

THE BRYDE'S WHALE
Balaenoptera edeni Anderson, 1878

Identifying Features. Bryde's Whale is very difficult to identify at sea because it resembles the Sei whale (*B. borealis*) very closely. It is somewhat smaller and more slender than the sei whale and has 3 longitudinal, parallel ridges atop the head and forward of the blowhole, while the sei whale has but a single median ridge. In addition, Bryde's whale does not have the strange, light-colored area on the lower right lip.

Size and Shape. The body of Bryde's Whale is long, slender, and spindle-shaped. It will reach a length of about 14 meters (46 ft.) which is about 1.5 meters (5 ft.) shorter than the sei whale. Most specimens, however, measure nearer 12 meters (39.4 ft.) in length. The throat and belly contain between 40 and 69 ventral grooves which, in this species, extend backward to the navel or just beyond. Some scholars recognize two groups of *B. edeni;* they describe them as an inshore form and an offshore form. In the offshore form, the skull has a very flat rostrum and the baleen plates are shorter and broader.

Color. Bryde's whale is described as a "dark smokey gray color" or a dark bluish gray. The darker color of the back shades gradually to a lighter gray on the sides and belly. They will occasionally exhibit a light area on the back of the body on each side just forward of the dorsal fin. The back sides of the flippers are gray in color.

Distribution. Bryde's whale prefers warmer water and is never found in the cooler regions of the world. It inhabits the warm temperate and tropical waters of the Pacific, Indian, and Atlantic Oceans between about 40° N.L. and 40° S.L. It apparently does not like waters which are much cooler than 20°C. (68° F.). In the western Pacific Ocean, it does not enter the Sea of Okhotsk, the Sea of Japan, or Korean waters.

Migration. Bryde's whale is not truly a migratory species, although it does gather into groups of as many as 100, at which times they are presumed to be enroute to their feeding or breeding grounds. In Japan, they have been observed moving northward in April and May. Some scholars regard them as being "local whales" which stay within the confines of their warm-water habitat.

Fins and Flippers. The dorsal fin is placed on the midline of the back about one-third or more of the body length forward of the tail. It is curved on both its anterior and posterior margins and terminates in a tip which is pointed backward. It is often notched and frayed on its posterior margin from unknown causes. It will measure about 45 cm. (18 in.) in height.

The flippers, which resemble those of the sei whale, are slender and terminate in a point.

The flukes of the tail are wide, have a nearly straight posterior margin, and have a distinct notch at the midpoint of their posterior border.

Baleen. The baleen plates are a slate gray color and are fringed with stiff, coarse bristles. They are somewhat lighter in color toward the front of the mouth. These plates will number from about 250 to about 370 on each side of the mouth. In a large specimen, the longest of these plates will measure from 40 to 50 cm. (16 to 20 in.) in length and as much as 25 cm. in width.

Skeletal Notes. The vertebrae are distributed approximately as follows: C 7 + D 13 + L 13 + Ca 21-22 = 54-55. The ribs are usually 13 in number, although an occasional individual will possess 14 ribs. The first rib has two heads; this feature is found only in the sei and Bryde's whale and is different from most whales. Only one pair of ribs articulates with the sternum. The two pelvic bones are about 27.5 cm. (10.8 in.) in length and are accompanied by a much smaller rudimentary femur. The bones of the fingers (phalanges) are distributed as follows: I (6), II (5), IV (5), V (3). The third finger is missing.

Other Anatomical Notes. Sensory hairs are present along the outsides of the central head ridge, on the upper jaw, and on both the front and sides of the lower jaw. The uterus has two horns. The caecum is present.

Food. Bryde's whale eats a wide variety of food, including fishes, squid, and plankton.

Swimming and Diving. This species does not often gather into large groups and is most often seen in small groups of 5 or 6 or fewer individuals. The swimming speed of the Bryde's whale is less than that of the sei whale (*B. borealis*), and is therefore more easily captured. When at the surface, they usually take a series of 2 or 3 shallow dives; these are usually followed by a deep dive. Unlike many other whales, Bryde's whale does not lift its tail flukes above the surface of the water at the beginning of its deep dives. Their spout is single and vertical. These whales exhibit some curiosity about ships and will occasionally approach large vessels.

Reproduction. There is little difference between the mating habits of this species and those of the other rorquals (*Balaenopteridae*). They appear to breed in a two-year cycle which has been described as "a year of gestation, half a year of nursing, and half a year of resting." The young will measure about 4 meters (13 ft.) at birth. Mating has been reported in some instances to occur throughout the year. The life expectancy of this species is thought to approach about 50 years.

Abundance. This is one of the commoner species of the rorquals.

Economic Importance. This whale has not been hunted commercially until recent times. With the shift of whaling to the smaller whales, it has becomes as vulnerable as any other species.

Miscellaneous. Anderson named this species *B. edeni* in honor of Ashley Eden, Chief Commissioner of Burma and the gentleman who called his attention to a specimen stranded in a stream in Burma in 1871. The common name of Bryde's Whale honors Johann Bryde, the Norwegian consul in South Africa after whom Olson in 1913 named and described this whale for a second time as *B. brydei;* this scientific name was a duplicate or synonym and was therefore abandoned, but the name of "Bryde" has remained as the common name.

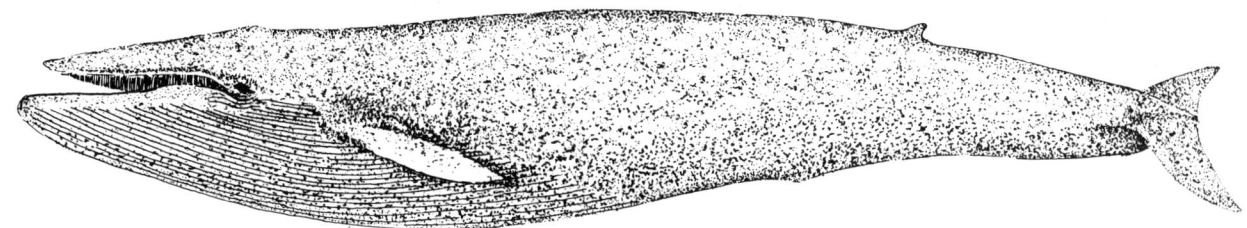

THE BLUE WHALE
Also known as The Sulphur-bottom Whale
and Sibbald's Rorqual
Balaenoptera musculus (Linnaeus, 1758)

Identifying Features. The most useful feature in identifying the blue whale at sea is its unusually long back. When surfacing, the head will appear with its spout and then submerge to be followed by a long, low back; finally a very small dorsal fin will appear, often followed by a fleeting glimpse of the tail. This sequence is characteristic of the blue whale.

Size and Shape. The blue whale is the largest animal to ever live on the planet Earth. Large specimens will reach a length of 30 meters (98.4 ft.) and weigh as much as 160 tons. A specimen measuring 105 feet (32 meters) seems to have been the largest whale recorded. Although individuals have been measured in excess of 100 feet in length, the average length of specimens today is nearer 25 or 26 meters (82 to 85.3 ft.). A specimen which measured 89 feet (27.12 m.) in length is reported to have weighed 136,400 kg. (300,707 lbs.).

The body of the blue whale is uniformly cylindrical, exceedingly long, tubular, and spindle-shaped and tapers very uniformly toward the head and tail. The upper jaw is the widest of the rorquals *(Balaenopteridae)* and bears a single, median ridge extending from its blowhole forward to the snout. The blowholes lie in a slight depression in the dorsal profile and, when at the surface, are surrounded on the front and sides by expanded fleshy crests. The throat and belly bear a series of 55 to 94 long, parallel, longitudinal grooves which extend from the chin to just beyond the navel.

Color. Although no two blue whales are the same color, they are in general a slaty, grayish blue color over the back and sides of the body and white to whitish beneath. Both the upper and lower sides of the body are covered in a mottled pattern by small grayish spots. The belly of the whale often has a yellowish color due to a coat of diatoms which it acquires on its northern or southern feeding grounds; this color fades away in warmer waters. The dorsal fin is often of a whitish color.

Distribution. The blue whale occupies all of the oceans of the globe from the tropics to the polar ice caps. In the North Atlantic Ocean, they go northward to the drift ice or to the Arctic Circle.

In the North Pacific Ocean, they go as far north as the Aleutian Islands; here they are distributed from the Gulf of Alaska westward to Kamchatka, but they do not often enter the Bering Sea.

In the South Pacific Ocean, they go southward to the edge of the ice, but usually return northward in the southern winter, although a few may linger in the Antarctic area.

Migration. Most blue whales migrate either northward or southward in the summer months, feed for a few months, and then return to warmer latitudes during the winter seasons. Not all whales follow this migratory pattern, because many individuals are observed at locations and at times which do not coincide with their usual migratory habits.

Fins and Flippers. The dorsal fin is very small for such a large whale and will measure only about one-third meter (13 in.) in height. In addition to being short and low, it is set three-fourths of the body length back from the head. Its shape varies from triangular to falcate.

The flippers measure from about one-seventh to one-tenth of the body length; they are small, long, slender, tapered, curved on their anterior margin, and terminate in a point. They are a light grayish blue or white color beneath.

The flukes of the tail are wide and may measure nearly one-fourth of the body length. They have a fairly straight posterior margin and bear a notch at the midline where they meet.

Baleen. The baleen plates together with the tongue, palate, and the entire inside of the mouth are a deep black color. These baleen plates will number from about 260 to 395 on each side of the mouth; the longest plates will reach a length of about 1 meter (39 to 40 in.) and a maximum width of as much as 55 cm. (21.6 in.).

Skeletal Notes. The vertebrae are distributed approximately as follows: C 7 + D 15-16 + L 14-16 + Ca 26-28 = 63-65. There are 15 pairs of ribs of which only one pair articulates with the sternum. Of the 15 pairs of ribs, the 1st rib has but a single head, the 2nd and 3rd ribs have two heads, and the 4th rib shows a single head with a rudiment of the 2nd head; all succeeding ribs have but a single head. The sternum is small. There is no evidence of the existence of a femur. The bones of the fingers are distributed approximately as follows: I (4-5), II (5-8), IV (5-7), V (3-4). The third finger is missing in this family.

Other Anatomical Notes. The eye, which lies above and behind the mouth, is about 12 cm. (5 in.) in diameter, is oval in shape, and has a brown iris. There are a few (possibly 4) hairs on the upper lip and about 40 on the lower lip. The uterus has 2 horns. A caecum, 20 cm. (8 in.) in length, is present. The penis will measure about 3 meters (9.8 ft.) in length. The diameter of the large intestine is about 20 cm. (8 in.).

In a female blue whale, which measured about 18.6 meters (61 ft.) in length, mammary slits measured about 38 cm. (15 in.) in length. One or more additional slits often lie parallel to the mammary slit; these slits may be smaller, equal, or occasionally slightly longer than the mammary slits.

In a male blue whale, which measured 21.6 meters (71 ft.) in length, the non-functional mammary slits measured 40.6 cm. (16 in.) and 48.2 cm. (19 in.) in length. In this same specimen, the penis measured 1.83 meters (6 ft.) in length. A single testis measured 68.6 cm. (27 in.) in length and 25.4 cm. (10 in.) in width in a specimen measuring about 20 meters (65 ft., 11 in.) in length. A single specimen, which was reported to weigh 50,904 kg., was reported to possess a brain which weighed 3,636 grams.

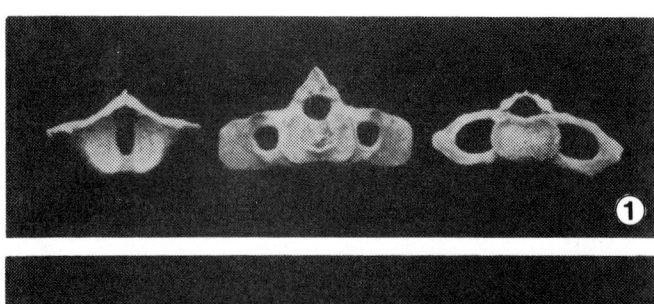

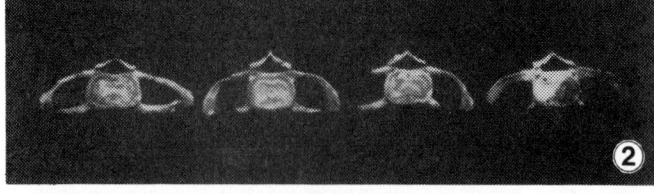

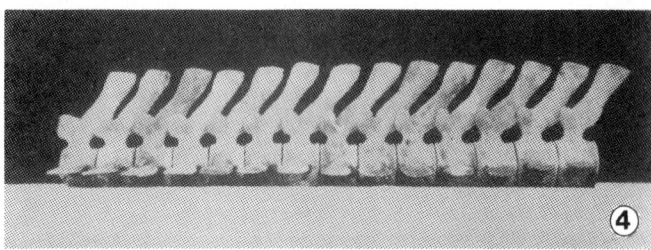

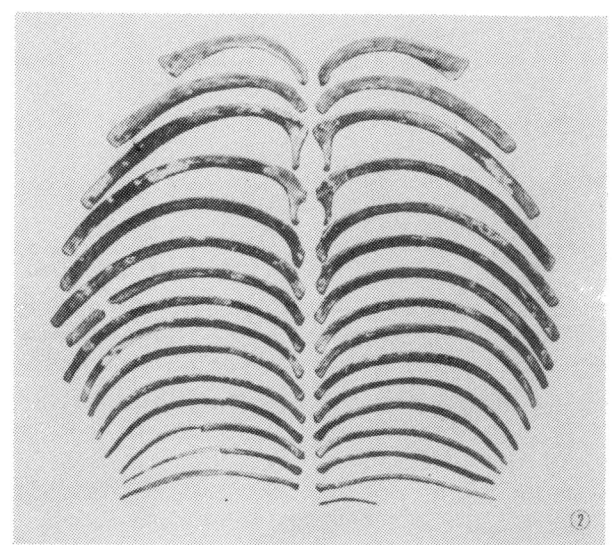

Photo of the ribs of the "pigmy" blue whale, *Balaenoptera musculus brevicauda.*
Photo by Omura, Ichihara, and Kasuya.

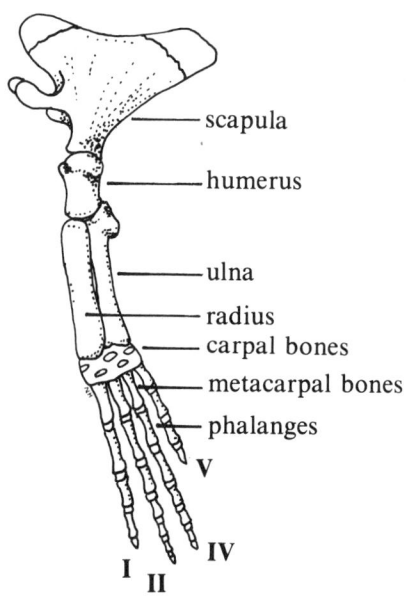

The vertebrae of the "pigmy" blue whale, *Balaenoptera musculus brevicauda* (Mysticeti: Balaenopteridae).

First row from left to right: atlas, axis, and 3rd cervical vertebra.

Second row from left to right: 4th, 5th, 6th, and 7th cervical vertebrae.

Third row from left to right: 15 dorsal or thoracic vertebrae.

Fourth row from left to right: 14 lumbar vertebrae including the sacral vertebrae.

Fifth row from left to right: 26+ caudal vertebrae. The chevron bones beneath the caudal vertebrae do not show.
Photos by Omura, Ichihara, and Kasuya.

Diagram of the left pectoral girdle and appendage of the blue whale, *Balaenoptera* sp. (Mysticeti: Balaenopteridae).
Drawn from Howell.

From: Alfred Brazier Howell — AQUATIC MAMMALS. 1931. Courtesy of Charles E. Thomas, Publishers. Springfield, Ill.

Food. The food of the blue whale consists almost exclusively of krill (*Euphausia superba* Dana), a euphausid crustacean which lives in the plankton of the Antarctic Seas. This crustacean requires about 2 years to reach an adult length of about 3 inches; it is abundant in quantities beyond the imagination. In northern latitudes, two species of krill, *Thysanoessa inermis* of the North Pacific Ocean and *Meganyctiphanes norvegica* of the North Atlantic Ocean, seem to form the basic diet of the blue whale and other species. In addition, they will consume other crustacea in the plankton plus any small available fishes. Adult whales, in areas with an abundance of krill, will ingest about 3 or 4 tons of food per day.

Swimming and Diving. Blue whales may be observed singly, in pairs, or more usually in small groups of 3 or 4 individuals; when feeding in colder climates or when they have gathered for breeding, they may congregate in much larger numbers. Blue whales normally swim at a speed of about 10 to 12 knots, but when frightened may exceed 14 knots or more. In general, they are shallow divers and will make a series of about a dozen shallow dives of 12 to 15 seconds following each deep dive. At the beginning of each deep dive, this whale will lift its tail in the air and then submerge for a period of about 10 to 20 minutes.

The spout of the blue whale is high, slender, vertical, and columnar in shape; it may reach a height of about 9 to 12 meters (29.5 to 39.4 ft.).

Reproduction. The young whales are born in warm water in the lower latitudes after the whales have returned from their cold-water feeding grounds. The gestation period lasts about 11 or 12 months and the young, when born, will measure about 7 or 8 meters (23 to 26 ft.). They are nursed for a period of about 7 or 8 months and, when weaned, will measure about 16 meters (52 ft.) In addition to doubling their length, it is estimated that these young whales will increase their weight nine times. The young whales will be sexually mature at about 8 or 9 years of age or older and will mate and produce young ever 2 or possibly 3 years thereafter. Occasionally a female whale will give birth to twin calves. Their life span is somewhere between 25 and 50 years.

Abundance. This whale was once abundant and was subsequently reduced in numbers by uncontrolled whaling until it faced extinction; it is partially protected and is slowly increasing in numbers.

Economic Importance. Because the blue whale was the largest of the whales and, when captured, yielded about 70 to 80 barrels of oil, it was of great importance to the whaling industry. Only the sperm whale approached it in economic importance.

Miscellaneous. The blue whale has developed at least three distinct sub-species which inhabit distinctly different areas of the ocean and which do not interbreed or intermingle in any way. In addition, there are other populations of blue whales off Peru and Chile and in the northern Indian Ocean which are not included among those sub-species currently recognized. The three recognized and established sub-species are listed below.

1. *Balaenoptera musculus musculus* (Linnaeus, 1758).
   THE NORTHERN BLUE WHALE
   This blue whale is a smaller form than *B. m. intermedia*. It occurs in the North Atlantic and North Pacific Oceans.

2. *Balaenoptera musculus intermedia* Burmeister, 1871.
   THE ANTARCTIC BLUE WHALE
   This blue whale is the largest of the three sub-species. Its distribution is limited to the southern hemisphere.

3. *Balaenoptera musculus brevicauda* Ichihara, 1966.
   THE PIGMY BLUE WHALE
   This blue whale is the smallest of the three sub-species. It inhabits the southern Indian Ocean near the Kerguelen Archipelago (50° S.L., 70° E.L.). It is sometimes listed as *B. m. brevicauda* Zemsky and Boronin, 1964. This sub-species has somewhat different body proportions than other blue whales; there are more caudal vertebrae, although the tail region seems shorter and the trunk region longer and heavier than the other sub-species. The baleen blades are also disproportionately larger.

Class Mammalia — The Mammals
Order Cetacea — The Whales
Suborder Mysticeti — The Whalebone Whales
Family Balaenopteridae — The Rorquals
or True Fin-backed Whales

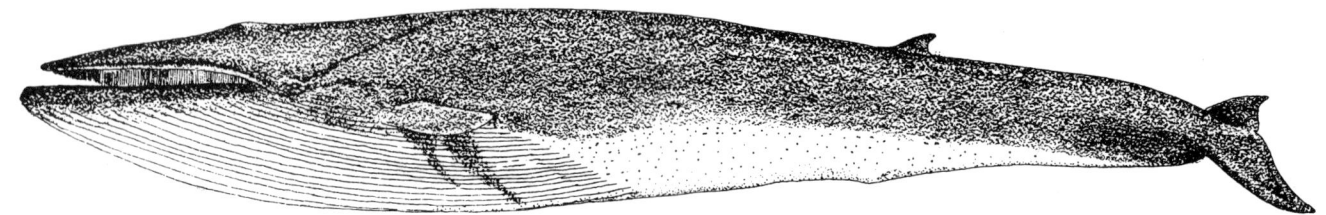

THE FIN WHALE
Also known as The Fin-backed Whale,
The Razor-back Whale, and The Common Rorqual
Balaenoptera physalus (Linnaeus, 1758)

Identifying Features. The fin whale may be recognized by a combination of several features. The head is flat on top and bears a single, high ridge which extends from the blowholes forward about half way to the snout. This ridge is formed by the union of the fleshy crests which lie lateral to the blowholes; these crests are quite high and join in front of the blowholes to form the beginning of this median ridge; this ridge decreases in height as it continues forward. A light chevron-shaped mark with the arms pointing toward the tail is often visible on the back behind the head. The right lower lip is whitish in color, while the left side is uniformly darker; this feature is often visible at sea and will establish the identity of a fin whale.

Size and Shape. The fin whale is the 2nd largest of the rorquals and is exceeded in size only by the blue whale. A record exists of a fin whale which measured 26.8 meters (87.9 ft.); this is exceptionally large in view of the fact that most fin whales today measure about 19 meters (62.33 ft.) in length. The body of this species has a very long, slender, and spindle-shaped profile; it tapers uniformly at the extremities to end in a long, conical snout and a conical tail stock. The head is flat on top and V-shaped when viewed from above and the mouth is large. There is a sharp ridge along the midline of the back posterior to the fin which has given this species the common name of "razor-back." The tail stock is strongly compressed laterally. The throat and belly bear a series of parallel, longitudinal grooves which vary in number between about 56 and 100; they begin at the tip of the jaw and extend as far back as the navel.

Color. The body is black or brownish gray above and changes gradually downward on the sides to white on the belly. The lower side of both the flippers and the tail flukes are also white in color. The brownish color is due to diatoms which grow on the body in cooler climates. There is no mottling on the body as in the blue whale. The color or pigmentation is not symmetrical on the head. The right lower lip and jaw are white in color, together with the inside of the mouth. This area of white sometimes extends onto the upper right lip and sometimes backward to include some areas of the neck. Occasionally a very light-colored, forward-pointing chevron is observed upon the back. Two faint, narrow, diagonal bands, one dark, one light, extend from behind the eye upward and backward onto the body. A few individuals have been reported which were entirely white in color.

Distribution. The fin whale is worldwide in distribution and inhabits all of the oceans of the world, although it is uncommon in the tropics and in polar seas with ice. In the North Pacific Ocean, these whales go north to the Aleutian Islands and into the Bering Sea and occasionally enter the Arctic Ocean. In general, they prefer to live at some distance from the land. They have been recorded from the Adriatic Sea.

Migration. Fin whales migrate with the seasons; they go into cooler temperate and polar waters to feed during the summer months and return to warmer waters for the winter.

Fins and Flippers. The dorsal fin will measure as much as 65 cm. (26 in.) in height. It is variously shaped, concave on its posterior margin, and with a tip which is strongly directed backward. It is located directly above the anus and about two-thirds of the body length behind the head.

The flippers are slender, tapering, pointed, and white beneath. They measure about one-eleventh of the body length.

The tail flukes are wide and measure between about one-fourth and one-fifth of the body length. Their posterior margin is slightly concave and bears a deep notch where the flukes meet at the midline.

Baleen. The anterior third of the baleen in the right front side of the mouth is white or yellowish in color, while the remainder is usually striped with yellowish white and a dark lead or bluish gray color. All of the plates on the left side of the mouth are dark in color. These plates will number from about 260 to 473 on each side of the mouth and will measure from 70 to 90 cm. (27 to 35 in.) in length at their longest point; at their widest point they may measure from 30 to 50 cm. (11.8 to 19.7 in.) in width.

Skeletal Notes. The vertebrae of the backbone are distributed approximately as follows: C 7 + D 15 + L 14-16 + Ca 25-27 = 60-63. The neck bones are separate and distinct in this family, however, in this species, the first 2 or 3 cervical vertebrae may be partially fused together. There are 15 pairs of ribs; of these, the 15th and last pair are "floating" ribs and do not articulate with the vertebral column. The 1st chevron bone is small; the 2nd is very large, after which they decrease gradually in size.

The sternum shows great variation in shape and size. It is fundamentally a wide, crude cross which is usually wider than long and often lacks symmetry.

The bones of the fingers (phalanges) are distributed approximately as follows: I (4), II (6-7), IV (5-7), V (3-4). The third finger is missing in this family (*Balaenopteridae*).

Other Anatomical Notes. The eyes are small and are located above and behind the corners of the mouth. The eyeball measures about 12.7 cm. (5 in.) in diameter; it has a brown iris and an oval, horizontal pupil about 2 cm. (.75 in.) in diameter. The external opening of the ear is located about 3 feet behind the eye on the same level.

There are about 50 to 100 sensory hairs around the nostrils and the upper and lower jaws. About 20 hairs, .5 inch in length, form a row on the front edge of the lower jaw. The gall bladder is absent and the bile ducts empty directly into the duodenum. In a specimen which might weigh between about 25,000 to 45,000 kg. (55,125 to 99,225 lbs.), the brain might weigh between about 6.5 kg. and 7.5 kg. (14.3 to 16.5 lbs.). A caecum is present. The uterus has 2 horns.

Miscellaneous organs and parts of a single fin whale, captured in 1941, were weighed prior to processing the carcass at the whaling station at Fields Landing, California. These weights* are recorded below.

THE WEIGHT OF A FIN WHALE
(A Female Specimen — 71 Feet In Length)

Part of Body	Weight		Percent of Body Weight
	Pounds	Kilograms	
Total Body Weight	130,942**	59,394.	
Adrenal Glands	1.614	0.732	.0012
Thyroid Gland	8.752	3.970	.0066
Brain	18.353	8.325	.014
Kidney (one)	461.	209.	.35
Liver	1,783.	809.	1.36
Heart	842.	382.	.64
Lung	868.	394.	.66
Spleen	15.	6.800	.0114
Eye (one)	3.792	1.720	.0029
Ovaries	11.33	5.15	.0086
Ovaries, oviducts, and uterus (non-pregnant)	215.	98.	.164
Stomach	685.	310.	.523
Intestine	2,255.	1,009.	1.722
Diaphragm	552.	250.	.421
Muscle	21,780.	9,863.	16.633
Tongue	2,705.	1,227.	2.065
Fat and Muscle Bits	27,319.	12,391.	20.86
Blubber	25,581.	11,603.	19.536
Skeleton	19,651.	8,913.	15.007

From the Jour. of Mammalogy 24:1, 1943, pp. 39-45.
**Includes an added 20% for blood and body fluids.*

Food. The food of the fin whale includes a wide variety of animals, including crustacea, squid, and fishes. In Antarctic Seas, they consume large quantities of schizopods (*Schizopoda: Mysidae*), a small crustacean which lives in the plankton.

Swimming and Diving. Fin whales live in groups of 6 or 7, but may gather into larger groups of 50, 100, or more individuals. They usually swim at a leisurely speed of about 5 knots; when frightened, they are reported to be able to swim at a speed of 18 knots for as long as 30 minutes and can even achieve a speed of 20 knots (37 km. per hr.) for short spurts.

When beginning a deep dive, this whale usually arches its back, but it does not usually expose the flukes at that time; these deep dives usually last for 20 to 30 minutes. Some deep dives have been known to reach a depth of 230 meters (755 ft.) or more. Occasionally, these whales will leap from the water and fall back with a splash.

When catching schools of small fishes, the fin whale is reported to charge into the school with its white, right side downward and with its right fin downward; the left fin meanwhile is held above the water. In this position, the white color of the right lip is less frightening to the small fishes and the downward flipper helps to change directions in pursuit of the fishes.

The spout of this species is a vertical, narrow, inverted, cone-shaped column of mist which rises to a height of 4 to 6 meters (13 to 20 ft.); it is accompanied by a whistling sound.

Reproduction. These whales mate in warmer latitudes during the winter months, although a few do mate at other times of the year. The females are pregnant for a period of 11 or 12 months and thereafter nurse the young whale for a period of about 6 months. At birth, the young will measure about 6 meters (19.7 ft.) or more and will weigh about 3,500 to 3,600 kg. (7717.5 to 7938 lbs.); they will grow very rapidly during their first 6 months and, when weaned at this time, will measure between about 12 and 13 meters (39.3 to 42.6 ft.). Females will rear a calf every 2 or 3 years. They will reach sexual maturity probably at about 3.5 to 4 years of age, but will continue to grow for about 20 years and will reach their full size at about 25 to 30 years of age. Their life span is uncertain, but some scholars, after studying their ears, have suggested that they may live to be 90 to 100 years old; this is doubtful.

Abundance. This has been an abundant species; its future depends upon the activity of the whaling industry and upon much better protection.

Economic Importance. The fin whale has always constituted a large part of the whaling industry's catch. With the protection of the blue whale, whalers increased their hunting for fin whales with the result that their numbers have declined rapidly. Northern fin whales will yield 5 or 6 tons of oil, while the southern fin whales will yield about 9 tons of oil per carcass; this is about one-half the yield of a blue whale.

Miscellaneous. The fin whale has developed at least two distinct sub-species which inhabit different areas of the ocean and which do not interbreed or intermingle in any way.

The two recognized sub-species are listed below:

1. *Balaenoptera physalus physalus* (Linnaeus, 1758).
   This sub-species is the smaller form. It is distributed in the oceans of the northern hemisphere.

2. *Balaenoptera physalus quoyi* (Fischer, 1829).
   This sub-species is the larger form. It is distributed in the oceans of the southern hemisphere. The name *"quoyi"* honors Jean Rene Constant Quoy (1790-1869), a French zoologist, who with Joseph Paul Gaimard (1790-1858), a biologist, accompanied the French explorer, Jean Francois de Galaup compte de la Perouse, on his expedition (1826-1829) of discovery in the Pacific Ocean aboard the ships *l'Astrolabe* and the *Broussole*.

In addition to the two sub-species listed above, a third group of whales, sometimes called *Balaenoptera physalus chinensis*, occurs in the South China Sea.

THE HUMP-BACKED WHALES
Genus *MEGAPTERA* Gray, 1846

The principal anatomical feature which separates this genus from the other fin-backed whales (*Balaenoptera*) is the presence of the great, long flippers. The name of *Megaptera*, which means "great wing," refers to these large flippers.

Studies of these whales by various scholars indicate that several names of species appearing in older books are really duplicate names or synonyms of other previously named species.

The following list indicates the older names and the more correct and current names of these species.

Old Name		Name Currently In Use
Megaptera americana	is now	*Megaptera novaeangliae*
Megaptera bellicosa	is now	*Megaptera novaeangliae*
Megaptera boops	is now	*Megaptera novaeangliae*
Megaptera longimanna	is now	*Megaptera novaeangliae*
Megaptera longipinna	is now	*Megaptera novaeangliae*
Megaptera nodosa	is now	*Megaptera novaeangliae*
Megaptera osphyia	is now	*Megaptera novaeangliae*
Megaptera poeskop	is now	*Megaptera novaeangliae*

This genus includes the single living species listed below.

Megaptera novaeangliae (Borowski, 1781)
THE HUMP-BACKED WHALE . . . . See page 290

Class Mammalia — The Mammals
Order Cetacea — The Whales
Suborder Mysticeti — The Whalebone Whales
Family Balaenopteridae — The Rorquals
or True Fin-backed Whales

THE HUMP-BACKED WHALE
Megaptera novaeangliae (Borowski, 1781)

Identifying Features. The flippers provide certain identification of this species. These flippers are nearly one-third the length of the body and have an irregular border. The snout is covered with lumps, the dorsal fin is small, and the tail flukes have an irregular posterior margin. On diving, the tail flukes are lifted into the air revealing their irregular margin and white markings.

Size and Shape. The body of this whale is robust, short, and fat and narrows rapidly toward the tail. Most adult hump-backed whales measure 15 or 16 meters (49.2 to 52.4 ft.) in length, although some have been known to reach a length of 19 meters (62.3 ft.).

The throat and belly are occupied by about 14 to 24 large ventral grooves which extend backward to the navel; of these, those grooves which are nearest to the sides turn upward onto the sides of the body in the area of the flippers, the eyes, and the ends of the mouth.

The head and jaws are covered with lumps or callosities about the size of a human fist; some of these are in rows, others appear to be placed at random, and all have one sensory hair. The row extending from the blowholes to the tip of the snout may have between 5 to 8 lumps; a lateral row down each outer edge of the top of the head will have from 5 to 15 lumps, and there are between 10 and 15 lumps on each side of the lower jaw plus a few at the very front of the lower jaw.

Color. The body is black in color above and white beneath; however, the amount of these colors varies. The whales in the North Pacific Ocean have less white than those of the southern oceans and a few have been observed which were totally black. Color patterns are inherited and can be used to identify groups.

Distribution. The humpbacked whale inhabits nearly all of the temperate and tropical seas of the world. In the northern hemisphere, the hump-backed whale is distributed from the equator to about 70° N.L. In the southern hemisphere, the hump-backed whales occur from the equator southward to the pack ice of the Antarctic Ocean.

Migration. The hump-backed whale is a migratory species which travel northward and southward with the seasons. They feed in the cooler latitudes and breed and give birth to their young in the warmer latitudes. In the North Pacific Ocean, they gather during the months of July through September in the Aleutian Islands. Some remain in the area of the Aleutian Islands, while others go northward into the Bering Sea and a few go on northward to the Chukchi Sea. They start southward in September and October and arrive at their winter breeding ground in late fall and early winter. A few of these routes follow shorelines. In the North Pacific Ocean, the whales seem to winter in three areas: (1) the area between the Bonin Islands, the Marianas Islands, the Ryukyu Islands, and Taiwan; (2) the Hawaiian Islands; and (3) along the coast of Mexico. In addition, there are migration routes along both sides of the North Atlantic Ocean and many migration routes between Antarctica and the shores of Australia, New Zealand, Africa, and South America. Since the migrations of the northern and southern hemispheres are 6 months apart, the whales of these groups do not appear to mix or interbreed.

Fins and Flippers. The dorsal fin is small in size and varies considerably in shape. It is located slightly more than two-thirds of the body length from the head and just posterior to the anus. This fin is mounted upon a hump, a feature found in no other whalebone whale. The flippers are very long and large and will measure between one-fourth and one-third of the body length; they will reach a length of about 5 meters (16.4 ft.) in an adult whale. They have an irregular, knobby margin on their leading edge and are usually black above and white beneath. The flukes of the tail are large and wide and approach one-third of the body length in width. The posterior margin of each fluke has a curved, irregular border; the two flukes meet at the midline to form a deep notch. The flukes are usually white or partly white beneath.

The "hump" of the hump-backed whale, *Megaptera novaeangliae,* showing the dorsal fin.

Ore. Inst. Mar. Biol.

Baleen. The baleen plates are usually black in color, although in young whales they may be of a lighter color; occasionally the baleen plates are lighter toward the front of the mouth and some are streaked. They will number between about 270 and 400 on each side of the mouth and will reach a length of 80 to 85 cm. (31.5 to 33.5 in.); their width may reach 15 cm. (6 in.) at their widest point.

Skeletal Notes. The vertebrae are distributed approximately as follows: C 7 + D 14 + L 10-14 + Ca 21-22 = 52-53. The cervical vertebrae are distinct and separate in this family (*Balaenopteridae*). The chevron bones may number from about 9 to 12. Of 14 pairs of ribs, only one pair articulates directly with the sternum. The bones of the fingers (phalanges) are distributed approximately as follows: I (2-4), II (6-8), IV (5-7), V (3). The third finger is missing in this family (*Balaenopteridae*).

Photo of a young, newly-born, hump-backed whale, *Megaptera novaeangliae,* beached at Waikiki off the end of Kapahulu Avenue on the morning of Saturday, March 14, 1936. **Photo by Tinker.**

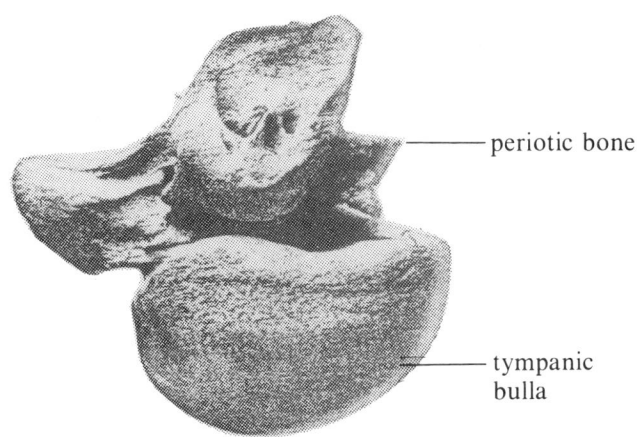

— periotic bone

— tympanic bulla

Photo of the interior face of the left periotic bone with the tympanic bulla attached of the hump-backed whale, *Megaptera novaeangliae* (Mysticeti: Balaenopteridae).

From Brit. Mus. (Nat. Hist.).

The Weight of Hump-backed Whales

Sex and Length	Male — 41 feet (12.5 m.)		Male — 44 feet (13.4 m.)		Male — 45 feet (13.7 m.)	
	Weight		Weight		Weight	
	Pounds	Kilograms	Pounds	Kilograms	Pounds	Kilograms
Total Body Weight	82,000	37,195	88,000	39,916	90,000	40,823
Adrenal Gland					2.66	1.210
Thyroid Gland	7.13	3.237			6.52	2.960
Brain	11.66	5.288	15.	6.800	15.94	7.229
Kidney (one)	424.	192.				
Liver	1,050.	476.	800.	363	1,400.	635.
Heart	472.	214.	400.	181.	425.	193.
Spleen	13.33	6.041				
Eye (one)					2.16	.980

*From the Jour. of Mammalogy 24:1, 1943, pp. 39-45.

Other Anatomical Notes. The lower jaw is longer than the upper jaw and bears a spherical projection at its tip. The pupils of the eyes are kidney-shaped; the iris is brown in color. The stomach is quite large. The intestine is thin and short. The caecum is present, but of moderate size.

In a specimen which might weigh between about 35,000 and 40,000 kg., the brain might weigh between about 5,000 and 7,000 grams.

The weights of three hump-backed whales, which were captured off California and processed in the whaling station at Fields Landing, California, in 1941, are shown above.

Food. Hump-backed whales eat a wide variety of foods, including all of the small animals in the plankton and, in addition, fishes, squid, etc. The major part of their diet has to consist of the various small pelagic crustaceans which abound in the plankton of the cooler latitudes.

Swimming and Diving. Hump-backed whales usually travel in small groups of 3 or 4 individuals, although they are often seen in groups containing a dozen or more. Hump-backed whales are slow swimmers and will cruise along at 3.5 to 5 knots. When preparing for a deep dive, they will bend the body and finally lift the tail flukes above the water. These deep dives will last from 15 to 20 minutes and are followed by 4 to 8 shallow dives of 15 to 20 seconds each. When resting at the surface, this whale may lie upon its side with the upper flipper in the air. The spout of this whale is between 3 and 5 meters (9.8 to 16.4 ft.) in height and is very wide in proportion to its height; it may even appear as a double spout.

Hump-backed whales show neither a great fear of boats nor any interest in their approach or presence. This whale is a playful species and will perform various antics for its delight, including leaping from the water (breaching), hitting the surface with a flipper (finning), hitting the surface of the water with the tail while the head is down (lob-tailing), and other forms of play.

Reproduction. Hump-backed whales breed in warm water during the winter months and then go to the cooler latitudes in the summer to fatten on the plankton. They return in the late fall and early winter in order to give birth to their young in warmer water after a gestation period of about 10 or 11 months. The young, when born, will measure about 4.5 to 5 meters (14.7 to 16.4 ft.) and will weigh about 1,300 to 1,400 kg. (2866.5 to 3087 lbs.). They are nursed for a period of 6 or more months during which time they will double their length. The young will then follow its mother to the feeding grounds, where it will become a feeder on plankton. This species will reach sexual maturity at possibly 7 or 8 years of age. Their life expectancy is estimated at 45 to 50 years.

Abundance. The hump-backed whale was once an abundant species. Its number have been greatly reduced by uncontrolled whaling. It needs continued and intense protection.

Economic Importance. Hump-backed whales once supplied a sizeable proportion of the whaling catch. Because its migration routes followed some shorelines, it was hunted by shore whaling stations. The blubber of this whale was thicker than that of the other rorquals, but it had one disadvantage, namely, when it was killed, it would sink.

Miscellaneous. Hump-backed whales sometimes come into shallow water to rub the barnacles from their backs. Hump-backed whales produce weird and eerie songs which they sing in repeated sequences of 10 or 15 minutes; this is a very interesting and unique accomplishment of this species.

THE RIGHT WHALE FAMILY
Family *BALAENIDAE* Gray, 1825

The right whale family includes three species of whalebone whales which inhabit cooler water. Of these, two species (*Balaena*) are of large size and the third species (*Caperea*) is a smaller whale. The whales of this family do not possess a dorsal fin (except in *Caperea*) and also lack the longitudinal grooves in the skin below the throat. These whales all have very large heads which comprise between one-fourth and one-third of the body. The skull bears a great, narrow, arching upper jaw which ends in a narrow rostrum from which the whalebone blades are suspended. The whalebone plates are long, thin, and flexible and are more numerous than in the other families of whalebone whales. The cleft of the mouth presents a great arched curve when viewed from the side.

It is interesting to note that the seven neck (cervical) vertebrae in this family are fused together into a single bony unit, while these same cervical vertebrae in the *Eschrichtiidae* and the *Balaenopteridae* are separate and distinct.

This family is known from the Lower Miocene Epoch to the Holocene (Recent) Epoch.

This family is usually divided into the two genera listed below.

Balaena Linnaeus, 1758 (2+ species)
    THE RIGHT WHALES . . . . See page 293
Caperea Gray, 1864 (1 species)
    THE PIGMY RIGHT WHALES . . . . See page 299

THE RIGHT WHALES
Genus *BALAENA* Linnaeus, 1758

The right whales are very large species with gigantic, grotesque heads which comprise about one-third the length of the body. Their mouths are gigantic with a great opening in front which is bordered below by a broad lower jaw and above by a slender, narrow, arched rostrum from which the whalebone blades descend. These whalebone blades reach their longest in the bowhead whales and have been known to measure as much as 14 feet in length. The two species of this genus lack a dorsal fin near the middle of the back. In this genus, there are five fingers within the flippers.

Fossils of this genus are known from as far back as the Early Miocene Epoch. In Europe, it is known from the Lower Pliocene Epoch to the Upper Pliocene Epoch. In South America, it is known from the Pleistocene Epoch to the Holocene (Recent) Epoch.

Studies of these whales by various scholars indicate that several names of species appearing in older books are really duplicate names or synonyms of other previously named species.

The following list indicates the older names and the more correct and current names of these species.

Old Name		Name Currently In Use
Balaena albicans	is now	*Delphinapterus leucas*
Balaena ampullata	is now	*Hyperoodon ampullatus*
Balaena australis	is now	*Balaena glacialis*
Balaena gibbosa	is now	*Eschrichtius robustus*
Balaena japonica	is now	*Balaena glacialis*
Balaena marginata	is now	*Caperea marginata*
Balaena maximus	is now	*Balaenoptera musculus*
Balaena musculus	is now	*Balaenoptera musculus*
Balaena novaeangliae	is now	*Megaptera novaeangliae*
Balaena physalus	is now	*Balaenoptera physalus*
Balaena rostrata	is now	*Balaenoptera acutorostrata*
Balaena sieboldi	is now	*Balaena glacialis*
Eubalaena	is now	*Balaena*
Eubalaena glacialis	is now	*Balaena glacialis*

This genus includes the two living species listed below; the first of these is usually divided into three geographical sub-species.

Balaena glacialis Muller, 1776
    THE RIGHT WHALE . . . . See page 294
Balaena mysticetus Linnaeus, 1758
    THE BOWHEAD WHALE . . . . See page 296

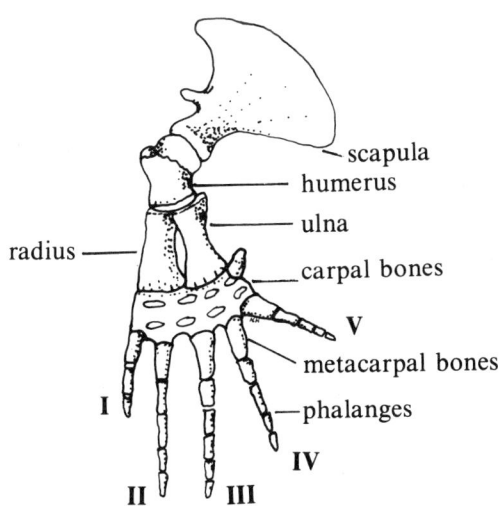

Diagram of the left pectoral girdle and appendage of *Balaena* sp. (Mysticeti: Balaenidae).

Drawn from Howell.

From: Alfred Brazier Howell — AQUATIC MAMMALS. 1931. Courtesy of Charles E. Thomas, Publishers. Springfield, Ill.

THE RIGHT WHALE
Also known as The Black Right Whale,
The Northern Right Whale, and The Pacific Right Whale
Balaena glacialis Muller, 1776

Identifying Features. The right whales can be recognized by their robust body, the absence of a dorsal fin, and their large head with its horny "bonnet" on top.

Size and Shape. The body of the right whale is very heavy, fat, robust, and rounded. It will reach a length of 15 to 18 meters (49.2 to 59.0 ft.). The males may weigh about 55,000 kg. (121,275 lbs.) and the females, which are larger and heavier, may weigh as much as 95,000 kg. (209,475 lbs.). The head is very large and comprises about one-fourth of the body length. The upper jaw is long, narrow, and arched upward; the lower lip is very large and fleshy and the tongue within it is likewise large and gray or bluish in color. A very unusual structure, known as the "bonnet," covers the outer surface of the head at the tip of the upper jaw. It is a somewhat yellowish horney excrescence or callosity which grows from the skin of the upper jaw and is full of whale lice, barnacles, and other parasites. In some whales, small bits of the bonnet will be found around the eyes, the lower jaw, and the blow holes. The throat and belly of the right whales (*Balaenidae*) do not possess any longitudinal folds of skin as do the rorquals *(Balaenopteridae).*

Color. The young right whales are a bluish gray color; however, as they grow older they become entirely black, grayish black, or brownish. Many of these whales have irregular white spots on the belly near the navel and about one whale in five has a large, white, ventral area which extends from the throat to the belly. Individuals of this species which were pure white in color have been reported from southern seas.

Distribution. In ancient times, the right whales occupied the temperate and cooler seas of the world. Their distribution in the Northern Hemisphere ranged between 20° and 70° N.L.

In the North Atlantic Ocean, they ranged from the entire Arctic region southward to the Bay of Biscay (Spain) and the Azores and along the eastern coasts of Canada and the United States as far south as Bermuda, Florida, and the Gulf of Mexico.

In the North Pacific Ocean, they occupied the waters of both the American and Asiatic coasts and migrated regularly into the Bering Sea and the Sea of Okhotsk.

On the American side of the North Pacific Ocean, they come southward along the coasts of British Columbia, Washington, and Oregon, and on rare occasions are seen along the coast of California.

This whale does not occur in the tropics or in warm temperate waters.

In the southern hemisphere, these whales were distributed rather evenly around the globe between 20° and 50° S.L.; today, they are scarce and their appearance is sporadic. Despite their scarcity in recent years, they have been observed as far north as Rio de Janeiro (23° S.L.).

The right whale and the bowhead whale occupy quite separate areas. The bowhead lives in colder waters than the right whale and does not often appear in temperate latitudes. Both species occur in the Bering Sea, but probably do not often meet because both go northward in the summer and southward in the winter.

Migration. These whales follow the same seasonal migration patterns as other baleen species. They go into higher latitudes in the summer seasons to feed on the immense quantities of plankton in cooler waters and return again to temperate seas during the winter months. Their migration routes were many and some in the southern hemisphere are not completely known.

Fins and Flippers. The dorsal fin is entirely absent in the two species of the genus *Balaena* and there is no dorsal ridge. The flippers are large, heavy, and broad, and of variable shapes. They are often damaged along their margins, possibly by the bites of killer whales. The caudal flukes together form a tail fin which is quite wide, deeply concave on its posterior margin, and which contains a deep notch where the flukes join at the midline. The posterior margin of the tail is smooth; the ends are pointed.

Baleen. The baleen of the right whale is very long and slender and, near the middle of the jaw, will reach a length of 2.8 meters (9 ft.) in large specimens; the great length of these baleen plates is due to the greatly arched upper jaw. The width of the baleen plates may reach as much as 30 cm. (11.8 in.). It is variously colored from yellowish through brown and gray and black. These baleen plates are reported to number between 206 and 268 on one side of the mouth.

Skeletal Notes. The vertebrae are distributed approximately as follows: C 7 + D 14-15 + L 10-12 + Ca 25 = 56-57. All 7 of the neck vertebrae are fused together into a single unit. There are about 12, 13, or more chevron bones present. There are 14 or 15 pairs of ribs. The sternum measures about 50 cm. (20 in.) in length and about 38 cm. (15 in.) in width. The bones (phalanges) of the fingers are distributed approximately as follows: I (3), II (5), III (6), IV (4-5), V (4).

Other Anatomical Notes. The skin is about 40 cm. (16 in.) thick on the chest and yields a good grade of oil. The flesh of the right whale is dark red with coarse fibers. The penis is long and slender and, when erect, will reach a length of about 3 meters (9.8 ft.). The caecum is absent in this species.

They do not possess acorn barnacles because they do not pass through the warmer waters where the larvae of these species may be acquired.

Food. The right whales feed upon all manner of small animals in the plankton. Their basic food consists of small crustaceans, principally copepods and euphausids (krill), and pteropods.

Swimming and Diving. Right whales usually travel in small groups of 5 or 6 or fewer. They are slow swimmers and cruise along at speeds of 2 to 3 knots. They are quite tame and will float at the surface during which time they may be approached. They will make deep dives lasting from 15 to 20 minutes at which time they will reach a depth of about 50 meters (164 ft.) or less; when beginning a dive, this whale will lift the tail flukes above the surface and then descend directly downward. Deep dives are usually followed by a series of 5 or 6 shallow dives at the rate of 2 or 3 per minute. It is able to remain under water for as long as 50 minutes.

The spout of this whale is double, wide, and V-shaped; it will reach a height of 4 to 8 meters (13.1 to 26.2 ft.) and is directed slightly forward.

Reproduction. In the northern hemisphere, the right whales mate in protected coastal waters during the months of February, March, and April. The young are born the following spring after a gestation period of about a year; at birth, they will measure about 5 to 6 meters (16.4 to 19.6 ft.) in length. The young are lighter in color at birth, are nursed for about 6 or 7 months, and are weaned thereafter by which time they have doubled their body length.

Abundance. This whale has been hunted to the verge of extinction. It is very scarce in nearly all of the regions which it formerly occupied.

Economic Importance. This whale was first hunted by the Europeans in the Bay of Biscay (Spain), beginning about 1100 A.D. and continuing to about 1800 A.D. It was the "right whale" to catch because it was a slow swimmer, floated when dead, and had a large yield of oil and whalebone; the latter was used to make whips, hoop skirts, various stays, umbrellas, etc. It was a lucrative species to hunt and this led to its ultimate scarcity.

Miscellaneous. Although there is doubtless only one species of the right whale, some scholars like to divide this species into three or more sub-species which inhabit different areas of the ocean; these groups of whales do not intermingle or interbreed in any way, although the North Pacific and the North Atlantic forms appear to be identical. These sub-species are listed below:

1. *Balaena glacialis glacialis* Muller, 1776.
   THE NORTH ATLANTIC RIGHT WHALE.
   This sub-species inhabits the North Atlantic Ocean from the Davis Strait (west of Greenland), Iceland, and Spitzbergen southward to Texas, Florida, Bermuda, and Madeira.
2. *Balaena glacialis japonica* Lacepede, 1818.
   THE NORTH PACIFIC RIGHT WHALE.
   This sub-species was originally distributed from the Bering Sea southward to Baja, California, and from the Sea of Okhotsk southward to Taiwan. Some scholars have used the name of *B. g. japonica* Gray, 1864 for these whales; they appear to be identical to *B. g. glacialis* mentioned above.
3. *Balaena glacialis australis* Desmoulins, 1822.
   THE SOUTHERN RIGHT WHALE.
   This sub-species occupies the southern latitudes from the Antarctic Seas and the Antarctic Circle northward to Chile, Brazil, Australia, and Africa.

THE BOWHEAD WHALE
Also known as The Greenland Right Whale,
The Arctic Right Whale, and The Great Polar Whale
Balaena mysticetus Linnaeus, 1758

Identifying Features. In the bowhead whale, the head is very large, the spout or blow is in two columns, the dorsal fin is totally absent, and the profile of the back consists of two upward curves which meet at the constriction of the neck. The chin is white and a white band sometimes encircles the posterior end of the tail stock.

Size and Shape. The bowhead (bṓ-hĕd) whale is a very robust species with a very large head which measures nearly one-third the length of the body. It will reach a maximum length of 18 to 20 meters (59.0 to 65.6 ft.), but most specimens are smaller and will measure between 15 and 18 meters (49.2 to 59.0 ft.) in length. The head is triangular in shape when viewed from above and contains no "bonnet" or other callosities. The upper jaw is arched and narrow in front; the lower jaw is wide and appears to cover the upper jaw when the mouth is closed. There are no longitudinal grooves of skin along the throat and belly. There is a slight constriction at the neck which is apparent in the dorsal profile.

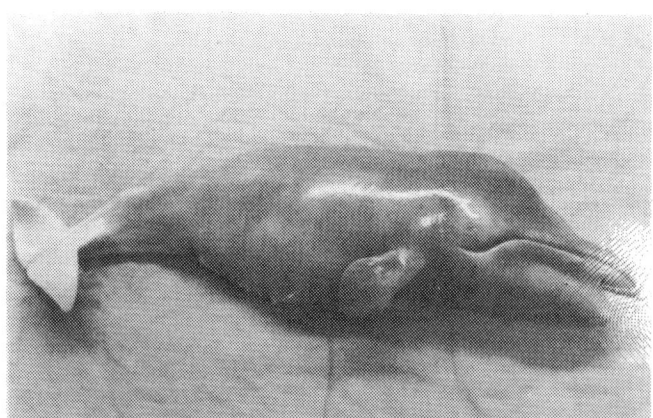

The fetus of a bowhead or Greenland right whale *(Balaena mysticetus)* taken in 1978 at Wainwright, Alaska (70° 30′+ N.L.). It measured 37.5 cm. (14.8 in.) in length.

Photo by Rockhill.

Color. The body is a dark blue-gray to black over the back and sides. The front end of the lower jaw or chin is white in color and occasionally this white area will extend backward onto the chin and belly. There is a white to grayish area of varying intensity at the end of the tail stock; it lies just forward of the tail flukes, where it forms a light colored band which completely encircles the tail stock. There are no callosities on the skin. The young whales are bluish in color. At least one individual has been reported which has a "creamy white" color and was without any black pigment on the back and sides of the body; it was sighted in waters off Wainwright, Alaska.

Distribution. The bowhead whale occurs only in the Arctic waters across the northern sides of North America, Europe, and Asia. In the Pacific Ocean, it comes as far south as the Aleutian Islands and stragglers have been observed as far south as California. A few live in the Sea of Okhotsk. In the Atlantic Ocean, it does not go much farther south than the coasts of Labrador and Newfoundland. It is rarely seen south of 50° N.L.

Migration. Bowhead whales spend their summers near the drifting ice and are always found in the regions just south of it. In the North Pacific Ocean, the bowhead whales move northward during the months of March, April, and May from their wintering ground in the western Bering Sea; they pass through the Bering Straight into the Chukchi Sea and then to the northeast into the Beaufort Sea. With the approach of colder weather, they reverse their direction and return southward into the Bering Sea between late August late October.

In the western Atlantic Ocean, they travel between the many islands to the west of Greenland and the coast of Labrador to the south. A third group of whales which formerly spent the winter along the eastern coast of Greenland and their summers in the seas near Spitzbergen, Franz Joseph Land, and Novaya Zemlya appears to have been exterminated in these areas.

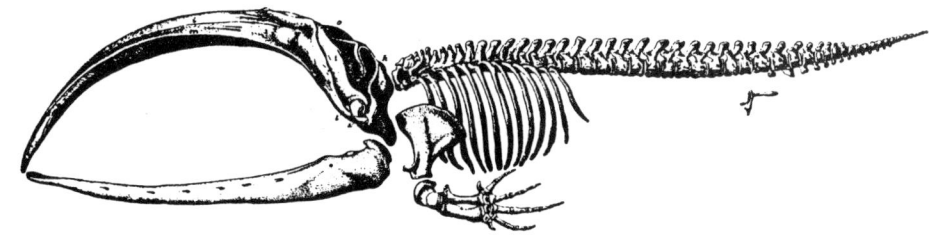

Drawing of the skeleton of the bowhead whale, *Balaena mysticetus* (Mysticeti: Balaenidae), showing the gigantic jaws, the general proportions of the body, and the remaining rudiments of the pelvis.

From Scammon.

Fins and Flippers. The dorsal fin is entirely absent in the two species of the genus *Balaena*. The flippers, which measure about one-sixth to one-eight of the body length, are large, flat, wide, rounded, and exhibit an obtuse tip. The caudal flukes are large and wide (6-8 meters wide; 2 meters front to back); they are tapered at their tips, concave along their rear margins, and exhibit a deep notch where they meet at the midline.

Baleen. The baleen plates reach their greatest length in the bowhead whale. The longest baleen plate known measured 4.5 meters (14.76 ft.) in length and doubtless came from a very large whale; most baleen will measure 2 to 3 meters (6.56 to 9.8 ft.) in length and may reach a maximum width of about 40 cm. (15.7 in.). The baleen plates number between 230 and 360 on each side of the mouth. They range in color from dark gray to black and are bordered by lighter colored fringes.

Skeletal Notes. The vertebrae are distributed approximately as follows: C 7 + D 12-13 + L 12-13 + Ca 22-23 = 53-55. The seven bones of the neck are fused into a single unit. There are 12 pairs of ribs of which 10 pairs have 2 heads and 2 pairs have 1 head each. One pair of ribs is attached directly to the sternum. The bones (phalanges) of the fingers are distributed approximately as follows: I (1), II (3-4), III (4-5), IV (3-4), V (2-3). Small vestigial remnants of pelvic bones and bones of the hind legs are occasionally found buried in the flesh of this species, indicating its affinities to its ancient 4-legged ancestors.

Other Anatomical Notes. The tongue is large, flabby, almost immobile, and white in color. The eye is small.

Food. The bowhead whale is a plankton feeder and eats nearly any and all forms which occur in the cooler surface waters. These include various small pelagic crustacea (amphipods, copepods, euphausids, and mysids) and pelagic mollusca (pteropods). This whale does not usually eat fishes.

Swimming and Diving. This species is a slow, sluggish swimmer, probably because food is everywhere and enemies are not numerous. They travel in small groups of 2, 3, 4, or more at a cruising speed of about 4 knots, but, when wounded, they are known to swim at speeds between 7 and 9 knots. They are known to take long dives lasting as much as 40 or more minutes and, when wounded, are able to stay down for

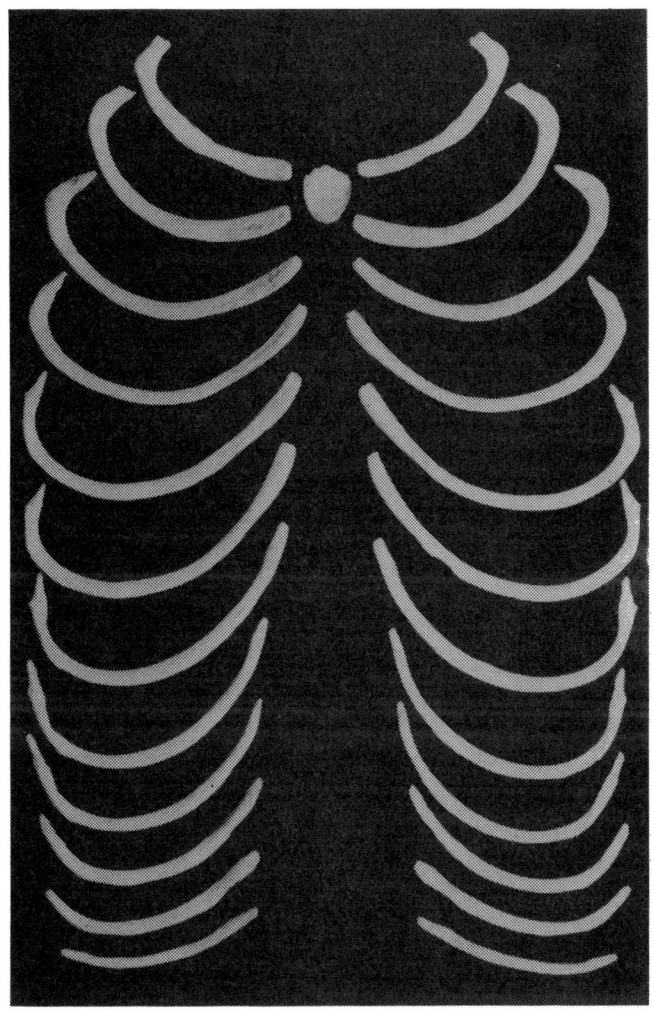

The ribs and sternum of the bowhead whale *(Balaena mysticetus).*

Photo by Nishiwaki and Kasuya.

periods approaching an hour. These whales will occasionally leap from the water (breeching) and engage in other antics common to whales. The spout is double and consists of two jets which diverge at an angle of 35 to 45° and which will reach a height of about 4 to 7 meters (13.1 to 22.9 ft.). The tail flukes are lifted clear of the water at the beginning of each dive. They show no fear of small boats.

Reproduction. Bowhead whales mate from early spring to the end of summer. The gestation period is presumed to be about a year or less in length. The young are born in the spring months of February, March, April, and May and are nursed for a period reported to be as long as 12 months. At birth, they will usually measure between 3 and 4.5 meters (9.8 to 14.76 ft.) in length and at the end of a year will measure about 9 meters (29.5 ft.) in length. This whale is reported to grow slowly and to reach its full size in about 20 years. At 12 years of age, the baleen is reported to be only about 6 feet in length.

Abundance. The population of this whale has been reduced by whaling to the point where it is nearing extinction. It is truly an endangered species.

Economic Importance. The bowhead whale was an important factor in the early development of whaling in western Europe and eastern North America. The animals were reasonably close, they were easy to hunt and capture, they floated when dead, and the yield was large. One whale would usually produce about 70 to 90 barrels of oil together with 1500 to 1700 pounds of whalebone; the capture of one whale was therefore enough to pay for a whaling expedition in the North Atlantic Ocean. It was the depletion of this whale and other species in the North Atlantic which caused the whaling industry to enter the Pacific Ocean in search of better whaling grounds. Today, this whale is hunted by a very few native people.

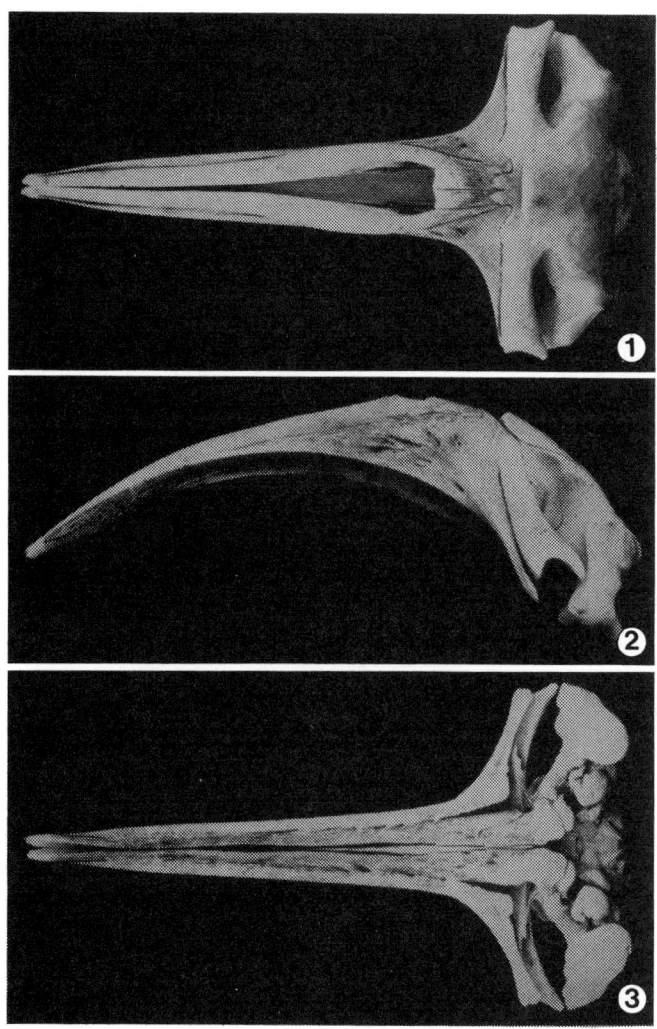

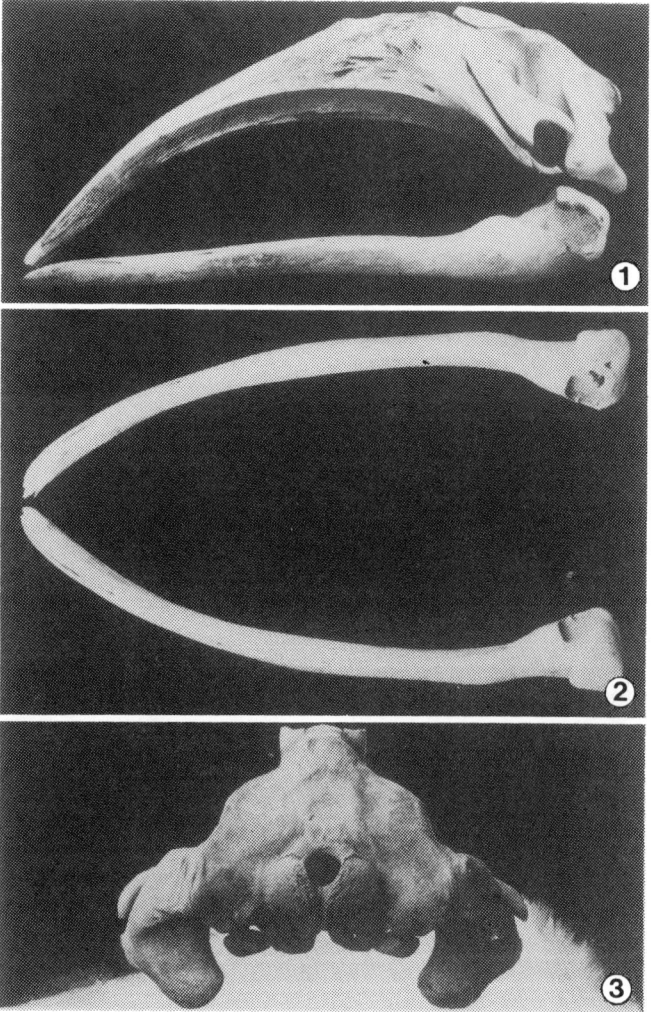

The skull of the bowhead or Greenland right whale *(Balaena mysticetus).* **The skull measured 198 cm. (78 in.) in length. The entire whale measured 6.4 m. (21 ft.) in length.**
Photos by Nishiwaki and Kasuya.

1. The bowhead skull in dorsal view.
2. The bowhead skull in lateral view.
3. The bowhead skull in ventral view.

The skull and jaws of the bowhead or Greenland right whale *(Balaena mysticetus).* Photos by Nishiwaki and Kasuya.

1. The skull and jaws in lateral view.
2. The jaws in dorsal view.
3. The skull in posterior view.

THE PIGMY RIGHT WHALES
Genus *CAPEREA* Gray, 1864

The pigmy right whale is separated from the Genus *Balaena* by its smaller size, by its smaller head which is about one-fourth the length of the body, by its small, irregular, curved dorsal fin, and by various skeletal features. The skeleton of this whale is quite unusual; the ribs are broad and are more numerous than in any other living species of whales, and the thorax and its rib cage are dorso-ventrally flattened. The flippers are small and contain only four digits. Only two longitudinal grooves are present on the throat.

This genus is known only from the Holocene Epoch (Recent).

The Genus *Neobalaena* is a synonym and should be replaced by the Genus *Caperea*.

This genus includes the single living species listed below.

Caperea marginata (Gray, 1846)

Class Mammalia — The Mammals
Order Cetacea — The Whales
Suborder Mysticeti — The Whalebone Whales
Family Balaenidae — The Right Whales

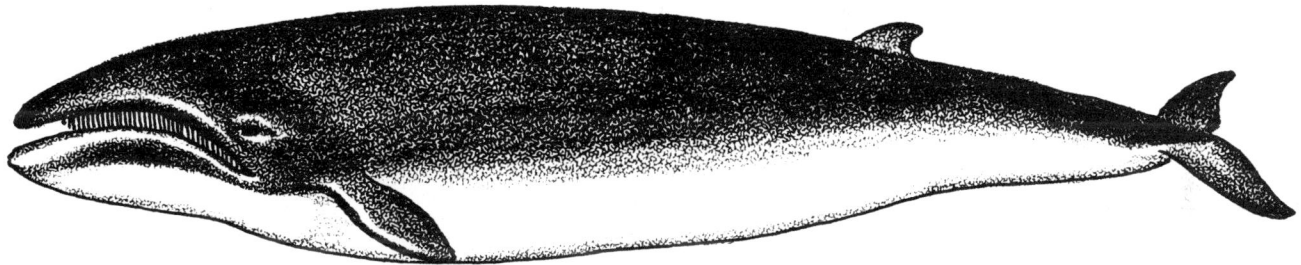

THE PIGMY RIGHT WHALE
Caperea marginata (Gray, 1846)

Identifying Features. The identification of this whale at sea is almost impossible. In addition to being a very rare and unseen species, it resembles the Lesser Rorqual or Minke Whale (*Balaenoptera acutorostrata*) to such an extent that positive identification could probably be made only on land.

Size and Shape. The pigmy right whale is the smallest and rarest of the 10 whalebone whales. The body is slender and spindle-shaped and will reach a length of 6.4 meters (21 ft.). The upper jaw is arched more than in the rorquals (*Balaenoptera*) but less than in the right whales (*Balaena*) and the lower jaw is likewise arched. The head measures about one-fourth the body length, lacks the "bonnet" found in the right whale (*Balaena glacialis*), and is without the many, long, longitudinal grooves found on the throats of the rorquals (*Balaenopteridae*).

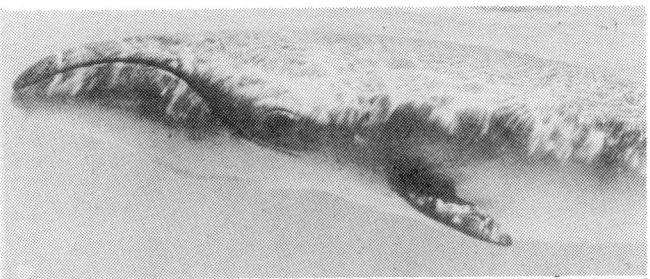

Photo of the pigmy right whale, *Caperea marginata,* taken in South Africa.

From Ross, Best, and Donnelly.

Reproduced by permission of the Dept. of Fisheries and Oceans, Dominion of Canada, from the Jour. Fish. Res. Bd. of Canada 32:7, July, 1975.

Photo of a pigmy right whale, *Caperea marginata,* **stranded in January, 1966, at Port Underwood, New Zealand.**
Photo by N.F. Herron.

From: "Whales and Dolphins of New Zealand and Australia" by A.N. Baker. Victoria University Press, Wellington, 1983. Courtesy A.N. Baker.

Color. The body is blue-gray to black in color above and shades gradually to a whitish color beneath. A vague darker area extends from the base of the flipper to the eye; a narrow, lighter, diagonal stripe marks the side of the body behind the eye.

Distribution. The pigmy right whale is distributed only in the cooler temperate waters of the southern oceans between about 30° and 60° S.L. and north of the Antarctic Convergeance.* They have been recorded from Tasmania, southeastern and southwestern Australia, southern New Zealand, the Falkland Islands, South Africa, and various islands in the southern ocean. They are often found stranded on beaches after heavy storms.

Migration. The migratory habits of this whale are not well known.

Fins and Flippers. A small dorsal fin is present. It is variously shaped and will measure about 15 cm. (5.9 in.) in height. The flippers are small and narrow, and terminate in a slightly rounded tip; they are dark in color. The flukes of the tail are quite wide, are gently concave on their posterior margins, and possess a deep notch where they join at the midline.

Baleen. The baleen blades are strong and flexible and are long compared to their width; of these; the longest blades will reach a length of about 70 cm. (27.5 in.); their maximum width is about 10 cm. (4 in.). In color, the baleen blades are a yellowish white or ivory white and are marked with blackish or brownish color along their outer margins. The number of blades varies from about 230 to 250 on each side of the mouth. The entire inside of the mouth and tongue is white in color.

Skeletal Notes. The most unusual features of this whale are found in its skeleton. The vertebrae are distributed approximately as follows: C 7 + D 17 + L 2 + Ca 14-15 = 40-41. There are 17 thoracic vertebrae and 17 pairs of ribs; this is more than in any other whale. Only one pair of ribs articulates directly with the sternum. The 1st rib has a single head and ribs 2 through 4 have 2 heads each. The ribs are unusually wide and strong and the rib cage is flattened in a dorso-ventral direction; these are features found only in this whale. The 7 neck vertebrae are fused into a single immobile unit. There are but 4 fingers in the hand of the flipper and there is some evidence of vestigial hind legs.

Other Anatomical Notes. The eye is black in color. A caecum, measuring about 20 cm. (8 in.) in length, is present. The small intestine measured 40 meters (131.24 ft.) in length in a whale 3.3 meters (10.8 ft.) in length; this is about 12 times the body length. The large intestine is 1.7 meters (5.57 ft.) in length. The tongue has been described as white in color and "strangely feathered at the tip."

Food. This whale is a plankton feeder and eats various forms including the copepods of the Genus *Calanus.*

Swimming and Diving. This small whale is often associated with other whales including dolphins, sei whales, and pilot whales; it is also known to gather into small schools. Very little is known about its habits. Its spout is difficult to observe.

Reproduction. These whales are believed to mate in late summer and autumn and the young are born in the spring months of September and October. At birth, the young are estimated to measure about 1.9 meters (6.23 ft.) in length and to be weaned about 5 or 6 months later at a length of about 3.5 meters (11.48 ft.).

Abundance. This seems to be the rarest and least known of the whalebone whales.

Economic Importance. This species is too scarce and too small to be of any commercial value.

---

*The Antarctic Convergence is an area which stretches around the earth as an irregular band of water just north of the Antarctic continent; here the colder, northward flowing waters from the Antarctic meet and sink beneath the warmer sub-Antarctic waters; it is an area of abundant marine life.

BIBLIOGRAPHY

A great many books have been published on the whales and many extensive bibliographies have been included within them. A large bibliography will not be included here; however, a few authoritative sources will be listed, most of which include bibliographies. Unfortunately, most of these references will only be included in the collections of the larger libraries. The following references may be helpful.

1. Anderson, Harald T. (editor) — THE BIOLOGY OF MARINE ANIMALS. 1969. 511 pages. Measures 6x9 inches.
   This book is a collection of eleven chapters by various authors on eleven different subjects. Each chapter has its own bibliography.

2. Anderson, S. and J.K. Jones, Jr. (editors) — RECENT MAMMALS OF THE WORLD: A Synopsis of Families. 1967. 453 pages.

3. Baker, Alan N. — WHALES AND DOLPHINS OF NEW ZEALAND AND AUSTRALIA. 1983. Wellington: Victoria University Press. 133 pages and 191 illustrations. Measures 5½ x 8¾ inches; sewn, with flexible cover. This is a very good book.

4. Bonner, W. Nigel — WHALES. 1980. 278 pages. Measures 5¾ x 8½ inches.
   It may also be listed under the Blandford Mammal Series: Whales. Pub. by Blandford Press, Dorset, England. It includes a bibliography and an index.

5. Ellis, Richard — THE BOOK OF WHALES. 1980. 202 pages. Measures 9x12 inches.
   Each species is illustrated by black and white drawings; there are also colored plates. This book contains a bibliography which is arranged by species. It is a companion volume to the book listed below.

6. Ellis, Richard — DOLPHINS AND PORPOISES. 1982. 270 pages. Measures 9x12 inches.
   This book includes only the smaller species of whales. Each species is illustrated in black and white; it also includes nine large color plates. It has a bibliography in the rear which is divided according to species. It is well indexed. This is a companion volume to the book listed above.

7. Gaskin, D.E. — WHALES, DOLPHINS, AND SEALS, With Special Reference to The New Zealand Region. 1972. 200 pages. Measures 8½ x 11 inches. This book contains an extensive bibliography.

8. Gaskin, David Edward — THE ECOLOGY OF WHALES AND DOLPHINS. 1982. 434 pp. plus 4 indices. Measures 6x9 inches. This book has ten chapters, each of which has its own bibliography. It is a very good book, although expensive.

9. Hall, E.R. and E.R. Kelson — THE MAMMALS OF NORTH AMERICA. 1959. 2 vols. About 1200 pages. Measures 8½ x 11 inches. This book is a taxonomic treatment of only those mammals which are found in North America and adjoining waters. The whales of other areas are not included. It is a very good reference. It includes a large bibliography and an index.

10. Harrison, R.J. (editor) — FUNCTIONAL ANATOMY OF MARINE ANIMALS. Vol. 1. 1972. 451 pages. Measures 6x9 inches. This book contains a collection of eight chapters by various authors on eight different subjects. Each chapter has its own bibliography.

11. Harrison, R.J. (editor) — FUNCTIONAL ANATOMY OF MARINE MAMMALS. Vol. 2. 1974. 366 pages. Measures 6x9 inches. This book is a collection of eleven chapters by various authors on eleven different subjects. Each chapter has its own bibliography.

12. Hershkovitz, Philip — CATALOG OF THE LIVING WHALES, U.S.N.M. Bull. 246. 1966. 259 pages. Measures 6x9¼ inches. This book is difficult reading for beginners. It is mostly synonymy (duplicate names) and bibliography.

13. Howell, A. Brazier — AQUATIC MAMMALS: Their Adaptations To Life In The Water. 1930. 338 pages. Measures 5½ x 8 inches.

14. Journal of Mammalogy. Published by the American Society of Mammalogists.
    This journal includes a wide variety of articles and book reviews.

15. Kellogg, Remington — A REVIEW OF THE ARCHAEOCETI. 1936. 366 pages and 37 plates. Measures about 8½ x 11 inches. Pub. by the Carnegie Institution of Washington.
    It contains photos and drawings of whale fossils and a bibliography.

16. Kellogg, Remington — WHALES: Giants of the Sea. Natl. Geog. Mag. 77:1, Jan. 1940, pp. 35-90. Measures 7 x 10 inches.
    This is a popular article with many colored illustrations and a text on many species. It is simply written.

17. Leatherwood, Stephen, et alii — WHALES, DOLPHINS, AND PORPOISES OF THE WESTERN NORTH ATLANTIC: A Guide to Their Identification. NOAA Technical Report, NMFS Circular 396. 1976. 176 pages. Measures 8½ x 11 inches.
    This is a good book, written in simple language; it contains many black and white pictures.

18. Leatherwood, Stephen, et alii — WHALES, DOLPHINS, AND PORPOISES OF THE EASTERN NORTH PACIFIC AND ADJACENT ARCTIC WATERS: A Guide To Their Identification. NOAA Tech. Report, NMFS Circ. 444. 1982. 245 pages. Measures 8½ x 11 inches. Short bibliography. This is a very good book. Like the book above it, this is a government publication and is not widely distributed.

19. Matthews, Leonard Harrison (editor) — THE WHALE. 1968. 287 pages. Measures 9½ x 10½ inches, height and width, respectively. Published in England by George Allen and Unwin, London.
This book includes eight chapters on whales and whaling. It is a well-illustrated, popular book and includes a short bibliography.

20. Minisian, Stanley, Kenneth Balcomb, and Larry Foster. — THE WORLD'S WHALES. 1984. 224 pages. Measures 10x10 inches. This book lists 76 species which are illustrated with many drawings, paintings, and both black-and-white and colored photographs. This is a popular book with a scientific basis and makes a very good presentation of the world's whales.

21. Mitchell, Edward (Special Editor) — "Review of Biology And Fisheries For Smaller Cetaceans." JOURNAL OF THE FISHERIES RESEARCH BOARD OF CANADA, vol. 32:7, July, 1975, pp. 875-1240. Measures 7½ x 10 inches. This article contains many photos and tables and several bibliographies. It discusses 66 species and is a very good source of information on the smaller cetaceans. This publication has a limited circulation and is difficult to obtain.

22. Nishiwaki, Masaharu — WHALES AND PINNIPEDS. 1965. 439 pages. Published by the Univ. of Tokyo. In Japanese. Measures 6x8½ inches.
Includes a pen drawing of each species.

23. Nishiwaki, Masaharu — DISTRIBUTION AND MIGRATION OF MARINE MAMMALS IN THE NORTH PACIFIC AREA. 1966. 49 pages. Measures 7x10 inches. Pub. by The Eleventh Pacific Science Congress — Symposium No. 4 (August 24, 1966).
The species are illustrated with pen drawings. In English. This is a very good pamphlet, but it is very scarce. It includes a bibliography.

24. Norris, Kenneth S. (editor) — WHALES, DOLPHINS, AND PORPOISES. 1966. 789 pages. Measures 6½ x 9¾ inches.
This book is a collection of 39 articles dealing with classification, anatomy, physiology, and behavior. Each article has its own bibliography.

25. Pilleri, Giorgio (editor) — INVESTIGATIONS ON THE CETACEA.
This is a continuing series of volumes on whales. It includes a variety of articles on anatomy and physiology. It is published in English by the Brain Anatomy Institute of the Univ. of Berne, Switzerland.

26. Rice, Dale W. — A LIST OF THE MARINE MAMMALS OF THE WORLD. NOAA Tech. Report, NMFS SSRF-711. 1977. 15 pp. Measures 8x10¼ inches. Includes a limited bibliography. This is an excellent guide to the species. No pictures.

27. Slijper, Everhard J. — WHALES. 1958, 1962. 475 pages. Measures 6x9 inches.
This book is an excellent treatment in simple language of the many aspects of whales. It has a good bibliography.

28. Tomilin, Avenir G. — MAMMALS OF THE USSR AND ADJACENT COUNTRIES. Vol. IX: CETACEA. 1967. About 738 pages. Measures 6½ x9½ inches.
A bibliography is listed for each species.

29. Van Valen, Leigh — "Monophyly Or Diphyly In the Origin of Whales." EVOLUTION, vol. 22, March, 1986. pp. 37-41.

30. Walker, Ernest P. — MAMMALS OF THE WORLD (in 3 volumes). 1964. Volumes 1 and 2 treat of the mammals, while volume 3 is an extensive bibliography.

31. Watson, Lyall — SEA GUIDE TO WHALES OF THE WORLD, 1981. 302 pages. Measures 8x9½ inches.
This is a very good book, although expensive, and is very well illustrated. It contains many historical notes, colored illustrations, a good bibliography, and an index.

32. Yablokov, A.V., V.M. Bel'kovich, and V.I. Borisov — WHALES AND DOLPHINS. 1972. 472 pages.
This book has been translated into English and is now available at the U.S. Dept. of Commerce, National Technical Information Service.

To obtain a copy, write to the
Joint Publications Research Service
1000 North Glebe Road
Arlington, Virginia 22201.
This translation measures 8½ x 11 inches, has 528 pages, and includes a bibliography of 1151 items.

Students who wish to wander through the shelves of libraries will find the books on whales included among those on mammals within the section on zoology.

In the libraries which use the Dewey Decimal System, the whales will be classified under the number 599.5. In this classification scheme, the zoological sciences are represented by the 590 numbers, the mammals by the 599 numbers, and the whales by 599.5.

In the larger libraries, which use the Library of Congress catalogue system, the whales will be classified as QL/737/.C4, representing zoology/mammals/whales, respectively.

APPENDIX

PROTECTION OF CETACEANS

Marine mammals are protected by the (U.S.) Marine Mammals Protection Act of 1972. This includes living mammals, dying mammals and the carcasses of dead mammals. Under this law, the living mammals are protected from all forms of molestation. Individuals are also prohibited from removing the carcasses of dead marine mammals or any part of them from their location without a permit from an official of the (U.S.) National Marine Fisheries Service. Violation of this Act is a Federal offense and is prosecuted in a U.S. Federal Court. However, it is permissible to photograph, measure, and sketch marine mammals.

BODY MEASUREMENTS

The following diagrams show the various measurements which scholars may wish to make on the carcasses of stranded whales. It is suggested that these blank forms be reproduced for work in the field, thereby preserving this original chart in a clean condition for future use. The figures on the following diagrams correspond to the figures on the Cetacean Data Record.*

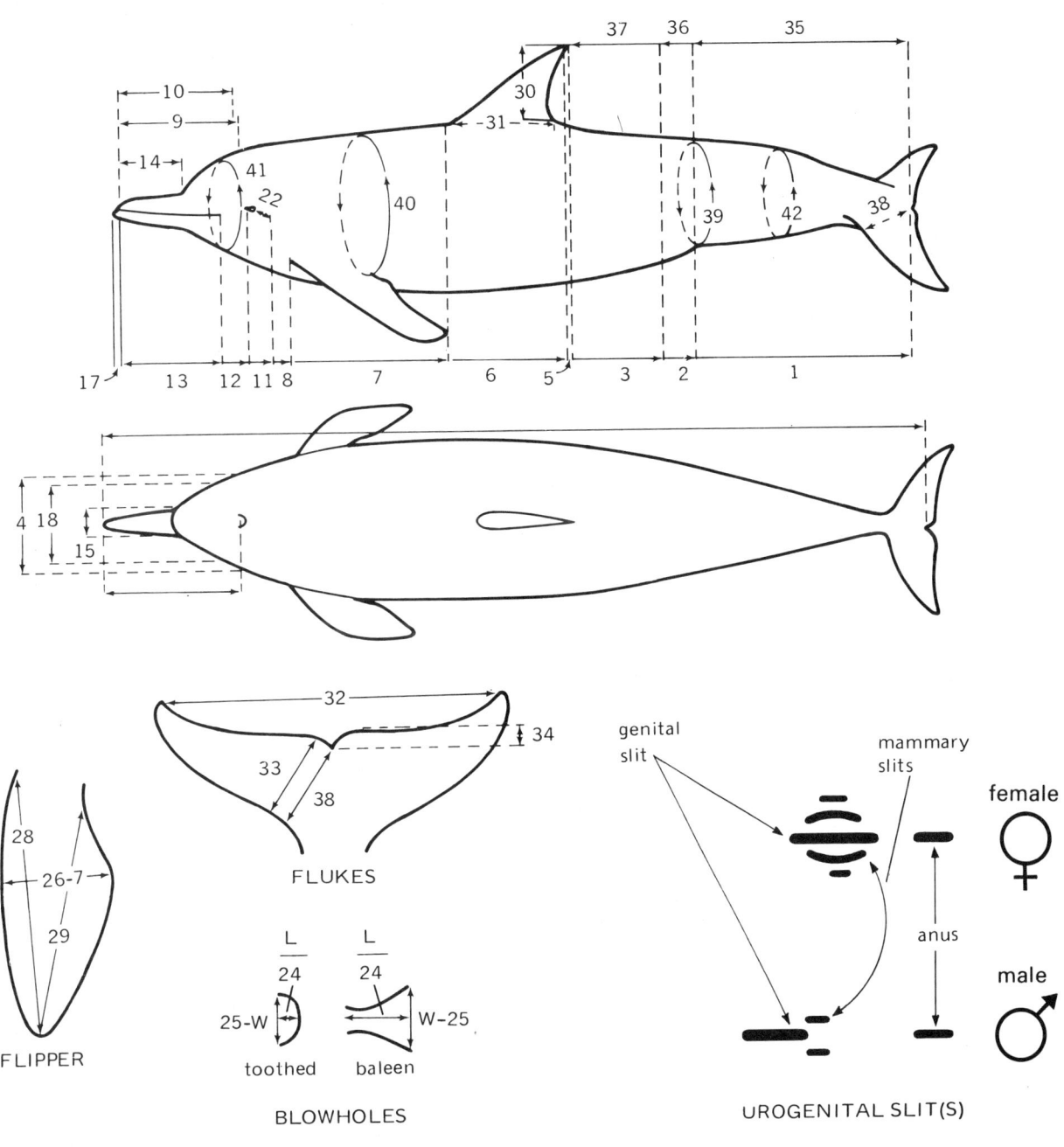

FLIPPER

FLUKES

toothed   baleen

BLOWHOLES

genital slit

mammary slits

female

anus

male

UROGENITAL SLIT(S)

*From Technical Report NMFS Circ. 396. Dept. of Commerce, U.S.A. 1976. pp. 169-176.

CETACEAN DATA RECORD*

SPECIES_____SEX_____LENGTH_____WEIGHT _____

DATE/TIME STRANDED_____DATE/TIME DATA COLLECTED _____

LOCATION OF COLLECTION _____

OBSERVER NAME/ADDRESS _____

		Distance In A Straight Line	Distance Point to Point
MEASUREMENTS:			
1.	Tip of upper jaw to deepest part of fluke notch	_____	_____
2.	Tip of upper jaw to center of anus	_____	_____
3.	Tip of upper jaw to center of genital slit	_____	_____
4.	Tip of lower jaw to end of ventral grooves		_____
5.	Tip of upper jaw to center of umbilicus	_____	_____
6.	Tip of upper jaw to top of dorsal fin	_____	_____
7.	Tip of upper jaw to leading edge of dorsal fin	_____	
8a.	Tip of upper jaw to anterior insertion of flipper (right)	_____	_____
b.	Tip of upper jaw to anterior insertion of flipper (left)	_____	_____
9.	Tip of upper jaw to center of blowhole(s)	_____	_____
10.	Tip of upper jaw to anterior edge of blowhole(s)	_____	_____
11a.	Tip of upper jaw to auditory meatus (right)	_____	_____
b.	Tip of upper jaw to auditory meatus (left)	_____	_____
12a.	Tip of upper jaw to center of eye (right)	_____	_____
b.	Tip of upper jaw to center of eye (left)	_____	_____
13.	Tip of upper jaw to angle of gape		_____
14.	Tip of upper jaw to apex of melon	_____	
15.	Rostrum - maximum width		_____
16.	Throat grooves - length	_____	_____

*From Technical Report NMFS Circ. 396. Dept. of Commerce, U.S.A.
1976. pp. 169-170.

		Distance In A Straight Line	Distance Point to Point

MEASUREMENTS:

17. Projection of lower jaw beyond upper (if reverse, so state) _____

18. Center of eye to center of eye _____

19a. Height of eye (right) _____

 b. Height of eye (left) _____

20a. Length of eye (right) _____

 b. Length of eye (left) _____

21a. Center of eye to angle of gape (right) _____ _____

 b. Center of eye to angle of gape (left) _____ _____

22a. Center of eye to external auditory meatus (right) _____ _____

 b. Center of eye to external auditory meatus (left) _____ _____

23a. Center of eye to center of blowhole (right) _____ _____

 b. Center of eye to center of blowhole (left) _____ _____

24. Blowhole length _____

25. Blowhole width _____

26. Flipper width (right) _____

27. Flipper width (left) _____

28a. Flipper length - tip to anterior insertion (right) _____

 b. Flipper length - tip to anterior insertion (left) _____

29a. Flipper length - tip to axilla (right) _____

 b. Flipper length - tip to axilla (left) _____

30. Dorsal fin height _____

31. Dorsal fin base _____

32. Fluke span _____

33. Fluke width _____

34. Fluke depth of notch _____

*From Technical Report NMFS Circ. 396. Dept. of Commerce, U.S.A.
1976. pp. 169-176.

	Distance In A Straight Line	Distance Point to Point

MEASUREMENTS:

35. Notch of flukes to center of anus _____

36. Notch of flukes to center of genital aperture _____ _____

37. Notch of flukes to umbilicus _____

38. Notch of flukes to nearest point on leading edge of flukes _____

39. Girth at anus _____

40. Girth at axilla _____

41. Girth at eye _____

42. Girth _____ cm in front of notch of flukes _____

43a. Blubber thickness (middorsal) _____

  b. Blubber thickness (lateral) _____

  c. Blubber thickness (midventral) _____

44. Width of head at post-orbital process of frontals _____

45. Tooth counts: right upper _____

   right lower _____

   left upper _____

   left lower _____

46. Baleen counts: right upper _____

   left upper _____

47. Baleen plates, length longest _____

48. Baleen plates, no. bristles/cm over 5 cm _____

49a. Mammary slit length (right) _____

  b. Mammary slit length (left) _____

50. Genital slit length _____

51. Anal slit length _____

*From Technical Report NMFS Circ. 396. Dept. of Commerce, U.S.A.
1976, pp. 169-176.

INDEX